INFECTIOUS AND PARASITIC DISEASES OF WILD BIRDS

Edited by

John W. Davis, D.V.M., M.S., Ph.D.

Roy C. Anderson, M.A., Ph.D.

Lars Karstad, D.V.M., M.S., Ph.D.

Daniel O. Trainer, M.S., Ph.D.

THE IOWA STATE UNIVERSITY PRESS, AMES, IOWA, U.S.A.

© 1971 The Iowa State University Press
Ames, Iowa 50010. All rights reserved
Composed and printed by
The Iowa State University Press

First edition, 1971

International Standard Book Number: 0–8138–0425–6
Library of Congress Catalog Card Number: 71–88003

◆ THE AUTHORS

Graham ±sd Falcons

J. Frederick Bell, M.D.
Medical Director, National Institute of Allergy and Infectious Diseases
Rocky Mountain Laboratory
Hamilton, Montana

Edith D. Box, B.S., Sc.D.
Associate Professor
University of Texas Medical Branch
Galveston, Texas

Robert L. Burkhart, V.M.D.
Technical Service Manager
American Cyanamid Company
Princeton, New Jersey

Robert S. Cook, B.S., M.S., Ph.D.
Assistant Professor of Biology
University of Wisconsin—Green Bay
Green Bay, Wisconsin

Robert T. DuBose, B.S., M.S., D.V.M.
Professor of Veterinary Science
Department of Veterinary Science
Virginia Polytechnic Institute
Blacksburg, Virginia

Warren C. Eveland, A.B., M.S.P.H., Ph.D.
Professor of Epidemiology
School of Public Health
University of Michigan
Ann Arbor, Michigan

Nathan B. Gale, B.S., D.V.M., M.P.H.
Assistant Director
Los Angeles Zoo
Los Angeles, California

Mildred M. Galton, Sc.M.
(Deceased March 19, 1968)
Formerly Chief, Veterinary Public Health
Laboratory
National Communicable Disease Center
Atlanta, Georgia

Datus M. Hammond, B.S., M.A., Ph.D.
Professor and Head of Zoology
Utah State University
Logan, Utah

Rolf Hartung, B.S., M.W.M., Ph.D.
Associate Professor, Environmental and Industrial Health
University of Michigan
Ann Arbor, Michigan

Carlton M. Herman, B.S., M.S., Sc.D.
Supervisory Biologist
Patuxent Wildlife Research Center
Laurel, Maryland

Lars Karstad, D.V.M., M.S., Ph.D.
Professor, Section of Zoonoses and Wildlife
Diseases
Ontario Veterinary College
University of Guelph
Guelph, Ontario, Canada

Richard M. Kocan, B.A., M.S., Ph.D.
Research Parasitologist
Patuxent Wildlife Research Center
Laurel, Maryland

Louis Leibovitz, B.A., B.S., V.M.D.
Avian Pathologist, Duck Research Laboratory
Cornell University
Eastport, New York

David C. O'Meara, A.B., M.S.
Associate Animal Biologist
University of Maine
Orono, Maine

Leslie Andrew Page, BA., M.A., Ph.D.
Principal Research Microbiologist
National Animal Disease Laboratory
Ames, Iowa

Steven F. Palmer, B.S., M.S.
Research Assistant, Veterinary Science Department
University of Wisconsin
Madison, Wisconsin

Malcolm C. Peckham, B.S., D.V.M.
Professor of Avian Diseases
Cornell University
Ithaca, New York

Merton N. Rosen, B.S., M.A.
Wildlife Pathologist
California Department of Fish and Game
Sacramento, California

Vance L. Sanger, A.B., D.V.M., M.S., Ph.D.
Professor, Pathology
Michigan State University
East Lansing, Michigan

v

Richard D. Shuman, B.S., D.V.M.
Veterinary Medical Officer
National Animal Disease Laboratory
Ames, Iowa

James H. Steele, D.V.M., M.P.H.
Chief, Office of Veterinary Public Health
    Services and Assistant Surgeon General,
    Public Health Service
National Communicable Disease Center
Atlanta, Georgia

Kenneth S. Todd, Jr., B.S., M.S., Ph.D.
Assistant Professor of Veterinary Parasitology
University of Illinois
Urbana, Illinois

Daniel O. Trainer, M.S., Ph.D.
Professor, Department of Veterinary Science
    and Wildlife Ecology
University of Wisconsin
Madison, Wisconsin

E. C. Turner, Jr., B.S., Ph.D.
Professor of Entomology
Virginia Polytechnic Institute
Blacksburg, Virginia

Everett E. Wehr, B.S.A., M.S.A., Ph.D.
Principal Parasitologist (Retired)
USDA, Animal Disease and Parasite Division
Beltsville, Maryland

Theodore Francis Wetzler, B.S., M.P.H., Ph.D.
Assistant Professor in Environmental Health
University of Michigan
Ann Arbor, Michigan

J. Franklin Witter, B.S., D.V.M.
Professor of Animal Pathology
University of Maine
Orono, Maine

◆ CONTENTS

PART FOUR ● NEOPLASTIC DISEASES

PART FIVE ● TOXINS

◆ PREFACE

DISEASE is an important ecologic factor affecting wild populations. Interest in and importance of infectious and parasitic diseases in wild birds have undoubtedly increased in recent years as witnessed by the amount of material published in various scattered journals throughout the world. That such interest did not suddenly skyrocket was principally because sources of specific information were lacking. Textbooks on bacteriology, parasitology, pathology, and zoology devote only a meager amount of space to diseases of animals not classified as domestic.

This first edition is an experimental effort in summarizing and correlating available knowledge in infectious and parasitic diseases of wild birds.

Preparation of this book was undertaken in response to inquiries and suggestions by students, research workers in animal diseases, wildlife specialists, veterinarians, laboratory workers, public health personnel, and teachers of infectious diseases in various areas of medicine. The chapters are arranged by disease and are based on the experience of the contributing author or authors and their interpretation of the available and pertinent world literature. In many instances the chapters are not a complete survey of the subject matter but they do provide a basic knowledge of the disease in question, which includes its etiology, history, distribution, epizootiology, signs, pathology, immunity, diagnosis, treatment, and control.

Each chapter is accompanied by a bibliography so designed that a reader may further his knowledge of the subject to the extent he desires. Also, an index has been assembled and designed to facilitate ease of finding subject matter and to provide a collection of related signs, lesions, and other data to hasten a diagnosis.

In writing this book we have been aware that we are dealing with a large, unexplored area of science and that our knowledge in this area is expanding very rapidly.

We trust this work will stimulate the interest of the young scientist and keep the interest of the mature scientist in the field of wildlife diseases, where so many obvious fundamental as well as applied problems await solution.

To all who have helped we extend our hearty thanks.

PART ONE

VIRAL DISEASES

1 ◆ NEWCASTLE DISEASE

- ● STEVEN F. PALMER
- ● DANIEL O. TRAINER

SYNONYMS: Avian pneumoencephalitis, avian pest, pseudo-fowl pest, avian distemper, Ranikhet disease, Doyle's disease. In Great Britain the term "fowl pest" officially includes both fowl plague and Newcastle disease.

NEWCASTLE DISEASE (ND) is a very contagious viral disease, primarily of avian species. In birds the infection can vary from subclinical to fatal, with degrees of systemic or localized nervous, respiratory, or gastrointestinal involvement.

◆ HISTORY. Newcastle disease was first recognized as a clinical entity in Indonesia, England, and Korea in 1926. The disease was extremely contagious and pathogenic for poultry. Although eliminated from England, the disease spread throughout the Far East, and subsequently most of the world. Newcastle disease virus (NDV) was probably present in California poultry in or before 1935, but because of the mild disease produced, was not identified in the United States until 1944. Recent historical reviews have been compiled by Brandly (1964), Levine (1964), Brandly and Hanson (1965), and Lancaster (1966).

In addition to domestic chickens, turkeys, and guinea fowl, numerous other avian species are susceptible to experimental or natural NDV infection (Tables 1.1 and 1.2). Although domestic anatids appear to be resistant to overt ND when experimentally exposed by natural routes and sometimes by direct experimental routes, field epizootics, a few with high mortality, have been observed in domestic waterfowl. Beaudette (1943) and Lancaster (1966) have reviewed the subject of natural and experimental NDV infections of domestic waterfowl.

Serologic studies in California by Quortrup et al. (1957) have revealed apparent NDV antibody in wild pintails (*Anas acuta tzitzihoa*) and wigeons (*Mareca americana*). Subsequent experimental exposure of pintails resulted in a low antibody response and no ND-associated death. Bradshaw and Trainer (1966) reported serologic evidence of ND in wild Canada geese (*Branta canadensis interior*) and mallards (*Anas platyrhynchos*) in the Mississippi flyway. NDV has been isolated from a swan in Europe (Vrtiak, 1958) and a Canada goose in Wisconsin (Palmer, 1969).

A variety of gallinaceous species has been reported susceptible to natural (Table 1.1) or experimental (Table 1.2) NDV infection. Newcastle disease has been reported in wild pheasants in Italy (Mantovani and Ceretto, 1953) and Great Britain (McDiarmid, 1965). In addition to natural occurrences of ND in ring-necked pheasants listed in Table 1.1, ND has been diagnosed in pheasants of various species by numerous investigators (Bianchi, 1941; Jansen et al., 1949; Liebengood, 1949; Moynihan et al., 1951; Jansen and Kunst, 1952; Wiedenmuller and Osthoff, 1953; Placidi and Santucci, 1954; Skoda and Zuffa, 1956; Mansjoer, 1961; Uzieblo, 1961; Jones, 1964). Three Italian investigators reported ND in pheasants associated with poultry epizootics (Brandly et al., 1946). In Iowa 174 wild pheasants (Andrews et al., 1963) and 2,000 game-farm pheasants (Roslien, 1966) were serologically negative for NDV hemagglutination-inhibiting antibody. Toth et al. (1966) reported fatal infection of pheasants by subcutaneous and

TABLE 1.1. Wild Avian Species Naturally Infected with NDV

Common Name	Scientific Name	Habitat	Reference
American widgeon	*Mareca americana*	W	Quortrup et al., 1957
Canada goose	*Branta canadensis*	WD	Page, 1958; Bradshaw and Trainer, 1966
Chinese spotted dove	*Streptopelia chinensis*	D	Hanson and Sinha, 1952
Cormorant	*Phalacrocorax carbo*	W	Blaxland, 1951
Cuckoo, koel	*Eudynamis scolopaceus*	W	Shah and Johnson, 1959
Dwarf turtledove	*Streptopelia humulis*	D	Hanson and Sinha, 1952
European house martin	*Delichon urbica*	W	Winmill and Weddell, 1961
European starling	*Sturnis vulgaris*	W	Gillespie et al., 1950
Gannet	*Sula bassana*	W	Wilson, 1950
Giant kingfisher	*Dacelo gigas*	Z	Kloppel, 1963; Schoop et al., 1955
Gray parrot	*Psittacus erithicus*	Z	Scott and Winmill, 1960
Great-horned owl	*Bubo virginianus* v.	Z	Ingalls et al., 1951
Hornbill	N.R.	Z	Kloppel, 1963; Schoop et al., 1955
House sparrow	*Passer domesticus*	W	Gustafson and Moses, 1953a; Monda et al., 1960; Keymer, 1961
Jackdaw	*Corvus monedula*	W	Baczynski, 1960a; Keymer, 1961
Jungle fowl	*Gallus* sp.	Z	Cavrini and Cabassi, 1960
King penguin	*Aptenodytes patachonica*	Z	Krauss et al., 1963
Laughing dove	*Streptopelia senegalensis*	D	Hanson and Sinha, 1952
Little owl	*Athene nocutra*	Z	Kloppel, 1963; Schoop et al., 1955
Macaw	*Ara severa*	Z	Cavrini and Cabassi, 1960
Mallard	*Anas platyrhynchos*	W	Bradshaw and Trainer, 1966
N.R.	*Streptopelia semitorquata*	D	Hanson and Sinha, 1952
Osprey	*Pandion haliaetus*	Z	Zuydam, 1952
Ostrich	N.R.	Z	Kloppel, 1963; Schoop et al., 1955
Ostrich	*Struthio camelus*	Z	Kauker and Siegert, 1957
Parrot	*Amazona orchocephala*	Z	Cavrini and Cabassi, 1960
Partridge	*Perdix perdix*	D	Torlone, 1954; Thompson, 1955
Peacock	*Pavo* sp.	Z	Cavrini and Cabassi, 1960
Peacock	N.R.	Z	Jansen and Kunst, 1952
Pigeon	*Columba livia*	D	Iyer, 1939; Hanson and Sinha, 1952
Pintail	*Anas acuta tzitzihoa*	W	Quortrup et al., 1957
Raven	*Bucovorus* sp.	Z	Kloppel, 1963; Schoop et al., 1955
Ringed dove	*Streptopelia risoria*	D	Hanson and Sinha, 1952
Ring-necked pheasant	*Phasianus colchicus*	D	Levine et al., 1947; Torlone, 1954
Shag	*Phalacrocorax aristotelis*	W	Blaxland, 1951
Secretary bird	N.R.	Z	Kloppel, 1963; Schoop et al., 1955
Toucan	*Ramphastos dicolorus*	Z	Kauker and Siegert, 1957
Vulture	*Pseudogyps africanus*	Z	Kauker and Siegert, 1957
White-tailed eagle	*Haliaetus albicilla*	Z	Kloppel, 1963; Schoop et al., 1955

SOURCE: Modified from Gustafson and Moses (1953b), with the permission of the American Veterinary Medical Association.
NOTE: D = game farm or aviary; W = wild; Z = zoo; N.R. = name not reported.

contact exposure. Beach (1942) reported that both California quail and Mongolian pheasants were as susceptible to ND as chickens, but Chelidze (1964) found quail to be less susceptible than chickens to intramuscular and intranasal exposure. A flock of 35 Indian partridges was fatally infected during a zoological garden epizootic (Parnaik and Dixit, 1953). In addition to the gallinaceous species listed in Table 1.2, grouse have been experimentally infected (Pomeroy and Fenstermacher, 1948).

Although ND of pigeons and doves has been reported (Picard, 1928; Vrtiak, 1958; Marastoni and Sidoli, 1959; Ulbrich and Sodan, 1965), other observers have noted a lack of apparent infection of pigeons and doves subject to probable natural exposure (Crawford, 1931; Bianchi, 1941; Orr and John, 1946; Adler et al., 1951). Pigeons are apparently less susceptible to overt ND than are chickens (Beach, 1942). Pigeons and doves are usually resistant to overt disease by experimental oral or contact exposure (Kee, 1928; Adler et al., 1951; Placidi and Santucci, 1953; Baczynski, 1960a;

TABLE 1.2. Wild Birds Experimentally Susceptible to NDV

Common Name	Scientific Name	Reference
American crow	*Corvus brachyrhynchos*	Karstad et al., 1959
Bobwhite quail	*Colinus virginianus*	Fenstermacher et al., 1946
Bondol	*Munia ferriginosa*	Collier and Dinger, 1950
Bondol	*Munia maja zaperena*	Collier and Dinger, 1950
California quail	*Lophortyx californica*	Beach, 1942
Canada goose	*Branta canadensis*	Page, 1958; Bradshaw, 1965
Cape pheasant	*Francolineus capensis*	Kaschula, 1950
Cape sparrow	*Passer melanurus*	Kaschula, 1950
Chukar partridge	*Alectoris graeca*	Fenstermacher et al., 1946
Cormorant	*Phalacrocorax carbo*	MacPherson, 1956
Dove	*Streptopelia* (hybrids)	Hanson and Sinha, 1952
English sparrow	*Passer domesticus*	Gustafson and Moses, 1953a; Mansjoer, 1961
Forest turtledove	*Streptopelia turtur*	Placidi and Santucci, 1953
Glatik	*Padda oryzivora*	Collier and Dinger, 1950
Hungarian partridge	*Perdix perdix*	Fenstermacher et al., 1946
Jackdaw	*Corvus monedula*	Baczynski, 1960a; Keymer, 1961
Japanese dove	*Geopelia striata*	Collier and Dinger, 1950; Mansjoer, 1961
Laughing dove	*Streptopelia senegalensis*	Kaschula, 1950
Manyar	*Ploceus manyar*	Collier and Dinger, 1950
Mourning dove	*Zenaidura macroura*	Jezierski, 1950
Pigeon	*Columba livia*	Beach, 1942; Fenstermacher et al., 1946; Hanson and Sinha, 1952; Placidi and Santucci, 1953
Prit	*Munia punctulata misoria*	Collier and Dinger, 1950
Prit	*Uroloncha leucogastra leuco- gastroides*	Collier and Dinger, 1950
Ringed dove	*Streptopelia risoria*	Kaschula, 1950
Ringed pigeon	*Columba palumbus*	Placidi and Santucci, 1953
Ring-necked pheasant	*Phasianus colchicus*	Fenstermacher et al., 1946
Silver pheasant	*Gennaeus nycthemerus*	Beach, 1942
Spotted dove	*Streptopelia chinensis tigrina*	Martini and Kurjana, 1950
Stilt bird	*Bulbulcus ibis*	Placidi and Santucci, 1953
Stone pigeon	N.R.	Mansjoer, 1961; Collier and Dinger, 1950
Striped ground dove	N.R.	Kraneveld and Mansjoer, 1950a; Martini and Kurjana, 1950

SOURCE: Modified from Gustafson and Moses (1953b), with the permission of the American Veterinary Medical Association; and Lancaster (1966), with the permission of the Queen's Printer, Ottawa, Canada.

Reuss, 1961a). Authors other than those listed in Table 1.2 have reported clinical or inapparent infection of pigeons by various experimental routes of exposure (Popovic, 1951; Placidi and Santucci, 1953; Walker et al., 1954; Reuss, 1961a).

NDV has been isolated from wild house sparrows *(Passer domesticus)* (Table 1.1). This species is also susceptible to experimental ND (Gustafson and Moses, 1952a, 1952b, 1953a; Moses and Gustafson, 1952). Sparrows *(Passer sp.)* were infected by intramuscular, intranasal, and contact exposure (Chelidze, 1964); however, Popovic (1951), Placidi and Santucci (1953) and Baczynski (1960a) failed to experimentally infect sparrows.

Gustafson and Moses (1953b) experimen-

tally exposed cowbirds *(Molothrus ater),* starlings *(Sturnus vulgaris),* and grackles *(Quisicalus quisicalus aenus)* to aerosol NDV with equivocal results. Chelidze (1964) reported experimental infection of magpies, and Farinas (1930) reported fatal infection of several captive Philippine birds.

NDV isolated in India from crows with "typical" ND symptoms was infective for poultry (Haddow, 1941). Authors have noted mortality of crows during poultry epizootics in India (Cooper, 1930; Sahai, 1937a), Indonesia (Picard, 1928), and Ceylon (Crawford, 1931). Scott and Winmill (1960) cited a report of possible NDV infection of Australian parrots and redheaded lovebirds *(Agraporius pullaria pul-*

laria) during a poultry epizootic in the Middle Congo, and ND has appeared concurrently with ornithosis in captive parakeets *(Paleornis* sp.) (Zuydam, 1952). The virus has been recovered from a naturally infected canary (Monda et al., 1960). Mansjoer (1961) reported fatal ND in lyrebirds, paradise birds, and ricebirds in an Indonesian zoological garden. Several other epizootics in zoological gardens have been reviewed by Lancaster (1966). A bearded vulture *(Gypactus barbatus aureus)* (Placidi and Santucci, 1953), ricebirds (Kee, 1928), and rooks (Baczynski, 1960a) have been reported resistant to experimental infections.

◆ **DISTRIBUTION.** Newcastle disease virus, as an antigenic entity, is of virtually worldwide distribution. Since 1961 ND has been reported for the first time in Argentina, Denmark, and Luxemburg. Although eradicated in Australia in 1933, ND has recently recurred (Forbes and Row, 1966). A comprehensive review of the geographic distribution of ND is presented by Lancaster (1966).

◆ **ETIOLOGY.** Newcastle disease virus was isolated from poultry in 1926 and was proved to be a filterable agent (Doyle, 1927). The virus has since been characterized by numerous investigators and placed taxonomically in the parainfluenza group of the myxoviruses on the basis of chemical and morphological properties (Cruickshank, 1964).

The virion consists of a pleomorphic, membranous envelope, 150 to 200 mμ in size, which surrounds a single-strand helix of ribonucleoprotein. The envelope is covered with a pattern of projections which confer specificity on hemagglutination-inhibiting and virus-neutralizing antibodies. Components of the envelope are also responsible for the ability of NDV to agglutinate and enzymatically elute from the erythrocytes of all amphibia, reptiles, birds, and some mammals (Cruickshank, 1964; Brandly and Hanson, 1965). The structure of NDV has recently been discussed in detail by Waterson (1964).

Because of the importance of NDV to the world poultry industry, many strains of the virus have been well characterized. There are currently more than 125 strains in the world NDV repository at the University of Wisconsin, Madison (Hanson, 1968). Strains of NDV may be differentiated into three groups—velogenic, mesogenic, and lentogenic—on the basis of virulence for embryonated eggs, day-old chicks, and 6- to 10-week-old chickens (Hanson and Brandly, 1955).

Velogenic strains cause severe, often terminal, disease in susceptible mature chickens when introduced by any route, while mesogenic strains cause severe disease and death only when inoculated into the nervous system. Chickens exposed to mesogenic strains by more natural, peripheral routes develop mild, seldom fatal disease. Lentogenic strains produce only mild to subclinical disease by any route (Brandly and Hanson, 1965). Chicken embryos die in about 50 hours when exposed to one minimum lethal dose of velogenic strain. One minimum lethal dose of a mesogenic strain kills embryos in 50 to 60 hours. Characteristics used to differentiate strains of NDV include mean death time of embryonated eggs, intracerebral pathogenicity index in day-old chicks, mammalian hemagglutinins, adsorption on suspended chicken-embryo brain cells, pH and thermostability, and gel precipitation by specific antibodies *(Methods for the Examination of Poultry Biologics,* 1963; Brandly and Hanson, 1965).

◆ **TRANSMISSION.** Among poultry, NDV is transmitted via exudates, excreta, eggs, and offal of infected birds. Respiratory and alimentary systems are the primary portals of virus entry, but other routes may be involved. The long-term carrier state is uncommon in chickens but not in turkeys. Shipments of live poultry and dressed carcasses have been incriminated in ND spread. Recent reviews by Brandly and Hanson (1965) and Lancaster (1966) discuss ND transmission in detail. Since NDV is relatively resistant to environmental inactivation, indirect transmission is a hazard. NDV infectivity has survived as long as 1 week at pH 3 and 11 (Moses et al., 1947) and 22 days in loam at 100% relative humidity (Boyd and Hanson, 1958). The virus has survived on down for 123 days at 20° to 30° C, 255 days at temperatures which fluctuated from −11° to 36° C, and 538 days at 3° to 6° C (Olesiuk, 1951). Although virus remained viable 19 days in sterile lake water at room temperature, infectivity was rapidly lost in aerated lake water (Boyd and Hanson, 1958). Survival time in earthworms, planaria, and feather mites is dependent primarily upon temperature (Boyd and Hanson, 1958; Baczynski, 1960b; Rotov, 1964). Experimental transmission with arthropod vectors has generally failed; however, Rotov (1964) has reported transmission from chicken to chicken by the feather mite *(Dermanyssus gallinae)*.

Partridges (Placidi and Santucci, 1953) and wild pheasants (Jerabek, 1961) have been circumstantially implicated in the spread of ND. Reid (1961) reported large outbreaks in pheasants penned near poultry but found no evidence that pheasants were an important reservoir.

A carrier state has been detected in adult domestic ducks (Vrtiak, 1958; Winmill and Haig, 1961) and a swan (Vrtiak, 1958), and suspected in geese (Heller, 1957), but has not been observed in some other investigations (Iyer, 1945; Asplin, 1947). Experimental contact infection of a chicken by 2 NDV-infected ducks has been reported (Doyle, 1927). Asplin (1947) detected NDV in feces of artificially exposed ducks and a goose 3 to 4 days following noninfective periods of up to 4 days.

Experimentally infected spotted doves, striped ground doves, house sparrows, and java sparrows developed subclinical ND which was transmittable to poultry by contact (Kraneveld and Mansjoer, 1950b). Infection of pigeons and doves by aerosol resulted in both clinical and subclinical disease (Hanson and Sinha, 1952). These experimental results enhanced the possibility that columbids may have a role in

NDV dissemination. Others have detected the excretion of NDV in the feces of pigeons after various methods of artificial exposure (Schyns and Florent, 1951; Kaschula. 1952; Walker et al., 1954; Reuss, 1961a, 1961b). Popovic (1951) observed contact transmission from pigeon to pigeon but not to sparrows or chickens.

Experimental transmission of NDV between English sparrows and chickens indicated the potential of wild sparrows as carriers of NDV (Gustafson and Moses, 1953a, 1953b). The experimental results of Gustafson and Moses have been confirmed by Hartwigk and Nitsch (1957) but contradicted by Maglione (1956).

Baczynski (1960a) could not recover NDV from perorally exposed rooks, jackdaws, sparrows, and pigeons, but Karstad et al. (1959) recovered virus from the feces of a crow 24 hours after peroral exposure. Karstad et al. speculated that wild birds, such as crows, which sometimes develop subclinical ND upon intravascular introduction of the virus could serve as virus reservoirs for arthropod vectors.

Because ND outbreaks in 1949–51 were scattered along the coast of Great Britain and on isolated off-shore islands, wild sea birds were suspected disseminators (Wilson, 1950; Blaxland, 1951; Reid, 1955; MacPherson, 1956). Many individual poultry epizootics began after the birds fed upon viscera of shags and cormorants shot by flock owners (Blaxland, 1951; MacPherson, 1956). NDV was isolated from naturally infected cormorants (Blaxland, 1951) and a gannet (Wilson, 1950) during the epizootic. Several hypotheses were offered to explain infection of the sea birds. The fish-eating shags and cormorants may have been infected by contact with poultry-scavenging gulls or may have mistaken floating poultry viscera for fish or eels (Blaxland, 1951). Sea birds may have eaten fish which had consumed infective poultry offal (MacPherson, 1956). MacPherson recovered NDV from feces of 2 cormorants 1 month after intranasal exposure and 2 others 5 and 6 days after peroral exposure. He concluded that because of the inapparent character of ND in these birds, cormorants may be a primary host to which the virus has adapted. MacPherson also presented evidence that ND epizootics in Asia, Australia, Africa, and, in 1898, Great Britain, originated in costal areas—regions frequented by sea birds.

Wild birds have been suggested as disseminators of NDV in India (Sahai, 1937a, 1937b; Seetharaman, 1951), the Middle Congo (Brandly et al., 1946), and Great Britain (Callander, 1958; Keymer, 1958; Locke, 1960). Migratory birds may have introduced NDV into Cyprus (Crowther, 1952) and Kenya (Winmill and Weddell, 1961).

Brandly (1946) has reviewed evidence that wild birds are one of the major factors in the spread of NDV. Skoda and Zuffa (1956) have also discussed the role of wild birds. Gustafson and Moses (1953b) have discussed the effect of behavior patterns on dissemination of NDV by wild birds. ND is probably not an important cause of mortality in most wild avian populations, but the role of these populations in the epizootiology of the disease among domestic poultry is of potential significance.

Transfer of NDV over long distances in shipments of infected game birds and live zoological specimens has frequently occurred (Zuydam, 1949, 1950, 1952; Anonymous, 1950; Adler et al., 1951; Jansen and Kunst, 1952; Thompson, 1955; Cavrini and Cabassi, 1960; and others).

♦ **SIGNS.** Signs of ND in poultry vary with both the virulence and tropic tendency of the infective strain. In Europe, Asia, and Africa virulent strains are usually viscerotropic, while in North America pneumotropic strains predominate. Both types may cause nervous signs if the disease is not quickly terminated. Most NDV isolates from wild birds have been velogenic or mesogenic, probably because most lentogenic NDV infections would be inapparent and undetected. The virulence of poultry lentogenic strains in wild birds, other than pheasants, has not been extensively studied.

In young chickens ND may be mani-

fested by coughing, hoarseness, or aphonia, followed by degrees of leg and wing paralysis, tremors, neck contortions, emprosthotonos, and a variety of abnormal locomotory movements. Laying poultry may have respiratory distress, depression, inappetence, near cessation of egg production with reduction of egg quality, and profuse diarrhea. Nervous signs are similar to those exhibited by younger birds, but less common (Brandly and Hanson, 1965). Overt signs of ND in domestic turkeys are similar to those seen in chickens (Hinshaw, 1965). Leg paralysis, ataxia, head tremors, and general depression have been observed in domestic ducks during epizootics of ND.

Signs of ND in game-farm pheasants were similar to those of chickens (Levine, 1947; Liebengood, 1949; Weidenmuller and Osthoff, 1953). Although partridges naturally infected with a viscerotropic, velogenic strain were not overtly affected prior to death, survivors suffered nervous sequelae typical of poultry (Thompson, 1955). Approximately 72 to 96 hours after partridges were exposed intramuscularly to a velogenic strain, depression appeared, followed in 20 hours by wing and leg weakness. Soon ability to walk was lost, and the birds rested with keel on the floor, and neck constantly raised and lowered. Signs in intratracheally exposed partridges were either similar to those in intramuscularly exposed birds, but with later onset, or consisted of leg weakness and other nervous signs which began at 240 hours and were followed by recovery (Fenstermacher et al., 1946).

Despite the route of exposure, pigeons primarily developed central nervous system signs, including incoordination, opisthotonos, torticollis, emposthotonos, paralysis, tremors, and somnolence. Although respiratory distress was not as marked as in poultry, some pigeons breathed with increased respiration rate and parted mandibles. Feathers of the nasal fossae became soiled with nasal discharge (Iyer, 1939; Dobson, 1952; Hanson and Sinha, 1952; Walker et al., 1954). Diarrhea accompanied nervous signs in pigeons artificially exposed to a Malayan NDV strain (Orr and John, 1946). Signs in doves *(Streptopelia* sp.) resembled those in pigeons (Hanson and Sinha, 1952).

Gustafson and Moses (1953a) observed nervous signs in 2 of 9 English sparrows 48 hours after aerosol exposure. One bird had clonic spasms of the cervical musculature approximately every second, and the other exhibited clonic opisthotonos at 5-second intervals. When held, both sparrows trembled like chickens infected with avian encephalomyelitis. Sparrows infected by peroral and intramuscular exposure, however, did not develop typical ND signs (Hartwigk and Nitsch, 1957).

NDV was isolated from a jackdaw which was unable to fly (Keymer, 1961) and a nestling European starling which exhibited incoordination and tremors (Gillespie et al., 1950). Virus was also isolated from a 25-day-old koel which suffered unilateral leg paralysis (Shah and Johnson, 1959). A peacock developed an unsteady gait and marked headshaking before death (Jansen and Kunst, 1952), and a peacock, parrots *(Amazona orchrocephala),* and a guinea fowl showed nervous symptoms during another epizootic (Cavrini and Cabassi, 1960). In gray parrots, respiratory signs along with profuse ocular and nasal discharge, but no nervous signs, were observed. Birds kept their eyes closed, and feathers were ruffled (Scott and Winmill, 1960). Nervous signs characterized by torticollis and opisthotonos were observed in a naturally infected great-horned owl (Ingalls et al., 1951). An osprey, from which NDV was isolated, had no clinical signs (Zuydam, 1952), and shags and cormorants appeared to develop asymptomatic infections (Blaxland, 1951; MacPherson, 1956). Intracardial or peroral exposure to NDV did not cause signs in crows, but intracerebral inoculation resulted in incoordination, nystagmus, clonic spasms, and death. Only depression preceded death of subcutaneously exposed crows (Karstad et al., 1959).

◆ **PATHOGENESIS.** The pathogenesis of ND in avian hosts is dependent upon nu-

merous factors, including susceptibility of the host species, immune status of the host, age and environment of the host, the virulence and tropic tendencies of the NDV strain involved, and the magnitude and route of exposure. Jungherr (1964) has thoroughly discussed the pathogenicity of NDV for chickens, and Bang (1964) the pathogenesis in chicken embryos. Little research has evolved to determine the pathogenesis of ND in wild birds; however, knowledge of domestic fowl may be extrapolated in various degrees to the study of NDV in wild avian hosts.

NDV is essentially a pantropic virus in poultry, although the limited invasive powers of a strain or the immune response of a host may limit virus spread. Sinha et al. (1952) detected a viremia associated with infection by each of three lethal and three nonlethal strains. Lethal strains produced higher blood virus titers of longer duration. Subcutaneously inoculated velogenic strains have been recovered from blood, spleen, liver, lung, trachea, and intestinal contents within 24 hours (Hofstad, 1951; Asdell and Hanson, 1960). Nervous tissues contained virus after 48 hours, and all other tissues contained virus after 72 hours. Primary virus multiplication occurred between 18 and approximately 40 hours after inoculation. There was then a marked decrease in virus titer until about 48 hours after inoculation; then titer increased until death of the chicken. The decrease in virus titer was postulated to be a nonspecific host response to foreign protein (Asdell and Hanson, 1960). In nonlethal infections, detectable virus had disappeared from the brain, blood, and intestinal contents by 144 hours and from the spleen and trachea by 168 hours after exposure of the birds to NDV (Hofstad, 1951).

A velogenic strain of NDV had a greater replication rate than a lentogenic strain in nervous tissues, but the growth rates in extraneural tissues were similar (Karzon and Bang, 1951). Karzon and Bang concluded that extraneural growth rate does not determine the lethality of a strain. A "blood-brain barrier" has been hypothesized to explain the lag in infection of the brain. The development of this barrier with the growth of the bird, and the effect of the barrier on the infection of nervous tissue, have been studied by Vadlamudi and Hanson (1966). The blood-brain barrier does not have an absolute effect on the neuropathogenicity of NDV strains, since even nonlethal strains may reach moderate titers in brain tissue (Sinha et al., 1952). Virus level in the brain may (Sinha et al., 1952) or may not (Karzon and Bang, 1951) be correlated with the presence of nervous symptoms.

◆ **PATHOLOGY.** The pathogenicity of NDV for chickens depends primarily on the characteristics of the virus strain. The pathologic changes in chickens, caused by any individual NDV strain, are extremely variable among age groups and among individual birds. Gross and microscopic lesions of the disease in chickens, usually hemorrhagic and inflammatory, have been reviewed by Beaudette (1943), Jungherr et al. (1946), Brandly and Hanson (1965), Lancaster (1966), and others.

Most investigators have noted a general lack of gross lesions in domestic ducks and geese (Albiston and Gorrie, 1942; Asplin, 1947). Craig (1950), however, reported severe exudative airsacculitis associated with a possible ND epizootic in a flock of assorted domestic and semiwild waterfowl.

Fenstermacher et al. (1946) did not observe gross lesions in Hungarian partridges *(Perdix perdix perdix)* after fatal experimental infections. Partridges *(Perdix perdix),* naturally infected with a European viscerotropic strain, had small intestinal ulcers which were grossly visible through the intestinal walls as white foci (Thompson, 1955). Other gross pathological changes observed in naturally infected partridges included lesions in the ceca (Tropilo, 1964), obvious hemorrhages on the serous coat of the gizzard (Parnaik and Dixit, 1953), enteritis, and slight hemorrhage at the entrance of the proventriculus (Lucas and Laroche, 1958).

Pheasants which succumbed to natural infection by Asian NDV strain had slight enteritis and hemorrhages under the horny gizzard lining (Jansen and Kunst, 1952). Purchase (1931) observed petechial hemorrhages in the proventriculus and serogelatinous fluid in the pericardial sac of a pheasant inoculated intramuscularly with an Egyptian strain of NDV. The lesions of ND in pheasants during an outbreak in Poland resembled those reported for domestic fowl (Tropilo, 1964). Weidenmuller and Osthoff (1953) discussed gross and histopathologic lesions observed during a destructive ND epizootic among pheasants in Germany.

Seven mature English sparrows, experimentally exposed to an aerosol of a velogenic North American strain, developed hemorrhagic enteritis during terminal stages of the infections (Gustafson and Moses, 1953a). Eight English sparrows which died after peroral inoculation with velogenic NDV developed hepatic lesions which included diffuse leukocytic infiltration, enlarged lymphoid foci, early degeneration of hepatic cells, passive congestion, and focal central necrosis. Other observed pathologic changes included enlarged spleen, albuminous degeneration and desquamation of kidney-collecting tubule epithelium, and pneumonia with cellular exudate in the alveoli and leukocytic infiltration of perialveolar connective tissue (Gustafson and Moses, 1952a).

ND lesions reported in pigeons resemble those in fowl (Ulbrich and Sodan, 1965). Keymer (1961) reported both visceral and respiratory involvement in a naturally infected jackdaw. Lesions included edema and patchy congestion in the lungs, cloudy thickened air sacs, large ecchymotic hemorrhages on an enlarged spleen, and small, discrete necrotic areas and congestion in the liver. Although Gillespie et al. (1950) isolated Newcastle disease virus from a nestling European starling, no gross lesions were observed. A naturally infected great-horned owl had exudative airsacculitis but no other gross lesions (Ingalls et al., 1951). Postmortem examination of a king penguin, infected in a zoological garden, revealed petechial hemorrhages in the epicardium, an enlarged liver, and catarrhal pneumonia (Krauss et al., 1963). NDV was isolated from an osprey which had pneumonia, with gray foci about 1 mm in diameter scattered throughout the lung tissue. The liver capsule was irregular and dull, with valleylike lesions about 0.5 cm wide (Zuydam, 1952). Marked vascular congestion and slight meningitis were the primary histopathological changes in the brains of crows which died after experimental NDV exposure (Karstad et al., 1959).

Wilson (1950) observed severe nephritis with some subcapsular petechiae in a gannet from which the NDV was isolated. MacPherson (1956) did not find gross lesions in a cormorant after fatal experimental infection.

Scott and Winmill (1960) found few lesions in gray parrots fatally infected in a Newcastle disease outbreak. Microscopic examination of tissues from fatally infected parakeets did not reveal pathologic changes (Zuydam, 1952).

◆ **DIAGNOSIS.** Since NDV elicits variable clinical response in the different hosts, clinical observation must be supplemented by other diagnostic procedures. Reviews by Lancaster (1966) and Brandly and Hanson (1965) have described methods of serological detection and virus isolation, and *Methods for the Examination of Poultry Biologics* (1963) details laboratory diagnostic procedures. The virus may be demonstrated, if present in large quantities, by hemagglutination techniques, or low levels may be detected by inoculation of tissue or exudate suspensions into susceptible chickens, tissue culture systems, or 9- to 11-day-old embryonated chicken eggs. Treatment of inocula with streptomycin and penicillin is advantageous. Host antibody response to NDV, detectable approximately 5 to 10 days after infection, may be studied by use of hemagglutination-inhibition, gel precipitation, and virus neutralization tests (Lancaster, 1966).

ND must be differentiated from fowl plague and other avian influenzas, infectious bronchitis, infectious laryngotracheitis, the encephalitides, chronic respiratory disease, avian pasteurellosis, ornithosis, and other bacterial diseases, nutritional deficiencies, and food toxins. Lancaster (1966) has recently reviewed the differential diagnosis of Newcastle disease.

◆ **IMMUNITY.** Poultry infected with NDV usually develop substantial, long-lasting immunity, and passive congenital immunity may persist up to 4 weeks in chicks (Lancaster, 1966). Most wild avian species probably develop comparable immunity to NDV. Although serologically detected antibody response of cormorants (MacPherson, 1956) and domestic ducks (Asplin, 1947) has been lower than that of chickens, these observations are not necessarily indicative of the immune status of the birds.

◆ **TREATMENT AND CONTROL.** There is no known effective treatment for ND.

The administration of NDV vaccines and the relative merits of various types of vaccines have been discussed by Lancaster (1966). Several effective commercial poultry vaccines are available, and vaccination of pigeons and doves (Hanson and Sinha, 1952; Kaschula, 1952) and pheasants (Toth et al., 1966) has produced satisfactory results. Grain soaked in live-virus vaccine was distributed to wild birds in an attempt to control an epizootic in pheasants in Czechoslovakia (Jerabek, 1961). In most cases, however, control of a ND epizootic in wild birds would not be practical.

Game-farm birds to be released should be closely observed to prevent release of diseased stock. Game-farm pheasants have developed ND only 2 days prior to planned release (Levine et al., 1947).

◆ **REFERENCES**

Adler, H. E., Willers, E. H., and Campbell, J. Newcastle disease (avian pneumoencephalitis) in Hawaii. *Am. J. Vet. Res.* 12:44, 1951.

Albiston, H. E., and Gorrie, C. J. R. Newcastle disease in Victoria. *Australian Vet. J.* 18:75, 1942.

Andrews, R. D., Haugen, A. O., and Quinn, L. Y. Antibodies of pullorum and Newcastle disease virus in pheasants. *J. Wildlife Management* 27:220, 1963.

Anonymous. Asiatic form of avian pneumoencephalitis. *J. Am. Vet. Med. Assoc.* 117:351, 1950.

Asdell, M. K., and Hanson, R. P. Sequential changes in the titer of Newcastle disease virus in tissues—A measure of the defense mechanism of the chicken. *Am. J. Vet. Res.* 21:128, 1960.

Asplin, F. D. Newcastle disease in ducks and geese. *Vet. Rec.* 59:621, 1947.

Baczynski, Z. Nosicielstwo i siewstwo wirusa rzekomego pomoru drobiu (Newcastle disease). II. Ptaki wolno zyjace. (Dissemination of Newcastle disease. II. Role of wild birds.) *Med. Weterynar.* 16:17, 1960a. Abstr. *Vet. Bull.* 30:449, 1960.

——. Nosicielstwo i siewstwo wirusa rzekomego pomoru drobiu (Newcastle disease). III. Dzdzownice. (Dissemination of Newcastle disease. III. Earthworms.) *Med. Weterynar.* 16:656, 1960b. Abstr. *Vet. Bull.* 31:327, 1961.

Bang, F. B. Pathogenesis in the embryo. In R. P. Hanson, ed., *Newcastle disease virus: An evolving pathogen,* p. 247. Madison: Univ. Wis. Press, 1964.

Beach, J. R. Avian pneumoencephalitis. *Proc. Ann. Meeting U.S. Livestock Sanit. Assoc.* 46:203, 1942.

Beaudette, F. R. A review of the literature on Newcastle disease. *Proc. Ann. Meeting U.S. Livestock Sanit. Assoc.* 47:122, 1943.

Bianchi, E. Sulla natura del virus dell' attuale moria del pollame. (Nature of the poultry disease at present occurring in Italy.) *Clin. Vet.* 64:323, 1941. Abstr. *Vet. Bull.* 13:129, 1943.

Blaxland, J. D. Newcastle disease in shags and cormorants and its significance as a factor in the spread of this disease among domestic poultry. *Vet. Rec.* 65:731, 1951.

Boyd, R. J., and Hanson, R. P. Survival of Newcastle disease virus in nature. *Avian Diseases* 2:82, 1958.

Bradshaw, Judith E. A study of waterfowl disease in the Mississippi flyway. Unpublished M.S. thesis, Univ. Wis., Madison, 1965.

Bradshaw, Judith E., and Trainer, D. O. Some infectious diseases of waterfowl in the Mississippi flyway. *J. Wildlife Management* 30: 570, 1966.

Brandly, C. A. Recognition of Newcastle disease as a new disease. In R. P. Hanson, ed., *Newcastle disease virus: An evolving pathogen.* Madison: Univ. Wis. Press, 1964.

Brandly, C. A., and Hanson, R. P. Newcastle disease. In H. E. Biester and L. M. Schwarte, eds., *Diseases of poultry,* 5th ed. Ames: Iowa State Univ. Press, 1965.

Brandly, C. A., Moses, H. E., Jones, E. Elizabeth, and Jungherr, E. L. Epizootiology of Newcastle disease of poultry. *Am. J. Vet. Res.* 7:243, 1946.

Callander, E. R. Newcastle disease and its control in Great Britain. *Vet. Rec.* 70:907, 1958.

Cavrini, C., and Cabassi, N. Pseudopeste spontanea in pappagalli della specie *Amazona ochrocephala.* (Outbreak of Newcastle disease in parrots.) *Nuovo Vet.* 36:123, 1960. Abstr. *Vet. Bull.* 31:326, 1961.

Chelidze, G. T. Susceptibility of some wild birds to Newcastle disease virus under experimental conditions. *Vopr. Vet. Virus* 1:395. Abstr. *Vet. Bull.* 34:597, 1964.

Collier, W. A., and Dinger, J. E. Research on Newcastle disease 1940–1942. *Doc. neer 1. Ind. Morb. Trop.* 2:189, 1950. Cited in J. E. Lancaster, *Newcastle disease. A review 1926–1964.* Can. Dept. Agr., 1966.

Cooper, H. Ranikhet disease. A new disease of fowls in India due to a filter-passing virus. *Proc. World's Poultry Congr.,* London 4: 489, 1930.

Craig, F. R. Newcastle disease. *Wildlife N.C.* 14(12):17, 1950.

Crawford, M. Ranikhet disease. *Rept. Gov. Vet. Surg. for 1930,* Columbo, Ceylon, p. 47, 1931. Cited in J. E. Lancaster, *Newcastle disease. A review 1926–1964.* Can. Dept. Agr., 1966.

Crowther, R. W. Newcastle disease in Cyprus. *Vet. Rec.* 64:91, 1952.

Cruickshank, J. G. The structure of myxoviruses and its biological significance. In G. E. W. Wolstenholme, ed., *Cellular biology of myxovirus infections.* Boston: Little, Brown, 1964.

Dobson, N. Newcastle disease. *World's Poultry Sci. J.* 8:107, 1952.

Doyle, T. M. A hitherto unrecorded disease of fowls due to a filter-passing virus. *J. Comp. Path.* 40:144, 1927.

Farinas, E. C. Avian pest, a disease of birds hitherto unknown in the Philippine Islands. *Philippine J. Agr.* 1:311, 1930.

Fenstermacher, R., Pomeroy, B. S., and Malmquist, W. A. Newcastle disease in Minnesota. *Proc. Ann. Meeting U.S. Livestock Sanit. Assoc.* 50:151, 1946.

Forbes, A. J., and Row, J. A. Newcastle disease in poultry. *Australian Vet. J.* 42:138, 1966.

Gillespie, J. H., Kessel, B., and Fabricant, S. The isolation of Newcastle disease virus from a starling. *Cornell Vet.* 40:93, 1950.

Gustafson, D. P., and Moses, H. E. Some effects of oral exposure of English sparrows to Newcastle disease virus. *Am. Vet. Res.* 13: 566, 1952a.

———. Some effects of Newcastle disease virus on the English sparrow. *Proc. Am. Vet. Med. Assoc.* 89:147, 1952b.

———. The English sparrow as a natural carrier of Newcastle disease virus. *Am. Vet. Res.* 14:581, 1953a.

———. Wild birds as possible spreaders of Newcastle disease. *Proc. Ann. Meeting Am. Vet. Med. Assoc.,* Toronto 90:281, 1953b.

Haddow, J. R. Ranikhet disease: The present position. *Indian Farming* 2:345, 1941. Cited in J. E. Lancaster, *Newcastle disease. A review 1926–1964.* Can. Dept. Agr., 1966.

Hanson, R. P. Personal communication, 1968.

Hanson, R. P., and Brandly, C. A. Identification of vaccine strains of Newcastle disease virus. *Science* 122:156, 1955.

Hanson, R. P., and Sinha, S. K. Epizootic of Newcastle disease in pigeons and studies on transmission of the virus. *Poultry Sci.* 31:404, 1952.

Hartwigk, H., and Nitsch, G. Zur Frage der Empfanglichkeit von Sperlingen fur atypische geflugelpest (Newcastle disease). (Susceptibility of sparrows to Newcastle disease.) *Berliner Muench. Tieraerztl. Wochschr.* 70:285, 1957. Abstr. *Vet. Bull.* 27:523, 1957.

Heller, V. O. Beitrag zur Epidemiologie der Huehnerpest: Gaense alslatente Virustraeger. (Epidemiology of Newcastle disease: Geese as latent carriers.) *Mh. Vet. Med.* 12:218, 1957.

Hinshaw, W. R. Diseases of the turkey. In H. E. Biester and L. H. Schwarte, *Diseases of poultry,* 5th ed., p. 1253. Ames: Iowa State Univ. Press, 1965.

Hofstad, M. S. A quantitative study of Newcastle disease virus in tissues of infected chickens. *Am. J. Vet. Res.* 12:334, 1951.

Ingalls, W. A., Versper, R. W., and Mahoney. Ann. Isolation of Newcastle disease virus from the great horned owl. *J. Am. Vet. Med. Assoc.* 119:71, 1951.

Iyer, S. G. Paralysis in a pigeon due to Doyle's (Ranikhet) disease virus. *Indian J. Vet. Sci.* 9:379, 1939.

———. The susceptibility of ducks to Newcastle (Ranikhet) disease. *Indian J. Vet. Sci.* 15:165, 1945.

Jansen, J., and Kunst, H. Newcastle disease in peacocks. *J. Am. Vet. Med. Assoc.* 120:201, 1952.

Jansen, J., Kunst, H., VanDorssen, C. A., and Van Der Berg, H. A. Newcastle disease in pheasants from Calcutta. *Tijdschr. Dier-geneesk.* 74:333, 1949. Cited in J. E. Lancaster, *Newcastle disease. A review 1926–1964.* Can. Dept. Agr., 1966.

Jerabek, J. Nekolik poznamek o prubehu moru v chovu drubeze. (Report on an outbreak of Newcastle disease.) *Veterinarstvi* 11:416, 1961. Abstr. *Vet. Bull.* 32:222, 1962.

Jezierski, A. La peste aviaire et la maladie de Newcastle au Congo Belge. (Fowl pest and Newcastle disease in the Belgian Congo.) *Bull. Agr. Congo Belge* 41:141, 1950.

Jones, M. B. Fowl pest (Newcastle disease) in pheasants. In B. W. deCourcy-Ireland, ed., *The Game Research Association/Annual report for 1963, 1964.*

Jungherr, E. L. Pathogenicity of Newcastle disease virus for the chicken. In R. P. Hanson, ed., *Newcastle disease virus: An evolving pathogen,* p. 257. Madison: Univ. Wis. Press, 1964.

Jungherr, E. L., Tyzzer, E. E., Brandly, C. A., and Moses, H. E. The comparative pathology of fowl plague and Newcastle disease. *Am. J. Vet. Res.* 7:250, 1946.

Karstad, L., Spalatin, J., and Hanson, R. P. Experimental infection of wild birds with the viruses of eastern equine encephalitis, Newcastle disease and vesicular stomatitis. *J. Infect. Diseases* 105:188, 1959.

Karzon, D. T., and Bang, F. B. The pathogenesis of infection with a virulent (Cg 179) and an avirulent (B) strain of Newcastle disease virus in the chicken. I. Comparative rates of viral multiplication. *J. Exptl. Med.* 93:267, 1951.

Kaschula, V. R. The epizootiology of Newcastle disease and its control by vaccination. *J. S. African Vet. Med. Assoc.* 21:134, 1950.

———. The domestic pigeon as a possible carrier of Newcastle disease. *Onderstepoort J. Vet. Res.* 25:25, 1952.

Kauker, E., and Siegert, R. Newcastle-Virus-Infektion beim Afrikanischen Strauss (*Struthio camelus* L.), Zwerggansegeier (*Pseudogyps africanus* Salvad.) und Bunttukan (*Ramphastos dicolorus* L.). (Newcastle disease in ostriches, vultures and toucans in a zoological garden.) *Mh. Tierheilk.* 9:64, 1957. Abstr. *Vet. Bull.* 28:76, 1958.

Kee, F. G. Notes on an outbreak of poultry epidemic. *Philippine Agriculturist* 17:263; 74:1140, 1928.

Keymer, I. F. A survey and review of the causes of mortality in British birds and the significance of wild birds as disseminators of disease. Part III. *Vet. Rec.* 70:736, 1958.

———. Newcastle disease in the jackdaw (*Corvus monedula*). *Vet. Rec.* 73:119, 1961.

Kloppel, G. Newcastle disease in ostriches.

Kleintier-Praxis 8:10, 1963. Abstr. *Vet. Bull.* 33:563, 1963.

Kraneveld, F. C., and Mansjoer, M. Newcastle disease. Wild birds as a source of infection. *Hemera Zoa.* 57:166, 1950a. Cited in S. E. Lancaster, *Newcastle disease. A review 1926–1964.* Can. Dept Agr., 1966.

———. Twee mogelijkheden tot besmetting van pluimveebedrijven met pseudovogelpest. (Newcastle disease. Wild birds as a source of infection.) *Hemera Zoa.* 57:166, 1950b. Abstr. *Vet. Bull.* 21:366, 1951.

Krauss, H., Paulick, C., Huchzermeyer, F., and Gylstorff, I. Newcastle disease in a king penguin. *Deut. Tierarztl. Wochschr.* 70:307, 1963. Abstr. *Vet. Bull.* 34:27, 1964.

Lancaster, J. E. *Newcastle disease. A review 1926–1964.* Can. Dept. Agr., 1966.

Levine, P. P. World dissemination of Newcastle disease. In R. P. Hanson, ed., *Newcastle disease virus: An evolving pathogen,* p. 65. Madison: Univ. Wis. Press, 1964.

Levine, P. P., Fabricant, J., and Mitchell, G. B. Newcastle disease in ring-necked pheasants. *Cornell Vet.* 37:265, 1947.

Liebengood, D. M. Avian pneumoencephalitis in pheasants. *Vet. Med.* 44:443, 1949.

Locke, R. D. Newcastle disease in pheasants. British Ministry of Agriculture, Fisheries and Food. (Unpublished report.) 1960. Cited in J. E. Lancaster, *Newcastle disease. A review 1926–1964.* Can. Dept. Agr., 1966.

Lucas, A., and Laroche, M. La maladie de Newcastle chez la perdrix (pseudo-peste aviaire). (Newcastle disease in partridges.) *Rec. Med. Vet.* 134:162, 1958. Abstr. *Vet. Bull.* 28:645, 1958.

McDiarmid, A. Modern trends in animal health and husbandry. Some infectious diseases of free-living wildlife. *Brit. Vet. J.* 121:245, 1965.

MacPherson, L. W. Some observations on the epizootiology of Newcastle disease. *Can. J. Comp. Med.* 20:155, 1956.

Maglione, E. Ricerche sulla pseudopeste aviare nel passero. Rapporti fral'infezione pseudopestosa notr dei passeri e la pseudopeste dei polli. (Newcastle disease in sparrows. Relationship between the infection in sparrows and in fowls.) *Ann. Fac. Med. Vet. Torino* 6:63, 1956. Abstr. *Vet. Bull.* 27:577, 1957.

Mansjoer, M. Newcastle disease in Indonesia. I. Its present situation, epizootiology and combat. *Commun. Vet. Bogor.* 5:1, 1961. In J. E. Lancaster, *Newcastle disease. A review 1926–1964.* Can. Dept. Agr., 1966.

Mantovani, G., and Ceretto, F. Osservazioni sulle forme morbose della selvaggina in Piemonte. (Causes of death amongst wild animals and birds in the Piedmont region of Italy.) *Atti. Soc. Ital. Sci. Vet.* Sanremo 1952, 6:571, 1953. Abstr. *Vet. Bull.* 25:80, 1955.

Marastoni, G., and Sidoli, L. Un focolaio di pseudo-peste spontanea nel piccione. (An outbreak of Newcastle disease in pigeons.) *Vet. Ital.* 10:349, 1959. Abstr. *Vet. Bull.* 29: 686, 1959.

Martini, I., and Kurjana, R. Newcastle disease (Pseudovogelpest). Experiments on an attenuated Indonesian virus. *Hemera Zoa.* 57: 557, 1950. Cited in J. E. Lancaster, *Newcastle disease. A review 1926-1964.* Can. Dept. Agr., 1966.

Methods for the Examination of Poultry Biologics, 2nd ed. (revised). Rept. Poultry Disease Subcommittee on Animal Health, Agr. Bd., Div. Biol. and Agr., Nat. Acad. Sci., Nat. Res. Council, Washington, D.C. Publ. 1038, 1963.

Monda, V., Tanga, G., and Guarino, C. Antigenic properties of Newcastle disease virus isolated from a sparrow and a canary. *Atti. Soc. Ital. Sci. Vet.* 14:736, 1960. Cited in J. E. Lancaster, *Newcastle disease. A review 1926–1964.* Can. Dept. Agr., 1966.

Moses, H. E., and Gustafson, D. P. Review work with Newcastle disease. *Ann. Rept.,* Lafayette, Indiana: Purdue Univ. Agr. Exp. Sta. 65:71, 1952.

Moses, H. E., Brandly, C. A., and Jones, E. E. The pH stability of the viruses of Newcastle disease and fowl plague. *Science* 105:477, 1947.

Moynihan, I. W., Landon, G. I., and McMillan, R. H. Newcastle disease in British Columbia. *Proc. 9th World's Poultry Congr.* 3:108, 1951.

Olesiuk, O. M. Influence of environmental factors on viability of Newcastle disease virus. *Am. J. Vet. Res.* 12:152, 1951.

Orr, W., and John, K. T. A Malayan virus of fowls. *Vet. Rec.* 58:117, 1946.

Page, C. A. Antibody response of the Canada goose to the Newcastle disease virus. *Avian Diseases* 2:365, 1958.

Palmer, S. F. Some potential pathogens of Canada geese. Unpublished M.S. thesis. Univ. Wis., Madison.

Parnaik, D. T., and Dixit, S. G. Ranikhet disease in Indian partridges. *Indian Vet. J.* 30: 145, 1953. Cited in J. E. Lancaster, *Newcastle disease. A review 1926-1964.* Can. Dept. Agr., 1966.

Picard, W. K. Pseudo-fowl pest. *Veeartsenijkundige Mededeeling* 65:1, 1928. Cited in J. E. Lancaster, *Newcastle disease. A review 1926–1964.* Can. Dept. Agr., 1966.

Placidi, L., and Santucci, J. Sur la receptivite de certaines especes au virus de la maladie de Newcastle. (Susceptibility of various species of birds to Newcastle disease.) *Ann. Inst. Pasteur* 84:588, 1953. Abstr. *Vet. Bull.* 24: 71, 1954.

———. Observations epidemiologiques sur la maladie de Newcastle. Evolution de l'infection dans un parc zoologique. (Epidemiology of Newcastle disease in a zoological garden.) *Bull. Acad. Vet. France* 27:255, 1954. Abstr. *Vet. Bull.* 25:171, 1955.

Pomeroy, B. S., and Fenstermacher, R. Newcastle disease is spreading. *U.S. Egg and Poultry Mag.* 54:18, 1948.

Popovic, B. Pigeons and sparrows and the spread of Newcastle disease. *Acta Vet. Belgrade* 1:168, 1951. Abstr. *Vet. Bull.* 23:414, 1953.

Purchase, H. S. An atypical fowl plague virus from Egypt. *J. Comp. Pathol.* 44:71, 1931.

Quortrup, E. R., Goetz, M. E., Dunsing, J. W., and Rosen, M. N. Studies on the incidence of poultry diseases in wild ducks. *Calif. Fish Game* 43:139, 1957.

Reid, J. Fowl pest. *Agriculture,* London 61:465. 1955.

———. The control of Newcastle disease in Great Britain. *Brit. Vet. J.* 117:275, 1961.

Reuss, U. Die Empfanglichkeit der Haustauben fuer die Atypische Gefluegelpest. (Susceptibility of pigeons to Newcastle disease.) *Mh. Tierheilk.* 13:153, 1961a. Abstr. *Vet. Bull.* 31:711, 1961.

———. Role of pigeons in the dissemination of Newcastle disease. *Arch. Gefluegelk.* 25:398, 1961b.

Roslein, D. J. Incidence of disease antibodies in pheasants and pheasant management on game farms and shooting preserves in Iowa. Unpublished Ph.D. dissertation. Iowa State Univ., Ames, 1966.

Rotov, V. I., Litvrishko, N. T., Dunaev, G. V., Gonchazov, A. P., Nazarenko, E. N., Dashkevich, S. M. Poultry tick—*Dermanyssus gallinae*—as vector of the Newcastle disease virus. *Vopr. Vet. Virusol.* 1:397, 1964.

Sahai, L. Doyle's disease of fowls: Its diagnosis and control. *Agr. Livestock India* 7(Part 1): 11, 1937a.

———. The diagnosis and control of Doyle's disease (Newcastle disease) of fowls. *Proc. Animal Husb. Res. Workers Conf., India, 1936,* p. 64; discussion, p. 69, 1937b.

Schoop, G., Siegert, R., Glassi, D., and Kloppel, G. Newcastle-Infektionen beim Steinkauz *(Athene noctura),* Hornraben *(Bucorvus* sp.), Seeadler *(Haliaetus albicilla)* und Rieseneisvogel *(Dacelo gigas).* (Newcastle disease in the little owl, raven, white-tailed eagle and giant kingfisher in a zoological garden.) *Mh. Tierheilk.* 7:223, 1955. Abstr. *Vet. Bull.* 26: 272, 1956.

Schyns, P., and Florent, A. Does the pigeon play any part in spreading fowl pest amongst poultry? *Proc. 9th World's Poultry Congr.,* Paris 3:14, 1951.

Scott, G. R., and Winmill, A. J. Newcastle disease in the grey parrot *(Psittacus erithacus* L.). *J. Comp. Pathol. Therap.* 70:115, 1960.

Seetharaman, C. Ranikhet (Newcastle) disease. Review of work done, with special reference to vaccination, at the Indian veterinary research institute, Mukteswar-Kumaun, U-P. *Indian Vet. J.* 37:331, 1951.

Shah, K. V., and Johnson, H. N. Isolation of Ranikhet (Newcastle) virus from a fledgeling koel, *Eudynamis scolopaceus s.* (Linnaeus), by intracerebral inoculation in mice. *Indian J. Med. Res.* 47:604, 1959.

Sinha, S. K., Hanson, R. P., and Brandly, C. A. Comparison of the tropisms of six strains of Newcastle disease virus in chickens following aerosol infection. *J. Infect. Diseases* 91: 276, 1952.

Skoda, R., and Zuffa, A. Newcastelska choroba u bazantov. (Newcastle disease in pheasants.) *Vet. Casopis* 5:441, 1956. Abstr. *Vet. Bull.* 27:466, 1957.

Thompson, C. H., Jr. Virulent foreign Newcastle disease in partridges. *Vet. Med.* 50:399, 1955.

Torlone, V. Studio di due ceppi di virus della pseudopeste isolati dal fagiano *(Phasianus colchicus)* e dalla starna *(Perdix perdix).* (Strains of Newcastle disease virus from the pheasant and partridge.) *Vet. Ital.* 5:107, 1954. Abstr. *Vet. Bull.* 24:559, 1954.

Toth, B., Molnar, I., and Vass, G. Susceptibility of pheasants to Newcastle disease and the possibility of immunizing them with LaSota vaccine. *Magy. Allatorv. Lapja* 21:271, 1966. Abstr. *Vet. Bull.* 37:306, 1967.

Tropilo, J. Newcastle disease in partridges and pheasants. *Med. Weterynar.* 20:164, 1964.

Ulbrich, F., and Sodan, U. Natural infection in pigeons with Newcastle disease virus. *Mh. Vet. Med.* 20:340, 1965. Abstr. *Vet. Bull.* 35: 774, 1965.

Uzieblo, B. Pomor vzekomy ptakow w bazaniarni w wojewodztwie szczecinskim. (Newcastle disease in a pheasant farm.) *Med. Weterynar.* 17:587, 1961.

Vadlamudi, S., and Hanson, R. P. Invasion of the brain of chicken by Newcastle disease virus. *Avian Diseases* 10:122, 1966.

Vrtiak, J. Epizootologicke zvlastnosti Newcastlskej choroby na vychodnom slovensku. *Sb. Cesk. Akad. Zemedel. Ved.* 31(3):437, 1958.

Walker, R. V. L., McKercher, P. D., and Bannister, G. L. Studies in Newcastle disease.

VII. The possible role of the pigeon as a carrier. *Can. J. Comp. Med.* 18:244, 1954.

Waterson, A. P. The morphology and composition of Newcastle disease virus. In R. P. Hanson, ed., *Newcastle disease virus: An evolving pathogen,* p. 119. Madison: Univ. Wis. Press, 1964.

Weidenmuller, M., and Osthoff, F. Untersuchungen ueber die Atypische Huehnerpest beim Fasan. (Newcastle disease in pheasants.) *Zentr. Vet. Med.* 1:105, 1953.

Wilson, J. E. Newcastle disease in a gannet *(Sula bassana).* A preliminary note. *Vet. Rec.* 62:33, 1950.

Winmill, A. J., and Haig, D. A. Observations on Newcastle disease in Kenya. *Bull. Epizoot. Diseases Africa* 9:365, 1961.

Winmill, A. J., and Weddell, W. A Newcastle disease vaccine inactivated by beta-propiolactone. *Res. Vet. Sci.* 2:381, 1961.

Zuydam, D. M. Pseudovogelpest (Newcastle disease) bij in nederland geimporteerde fazanten. (Newcastle disease in imported pheasants.) *Tijdschr. Diergeneesk.* 74:481, 1949. Abstr. *Vet. Bull.* 21:366, 1951.

———. Pseudovogelpest (Newcastle disease) bij in nederland geimporteerde fazanten. (Newcastle disease in imported pheasants in the Netherlands.) *Tijdschr. Diergeneesk.* 75:158, 1950. Abstr. *Vet. Bull.* 21:616, 1951.

———. Isolation of Newcastle disease virus from the osprey and the parakeet. *J. Am. Vet. Med. Assoc.* 120:88, 1952.

2 ◆ ARBOVIRUSES

● LARS KARSTAD

As a GENERAL RULE, overt disease associated with arbovirus infection is uncommon in birds. The American arboviruses, eastern encephalitis virus (EEV), and western encephalitis virus (WEV) cause illness and fatal infections in several species of introduced birds, while species indigenous to the Americas generally carry infections without signs of disease. This is, apparently, an example of host-parasite adaptation, the end result of ages of natural selection.

EASTERN ENCEPHALITIS VIRUS

◆ **HISTORY.** Although the natural occurrence of EEV in birds had been predicted earlier, it was not until 1938 that Tyzzer and his associates proved infection by the isolation of EEV from a pheasant *(Phasianus colchicus)* and Fothergill and Dingle (1938) isolated EEV from a domestic pigeon *(Columba livia)*. Fatal EEV infections have now been seen also in chukar partridges *(Alectoris graeca)* and domestic white Pekin ducklings (Luginbuhl et al., 1958; Dougherty and Price, 1960; Moulthrop and Gordy, 1960).

Infections, both natural and experimental, and usually subclinical, have been reported in a very large number of indigenous birds. The information on such infections up to 1963 was reviewed by Stamm (1963). He listed 51 species of wild birds in which infection has been detected or induced experimentally.

◆ **DISTRIBUTION.** The geographic distribution of EEV is known to include eastern North America, Central America, and several South American countries, particularly areas bordering the Caribbean Sea.

◆ **ETIOLOGY AND TRANSMISSION.** EEV is a member of arbovirus group A (Wilner, 1965). It is transmitted in nature by several species of vector mosquitoes. The most important biological vector among birds is *Culiseta melanura,* a swamp-breeding mosquito with definite preference for bird blood.[1] Epizootics occur only in the summer and autumn. It has been suggested that overwintering and interepizootic survival of EEV may occur in freshwater swamps of the southeastern United States, where *Culiseta melanura* breeds and where mild winter weather permits vector transmission among resident wild birds. Several other species of mosquitoes, particularly *Aedes* spp., have been shown to be able to act as biological vectors of EEV, probably transmitting the virus from swamp-dwelling birds to birds which frequent farm and urban areas, and from these birds to horses and man. Extensive outbreaks in horses, man, and pheasants have occurred following hurricanes along the Atlantic coast. These storms increase the number of surface pools for mosquito breeding and often blow large numbers of salt-marsh mosquitoes far inland.

Transmission among flocks of penned birds, such as pheasants, may occur through the cannibalistic habits which the birds develop. In outbreaks investigated in Connecticut, feather-picking by penned pheasants was believed to be an important means of bird-to-bird transmission (Satri-

---

For a general discussion of arboviruses, see Karstad (1970) and Casals and Reeves (1965).

1. Biological vectors are those which support multiplication of a virus, as opposed to mechanical vectors which do not become infected but are merely contaminated with the virus.

ano et al., 1958). In the same studies EEV was found in the feces of infected pheasants. Karstad et al. (1959) found EEV in the feces of crows (Corvus brachyrhynchos) infected by feeding upon infected chicken embryos. Pen contact was found to be sufficient for transmission among infected ducklings (Dougherty and Price, 1960).

Wild birds are considered to be an important reservoir of EEV, from which infection is disseminated to horses and man during epidemics. Because of the transient nature of infection in birds, however, and because of the regularity of appearance of EEV in summer epizootics in northern areas, a search was made among reptiles for sources of EEV (see also comments on western encephalitis in garter snakes on page 19). Antibody to EEV was found among reptiles of 5 species in Georgia, and snakes, turtles, lizards, and alligators were found susceptible to infection (Karstad, 1961; Hayes et al., 1964). Reptiles should be studied further as possible overwintering reservoirs of EEV.

◆ **SIGNS.** EEV in birds may vary from clinically inapparent to fatal infections. In cases in which the virus successfully invades the central nervous system, affected birds become depressed and lethargic and show incoordination, paralysis, and abnormal postures, especially of the head and neck. Tremors are sometimes seen and torticollis is a common sign. Some birds show head retraction, retropulsion, or circling (Jungherr et al., 1958). In some cases the only signs are profound depression, leading to coma and death.

It must be understood that severity of clinical signs bears no relationship to the success or failure of EEV to invade and multiply. Many indigenous species of birds are highly susceptible to infection and may circulate virus in high titer in their bloodstreams for several days without showing any signs of illness (Kissling et al., 1954). Such birds are of the greatest epizootiological importance, since they provide large quantities of infected blood for vector transmission, yet they remain normally mobile and may transport the virus long distances. Introduced species of birds, on the other hand, such as pheasants and pigeons, usually suffer severe, frequently fatal infections.

◆ **PATHOLOGY.** The major lesions caused by EEV are those of nonsuppurative encephalitis. They consist of vasculitis, focal or patchy necrosis, perivascular leukocyte infiltrations, swelling and proliferation of glial cells, meningitis and degeneration, and necrosis of neurones (Jungherr et al., 1958). These changes are not specific for EEV and therefore are of limited diagnostic value.

◆ **DIAGNOSIS.** Diagnosis is based on isolation and identification of the virus or demonstration of a rise in specific serum antibody during convalescence (Hammon, 1956).

For isolation of virus, either blood taken during the stage of viremia or a suspension of brain tissues may be inoculated into the allantoic chambers of embryonating hens' eggs, intracerebrally inoculated into suckling or weanling laboratory mice, or inoculated into susceptible cell cultures —for example, cultures of chicken embryo fibroblasts. Presence of EEV will cause deaths of chicken embryos and mice and marked cytopathic effects in cell cultures. Bacterial contamination must be minimized. When it occurs, bacteria must either be inhibited by addition of antibiotics to the inocula or removed by filtration procedures. Viral isolates are identified by neutralization with specific antisera (Hammon, 1956).

◆ **IMMUNITY.** Birds which survive EEV infection become solidly immune. Hemagglutination-inhibiting (HI), complement-fixing (CF), and virus-neutralizing (VN) antibodies can be demonstrated. CF antibodies persist for several weeks; VN antibodies persist for months or years.

Vaccines prepared from infected chicken embryos, which are commercially available for vaccination of horses, may be used to vaccinate pheasants. One-half ml of vaccine injected into the breast muscles was shown to stimulate immunity to subsequent challenge with a virulent inoculum. Use of vaccine would be indicated to stop outbreaks among penned pheasants. In Wisconsin, vaccination has been used in attempts to improve the survival rate of pen-reared pheasants released for hunting.

◆ **CONTROL.** Control is based on attempts to break the cycle of vector transmission from reservoir species to other susceptible birds. Control of vectors should be aimed at drainage or destruction of mosquito-breeding sites, screening of pens or houses, and if necessary, use of chemical insecticides. Control of indigenous wild birds, which may become infected and serve as amplifier hosts without showing signs of disease, is usually difficult or impractical. Apart from this, destruction of indigenous wild birds to protect susceptible introduced species could not be defended as sound conservation practice.

WESTERN (EQUINE) ENCEPHALITIS VIRUS

◆ **HISTORY.** Western encephalitis virus (WEV) was first isolated in California in 1930 from the brains of horses with encephalitis (Meyer et al., 1931). In 1938 both EEV and WEV were proved by virus isolation to be causes of fatal human encephalitis (Fothergill et al., 1938; Howitt, 1938). In 1941 Cox and his associates isolated WEV from a naturally infected prairie chicken *(Tympanuchus cupido)* during a field investigation of encephalitis in horses and man in North Dakota. Since that time it has been repeatedly isolated from many species of wild birds. Stamm (1963) lists 52 avian species in which natural or experimental infections have been demonstrated.

◆ **DISTRIBUTION.** Until 1953 it was thought that WEV was largely restricted to parts of North America west of the Mississippi River. In 1953, however, and again in 1956, isolations of WEV were made from birds in New Jersey (Holden, 1955; Dardiri et al., 1957; Stamm, 1958). WEV occurs also in parts of South America, notably in Argentina, where it was first isolated in 1933.

◆ **ETIOLOGY AND TRANSMISSION.** Like EEV, WEV is a member of arborvirus group A. Several species of mosquitoes are known to be able to serve as biological vectors. The most important vector of WEV, judging from numbers of virus isolations from field-caught mosquitoes, is *Culex tarsalis*. *Culex tarsalis* feeds readily on both birds and mammals; thus it is able to transmit WEV from wild birds, the important reservoirs of WEV in epizootics, to man and horses, species which are "dead-end hosts." In the laboratory, *Culex tarsalis* has been observed to transmit EEV from infected chickens to garter snakes and back to chickens again. Garter snakes *(Thamnophis* spp.) are considered to be potential overwintering reservoirs of WEV (Thomas and Eklund, 1960; Spalatin et al., 1964).

Birds are generally considered to be unable to carry WEV for long periods of time, since they usually have pronounced but brief viremia, followed by a prompt and enduring antibody response. Reeves et al. (1958), however, were able to demonstrate chronic latent WEV infections in several birds.

◆ **SIGNS.** WEV infections in wild birds are usually clinically inapparent. It is probable that natural WEV infections can on occasion result in severe encephalitis and death. Johnson (1960) reported isolations of WEV from 15 sparrow nestlings *(Passer domesticus),* 3 of which were found dead in the nest. Faddoul and Fellows (1965) reported isolation of WEV from the brain of a dead impeyan pheasant in Massachusetts.

◆ **PATHOLOGY.** The lesions produced by WEV are similar to those of EEV, constituting acute nonsuppurative encephalitis. Such changes are not specific for WEV and are therefore of limited diagnostic value.

◆ **DIAGNOSIS.** Diagnosis is usually based upon isolation and identification of the virus. Early in the disease, virus may be found in the blood; later, the brain is a more dependable source of virus. Blood or brain suspensions are inoculated intracerebrally into suckling or weanling mice, embryonating eggs, or susceptible cell cultures, such as cultures of chicken embryo fibroblasts. The specific viral effects—that is, death of mice or embryos, or cytopathic effects in cell cultures—must be neutralized with specific WEV antiserum in order to confirm the presence of WEV.

Diagnosis of WEV infection in nonfatal cases can sometimes be made serologically by demonstration of marked elevation in titers of specific antibody in paired sera collected during the acute and convalescent phases of the disease (Hammon, 1956).

◆ **CONTROL.** Control of WEV is possible by any of three methods:

1. Limiting the numbers of susceptible hosts by vaccination. Effective vaccines have been developed for horses and man.
2. Limiting the populations of vector mosquitoes. This is most satisfactorily accomplished by destruction of breeding sites or, in the case of captive birds, by screening. Chemical insecticides may be used.
3. Limiting the numbers of reservoir hosts. This is usually most difficult, since one is dealing with free-flying wild birds. From the conservation point of view it is distasteful, and should be a last resort for control of WEV.

◆ **REFERENCES**

Casals, J., and Reeves, W. C. The arboviruses. In F. L. Horsfall and I. Tamm, eds., *Viral and rickettsial infections of man,* 4th ed., p. 580. Philadelphia: J. B. Lippincott, 1965.

Cox, H. R., Jellison, W. L., and Hughes, L. E. Isolation of western equine encephalomye- litis virus from a naturally infected prairie chicken. *Public Health Rept.* 56:1905, 1941.

Dardiri, A. H., Yates, V. J., Chang, P. W., Wheatley, G. H., and Fry, D. E. The isolation of eastern equine encephalomyelitis virus from brains of sparrows. *J. Am. Vet. Med. Assoc.* 130:409, 1957.

Dougherty, E., and Price, J. I. Eastern encephalitis in white Pekin ducklings on Long Island. *Avian Diseases* 4:247, 1960.

Faddoul, G. P., and Fellows, G. W. Clinical manifestations of eastern equine encephalomyelitis in pheasants. *Avian Diseases* 9:530, 1965.

Fothergill, L. D., and Dingle, J. H. A fatal disease of pigeons caused by the virus of the eastern variety of equine encephalomyelitis. *Science* 88:549, 1938.

Fothergill, L. D., Dingle, J. H., Farber, S., and Connerley, M. L. Human encephalitis caused by the virus of the eastern variety of equine encephalomyelitis. *New Engl. J. Med.* 219: 411, 1938.

Hammon, W. McD. Encephalitis. In *Diagnostic procedures for virus and rickettsial diseases,* 2nd ed., p. 169. New York: Am. Public Health Assoc., 1956.

Hayes, R. O., Daniels, J. B., Maxfield, H. K., and Wheeler, R. E. Field and laboratory studies on eastern encephalitis in warm- and cold-blooded vertebrates. *Am. J. Trop. Med. Hyg.* 13:595, 1964.

Holden, P. Recovery of western equine encephalomyelitis virus from naturally infected English sparrows of New Jersey, 1953. *Proc. Soc. Exptl. Biol. Med.* 88:490, 1955.

Howitt, B. Recovery of the virus of equine encephalomyelitis from the brain of a child. *Science* 88:455, 1938.

Johnson, H. Public health in relation to birds: Arthropod-borne viruses. *Trans. 25th N. Am. Wildlife Conf.,* p. 121, 1960.

Jungherr, E. L., Helmboldt, C. F., Satriano, S. F., and Luginbuhl, R. E. Investigation of eastern equine encephalomyelitis. III. Pathology in pheasants and incidental observations in feral birds. *Am. J. Hyg.* 67:10, 1958.

Karstad, L. Reptiles as possible reservoir hosts for eastern encephalitis virus. *Trans. 26th N. Am. Wildlife Conf.,* p. 186, 1961.

——. Arboviruses. In Davis et al., eds., *Infectious diseases of wild mammals.* Ames: Iowa State University Press, 1970.

Karstad, L., Spalatin, J., and Hanson, R. P. Experimental infections of wild birds with the viruses of eastern equine encephalitis, Newcastle disease and vesicular stomatitis. *J. Infect. Diseases* 105:188, 1959.

Kissling, R. E., Chamberlain, R. W., Sikes, R. K., and Eidson, M. E. Studies on the

North American arthropod-borne encephalitides. III. Eastern equine encephalitis in wild birds. *Am. J. Hyg.* 60:251, 1954.

Luginbuhl, R. E., Satriano, S. F., Helmboldt, C. F., Lamson, A. L., and Jungherr, E. L. Investigation of eastern equinine encephalomyelitis. II. Outbreaks in Connecticut pheasants. *Am. J. Hyg.* 67:4, 1958.

Meyer, K. F., Haring, C. M., and Howitt, B. The etiology of epizootic encephalomyelitis of horses in the San Joaquin Valley, 1930. *Science* 74:227, 1931.

Moulthrop, I. M., and Gordy, B. A. Eastern viral encephalomyelitis in chukar (*Alectoris graeca*). *Avian Diseases* 4:380, 1960.

Reeves, W. C., Hutson, G. A., Bellamy, R. E., and Scrivani, R. P. Chronic latent infections of birds with western equine encephalomyelitis virus. *Proc. Soc. Exptl. Biol. Med.* 97:733, 1958.

Satriano, S. F., Luginbuhl, R. E., Wallis, R. C., Jungherr, E. L., and Williamson, L. Q. Investigation of eastern equine encephalomyelitis. IV. Susceptibility and transmission studies with virus of pheasant origin. *Am. J. Hyg.* 67:21, 1958.

Spalatin, J., Connell, R., Burton, A. N., and Gollop, B. J. Western equine encephalitis in Saskatchewan reptiles and amphibians, 1961–1963. *Can. J. Comp. Med. Vet. Sci.* 28:131, 1964.

Stamm, D. D. Studies on the ecology of equine encephalomyelitis. *Am. J. Public Health* 48:328, 1958.

———. Susceptibility of bird populations to eastern, western and St. Louis encephalitis viruses. *Proc. 13th Intern. Ornithological Congr.*, p. 591, 1963.

Thomas, L. A., and Eklund, C. M. Over-wintering of western equine encephalomyelitis virus in experimentally infected garter snakes and transmission by mosquitoes. *Proc. Soc. Exptl. Biol. Med.* 105:52, 1960.

Tyzzer, E. E., Sellards, A. W., and Bennett, B. L. The occurrence in nature of equine encephalomyelitis in the ring-necked pheasant. *Science* 88:505, 1938.

Wilner, B. I. *A classification of the major groups of human and other animal viruses,* 3rd ed. Minneapolis: Burgess, 1965.

3 ◆ DUCK PLAGUE

● LOUIS LEIBOVITZ

SYNONYMS: Duck virus enteritis, Dutch duck plague, eendenpest, peste du canard, entenpest.

DUCK PLAGUE is an acute, contagious herpesvirus infection of ducks, geese, and swans that is characterized by vascular damage with tissue hemorrhages and free blood in the body cavities, enanthematous lesions of the digestive mucosal surface, lesions of the lymphoid organs, and retrograde changes of the parenchymatous organs.

◆ HISTORY AND DISTRIBUTION.

Because of the similarity of the lesions of this disease to fowl plague, early outbreaks in the Netherlands were diagnosed as the latter disease. Baudet in 1923 and DeZeeuw in 1930 reported outbreaks of a disease that probably were duck plague. In 1942 Bos concluded that these outbreaks were not fowl plague but a new specific viral infection of ducks. These observations were further supported by more detailed studies of Jansen and Kunst (1949a, 1949b). Since recognition of the disease, Jansen and Jansen et al. have published extensively on their observations, experimental studies, virus propagation, and incidence, pathology, and immunity of the disease.

Duck plague has been suspected in France (Lucam, 1949) and China (Jansen and Kunst, 1964). It has been confirmed in Belgium (Devos, 1964) and India (Mukerji et al., 1963a, 1963b). In 1967 the first reported outbreak on the American continent was observed in white Pekin ducks in the concentrated duck-producing area of Long Island (Leibovitz and Hwang, 1968b).

Since this report, the disease has been detected on 12 other commercial duck farms on Long Island (Urban, 1968). In addition, outbreaks in wild, free-flying waterfowl on Long Island have occurred at seven different locations (Leibovitz, 1968; Leibovitz and Hwang, 1968a). The disease has also been detected at two localities in central New York State (Peckham, 1968), one in Pennsylvania (Locke, 1968), and one in Maryland (Locke, 1968). Whether these reports represent extension of an emerging exotic infection or previous unreported enzootic infection on the American continent is unknown.

◆ ETIOLOGY.

The duck plague virus has been classified in the herpesvirus group. The mature virus particle has an outer diameter of approximately 180 mμ and a dense DNA inner core of about 75 mμ. The virus develops initially as intranuclear particles that mature and move into the cytoplasm and extracellular spaces (Breese and Dardiri, 1968).

Although duck plague virus can be adapted by serial passage to grow in embryonated chicken eggs, primary isolation of the virus cannot be made in this medium. Initial isolation can best be made by cultivation of the virus on the chorioallantoic membrane of 12-day-old embryonated duck eggs (Jansen, 1949). The virus has also been propagated in duck embryo cell cultures (Kunst, 1967; Dardiri and Hess, 1968).

A variation in the degree of virulence has been noted in selected strains of virus; however, all strains appear interrelated and are neutralized by specific antisera for any given strain. The virus appears immunologically distinct from all other avian viruses, including those of Newcastle disease, fowl plague, and duck virus hepatitis. The virus does not produce hemagglutination or hemadsorption. Inactivation of the agent occurs in 10 minutes at 56° to 60° C, and in 2 hours at 50° C. At room temperature infectivity is lost in 30 days. The virus has been found to be stable at a pH range of 5 to 9, and inactivated at a pH of 3 and 11 (Dardiri et al., 1967).

◆ **TRANSMISSION.** Duck plague can be transmitted directly by contact between infected and susceptible birds, and indirectly by contact with a contaminated environment. Since waterfowl are dependent upon an aquatic medium that provides a common vehicle for feeding, drinking, and body support, water appears to be the natural medium of transmission of the virus from infected to susceptible individuals. Support of this concept is found in the history of new outbreaks of the disease in domestic ducks which have been limited to birds having access to open bodies of water cohabited by wild, free-flying waterfowl. Once infection is established, however, it can be maintained in the absence of open water or infected birds, if susceptible populations are moved into recently contaminated premises.

New loci of infection can be established by the movement of infected waterfowl onto bodies of water previously free of virus contamination. Once virus dispersion occurs, environmental contamination can be increased and sustained by the recycling of infection through new susceptible populations that arrive at the infected aquatic premises. Accordingly, the course and duration of the infection is defined by population densities and the rate of transmission between infected and susceptible waterfowl. Since selected anseriform population densities are comparable to those of domestication, the potential of mass and sustained infection in large migrating flights of waterfowl should be considered.

The disease can be transmitted experimentally via the oral, intranasal, intravenous, intraperitoneal, intramuscular, and cloacal routes of administration. Potential transmission by bloodsucking arthropods is suggested by the viremic character of the disease.

In the Netherlands a higher incidence was noted in the spring of the year (Jansen, 1963); however, in the concentrated white Pekin duck-producing area of Long Island, no seasonal increase was noted. A higher incidence, in wild, free-flying Anseriformes on Long Island was noted in the fall of the year 1967 (Leibovitz, 1968).

◆ **HOSTS.** To date, reported susceptibility to duck plague has been limited to members of the family Anatidae (ducks, geese, and swans) of the order Anseriformes. Because the virus can be adapted by serial passage to grow in embryonating chicken eggs and even chickens up to 2 weeks of age, Jansen (1964a, 1964b) suggests a wider host range than reported. Natural outbreaks of the disease have been noted in a variety of domestic ducks *(Anas platyrhynchos domesticus)*, including the white Pekin, Khaki Campbell, Indian runner, hybrids, and native ducks of mixed breeding. Grey call ducks have been found resistant to lethal infection (Van Dorssen and Kunst, 1955). Outbreaks have been noted in muscovy ducks *(Cairina moschata)* and domestic geese *(Anser anser domesticus)* (Jansen and Wemmenhove, 1965).

Because domestic ducks are maintained in large numbers in concentrated duck-producing areas by economically concerned individuals, surveillance for the presence and diagnosis of duck diseases is constantly in effect. Accordingly, the comparative reported incidence of duck plague in domestic ducks to that of wild waterfowl may be misleading. An appraisal of the importance of this disease to wild waterfowl has not been made.

Van Dorssen and Kunst (1955) studied the susceptibility of various species of Anseriformes to duck plague (Table 3.1). The first reported outbreaks of the spontaneous disease in wild waterfowl were noted in the state of New York on Long Island (Leibovitz and Hwang, 1968a; Leibovitz, 1968).

TABLE 3.1. Reported Susceptibility of Members of the Order Anseriformes to Experimental and Natural Duck Plague Infection

Common Name	Scientific Name	Experimental	Natural
Subfamily Anatinae			
Black duck	*Anas rubripes*	o	+
European teal	*Anas crecca*	—	o
European widgeon	*Anas penelope*	+	o
Gadwall	*Anas strepera*	+	o
Garganey teal	*Anas querquedula*	+	o
Mallard	*Anas pl. platyrhynchos*	+	+
Pintail	*Anas acuta*	—	o
Shelduck	*Tadorna tadorna*	+	o
Shoveler	*Spatula clypeata*	+	o
Wood duck	*Aix sponsa*	+	o
Subfamily Anserinae			
Bean goose	*Anser fabalis*	+	o
Canada goose	*Branta canadensis*	o	+
White-fronted goose	*Anser albifrons*	+	o
Subfamily Aythyinae			
Bufflehead	*Bucephala albeola*	o	+
Common eider	*Somateria mollissima*	+	o
Common pochard	*Aythya ferina*	+	o
Greater scaup	*Aythya marila*	o	+
Tufted duck	*Aythya fuligula*	+	o
Subfamily Cygninae			
Mute swan	*Cygnus olor*	+	+

SOURCES: Van Dorssen and Kunst (1955) (experimental infection); Leibovitz and Hwang (1968a) and Leibovitz (1968) (natural infection).

NOTE: + = died of duck plague; — = resisted lethal infection but produced antibodies against duck plague; o = not reported.

It is difficult to accept that outbreaks in other areas of the world were limited to domestic waterfowl in localized geographic areas. The possibility exists that outbreaks in wild waterfowl in these areas were not detected. Table 3.1 indicates reported experimental susceptibility and natural infection of Anseriformes. Van Dorssen and Kunst found European teal and pintails resisted fatal infection but produced antibodies against the agent following infection.

Herring gulls *(Larus argentatus)* and black-headed gulls *(Larus ridibundus)* were not susceptible to experimental infection and failed to produce antibodies against the virus (Van Dorssen and Kunst, 1955).

♦ **SIGNS.** The specific pathologic response to duck plague virus is dependent upon the species, age, sex, and susceptibility of the affected host, the stage of the infection, the virulence, and the intensity of virus exposure.

In domestic ducks the incubation period ranges from 3 to 7 days. Once overt signs of the disease appear, death usually follows within 1 to 5 days. Since natural infection has been observed in ages ranging from 7-day-old ducklings to old breeder ducks, all ages are susceptible.

In domestic breeder ducks sudden high and persistent flock mortality is often the first reported observation. Mature ducks die in good flesh. Prolapse of the penis may be evident in dead mature male breeders. In laying flocks a drop in egg production of 25 to 40% may be noted during the period of greatest mortality.

As the disease progresses within a flock, more signs are observed. Photophobia (associated with half-closed, pasted eyelids), inappetence, extreme thirst, droopiness, ataxia, ruffled feathers, nasal discharge, soiled vents, and a watery diarrhea appear. Affected ducks are unable to stand, and they maintain a posture with drooping outstretched wings and heads down, suggesting weakness and depression. Sick ducks forced to move may evidence tremors of the head, neck, and body.

Young market ducklings, 2 to 7 weeks of age, evidence dehydration, loss of weight, blue beaks, and often a blood-stained vent.

Total mortality in outbreaks in domestic ducks has ranged from 5 to 100%. Adult breeder ducks tend to experience greater percentage mortality than do young ducks.

In the limited detection of the disease in wild, free-flying waterfowl, dead mallards and black ducks, a mute swan, and a Canada goose were found dead, floating among the vegetation in the shallow water along the banks of creeks and rivers. When the dead black ducks and mallards were observed on the surface of the water, the back of the head, extended neck, partially flexed wings, back and extended feet, with the plantar surface of the web uppermost, were visible. The beak and the face were submerged. Some of the male mallards evidenced prolapse of the penis (Fig. 3.1). When the ducks were picked up and suspended by their feet, a dark brown, tarry fluid (blood mixed with ingesta) flowed from their mouths. Ducks died in good flesh and were devoid of other external changes noted in domestic ducks. Although eye alterations were not noted, it is likely that a photophobia was present, as indicated by the retreat of ducks into the more shaded vegetated areas prior to death.

The mortality of the various susceptible species in waterfowl die-offs appeared related to the population density of a given species rather than the selective action of the virus upon specific hosts. No estimates of total losses have been made in individual outbreaks.

The lesions of duck plague (Fig. 3.2) are those of vascular damage, as expressed in tissue hemorrhage and the presence of free blood in body cavities, enanthematous lesions in specific locations on the mucosal surface of the gastrointestinal tract, lesions of lymphoid organs, and retrograde sequela in parenchymatous organs. These lesions are pathognomonic of duck plague. The presence of limited pathologic alterations restricts the ability to diagnose the disease upon the basis of necropsy alone and may be related to inadequate sampling, the stage of infection, and the more qualified response of specific anseriform hosts.

Domestic ducks and mallards exhibit similar necropsy findings. Pinpoint and larger hemorrhages may be found in the

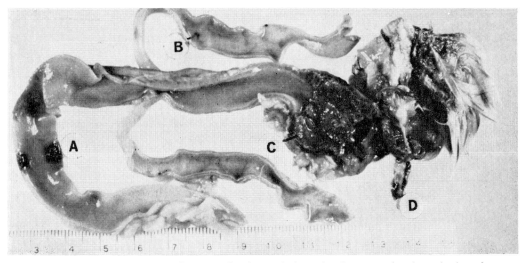

FIG. 3.1. Duck plague lesions in the posterior intestinal and reproductive tracts of a mature mallard: *(A)* posterior ileal annular band, *(B)* cecal macules, *(C)* cloacal lesions, *(D)* prolapse of penis.

FIG. 3.2. Sketch of duck plague lesions in a mature mallard: *(A)* enanthematous lesions of the esophagus, *(B)* myocardial paint-brush hemorrhages, *(C)* hemorrhages and white spots on the liver, *(D)* annular band lesions, *(E)* intestinal pinpoint hemorrhage, *(F)* prolapse of the penis, *(G)* cloacal lesion, *(H)* rectal and cecal enanthematous lesions, *(I)* hemorrhage under gizzard lining, *(J)* small dark spleen, *(K)* proventricular hemorrhage, *(L)* proventricular-esophageal sphincter hemorrhage, *(M)* dark brown fluid from mouth.

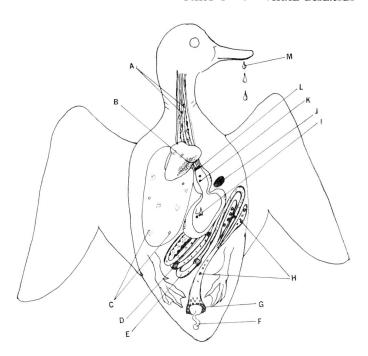

heart, other visceral organs, and their supporting structures, including the mesentery. On the external surface of the heart, especially within the coronary grooves, closely packed collections of small hemorrhages give the surface a red paint-brushed appearance. Hemorrhages may also be found within the chambers of the heart and its valves. The surface of the liver, pancreas, intestine, lung, and kidney may also be dotted with small hemorrhages. In mature laying females, a fully formed egg may be found in the oviduct at the time of the fatal hemorrhage. The lumen of the intestine is often filled with blood, and the esophageal-proventricular sphincter appears as a red ring at the junction of the two organs.

Specific enanthematous mucosal lesions of the digestive tract are found in the esophagus (Figs. 3.2, 3.3), cecum, rectum, and cloaca (Figs. 3.1, 3.2). They occur parallel to and above the vascular supply to these organs. Each of these lesions undergoes progressive alterations during the course of the disease. Initially, macular surface hemorrhages appear which are later covered by elevated yellowish white plaques. If the bird survives, these lesions subsequently become organized into a green, superficial scab devoid of its former hemorrhagic base. These lesions range in size from approximately 1 mm to 1 cm in length. In the esophagus and cloaca, these lesions may become confluent; however, close inspection will reveal their composite structure.

In the esophagus the macules occur parallel to the longitudinal folds. When the macular concentrations are great, the smaller lesions may merge to form larger ones, suggesting a patchy diphtheritic membrane. In young ducklings individual lesions are less frequent, sloughing of the entire mucosa tends to occur, and the lumen becomes lined with a thin, yellowish white membrane.

In the ceca the macular lesions are singular, separated, and well-defined between folds of the mucosal surface. The external surface of the affected ceca presents a barred and congested appearance.

Rectal lesions are usually few in number, with greatest concentration in the pos-

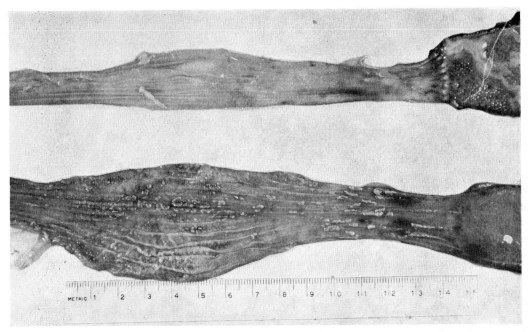

FIG. 3.3. Esophagus and portion of the proventriculus of a normal mature mallard duck (above); esophagus and proventriculus of a mature mallard affected with duck plague (below).

terior portion of the rectum, adjacent to the cloaca.

In the cloaca (Fig. 3.1) macular lesions are densely packed, and initially the entire lumen appears reddened. Later the individual plaquelike elevations become green in color and form a continuous scalelike band lining the lumen of the organ.

All lymphoid organs are affected. The spleen tends to be normal or smaller in size, dark in color, and mottled. The lobes of the thymus have multiple pinpoint hemorrhages and yellow spots, both on their surface and when cross-sectioned, and they are surrounded by a zone of clear yellow fluid that infiltrates and discolors the subcutaneous tissues of the adjacent cervical region. The bursa of Fabricius, during early infection, is intensely reddened. The exterior becomes surrounded by a clear yellow fluid that discolors the adjacent tissue of the pelvic cavity. When the lumen of the bursa is opened, pinpoint yellow spots are found on an intensely reddened surface. Later during the course of the infec-

tion, the walls of the bursa become thin and dark in color, and its cavity fills with a white coagulated exudate. The intestinal annular bands[1] (Fig. 3.2 and Fig. 3.4) appear as intensely reddened rings, visible from the external surface as well as from the internal surface of the intestine. Yellow, pinpoint spots can be observed on the mucosal surface, and later in the infection the entire band becomes a dark brown color and tends to separate at its margins from the internal surface of the intestines.

Of the parenchymatous organs, the liver

1. The annular bands (AB) are 4 normal, regularly spaced lymphoid organs that are located in the anterior and posterior portions of those regions of the avian intestines commonly referred to in mammals as the jejunum and ileum. The bands are approximately 1 cm wide. When viewed from the serosal surface, they give the appearance of ringlike transverse dilations of the intestinal wall. Inside the lumen of the organ they form slight elevations of the mucosal circumference. The posterior ileal AB can be found on that portion of the ileum located between the 2 attached ceca and is usually an incomplete ring. The anterior ileal and posterior jejunal AB are well-defined, complete rings, while the anterior jejunal AB is faint and poorly defined.

offers the greatest surface area for examination. During early infection in domestic ducks affected with duck plague, the entire surface is a pale copper color with the admixture of irregularly distributed pinpoint hemorrhages and white spots, which give the surface a heterogeneous speckled appearance. Although mallards exhibit similar changes in duck plague to those found in domestic ducks, they differ in liver lesions. The liver of the mallard is normally darker than that of domestic ducks. Early in the infection the affected mallard liver is a dark copper color, and surface hemorrhages are more difficult to detect. Late stages of infection for both the mallard and domestic duck are characterized by dark bronze or bile-stained livers without the previously noted hemorrhages, and surface white spots are larger and more distinct on this darkened background.

The tubules of the kidney are outlined as minute, white, circular areas in a dark red background, and occasionally surface hemorrhages can be seen. The lungs may appear congested.

While the above lesions are representative of the general findings in domestic and mallard ducks, each age group responds distinctively. In ducklings, tissue hemorrhages are less and lymphoid lesions are greater. In older ducks, the lymphoid organs, especially the thymus and the bursa, have completely regressed and lesions of these organs are absent. Since most wild bird specimens are mature birds, lesions of lymphoid organs are infrequently observed. In older domestic ducks and mallards, tissue hemorrhages and reproductive changes dominate duck plague manifestations.

In black ducks, the differential feature of the disease is the relative absence of esophageal and cloacal lesions. The limit of esophageal involvement is usually one or two solitary elevated yellow plaques; cloacal changes when present are limited to a few plaquelike lesions at the posterior margins. The intestinal response, while similar to that described for domestic ducks and mallards, differs by the individualized response of each black duck. Some black ducks exhibit a few large enanthematous lesions throughout the intestines, while others evidence diffuse pinpoint enanthematous lesions in the same locations. Like the mallard, the early affected liver also is dark copper colored, and surface hemorrhages or white spots are difficult to detect.

To date, reported natural infection in diving ducks (Aythyinae) has been limited to a single bufflehead and a greater scaup. No duck plague lesions were found in these birds. Both evidenced gunshot wounds and traumatic injuries.

In a single immature Canada goose that died of the infection, the features of the disease were the presence of lymphoid lesions, associated with the age of the bird, and the specific character of the lesions of the intestinal lymphoid discs[2] (Fig. 3.5), resembling buttonlike ulcers. The intestinal lymphoid discs of geese are analogous to the annular bands found in ducks. Similar intestinal lesions have been observed by Locke (1968) in an outbreak of duck plague in Canada geese.

In a single infected mute swan, a severe hemorrhagic enteritis with free blood throughout the intestinal lumen was found.

◆ **PATHOLOGY.** The initial injury produced by the duck plague virus is an alteration of the walls of blood vessels. Although alterations can be noted in the larger blood vessels, the smaller blood vessels, venules, and capillaries are more

---

2. Intestinal annular bands as described previously in mallards and black ducks are absent in geese and swans. In geese, suggestive corresponding structures are referred to here as intestinal lymphoid discs (ILD). These are multiple, slightly raised, disc-shaped areas of varying dimensions, arranged in groups on the small intestinal mucosa, ranging in length from approximately 0.5 to 1.5 cm. These groupings are found in the same general anatomic portions of the small intestines where the analogous AB are located. In normal geese the ILD are not visible from the external (serosal) surface and can only be observed by careful examination of the washed mucosal surface of the small intestines. When diseased, however, the discolored ILD often stand out in sharp contrast to the surrounding mucosal surface.

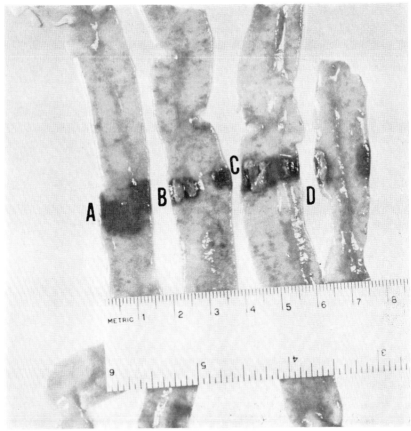

FIG. 3.4. Hemorrhagic and necrotic intestinal annular bands of a spontaneously infected 4-week-old white Pekin duckling: (A) anterior jejunal annular band, (B) posterior jejunal annular band, (C) anterior ileal annular band, (D) split posterior ileal annular band. Note pinpoint hemorrhages on other portions of the intestines. (Courtesy of the AVMA.)

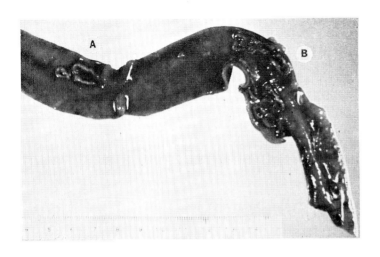

FIG. 3.5. Button-ulcer-like lesions of the intestinal lymphoid discs of a Canada goose: (A) region of posterior jejunum, (B) region of anterior ileum.

markedly involved. The endothelial lining is broken, and the connective tissue elements of the wall become less compact, with visible separations at those points where extravasations of the blood elements pass from the lumen through the thin, ruptured wall into the tissue proper. The suggestion that this effect is related to viral concentration is found in the gross pathologic alterations in the vicinity of lymphoid organs. It is likely that viral concentrations are high in the lymphoid tissues, and the clear fluids observed around the thymus and bursa are representations of the lytic action of the virus upon adjacent tissues. The permanent discolorations of the subcutaneous tissues of the neck about the thymus and in the pelvic cavity surrounding the bursa are evidence of the intense lysis of tissue. A similar effect can be achieved by experimental subcutaneous inoculations of concentrated virus preparations. It is quite likely that such a process occurs at a microscopic level, with lower virus concentrations during the viremic stage of the disease. The alterations produced by the circulating agent can best be manifested in the more yielding, smaller blood vessels, and can best be seen grossly where these vessels are most superficial. The results of this initial blood loss and interruption of vital circulation produce the related sequela, destruction of tissue, and finally death of the host.

In contrast to the generalized circulatory changes, the cycle of specific cellular response to duck plague virus is altered staining properties, cellular swelling, division of the cytoplasm into subunits that are discharged through a ruptured cell surface, and the formation of intranuclear inclusion bodies. The cell is finally represented by a delicate remaining outer wall and a nuclear membrane surrounding an intranuclear inclusion body (Fig. 3.6). The cytoplasmic alterations are distinctive and of short duration. Since intranuclear inclusion bodies are the terminal persistent cellular response, they are observed for longer periods of time in affected tissue. Although these cellular changes are observed in occasional scattered groups of epithelial cells within lesions of the esophagus, cloaca, liver, and pancreas, they are found as a uniform response in the reticular cells of lymphoid tissue (Leibovitz and Hwang, 1969).

Bacterial organisms can frequently be recovered from the internal organs of birds that have died of duck plague. Bacteria can also be demonstrated in histopathologic sections of these birds. It is likely that destruction of the reticuloendothelial system permits these organisms to enter as secondary invaders.

◆ **DIAGNOSIS.** Complete gross lesions found at necropsy are diagnostic of duck plague. Histopathologic studies can further support these findings. The isolation and the identification of the virus provide a confirmation even in the absence of diagnostic morphologic alterations. The isolation of a virus that fails to propagate in chick embryos, that grows when inoculated upon the chorioallantoic membrane of 9- to 14-day-old embryonated duck eggs, and produces the characteristic lesions and mortality when inoculated into susceptible day-old ducklings is highly suggestive of the duck plague virus. The neutralization of such an isolate by known duck plague antisera confirms the identification.

◆ **PROGNOSIS.** No treatment is known for duck plague. Outbreaks within a fixed population are self-limiting. Mortality may persist 3 to 5 weeks following initial infection. If new susceptible populations are added to infected environments or flocks, the infection will persist for a longer period of time. Survivors of outbreaks are immune to the disease. Little is known about the carrier state of recovered birds. Since water is an important vehicle for disseminating the virus, removal of infected birds from swimming areas, ponds, or open bodies of water limits the spread of disease. The presence of other stresses, such as crowding, secondary infections, drake damage, and severe weather conditions, accentuates mortality.

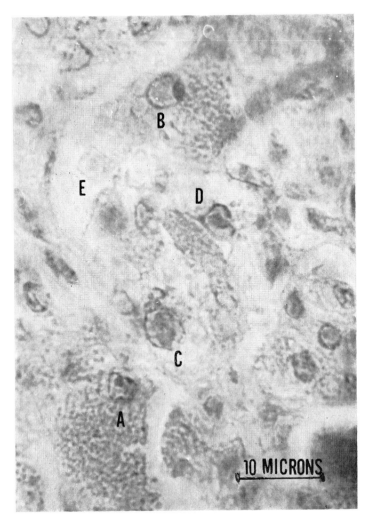

FIG. 3.6. Microscopic lesions of the liver of an experimentally infected 3-week-old white Pekin duckling 96 hours postinoculation: *(A)* more normal hepatic cell, *(B)* hepatic cell with intranuclear inclusion body and spherical bodies within the cytoplasm, *(C)* swollen hepatic cell with intranuclear inclusion body and disrupted cytoplasm, *(D)* hepatic cell with intranuclear inclusion body and discharged cytoplasmic contents, *(E)* empty hepatic cell with delicate remaining vestige of intranuclear inclusion body and cell wall. (Courtesy of the AVMA.)

◆ **IMMUNITY AND VACCINATION.** Birds recovered from duck plague are immune to reinfection. All reported strains have been shown to be immunologically identical, and immunity to one strain will protect against others (Jansen, 1968). A chicken-embryo-adapted strain of duck plague virus that is avirulent for domestic ducks has been developed by Jansen (1964a, 1964b). This modified live virus has been extensively employed with good success in the Netherlands and experimentally on commercial duck farms on Long Island for the prevention of the disease. The chicken-embryo-adapted modified live virus has also been propagated on tissue cultures and assayed (Dardiri and Hess, 1968). An inactivated virus vaccine and a live chicken-embryo-adapted vaccine have been studied experimentally (Butterfield and Dardiri, 1968).

Jansen (1964a, 1964b) has reported an interference phenomenon following vaccination. Experimentally vaccinated birds acquired a resistance to infection as early as the first day following vaccination. In Long Island outbreaks on commercial duck farms, the protection afforded by the interference phenomenon has not been as dramatic as Jansen reported, and field infections have been observed in a small percentage of individuals in vaccinated flocks. Parental (egg-transmitted) immunity may interfere with response to the live virus vaccine (Toth, 1968). To date the modified chicken-embryo-adapted vaccine has been limited to experimental use and has not been authorized for general distribution in the United States. It has been used experimentally in treating outbreaks of the disease in domestic white Pekin ducks on Long Island. The vaccine has been administered in ½-cc doses by the subcutaneous route in domestic ducklings over 2 weeks of age.

The practicality of employing this vaccine as a preventive measure in outbreaks of the disease in wild waterfowl is questionable. The safety of the vaccine for wild species has not been reported. Since the value of the vaccine is of a preventive nature, protection for wild species would have to be established early in the outbreak. Vaccine use in wild waterfowl may have value in preventing the disease in susceptible migratory birds moving into known infected localities.

◆ **CONTROL.** The disease can be controlled in domestic ducks by depopulation, sanitation, disinfection, and removal of the birds from the infected environment. All possible measures should be taken to prevent dissemination of the virus by free-flowing water.

Control of the disease in wild waterfowl poses a serious and difficult problem. The importance of such control is dependent upon its impact on wild waterfowl populations. Unfortunately, the latter is not known. In the event this disease produces high mortality, serious study of its control in wild waterfowl populations should be undertaken. If the disease is not an enzootic infection, and is truly exotic, measures should be taken to further prevent the entry and dissemination of the disease. This would include specific examination for duck plague in imported birds, populations maintained by aviculturists, and domesticated waterfowl. Efforts should be made to increase the efficiency of detection of duck plague by laboratory workers and waterfowl specialists in order that the

status and importance of this disease be better defined.

◆ **REFERENCES**

Baudet, A. E. R. F. Een sterfte onder eenden in Nederland, veroorzaakt door een filtreerbaar virus (vogelpest). (Mortality in ducks in the Netherlands caused by a filtrable virus; fowl plague.) *Tijdschr. Diergeneesk.* 50:455, 1923.

Bos, A. Weer nieuwe gevallen van eendenpest. (Some new cases of duck plague.) *Tijdschr. Diergeneesk.* 69:372, 1942.

Breese, S. S., Jr., and Dardiri, A. H. Electron microscopic characterization of duck plague virus. *Virology* 34:160, 1968.

Butterfield, W. K., and Dardiri, A. H. Serologic and immunologic response of ducks to inactivated and attenuated duck plague virus. *Proc. Ann. Meeting Am. Soc. Microbiol.,* Detroit, May 1968.

Dardiri, A. H., and Hess, W. R. A plaque assay for duck plague virus. *Can. J. Comp. Med.* 32:505, 1968.

Dardiri, A. H., Hess, W. R., Breese, S. S., Jr., and Seibold, H. R. Characterization of duck plague virus from a duck disease outbreak in the United States. *Proc. 39th Northeastern Conf. Avian Diseases,* State Univ. N.Y., Stony Brook, June 17–20, 1967.

Devos, A., Viaene, N., and Staelens, M. Eendenpest in Belgie. (Duck plague in Belgium.) *Vlaams Diergeneesk. Tijdschr.* 33: 260, 1964.

DeZeeuw, F. A. Nieuwe gevallen van eendenpest en de specificiteit van het virus. *Tijdschr. Diergeneesk.* 57:1095, 1930.

Jansen, J. Discussion. *Rept. 14th Intern. Vet. Congr., London* 2:385, 1949.

———. Over het voorkmen van eendenpest. (About the incidence of duck plague.) *Tijdschr. Diergeneesk.* 88:1341, 1963.

———. Het interferentie fenomeen bij de enting tegen eendenpest. (The interference phenomenon in vaccination against duck plague.) *Tijdschr. Diergeneesk.* 89:376, 1964a.

———. The interference phenomenon in the development of resistance against duck plague. *J. Comp. Pathol. Therap.* 74:3, 1964b.

———. Duck plague. *J. Am. Vet. Med. Assoc.* 152(7):1009, 1968.

Jansen, J., and Kunst, H. Is duck plague related to Newcastle disease or to fowl plague? *Proc. 14th Intern. Vet. Congr.* 2:363, 1949a.

———. Is eendenpest verwant aan hoenderpest of pseudo hoenderpest? (Is duck plague related to fowl plague or Newcastle disease?) *Tijdschr. Diergeneesk.* 74:705, 1949b.

———. The reported incidence of duck plague in Europe and Asia. *Tijdschr. Diergeneesk.* 89:765, 1964.

Jansen, J., and Wemmenhove, R. Eendenpest bij tamme ganzen *(Anser anser).* (Duck plague in domesticated geese [*Anser anser*].) *Tijdschr. Diergeneesk.* 90:811, 1965.

Kunst, H. Isolation of duck plague virus in tissue cultures. *Tijdschr. Diergeneesk.* 92:713, 1967.

Leibovitz, L. Progress report: Duck plague surveillance of American Anseriformes. *Bull. Wildlife Disease Assoc.* 4(3):87, 1968.

———. Comparative pathology of duck plague in wild Anseriformes. *J. Wildlife Management* 33(2):294, 1969.

Leibovitz, L., and Hwang, J. Duck plague in American Anseriformes. *Bull. Wildlife Disease Assoc.* 4 (1): 13, 1968a.

———. Duck plague on the American continent. *Avian Diseases* 12(2):361, 1968b.

———. The histopathology of duck plague in White Pekin ducklings. *Proc. 4th Congr.* *World Vet. Poultry Assoc., Belgrade, Yugoslavia,* Sept. 15–17, 1969.

Locke, L. Personal communication, 1968.

Lucam, F. La peste aviaire en France. *Rept. 14th Intern. Vet. Congr., London* 2:380, 1949.

Mukerji, A., Das, M. S., Ghosh, B. B., and Ganguly, J. L. Duck plague in West Bengal. I. *Indian Vet. J.* 40:457, 1963a.

———. Duck plague in West Bengal. II. *Indian Vet. J.* 40:753, 1963b.

———. Duck plague in West Bengal. III. *Indian Vet. J.* 42:811, 1965.

Peckham, M. Personal communication, 1968.

Toth, Thomas. Personal communication, 1968.

Urban, W. D. Current status of duck virus enteritis (duck plague). *Proc. 40th Northeastern Conf. Avian Diseases,* Storrs, Conn., June 24–26, 1968.

Van Dorssen, C. A., and Kunst, H. Over de gevoeligheid van eenden en diversr andere watervogels voor eendenpest. (Susceptibility of ducks and various other waterfowl to duck plague virus.) *Tijdschr. Diergeneesk.* 80:1286, 1955.

4 ◆ POX

● LARS KARSTAD

SYNONYMS: Fowl pox, avian diptheria, contagious epithelioma, molluscum contagiosum, Geflugelpocken, viruela aviare, variole aviaire.

AVIAN POX is a viral infection of birds, characterized by discrete, proliferative lesions on the skin and/or mucous membrane of the mouth and upper respiratory tract. It is comparable to the pox infections of man and domestic mammals—for example, smallpox, vaccinia, and sheep and swine poxes.

◆ HISTORY AND DISTRIBUTION.
Because they produce obvious lesions, pox infections in both domestic and wild birds were among the earliest described avian diseases. It was not until around the turn of the century, however, that studies of pox in wild birds were described in which histopathology and cultural methods were employed to confirm the diagnoses.

The geographic distribution of the avian poxes appears to be worldwide.

◆ ETIOLOGY.
Avian pox is caused by a virus of the pox group (Wilner, 1965). The virus particle is large, oval, or brick-shaped, about 150 to 200 mμ by 265 to 350 mμ in size. It is a DNA-containing, enveloped virus, which develops in the cytoplasm of infected epithelial cells. Infected cells characteristically contain large acidophilic intracytoplasmic inclusions (Bollinger bodies). Electron microscopy of avian-pox inclusions reveals viral particles embedded in a rather homogeneous matrix, typical of poxviruses in general (Fig. 4.1).

Avian poxviruses have been classified according to their hosts of origin (Cunningham, 1965). There seems to be no valid argument, however, for considering strains adapted to different avian hosts as different poxvirus species, since their basic viral characteristics appear to be identical. In the light of present knowledge, it seems justified to regard all avian poxviruses as strains of *Poxvirus avium*.

◆ TRANSMISSION.
Poxvirus avium is transmitted directly by contacts between infected and susceptible birds, and indirectly by contact with contaminated objects, such as perches, and by means of insect vectors, such as mosquitoes. Mosquitoes have been shown to be mechanical vectors only, transferring virus from infected to susceptible birds by contamination of their skin-piercing mouth parts.

Poxvirus is unable to penetrate unbroken skin, but small abrasions are sufficient to permit infection. Burnet (Kirmse, 1967a) found that lesions developed at sites of minor experimental skin injury in birds inoculated intravenously.

Fowl pox in chickens is reported to appear most often in young birds during fall and winter months, often about the time they are housed in laying quarters. During the fall and early winter the cutaneous form is most common, while later in the winter the diphtheritic form is said to predominate (Cunningham, 1965). Infections in wild birds have been observed at all seasons of the year.

◆ HOSTS.
Most, if not all, avian species are susceptible to one or more pox strains. On the basis of host specificity, strains have been classified as mono-, bi-, or tri-pathogenic. A strain from a yellow-shafted flicker (*Colaptes auratus*) was a good exam-

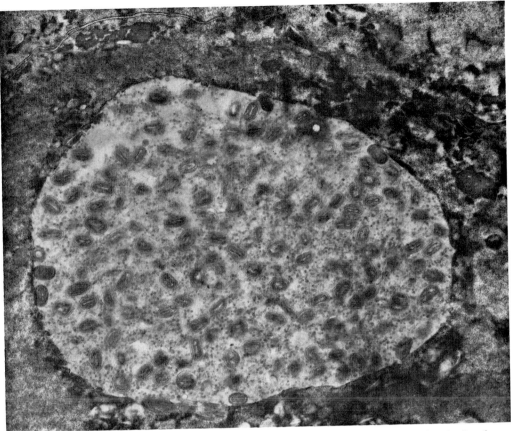

FIG. 4.1. Electron micrograph of a cytoplasmic inclusion body of pox in a yellow-shafted flicker. Note numerous oval virus particles. ×19,952. (From Kirmse, *Bull. Wildlife Disease Assoc.* 3:18, 1967.)

ple of a monopathogenic strain, since among 19 species of inoculated wild and domestic birds only flickers were found susceptible to infection (Kirmse, 1966). More often, avian-pox strains are pathogenic for several species. It is interesting to speculate upon the role of the tree-hole nesting habits of flickers and their general lack of contacts with other species in permitting a degree of isolation of the flicker virus as a monopathogenic strain. Naturally occurring pox infections have been reported in some 60 species of wild birds, comprising 20 families (Kirmse, 1967a). It is interesting that pox has not yet been observed in wild waterfowl, although domestic ducks and geese are susceptible (Kirmse, 1967b).

Kirmse (1967c) attempted to infect chickens with strains of pox from the yellow-shafted flicker, slate-colored junco (*Junco hyemalis*), song sparrow (*Melospiza melodia*), field sparrow (*Spizella pusilla*), and domestic canary. Only the field-sparrow strain produced lesions in chickens. Conversely, three strains of fowl pox were pathogenic for chickens but not for several species of wild birds, including the red-winged blackbird (*Agelaius phoeniceus*), starling (*Sturnus vulgaris*), oriole (*Icterus galbula*), catbird (*Dumetella carolinensis*), song sparrow, house sparrow (*Passer domesticus*), white-throated sparrow (*Zonotrichia albicollis*), robin (*Turdus migratorius*), evening grosbeak (*Hesperiphona vespertina*), indigo bunting (*Passerina cyanea*), goldfinch *(Spinus tristis)*, brown thrasher *(Toxostoma rufum)*, kingbird *(Tyrannus tyrannus)*, and grackle *(Quiscalus versicolor)*. These results may be taken as evidence of host specificity and suggest that pox infections in small migratory birds do not constitute a threat to the poultry industry.

♦ **SIGNS.** Avian pox occurs in two forms, the diphtheritic form, in which moist, necrotic lesions develop on the mucous membranes of the mouth and upper respiratory tract, and the more common skin form, in which discrete, warty, proliferative lesions develop on the skin. Lesions are most common on the unfeathered parts of the body—the legs, feet, eyelids, base of the beak, and the comb and wattles of gallinaceous birds. In some cases lesions are present on both mucous membranes and skin.

The incubation period varies with the strain and host species from 4 to 14 days in chickens (Cunningham, 1965) to 1 month in the flicker (Kirmse, 1966). Duration of the disease is equally variable. Fowl pox in chickens persists in individual birds for about 4 weeks. Most records of pox in wild birds show longer duration: several months in chipping sparrows *(Spizella passerina)* (Musselman, 1928); 82 days in a mourning dove *(Zenaidura macroura)* (Kossack and Hanson, 1954); more than 81 days in a slate-colored junco and 13 months in a flicker (Kirmse, 1966, 1967c); and more than 109 days in a slate-colored junco (Hood, 1967).

Pox lesions heal, following degeneration and sloughing of the abnormally proliferated epithelium.

Little is known about mortality rates in naturally infected, free-flying wild birds. In chickens the diphtheritic form of pox warrants a less favorable prognosis, mortality rates being usually higher than in birds with cutaneous pox. Captive pheasants are probably similar to chickens with regard to the severity and course of pox infections. Dobson (1937) reported extensive losses in pheasants *(Phasianus colchicus)* affected by the diphtheritic form of pox. Eyelid le-

sions, which completely covered the eyes and thus prevented feeding, were responsible for extensive losses among impeyan pheasants (Karstad, 1965). The outbreak occurred in the fall and subsided after frosts had reduced mosquito populations. Gallagher (1916) reported 85% mortality in quail (of unstated species) imported from Mexico. In these birds lesions were present on the unfeathered skin and in the mouth. Most reports of pox in wild birds have indicated that the disease is mild and self-limited. Often the lesions are few in number, appearing as innocuous warty growths on one or two toes (Fig. 4.2), at the base of the bill (Fig. 4.3), or on an eyelid. Large persistent pox lesions are subject to trauma, resulting in hemorrhage, necrosis, and portals of entry for bacteria and fungi. Locke et al. (1965) described deaths in red-tailed tropic birds *(Phaethon rubricauda)* in which pox was complicated by secondary mycotic infections. Histologic sections of cutaneous pox lesions usually reveal areas of necrosis on or near the surface, in which masses of bacteria or fungi

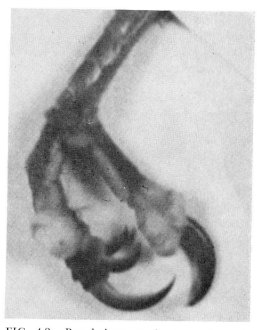

FIG. 4.2. Pox lesions on the toes of a red-capped manakin *(Pipra mentalis)* from Panama. (Courtesy P. Kirmse.)

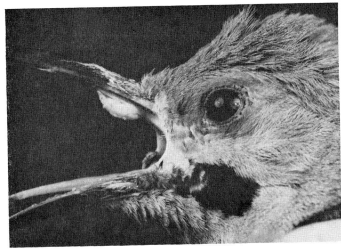

FIG. 4.3. Pox lesion on the palate of a yellow-shafted flicker. (From Kirmse, *Bull. Wildlife Disease Assoc.* 3:17, 1967.)

are seen. There are usually no obvious systemic effects of these secondary bacterial or mycotic infections.

Pox in canary aviaries may be associated with extensive losses (Bigland et al., 1962). Transmission is facilitated by the housing of large numbers of birds in close quarters. In such situations transmission may occur by contacts, direct and indirect, and also by inhalation of virus-laden dust. Poxviruses are very resistant to inactivation by drying, and therefore dust which contains contaminated particles of feathers, skin, or scabs may be highly infective. Under conditions of aerosol exposure, canaries may die with rather acute, apparently generalized systemic infections.

In experimentally infected domestic ducks and geese, pocks appeared along the ramifications of blood vessels in the foot webs, much like the distribution of leaves on branches of a tree (Fig. 4.4). Focal epi-

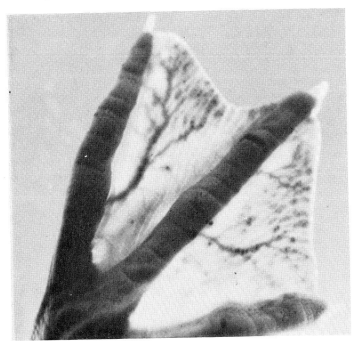

FIG. 4.4. Early lesions resulting from experimental fowlpox infection in a domestic goose. (From Kirmse, *Avian Diseases* 11:210, 1967.)

FIG. 4.5. Spherical elevations on feet of domestic duckling experimentally infected with fowlpox virus. (From Kirmse, *Avian Diseases* 11:211, 1967.)

thelial proliferation and later necrosis and sloughing occurred mainly on the plantar surfaces of the webs and toes (Fig. 4.5). When fully developed, these lesions appeared as circular pocks, 3 to 5 mm in diameter, with central areas of necrosis, bordered by zones of erythema.

◆ **PATHOLOGY.** Avian-pox infections cause localized proliferations of epithelial cells. Affected cells become hyperplastic and hypertrophic. The increased rate of multiplication occurs in the basal germinal layer of cells in the epithelium. Hypertrophy and the appearance of large granular acidophilic intracytoplasmic inclusions appear as the cells mature in layers of the epithelium above the stratum germinativum (Fig. 4.6). The piling up of infected epithelial cells to form "pocks" occurs at variable rates, and lesions may persist for different lengths of time in different species.

In chickens, cutaneous lesions are said to become inflamed and hemorrhagic about their bases, just prior to regression. Desiccation and scab formation then follow,

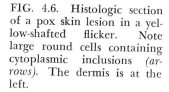

FIG. 4.6. Histologic section of a pox skin lesion in a yellow-shafted flicker. Note large round cells containing cytoplasmic inclusions *(arrows)*. The dermis is at the left.

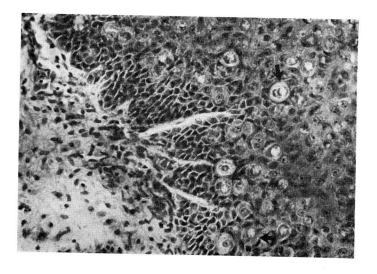

with eventual sloughing and replacement by normal skin. In wild birds, cutaneous lesions may be few, sometimes only one or two, and the whole process of development, regression, and healing of these lesions may be much prolonged. Perhaps this occurs because of a fairly high natural resistance to infection, combined with minimal host response. Whatever the reasons, it is obvious that a rather good host-parasite relationship exists in such infections, and that it is beneficial to survival of the virus for it to be carried for a long period of time by an individual host.

The secondary infections with bacteria and fungi have nothing specific about them, occurring as they would in any skin surface where abrasion and contamination occur. Elevated pox lesions predispose the skin surfaces to trauma. Bird banders find that birds with pox lesions usually become entangled in mist nets in such a way that the warty pox lesions are injured and made to bleed.

Diphtheritic lesions are relatively infrequent in wild bird pox infections. Table 4.1 contains a summary of lesions occurring in 27 species, of which only 5 reports of diphtheritic lesions were found. This information is drawn mainly from references cited by Kirmse (1967a). Cunningham (1965) describes lesions on the mucous membranes of chickens as white, opaque, slightly elevated nodules, which rapidly

TABLE 4.1. Distribution of Lesions of Pox Infection in Some Wild Birds

Family and Species	Cutaneous Lesions		Diphtheritic Lesions
	Feet	Head	
Certhiidae			
brown creeper	X		
Corvidae			
crow	X		
Fringillidae			
bullfinch		X	X
chaffinch	X		
chipping sparrow	X		
field sparrow	X		
slate-colored junco	X		
song sparrow	X		
towhee	X		
tree sparrow	X		
white-throated sparrow	X		
Icteridae			
cowbird	X	X	
grackle	X		
Mimidae			
mockingbird	X		
Parulidae			
Cape May warbler	X		
yellow-breasted chat	X		
yellowthroat	X		
Phasianidae			
pheasant		X	X
quail	X	X	X
Picidae			
flicker	X	X	
Sturnidae			
starling		X	X
Tetraonidae			
ruffed grouse		X	X
sage grouse	X	X	
Turdidae			
American robin	X		
gray-cheeked thrush	X		
Swainson's thrush	X		
wood thrush	X		

increase in size, often coalescing to form a yellowish, cheesy, necrotic material which has the appearance of a pseudomembrane. He says the condition is aggravated by invasion of contaminating bacteria and that it may extend to involve the sinuses and pharynx, causing respiratory distress.

The pathology of canary pox is sometimes quite different. Lesions frequently seen are fibrinous inflammation of serous membranes, liver degeneration or necrosis, edema and hyperemia of the lungs, and fibrinous pneumonitis. Such lesions are seen in canaries with the acute systemic form of the disease. In other cases, cutaneous lesions or diphtheritic lesions may predominate. Canaries may have cutaneous lesions also on the feathered portions of the body.

Goodpasture and Anderson (1962) described strains of pox isolated from the slate-colored junco and from a wood thrush which were characterized by the development of intranuclear as well as intracytoplasmic inclusions. Both types of inclusions occurred in the original junco host as well as in chickens infected with the junco strain. Beaver and Cheatum (1963) studied the cytopathology of this strain by electron microscopy. The nuclear inclusion was seen to be devoid of viral particles and was composed of a loose array of irregularly branching filaments.

In pox-infected juncos studied by the author, 1 of 4 had intranuclear as well as typical intracytoplasmic inclusions. This bird was submitted in formalin, so that virus isolation was not attempted. Intranuclear inclusions were seen also in a formalin-fixed cutaneous lesion from a mockingbird *(Mimus polyglottos)* which had intracytoplasmic inclusions in hypertrophied epithelial cells, typical of avian-pox infection. Furthermore, 1 of 6 yellow-shafted flickers with cutaneous pox lesions had small, eosinophilic, rod-shaped inclusions in the nuclei of cells which also contained typical Bollinger bodies.

Histologic examination of a pox lesion from a Savannah sparrow *(Passerculus sandwichensis)* revealed rod- or brick-shaped inclusions in the cytoplasm of hypertrophic epithelial cells which bore typical Bollinger bodies.

◆ **DIAGNOSIS.** Histopathologic examination, with demonstration of typical intracytoplasmic inclusions, is usually sufficient for a diagnosis of avian-pox infection. Isolation and propagation of virus on chorioallantoic membranes of chicken embryos should be attempted (Cunningham, 1965). Some strains of wild bird pox do not grow readily in chicken embryos. In such cases demonstration of typical poxvirus particles by electron microscopy may provide confirmation of pox infection (Kirmse, 1966).

◆ **PROGNOSIS.** The majority of wild bird pox infections are mild and self-limiting. Preponderance of lesions of the eyelids, however, may cause heavy mortality. This has been the outcome of such lesions in graniferous birds, such as pheasants, which become unable to see to find food. Lesions of the mucous membranes of the mouth and upper air passages also warrant a less favorable prognosis. In canaries acute systemic infections are commonly associated with high mortality.

◆ **IMMUNITY AND VACCINATION.** Birds recovered from pox infection usually are immune to reinfection with that strain.

Cross-immunity is proved for several strains of avian pox. For example, chickens may be vaccinated with live pigeon pox strains, since they stimulate immunity to typical fowl-pox strains without causing serious disease. Many of the wild bird poxes are not pathogenic for chickens. On occasion it may be useful to try vaccination in situations where pox occurs in captive wild birds. Ideally one should select for vaccination a pox strain which causes a mild infection limited to the skin at the site of vaccine application. For techniques of vaccination, see Cunningham (1965).

Strains isolated from a single host species may vary in pathogenicity for other species. For example, a strain of pox from the canary has been found which will infect chickens, quail, and turkeys but not house sparrows and pigeons; another canary-pox strain infected chickens, pigeons, and sparrows. Irons (1934) found a strain of pox from the pigeon which produced lesions in house sparrows after a series of blind passages. It seems probable that avian pox exists in a spectrum of continuous adaptation to various avian species.

Dobson (1937) has described a pox strain isolated from pheasants which was transmissible to chickens and pigeons. Pigeon poxvirus immunized against this pheasant strain. DuBose (1965) reported reciprocal immunization between a pox strain from the sage grouse *(Centrocercus urophasianus)* and a fowl-pox strain. Similarly Syverton and Cowan (1944) reported immunization of chickens against fowl pox with a strain of pox isolated from the sooty grouse *(Dendragapus fuliginosus).*

◆ **CONTROL.** In outbreaks in which virus is transmitted by mosquito vectors, control should be aimed at destruction of mosquitoes or preventing their access to captive birds by screening. If infection is dust-borne, as it may be in aviaries, control of dust may be an important factor. In aviaries diseased and healthy birds should be separated and the diseased birds kept in separate screened cages. Cannibalism or feather picking should be discouraged by providing ample cage space and feeding a suitably varied diet. Vaccination may be practicable in certain situations.

◆ **REFERENCES**

Beaver, D. L., and Cheatum, W. J. Electron microscopy of junco pox. *Am. J. Pathol.* 42:23, 1963.

Bigland, C. H., Whenham, G. R., and Graesser, F. E. A pox-like infection of canaries: Report of an outbreak. *Can. Vet. J.* 3:347, 1962.

Cunningham, C. H. Fowl pox. In H. E. Biester and L. H. Schwarte, eds., *Diseases of poultry,* 5th ed. Ames: Iowa State Univ. Press, 1965.

Dobson, N. Pox in pheasants. *J. Comp. Pathol.* 50:401, 1937.

DuBose, R. T. Pox in the sage grouse. *Bull. Wildlife Disease Assoc.* 1:6, 1965.

Gallagher, B. Epithelioma contagiosum of quail. *J. Am. Vet. Med. Assoc.* 50:366, 1916.

Goodpasture, E. W., and Anderson, K. Isolation of a wild avian pox virus inducing both cytoplasmic and nuclear inclusions. *Am. J. Pathol.* 40:437, 1962.

Hood, L. L. Personal communication, 1967.

Irons, V. Cross-species transmission studies with different strains of bird pox. *Am. J. Hyg.* 20:329, 1934.

Karstad, L. An outbreak of pox in impeyan pheasants. *Bull. Wildlife Disease Assoc.* 1:3, 1965.

Kirmse, P. Host specificity and long persistence of pox infection in the flicker *(Colaptes auratus). Bull. Wildlife Disease Assoc.* 3:14, 1966.

———. Pox in wild birds: An annotated bibliography. *Wildlife Diseases,* no. 49, 1967a.

———. Experimental pox infection in waterfowl. *Avian Diseases* 11:209, 1967b.

———. Personal communciation, 1967c.

Kossack, C. W., and Hanson, H. C. Fowl pox in the mourning dove. *J. Am. Vet. Med. Assoc.* 124:199, 1954.

Locke, L. N., Wirtz, W. O., and Brown, E. E. Pox infection and a secondary cutaneous mycosis in a red-tailed tropic bird *(Phaeton rubricauda). Bull. Wildlife Disease Assoc.* 1:60, 1965.

Musselman, T. E. Foot disease of chipping sparrows *(Spizella passerina). Auk* 45:137, 1928.

Syverton, J. T., and Cowan, I. M. Bird pox in the sooty grouse *(Dendragapus fuliginosus)* with recovery of the virus. *Am. J. Vet. Res.* 5:215, 1944.

Wilner, B. K. *A classification of the major groups of human and other animal viruses,* 3rd ed. Minneapolis: Burgess, 1965.

5 ◆ QUAIL BRONCHITIS

● ROBERT T. DU BOSE

SYNONYMS: Although first referred to as quail disease (Olson, 1950), the name quail bronchitis, suggested by the title of Olson's report and used by Yates and Fry (1957), has become generally accepted (DuBose and Grumbles, 1959; Hofstad, 1965a; Wilner, 1965; DuBose, 1967).

QUAIL BRONCHITIS (QB) is an acute, highly contagious, respiratory disease of bobwhite quail *(Colinus virginianus* Linne). The disease was reviewed by Hofstad (1965a) and by DuBose (1967). The causative agent, quail bronchitis virus (QBV), is an avian adenovirus (Cabasso, 1965; Wilner, 1965).

◆ **HISTORY.** Studies on QB have resulted from occurrence of the disease in quail on game-bird farms. Its importance in wild quail is not known. QB was first described by Olson (1950), who isolated the causative agent from quail in West Virginia, identified it as a virus, and reproduced the disease in quail. Personal communications cited by Olson (1950) indicate that the disease may have been observed in the United States as early as 1933. DuBose et al. (1958) studied a similar disease of quail in 1956, compared its causative virus with Olson's quail virus, and concluded they were the same agent. Additional epornitics were observed in Texas in 1957 (DuBose et al., 1960) and in Virginia in 1959 (DuBose, 1967).

Chukar partridges, pheasants, chickens, and "Japanese" quail *(Coturnix coturnix)* were on the premises with affected quail but did not show signs of disease (Olson, 1950; DuBose et al., 1958; DuBose, 1967). Chickens and turkeys inoculated with QBV did not exhibit signs of disease (Olson, 1950; DuBose et al., 1958) but the agent was reisolated from both species (Olson, 1950).

Yates and Fry (1957) isolated an endogenous virus from embryonating chicken eggs that had been inoculated with unrelated materials and named it chicken embryo lethal orphan virus (CELO). They established its similarity to QBV by the lesions and death pattern induced in chicken embryos and by its serological characteristics. These similarities were confirmed by DuBose and Grumbles (1959). The latter also confirmed the endogenous occurrence of either QBV or CELO by isolating it from uninoculated embryonating chicken eggs. In addition they reproduced bronchitis in quail by inoculation and by exposure to cagemates infected with QBV from natural outbreaks on one hand and with early-passage CELO (Phelps strain) obtained from Yates on the other. Yates (1960) also produced the disease in quail by inoculation with the Phelps strain of CELO. Yates and Fry (1957) demonstrated widespread occurrence of their CELO viruses by detecting antibodies in sera from chickens in many parts of the United States.

In this chapter, the name *quail bronchitis virus* will be used for the isolates obtained from bobwhite quail and the name *chicken embryo lethal orphan virus* will be used for the isolates so designated by other investigators.

◆ **DISTRIBUTION.** Since 1933 QB has been observed in New York and New Jersey (personal communications cited by Olson, 1950), West Virginia (Olson, 1950), Texas (DuBose et al., 1958, 1960), Virginia (DuBose, 1967), and Maryland (Locke, 1967). In addition, information from state diagnostic laboratories indicates occurrence in South Carolina, Georgia, and Florida during the 1960s. Lack of information on the disease in other than the Atlantic and southern regions may reflect absence of the disease, lower numbers of bobwhite quail (both free-living and captive), failure of game-bird breeders to submit cases, or limited distribution of state or regional reports of the disease.

Infection with the similar virus, CELO, apparently occurs in chickens over most of the United States (Yates and Fry, 1957). Although one isolate of CELO virus was shown to cause QB in bobwhite quail (DuBose and Grumbles, 1959; Yates, 1960), it is not known what proportion of these agents that commonly infect chickens is capable of causing bronchitis in bobwhite quail. If the majority are pathogenic for the quail, then a reservoir for QB exists in commercial poultry over most of this country. If antibodies against CELO found in sera from pheasants, redwing blackbirds, and swan (V. Srikrishnan, personal communication cited by Yates, 1960) indicate earlier infection with virus capable of causing bronchitis in quail, then wild birds may constitute an additional widespread reservoir in the Western Hemisphere.

◆ **ETIOLOGY.** QBV is classified as an avian adenovirus (Cabasso, 1965; Wilner, 1965). Electron micrographs by Dutta and Pomeroy (1967) revealed large particles with cubic, icosahedral symmetry, 252 solid capsomeres, no envelope, and a diameter of 70 to 75 mμ. Smaller particles, fewer but still abundant, were observed to be polyhedral with cubic symmetry, no envelope, solid capsomeres (number not determined), and of 20 to 24 mμ in diameter.

Comparing their results with an earlier study of CELO virus (Dutta and Pomeroy, 1963), they concluded that only the large particle of the QBV preparation could be considered identical structurally to the CELO virus. The significance of the small particle was not determined. The authors indicated that further studies would be made on the character and pathogenicity of the large and small QBV particles.

QBV grows readily in inoculated chicken embryos, causing lesions and mortality patterns similar to those caused by infectious bronchitis virus of chickens. The virus in chick embryo allantoic fluid does not agglutinate washed chicken red blood cells. It can be differentiated from infectious bronchitis virus by serological differences, by its much greater resistance to heat, and by its infectivity for quail (DuBose and Grumbles, 1959; DuBose et al., 1960). Yates (1960) suggested that 37.0° or 37.5° C for several days might be better for differentiation of QBV or CELO from infectious bronchitis virus rather than the 56° C for shorter periods used by DuBose et al. (1960). QBV is filterable and has been stored successfully for 4 years at —20° C plus 4 years at —50° C, with at least one inadvertent thawing in the latter period (DuBose, unpublished evidence).

CELO virus is similar to QBV in the above characteristics (Yates and Fry, 1957; DuBose and Grumbles, 1959), but there have been few trials to compare QBV and the viruses designated CELO in their pathogenicity for bobwhite quail.

◆ **TRANSMISSION.** In bobwhite quail, only contact transmission of the virus has been demonstrated experimentally (Olson, 1950; DuBose and Grumbles, 1959), but evidence based on flock histories in a series of outbreaks suggests that airborne and mechanical transmission are factors in the spread of the disease (DuBose, 1967). Although circumstantial in nature, the indications that chickens, turkeys, adult quail, game birds of other species, and wild birds may serve as reservoirs of infection for QB should be kept in mind. The sudden onset, rapid spread, and high morbidity reported in most of the natural outbreaks emphasize the highly contagious nature of QB.

◆ **SIGNS.** QB was described by Olson (1950), DuBose et al. (1958), DuBose and Grumbles (1959), and DuBose (1967). The natural infection in quail under 4 weeks of age is characterized by a sudden onset and the rapid spread of tracheal rales, coughing, and sneezing. Depression, huddling, and ruffled feathers may be observed, and neural signs—twisting or bending the neck over the back or between the legs—may appear in a few birds. Signs persist 1 to 3 weeks and mortality ranges from 10 to 100%, often being over 50%. Conjunctivitis was observed in a natural infection (DuBose, unpublished diagnostic accession) and in experimentally infected quail (DuBose and Grumbles, 1959). In some birds oral respiration and a bellowing in and out of the skin over the infraorbital sinus may result from congestion of the nasal passages, but an external nasal discharge usually is not seen. Spread may be slower and the signs and mortality markedly less in older birds.

The incubation period in experimentally infected quail has ranged from 2 to 7 days (Olson, 1950; DuBose and Grumbles, 1959).

◆ **PATHOGENESIS.** The most probable route of infection with QBV is the respiratory tract; the conjunctiva and the alimentary tract also are possible routes. In natural infections in quail, virus has been isolated from the trachea, lungs, and air sacs, but in most instances these were the only organs from which recovery was attempted (Olson, 1950; DuBose et al., 1958). In addition to the above, QBV and/or the Phelps strain of CELO have been obtained from the brain, spleen, conjunctiva, and aqueous humor of experimentally infected quail (DuBose and Grumbles, 1959; Yates, 1960). Persistence of virus in different organs has not been adequately studied, but DuBose and Grumbles (1959) obtained QBV from aqueous humor and tracheae of quail 48 days after they were placed with inoculated cagemates.

From inoculated chickens, Yates (1960) reisolated the Phelps strain of CELO virus from the blood, muscle, lungs, spleen, liver, aqueous humor, and intestines.

◆ **PATHOLOGY.** Tracheitis and bronchitis (evidenced by excess mucus and/or bronchial plugs) and inflammation of the air sacs (cloudiness, mucoid exudate) are usually, but not always, seen in QB (Olson, 1950; DuBose et al., 1958; DuBose, 1967). Cloudy corneas (Olson, 1950) or conjunc-

tivitis and congestion of the nasal or infraorbital sinuses may be observed (DuBose and Grumbles, 1959).

The virus has been isolated from young quail which showed no gross lesions or signs of infection (DuBose and Grumbles, 1959).

Information on microscopic lesions of QB needs to be obtained.

◆ **DIAGNOSIS.** In the absence of signs or lesions pointing to other diseases, a presumptive diagnosis of QB may be based on a sudden onset and rapid spread of rales, sneezing or coughing, and change of voice, accompanied by a high mortality within a 2-week period. Neural disorders may or may not occur in a few birds of a group. In birds over 4 weeks of age, the signs may be less severe, the spread slower, and the mortality less than 10%. Necropsies during the first 10 days should reveal excess mucus in the tracheae, bronchi, and air sacs, and cloudiness of the air sacs.

Although Newcastle disease has caused similar signs and lesions in other species (Brandly and Hanson, 1965), to the author's knowledge Newcastle disease has not been described in *bobwhite* quail.

An accurate diagnosis is based on isolation and identification of QBV. The methods described for infectious bronchitis (Cunningham, 1963; NAS-NRC Pub. No. 1038, 1963; Hofstad, 1965b) have been effective. Suspensions of aqueous humor (DuBose and Grumbles, 1959), tracheae, air sacs, and/or lungs (Olson, 1950; DuBose et al., 1958) from affected quail are injected into the allantoic sacs of chicken embryos at 9 to 11 days of incubation. QBV usually causes deaths within the first three embryo passages, often in the first passage, and the mortality rate increases with the number of passages. Curling and stunting of the embryos, thickening of the amnionic membrane, necrotic foci or patches in the liver, and urate collections in the kidneys are typical effects of QBV infection but are not pathognomonic. Similar embryo lesions are caused by infectious bronchitis virus (not known to infect quail) and by CELO virus which could be endogenous to the chicken embryos (Yates and Fry, 1957; Yates, 1960). Allantoic fluid harvested from each embryo passage should be checked for Newcastle disease virus by the hemagglutination test (Brandly and Hanson, 1965). Newcastle disease virus agglutinates washed chicken red blood cells; infectious bronchitis virus, QBV, and CELO do not. Eggs for virus isolations should be from CELO-free or QBV-free chicken flocks.

Final identification of the QBV is based on neutralization of its infectivity for chicken embryos by specific QBV antiserum or by CELO antiserum known to neutralize QBV.

◆ **PROGNOSIS.** Mortality in bobwhite quail under 4 weeks of age has reached 100%, but usually ranges from 10 to 80%. Information from case histories indicates that resistance increases with age and that adult quail may have only transitory respiratory distress, but it was not demonstrated that these older birds had no level of acquired immunity from a previous infection with QBV.

In the absence of secondary complications, quail that survive the course of respiratory signs apparently recover fully. There are insufficient data for predicting the outcome in individuals that show neural disorders.

◆ **IMMUNITY.** The degree and duration of immunity after recovery from QB have not been satisfactorily established. Significant levels of specific antibodies against QBV were demonstrated in sera from quail that recovered from the disease (DuBose and Grumbles, 1959), but antibody levels are not necessarily an efficient measure of degree of resistance against reinfection by a virulent strain of homologous virus. In limited trials quail resisted challenge 2 months after experimental infection (Olson, 1950) and 6 months after a natural infection (DuBose et al., 1958). The challenge virus, however, had been propagated in chicken embryos and did not cause high mortality in young, susceptible quail. Age

resistance to QB, suggested by Yates (1960) and supported by lack of mortality in older quail in the outbreaks reviewed by DuBose (1967), may be a resistance to overt pathogenic effects, not a resistance to infection per se.

To obtain more definite information on degree and duration of immunity, quail chicks could be infected by natural routes with a non-embryo-propagated QBV that causes high mortality, and the survivors challenged in groups at various intervals by natural routes with the same virus. Initial infection of the subjects by penmate or cagemate contact with chicks that were inoculated via the respiratory tract probably would approximate the route of transmission that occurs within a flock in natural outbreaks. Infection in a similar manner of adult quail that had never been exposed to the virus, with a non-embryo-propagated QBV of proved virulence and pathogenicity for quail chicks, would demonstrate whether or not an age resistance to pathogenic effects existed. In the absence of overt signs, reisolation of QBV would then show the occurrence of inapparent infections in adult quail that had no acquired immunity.

◆ **TREATMENT.** There is no specific treatment for QB. Avoidance of crowding, adequate ventilation without drafts, ample feeder and water space, and increased warmth in the brooder and house are measures that may lower the mortality rate and decrease the chances of complicating secondary infections.

◆ **PREVENTION.** The basic measure in prevention of QB is the isolation of susceptible birds from possible sources of QBV (or CELO). Steps should be directed toward (1) preventing entry of the agent onto the premises, and (2) preventing transmission of the agent from one group of birds to another. Fortunately the same steps contribute to prevention of other infectious diseases.

To prevent mechanical transmission, rubber boots should be worn by the owner, attendants, and necessary visitors, and should be dipped in disinfectant before going from one group of birds to another. Pets and casual visitors should be kept from the premises. To minimize chances of air transmission, as much space as feasible should be provided between different age groups of the birds. To protect the most susceptible age groups, hatchers and brooder units should be placed on the side of the prevailing wind and the pens for older groups successively downwind. Until more evidence to the contrary is obtained, owners should assume that mature quail can become reinfected even though they survived the disease as chicks, that the infection may be mild or inapparent, and that inapparently infected quail may transmit QBV to susceptible quail. If quail are purchased, they should be kept in quarantine pens and observed for 1 month before being placed with or in proximity to other birds. A definite program for the cleaning and disinfecting of incubators, hatchers, brooders, pens, and related equipment should be planned and consistently carried out. Management practices which emphasize methods of blocking transmission of disease agents have been described in detail by Hinshaw (1965) and by Gross and DuBose (1963a, 1963b).

Other species of birds may show no signs of disease yet be infected and serve as sources for transmission of QBV to bobwhite quail. Such inapparent infections have been demonstrated in chickens and turkeys (Olson, 1950; Yates, 1960) and varying types of evidence suggest that similar infections occur in other game birds and in wild birds (Yates, 1960; DuBose, 1967). Therefore, keeping other species in proximity to bobwhite quail should be avoided. Pens and buildings should be provided with sparrow-proof wire, and to discourage predominantly ground-dwelling birds the premises should be surrounded by fencing through which free-living quail cannot pass. Such fencing would also be helpful between breeder pens, growing pens, and brooder houses to slow down the movement of escaped birds and facilitate their capture.

A vaccine against QB is not currently available. Should a modified *live-virus* vaccine be developed, it should not be adopted for general use until careful studies are made of the vaccine reaction and its effect on other infections in quail. Live-virus vaccine reactions in chickens sometimes precipitate serious respiratory diseases caused by other agents (Hofstad, 1965b).

◆ **CONTROL.** A presumptive diagnosis of QB is sufficient basis for immediately instituting a control program. Measures to prevent transmission between groups of birds and to confine the agent to the premises should be strengthened. The recommendations noted under Treatment should be applied to affected groups. Deferring hatching operations until at least 2 weeks after all signs of infection have disappeared will provide a gap in the presence of the most susceptible age group. A final diagnosis based on isolation and identification of the causative agent should be obtained.

More stringent measures should be tailored to the individual farm and outbreak, keeping in mind that airborne transmission is a possibility. Decisions should be based on an estimation of the chances of restricting the virus to already infected birds, taking into consideration the size and physical arrangement of the farm, morbidity and mortality in infected groups, amount of time left in the hatching season, number and ages of groups of quail on the farm, and perhaps most important, the ability of personnel to apply control measures. Various actions taken in the 7 outbreaks reviewed by DuBose (1967) included deferral of all hatching operations until 6 weeks after disappearance of signs, slaughter of all quail in affected groups and deferral of hatching for 3 or 4 weeks, closing down hatching for the balance of the year, and depopulation of all quail on the farm for the balance of the year.

◆ **REFERENCES**

Brandly, C. A., and Hanson, R. P. Newcastle disease. In H. E. Biester and L. H. Schwarte, eds., *Diseases of poultry*, 5th ed. Ames: Iowa State Univ. Press, 1965.

Cabasso, V. J. The emerging classification of animal viruses—A review. *Avian Diseases* 9:471, 1965.

Cunningham, C. H. *A laboratory guide in virology,* 5th ed. Minneapolis: Burgess, 1963.

DuBose, R. T. Quail bronchitis. *Bull. Wildlife Disease Assoc.* 3:10, 1967.

DuBose, R. T., and Grumbles, L. C. The relationship between quail bronchitis virus and chicken embryo lethal orphan virus. *Avian Diseases* 3:321, 1959.

DuBose, R. T., Grumbles, L. C., and Flowers, A. I. The isolation of a nonbacterial agent from quail with a respiratory disease. *Poultry Sci.* 37:654, 1958.

———. Differentiation of quail bronchitis virus and infectious virus by heat stability. *Am. J. Vet. Res.* 21:740, 1960.

Dutta, S. K., and Pomeroy, B. S. Electron microscopic structure of chicken embryo lethal orphan virus. *Proc. Soc. Exptl. Biol. Med.* 114:539, 1963.

———. Electron microscopic studies of quail bronchitis virus. *Am. J. Vet. Res.* 28:296, 1967.

Gross, W. B., and DuBose, R. T. Security management, a method for disease prevention. *Circ. 848, Coop. Agr. Ext. Serv.,* Va. Polytechnic Inst., Blacksburg, 1963a.

———. Security management, procedures for poultry farm visitors. *Leaflet 161, Coop.*

Agr. Ext. Serv., Va. Polytechnic Inst., Blacksburg, 1963b.

Hinshaw, W. R. Principles of disease prevention. In H. E. Biester and L. H. Schwarte, eds., *Diseases of poultry,* 5th ed. Ames: Iowa State Univ. Press, 1965.

Hofstad, M. S. Quail bronchitis. In H. E. Biester and L. H. Schwarte, eds., *Diseases of poultry,* 5th ed. Ames: Iowa State Univ. Press, 1965a.

———. Infectious bronchitis. In H. E. Biester and L. H. Schwarte, eds., *Diseases of poultry,* 5th ed. Ames: Iowa State Univ. Press, 1965b.

Locke, L. N. Personal communication, 1967.

NAS–NRC Pub. No. 1038, *Methods for the examination of poultry biologics,* 2nd ed. Washington, D.C.: NAS–NRC, 1963.

Olson, N. O. A respiratory disease (bronchitis) of quail caused by a virus. *Proc. 54th Ann. Meeting U.S. Livestock Sanit. Assoc.,* p. 171, 1950.

Wilner, B. I. Adenoviruses. *A classification of the major groups of human and other animal viruses,* 3rd ed. Minneapolis: Burgess, 1965.

Yates, V. J. Characterization of the chicken–embryo–lethal–orphan (CELO) virus. Thesis, Univ. Wis., Madison, 1960.

Yates, V. J., and Fry, D. E. Observations on a chicken embryo lethal orphan (CELO) virus. *Am. J. Vet. Res.* 18:657, 1957.

6 ◆ PUFFINOSIS

● LARS KARSTAD

PUFFINOSIS is a disease of shearwaters and gulls, seen on islands near the coast of Wales (Dane, 1948; Miles and Stoker, 1948). It is characterized by the development of vesicles in the skin of the feet. Other signs described are conjunctivitis and spastic extension of the legs. The disease is reported to occur in shearwaters *(Puffinus puffinus)* and herring gulls *(Larus argentatus)*.

Jennings and Soulsby (1956) described a similar disease in common gulls *(Larus canus)* and black-headed gulls *(Larus ridibundus)*, which they called vesicular dermatitis. Kirmse (1967) has described similar lesions in ring-billed gulls *(Larus delawarensis)*.

The cause of the shearwater disease was shown to be a small filterable virus which could be propagated in chicken embryos (Stoker and Miles, 1953). The virus was transmitted also to domestic ducks and pigeons.

◆ REFERENCES

Dane, D. S. A disease of Manx shearwaters *(Puffinus puffinus)*. *J. Animal Ecology* 17: 158, 1948.

Dane, D. S., Miles, J. A. R., and Stoker, M. G. P. A disease of Manx shearwaters: Further observations in the field. *J. Animal Ecology* 22:123, 1953.

Jennings, A. R., and Soulsby, E. J. L. Diseases in wild birds, third report. *Bird Study* 3: 270, 1956.

Kirmse, P. Experimental pox infection in waterfowl. *Avian Diseases* 11(2):209, 1967.

Miles, J. A. R., and Stoker, M. G. P. Puffinosis, a virus epizootic of the Manx shearwater *(Puffinus puffinus)*. *Nature* 161:1016, 1948.

Stoker, M. G. P., and Miles, J. A. R. Studies on the causative agent of an epizootic amongst Manx shearwaters *(Puffinus puffinus)*. *J. Hyg.* 51:195, 1953.

PART TWO

BACTERIAL, RICKETTSIAL, AND MYCOTIC DISEASES

7 ◆ SALMONELLOSIS

- **JAMES H. STEELE**
- **MILDRED M. GALTON**

- **JAMES H. STEELE**
- **MILDRED M. GALTON**

SYNONYMS: Paratyphoid infections, bacillary white diarrhea, fowl typhoid.

SALMONELLOSIS is the term applied to infection caused by any one of a group of more than 1,100 microorganisms, members of the genus *Salmonella*. All members of the genus are considered to be potential pathogens for man and animals; however, some serotypes differ widely in their host adaptations and pathological syndromes produced. Salmonellosis usually occurs as an intestinal infection which may result in enteritis and diarrhea and terminate in septicemia and death, or the organisms may exist in the host as commensals (Edwards et al., 1964).

◆ **HISTORY.** The occurrence of salmonellae in avian species was recorded first in 1889 when Klein (1889) isolated *Salmonella gallinarum,* the causative organism of "fowl typhoid." A few years later, during investigations to determine the cause of "bacillary white diarrhea" in young chicks, Rettger (1909) recovered *Salmonella pullorum*. Subsequently, many other *Salmonella* serotypes have been found in poultry (Edwards et al., 1948; Hinshaw and McNeil, 1951; International Microbiological Congress, 1963; U.S. Public Health Service, 1964, 1965), and their importance as a cause of economic loss and a health hazard in man is well recognized.

Comparatively little attention was given to the presence of these microorganisms in wild birds until the 1930s, and even now, in spite of numerous surveys, relatively

This chapter is the last manuscript Mildred Galton worked on before her death March 19, 1968.

few positive reports have been recorded (McDiarmid, 1962; Wilson and MacDonald, 1967). However, outbreaks of salmonellosis among birds in large flocks have been reported in which a high percentage were infected (Faddoul et al., 1966). In 1935 Van Dorssen isolated *Salmonella typhimurium* from sea gulls. Kumerloeve and Steiniger (1952) recovered *Salmonella paratyphi* B from the same species. Because of their habit of scavenging, sea gulls were suspected as a possible source of salmonellae in domestic poultry (Nielsen, 1960). Following the recovery of *S. typhimurium* from 2 black-headed gulls *(Larus fascus)* found dead at a Copenhagen cannery, 249 apparently healthy gulls were shot, and examination revealed the same serotype in 4. Investigations at a Danish duck farm during an outbreak of *S. typhimurium* infection in ducklings suggested that wild mallards were the most likely source (Nielsen, 1960).

An epidemic of *S. typhimurium* infections among black-headed gulls *(Larus ridibundas)* and common gulls *(Larus canus)* on islands in the Baltic Sea was described by Schmidt (1954). During a 6-year survey (1952–58), Jennings (1961) examined 734 birds and found only a black-headed gull positive for *Salmonella* (serotype not identified). In another survey conducted by Keymer (1958), 460 specimens were examined and *S. typhimurium* was recovered from a tufted duck *(Aythya fuligula)*. In contrast, this same serotype has been reported in up to 26% of samples from feral pigeons in London (Farrant et al., 1964) and in 30% in Hamburg (Muller, 1965).

From 1939 to 1959 Wilson examined 1,573 birds of 74 different species in the

United Kingdom. *Salmonella typhimurium* was isolated from 8 specimens which included a feral pigeon *(Columba livia),* a greenfinch *(Chloris chloris),* a tawny owl *(Strix aluco),* a hooded crow *(Corvus cornix),* a rook *(Corvus frugelegus),* a red-throated diver *(Colymbus stallatas),* a mallard *(Anas platyrhynchos),* and a mute swan *(Cygnus olor).* This serotype was also isolated from the viscera of 2 mice found in the gizzard of the tawny owl. *Salmonella london* was recovered from a red grouse *(Lagopus scoticus).* From 1962 to 1965 additional studies by Wilson and MacDonald (1967) revealed *S. paratyphi* B or *S. typhimurium* in a variety of species, including herring gulls, wood pigeons *(Columba palumbus),* gannets *(Sula bassana),* starlings *(Sturnus vulgaris),* and house sparrows *(Passer domesticus).*

More recently, Wilson and MacDonald (1967) investigated 4 outbreaks of *S. typhimurium* infection because of mortality in wild flocks. Three of these outbreaks occurred in greenfinches and 1 in sparrows.

In the United States Faddoul et al. (1966) examined 187 specimens of 29 different species of wild birds submitted to determine the cause of death. The brown-headed cowbird *(Molothrus ater)* was found infected more frequently with *S. typhimurium* than any other species. This serotype was also recovered from the hornbill and from sparrows. *Salmonella derby* was isolated from a herring gull, *S. chester* from a swan, *S. anatum* from chukar partridges *(Alectoris graeca),* and *S. blockley* from a pigeon (Faddoul and Fellows, 1966). Although for many years *S. pullorum* and *S. gallinarum* were a problem in domestic poultry, there have been relatively few reports of isolations from wild birds. In most cases when these serotypes have been recovered, evidence suggests an outbreak in domestic poultry as the probable source. Both of these serotypes have decreased in the western world to almost negligible incidence, due to long and intensive programs.

In captive birds salmonellosis has been observed in various species in zoological park collections. It can occur at any time in any species.

◆ **DISTRIBUTION.** It is well known that salmonellae inhabit most species of warm-blooded animals and many cold-blooded vertebrates throughout the world. However, salmonellae are probably recovered more frequently from domestic avian species than from any other animal source. The high isolation rate in domestic poultry may be attributed, in part, to the pullorum disease control programs which frequently involve the examination of reactor birds. While numerous surveys show wild birds to be infected in many areas of the world, the reported incidence has been much lower than in domestic species.

Reported *Salmonella* serotypes isolated from various wild avian species are summarized in Table 7.1.

In the United States during 1965, 3,842 *Salmonella* isolations of 58 serotypes from fowl or their environment were reported to the Salmonella Surveillance Unit, National Communicable Disease Center (U.S. Public Health Service, 1966). Of these, only 55 were from wild birds, and of these, more than half were from pheasant and quail which are frequently raised under domestic poultry conditions for commercial purposes. *Salmonella typhimurium* was the most common of 17 serotypes reported.

◆ **ETIOLOGY.** The etiologic agents of salmonellosis belong to the large group of antigenically related microorganisms in the genus *Salmonella.* Numerous definitions of the genus have been proposed (Kauffmann, 1937; Breed et al., 1957; International Microbiological Congress, 1963; Kauffmann, 1964). The recent definition of Kauffmann (1964) in which he proposed subdivision into subgenera I, II, and III was summarized and discussed by Edwards and Galton (1967). The genus is composed of gram-negative, aerobic, non-spore-forming rods that grow well on artificial media and reduce nitrate to nitrite. The majority are motile with peritrichous flagella, although

TABLE 7.1. *Salmonella* Serotypes Reported in Various Species of Wild Birds

Serotype	Avian Species		Reference
	Common name	Scientific name	
S. anatum	chukar partridge	Alectoris graeca	Francis et al., 1963
	gull		Muller, 1965
S. blockley	pigeon		Faddoul and Fellows, 1966
	gull		Muller, 1965
S. bovis-morbificans	gull		Muller, 1965
S. braenderup	gull		Muller, 1965
S. chester	pheasant		Faddoul and Fellows, 1966
S. derby	chukar partridge	Alectoris graeca	Faddoul et al., 1966; Francis et al., 1963
	herring gull	Larus argentatus	Muller, 1965
	pheasant		Muller, 1965
S. duisburg	gull		Muller, 1965
S. enteritidis	herring gull		Steiniger and Hahn, 1953
S. gallinarum	blackbird	Turdus merula	Wilson and MacDonald, 1967
	curlew	Numenius arguata	Wilson and MacDonald, 1967
	goldfinch	Carduelis carduelis	Wilson and MacDonald, 1967
	house sparrow		Wilson and MacDonald, 1967
	jackdaw	Corvus monedula	Wilson and MacDonald, 1967
	partridge	Perdix perdix	Wilson and MacDonald, 1967
	red grouse		Wilson and MacDonald, 1967
	rook		Wilson and MacDonald, 1967
	tawny owl		Wilson and MacDonald, 1967
	wood pigeon		Wilson and MacDonald, 1967
S. hessarek	coot	Fulica americana	Faddoul et al., 1966
S. infantis	gull		Muller, 1965
S. london	red grouse	Lagopus scoticus	Wilson and MacDonald, 1967
S. manchester	gull		Muller, 1965
S. montevideo	gull		Muller, 1965
S. muenchen	gull		Muller, 1965
S. newport	gull		Muller, 1965
S. panama	gull, herring gull		Muller, 1965; Steiniger and Hahn, 1953
S. paratyphi B	barnacle goose	Branta leucopis	Wilson and MacDonald, 1967
	black-headed gull	Larus fuscus	Wilson and MacDonald, 1967
	common gull	Larus canus	Nielsen, 1960
	guillemot	Uria aalge	Steiniger and Hahn, 1953
	herring gull	Larus argentatus	Wilson and MacDonald, 1967; Steiniger and Hahn, 1953
	lesser black-headed gull	Larus fuscus	Steiniger and Hahn, 1953
	razorbill	Alca torda	Steiniger and Hahn, 1953
S. pullorum	coot	Fulica americana	Faddoul et al., 1966
	magpie	Pica pica	Wilson and MacDonald, 1967
	partridge		Wilson and MacDonald, 1967
	sparrow		Wilson and MacDonald, 1967
	wild pheasant	Phasianus colchicus	Faddoul et al., 1966
S. san-diego	gull		Muller, 1965
S. senftenberg	gull		Muller, 1965
S. stanley	gull		Muller, 1965
S. thompson	common gull		Steiniger and Hahn, 1953
	laughing gull		Steiniger and Hahn, 1953
S. typhi	herring gull	Larus argentatus	Steiniger and Hahn, 1953
	laughing gull		Steiniger and Hahn, 1953
	razorbill	Alca torda	Steiniger and Hahn, 1953
S. typhimurium	black-headed gull		Schmidt, 1954
	brown-headed cowbird	Molothrus ater	Faddoul et al., 1966; Faddoul and Fellows, 1966

TABLE 7.1. *Salmonella* Serotypes Reported in Various Species of Wild Birds *(cont.)*

| Serotype | Avian Species | | Reference |
	Common name	Scientific name	
S. typhimurium (cont.)	canary		Faddoul and Fellows, 1966
	common gull		Steiniger and Hahn, 1953
	coot		Faddoul et al., 1966
	gannet	*Sula bassana*	Wilson and MacDonald, 1967
	greenfinch	*Chloris chloris*	Wilson and MacDonald, 1967
	heron		Steiniger and Hahn, 1953
	herring gull		Wilson and MacDonald, 1967; Steinger and Hahn, 1953
	hooded crow	*Corvus cornix*	Wilson and MacDonald, 1967
	hornbill		Faddoul and Fellows, 1966
	house sparrow	*Passer domesticus*	Wilson and MacDonald, 1967; Faddoul et al., 1966
	laughing gull		Steiniger and Hahn, 1953
	mallard	*Anas platyrhynchos*	Nielsen, 1960; Wilson and MacDonald, 1967
	mute swan	*Cygnus olor*	Wilson and MacDonald, 1967
	pheasant		Faddoul and Fellows, 1966
	pigeon (feral)	*Columba livia*	Wilson and MacDonald, 1967
	red-throated diver	*Colymbus stellatus*	Wilson and MacDonald, 1967
	rook	*Corvus frugilegus*	Wilson and MacDonald, 1967
	rusty blackbird		Hudson and Tudor, 1957
	starling	*Sturnus vulgaris*	Wilson and MacDonald, 1967
	tawny owl	*Strix aluco*	Wilson and MacDonald, 1967
	tufted duck		Keymer, 1958
	white-throated sparrow	*Zonotrichia albicollis*	Faddoul et al., 1966
	wood pigeon	*Columba palumbus*	Wilson and MacDonald, 1967
S. typhimurium var. *copenhagen*	common tern	*Sterna hirundo*	Faddoul et al., 1966
	pigeon		Faddoul and Fellows, 1966

atrichous and nonmotile flagellated variants may occur. They ferment glucose but do not ferment adonitol or sucrose, do not form indol, and do not produce urease. The Voges-Proskauer test is negative, and methyl red reaction is positive. Delayed fermentation of salicin may occur rarely. The Arizona group of microorganisms appears in the simplified Kauffman-White schema as subgenus III (of the genus *Salmonella*), that is, *S. arizonae*. Strains belonging to subgenera I and II usually do not ferment lactose, but those of subgenus III may ferment lactose rapidly, slowly, or not at all.

There is considerable disagreement regarding speciation and nomenclature, but the majority of investigators regard the serotypes as subspecific or infrasubspecific entities (Edwards and Galton, 1967). All members of the genus are potentially pathogenic for man and animals.

♦ **TRANSMISSION.** The literature abounds with reports documenting the methods of spread of *Salmonella* infections from domestic and wild mammals and fowls to man (Hedstrom, 1941; Hinshaw et al., 1944; Clarenburg et al., 1952). Evidence indicates that these microorganisms are transmitted either directly from animals or indirectly through food products of animal origin. Furthermore, it is well known that animal feeds and feed ingredients are heavily contaminated with salmonellae and provide a means for the extensive spread of infection now apparent in domestic animals and fowl.

Steiniger and Hahn (1953) examined fecal droppings from wild birds and recovered *S. paratyphi* B from guillemots *(Uria aalge)*, razorbills *(Aleoa torda)*, and lesser black-backed gulls *(Larus fuscus)*. This survey was undertaken as part of an epidemiological investigation of an outbreak of *S.*

paratyphi B infection involving 800 human cases. The outbreak was associated with the use of sea water to cool cooked crabs. The water, where many sea birds feed, was heavily contaminated with *S. paratyphi* B. It was suggested that the birds rather than sewage may have contaminated the water. Subsequently, more than 1,000 samples of fecal droppings from gulls were collected in the area of the Hamburg, Germany, sewage disposal works, in the port, and in the city streets (Muller, 1965). Salmonellae were recovered from 78% of the samples from the sewage disposal works, 66% of the samples obtained in the port, and 28% of the samples in the city. Again, *S. paratyphi* B was the most common. However, samples taken from sewage-free areas were consistently negative. Other serotypes isolated from the droppings of these birds included *S. typhimurium, S. manchester, S. montevideo, S. infantis, S. duisburg, S. senftenberg, S. anatum, S. stanley, S. newport, S. branderup, S. san-diego, S. muenchen, S. blockley, S. bovis-morbificans* and *S. panama,* all of which were recovered also from the waters around Hamburg. Examination of other birds in the Hamburg area (Muller, 1965) revealed wide differences in the proportion harboring salmonellae. For example, salmonellae were recovered from 30% of the pigeons and 16% of the ducks, but only 0.2% of the sparrows and 0.15% of the thrushes.

From the results of the outbreaks of salmonellosis studied by Wilson and Mac-Donald (1967), it appeared that greenfinches and sparrows were highly susceptible to *S. typhimurium* infection, but the occurrence of large outbreaks was attributed primarily to their habit of gathering in large groups to feed. It was suggested that the food also attracted rats and mice which may have been carrying *S. typhimurium.*

In Switzerland Bouvier et al. (1955) isolated *S. typhimurium* from a sparrow and suggested the possibility that the bird had become infected from eating cultures used for rat control. Cultures of both *S. typhimurium* and *S. enteritidis* have been used to control rodents for many years in Europe and are still used in some parts of Eastern Europe, although the World Health Organization Expert Committees on Plague (WHO, 1950) and Zoonoses (WHO, 1967) condemned the procedure as hazardous to man and domestic animals and recommended that it be discontinued. Broth cultures of *S. enteritidis* for this purpose, however, were available from the Pasteur Institute, Paris, in 1966.

It appears from the data available that *Salmonella* infections in wild birds are acquired primarily from their environment and that these infected birds play relatively little part in the transmission of the disease to domestic animals and man. The paucity of reports of *S. pullorum* and *S. gallinarum* infection in wild birds suggests that they possess a natural resistance to these serotypes or that they are exposed infrequently.

◆ **SIGNS.** Salmonellosis in wild birds as in domestic fowl may vary from acute, septicemic to chronic, localized, or subclinical. Clinical signs are also extremely variable. Acute disease occurs more frequently in young birds. Young pigeons are often retarded in growth, underweight, and listless. Diarrhea usually occurs. Temperature may be elevated or subnormal, depending upon the severity and duration of infections. A chronic arthrosynovitis, characterized by pain, stiffness, or soft swelling, may involve certain joints, particularly the humero-ulnar or the tibial-metatarsal. Chronically affected adult birds often become emaciated and weak (Faddoul and Fellows, 1965). Angstrom (cited by Faddoul and Fellows, 1965) noted an extensive panophthalmitis in pigeons. Panophthalmitis was also observed in greenfinches but not in sparrows during outbreaks of *S. typhimurium* (Wilson and MacDonald, 1967). The eyeball was replaced by a mass of inspissated white pus from which the salmonellae were isolated. In gulls, enteritis may frequently be the only sign (Nielsen, 1960). Mild forms of the infection, accompanied by vague signs, occur. Many species acquire the organisms and become intestinal carriers without exhibiting any visible signs.

◆ **PATHOLOGY AND PATHOGENESIS.** Similar pathologic changes have been reported in sparrows, cowbirds, gulls (Faddoul and Fellows, 1966), greenfinches, and other species of wild birds (Wilson and MacDonald, 1967). In most wild bird species with *Salmonella* septicemia, marked pathologic changes may occur. Enlargement and congestion of the liver and spleen are usually observed. Congestion may also appear in the lungs and kidneys. Pericarditis may be present. Severe ulceration of the esophagus with perforation in the subcutaneous tissue of the neck or lower cervical region has been observed in greenfinches. In cowbirds, ulceration of the intestinal tract has been noted.

The fact that *S. typhimurium* is the most common type reported in wild avian species follows the predominance of this serotype in all other species, including man, throughout the world. However, the rarity in wild avian species of the host-adapted serotypes *S. pullorum* and *S. gallinarum* to which young domestic poultry are highly susceptible suggests a natural resistance of wild bird species or a failure to encounter these serotypes in their environment.

◆ **DIAGNOSIS.** Isolation and identification of *Salmonella* microorganisms is the only certain method on which a diagnosis of infection can be based. Salmonellae are relatively easy to isolate from fecal material of infected birds or from the blood and tissues if in the septicemic stage. A portion of the specimen may be streaked directly onto a selective plating medium such as brilliant green, bismuth sulfite, or SS agars. After incubation, suspicious colonies may be picked to a differential medium (Triple Sugar Iron agar or Gillies I and II media). Organisms which show reactions characteristic of the salmonellae may then be identified serologically.

For detection of the organisms in ap-

parently healthy carrier birds, fecal droppings should be placed first into selective enrichment media, such as tetrathionate brilliant green broth or selenite-cystine broth, and incubated at 37° C for 24 hours before streaking to selective agars. For a detailed description of the methods of isolating salmonellae, the reader is referred to any of the several recent books and manuals on *Salmonella* procedures (Edwards and Ewing, 1962; Edwards and Galton, 1967).

◆ **PROGNOSIS.** The course and outcome of the disease are extremely variable and depend largely upon the clinical syndrome produced and the age and susceptibility of the particular avian host. Acute septicemic infections may last for one to several weeks, or they may terminate in death. Young birds are more susceptible to acute infections, and mortality is higher. Certain predisposing stress factors, such as lowered nutrition and exposure to extreme temperatures, lower the resistance of older birds. Survivors of acute septicemias and enteritis may become healthy carriers and remain so for long periods.

◆ **IMMUNITY.** Vaccines in domestic avian species have been tried unsuccessfully (Van Roekel, 1959). A live vaccine prepared from a rough variant of *S. dublin* has recently been reported to protect calves against infection. This vaccine has also been observed to provide some degree of protection against *S. typhimurium* in cattle (Smith, 1965). The same vaccine was found to confer immunity against *S. typhimurium* and *S. choleraesuis* infection in mice and later in guinea pigs (Smith and Halls, 1966). Immunization of wild bird species would not be a practical procedure, but the recent findings with one serotype in which cross protection was observed in cattle and laboratory animals suggest that trials with the same vaccine in captive avian species might be worthwhile.

◆ **TREATMENT.** No drugs or antibiotics have proved to be entirely effective for the treatment of salmonellosis in any species, avian or mammalian. Certain drugs, such as sulfaguanidine and nitrofurazone, and some of the antibiotics, including oxytetracycline, polymyxin, and chloramphenicol, may have limited and irregular effect.

◆ **CONTROL.** Prevention and control of any infectious disease in wild animals and birds are always difficult problems. Fortunately, the reported incidence of *Salmonella* infections in the general wild bird population is extremely low, so they do not pose a major threat as a natural reservoir and source of infection for man and/or domestic animals. In certain circumstances, where large flocks of wild birds gather to feed in areas where domestic animals are raised, outbreaks may occur and the surviving wild carriers of *Salmonella* may transmit infection to domestic animals on other farms. Seabirds that feed in sewage-contaminated waters have been shown to be heavily infected and may serve as carriers.

There is some evidence to suggest that the infection rate is higher in large flocks during winter months, but more information is needed to determine whether this is due to environmental conditions or to the birds flocking together at feeding stations and roosting areas (Faddoul et al., 1966).

Husbandry practices now used widely in the raising of domestic poultry help prevent wild birds from sharing their feed. However, gathering of cattle in feedlots during the winter attracts large numbers of birds, particularly when the ground is covered with snow. Information on specific control practices in the wild population is at present unavailable and unnecessary.

◆ **REFERENCES**

Bouvier, G., Burgisser, H., and Schneider, P. A. Observations sur les maladies due gibier, des oiseaux et des poissons faites en 1953 et 1954. *Schweiz. Arch. Tierheilk.* 97:318, 1955.

Breed, R. S., Murray, E. G. D., and Smith, N. *Bergey's manual of determinative bacteriology,* 7th ed. Baltimore: Williams & Wilkins, 1957.

Clarenburg, A., Hemmes, G. D., and Wagenvoort, W. On the occurrence of *Salmonella bareilly* in man and animals and the mode of transmission of the salmonellosis caused by this species. *Antonie Leeuwenhoek* 18:171, 1952.

Edwards, P. R., and Ewing, W. H. *Identification of enterobacteriaceae,* 2nd ed. Minneapolis: Burgess, 1962.

Edwards, P. R., and Galton, M. M. Salmonellosis. *Advan. Vet. Sci.,* p. 1, 1967.

Edwards, P. R., Bruner, D. W., and Moran, A. B. The genus *Salmonella:* Its occurrence and distribution in the United States. *Ky. Agr. Exp. Sta. Bull.* 525, 1948.

Edwards, P. R., Galton, M. M., Brachman, P. S., and McCall, C. E. A perspective of salmonellosis. National Communicable Disease Center, Atlanta, Ga., p. 1, 1964.

Faddoul, G. P., and Fellows, G. W. Clinical manifestations of para-typhoid infection in pigeons. *Avian Diseases* 9:377, 1965.

———. A five-year survey of the incidence of salmonella in avian species. *Avian Diseases* 10:296, 1966.

Faddoul, G. P., Fellows, G. W., and Baird, J. A survey on the incidence of *Salmonella* in wild birds. *Avian Diseases* 10:89, 1966.

Farrant, W. N., Phillips, A. G., and Rogers, S. M. *Salmonella typhimurium* in London pigeons. *Monthly Bull. Ministry Health,* London 23:231, 1964.

Francis, D. W., Campbell, H., and Newton, G. R. A study of a *Salmonella* infection in a flock of chukar partridges. *Avian Diseases* 7:501, 1963.

Hedstrom, H. *Salmonella typhimurium* infection in poultry and transmission of infection to man. *Skand. Vet. Tidskr.* 31:98, 1941.

Hinshaw, W. R., and McNeil, E. *Salmonella* infection as a food industry problem. *Advan. Food Res.* 3:209, 1951.

Hinshaw, W. R., McNeil, E., and Taylor, T. J. Avian salmonellosis. Types of *Salmonella* isolated and their relation to public health. *Am. J. Hyg.* 50:264, 1944.

Hudson, C. G., and Tudor, D. C. *Salmonella typhimurium* infection in feral birds. *Cornell Vet.* 47:394, 1957.

International Microbiological Congress, Report of the Subcommittee on Taxonomy of the Enterobacteriaceae. *Intern. Bull. Bacteriol. Nomenclature Taxon.* 13:69, 1963.

Jennings, A. R. An analysis of 1,000 deaths in wild birds. *Bird Study* 8:25, 1961.

Kauffmann, F. Ueber eine lactosespaltende Salmonella-Variante sowie die Definition der Salmonella Gruppe. *Z. Hyg. Infektionskrankh.* 119:252, 1937.

———. Dos Kauffmann-White schema. *The*

world problem of salmonellosis, p. 21. The Hague: Dr. W. Junk Publishers, 1964.

Keymer, I. F. A survey and review of the causes of mortality in British birds as disseminators of disease. *Vet. Rec.* 70:713, 1958.

Klein, F. Ueber eine epidemische krankheit der huhner, veriersacht durch einen bacillus, *Bacillus gallinarum. Zentr. Bakteriol.* 5:689, 1889.

Kumerloeve, H., and Steiniger, F. Ueber das Krankheitsbild des Paratyphus B (Schott-muller) bei der Silbermowe. *Deut. Tierarztl. Wochschr.* 59:312, 1952.

McDiarmid, A. Diseases of free-living wild animals. *Food Agr. Organ. UN* no. 57, p. 16, 1962.

Muller, G. Salmonella in bird faeces. *Nature* 207:1315, 1965.

National Communicable Disease Center, *Salmonella Surveillance Rept., 1963 Ann. Summary,* 1964.

National Communicable Disease Center, *Salmonella Surveillance Rept., 1964 Ann. Summary,* 1965.

National Communicable Disease Center, *Salmonella Surveillance Rept., 1965 Ann. Summary,* 1966.

Nielsen, B. B. *Salmonella typhimurium* carriers in seagulls and mallards as a possible source of infection to domestic animals. *Nord. Veterinaermed.* 12:417, 1960.

Rettger, L. F. Further studies of fatal septicemia in young chickens, or "white diarrhea." *J. Med Res.* 21:115, 1909.

Schmidt, U. Massensterben von Mowen infolge Bacterium enteritidis Breslau-Infektion. *Zentr. Bakteriol. I. Orig.* 160:487, 1954.

Smith, H. W. The immunization of mice, calves and pigs against *Salmonella dublin* and *Salmonella cholerae-suis* infections. *J. Hyg.* 63:117, 1965.

Smith, H. W., and Halls, S. The immunity produced by a rough *Salmonella dublin* variant against *Salmonella typhi-murium* and *Salmonella cholerae-suis* infection in guinea-pigs. *J. Hyg.* 64:357, 1966.

Steiniger, F., and Hahn, E. Ueber den Nachweis von Keimen der Typhus-Paratyphus-Enteritis-Gruppe aus Vogelkot von der Stora Karlso, Sweden. *Acta Pathol. Microbiol. Scand.* 33:401, 1953.

Van Dorssen, C. A. *Salmonella typhi-murium* infectie bij een kleine zeemeeuw *(Larus canus). Tijdschr. Diergeneesk* 62:1263, 1935.

Van Roekel, H. Pullorum disease. In H. E. Biester and L. H. Schwarte, eds., *Diseases of poultry*, p. 162. Ames: Iowa State Univ. Press, 1959.

Wilson, J. E., and MacDonald, J. W. *Salmonella* infections in wild birds. *Brit. Vet. J.* 123:212, 1967.

World Health Organization, WHO Expert Committee on Plague, First Session. *WHO Tech. Rept. Ser. 11,* 1950.

World Health Organization, Joint FAO/WHO Expert Committee on Zoonoses, Third Report. *WHO Tech. Rept. Ser. 378,* 1967.

8 ◆ AVIAN CHOLERA

● MERTON N. ROSEN

SYNONYMS: Fowl cholera, avian pasteurellosis, chicken cholera.

AVIAN CHOLERA is an infectious disease caused by the bacterium *Pasteurella multocida.* A wide variety of wild and domestic birds is susceptible. Wild birds usually have an acute to peracute septicemia, with a resultant high mortality rate. Epornitics of avian cholera are not uncommon among wild waterfowl.

◆ **HISTORY.** Avian cholera has been recognized as a distinct disease for almost 200 years. The first known study was in 1782 by Chabert in France (Gray, 1913). Maillet in 1836 applied the term "fowl cholera" to the disease because of its explosive onset, accompanying diarrhea, and high mortality rate. The highly contagious nature of avian cholera was demonstrated experimentally in the mid-1800s. Toussaint described a bacteremia in fowls in 1879, and a year later both he and Pasteur (1880a) isolated the causative organism. In 1887 Trevisan named the causative organism of avian cholera "Pasteurella" in honor of Pasteur and separated three species: *P. cholerae gallinarium, P. davianei,* and *P. suilla.* The animal of origin was the basis of the taxonomy submitted by Flugge in 1897: *P. aviseptica, P. boviseptica, P. suiseptica,* etc. (Hutyra et al., 1949). Topley and Wilson (1931) combined these forms as *P. septica* which has been, until recently, the accepted designation throughout the British Commonwealth. Rosenbusch and Merchant (1939) introduced the now-accepted name *P. multocida* Trevisan for the etiologic agent of avian cholera and as the type species of the genus *Pasteurella.* The

hemorrhagic septicemia syndromes were designated "Pasteurelloses" (Trevisan, 1887; Lignieres, 1901).

There is considerable literature pertaining to avian pasteurellosis in domestic poultry. On the other hand, there are few reports referring to the disease in wild birds. A summary of wild avian hosts of avian cholera is presented in Table 8.1.

Game-farm pheasants have been infected by *P. multocida,* undoubtedly on more occasions than the three reported (Hudson, 1944; Alberts and Graham, 1951; Jaksic et al., 1964). Only one occurrence of avian cholera in captive valley quail *(Lophortyx californica)* has been described (Hinshaw and Emlen, 1943). Concern about the effect of an epornitic of this disease in wild game was expressed when *P. multocida* was isolated from wild ruffed grouse *(Bonasa umbellus)* (Green and Shillinger, 1936). Jennings (1955) isolated *P. multocida* from red grouse *(Lagopus scoticus)* and reported that heavy losses occurred among them on the moor in Scotland. However, wild waterfowl have had far greater losses from avian cholera than any other avian species.

The first reported epizootic of avian pasteurellosis in wild waterfowl occurred at Lake Nakuru in Kenya during February 1940 (Hudson, 1959). Forty Egyptian *(Alopochen aegyptiacus)* and spur-winged geese *(Plectropterus gambensis)* died during the outbreak. Wild ducks migrating through Holland in 1945 died of the disease, and transmission to the domestic poultry flocks occurred (Van den Hurk, 1946). Zuydam (1952) reported that wild ducks transmitted pasteurellosis to domestic geese in Holland.

Quortrup et al. (1946) were the first to record an outbreak of pasteurellosis in wild

TABLE 8.1. The Occurrence of Avian Pasteurellosis in Wild Birds

Common Name	Scientific Name	Location	Reference
Whistling swan	*Olor columbianus*	California	Rosen and Bischoff, 1949; Rosen and Morse, 1959
Trumpeter swan	*Olor buccinator*	Montana	Gritman and Jensen, 1965
Canada goose	*Branta canadensis leucopareia*	Texas	Petrides and Bryant, 1951
	Branta c. hutchinsii	Missouri	Vaught et al., 1967
	Branta c. minima	California	Rosen, 1967
	Branta c. parvipes	California	Rosen, 1967
White-fronted goose	*Anser albifrons*	California	Rosen, 1967
		Missouri	Rosen and Morse, 1959
Snow goose	*Chen hyperborea*	California	Rosen and Morse, 1959
		Missouri	Vaught et al., 1967
Blue goose	*Chen caerulescens*	Missouri	Vaught et al., 1967
Ross' goose	*Chen rossii*	California	Rosen, 1967
Egyptian goose	*Alopochen aegyptiacus*	Kenya	Hudson, 1959
Spur-winged goose	*Plectropterus gambensis*	Kenya	Hudson, 1959
Mallard	*Anas platyrhynchos*	Texas	Quortrup et al., 1946; Petrides and Bryant, 1951
		California	Rosen and Bischoff, 1949
		Missouri	Vaught et al., 1967
Black duck	*Anas rubripes*	Missouri	Vaught et al., 1967
Gadwall	*Anas strepera*	California	Rosen, 1967
Pintail	*Anas acuta*	Texas	Quortrup et al., 1946; Petrides and Bryant, 1951
		California	Rosen and Bischoff, 1949
		Missouri	Vaught et al., 1967
Green-winged teal	*Anas carolinensis*	Texas	Quortrup et al., 1946; Petrides and Bryant, 1951
		California	Rosen, 1967
		Missouri	Vaught et al., 1967
Cinnamon teal	*Anas cyanoptera*	California	Rosen, 1967
American widgeon	*Mareca americana*	California	Rosen and Bischoff, 1949; Rosen and Morse, 1959
		Texas	Petrides and Bryant, 1951
		Missouri	Vaught et al., 1967
Shoveler	*Spatula clypeata*	California	Rosen and Bischoff, 1949, 1950
		Texas	Petrides and Bryant, 1951
Wood duck	*Aix sponsa*	California	Rosen, 1967
Canvasback	*Aythya valisineria*	California	Rosen and Bischoff, 1949
Greater scaup	*Aythya marila*	California	Rosen, 1967
Lesser scaup	*Aythya affinis*	Texas	Petrides and Bryant, 1951
Common eider	*Somateria mollissima*	Maine	Gershman et al., 1964; Reed and Cousineau, 1967
Ruddy duck	*Oxyura jamaicensis*	Texas	Petrides and Bryant, 1951
Eared grebe	*Podiceps caspicus*	California	Rosen, 1967
Brown pelican	*Pelecanus occidentalis*	California	Rosen, 1967
Great blue heron	*Ardea herodias*	California	Rosen and Bischoff, 1949
Marsh hawk	*Circus cyaneus hudsonius*	California	Rosen and Morse, 1959
Sparrow hawk	*Falco sparverius*	California	Rosen, 1967
Ruffed grouse	*Bonasa umbellus*	Minnesota	Green and Shillinger, 1936
Red grouse	*Lagopus scoticus*	Scotland	Jennings, 1955
Hungarian partridge	*Perdix perdix*	England	Jennings, 1954
California valley quail	*Lophortyx californica*	California	Hinshaw and Emlen, 1943
Ring-necked pheasant	*Phasianus colchicus*	New Jersey	Hudson, 1944
		Illinois	Alberts and Graham, 1951
		California	Rosen and Morse, 1959
		Massachusetts	Faddoul et al., 1967
Sandhill crane	*Grus canadensis*	California	Rosen, 1967

NOTE: Several other species have been reported with infections of *Pasteurella multocida* in zoos.

TABLE 8.1. The Occurrence of Avian Pasteurellosis in Wild Birds *(cont.)*

Common Name	Scientific Name	Location	Reference
American coot	*Fulica americana*	California	Rosen and Bischoff, 1949, 1950; Rosen and Morse, 1959; Raggi and Stratton, 1954
		Texas	Petrides and Bryant, 1951
		Missouri	Vaught et al., 1967
Least sandpiper	*Erolia minutilla*	California	Rosen and Bischoff, 1949
Phalarope	*Phalaropodidae*	California	Rosen and Bischoff, 1949
Glaucous-winged gull	*Larus glaucescens*	California	Rosen and Bischoff, 1949, 1950
Western gull	*Larus occidentalis*	California	Rosen and Bischoff, 1949, 1950
California gull	*Larus californicus*	California	Rosen and Bischoff, 1949, 1950
Gull	*Larus dominicanus*	S. Africa	Kaschula and Truter, 1951
Puffin	(no spp. given)	Argentina	Suarez and Ilazabal, 1941
Owl	*Otus choliba choliba*	Brazil	Brada and Campelo, 1960
Screech owl	*Otus asio*	Massachusetts	Faddoul et al., 1967
Short-eared owl	*Asio flammeus*	California	Rosen and Morse, 1959
Snowy owl	*Nyctea scandiaca*	California	Hunter, 1967
Common raven	*Corvus corax*	Utah	Locke, 1966
Fish crow	*Corvus ossifragus*	Florida	Sanders, 1938
Robin	*Turdus migratorius*	New Jersey	Bivins, 1955
		Massachusetts	Faddoul et al., 1967
Starling	*Sturnus vulgaris*	New Jersey	Bivins, 1953
		England	Jennings, 1954
		Massachusetts	Faddoul et al., 1967
Common grackle	*Quiscalus quiscula*	New Jersey	Bivins, 1955
		Massachusetts	Faddoul et al., 1967
Baltimore oriole	*Icterus galbula*	Massachusetts	Faddoul et al., 1967
Evening grosbeak	*Hesperiphona vespertina*	Massachusetts	Faddoul et al., 1967

ducks of North America. This epornitic occurred in the Texas Panhandle at the Muleshoe National Wildlife Refuge in February 1944, with a loss of 307 ducks. An estimated 40,000 swans, geese, ducks, and coots, as well as some shorebirds, succumbed to avian cholera in the San Francisco Bay area in the winter of 1948–49 (Rosen and Bischoff, 1949, 1950). During the winter of 1956–57 more than 60,000 waterfowl perished at the Muleshoe Refuge, Texas (Jensen and Williams, 1964). In January 1964 more than 1,100 lesser snow geese *(Chen hyperborea)* and blue geese *(Chen caerulescens)* died at Squaw Creek National Wildlife Refuge, Missouri, in one night (Vaught et al., 1967). During the period from December 1963 to mid-April 1964, 5,615 mallards *(Anas platyrhynchos)*, 23 black ducks *(Anas rubripes)*, 23 American widgeon *(Mareca americana)*, 38 green-winged teal *(Anas carolinensis)*, 48 wood ducks *(Aix sponsa)*, one pintail *(Anas acuta)*, and one canvasback *(Aythya*

valisineria) were picked up. In that same April, 80 snow geese and 23 other waterfowl were found dead 43 miles northwest of Squaw Creek Refuge, and the cause of death was avian cholera (McDougle et al., 1965). They speculated that this same disease may have been responsible for waterfowl losses in 1950 and 1964 on the Platte River in Nebraska and at Squaw Creek Refuge during the 1956–57 winter.

Only two enzootic areas of pasteurellosis in waterfowl exist in the world—the Muleshoe National Wildlife Refuge in Texas and north central California. Both locations have had periodic winter outbreaks since 1944 and possibly the disease was present prior to that time but was either unrecognized or mistakenly diagnosed as "winter botulism," lead poisoning, or aspergillosis.

California has had a long siege of avian cholera in wintering waterfowl since it was first noted during 1944 in the lower delta of the Sacramento and San Joaquin rivers where approximately 1,000 coots died (Rosen and Bischoff, 1949). Four years later 40,000 waterfowl, including geese, ducks, and coots, succumbed to the disease. No losses were recorded the following year, but thereafter pasteurellosis occurred annually. The severity of the epornitics has fluctuated both in numbers and in the composition of the species affected. In 1961 about 1,300 whistling swans *(Olor columbianus)* succumbed, while there were less than 250 deaths among other waterfowl species. In the winter of 1965–66 the largest epornitic of avian cholera ever recorded occurred. The combined waterfowl die-off exceeded 70,000 birds, and the mortality extended from the Salton Sea in southern California to the Tule Lake National Wildlife Refuge on the Oregon border. In north central California wherever there were water and waterfowl, dead birds could be found. The principal species affected were snow geese and white-fronted geese, baldpate ducks, pintail ducks, green-winged teal, and coots. The mortality in 1966–67 decreased from the previous year to an estimated 2,000 waterfowl despite an increase of 16% in the number of wintering ducks, twice the goose population, and 73% more coots.

Two conclusions seem to be indicated by California's epornitic data. First, there is no correlation between the size of the population and the number of birds that die. The 1962 episode that claimed 1,300 whistling swans happened at a time when the total swan population in California was at a low point (Rosen, 1969), and the mortality of the greater wintering population of waterfowl in 1966–67 was a fraction of the loss suffered by them during the preceding year. Second, the mortality rate does not vary by species according to body size as suggested by Petrides and Bryant (1951). Some years whistling swans may be affected more than other waterfowl, and in other years the snow and white-fronted geese die at approximately an equal rate to the baldpate and pintail ducks. The comparative susceptibilities and resulting mortalities are probably the result of a combination of ecological factors, particularly the subhabitats of the individual species—for example, less exposure of mallards which are in heavier cover than baldpates and pintails and consequently the mallards are more dispersed. The virulence of the organism may be another factor which exerts an influence on mortality rates during different years and for individual species of waterfowl.

What is the relative importance of pasteurellosis to waterfowl in California? As a result of avian cholera, in certain years approximately 2% less ducks and 6% less swans migrate northward to the breeding grounds. Regardless of its statistical significance, the avian cholera mortality adds yet another factor that diminishes the waterfowl resource, not to mention the potential effect on breeding success of exposed birds. Furthermore the possibility exists that the disease may be carried by the whistling swans from Tule Lake to precipitate an epizootic among the trumpeter swans at Malheur Refuge in Oregon, and the trumpeter swan is a species which has been in danger of extinction.

♦ **ETIOLOGY.** *Pasteurella multocida* is a small, occasionally pleomorphic, gram-negative coccobacillus. Typically, it is 0.3 to 1.25μ long, and usually single, but it may occur in pairs, infrequently in short chains, and rarely in filaments. The organism is encapsulated, although it may lose its capsule, and is nonmotile. Wright's, Giemsa's, methylene blue, or carbol-fuchsin stains will show the characteristic bipolar morphology of the organism which Gram's stain may obscure.

Pasteurella multocida will grow on ordinary nutrient agar; however, more luxuriant growth may be obtained on enriched media such as tryptose heart infusion agar. Serum added to the medium will enhance growth, but whole blood may inhibit its development. The colonies on agar are small, round, and translucent. In broth an even turbidity throughout the medium is evident for several weeks before the organisms precipitate.

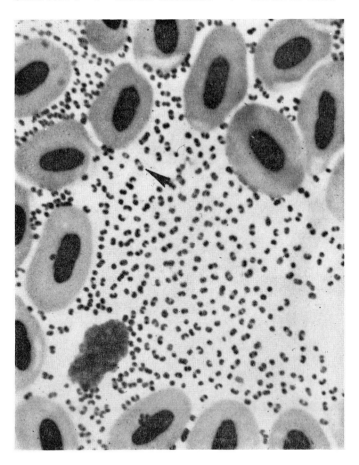

FIG. 8.1. Bacteremia in swan blood with typical "safety pin" characteristics *(arrow)* of *Pasteurella multocida* when treated with Wright's stain. ×2,000. (Photo by John Azevedo.)

The optimum temperature for *P. multocida* is 37° C, but it will grow from 20° to 45° C. This species is aerobic to facultatively anaerobic, and will tolerate pH 6.0 to 8.5, with an optimum pH 7.2.

Pasteurella multocida is not hemolytic (Breed et al., 1957). The sugars fermented without gas are glucose, sucrose, mannitol, and xylose. Sorbitol, arabinose, and lactose are variable. Raffinose and rhamnose are negative.

In addition the organism is catalase positive, oxidase positive, indol positive, urease negative, and it will reduce nitrates to nitrites, and will not grow on MacConkey medium (King, 1964). Sulfide is not detectable other than on lead acetate paper. Other characterizations useful in the identification of *P. multocida* are: citrate utilization negative, MR-VP negative, lysine decarboxylase negative, positive for ornithine decarboxylase, growth in potassium cyanide broth, and negative in malonate (Cowan and Steel, 1965).

Differentiation of strains was originally based on the host species from which the pathogen was isolated, but this was replaced in favor of fermentation reactions when Khalifa (1934) distinguished 3 strains of the organism by their action in media containing the sugars xylose, arabinose, and mannitol. Rosenbusch and Merchant (1939) also separated 3 groups of *P. multocida*, but on the basis of each strain's capability to ferment xylose, arabinose, and dulcitol. They had reservations on this separation when serologic tests gave cross-reactions between the strains. Other workers have shown that considerable fermentation variation exists; thus they claimed there may not be a natural grouping from biochemical studies alone (Russo, 1939; Das, 1958). Bain (1957) suggested that it is not necessary for the biochemical and serological results to coincide in strain grouping.

There are many combinations of the fermentation reactions of *P. multocida* strains. Addition of the strain source as another variable increases these combinations, so for simplification all the factors have been compared by electronic computer analysis (Talbot and Sneath, 1960). A comparison of many biochemical activities of the isolates may be used epidemiologically to directly relate transmission or animal associations (Smith, 1958; Talbot and Sneath, 1960).

Pasteurella multocida generally is encapsulated when directly isolated from an animal that has succumbed to pasteurellosis. However, after continuous subculture on artificial media the organisms tend to lose their capsule. Restoration of the capsule may be accomplished by serial passage of the bacteria in mice.

Lyophilization or suspension of the organisms in normal serum and storing at −20° C or lower will insure viability as well as encapsulation. One strain isolated from a wild duck and lyophilized in 1948 was restored in 1963 and was as virulent as it had been 15 years previously. This agrees with the conclusions on storage made by Stein et al. (1949) and Bain (1954).

Colonial morphology is influenced by the presence or lack of a capsule and its size and composition. A variety of descriptive terms have been used in the past which have now been standardized as large mucoid, smooth small iridescent, smooth gray-blue noniridescent, and rough (Braun, 1953; Carter, 1957). The mucoid colonies are not only the largest, but are composed of organisms having large capsules. Virulence is related to the colonial morphology of *P. multocida;* for example, rough colonies have a low virulence for mice (Carter, 1967).

There is considerable variation in virulence of strains of organisms for different species of animals. For example, an isolate

from a black-tailed deer *(Odocoileus hemionus)* would not infect coots or ducks but was pathogenic for laboratory mice. All isolates from avian cholera epizootics have been extremely virulent for mice. These were all iridescent colonies on primary isolation. According to Carter and Bigland (1953), the mucoid variants obtained from most chronic cases of pasteurellosis are weakly to moderately virulent for mice. Our attempts to determine carrier states in wild ducks and geese by the inoculation of mice with suspensions of lungs and washings of the respiratory passages may have failed due to this lack of virulence for mice which Carter and Bigland hypothesized as characteristic of the mucoid mutants in carrier birds.

Heavy losses in domestic poultry and livestock from pasteurellosis prompted the search for effective immunizing antigens. Failure to induce immunity with some strains led workers to attempt serologic typing of strains. Practical application of serologic typing for effective vaccine production is but one consideration; another is to aid in the investigation of the epizootiology of the disease. A wide variety of methods were tried: plate and tube agglutination; precipitin testing; capsular swelling test; complement fixation; indirect hemagglutination; bacteriophage; fluorescent antibody; mouse serum protection; Ouchterlony double diffusion; and immunoelectrophoresis (Roberts, 1947; Carter, 1953, 1955; Kirchner and Eisenstark, 1956; Carter and Bain, 1960; Prince and Smith, 1966a, 1966b, 1966c).

Little and Lyon (1943) claimed to have separated 3 serotypes of *P. multocida* by the plate agglutination test, none of which was related either to virulence or host origin. Carter (1958) refuted their claim on the basis of autoagglutination in saline and interference by the capsule of the bacteria, but some workers continued to rely on it (Namioka and Murata, 1961a; Dorsey, 1963a, 1963b; Heddleston, 1966). Roberts (1947) separated 4 groups on the basis of the serum protection test for mice. His groupings were confirmed by Carter (1955,

1964) with a hemagglutination test in which the capsular antigen was used to sensitize human type O erythrocytes. The recognized grouping of the strains, according to Carter (1963a, 1963c), is A, B, D, and E.

Namioka and Murata (1961b, 1961c) treated the bacteria with 1.0 N HCl to produce a satisfactory somatic antigen for agglutination tests. Specific serological types were elucidated using cross-absorption tests. Carter (1963c) proposed adoption of the capsular groups A, B, D, and E, and the numerical type designations of Namioka and Bruner (1963), which included 10 varieties (11 as of 1964, Namioka et al., 1964). Avian cholera strains are predominantly 5:A, 8:A, and 9:A (Namioka et al., 1964). Some isolates from avian cholera epizootics in wintering waterfowl in California could not be typed inasmuch as they were either antigenically rough or had lost their capsule (Carter, 1963b).

The differentiation of strains by either the capsular or somatic designations has been challenged. Bain (1964) attempted to repeat work reported by Carter and Rappay (1963) in which a lipopolysaccharide extract was used for indirect hemagglutination, but he could not find any difference between groups B and E. Furthermore, the O antigen is not a true somatic antigen in the classical sense (Namioka et al., 1964). Prince and Smith (1966a, 1966b, 1966c) used various methods of antigen preparation and tested the fractions against heterologous and homologous sera by the Ouchterlony double diffusion and by immunoelectrophoresis. They identified 18 soluble antigens of *P. multocida*, 2 of which were capsular and designated α and β. The more deeply seated antigens were named *a* to *n*. They challenged the assumptions made in current typing techniques for determination of "capsular" and "O somatic" types.

It may be concluded that there are two ways of looking at the problem of classification. One is the viewpoint of the taxonomist who will use all of the available methods, including biochemistry and serology

and the exacting refinements of each, to differentiate the species, groups, types, and subtypes as has been done with the *Salmonella*. Another view is that of the epizootiologist who is interested in a facile technique by which strains may be distinguished for the study of carrier states, transmission, and spread of the etiologic agent. Until further studies elucidate a system, the capsular technique of Carter and the somatic method of Namioka may shed some light on the epizootiology.

◆ **TRANSMISSION.** The mode of transmission of avian cholera among waterfowl is unknown. The natural spread of the disease among domestic fowl has been theorized to be by ingestion, by arthropod vectors mechanically, and by inhalation. For wild birds the last premise seems to be the most likely, although there is evidence of oral transmission from diseased carcasses to predators and scavengering birds. When an outbreak of pasteurellosis occurs in waterfowl, gulls may eat dead coots, ducks, or geese. It was observed that during one epizootic in which mice *(Microtus montanus)* were infected, 44 short-eared owls *(Asio flammeus)* and 5 marsh hawks *(Circus cyaneus hudsonius)* died from avian cholera. The stomach contents of the owls and hawks contained remnants of *Microtus* (Rosen and Morse, 1959).

Immediately after death, ducks and geese that have succumbed to avian cholera have a catarrhal nasal discharge which contains tremendous numbers of *P. multocida*. As much as 15 ml has been collected from a single snow goose. Water from a pond was found to be infective for mice 3 weeks after the removal of dead geese (Rosen, 1969). Infective water aerosols created by the birds landing and wing-flapping immediately thereafter lend credence to a respiratory transmission of the organism. It is possible, however, transmission per os also could occur in this situation.

Gulls or rodents may harbor the organism (Schipper, 1947; Ponomareva and Rodkevich, 1964), but whether there are

FIG. 8.2. Dead waterfowl along a levee during an avian cholera outbreak. Whistling swan and two lesser Canada geese in the foreground.

FIG. 8.3. Remains of a shoveler and coot that had been scavengered by gulls.

FIG. 8.4. Carcass of a widgeon that had died of avian cholera and then had been eaten by gulls.

sufficient numbers to initiate outbreaks is doubted.

It has been found that "healthy" nasal carriers provide an enzootic focus of infection in chickens (Webster et al., 1927). Chickens that had been exposed during the preceding year provided the reservoir for acute avian cholera a year later (Pritchett et al., 1930a, 1930b; Pritchett and Hughes, 1932).

An argument against the avian carrier theory is that California and Texas alone have had annual occurrences. The flyway concept is not rigid. It is known that there is crossing over of birds between flyways, yet in the last 20 years there have been only 2 recorded outbreaks outside the Pacific and Central flyways—the Missouri epizootic among geese and ducks of the Mississippi flyway, and among coots in the Florida Everglades (Klukas, 1968). Additional research is needed not only on the carrier theory in wild waterfowl but on the enzootic focus idea as well.

◆ **SIGNS.** Outbreaks of peracute avian cholera in waterfowl have occurred annually in California, with one exception, for the past 20 years. The exception was observed by the author in ducks that had the infection during 1947. These birds either had ear or brain involvement that affected their flight coordination. Some flew in peculiar undulating patterns, sometimes upside down, and landed 2 or more feet above the surface, tumbled the intervening distance, and splashed in the water.

Regardless of the species of waterfowl, sick birds were rarely encountered during a peracute epornitic. On single ponds there were hundreds of dead birds, perhaps 4 to 6 moribund, and a thousand or more healthy-appearing waterfowl. Those that were symptomatic were in an agonal stage with torticollis as the head moved either backward over the shoulder or forward in a prostrate position as death ensued.

◆ **PATHOGENESIS AND PATHOLOGY.** Regardless of the portal of entry, *P. multocida* invades the systemic circulation and is carried to the various organs of the body. The fulminating infection of peracute avian cholera is probably due to the release of endotoxins by the autolyzing bacteria.

The most prominent gross lesions are petechial hemorrhages on the epicardium and myocardium and sometimes on the surface of the gizzard (Rosen and Bischoff, 1949). If the course of the disease is acute rather than peracute, the surface of the liver appears studded with numerous small necrotic foci. The spleen has no gross abnormalities, nor do the kidneys. There may be hemorrhagic consolidation of the

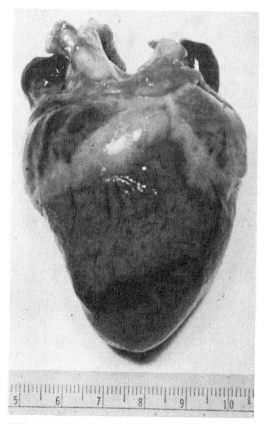

FIG. 8.5. Petechial hemorrhage in the middle aspect of the myocardium and coalesced hemorrhage below in the heart of a swan.

lungs. Rarely is there a catarrhal or hemorrhagic enteritis, but usually the proventriculus, gizzard, and intestinal tracts are empty or may contain a thin greenish fluid. With respiratory signs there is evidence of a catarrhal exudate that is most prominent in the upper trachea. The veins about the intestinal tract are enlarged and congested, and ecchymosis may be visible on the serosa (Harshfield, 1965). The air sacs appear clear and normal. The central nervous system has no lesions in peracute avian cholera.

The most evident histopathologic finding is hyperemia in most of the organs. This, coupled with cloudy swelling in the parenchyma of the liver and the tubules of the kidney, is indicative of a generalized toxic reaction as described by Rhoades

(1964), Shubin and Well (1963), and Weil and Spink (1958). There are islands of bacteria in the sinusoids of the liver, but in the other organs they seem to be restricted to the lumen of the swollen blood vessels. Again it must be emphasized that the peracute nature of the disease allows little time for the development of pathologic manifestations and disruption of the normal architecture of the tissues. The heterophilic infiltration of the liver, lung, and kidney described by Rhoades is either slight or missing in the tissues taken from waterfowl which succumb to peracute pasteurellosis.

◆ **DIAGNOSIS.** The presence of petechial hemorrhages in the epicardial adipose tissue and the myocardium, and especially with focal necrosis in the liver, is almost pathognomonic, particularly when associated with the sudden death of numerous waterfowl during the winter. A presumptive diagnosis is partially confirmed if the bipolar bacteria are observed in blood smears that have been stained with Wright's, Giemsa's, or methylene blue. Additional diagnostic support is gained by the death of mice following intraperitoneal inoculation of blood from the specimen and again finding bipolar bacteria in blood smears from the experimental animals.

A definitive diagnosis can only be based on isolation of the organism and its identification through biochemical reactions. This may be confirmed by fluorescent antibody techniques.

A pure culture of *P. multocida* may be obtained from the heart blood of a bird that has recently succumbed. If the specimen is not fresh or is decomposed, the organism may be recovered from the bone marrow or from the brain.

◆ **PROGNOSIS.** In peracute avian cholera outbreaks among waterfowl, the individual bird almost invariably dies within hours. However, a few recover to become chronic carriers (Vaught et al., 1967). When the resistance of these subacute or chronic carriers is lessened, they may de-

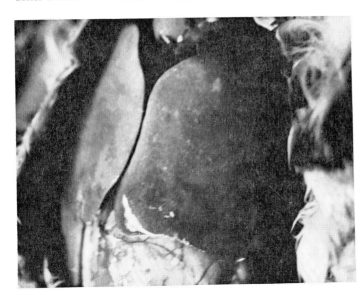

FIG. 8.6. Focal necrosis of the liver of a snow goose. Note the engorged blood vessels on the gizzard.

velop acute disease and die. It is known that during winter an outbreak of avian cholera will occur among the waterfowl of central California, and it is possible to predict that the epizootic will wane with the advent of spring as the birds migrate north. According to Ryder (1967) the Ross geese, after flying thousands of miles north, arrive on the breeding grounds in the finest physical condition of the year, and this phenomenon is believed to happen with the other waterfowl species as well. The turning point of the epizootic may be brought about by the birds' increased resistance as their physical condition improves.

Between the appearance and disappearance of the disease in waterfowl the birds continue to succumb as they migrate north from central California to Tule Lake. It is at Tule Lake in March that the epornitic will finally end.

◆ **IMMUNITY.** It is interesting to note that Pasteur's first experiments in the field of immunology were conducted with avian cholera (Pasteur, 1880b). He did succeed in protecting chickens with an attenuated strain of the organism that he had modified by serial passage in artificial media. However, his results were not often successfully duplicated because of strain variation. Almost all of the subsequent immunologic work was done to protect domestic stock against pasteurellosis.

Priestly (1936) thought that an effective vaccine could be prepared only with highly virulent encapsulated bacteria. However, Heddleston et al. (1966) disproved this concept with the production of potent vaccines from noncapsulated avirulent organisms. Their antigens were prepared by extraction with saline and high-speed centrifugation, and their protective properties were ascribed to an endotoxinlike nature that stimulated strain-specific antibodies (Rebers et al., 1967). An overdose of the vaccine produced many of the signs found in naturally occurring acute avian cholera and killed the recipients. Heddleston (1966) showed that no difference exists in the protective activity of serotypes 8:A, 8a:A, and 9:A, but asserted that 5:A and 9:A are both necessary for the production of a bivalent, effective avian cholera vaccine. Avian cholera vaccine with aluminum hydroxide as an adjuvant will provide immunity for about a year (Heddleston and Reisinger, 1960). Poultry were immunized per os (Heddleston and Rebers, 1968).

Immunization of wildlife is impractical. It is not known if natural immunity exists in wild populations, although there is one record of wildfowl sera containing antibodies to *P. multocida* (Donahue and Olson, 1969). No organisms were isolated from the serologically positive waterfowl. Observations made during an outbreak of the disease have given no indication of age resistance since there has been no significant difference in the proportion of dead young to dead adult waterfowl.

In game farms or with other captive wildlife there may be occasion to vaccinate against avian cholera, particularly when there may be exposure from an outside source.

♦ **TREATMENT.** Drug therapy applied to a wild population is generally futile, and in the case of peracute avian cholera in waterfowl it would be impossible. Against this form of the disease, drugs are more valuable as prophylactic than therapeutic agents and could only be administered to captive birds. Alberts and Graham (1951) reduced mortality among game-farm pheasants by the intramuscular injection of chlortetracycline, but there was no effect when the drug was administered orally. In poultry it has been observed that penicillin and streptomycin administered per os are ineffective in curbing losses, but chlortetracycline and oxytetracycline are capable of controlling mortality. Sulfaquinoxaline and sulfamerazine appear to be the drugs of choice for the prophylactic medication of birds (Alberts and Graham, 1951; Nelson, 1955; Dorsey and Harshfield, 1959). When sulfonamides are used for treatment, the losses are curbed but resume if treatment is discontinued (Carter, 1967).

♦ **CONTROL.** Efforts to stem the spread of an epornitic of pasteurellosis in waterfowl may be divided into three somewhat overlapping approaches toward control, depending on the stage and severity of the problem. The first of the three approaches is at onset of the epizootic when the disease is localized in an area such as one pond; second, when the epizootic is in widely scattered but circumscribed locations; and

third, if the areas have coalesced into a generalized outbreak throughout a large, contiguous region, encompassing thousands of square miles.

In the case of a localized epizootic every means possible to limit transmission should be employed immediately. Every carcass should be collected and burned. If the pond empties into a small drainage ditch that connects with a river in which contaminated water may be diluted, and if there is a ready source of clean water available, the pond should be flushed. But if the pond is one in a series and water from the site of the outbreak could contaminate the secondary impoundments, it is inadvisable to drain.

In the second instance, where there are widely separated areas of avian cholera, the individual sites may be handled as above. In addition, larger areas may call for an attempt to limit the scavengering activities of the gulls. The gull can act as a transmitter of avian cholera due to its resistance to this disease (Brunetti, 1952). Gulls can fly a considerable distance before they die; thus it might be advisable to remove them as vectors by shooting. However, such action must be weighed carefully, since indiscriminate shooting may disperse the gulls and thus provide new focal points of contamination. Uncontrolled shooting could also disperse the waterfowl among which may be birds that are in the incubation stage of the disease.

The separate contaminated areas generally include wetlands which are managed by private duck clubs. Appeals should be made to enlist the cooperation of these clubs to apply measures which would limit losses. The additional manpower could gather carcasses with subsequent incineration. Many of the private clubs have positive means of controlling water. Simple drainage could force the waterfowl in the prodromal stage to spread the contagion to new locations. On the other hand, if the number of dead waterfowl poses too great a problem of carcass removal in a flooded area, it may be that the best action to take is drainage. This is bolstered by the fact that dead birds floating on the water act as decoys, and lure more waterfowl into the infectious water. Regardless of the steps taken, the ducks and geese will move from place to place in their normal daily flight patterns.

One hypothesis which must be borne in mind with this as well as with many other diseases is that there may be dilution of disease in the wild. Ordinarily a single or even a few infected birds when mixed with a large population of susceptible birds would not have the close contact that exists in a static population such as pheasants on a game farm. In the Missouri outbreak there was undue concentration of waterfowl by the artificial maintenance of open water through pumping operations; in the subsequent years pumping was not done and pasteurellosis did not recur (Vaught et al., 1967). On the other hand, there are tremendous aggregations of waterfowl, especially snow geese, on the refuge in the California Gray Lodge Waterfowl Management Area without epizootics of avian cholera. The ecology of the enzootic focal points and the population composition both within and outside the enzootic locations need further investigation.

When a generalized outbreak of avian cholera encompasses thousands of square miles such as was experienced in California in 1965–66, any control measures attempted are futile. Token attempts to save some birds may be of help, but in the overall picture, those that are spared by such efforts constitute a small fraction of the total. Continued research is needed to learn more about the disease in nature, its transmission, immunity, etc., so that a method of limiting the loss of waterfowl to avian pasteurellosis can be realized.

◆ REFERENCES

Alberts, J. O., and Graham, R. An observation on aureomycin therapy of fowl cholera in pheasants. *Vet. Med.* 46:505, 1951.

Bain, R. V. S. Studies on haemorrhagic septicemia of cattle. I. Naturally acquired immunity in Siamese buffaloes. *Brit. Vet. J.* 110:481, 1954.

———. A note on some *Pasteurella* types in Australian animals. *Australian Vet. J.* 33:119, 1957.

———. Classification of the *Pasteurella* which causes haemorrhagic septicemia. South-East Treaty Organization, Bangkok, 1964.

Bivins, J. A. Pasteurellosis in a starling. *Cornell Vet.* 43:241, 1953.

———. Pasteurellosis in feral birds. *Cornell Vet.* 45:180, 1955.

Brada, W., and Campelo, J. C. F. Isolation of *Pasteurella multocida* from an owl (*Otus choliba choliba*). *Arquiv. Inst. Biol. Animal* (Rio de Janeiro) 3:117, 1960.

Braun, W. *Bacterial genetics.* Philadelphia: W. B. Saunders, 1953.

Breed, R. S., Murray, E., and Smith, N. R. *Bergey's manual of determinative bacteriology,* 7th ed. Baltimore: Williams & Wilkins, 1957.

Brunetti, O. Unpublished records, 1952.

Carter, G. R. A serological study of hemorrhagic septicemia *Pasteurella. Cornell Vet.* 43:223, 1953.

———. Studies on *Pasteurella multocida.* I. A hemagglutination test for the identification of serologic types. *Am. J. Vet. Res.* 16(60):481, 1955.

———. Studies on *Pasteurella multocida.* II. Identification of antigenic characteristics and colonial variants. *Am. J. Vet. Res.* 18(66):210, 1957.

———. Failure of the agglutination test to identify types of *Pasteurella multocida. Nature* 181:1138, 1958.

———. Immunological differentiation of type B and E strains of *Pasteurella multocida. Can. Vet. J.* 4:61, 1963a.

———. Personal communication, 1963b.

———. Proposed modification of the serological classification of *Pasteurella multocida. Vet. Rec.* 75:1264, 1963c.

———. Correlation between hemagglutinating antibody and mouse protection in antipasteurella (*Pasteurella multocida*) sera. *Can. J. Microbiol.* 10:753, 1964.

———. Pasteurellosis: *Pasteurella multocida* and *Pasteurella hemolytica. Advan. Vet. Sci.* 11:321, 1967.

Carter, G. R., and Bain, R. V. S. Pasteurellosis (*Pasteurella multocida*). A review stressing recent developments. *Vet. Rev. Annotations* 6:105, 1960.

Carter, G. R., and Bigland, C. H. Dissociation and virulence in strains of *Pasteurella multocida* isolated from a variety of lesions. *Can. J. Comp. Med. Vet. Sci.* 17(11):473, 1953.

Carter, G. R., and Rappay, D. E. A haemagglutination test employing specific lipopolysaccharide for the detection and measurement of *Pasteurella* antibodies to *Pasteurella multocida*. *Brit. Vet. J.* 119:73, 1963.

Cowan, S. T., and Steel, K. J. *Identification of medical bacteria*. New York: Cambridge Univ. Press, 1965.

Das, M. S. Studies on *Pasteurella septica (Pasteurella multocida)*. Observations on some biophysical characters. *J. Comp. Pathol. Therap.* 68:288, 1958.

Donahue, J. M., and Olson, L. D. Survey of wild ducks and geese for *Pasteurella* spp. *Bull. Wildlife Disease Assoc.* 5:201, 1969. *(Proc. Ann. Conf.)*

Dorsey, T. A. Studies on fowl cholera. I. A biochemic study of avian *Pasteurella multocida* strains. *Avian Diseases* 7:386, 1963a.

――――. Studies on fowl cholera. II. The correlation between biochemic classification and the serologic and immunologic nature of avian *Pasteurella multocida* strains. *Avian Diseases* 7:393, 1963b.

Dorsey, T. A., and Harshfield, G. S. Studies on control of fowl cholera. Tech. Bull. 23, S. Dak. Agr. Exp. Sta., 1959.

Faddoul, G. P., Fellows, G. W., and Baird, J. Pasteurellosis in wild birds in Massachusetts. *Avian Diseases* 11:413, 1967.

Gershman, M., Witter, J. F., Spencer, H. E., Jr., and Kalvaitis, A. Case report: Epizootic of fowl cholera in the common eider duck. *J. Wildlife Management* 28:587, 1964.

Gray, H. Avian cholera. In E. W. Hoare, ed., *A system of veterinary medicine*, vol. 1, p. 420. Chicago: Alexander Eger, 1913.

Green, R. G., and Shillinger, J. E. Progress report of wildlife disease studies for 1935. *Proc. North Am. Wildlife Conf.* 50: 469, 1936.

Gritman, R. B., and Jensen, W. I. Avian cholera in a trumpeter swan *(Olor buccinator)*. *Bull. Wildlife Disease Assoc.* 1:54, 1965.

Harshfield, G. S. Fowl cholera. In H. Biester and L. H. Schwarte, eds., *Diseases of poultry*, 5th ed. Ames: Iowa State Univ. Press, 1965.

Heddleston, K. L. Immunologic and serologic comparison of three strains of *Pasteurella multocida*. *Cornell Vet.* 56:235, 1966.

Heddleston, K. L., and Rebers, P. A. Fowl cholera: Active immunity induced in chickens and turkeys by oral administration of killed *Pasteurella multocida*. *Avian Diseases* 12:129, 1968.

Heddleston, K. L., and Reisinger, R. C. Studies on pasteurellosis. IV. Killed fowl cholera vaccine absorbed on aluminum hydroxide. *Avian Diseases* 4:429, 1960.

Heddleston, K. L., Rebers, P. A., and Ritchie, A. E. Immunizing and toxic properties of particulate antigens from two immunogenic

types of *Pasteurella multocida* of avian origin. *J. Immunol.* 96:124, 1966.

Hinshaw, W. R., and Emlen, J. T. Pasteurellosis in California valley quail. *Cornell Vet.* 33:351, 1943.

Hudson, C. B. Fowl cholera in ring-necked pheasants. *J. Am. Vet. Med. Assoc.* 109:211, 1944.

Hudson, J. R. In A. Stableforth and I. Galloway, *Infectious diseases of animals*, vol. 2, p. 413. London: Butterworths Scientific Publ., 1959.

Hunter, B. Isolation of *Pasteurella multocida* from a snowy owl *(Nyctea scandiaca)*—A new host record. *Calif. Fish Game* 53(3):213, 1967.

Hutyra, F., Marek, J., and Manninger, R. *Special pathology and therapeutics of the diseases of domestic animals*, vol. 1. Chicago: Alexander Eger Inc., 1949.

Jaksic, B. L., Dordevic, M., and Markovic, B. O koleri divljih ptica. *Vet. Glasnik* 18: 725, 1964.

Jennings, A. R. Diseases in wild birds. *J. Comp. Pathol. Therap.* 64:356, 1954.

――――. Diseases in wild birds. *Bird Study* 2:69, 1955.

Jensen, W. I., and Williams, C. In USDI, *Waterfowl tomorrow*, p. 333. Washington: USGPO, 1964.

Kaschula, V. R., and Truter, D. E. Fowl cholera in sea-gulls on Dassen Island. *J. S. African Vet. Med. Assoc.* 22:191, 1951.

Khalifa, I. A. B. In A. W. Stableforth and I. W. Galloway, *Infectious diseases of animals*, p. 333. London: Butterworths Scientific Publ., 1934.

King, E. O. The identification of unusual pathogenic gram-negative bacteria. Atlanta: DHEW, PHS, CDC, 1964.

Kirchner, C., and Eisenstark, A. Lysogeny in *Pasteurella multocida*. *Am. J. Vet. Res.* 17: 547, 1956.

Klukas, R. W. Personal communication, 1968.

Lignieres, J. In F. P. Gay, *Agents of disease and host resistance*. Baltimore: Charles C Thomas, 1935.

Little, P. O., and Lyon, B. M. Demonstration of serologic types within the non-hemolytic *Pasteurella*. *Am. J. Vet. Res.* 4:110, 1943.

Locke, L. Personal communication, 1966.

McDougle, H. C., Vaught, R., and Burgess, H. H. Mimeo. report, 1965.

Namioka, S., and Bruner, D. W. Serological studies on *Pasteurella multocida*. IV. Type distribution of the organisms on the basis of their capsule and O groups. *Cornell Vet.* 53:41, 1963.

Namioka, S., and Murata, M. Serological studies on *Pasteurella multocida*. I. A simplified method for capsule typing of the organism. *Cornell Vet.* 51:498, 1961a.

———. Serological studies on *Pasteurella multocida*. II. Characteristics of somatic (O) antigen of the organism. *Cornell Vet.* 51: 507, 1961b.

———. Serological studies on *Pasteurella multocida*. III. O antigenic analysis of cultures isolated from various animals. *Cornell Vet.* 51:522, 1961c.

Namioka, S., Murata, M., and Bain, R. V. S. Serological studies on *Pasteurella multocida*. V. Some epizootiological findings resulting from O antigenic analysis. *Cornell Vet.* 54: 520, 1964.

Nelson, C. L. The veterinarian in poultry practice. *Proc. 92nd Ann. Meet. Am. Vet. Med. Assoc.*, p. 306, 1955.

Pasteur, L. Sur les maladies virulents et en particulier sur la maladie appelee vulgairement cholera des poules. *Compt. Rend. Acad. Sci.* 90:239, 952, 1030, 1880a.

———. De l'attenuation du virus du cholera des poules. *Compt. Rend. Acad. Sci.* 91:673, 1880b.

Petrides, G. A., and Bryant, C. R. An analysis of the 1949–50 fowl cholera epizootic in Texas Panhandle waterfowl. *Trans. North Am. Wildlife Conf.* 16:193, 1951.

Ponomareva, T. N., and Rodkevich, L. V. *Pasteurella multocida* infection among rodents in a large city. *J. Microbiol.* 41:144, 1964.

Priestly, F. W. Experiments on immunization against *Pasteurella septica* infection. *J. Comp. Pathol. Therap.* 49:430, 1936.

Prince, G. H., and Smith, J. E. Antigenic studies on *Pasteurella multocida* using immunodiffusion techniques. I. Identification and nomenclature of the soluble antigens of a bovine haemorrhagic septicemia strain. *J. Comp. Pathol. Therap.* 76:303, 1966a.

———. Antigenic studies on *Pasteurella multocida* using immunodiffusion techniques. II. Relationships with other gram-negative species. *J. Comp. Pathol. Therap.* 76:315, 1966b.

———. Antigenic studies on *Pasteurella multocida* using immunodiffusion techniques. III. Relationships between strains of *Pasteurella multocida*. *J. Comp. Pathol. Therap.* 76:321, 1966c.

Pritchett, I. W., and Hughes, T. P. The epidemiology of fowl cholera. VI. The spread of epidemic and endemic strains of *Pasteurella avicida* in laboratory populations of normal fowl. *J. Exptl. Med.* 55:71, 1932.

Pritchett, I. W., Beaudette, F. R., and Hughes, T. P. Epidemiology of fowl cholera. IV. Field observations of the "spontaneous" disease. *J. Exptl. Med.* 51:249, 1930a.

———. Epidemiology of fowl cholera. V. Further observations of the "spontaneous" disease. *J. Exptl. Med.* 51:259, 1930b.

Quortrup. E. R., Queen, F. B., and Merovka, L. J. An outbreak of pasteurellosis in wild ducks. *J. Am. Vet. Med. Assoc.* 108 (827):94, 1946.

Raggi, L. G., and Stratton, G. S. Pasteurellosis in coots. *Cornell Vet.* 44:229, 1954.

Rebers, P. A., Heddleston, K. L., and Rhoades, K. R. Isolation from *Pasteurella multocida* of a lipopolysaccharide antigen with immunizing and toxic properties. *J. Bacteriol.* 93:7, 1967.

Reed, A., and Cousineau, J. G. Epidemics involving the common eider *(Somateria mollissima)* at Ile Blanche, Quebec. *Naturaliste Can.* 94:327, 1967.

Rhoades, K. R. The microscopic lesions of acute fowl cholera in mature chickens. *Avian Diseases* 8:658, 1964.

Roberts, R. A. An immunological study of *Pasteurella septica*. *J. Comp. Pathol. Therap.* 57:261, 1947.

Rosen, M. N. Species susceptibility to avian cholera. *Bull. Wildlife Disease Assoc.* 5:195, 1969. *(Proc. Ann. Conf.)*

Rosen, M. N., and Bischoff, A. I. The 1948–49 outbreak of fowl cholera in birds in the San Francisco Bay area and surrounding counties. *Calif. Fish Game* 35:185, 1949.

———. The epidemiology of fowl cholera as it occurs in the wild. *Trans. 15th North Am. Wildlife Conf.*, p. 147, 1950.

Rosen, M. N., and Morse, E. E. An interspecies chain in a fowl cholera epizootic. *Calif. Fish Game* 45:51, 1959.

Rosenbusch, C., and Merchant, I. A. A study of hemorrhagic septicemia pasteurellae. *J. Bacteriol.* 37:68, 1939.

Russo, E. Fermentation studies with cultures of *Pasteurella*. *Bol. Vet. Ener. Brazil* 6:127 (Abstr. *Vet. Bull.* 11:284), 1939.

Ryder, J. P. Personal communication, 1967.

Sanders, D. A. Univ. Fla. Agr. Exp. Sta. Tech. Bull. 322 (orig. not seen—cited by Bivins, 1953), 1938.

Schipper, G. J. Unusual pathogenicity of *Pasteurella multocida* isolated from the throats of common wild rats. *Bull. Johns Hopkins Hosp.* 81:333, 1947.

Shubin, H., and Well, M. H. Bacterial shock. *J. Am. Med. Assoc.* 185:850, 1963.

Smith, J. E. Studies on *Pasteurella septica*. II. Some cultural and biochemical properties of strains from different host species. *J. Comp. Pathol. Therap.* 68:315, 1958.

Stein, C. D., Mott, L. O., and Gates, D. W. Pathogenicity and lyophilization of *Pasteurella bubaliseptica*. *Vet. Med.* 44:336, 1949.

Suarez, J. G., and Ilazabal, L. L. Epidemie de choloera en los patos marinos. *Rev. Med. Vet.* Buenos Aires 23:145, 1941.

Talbot, J. M., and Sneath, P. H. A. A taxonomic study of *Pasteurella septica,* especially of strains isolated from human sources. *J. Gen. Microbiol.* 22:303, 1960.

Topley, W., and Wilson, G. *The principles of bacteriology and immunity.* New York: William Wood, 1931.

Trevisan, C. Real Instituto Lombardo di Scienze e lettere Rendiconto, Milan, p. 94, 1887.

Van den Hurk, C. F. G. W. Aanteekeningen by de epizootie van vogel cholera over Nederland in het najaar van 1945. *Tijdschr. Diergeneesk* 71:361, 1946.

Vaught, R. W., McDougle, H. C., and Burgess, H. H. Fowl cholera in waterfowl at Squaw Creek National Wildlife Refuge, Missouri. *J. Wildlife Management* 31:248, 1967.

Webster, L. T., Hughes, T. P., Pritchett, I. W., and Beaudette, F. R. *Pasteurella avisepticum* infection in poultry. *Proc. Soc. Exptl. Biol. Med.* 25:119, 1927.

Weil, M. H., and Spink, W. W. The shock syndrome associated with bacteremia due to gram-negative bacilli. *Arch. Internal Med.* 101:184, 1958.

Zuydam, D. M. Penicillin as therapeutic in fowl cholera. *Tijdschr. Diergeneesk* 77:256, 1952.

9 ◆ PSEUDOTUBERCULOSIS

◉ THEODORE F. WETZLER

SYNONYMS: Zoogleic tuberculosis, avian tuberculosislike syndrome, bird plague, bacillary pseudotuberculosis, canary cholera, infectious necrosis of canaries, avian paracholera, turkey parapest, avian pseudotuberculosis, and others (see Table 9.1).

PSEUDOTUBERCULOSIS IN wild birds, usually caused by *Pasteurella pseudotuberculosis* (syn. *Yersinia pseudotuberculosis*), has been manifested as an acute, rapidly fatal disease. Major epornitics have been reported in canaries, caged song birds, magpies, purple or common grackles, and stock doves. Generally only sporadic cases are involved, and in these cases, tremendous variations of environmental stress, virulence of the etiologic agent, and susceptibility of the host at risk make antemortem diagnosis quite impossible.

◆ **HISTORY.** Many terms were used to describe pseudotuberculosis in wild birds in the early literature, and concurrently, many names were proposed for the etiologic agent of the infectious disease. Incomplete descriptions of isolated agents in a few extant publications make interpretation difficult in today's terms. Synonymies for disease states, as well as for etiologic agents, are listed in Table 9.1.

It cannot be overemphasized that prior to 1930 most of the descriptions of avian pseudotuberculosis did not recognize the synonymy of *Pasteurella pseudotuberculo-*

TABLE 9.1. Synonymies in Avian Pseudotuberculosis Literature

Disease State	Reference	Etiologic Agent	Reference
Zoogleic tuberculosis	Nocard, 1885	*Bacterium canariensis necrophorus*	Meissner and Schern, 1908
Avian tuberculosis	Clarke, 1895		
Avian tuberculosislike syndrome	Bryner, 1906	*Bact. pfaffi*	Hadley et al., 1918
Bird plague	Clarke, 1895	*Paracholera bacillus*	Beck and Huck, 1925
Bird plague	Kinyoun, 1906	*Eberthella pfaffi*	Bergey et al., 1925
Bacillary pseudotuberculosis	Woronoff and Sineff, 1897	*Bact. pseudotuberculosis avium*	Lerche, 1927
Pseudotuberculosis	Muir, 1898	*Shigella pfaffi*	Weldin, 1927
Canary cholera	Kern, 1896	*Bact. parapestis*	Truche and Bauche, 1929
Infectious necrosis of canaries	Meissner and Schern, 1908		
Avian paracholera	Beck and Huck, 1925		
Parapestis	Lerche, 1927	*Bact. pseudotuberculosis rodentium*	Lesbouyries, 1934
Turkey parapestis	Truche and Bauche, 1929		
Avian pseudotuberculosis	Lesbouyries, 1934	Bacillus of Malassez and Vignal	Lesbouyries, 1934
		Shigella pseudotuberculosis	Haupt, 1935
		Pasteurella pseudotuberculosis	Topley and Wilson, 1936
		Cillopasteurella pseudotuberculosis	Prevot, 1948
		Yersinia pseudotuberculosis	Mollaret, 1965

sis rodentium and *Pasteurella pseudotuber-culosis avium.* As early as 1894 Preisz stated that the etiologic agents of pseudotuberculosis from both birds and animals were identical. By 1898 Muir had shown clearly the identity of the two. Nevertheless, well into the 1920s the etiologic agents of avian pseudotuberculosis continued to be confused with any number of fowl disease agents.

The early literature on pseudotuberculosis in birds has been examined and reviewed by several groups of scientists: Beaudette (1940), Truche and Bauche (1933), and in good detail by Stovell (1963). The implicit confusion on the exact disease state in the early literature can be eliminated by organizing the disease state terminology, and differentiating between natural disease in wild birds and experimental disease in birds (regardless of the original source of the etiologic agent).

The first reports of pseudotuberculosis in birds were those of Zuern (1884) in canaries (this seldom-cited reference may not exist anymore) and of Nocard (1885) in fowl. Rieck (1889) isolated the agent of pseudotuberculosis from canaries and experimentally established its virulence in both pigeons and sparrows. Kern (1896) isolated the etiologic agent from canaries in Budapest and established its virulence experimentally in other canaries as well as in linnets, sparrows, and pigeons. He proposed the term "canary cholera" for the syndrome he described in the diseased birds.

Muir (1898) published a comprehensive study of pseudo-tuberculosis [*sic*] in birds, with particular emphasis on the morphology, culture, virulence, and pathology of the etiologic agent in experimental hosts. He did not specify the kind of birds from which the agents were isolated other than to note they were small song birds and that the disease process was quite commonly found in such.

In Berlin, Wasielewski and Hoffmann (1903) isolated the etiologic agent from yellow buntings and experimentally proved the virulence of the isolate in canaries,

chaffinches, and pigeons. They described a hemorrhagic septicemia which has probably led to confusion of the agent with *Pasteurella multocida* (syn. *P. septica*). Bryner (1906) described a "tuberculosis-like" syndrome in avian disease states which must have been due to *P. pseudotuberculosis.* In the same year, in the United States, Kinyoun proposed the name "bird plague" for the disease state he investigated in canaries. Kinyoun established the virulence of his isolates by experimental passage or inoculation of canaries, finches, mockingbirds, pigeons, thrushes, parakeets, and sparrows.

Meissner and Schern (1908) offered the epithet *Bacterium canariensis* for the agent we know today as *P. pseudotuberculosis* and suggested that the syndrome of pseudotuberculosis in birds be called "infectious necrosis of canaries." In their 1918 monograph on paratyphoid and cholera in fowl, Hadley et al. suggested the epithet *Bacterium pfaffi* for the etiologic agent now known as *P. pseudotuberculosis.* Beck and Huck (1925) described pseudotuberculosis disease in fowl as "paracholera," while Lerche (1927) proffered the term "parapest" for the disease caused by *Bacterium pseudotuberculosis avium.* Truche and Bauche (1929) took issue with various publications on the disease states engendered by *P. pseudotuberculosis,* noting that the infections could not be paracholera since septicemia was an inconstant finding and that they could not be cholera for there were no vibrio-shaped bacteria. They finally suggested that the disease be called "parapest" and that the etiologic agent was *Bacterium parapestis.* Many of the observations made by Truche and Bauche were from turkeys.

Natural disease states wherein *P. pseudotuberculosis* was incriminated as the etiologic agent include Nocard (1885) in fowl; Rieck (1889) in canaries and experimental disease studied in pigeons and sparrows; Kern (1896) in canaries and experimental disease evaluated in canaries, sparrows, linnets, and pigeons; Pfaff (1905) in canaries and experimentally studied in canaries, sparrows, and hens; Wasielewski and Hoff-mann (1903) in yellow buntings and studied experimentally in canaries, chaffinches, and pigeons; Kinyoun (1906) in canaries and experimentally studied in canaries, finches, mockingbirds, pigeons, parakeets, and sparrows; Muir (1898) in "song birds" and studied experimentally in "small" birds, including canaries and linnets; Bryner (1906) in tiger finches, butterfly finches, and Japanese titmice and studied experimentally in canaries, chickens, and pigeons.

Isolations were made directly from pigeons by Dolfen (1916), Lesbouyries (1934), and others.

It is to be noted that the experimental disease states studied by Manfredi (1886) were performed in quail and sparrows; however, the strains were not isolated from birds. It is possible that Manfredi's isolates may have been corynebacteria. Studies reported by Nocard and Masselin (1889), although experimentally performed in pigeons, utilized an isolate from a diseased calf.

From 1932 to date, the worldwide literature is quite straightforward, with precise descriptions of the disease and of the etiologic agents whenever the latter were isolated or studied. It is rather interesting to note with respect to the recent literature (1930 to 1967) that the majority of the publications are limited mostly to three circumstances of disease: (1) explosive epornitics, (2) sporadic cases from already-described foci, and (3) pseudotuberculosis disease in museum or zoological garden specimen birds.

◆ **DISTRIBUTION.** Despite the fact that the world literature does not yet prove the point, it is reasonable to infer a worldwide distribution of pseudotuberculosis in wild birds. The incrimination of *P. pseudotuberculosis* from infectious disease states in birds gains a proper perspective when a sharp differentiation is made between a natural disease case and the experimental disease produced in a "normal" host.

Table 9.2 lists various wild birds from which *P. pseudotuberculosis* has been isolated. Table 9.3 lists those types of birds (either wild or caged song birds) which have been employed for experimental susceptibility studies.

◆ **ETIOLOGY.** The biological characteristics of *P. pseudotuberculosis* have been partially detailed by Wetzler (1970a). The biological and biochemical reactions of *P. pseudotuberculosis* are thoroughly treated by Mollaret (1962), and to a lesser extent by Thal (1956), Knapp (1963), Wetzler and Hubbert (1968a), and others.

Inasmuch as *P. pseudotuberculosis* seems to be the only etiologic agent for avian pseudotuberculosis yet reported in wild birds, very little more need be said. However, a realistic view of the extremely close relationships between *P. pseudotuberculosis* and *Yersinia enterocolitica* (cultural and colonial morphology, pathogenesis, mode of transmission, and routes of infection) leads one to suspect that the latter species should be expected in avian pseudotuberculosis. Rather complete descriptions of the biochemical reactions of *Y. enterocolitica* are a matter of recent record (Knapp and Thal, 1963; Frederiksen, 1964; Mollaret and Lucas, 1965; and Wetzler and Hubbert, 1968b).

Antigenic components of *P. pseudotuberculosis* may be distributed among the following general categories: (1) virulence factors, (2) protective factors, (3) flagellar "H" antigens, and (4) somatic smooth or rough, common or serotyping factors. Virulence factors and protective factors have been reviewed recently by Wetzler (1965), flagellar "H" antigens by Thal (1966), and somatic "O" antigens by Wetzler et al. (1968).

◆ **TRANSMISSION.** Much of the present-day information on modes of transmission of *P. pseudotuberculosis* (or other etiologic agents of pseudotuberculosis) has been obtained from natural outbreaks or experimental pathogenic studies in birds. As early as the major canary and song bird epornitics reported by Zwick (1908), the

TABLE 9.2. *Pasteurella pseudotuberculosis* in Wild Birds (1885–1967)

Order	Common Name	Scientific Name	Country Reported
Anseriformes			
	duck	. . .	France, Poland
	eider	*Somateria mollissima*	England
	swan	*Cygnus olor*	France
Charadriiformes			
	oyster catcher	*Haematopus ostralegus*	England
Columbiformes			
	dove, nonspecified		United States*
	dove, barbary	*Streptopelia decaocto*	England
	dove, collared	*Streptopelia risoria*	Germany
	dove, stock	*Columba oenas*	England
	pigeon, domestic	*Columba livia*	France, Germany, United States, Poland, Switzerland
	pigeon, wood	*Columba palumbus*	Denmark, England,† Germany
Galliformes			
	capercaille	*Tetrao urogallus*	Finland, Sweden
	grouse	*Lagopus* sp.	England
	partridge	*Perdix perdix*	Denmark, England, Sweden
	peacock, nonspecified		Sweden
	pheasant	*Phasianus colchicus*	Denmark, England, France, Italy, Sweden
	quail	*Coturnix coturnix*	England, Sweden
	quail, bobwhite	*Colinus virginianus*	England
Gruiformes			
	coot	*Fulica atra*	England
Passeriformes			
	bird of paradise	. . .	Sweden
	blackbird	. . .	United States
	bunting, snow	*Plectrophenax nivalis*	Denmark, England
	bunting, yellow	*Emberezia citrinella*	England, Germany
	canary	*Serinus canarius*	Canada,* Czechoslovakia,* England,* Germany,* Holland, Hungary,* United States, Switzerland*
	finch, nonspecified		Sweden
	finch, bull	*Pyrrhula pyrrhula*	Canada
	finch, butterfly	. . .	Switzerland
	finch, Cuban	*Tiaris canora*	England
	finch, tiger	*Estrilda formosa*	Switzerland
	flycatcher, pied	*Muscicapa hypoleuca*	Sweden
	grackle, purple	*Quiscalus quiscula*	United States*
	jackdaw	*Corvus monedula*	England
	lark	. . .	England
	martin, house	*Delichon ursica*	England, Sweden
	magpie	*Pica pica*	Australia,* England, Switzerland
	rook	*Corvus frugilegus*	England
	silver bill	*Euodice cantans cantans*	England
	sparrow	*Passer* sp.	England
	swallow	*Hirundo rustica*	England, Switzerland
	tanager, superb	*Tangara fastuosa*	England
	tit, great	*Parus major*	Sweden
	titmouse, Japanese	*Parus varius*	Switzerland
	wagtail	*Motacilla alba*	England
	waxwing	*Bombycilla garrulus*	Denmark
	wheatear	*Oenanthe oenanthe*	Sweden
	whydah	. . .	England
	wren	*Troglodytes troglodytes*	England

NOTE: Unless otherwise specified, deaths were sporadic in nature.

TABLE 9.2. *Pasteurella pseudotuberculosis* in Wild Birds (1885–1967) *(cont.)*

Order	Common Name	Scientific Name	Country Reported
Piciformes			
	toucan, nonspecified		England
	toucan	*Selenidera maculirostris*	Poland
	toucan	*Ramphastos cuivieri*	France
	toucan	*Ramphastos ariel*	France
Psittiformes			
	cockatoo	*Kakatoe galerita*	England
	parakeet, shell	*Amasona roseicapilla*	England, Poland
Strigiformes			
	owl, long-eared	*Asio otus otus*	Sweden

* Epornitic, or large "die off."
† In country specified, bacterium is epornitic in bird listed.

TABLE 9.3. Experimental Pseudotuberculosis in Wild Birds (1885–1945)

	Pasteurella pseudotuberculosis		
Order	Common Name	Scientific Name	Reference
Columbiformes			
	pigeons, nonspecified		Rieck, 1889; Kern, 1896; Muir, 1898; Wasielewski and Hoffmann, 1903; Kinyoun, 1906; Bryner, 1906; Nocard and Masselin, 1889
Galliformes			
	quail, nonspecified		Manfredi, 1886
Passeriformes			
	canary	*Serinus canarius*	Kern, 1896; Pfaff, 1905; Wasielewski and Hoffmann, 1903; Kinyoun, 1906; Bryner, 1906
	chaffinch	*Fringilla coelebs*	Wasielewski and Hoffmann, 1903
	finch, nonspecified		Kinyoun, 1906
	linnet	*Carduelis cannabina*	Kern, 1896; Muir, 1898
	mockingbird	*Mimus polyglottos*	Kinyoun, 1906
	sparrow, nonspecified		Rieck, 1889; Kern, 1896; Pfaff, 1905; Kinyoun, 1906; Manfredi, 1886
	thrush, nonspecified		Kinyoun, 1906
Psittiformes			
	budgerigar	*Amasona roseicapilla*	Kinyoun, 1906
	Corynebacterium pseudotuberculosis		
Passeriformes			
	magpie	*Pica pica*	Humphreys and Gibbons, 1942

79

mechanisms of transmission incriminated inert vehicles contaminated with feces of affected birds. Zwick indicated that contaminated fomites, carried or spread by human handlers, might have contributed largely to the outbreak. His study included a 500-bird loss from a total population of about 600 canaries. Stovell (1963) offers excellent experimental evidence which establishes transmission via contaminated food and shows fecal shedding rates and times of the etiologic agent.

There is no reason to believe that *P. pseudotuberculosis* strains are enhanced in virulence by animal (or bird) passage. Actually, it appears that the reverse is true if the major parasitic virulence factor is the VW antigen. It would seem, therefore, that either an extremely virulent strain of *P. pseudotuberculosis* must be disseminated among highly sensitive hosts or that a prestressing of the susceptible population must be assured, with or without an extremely virulent strain.

Examples of these concepts include the following:

1. *High virulence.* The outbreak of "pseudotuberculosis" reported by Murray-Pullar (1932) seems to fit this picture. A number of geographically separated sheep ranches were struck in rapid succession with an extremely serious epizootic of *P. pseudotuberculosis.* Sheep dying of the infection were pelted, and the skins were hung on fences to dry. Local magpies *(Pica pica)* pecked at or fed upon fragments of tissue adherent to the hides. A number of magpies died of *P. pseudotuberculosis* concurrently with the afflicted sheep.

2. *Prestressed susceptibles.* The massive die-off of common or purple grackles *(Quiscalus quiscula),* reported by Clark and Locke (1962), included a number of factors which might be considered as highly stressing: massive numbers of birds concentrated in a roost (estimated at one million birds over the winter months), limited forage, and freezing temperatures.

Paterson and Cook (1963) investigated the circumstances which lead to a massive epizootic in stock guinea pigs in Porton, England. Their observations and data clearly incriminated fecally infected green foods—that is, field kale—as the vehicle for dissemination of *P. pseudotuberculosis* to the sensitive guinea pig population. They further noted that the wood pigeon *(Columba palumbus)* of southern England is commonly infected with *P. pseudotuberculosis.* This would suggest that the wood pigeon may act as a carrier of *P. pseudotuberculosis,* although it is still uncertain whether or not this state occurs as an instance of microbial persistence or as a latency. Based on present knowledge concerning immune protection of the host obtained for all five serotypes of *P. pseudotuberculosis* by any one type, it is difficult to accept the concept of the introduction of an extremely virulent strain of *P. pseudotuberculosis* as the etiologic agent for "pseudotuberculosis" infection and death with the wood pigeon. Yet pigeons have been found dead of pseudotuberculosis. The better explanation might lie in the unknown "prestressing" of the relatively refractory host. In such an instance, humoral or cellular defenses might be overwhelmed and overt pathogenesis become established. This latter concept is analogous to the criteria thought reasonable for the cycling of plague *(P. pestis)* in natural endemic foci.

An inspection of Table 9.2 indicates the same trend which appears from Table 21.1 of Wetzler's chapter Pseudotuberculosis in *Infectious Diseases of Wild Mammals*—that is, the more likely the herbivorous diet, the more likely that pseudotuberculosis occurs. For ready comparison, the above-mentioned Table 21.1 is reproduced as Table 9.4.

Infected or dead canaries have been incriminated as sources of human pseudotuberculosis by Daniels (1961).

◆ **SIGNS.** For sporadic cases of avian pseudotuberculosis, little information on clinical signs is available. Considerable de-

TABLE 9.4. *Pasteurella pseudotuberculosis* in Wild Animals

Order	Genus and Species	Common Name
ARTIODACTYLA	. . .	boar, wild, nonspecified
	Dama dama	deer, fallow
	Odocoileus hemionus	deer, mule
	Cervus elaphus	deer, red
	Capreolus capreolus	deer, roe
	Odocoileus virginianus	deer, white-tailed
	. . .	gazelle, nonspecified
	Ovis aries (syn. *O. musimon*)	sheep, wild (mouflon)
CARNIVORA	*Dendrohydrax* sp.	badger, rock
	Vulpes vulpes	fox
	Vulpes sp.	fox, silver, nonspecified
	Felis leo	lion
	Martes sp.	marten
	Mustela vison	mink
	Felis pardalis	ocelot
	Lutra lutra	otter
	Procyon lotor	raccoon
INSECTIVORA	*Erinaceus europaeus*	hedgehog
	. . .	mole, nonspecified
	Suncus murinus	shrew
MARSUPIALIA	*Macropus melanops*	kangaroo, black-faced gray
PRIMATES	*Papio papio*	baboon, dog-faced
	Galago crassicaudatus	bushbaby
	Pan satyrus	chimpanzee
	Hylobates syndactylus	gibbon
	Papio hamadryas	hamadryad
	Happale jacchus	marmoset
		monkeys
	Cercopithecus althiops	African tree or guenon
	Macaca sylvana	Barbary ape
	Macaca irus	buffoon or crab-eating
	Cebus albifrons	capuchin or sapajous
	Macaca cynomolgus	cynomolgous
	Cercopithecus brazzae or *C. neglectus*	De Brazza
	Cercopithecus mona grayi	gray
	Cercopithecus callitrichus	green guenon
	Cercopithecus n. nictitans	large spot-nosed
	Cercocebus cristatus	mangabey
	Erythrocebus patas	patas
	Macaca rhesus, *M. mulatta*	rhesus
	Cercopithecus leucampyx	silver
	Cercopithecus ascanius	white-nosed African
RODENTIA	*Dasyprocta aguti*	agouti
	Castor canadensis	beaver
	Chinchilla laniger	chinchilla
	Lepus americanus, *L. californicus*, *L. europaeus*, *L. timidus*	hare
	Lemmus lemmus	lemming
	Apodemus sp., *Arvicola* spp., *Clethrionomys* spp., *Mus* sp., *Microtus* (to include *M. mexicanus*), *Pitymus* spp.	mice and voles

TABLE 9.4. *Pasteurella pseudotuberculosis* in Wild Animals *(cont.)*

Order	Genus and Species	Common Name
RODENTIA *(cont.)*	*Ondatra zibethica*	muskrat
	Myocastor coypus	nutria (rangodin) (coypu)
	Cynomys (either *gunnisoni* or *ludovicianus*	prairie dog
	Sylvilagus floridanus	rabbit
	Rattus exulans, R. norvegicus, R. rattus	rat
	Citellus leucurus	squirrel, white-tailed antelope

tails, however, have been afforded on those occasions wherein massive numbers of birds were involved and where the disease outbreak was spread over some reasonable time. Among the better descriptions of signs available are those given for experimental infection studies (Muir, 1898; Pallaske, 1933; Stovell, 1963).

As would be expected, the signs vary from bird type to bird type and by the circumstances and environments wherein the disease was studied. There are apparently three major syndromes: catarrh and pneumonia, enteritis, and generalized septicemia. In general, however, the following seem to be rather constant findings: rapid onset, usually rapid death following onset of signs, bronzing of skin, malaise, diarrhea, inappetence, anorexia, and occasionally arthralgia or lameness.

♦ **PATHOGENESIS.** The pathogenesis of *P. pseudotuberculosis* in the natural disease of wild birds probably differs little from that noted in experimental infections in these and other vertebrates. In the absence of evidence to the contrary, one must assume that the virulence factor of the bacterium in pathogenesis is the VW antigen of Burrows and Bacon (1960).

A review of the large epornitics in canaries, magpies, and common grackles leads to the conclusion that the prestressing of the susceptible populations is rather characteristic. This is quite consistent with laboratory observations that *P. pseudotuberculosis* tends to select toward increasingly avirulent populations with continuous exposures to temperatures of $35°$ to $37°$ C (Wetzler, 1965). This is readily explained by the loss of VW antigens. In such instances, either increasingly large inocula or prestressing of sensitive hosts, which attenuates cellular resistance, is required to obtain death. Experimental stressing has been accomplished with such techniques as urethane-barbital (Riha, 1958), cortisone (Shtel'man, 1960), or ferrous sulfate (Avanyan and Gubina, 1961).

The three recent canary epornitics reported by Stovell (1963) are examples of well-studied natural outbreaks. He incriminated winter conditions for the first canary outbreak (26 infected of 29 at risk), the stresses of reproductive periods for the second canary outbreak (58 infected of 68 at risk), and overheating and poor ventilation for the third epornitic (224 dead of 225 at risk). Some of the canaries in the third outbreak had been fed paprika, a bowel irritant held to enhance or deepen the bird's coloration. This might have been a predisposing factor for the eventual enteritis and visceral granulomas which characterize avian pseudotuberculosis.

Stovell also studied the fecal excretion of *P. pseudotuberculosis*. His data indicated that following oral inoculation 16 of 20 experimental canaries shed from $10^{4.3}$ to $10^{8.1}$ viable *P. pseudotuberculosis* per day, from 3 to 19 days. The 12 experimental birds which survived ceased shedding the bacteria by the 20th day following the last oral inoculation. The author's data led to the conclusions that canaries infect each other, that they are potential sources of disease for other species, including man, and that the most massive fecal shedders are those birds which develop cecal abscesses.

◆ **PATHOLOGY.** Most of the authors cited in Table 9.1, from Nocard (1885) through Lesbouyries (1934), have made careful pathologic descriptions of pseudotuberculosis. The following summarizes their observations: In natural disease states in wild birds, the characteristic millet-seed-sized nodules in spleen and liver are held to be pathognomonic for pseudotuberculosis. These are caseating granulomatous, or necrotizing, focal lesions.

The signs, as well as the gross and microscopic pathology, tend to mimic or incriminate several other syndromes: cholera, hemorrhagic septicemia, and paratyphoid. Catarrhal enteritis, when it occurs, may be mistaken for salmonellosis or coccidiosis. The caseating granulomas could be confused with those produced in listeriosis or vibrionic hepatitis.

Occasionally the focal lesions will occur in breast and other skeletal muscles and in the lungs as yellow-to-white nodules. The visceral organs are not encased particularly with fibrinous exudates. In rare instances cardiac hemorrhages or renal congestion may occur. There may be pleural or peritoneal ascites.

For most birds death has been observed within 4 days of the onset of clinical signs, and with other types (largely domesticated birds) from 8 to 10 days. At necropsy those birds which died rapidly after the onset of signs had few detectable gross lesions, and none were pathognomonic. With more chronic types of infection, or at least more time between onset of signs and death, most case histories reported coalescing miliary foci, especially in spleen, liver, and rarely in the lungs; catarrhal enteritis; peritoneal hemorrhages; and hypertrophied spleen. Given these latter findings, one usually obtains a picture of marked degeneration of both liver and kidney.

Histologically spleens and livers evince marked granulomatous reactions, and macrophages or monocytes predominate in the cellular reaction site. Numerous, discrete, scattered areas of eosinophilic caseated necrosis are found. The cellular response in the spleen is rather diffuse surrounding focal lesions, while in the liver, the necrotic foci seem to have intense cuffing perimeters. Liver cords in reaction areas are usually disrupted with marked degeneration of parenchyma. There is a notable monocytic accumulation.

◆ **DIAGNOSIS.** A positive and confirmed diagnosis of pseudotuberculosis caused by *P. pseudotuberculosis* requires direct laboratory isolation and identification of agents or indirect identification by serology.

The collection of suitable specimens for laboratory processing is not difficult, and the condition of the dead bird will dictate what is appropriate. If available in a moribund state or at death, a blood sample should be withdrawn aseptically for serologic studies. The tissues which are desired for culture include fragments of any or all of the following, as circumstances permit: spleen, liver, lung, and feces. Impression slides may be made for polyvalent fluor-labeled antiserum evaluation. These must be air dried, gently heat fixed, and stored in the cold until ready for processing. Very thin films are required.

If the carcass is badly decomposed, tissues should be collected in isotonic saline containing 50 μg/ml potassium tellurite and/or tetrathionate broth, incubated for several hours at 35° to 37° C, then promptly stored at refrigerator temperature until delivered to the laboratory. If the carcass is quite dessicated, isolation of the pseudotuberculosis agent may still be possible from marrow of the larger bones.

Pasteurella pseudotuberculosis and *Y. enterocolitica* are psychroduric, and analogous to *Listeria monocytogenes,* proliferate reasonably well at temperatures at or above 4° C. This property serves a useful purpose for cold storage "enrichment" techniques.

Typical flow patterns for isolation and identification of the etiologic agent at the laboratory level are available (Wetzler, 1970a). Biochemical reactions should be standardized, for example, to those detailed by Cowan and Steel (1965).

TABLE 9.5. Somatic Antigenic Schema of *Pasteurella pseudotuberculosis*

Serotype	Subtype	O Antigen
I	I A	1, 2, 3, 13*
	I B	1, 2, 4, 13
II	II A	1, 5, 6, 13
	II B	1, 5, 7, 13
III	toxic	1, 8, 13
	non-toxic	1, 8, 13
IV	IV A	1, 9, 11, 13
	IV B	1, 9, 12
V	. . .	1, 10, 13

* Serofactor 13 occurs irregularly in all serotypes.

Serologic identification may be done by whole-cell somatic O agglutination, which is the current practice in Europe (Thal, 1956) or by the hemagglutination of sensitized, nontanned sheep erythrocytes, which is current practice in the United States (Wetzler et al., 1968).

A peculiarity of the somatic serology of *P. pseudotuberculosis* lies in the fact that there are five serotypes, three of which are further subdivided. The smooth somatic O antigens which make up each individual serotype are quite independent of all other serotypes. This point is clearly delineated in Table 9.5.

Further complications lie in the fact that: (1) Serotype II of *P. pseudotuberculosis* shares a common antigen with *Salmonella* Type B (Schuetze, 1932; Thal, 1953); (2) Serotype IV of *P. pseudotuberculosis* shares a common antigen with *Salmonella* Type D (Knapp, 1955); (3) Serofactor 1 is a rough somatic antigen of *P. pseudotuberculosis*, which is shared by *P. pestis* (Davies, 1956, 1958; Schuetze, 1932), *Shigella flexneri*, *Sh. sonnei*, and *Escherichia coli* (Wetzler et al., 1968); and (4) Serofactor 13, which was proposed by Wetzler (1965) as a new, serotype-independent somatic smooth antigen, has been shown to cross with *Y. enterocolitica, Flavobacterium meningosep-*

ticum, Sh. flexneri, and *Bordetella bronchiseptica* (syn. *Alcaligenes bronchiseptica*), as reported by Wetzler et al. (1968).

We propose, therefore, that considerable attention must be given to the proper identification and interpretation of serologic results, and that many times one will have to perform considerable adsorption of antisera in order to define the etiologic agent with high precision.

The simplest serologic tests of great sensitivity and flexibility are those using the antigen-sensitized, nontanned erythrocyte hemagglutination systems of Currie (1965), Currie et al. (1966), and Wetzler (1965). Multiple antigens may be adsorbed to the erythrocytes at one time.

Fluorescein-isothiocyanate-labeled antibody techniques are suitable under limited circumstances but suffer in sensitivity and are subject to the obvious problems delineated above in the potential, multiple "shared" serofactors (Wetzler, 1965).

The definition of *Y. enterocolitica* into serotypes has not been sufficiently studied to date to permit adequate evaluation. It is most likely, however, that there will be at least eight serotypes (Winblad, 1968). At the moment, the best evidence which one can amass for diagnosis of this agent is the rather consistent biochemical characterization profile, its lack of inciting pathology in laboratory animals, its nonsensitivity to *P. pseudotuberculosis* bacteriophage, and identification with the various somatic O serofactors which are known at this time (Knapp and Thal, 1963; Mollaret and Chevalier, 1964; Wetzler and Hubbert, 1968b).

♦ **PROGNOSIS.** The course of *P. pseudotuberculosis* in pathogenesis in the few well-studied epornitics reported in the literature leaves one in an uncertain position regarding prognosis.

Natural outbreaks have suggested that the virulence of the etiologic agent is not the overriding criterion which logic dictates. Time and again stressing factors are postulated and sometimes evaluated, and considerable weight has been awarded to these real or hypothetical circumstances.

Still, an overall dispassionate view would acknowledge that there are self-limiting factors, that not all "susceptibles-at-risk" die or even show signs of overt infection. These observations cannot be explained away in terms of humoral immunity.

Except for the very rare epornitics reported wherein all the susceptibles were lost, avian pseudotuberculosis tends to burn itself out rapidly.

It is reasonable to believe that the innate virulence of the etiologic agent is primary and that this virulence is largely, but not necessarily exclusively, manifested by a VW antigenic expression (Burrows and Bacon, 1960). Strains isolated from rapidly fatal processes have been shown to be highly virulent when inoculated into experimental, susceptible hosts. Those isolates taken from chronic or delayed wasting processes are of markedly lower virulence in similar experimental hosts when injected in equivalent numbers.

It is our belief that given an inoculum of *P. pseudotuberculosis* having sufficient VW+ cells to overcome the susceptible hosts' threshhold minima, the prognosis is not good. Given an inoculum lower than the threshhold minima, in terms of numbers of cells possessing VW antigens, the prognosis is excellent.

◆ **IMMUNITY.** It is known that various wild birds may be quite refractory to *P. pseudotuberculosis* during natural outbreaks of the disease. Further, experimental avian pseudotuberculosis by this etiologic agent is often "route" dependent regardless of dose (numbers of VW+ cells).

The types of birds in which major epornitics have occurred include canaries, grackles, stock doves, magpies, buntings, and caged song birds. The remaining birds listed in Table 9.2 have been involved in sporadic cases of pseudotuberculosis.

If it is permissible to extrapolate data from mammalian pseudotuberculosis, one would expect circulating antibody levels to fall rapidly after an overt infection. But this has not been established yet for avian hosts.

Natural and acquired immunity to *P. pseudotuberculosis* remain largely unstudied in avian systems.

◆ **TREATMENT.** Where practicable and desirable, chemotherapy for specific treatment can readily be accomplished with the broad-spectrum antibiotics. It is likely that prophylactic measures can easily be obtained by the simple expedient of incorporating suitable antibiotics into the drinking water or by the addition of dilute elemental iodine solution into the drinking water to provide 5 to 6 mg/L free iodine.

◆ **CONTROL.** For managed and housed wild bird populations, the following control measures suggested by Stovell (1963) are applicable:

1. Clean, dry quarters
2. Controlled temperatures
3. Adequate ventilation
4. Rodent-proof quarters
5. Regular daily cleaning procedures
6. Exclusion of bird types known or suspected to be fecal shedders of *P. pseudotuberculosis*
7. Indoctrination of workmen or handlers concerning hygienic measures designed to minimize contact transmission
8. Storage of all foods in closed, rodent-proof containers
9. Prompt removal and/or incineration of all dead birds, wastes, and spilled foods outside the cages

There seem to be no realistic measures for control of pseudotuberculosis in non-managed wild bird populations. Awareness of the potential hazards of infected birds or fecal-shedders to economically important susceptible animals or to man can readily be achieved after the incidence of *P. pseudotuberculosis* is clearly established and accepted by those having responsibility in health-oriented areas.

◆ REFERENCES

Avanyan, L. A., and Gubina, N. E. The action of iron on the growth and virulence of *Pasteurella pestis*. *Zh. Mikrobiol. Epidemiol. Immunobiol.* 32:92, 1961.

Beaudette, F. R. A case of pseudotuberculosis in a blackbird. *J. Am. Vet. Med. Assoc.* 97:151, 1940.

Beck, A., and Huck, A. Enzootische Erkrankungen von Truthuener und Kanarienvoegeln durch Bakterien aus der Gruppe der Haemorrhagischen Septikaemie (Paracholera). *Zentr. Bakteriol. Parasitenk., Abt. I. Orig.* 95:330, 1925.

Bergey, D. H. *Bergey's manual of determinative bacteriology*, 2nd ed. Baltimore: Williams & Wilkins, 1925.

Bryner, A. Ein Beitrag zur Pseudotuberkulose der Vogel. Inaug. dissertation. Univ. Zurich, Switzerland, 1906.

Burrows, T. W., and Bacon, G. A. V and W antigens in strains of *Pasteurella pseudotuberculosis*. *Brit. J. Exptl. Pathol.* 41:38, 1960.

Clarke, E. H. On septic fever in birds. *Scottish Poultry J.*, July 19 and 26, 1895.

Clark, G. M., and Locke, L. N. Case report: Observations on pseudotuberculosis in common grackles. *Avian Diseases* 6:506, 1962.

Cowan, S. T., and Steel, K. J. *Manual for the identification of medical bacteria.* London: Cambridge Univ. Press, 1965.

Currie, J. A. A rapid micro-hemagglutination test for the differentiation of *Pasteurella pseudotuberculosis* types. M.S. thesis, Howard Univ., Washington, D.C., 1965.

Currie, J. A., Marshall, J. D., Jr., and Crozier, D. Rapid microhemagglutination test for the detection of *Pasteurella pseudotuberculosis* antibodies. *J. Infect. Diseases* 116:117, 1966.

Daniels, J. J. H. M. Enteral infection with *Pasteurella pseudotuberculosis*. Isolations of the organisms from human faeces. *Brit. Med. J.* 2:997, 1961.

Davies, D. A. L. A specific polysaccharide of *Pasteurella pestis*. *Biochem. J.* 63:105, 1956.

————. The smooth and rough somatic antigens of *Pasteurella pseudotuberculosis*. *J. Gen. Microbiol.* 18:118, 1958.

Dolfen, H. Ueber eine pseudotuberkulose, seuchenhafte Erkankung bei Tauben. *These Vet.*, Hannover, Germany, 1916.

Frederiksen, W. A study of *Yersinia pseudotuberculosis*-like bacteria *(Bacterium enterocoliticum* and *Pasteurella X). Proc. 14th Scand. Congr. Pathol. Microbiol.* Abt. 47:103, 1964.

Hadley, P., Elkins, M. W., and Caldwell, D. W. The colon typhoid intermediates as causative agents of disease in birds. I. The paratyphoid bacteria. *R.I. Agr. Exp. Sta. Bull.* 174, p. 1, 1918.

Haupt, H. *Bacterium pfaffi* Hadley 1918— *Bacillus pseudotuberculosis* Eisenberg 1891. *Zentr. Bakteriol. Parasitenk., Abt. I. Orig.* 132:349, 1934.

————. Zur Systematik der Bakterien. *Ergeb. Hyg. Bakteriol.* 17:175, 1935.

Humphreys, F. A., and Gibbons, R. J. Some observations on corynebacterial infections with particular reference to their occurrence in mule deer, *Odocoileus virginianus*, in British Columbia. *Can. J. Comp. Med. Vet. Sci.* 6:35, 1942.

Kern, F. Eine neue infektioese Krankheit der Kanarienvoegel (Kanariencholera). *Deut. Zt. Tiermed. Vergleich. Pathol.* 22:171, 1896.

Kinyoun, J. J. Bird plague (preliminary notes). *Science* 23:217, 1906.

Knapp, W. Die diagnostische Bedeutung der antigenen Beziehungen zwischen *Past. pseudotuberculosis* und der Salmonella Gruppe. *Zentr. Bakteriol. Parasitenk. Abt. I. Orig.* 164:57, 1955.

————. Klinisch-Bakteriologische und epidemiologische Befunde bei der Pseudotuberkulose des Menschens. *Arch. Hyg. Bakteriol.* 147:369, 1963.

Knapp, W., and Thal, E. Untersuchungen ueber die kulturellbiochemischen, serologischen Tierexperimentellen und immunologischen Eigenschaften einer vorlaufig *Pasteurella* X bennanten Bakterienart. *Zentr. Bakteriol. Parasitenk. Abt. I. Orig.* 190:472, 1963.

Lerche, M. Die "Paracholera" der Puten und ihre Beziehungen zur Pseudotuberkulose der Nagetiere. *Zentr. Bakteriol. Parasitenk. Abt. I. Orig.* 104:493, 1927.

Lesbouyries, G. Pseudo-tuberculose du pigeon. *Bull. Acad. Vet. France* 7:103, 1934.

Manfredi, L. Ueber einen neuen Micrococcus als pathogenes Agens bei infektiosen Tumoren. *Fortschr. Med. Berlin* 22:713, 1886.

Meissner and Schern. Die infektioese Nekrose bei den Kanarienvoegeln. *Arch. Wiss. Prakt. Tierheilk.* 34:133, 1908.

Mollaret, H. H. Le bacille de Malassez et Vignal. Caracteres culturaux et biochemiques. Ph.D. dissertation. Univ. Paris, 1962.

————. Sur la nomenclature et la taxinomie du bacille de Malassez et Vignal. *Intern. Bull. Bacteriol. Nomen. Tax.* 15:97, 1965.

Mollaret, H. H., and Chevalier, A. Contribution a l'etude d'un nouveau groupe de germes proches du bacille de Malassez et Vignal. *Ann. Inst. Pasteur* 107:121, 1964.

Mollaret, H. H. and Lucas, A. Sur les particularites biochimiques des souches de *Yersinia enterocolitica* isolees chez les lievres. *Ann. Inst. Pasteur* 108:121, 1965.

Muir, R. On pseudo-tuberculosis, with special reference to pseudo-tuberculosis in birds. *J. Pathol. Bacteriol.* 5:160, 1898.

Murray-Pullar, E. Pseudotuberculosis of sheep due to *B. pseudotuberculosis rodentium* (so-called "pyaemic hepatitis"). *Australian Vet. J.* 8:181, 1932.

Nocard, E. Sur une tuberculose zoogleique des oiseaux de basse-cour. *Bull. Soc. Centr. Med. Vet.* 39:207, 1885.

Nocard, E., and Masselin. Sur un cas de tuberculose zoogleique d'origine bovine. *Compt. Rend. Soc. Biol.* Paris 41:177, 1889.

Pallaske, G. Beitrag zur Patho- und Histogeneses der Pseudotuberkulose *(Bact. pseudotuberculosis rodentium)* der Tiere. *Zeit. Infekt. Haustiere* 44:43, 1933.

Paterson, J. S., and Cook, R. A method for the recovery of *Pasteurella pseudotuberculosis* from faeces. *J. Pathol. Bacteriol.* 85: 241, 1963.

Pfaff, F. Eine infektioese Krankheit der Kanarienvoegel. *Zentr. Bakteriol. Parasitenk. Abt. I. Orig.* 38:275, 1905.

Preisz, H. Recherches comparatives sur les pseudotuberculoses bacillaires et une novelle espece de pseudotuberculose. *Ann. Inst. Pasteur* 8:231, 1894.

Prevot, A. R. Manuel de classification et de determination des bacteries anaerobies. *Monograph Inst. Pasteur,* 2nd. ed., Masson, Paris, 1948.

Rieck, M. Eine infektioese Krankheit der Kanarienvoegel. *Deut. Zt. Tiermed. Vergleich. Pathol.* 15:68, 1889.

Riha, I. The influence of urethane-barbital narcosis on infection in passively immunized rats. *J. Hyg. Epidemiol. Microbiol. Immunol.* 30: 345, 1958.

Schuetze, H. Studies in *B. pestis* antigens. II. The antigenic relationship of *B. pestis* and *B. pseudotuberculosis rodentium. Brit. J. Exptl. Pathol.* 13:289, 1932.

Shtel'man, A. I. The use of cortisone for the detection of latent plague infection. *Zh. Mikrobiol. Epidemiol. Immunobiol.* 31:39, 1960.

Stovell, P. L. Epizootiological factors in three outbreaks of pseudotuberculosis in British Columbia canaries *(Serinus canarius).* M.S. thesis, Univ. British Columbia, Vancouver, 1963.

Thal, E. Untersuchungen ueber *Pasteurella pseudotuberculosis.* Proc. 15th Internationaler Tieraertzlicher Kongress, p. 1, *Gernandts Boktrycheriet,* Lund, Sweden, 1953.

———. Untersuchungen ueber *Pasteurella pseudotuberculosis* unter besonderen Beruecksichtigung ihres immunologischen Verhaltens. *Berlingska Boktrycheriet,* Lund (Sweden), 1956.

———. Weitere Untersuchungen ueber die thermolabilen Antigene der *Yersinia pseudotuberculosis* (Syn. *Pasteurella pseudotuberculosis). Zentr. Bakteriol. Parasitenk. Abt. I. Orig.* 200:56, 1966.

Topley, W. W. C., and Wilson, G. S. *Principles of bacteriology and immunity,* 2nd ed. London: E. Arnold, 1936.

Truche, M., and Bauche, J. La pseudo-tuberculose du dindon. *Bull. Acad. Vet. France* 2:162, 1929.

———. Le bacille pseudotuberculeux chez la poule et la faisan. *Bull. Acad. Vet. France* 6:43, 1933.

Wasielewski, V., and Hoffmann, W. Ueber eine seuchenhafte Erkrankung bei Singvoegeln. *Arch. Hyg.* 47:44, 1903.

Weldin. Cited by Haupt, H., 1935, 1927.

Wetzler, T. F. Antigens and factors affecting virulence of *Pasteurella pseudotuberculosis* and *Yersinia enterocolitica* with a description of a new strain. Ph.D. dissertation. Univ. Mich., Ann Arbor, 1965.

———. Pseudotuberculosis. In *Diagnostic procedures for bacterial mycotic and parasitic infections,* 5th ed. New York: Am. Public Health Assoc., p. 449, 1970a.

———. Pseudotuberculosis. In Davis et al., eds., *Infectious diseases of wild mammals.* Ames: Iowa State University Press, 1970b.

Wetzler, T. F., and Hubbert, W. T. *Pasteurella pseudotuberculosis* in North America. Presented at Reunion sur la Pseudotuberculose. Permanent Committee on Biological Standardization, Intern. Assoc. Microbiol. Soc., Inst. Pasteur, Paris, July, 1967a. *Symp. Ser. Immunobiol. Standardization* 9:33, 1968a (Karger, Basel).

———. *Yersinia enterocolitica* in North America. Presented at Reunion sur la Pseudotuberculose. Permanent Committee on Biological Standardization, Intern. Assoc. Microbiol. Soc., Inst. Pasteur, Paris, July, 1967b. *Symp. Ser. Immunolog. Standardization* 9:343, 1968b (Karger, Basel).

Wetzler, T. F., Eitzen, H. E., Currie, J. A., and Marshall, J. D., Jr. Lipopolysaccharide-like antigens from *Pasteurella pseudotuberculosis* shared by various genera of Enterobacteriaceae as demonstrated by hemagglutination tests. Presented at Reunion sur la Pseudotuberculose. Permanent Committee on Biological Standardization, Intern. Assoc. Microbiol. Soc., Inst. Pasteur, France, July, 1967. *Symp. Ser. Immunolog. Standardization* 9:155, 1968 (Karger, Basel).

Winblad, S. Studies on O-antigen factors of *Yersinia enterocolitica*. Presented at Reunion sur la Pseudotuberculose. Permanent Committee on Biological Standardization, Intern. Assoc. Microbiol. Soc., Inst. Pasteur, July 1967. *Symp. Ser. Immunolog. Standardization* 9:337, 1968.

Woronoff, A., and Sineff, A. Zur pathologischen Anatomie und Bakteriologie der Bacillaeren Pseudo-tuberculose. *Zentr. Allgem. Pathol. Bakt-Anat.* 8:622, 1897.

Zurn, F. A. *Blaetter Geflugelzucht,* Dresden, p. 236, 1884.

Zwick, W. Untersuchungen ueber eine Kanarienvoegel Seuche. *Zeit. Infekt. Parasit. Krank. Hyg. Haustiere* 4:33, 1908.

● NATHAN B. GALE

SYNONYMS: *Tuberculosis verrucosa cutis* (in parrots), lupus vulgaris, scrofuloderma (tuberculosis of the skin), scrofula (tuberculosis of the cervical lymph nodes), miliary tuberculosis, and tuberculous caseous pneumonia.

THE SPECIFIC ORGANISM responsible for the disease tuberculosis is *Mycobacterium tuberculosis;* three typical strains—human, bovine, and avian—are recognized. The pathogenic *Mycobacteria* cause chronic diseases with lesions of an infectious granuloma type, characterized by epithelioid and giant cells, and in fully developed lesions, caseation necrosis. Infection in birds with this organism produces variable clinical signs and lesions.

◆ HISTORY AND DISTRIBUTION.

Avian tuberculosis occurs most frequently in the North Temperate Zone (Feldman, 1959). It is present in most European countries, infrequent in Switzerland, rare in Italy, and nearly unknown in Greece. It was recognized in the United States around 1900, but was not reported until the early 1920s.

In 1869 at the Pathological Society of London, Crisp was the first to describe tuberculosis in fowl. He reported that hens confined in a damp, sheltered corner of his garden had become emaciated. At necropsy the liver, spleen, and peritoneal surface of the intestines of infected birds were enlarged and tuberculated. In 1872 Crisp suggested that avian tuberculosis was contagious. Sutton and Gibbes (1884) examined and found tuberculosis in a great variety of birds, including peafowl, guineafowl, pigeons, partridges, grouse, pheasants, storks, cranes, falcons, and an eagle. Some were wild birds, while others had originated from the Zoological Society of London.

Tuberculosis was later detected in wild geese, pheasants, swans, peafowl, pigeons, doves, canaries, finches, owls, and vultures (Sibley, 1890).

Stableforth (1929) reported infection of the human type in a parrot and believed it offered evidence as the first example of natural infection from a human source, since the owner of the bird had been tuberculous.

Tuberculosis in captive birds was reported by a number of early workers. Liston and Soparkar (1924) noted partridges *(Caccabis chukor)* and pigeons *(Goura coronata)* in the Bombay Gardens were infected. Griffith (1928) and Lovell (1929) recorded tuberculosis in captive doves, kingfishers, rails, egrets, an eagle, a gull, and a parrot *(Lorius roratus)*. All isolates were the avian strain except for the latter, a human strain of standard virulence.

In England tuberculosis was reported in rooks *(Corvus frugeleaus)*, jackdaws *(Corvus monedula)*, blackbirds *(Turdus merula)*, and starlings *(Sturnus vulgaris)* (Hare, 1932; Hignett and MacKenzie, 1940; Keymer, 1958; McDiarmid, 1964).

Tuberculosis has also been reported in crows *(Corvus brachyrhynchos)* from Canada (Mitchell and Duthie, 1929), in owls *(Asio flammeus)* and a sparrow hawk *(Accipiter n. nisus)* from England (Harrison, 1943; Harrison, 1948), golden eagles *(Aquila chrysaetos)* from Scotland (Wilson and MacDonald, 1965), and a falcon *(Falco berigora)* in Australia (Rac, 1951).

Grini (1944) and Hulphers and Lilleengen (1947) detected avian tuberculosis in wild and captive capercaillies *(Tetrao urogallus)*, captive black grouse *(Tetrao tetrit)*, wild pheasants, and a captive pygmy owl from Norway and Sweden. In Denmark 6% of the pigeons and 3.9% of the gulls examined had tuberculosis (Plum, 1942).

A series of studies of disease and mortality in wild English birds indicated tuberculosis in wild wood pigeons *(Columba palumbus)*, gulls *(Larus ridibundus)*, starlings *(Sturnus vulgaris)*, blackbirds *(Turdus merula)*, partridges, eiders *(Somateria mollissima)*, pheasants *(Phasianus colchicus)*, kestrels *(Falco tinnunculus)*, and sparrows *(Passer domesticus* and *P. montanus)* (Plum, 1942; McDiarmid, 1948; Jennings, 1954, 1959; Jennings and Soulsby, 1957; MacDonald, 1962, 1963).

Poulding (1957) reported a 10.3% infection among 97 gulls *(L. ridibundus* and *L. argentatus)* from England and Scotland. Lasky (1952) reported the death of 2 avocets *(Recurvirostra americana)* in California from 1 of which an acid-fast organism was recorded.

Tuberculosis was recorded in the gray plover *(Squatarola squatarola)*, green plover *(Vanellus vanellus)*, golden plover *(Pluvialis apricaria)*, and Knot *(Calidris canulus)* (Wilson, 1960).

McDiarmid (1956) indicated that tuberculosis was comparatively common in wild birds. Approximately 4% of the wood pigeons and starlings and about 1% of the rooks and jackdaws were infected. Cases in pheasants and partridges were rare and usually resulted from close contact with domestic fowl.

Tuberculosis of an Australian duck *(Querquedula gibberifrons)* was noted by Sankovic (1954) and has been reported in wild ducks *(Anas penelope, Tadorna tadorna,* and *Aythya fuligula)* from Britain by Randall and Harrison (1956), Harrison (1957), and Harrison and Harrison (1960).

In North America tuberculosis among wild ducks and swans was observed by Cowan (1941) through Francis (1958), Quortrup and Shillinger (1941), Garden (1960), and Karlson et al. (1962). Species involved included the American wigeon,

trumpeter swan, green-winged teal, red-headed duck, pin-tailed duck, mallard, shoveler, and whistling swan.

◆ **ETIOLOGY.** Synonyms of the etiologic agent are *Bacillus tuberculosis, Mycobacterium tuberculosis* var. *hominis,* var. *bovis,* and var. *avian* (Merchant and Packer, 1968).

Each of the three types of tubercle bacilli is infective to birds. The avian tubercle bacillus is primarily pathogenic to domestic fowl but is capable of infecting all species of birds. Chickens are said to be resistant to *Mycobacterium bovis,* while parrots and parrotlike birds are highly susceptible to infection. Parrots may also become infected with human strains after close association with a tuberculous person, while birds other than psittacines are resistant to infections by the human bacilli (Merchant and Packer, 1968).

◆ **TRANSMISSION.** It is generally supposed that tuberculosis in predatory birds has its origin in an alimentary tract infection, presumably from ingestion of an infected bird or mammal (Harrison, 1948). Wilson and MacDonald (1965) believed that tuberculous wood pigeons constituted a source of infection for golden eagles in Scotland.

Wilson (1960) concluded that tuberculosis in wild birds was frequently suggestive of prior contact with diseased poultry.

Cases of avian tuberculosis in pigs in England were associated with starlings and rooks at feeding troughs (McDiarmid, 1964). Plum (1942) recorded 40% prevalence of tuberculosis among sparrows in close association with pigs which were infected with avian tuberculosis, while sparrows from noninfected ranches were largely uninfected.

Poulding (1957) found a 10.3% prevalence of tuberculosis among a series of gulls and observed that a likely source of infection was the effluence from sewers emptying into rivers where gulls congregated in large numbers. In recording infection in wood pigeons, McDiarmid (1956) concluded that the disease among these birds was enzootic and had transferred from the brooding pigeon to the squab.

◆ **SIGNS.** Signs of infection of tuberculosis in Aves are variable. They may be nonexistent, as noted by Wilson (1960), who reported the death of a golden eagle that was seen to die suddenly after alighting, and by Condon (1951), who reported a hawk from Australia that was severely infected with tuberculosis although in good condition, with normal plumage.

Alteration of plumage, reported by McDiarmid (1948) and Harrison and Harrison (1956), is attributed to infection among wood pigeons with tuberculosis. The feathers are darker than those of normal birds and there is an abnormality of the feather structure, including atrophy and excessive melanin deposition. Emaciation appears to be the most frequent obvious external sign of infection in many birds (Randall and Harrison, 1956; Poulding, 1957).

Fox (1923) states that skin lesions often occur in birds. They may occur around the eye, at the wing joints, or on the legs. Parrots frequently exhibit nodular or diffuse growths around the eyes and at the commissure of the beak.

Hare (1932) observed a blackbird that progressively developed a large necrotic abscess on the side of its face.

◆ **PATHOGENESIS AND PATHOLOGY.** In tuberculous birds the liver and spleen are more commonly affected than is the lung. The alimentary system was the most common portal of entry in 60% of the cases reported by Fox (1923) and 78% by Scott (1930).

Intestinal tuberculosis occurs in three different forms in Aves (Fox, 1923): where the bacilli appear to be restricted to small nodules in the subperitoneal tissue; where ulceration of the mucous membrane occurs with no significant features; and in an upper intestinal tract form where the wall is thickened and the mucosa, except for some congestion, appears to be healthy.

Hinshaw et al. (1932) studied tuberculosis in domestic turkeys and noted lesions which indicated that the disease was contracted via the alimentary tract. The liver, spleen, intestine, lungs, ovaries, and thymus gland were found, in that order, to be the most commonly infected organs.

Quortrup and Shillinger (1941) observed tuberculosis in ducks and swans among necropsies of 3,000 wild birds from western United States. They noted that the liver was the primary organ involved.

Karlson et al. (1962) reported tuberculosis in a trumpter swan where the liver, spleen, lungs, and intestines contained many yellowish caseous nodules.

Harrison and Harrison (1960) examined an injured pochard *(Aythya fuligula)* and found an enlarged liver studded with small, hard, whitish nodules which were also present on the visceral surfaces of the gall-bladder and intestine. Histologically the liver presented a picture of miliary tuberculosis, with caseous areas largely destroying the central area of each liver lobule. It was apparent the disease had reached the central artery of each lobule as a blood-borne infection, and caseation developed peripherally, ultimately destroying the lobule. There was marked involvement of the air sacs and pericardium and of the skeletal system, with erosion of a portion of one rib.

Garden (1960) observed tuberculosis in 4 of 173 eiders where typical lesions indicated infection by way of the alimentary tract. Gordon et al. (1941) examined a series of ducks, 25.8% of which had lesions of tuberculosis, in which a striking feature was frequent involvement of the lungs, air sacs, and serous membranes. Lesions on the serous membranes of the thorax appeared as "grapelike" clusters of tubercles, resembling infections by the bovine strain. Smears from the lesions stained by Ziehl-Neelsen techniques showed acid-alcohol-fast bacilli in enormous numbers. Culture characteristics and laboratory animal inoculation indicated this was an atypical avian strain.

Skeletal involvement of a sparrow hawk

was noted by Harrison (1948) where lesions were found in the liver, lungs, and joints of the leg, with associated ligamentous and muscular structures.

Mitchell and Duthie (1950) studied crows over a 3-year period and reported a 9.5% incidence of tuberculosis. Of 25 infected crows, lesions were found in the livers of 23, in the spleens of 8, in the lungs of 2, and in other parts of the body in 4.

Scott (1930) observed that the disease most often seen in birds occurs as isolated nodules which appear so distinct that they give the impression of being encapsulated. He noted, however, that upon microscopic examination, there is no evidence of a true capsule. The reaction results in fibrosis with an increase in mononuclear cells and does not proceed to a softening and production of pus as it does in mammals, but rather undergoes a dry necrosis, developing a center which can easily be extracted from the encircling fibrous tissue.

In a variety of captive birds, Ratcliffe (1960) noted widely distributed foci of macrophages heavily "parasitized" by innumerable bacilli, usually without tubercle formation or necrosis. In some instances parasitized cells accumulated in the mucosa of the intestine and displaced 90% of the glandular epithelial tissue.

◆ **DIAGNOSIS.** Blount (1938) and Spears and Dobson (1941) described the avian tuberculin test as the injection of 0.1 ml of tuberculin intradermally into the tip of the wattle. The site of injection is examined for the characteristic swellings 48 to 72 hours after the time of injection. It is sometimes necessary to rely upon the sense of touch to make an evaluation. Lesions are found in 92 to 98% of the birds that show a positive reaction.

Hinshaw et al. (1932) reported that the intradermal tuberculin test was a less sensitive means of diagnosing tuberculosis in turkeys than in chickens. Shchepilov (1955) suggested tuberculosis testing of geese by the intradermal injection but gave no indication of the percentage of correlation be-

tween reactors and positive cases on necropsy.

Bacteriologic evidence of infection depends upon demonstration of tubercle bacilli in lesions. Clinical specimens collected aseptically may be inoculated directly into Middlebrook 7H-9 or Tween albumen liquid medium and later transferred to Lowenstein-Johnson coagulated egg medium or Middlebrook-Cohn 7H-10 agar-base medium for primary isolation. Contaminated specimens, other than fecal specimens, should be processed through a NALC-NaOH digestion-decontamination solution medium. Fecal specimens should be processed by the Petroff method (Kubica and Dye, 1967). The three strains of pathogenic tubercle bacilli can be differentiated by observation of relative virulence in laboratory animals (Merchant and Packer, 1968).

◆ **IMMUNITY.** To protect captive birds in the environment of a zoological garden, Vizy et al. (1964) developed a vaccine from killed, decapsulated bacilli which was administered subcutaneously and intraperitoneally. This was reported to give 100% immunity against both natural and artificial infection.

Vaccination of poultry with several products has been attempted, but results indicate that the disease as it occurs naturally in these birds cannot be controlled by this technique (Biester and Schwarte, 1965).

◆ **TREATMENT AND CONTROL.** Treatment of infected birds is not normally attempted. Control is directed toward elimination of infected individuals and removal of noninfected birds from infected premises where bacilli-laden soil and litter are the major sources of the disease (Biester and Schwarte, 1965).

◆ **REFERENCES**

Biester, H. E., and Schwarte, L. H. *Diseases of poultry,* 5th ed., Ames: Iowa State Univ. Press, 1965.

Blount, W. P. A note on the reliability of the

avian tuberculin test. *Vet. Rec.* 50:1772, 1938.

Condon, H. T. Tuberculosis in a hawk. *S. Australian Ornithol.* 20:24, 1951.

Crisp, E. Tubercle in the common fowl, from a damp atmosphere. *Trans. Pathol. Soc. London* 20:441, 1869.

———. On tubercle in the common fowl after vaccination. *Trans. Pathol. Soc. London* 23: 312, 1872.

Feldman, W. H. Tuberculosis of poultry. In H. E. Biester and L. H. Schwarte, eds., *Diseases of poultry*, p. 374. Ames: Iowa State Univ. Press, 1959.

Fox, H. *Diseases in captive wild mammals and birds.* Philadelphia: J. B. Lippincott, 1923.

Francis, J. *Tuberculosis in animals and man.* London: Cassell, 1958.

Garden, E. A. Tuberculosis in eiders. *Wildfowl Trust, 12th Annual Rept.,* p. 165, 1960.

Gordon, R. F., Garside, J. S., Dobson, N., and Reid, J. An extensive outbreak of tuberculosis in ducks. *Vet. Rec.* 53:575, 1941.

Griffith, A. S. Tuberculosis in captive wild animals. *J. Hyg.* 28:198, 1928.

Grini, O. A case of tuberculosis in a capercailzie. *Abstr. Vet. Bull.* 14, p. 1674, 1944.

Hare, T. Tuberculosis in a blackbird. *Proc. Roy. Soc. Med.* 25:1500, 1932.

Harrison, J. G. On a case of tuberculosis in a wild bird. *IBIS* 58:516, 1943.

———. Avian tuberculosis in a wild shelduck in association with an exceptional parasitic burden. *Bull. Brit. Ornithol.* 77:149, 1957.

Harrison, J. M. Tuberculosis in a wild sparrow hawk. *J. Pathol. Bacteriol.* 60:583, 1948.

Harrison, J. M., and Harrison, J. G. Plumage changes in wild tubercular wood pigeons. *Bull. Brit. Ornithol.* 76:76, 1956.

———. Tuberculosis in a wild pochard and remarks on the recognition of disease by predators. *Bull. Brit. Ornithol.* 80:40, 1960.

Hignett, S. L., and MacKenzie, D. A. *Vet. Rec.* 52:585, 1940.

Hinshaw, W. R., Niemann, K. W., and Busic, W. H. Studies of tuberculosis in turkeys. *J. Am. Vet. Med. Assoc.* 80:765, 1932.

Hulphers, G., and Lilleengen, K. Tuberculosis in wild mammals and birds. *Abstr. Vet. Bull.* 20:844, 1947.

Jennings, A. R. Diseases in wild birds. *J. Comp. Pathol. Therap.* 64:356, 1954.

———. Diseases of wild birds. *Bird Study* 6:19, 1959.

Jennings, A. R., and Soulsby, E. J. Diseases in wild birds. *Bird Study* 4:216, 1957.

Karlson, A. G., Davis, C. L., and Cohn, M. L. Skotochromogenic *Mycobacterium avium* from a trumpeter swan. *Am. J. Vet. Res.* 23: 575, 1962.

Keymer, I. F. Survey and review of the causes of mortality in British birds and the significance of wild birds as disseminators of disease. *Vet. Rec.* 70:713, 1958.

Kubica, G. P., and Dye, W. E. Laboratory methods for clinical and public health mycobacteriology. *Public Health Serv. Pub. 1547.* USGPO, Washington, D.C., 1967.

Lasky, W. R. A case of avian tuberculosis in an immature avocet. *Condor* 54:316, 1952.

Liston, W. G., and Soparkar, M. B. Bovine tuberculosis in India, an outbreak of tuberculosis among animals in the Bombay Zoological Gardens. *Indian J. Med. Res.* 2:671, 1924.

Lovell, R. The isolation of tubercle bacilli from captive wild animals. *J. Comp. Pathol.* 43:205, 1929.

McDiarmid, A. The occurrence of tuberculosis in the wild wood pigeon. *J. Comp. Pathol.* 58:128, 1948.

———. Some diseases of free-living wild birds in Britain. *Bull. Brit. Ornithol.* 76:145, 1956.

———. Tuberculosis in wild birds. *Proc. Roy. Soc. Med.* 57:480, 1964.

MacDonald, J. W. Mortality in wild birds with some observations on weights. *Bird Study* 9:147, 1962.

———. Mortality in wild birds. *Bird Study* 10:1, 1963.

Merchant, I. A., and Packer, R. A. *Veterinary bacteriology and virology.* Ames: Iowa State Univ. Press, 1968.

Mitchell, C. A., and Duthie, R. C. Tuberculosis in the common crow: A preliminary study. *A. Rev. Tuberc.* 19:134, 1929.

———. Tuberculosis of the common crow. *Can. J. Comp. Med.* 14:109, 1950.

Plum, N. Studies on the occurrence of avian tuberculosis among wild birds, especially gulls and sparrows and rats and hares. *Abstr. Vet. Bull.* 13:2802, 1942.

Poulding, R. H. Tuberculosis in gulls: A preliminary investigation. *Bull. Brit. Ornithol.* 77:144, 1957.

Quortrup, E. R., and Shillinger, J. E. 3,000 wild bird autopsies on western lake areas. *J. Am. Vet. Assoc.* 99:382, 1941.

Rac, I. C. Avian tuberculosis in an Australian brown hawk, *Falco berigora. Australian Vet. J.* 27:209, 1951.

Randall, K., and Harrison, J. G. A case of avian tuberculosis in a wild wigeon. *Bull. Brit. Ornithol.* 76, 1956.

Ratcliffe, H. L. *Rept. Penrose Res. Lab.,* Philadelphia Zoo, 1960.

Sankovic, B. Tuberculosis in a gray teal duck. *Australian Vet. J.,* p. 215, 1954.

Scott, H. H. Tuberculosis in man and lower

animals. *Spec. Rept. Ser. Med. Res. Council London,* p. 149, 1930.

Shchepilov, N. S. Tuberculin testing of geese and ducks. *Abstr. Vet. Bull.* 26:1112, 1955.

Sibley, W. K. Further observations on tuberculosis in fowls and other birds. *Trans. Pathol. Soc. London* 41:332, 1890.

Spears, H. N., and Dobson, N. The avian tuberculin test and its specificity. *Vet. Rec.* 53:365, 1941.

Stableforth, A. W. A bacteriological investigation of cases of tuberculosis in 5 cats, 16 dogs, a parrot and a wallaby. *J. Comp. Pathol.* 42:163, 1929.

Sutton, J. B., and Gibbes, H. Tuberculosis in birds. *Trans. Pathol. Soc. London* 35:477, 1884.

Vizy, L., Douza, I., and Pasztor, L. Uber immunisierungsversuche an verschiedenen Geflugelarten mit abgetoteten, entkapselten Tuberkelbazillen vom typus gallinaceus. *5th Intern. Symp. Diseases Zoo-Animals* 89:209, 1964.

Wilson, J. E. Avian tuberculosis—An account of the disease in poultry, captive birds and wild birds. *Brit. Vet. J.* 116:380, 1960.

Wilson, J. E., and MacDonald, J. W. Tuberculosis in wild birds. *Vet. Rec.* 77:177, 1965.

11 ◆ QUAIL DISEASE (ULCERATIVE ENTERITIS)

● MALCOLM C. PECKHAM

QUAIL DISEASE (ulcerative enteritis) is a highly infectious, extremely virulent disease of captive bobwhite quail, caused by a spore-forming anaerobic bacterium and characterized by intestinal ulcerations and liver necrosis.

◆ HISTORY AND DISTRIBUTION. Susceptible species are bobwhite quail *(Colinus virginianus)*, California quail *(Lophortyx californicus)*, mountain quail *(Oreotyx pictus)*, sharp-tailed grouse *(Pedioecetes phasianellus campestris)*, Gambel's quail *(Lophortyx gambeli)*, European partridge *(Perdix perdix)*, chukar partridge *(Alectoris graeca)*, wild turkey *(Meleagris gallopavo)* (Durant and Doll, 1941); ruffed grouse *(Bonasa umbellus)* (Levine, 1932); pigeon *(Columba livia)* (Glover, 1951; Peckham, 1963); pheasant *(Phasianus colchicus)*, blue grouse *(Dendragapus obscurus)* (Buss et al., 1958); crested quail *(Lophortyx c. californica)* (Harris, 1961). The disease was reported only in North America until Harris (1961) described it in England.

◆ ETIOLOGY. Published reports are not in agreement concerning the identity of the etiologic agent of ulcerative enteritis. Morley and Wetmore (1936) reported the isolation of a gram-positive, pleomorphic, aerobic, nonmotile rod which they designated *Corynebacterium perdicum*. Growth was accomplished in liquid media, but the organism lost its virulence for quail after several subcultures.

Bass (1941a, 1941b) described the isolation of a gram-negative, anaerobic bacillus from the intestine and liver of bobwhite quail *(C. virginianus)*. He grew the bacterium in thioglycollate with 0.1% agar and reproduced the clinical syndrome in quail by feeding thioglycollate cultures.

Peckham (1959, 1960) reported on the isolation of a gram-positive, spore-forming rod from the blood, liver, and intestine of infected bobwhite quail. The same organism was isolated from chickens *(Gallus gallus domesticus)* and turkeys *(M. gallopavo)*. Isolations were made by the yolk sac inoculation of 5-day embryonated eggs with liver suspension or whole blood. Yolk cultures from embryos dying following inoculation were pathogenic for bobwhite quail when administered by oral, intramuscular, and intraperitoneal routes. Primary isolation of the bacterium on artificial media was difficult, and embryo inoculation was more successful. Harvested yolk from inoculated embryos can be used as inoculum for thioglycollate enriched with 10% horse serum. After adaptation to artificial media the bacterium can be grown on yolk agar, PPLO agar (Difco) with 3% serum fraction, and 10% horse blood agar incubated under anaerobic conditions. The bacillus is 3 to 4μ long and occurs singly as a straight rod or a slightly curved rod with rounded ends. Spores occupy the terminal third of the cell and have a cylindrical form with rounded ends (Fig. 11.1). The organism has survived in yolk cultures for 8 years at $-20°$ C.

◆ TRANSMISSION. Under natural conditions the disease is transmitted by ingestion of feed, litter, or water that has been contaminated with the etiological bacteria. Experimentally the disease can readily be transmitted to quail by feeding suspensions of intestinal contents from infected chickens, turkeys, quail, and pigeons (Peckham, 1960).

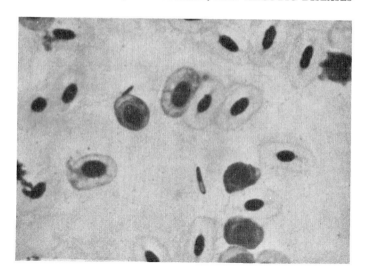

FIG. 11.1. Ulcerative enteritis. Blood smear showing two bacilli, one of which has a subterminal spore. ×1,512.

Peckham (1959, 1960) reported that yolk cultures were pathogenic for quail when administered by oral, intramuscular, or intraperitoneal routes. Intestinal ulcerations and liver necrosis occurred, following all methods of challenge. Mortality began 18 hours postinoculation.

◆ **SIGNS.** Quail enteritis may strike with explosive rapidity and quail chicks may sustain major losses within a few days. Birds dying acutely show no premonitory signs and are fat, heavily muscled, and may have feed in the crop. Chronically infected quail are listless, humped up, with the eyes partly closed, and the feathers are dull and ruffled. One of the first signs is a watery dropping containing urates. Infection causes a decrease in feed consumption, and emaciation of the birds rapidly occurs.

The course of the disease in a group of quail, following experimental infection, is approximately 3 weeks, with the peak of mortality between 5 and 14 days postinoculation.

◆ **PATHOLOGY**

● **Gross.** The nature and extent of the gross lesions in quail are dependent upon the time elapsing between infection and death. In birds dying acutely, lesions may be limited to the hemorrhagic enteritis in the upper portion of the intestine and punctate hemorrhages in the intestinal wall. In birds surviving more than a few days, the lesions become more prominent and extensive. Ulcerations may occur in any portion of the intestine and ceca (Fig. 11.2). The ileum and rectum are most

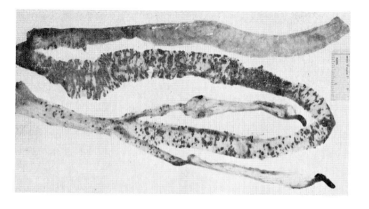

FIG. 11.2. Ulcerative enteritis. Intestine from a quail with extensive ulcerations.

FIG. 11.3. Ulcerative enteritis. Diphtheritic ulcerations in the intestine of a quail.

commonly affected. The ulcers originate as small yellow foci with a hemorrhagic border and are visible on the serosa and mucosal surfaces. The ulcers may be lenticular or roughly circular in outline and may be deep in the mucosa or sometimes coalescing to form large necrotic diphtheritic areas that may be superficial and have raised edges (Fig. 11.3). In the ceca the ulcers may have a central depression filled with dark-staining material that cannot be rinsed away readily. Perforation of the intestinal wall may occur, resulting in peritonitis and intestinal adhesions.

Liver lesions vary from light yellow mottling to large irregular yellow areas of necrosis along the edges of the liver. Other liver lesions are disseminated gray foci or small yellow circumscribed foci which are sometimes surrounded by a light yellow halo effect (Fig. 11.4). The spleen may be congested, enlarged, and hemorrhagic.

● **Histopathology.** A detailed description of the histopathology of ulcerative enteritis in quail was given by Durant and Doll (1941). Intestinal sections from acute cases revealed desquamation of mucosal epithelium and lymphocytic infiltration. The lumen of the intestine contained desquamated epithelium, blood cells, and fragments of mucosa. Early ulcers were small hemorrhagic necrotic areas involving the villi and penetrating into the submucosa. Cells adjacent to these areas exhibited coagulation necrosis with karyolysis and karyorrhexis. Lymphocytic and granulocytic infiltration occurred in the area adjacent to the necrosis. Small clumps of bacteria were present in the necrotic tissue. Older ulcers appeared as thick masses of granular acidophilic coagulated material mixed with cellular detritus and bacteria. Granulocytes and lymphocytes infiltrated the area surrounding the ulcer. In the sub-

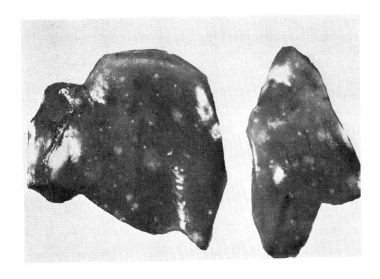

FIG. 11.4. Ulcerative enteritis. Focal necrosis in the liver of a quail.

mucosa and muscularis, small blood vessels near the ulcers were occasionally occluded by bacteria.

◆ **DIAGNOSIS.** A presumptive diagnosis of quail disease could be made on the basis of finding ulcerations in the ceca and intestine, accompanied by necrotic foci in the liver and an enlarged, hemorrhagic spleen. A positive diagnosis could be made by making a liver smear and demonstrating the gram-positive bacilli with subterminal spores.

◆ **PROGNOSIS.** The prognosis is poor for individuals showing signs, but it is good for the flock if treatment is started at the onset of the disease.

◆ **IMMUNITY.** Kirkpatrick et al. (1950, 1952a, 1952b) found that the survivors of a natural outbreak were completely refractory to challenge. However, after reexposure of one-half of the survivors in groups treated with streptomycin in the water, Kirkpatrick concluded that there were no marked differences in the development of immunity by variations in dosage of antibiotic, the time when treatment was given, or the duration of treatment.

◆ **TREATMENT AND CONTROL.** Control measures which have been tried include bacterins, serologic tests, and prophylactic and therapeutic chemotherapy. Bass (1941b) reported that he immunized quail by 2 intramuscular injections of a bacterin 5 days apart. The bacterin was prepared from 24- to 36-hour cultures grown in thioglycollate and killed with 1:10,000 dilution of Merthiolate. Birds thus immunized survived the feeding of several hundred times the infectious dose for nonimmune birds.

Peckham (1962) reported the results of 4 trials in which attempts were made to immunize quail by single and multiple intramuscular injections of heat-attenuated and untreated yolk cultures. Although some trials gave encouraging results, other

trials indicated no protection was given by the vaccination procedures.

Morris (1948) described in detail the technique of a complement-fixation test for the detection of ulcerative enteritis in quail. He stated that the chronic carrier was one of the most important factors in perpetuating the disease, and by the use of the complement-fixation test, carriers of the disease could be detected. Comparable serologic results were obtained in tests conducted on birds following artificial and natural infection.

Kirkpatrick et al. (1950, 1952a, 1952b) and Kirkpatrick and Moses (1953) reported that streptomycin administered by injection, water, or feed had a prophylactic and therapeutic value against ulcerative enteritis in quail. He also found that Chloromycetin, at a level of 500 g/ton of mash, gave complete protection. The majority of quail that survived in groups treated with streptomycin and Chloromycetin in the feed remained highly susceptible when reexposed to infectious material. Streptomycin at a level of 60 g/ton gave complete protection when medication was started prior to infection. The administration of streptomycin at a level of 1 g/gal of drinking water gave complete protection when administered prior to or concomitant with artificial infection. Kirkpatrick and Moses (1953) reported on the results of using streptomycin in the water against a natural outbreak of ulcerative enteritis on a game farm. On the first day of treatment, the concentration of streptomycin in the water was 5 g/gal, and 1 g/gal for the next 19 days. The untreated birds sustained a 21% mortality, and the treated birds 4%.

Peckham and Reynolds (1962) reported on the efficacy of chemotherapeutic drugs in the control of experimental ulcerative enteritis in quail. Their results confirmed those of Kirkpatrick et al. (1952b), and it was found that prophylactic administration of streptomycin (at a level of 2 g/gal of drinking water for 25 days) gave complete protection against experimental exposure.

Bacitracin, fed at a level of 100 g/ton of feed, also gave complete protection. In 1 drug trial, quail receiving streptomycin in the water or bacitracin in the feed were completely refractory to challenge after medication was discontinued. However, in another trial, 2 groups receiving bacitracin were 100% susceptible to challenge after medication was discontinued. These observations are in agreement with those of Kirkpatrick and Moses (1953), who also noted marked differences in the susceptibility of quail following medication.

In controlling outbreaks of ulcerative enteritis, strict isolation should be maintained between groups of infected and healthy quail. As survivors of an outbreak may be carriers of the disease, they should not be mixed with unexposed birds. The causative organism is extremely resistant, and this necessitates thorough cleaning and disinfecting of contaminated pens and equipment. Contaminated yards may remain infectious for long periods.

♦ REFERENCES

Bass, C. C. Quail disease—some important facts about it. *Louisiana Conservationist Rev.,* Summer 11, 1941a.

——. Specific cause and nature of ulcerative enteritis of quail. *Proc. Soc. Exptl. Biol. Med.* 46:250, 1941b.

Buss, I. O., Conrad, R. D., and Reilly, J. R. Ulcerative enteritis in the pheasant, blue grouse and California quail. *J. Wildlife Management* 22:446, 1958.

Durant, A. J., and Doll, E. R. Ulcerative enteritis in quail. *Mo. Agr. Exp. Sta. Res. Bull.* 325, 1941.

Glover, J. S. Ulcerative enteritis in pigeons. *Can. J. Comp. Med.* 15:295, 1951.

Harris, A. H. An outbreak of ulcerative enteritis amongst bobwhite quail *(Colinus virginianus). Vet. Rec.* 7:11, 1961.

Kirkpatrick, C. M., and Moses, H. E. The effects of streptomycin against spontaneous quail disease in bobwhites. *J. Wildlife Management* 17:24, 1953.

Kirkpatrick, C. M., Moses, H. E., and Baldini, J. T. Streptomycin studies in ulcerative enteritis in bobwhite quail. I. Results of oral administration of the drug to manually exposed birds in the fall. *Poultry Sci.* 29:561, 1950.

——. The effects of several antibiotic products in feed on experimental ulcerative enteritis in quail. *Am. J. Vet. Res.* 13:99, 1952a.

——. Streptomycin studies in ulcerative enteritis in bobwhite quail. II. Concentrations of streptomycin in drinking water suppressing the experimental disease. *Am. J. Vet. Res.* 13:102, 1952b.

Levine, P. P. A report on an epidemic disease in ruffed grouse. *Trans. 19th Am. Game Conf.,* p. 437, 1932.

Morley, L. C., and Wetmore, P. W. Discovery of the organism of ulcerative enteritis. *Proc. N. Am. Wildlife Conf.,* p. 471. Senate Comm. Print, 74th Congr., 2nd sess., Washington, D.C., 1936.

Morris, A. J. The use of the complement fixation test in the detection of ulcerative enteritis in quail. *Am. J. Vet. Res.* 9:102, 1948.

Peckham, M. C. An anaerobe, the cause of ulcerative enteritis (quail disease). *Avian Diseases* 3:471, 1959.

——. Further studies on the causative organism of ulcerative enteritis. *Avian Diseases* 4:449, 1960.

——. Immunization trials against ulcerative enteritis in quail. *Ann. Rept. N.Y. State Vet. Coll.* 1961–62, 1962.

——. Poultry diagnostic accessions. *Ann. Rept. N.Y. State Vet. Coll.* 1962–63, 1963.

Peckham, M. C., and Reynolds, R. The efficacy of chemotherapeutic drugs, in the control of experimental ulcerative enteritis. *Avian Diseases* 6:111, 1962.

12 ◆ BOTULISM

● MERTON N. ROSEN

SYNONYMS: Limberneck, western duck sickness, and duck disease.

BOTULISM is a paralytic disease induced by the ingestion of food which contains toxin from the anaerobe *Clostridium botulinum*. The peripheral nerves are affected, resulting in a flaccid paralysis of the voluntary muscles. Death occurs when the paralysis interferes with the normal functioning of the respiratory and/or cardiac musculature. Epizootics of botulism are sometimes responsible for tremendous losses in waterfowl populations, mortality in shorebirds, and a heavy toll of pheasants in game farms.

◆ **HISTORY.** Observations by western explorers early in the nineteenth century are singularly devoid of any mention of large waterfowl mortalities, although they do refer to great numbers of birds. The first report of possible botulism was in a geographical survey of 1876 in which many dead ducks were seen on the shore of Owens Lake (Kalmbach and Gunderson, 1934). Large numbers of dead ducks were found by hunters in the Great Salt Lake marshes in 1893 (Coale, 1911). This location and time of year (hunting season) correspond with the present occurrence of botulism.

The first investigation of the etiology of western duck sickness was begun by the California Fish and Game Commission in cooperation with the University of California in 1913 (Clarke, 1913). A year later the U.S. Bureau of Biological Survey initiated a study of the disease (Wetmore, 1915). The initial findings of the study implicated alkaline salts in the water. Consequently the emphasis of subsequent research was on soil chemistry and water analysis (Shaw, 1930).

In the late 1920s the California Fish and Game Commission, with the cooperation of the University of California, introduced a multipronged approach to the study of duck sickness by research not only in soil chemistry but also in the fields of parasitology, bacteriology, and pathology. The Bureau of Biological Survey intensified its efforts in 1929, with the cooperation of the Bureau of Animal Industry, by the assignment of several specialists to the problem. This increased multidisciplinary assault finally culminated in 1930 with the discovery that the cause of western duck sickness was *C. botulinum* type C (Giltner and Couch, 1930; Hobmaier, 1930; Kalmbach, 1930).

In years of higher than normal precipitation as rain or snow, the excess water floods specific areas, providing sites which are more dangerous as sources of botulism than ordinary marshes or lakes. The winter and spring of 1952 were extremely wet, and throughout the western United States it was estimated that between 4 and 5 million ducks perished from botulism. This severe mortality undoubtedly exerted a profound influence on the population dynamics governing waterfowl.

In 1922 Bengston described *C. botulinum* type C. It is significant that she isolated this organism from the fly larvae of the green bottle fly (*Lucilia caesar*) and pointed out its relationship with limberneck in chickens. In their comprehensive review of botulism in ducks, Kalmbach and Gunderson (1934) mentioned the involvement of the ring-necked pheasant during an outbreak among waterfowl in South

Dakota. Shillinger and Morley (1937) reported that pheasants are frequently affected with botulism in game farms where they eat blowfly larvae bred in the carcasses of dead birds. Its importance to pheasants on game farms was again emphasized in 1955, and in addition the occurrence of epizootics among pheasants in the wild was reported (Rosen and Mathey, 1955). Severe game-farm outbreaks of botulism in pheasants have not been restricted to western United States. In single episodes more than 8,000 pheasants were killed in New York (Cheatum et al., 1957), 10,000 in Wisconsin (Vadlamudi et al., 1959), and 3,000 in Ontario, Canada (Fish et al., 1967). California had one game-farm outbreak that resulted in the loss of 40,000 pheasants.

Reilly and Boroff (1967) reported that about 1,000 waterfowl, shorebirds, and gulls died of botulism in a New Jersey tidal estuary in 1959, and the causative organism was *C. botulinum* type C_β.

Recurrent losses of gulls and other water birds were noticed on the shores of the Great Lakes in 1959, 1960, and 1962 (Fay et al., 1965). However, no diagnosis was made until 1963 when type E botulism was indicated by demonstration of toxin in the blood of dead loons and gulls (Kaufmann and Fay, 1964). Approximately 7,700 gulls and loons died in 1963 and 4,900 in 1964.

◆ **DISTRIBUTION.** The initial term used to describe waterfowl botulism (western duck sickness) tended to relegate it to the western part of the United States. Subsequent reports have shown that type C botulism is not only found throughout North America but has been reported in Europe (Meyer and Dubovsky, 1922), South Africa (Blaker, 1967), Uruguay (Kalmbach and Gunderson, 1934), and Australia (Pullar, 1934). Nevertheless the greatest waterfowl mortalities have been in the western states and provinces, including in order of importance California, Utah, South and North Dakota, Oregon, Idaho, Texas, Nebraska, Saskatchewan, Alberta, Manitoba,

Nevada, Arizona, New Mexico, Minnesota, Montana, and Kansas. In California the outbreaks extend throughout the state, from the Salton Sea close to the Mexican border to the Tule Lake and Klamath National Wildlife Refuges on the Oregon border. Utah is a close second in botulism losses which occur among the concentration of the ducks about the Great Salt Lake, particularly in the Bear River marshes.

The distribution of affected species probably is a reflection of the composition of the population and the feeding habits of the individual species. It may be surmised that the diving ducks are not affected ordinarily since their habitat is deep water rather than shallow margins. Kalmbach and Gunderson (1934) list 69 species of 21 families of North American wild birds which have been afflicted with type C botulism. The duck involved most frequently is the pintail *(Anas acuta)*, 64%; followed by the green-winged teal, 23%; shoveller *(Spatula clypeata)*, 8%; cinnamon teal *(Anas cyanoptera)*, 2%; mallard, 2%; and miscellaneous species, 1% (McLean, 1946). In South Dakota the pintail again led the list of victims and accounted for 38% of the cases; followed by the shoveller, 29%; the blue-winged teal *(Anas discors)*, 19%; baldpate *(Mareca americana)*, 4%; gadwall *(Anas strepera)*, 4%; mallard, 2%; ruddy duck *(Oxyura jamaicensis)*, 2%; redhead *(Aythya americana)*, 1%; and green-winged teal, 1% (Batson, 1940). The shorebirds stricken most frequently are the avocets *(Recurvirostra americana)*, the black-necked stilts *(Himantopus mexicanus)*, and on occasion the least sandpipers *(Pisobia minutilla)*. The list by Kalmbach and Gunderson (1934) is complete with the exception of the American bittern *(Botaurus lentiginosus)*, fulvous tree duck *(Dendrocygna bicolor)*, and great blue heron *(Ardea herodias)*.

Mortality in the Lake Michigan epizootics from type E botulism had a species distribution estimated at 54% common loons *(Gavia immer)*; 34% herring gulls *(Larus argentatus)*; 5% ring-billed gulls

(L. delawarensis); 2% grebes, including pied-billed *(Podilymbus podiceps)*, horned *(Podiceps auritus)*, and red-necked grebes *(P. grisengena)*; 3% ducks, including old-squaws *(Clangula hyemalis)*, goldeneyes *(Bucephala clangula)*, ring-necked *(Aythya collaris)*, common mergansers *(Mergus merganser)*, red-breasted mergansers *(M. serrator)*, hooded mergansers *(Lophodytes cucullatus)*, buffleheads *(Bucephala albeola)*, greater scaups *(Aythya marila)*, and white-winged scoters *(Melanitta deglandi)*; 1% Bonaparte's gulls *(Larus philadelphia)*; and 1% miscellaneous birds, consisting of mourning doves *(Zenaidura macroura)*, Canada geese *(Branta canadensis)*, blue geese *(Chen caerulescens)*, short-eared owls *(Asio flammeus)*, and an unidentified hawk (Fay et al., 1965).

♦ **ETIOLOGY.** Almost 100 years ago, Mueller termed a paralytic syndrome of man that followed the eating of spoiled sausage "botulism" (Dolman, 1964). About 25 years later Van Ermengem (1897) isolated an anaerobic spore-forming bacillus from a toxin-laden ham that had been responsible for the death of 3 people and serious illness in 10 others. He found that a filtrate from a broth culture of the organism produced the same syndrome in animals that had been evinced in the human cases. He named the bacterium *Bacillus botulinus.* In 1919 the Association of American Bacteriologists classified the anaerobic members of the family Bacillaceae as the genus *Clostridium,* thus the accepted name became *Clostridium botulinum.* In 1910 Leuchs found that antitoxin produced by 2 strains of *C. botulinum* differed in that neutralization was accomplished only with the homologous toxin. In 1919 Burke substantiated this finding and labeled the 2 strains as types A and B (Table 12.1).

Almost simultaneously Bengston (1922) and Seddon (1922) isolated and identified a 3rd strain which was designated type C. Bengston recovered her organism from the larvae of *Lucilia caesar* and *L. serricata.* Seddon's bacillus was isolated from cattle in Australia. Theiler and Robinson (1927) cultured a toxigenic organism from a cattle disease "lamsiekte" in South Africa. The 3 strains exhibited some common characteristics. Bengston's strain (C_α) antitoxin neutralized the Seddon strain (C_β) toxin but the converse attempted neutralization was ineffective. All three isolates were nonproteolytic in contrast to types A and B which were most often proteolytic. Further investigations (Pfenninger, 1924; Meyer and Gunnison, 1928, 1929) resulted in the designations type C_α (Bengston), type C_β (Seddon), and type D (Theiler and Robinson).

Gunnison et al. (1936) examined 2 isolates from Russia that had been recovered from sturgeon in the Sea of Azov and reported type E for the first time. Moeller and Scheibel (1960) described type F from homemade liver paste in Denmark, and the same strain was found in silt of the coast of Alaska and from the intestines of a fish from an inland lake of British Columbia by Dolman and Murakami (1961).

Gunnison and Meyer (1929) separated the 6 types into 2 groups on the basis of their proteolytic properties—namely, the proteolytic as *C. parabotulinum* and nonproteolytic as *C. botulinum.* Thus the generally accepted classification is *C. botulinum* types B, C_α, C_β, D, and E, and *C. parabotulinum* types A, B, and F. The distinction between 2 groups is greater than their proteolytic activities; it extends to metabolic utilization of carbohydrates and other substrates, as well as colonial and individual morphology.

Clostridium botulinum bacilli are gram-positive rods with peritrichous flagella, occur singly, in pairs, and in short to long chains. The length of type C is 3 to 6μ (Breed et al., 1957). Types C and E spores are almost always subterminal, but occasionally are central to terminal. These bacilli are obligate anaerobes. Colonial morphology of types C and E toxigenic, wild types is characterized by a granular surface with a rhizoidal margin (Batty and Walker, 1965). These typical colonies are subject to considerable mutational change (Dolman, 1957). The biochemical charac-

TABLE 12.1. Main Features of the Different Types of *C. botulinum*

Type	Differentiated by	Year	Species Mainly Affected	Commonest Vehicles	Highest Geographic Incidence
A	Leuchs Burke	1910 1919	man, chickens (limberneck)	home-canned vegetables and fruits; meat and fish	Western United States Soviet Ukraine
B	Leuchs Burke	1910 1919	man, horses, cattle	prepared meats, especially pork products	France, Norway, East. United States
Cα	Bengston	1922	aquatic wild birds	fly larvae (*Lucilia caesar*)	West. United States and Canada, South America, South Africa, Australia
Cβ	Seddon	1922	cattle (midland cattle disease), horses (forage poisoning), mink	toxic forage; carrion; pork liver	Australia, South Africa, Europe, North America
D	Theiler and Robinson Meyer and Gunnison	1927 1929	cattle (lamziekte)	carrion	South Africa, Australia
E	Gunnison et al. Kushnir et al.	1936 1937	man	uncooked products of fish and marine mammals	Northern Japan, British Columbia, Labrador, Alaska, Great Lakes region, Sweden, Denmark, USSR
F	Moeller and Scheibel Dolman and Murakami	1960 1961	man	homemade liver paste	Denmark

SOURCE: Dolman (1964), p. 19.

teristics of the types are summarized in Table 12.2.

The optimal temperature for growth of *C. botulinum* is between 25° and 30° C, although this may vary among the different types. Production of toxin is best at 28° C. Dolman and Iida (1963) found that 1 strain of type E could form a considerable amount of toxin when grown at 6° C for a week. Type B *C. botulinum* spores germinated and formed toxin at 3.3° C after more than 109 days of incubation (Eklund et al., 1967). Quortrup (1953) reported that type C toxin was present when the environmental temperature was 5° C.

In addition to the organism, another distinct but related etiologic factor which must be considered is the toxin. The toxin is the end product of the organism (Raynaud and Second, 1949), and despite the earlier literature this "powerful exotoxin"

is not continually elaborated as a consequence of catabolism, but is probably released by enzymatic autolysis of the bacillus (Bonventre and Kemp, 1960). This toxin is the most potent of any poison known to man. Based solely on toxin-antitoxin reactions, the toxigenic types are antigenically distinct and specific with the exception of the one-sided cross-neutralization of the 2 subtypes of C.

Various techniques have been used to concentrate and purify the toxin of *C. botulinum* type C (Boroff et al., 1952; Katitch, 1952; Raynaud et al., 1953; Vinet and Raynaud, 1963, 1964) and type E (Gerwing et al., 1964). Only type A toxin has been reduced to crystalline form (Abrams et al., 1946; Lamanna et al., 1946). Investigation of the properties of toxins disclosed that they were simple proteins (Lamanna, 1959; Gerwing et al., 1964) and that type E

TABLE 12.2. Saccharolytic, Proteolytic, and Toxigenic Activities Types A to F *C. botulinum*

Type	A, B, F	E	E	A, B, E, F	B (nonproteolytic)		Cα	Cβ	D
Phase	TOX, TP	TP	TOX	OS	TOX	OS	TOX	TOX	TOX
Glucose	AG++	AG	AG++++	A	AG+++	A	AG	(AG)	A
Fructose	AG	AG	AG++++	A	AG++	A	AG	(AG)	(A)
Maltose	AG++	AG	AG++++	A	AG+++	A	AG	0	(A)
Sorbitol	AB	(AG)	AG++++	0	AG++	0	0	0	0
Sucrose	0	0	AG++++	A	AG	0	0	0	(A)
Glycerol	(AG)	(AG)	(AG)	A	(A)G	0	AG	0	A
Dextrin	(AG)	0	0	0	AG+++	0	AG	0	0
Salicin	(AG)	A (G)	0	0	(AG)	0	0	0	0
Inositol	0	0	0	0	0	0	AG	0	A(G)
Adonitol	0	0	(AG++)	0	AG	0	0	0	0
Galactose	0	0	0	A	0	0	AG	0	(A)
Gelatin	+	+	0(+)	0	+(late)	+	0	0	0(+)
Protein	+	+	0	0	0	+	0	0	0
H_2S	+++	+++	0	0	0	++	0	0	0(+)
Toxin	+	0	+	0	+	0	+	+	+

SOURCE: Dolman (1964), p. 44.

Cultures were grown for 48 hours at 37° C in air in beef infusion medium containing 1% Difco peptone and 0.2% sodium thioglycollate, and 1% carbohydrate Bromthymol blue indicator was added after incubation.

TOX = toxigenic; TP = transparent proteolytic; OS = opaque sporulating; O = no acid or gas; A = acid; AG = acid and gas; (A) = trace or sometimes acid; (AG) = traces or sometimes acid and gas; A(G) = acid and trace or sometimes gas; (A)G = trace or sometimes acid, and gas.

had a MW of 18,600 (Gerwing et al., 1964).

Heat, a pH of 11 or above, and strong oxidizing agents denature the toxin very quickly. In approximately neutral solution, a temperature of 40° C for 1 hour will not reduce the toxicity, but at 50° C about 1% of the original strength remains after 30 minutes, and at 60° C for 30 minutes only 0.1% is left (Cartwright and Lauffer, 1958). It must be borne in mind that the effect of heat is tempered by the amount of toxic material, the composition of the toxic material, pH, etc. It is suggested that boiling for 20 minutes is the minimum time necessary to render any suspect food safe for ingestion.

In the laboratory, activation of type A spores is accomplished by treatment at 75° C for 15 to 20 minutes (Treadwell et al., 1958). How this is accomplished in nature is unknown, and whether heat activation is necessary for type C is not known. The outgrowth of spores is influenced by the number present, particularly under unfavorable conditions. There will be no growth at a pH of 5.21 with 2 million spores, but with 20 million spores the tolerance is lowered to 5.03 (Segner et al., 1964). This change in tolerance also holds with other factors; for example, the limiting salt concentration is lowered as the pH or temperature becomes less favorable (Segner et al., 1964). The effect of the factors influencing spore germination, development, and outgrowth varies with the types. Most of the work on spores has been done with type E, following 4 occurrences of human botulism with this type (Roberts and Ingram, 1965).

Spores are extremely resistant to heat (Fahraeus, 1949), those of type E being considerably less resistant than the other types. There is also variation among strains within types (Esty and Meyer, 1922; Dolman and Chang, 1953; Foster and Sugiyama, 1966).

Clostridium botulinum, in addition to producing toxin, forms hemagglutinating substances which after separation from the toxin are readily adsorbed to a variety of materials, which adapts the substance to a hemagglutination technique (Lamanna, 1959).

◆ **TRANSMISSION.** The seasonal incidence of botulism is greatest in late summer and early fall, although it may extend throughout the winter. There are annual recurrences in California and Utah, but the morbidity is subject to wide fluctuations. Part of the variation in numbers of birds affected may be correlated with the size of the population, and water levels due to the amount of precipitation of the preceding spring. For example, in 1938 there were 50 sections of land flooded at Tulare Lake, California, and a population of 100,000 ducks, with losses to botulism estimated between 15,000 to 20,000; whereas in 1941, 125 sections were under water, with a population of 2,000,000 ducks of which approximately 250,000 died (McLean, 1946).

Given the right ecological conditions, it is possible to predict an outbreak of botulism in waterfowl. By manipulating the environment, an epizootic of botulism has been actually precipitated. These two statements suggest that the various factors responsible for an outbreak of botulism are known, but this is only partly true. A considerable amount of knowledge has been accumulated on the causative organism, its toxin, and some of the environmental elements, but the actual mode of transmission of toxin to waterfowl remains theoretical.

A typical sequence of factors precipitating an outbreak of botulism in western United States would include the following: (1) *C. botulinum* type C is a natural inhabitant of the soil, (2) flooding of agricultural lands produces large shallow expanses of water, (3) hot temperatures of July and August warm the water and the mud in the shallow areas, (4) a large flight of ducks moves into the area, and (5) within a few days sick ducks are observed. Sera from the sick ducks contains sufficient toxin to kill mice when inoculated with fractional amounts. The actual method of transition of the toxin from the environment to circulating toxin in the sick bird is subject to speculation.

A similar set of circumstances may initiate botulism in the Midwest, specifically Lake Michigan, but with the following changes: (1) *C. botulinum* type E is associated with a marine or lake environment rather than land proper (Bott et al., 1968), (2) low lake water levels in the hot dry summer, and (3) dead gulls and loons are observed. Again, the transfer of toxin from the environment to the birds has not been definitely proved.

Kalmbach and Gunderson (1934) advanced the hypothesis that dead organic matter is required by *C. botulinum* for growth and the production of toxin. The organic matter could be invertebrates, decomposed vertebrates, or submerged grain and possibly other plant material. This hypothesis was investigated by many workers (Hobmaier, 1932; Coburn and Quortrup, 1938; Prevot and Brygoo, 1950; Bell et al., 1955), and initially there was conflict as to whether decayed vegetation or animal matter was the natural medium of botulism. In the laboratory, animal matter is a superior substrate for toxin production (Bell et al., 1955). Kalmbach and Gunderson (1934) intimated that aquatic invertebrates could be the source of toxin consumed by ducks when they isolated the organism from invertebrates and produced toxin with insect debris.

The presence of large amounts of decomposing organic matter depletes the oxygen content of water and the underlying ooze, and thereby may provide a rich anaerobic environment for the development and growth of *C. botulinum* (Coburn and Quortrup, 1938) (Fig. 12.1). This has been termed the "sludge-bed hypothesis" by Bell et al. (1955). Their alternative suggestion is that the causative organism of botulism reproduces within particulate substances, that these substances are independent of the ambient medium for development of the organism, and that the toxin is contained within the bacteria rather than diffused in the water. They substantiated this "microenvironment concept" by dem-

FIG. 12.1. Ducks that died of botulism in a stagnant pothole. (Photo by Brian Hunter.)

onstrating that *C. botulinum* type C would germinate, reproduce, and synthesize toxin in the larvae of 2 orders of insects. However, their concept fails to explain all botulism epizootics such as the die-offs that immediately follow the flooding of grain fields (Jensen and Allen, 1960).

It is generally accepted that *C. botu-*linum type C toxin is released by autolysis of the cells. Boroff (1955) stated that the amount of toxin is minimal during the active growth phase of the organism, and maximal amounts of toxin are present at or after the equilibrium between reproduction and death of the bacteria has been reached. It is attractive to speculate that following the appearance of botulism during late summer, the residual morbidity that extends through the winter is the result of low levels of toxin being released as the residual vegetative forms of the bacteria slowly autolyze. It also could be theorized that smaller numbers of invertebrates containing toxin are being ingested by the ducks during the winter, and based on food-habit studies there is evidence that such is the case.

There is evidence that in addition to aquatic invertebrates many fly larvae found on the carcasses of dead waterfowl are toxic (Fig. 12.2). The maggots are ingested by ducks (Fig. 12.3), which results in their death and subsequently more fly larvae. This situation could be the reason for an increased prevalence as well as perpetuation of a botulism epornitic (Hunter et al., 1970).

The common source of botulism for pheasants in a game farm is the maggot

FIG. 12.2. Duck carcass with dislodged maggots in the water, one source of toxin available to waterfowl. (Photo by Phillip Coleman.)

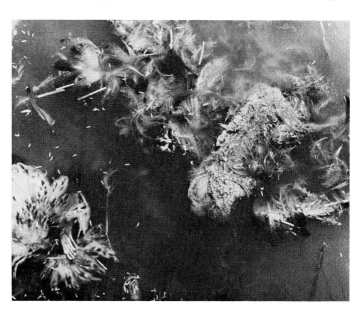

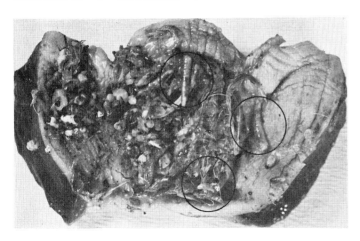

FIG. 12.3. Mallard gizzard containing ingested maggots. (Photo by Phillip Coleman.)

(Cheatum et al., 1957; Rosen, 1959; Vadlamudi et al., 1959; Fish et al., 1967). Game-farm outbreaks have been initiated following the death of pheasants from such causes as flying into the wire surrounding the pen or being killed by cannibalistic penmates. The green bottle fly *(Calliphora* spp.) deposits eggs on the pheasant carcasses, and these eggs soon develop into larvae which are sought avidly by the pheasants. Three or 4 larvae may contain sufficient toxin to kill an adult pheasant. Lee et al. (1962) estimated that 5,000 or more maggots could be found on a single pheasant carcass and that these would theoretically contain sufficient toxin to kill 200 to 300 birds. They also incriminated the adult blowfly in botulism by demonstrating that it contained toxin. Evidently toxin may persist through the metamorphosis into the pupal stage and even in adult flies. The removal of a carcass and the maggots would not necessarily cleanse a pen of its source of botulism, since the larvae and pupae would be in the moist soil beneath the surface and the pheasants could dig them out, ingest them, and become afflicted with the disease.

Large numbers of gulls and loons as well as some ducks died in 1963 and 1964 on Lake Michigan (Herman, 1964; Fay, 1966). Botulism was incriminated when it was found that the affected bird's blood was lethal for mice but mice could be protected by type E antitoxin (Kaufmann and

Fay, 1964; Fay et al., 1965). Additional indirect evidence was the composition of the diet of the birds, since fish and aquatic invertebrates are the main food items of many of these birds and *C. botulinum* type E has been found in fish and bottom samples of Lake Michigan (Bott et al., 1964, 1968). On the other hand, there have been some experiments performed in which 3×10^6 mouse lethal doses of type E toxin were force-fed to gulls without producing disease (Foster and Sugiyama, 1966; Locke, 1967). One possible explanation of these results was that the gulls had acquired an immunity to type E. This has been demonstrated in gulls experimentally (Kaufmann and Crecelius, 1967).

◆ **SIGNS.** Botulism has a syndrome characterized by neuromuscular involvement that produces a flaccid paralysis. In cases of mild intoxication the most noticeable effect is the loss of power to make a sustained flight. In more advanced cases the duck unsuccessfully attempts to fly, although it is able to propel itself on land and water with the aid of its wings. As the paresis progresses, the use of the leg muscles is lost, and muscular control of the nictitating membrane diminishes. In some cases dilation and contraction of the pupil occur so rapidly that the pupil appears to pulsate spasmodically. Complete immobility of the nictitating membrane ensues, and soon fluids collect beneath the lid, causing

FIG. 12.4. A mallard with flaccid paralysis of the cervical muscles, the condition termed "limberneck." (Photo by Robert Gretzner.)

FIG. 12.5. A pintail paralyzed by botulism, thus unable to lift its head from the water to prevent drowning. (Photo by John Cowan.)

a swollen condition. The fluids thicken and actually cement the eyelids together. The cervical muscles lose their tone and the typical limberneck posture is assumed, with the head and neck lying on the ground (Herman, 1955) (Fig. 12.4). If the duck is in the water at this time, death results from drowning. Difficulty in breathing is quite noticeable as the bird gasps for air as it lies on the ground, and the progressive paralysis affects the diaphragm and air sacs. The heartbeat lessens both in frequency and intensity with a concurrent irregularity of the pulse. The body temperature is lowered from a mean of about 106° F to less than 100° F. As with many other diseases and conditions, such as tuberculosis, aspergillosis, and plumbism, there is at first a greenish diarrhea which is followed by constipation and plugging of the vent. Signs of botulism in waterfowl vary according to the amount of toxin ingested, complete paralysis occurring with larger quantities. The waterfowl may die from drowning (Fig. 12.5), respiratory failure, lack of water, or exposure.

The most pronounced sign in shorebirds, particularly the avocet and blacknecked stilt, is loss of the use of their legs. Pheasants have paralysis of the legs and lie on their sides. The cannibalistic trait of

the species cause death of the birds by their penmates. In the wild the afflicted pheasant is easy prey for predators.

◆ **PATHOGENESIS.** Almost invariably the toxin of *C. botulinum* is taken into the body orally. The only recorded exceptions are 2 cases of man due to wound infections (Davis et al., 1951; Hampson, 1951). In oral cases the toxin passes through the mucous membranes of the intestinal tract into the lymph and then enters the general circulation in sufficient quantity to be demonstrable in the serum by mouse inoculation. There is conjecture that the toxin may increase the permeability of the intestinal membranes, thus explaining how such large undenatured protein molecules that are not dialyzable can be absorbed (Bell et al., unpublished reports).

The target of botulinum toxin in the body is the motor nerve end plate (Rosen, 1938; Ambache, 1949). Its effect is on the synapses of the efferent parasympathetic nerves and myoneural junction. It interferes with the release of acetylcholine at the presynaptic site. Although this has been demonstrated physiologically, no visual changes have been perceived even when the neuromuscular junctions have been studied with electron microscopy (Brooks, 1964).

◆ **PATHOLOGY.** It is contradiction in terminology to assert that in botulism the almost complete lack of pathology is pathognomonic, but this finding, with the signs of the disease, is highly indicative. There may be some pathologic findings that are secondary to the paralytic nature of the disease—for example, the swollen cemented eyelids and the plugged vent (Kalmbach and Gunderson, 1934). Usually, however, there is no characteristic pathology and the birds are in good flesh. When ducks are continually exposed to low-level doses of toxin, as often occurs toward the end of an outbreak, they may become chronic cases with emaciation. Inasmuch as the afflicted birds have not partaken of food, the gallbladder is distended with bile. Histologic examination is fruitless.

◆ **DIAGNOSIS.** A presumptive diagnosis of botulism may be made by observation of the typical flaccid paralysis, puffy lower eyelid, labored breathing, diarrhea with limited locomotor loss, and obstructed anus in advanced cases. However, lead poisoning may cause the bird to have many of the same signs (Rosen and Bankowski, 1960).

The proof of botulism is the mouse-protection test. The serum from a sick bird is inoculated intraperitoneally in 0.5- to 1.0-ml amounts into groups of mice, with a 3 per group minimum. One group of mice is protected by prior injection of 150 units of botulinum antitoxin type C, or if unavailable, with polyvalent antitoxin which is usually types A, B, and C. Another group of mice serve as controls and receive suspect serum only. The death of the mice that had not been given antitoxin and the survival of the antitoxin recipients confirm the diagnosis (Quortrup and Sudheimer, 1943; Quortrup, 1946). If a dead bird is presented for necropsy, it is often difficult to obtain sufficient serum to carry out the test in 6 mice. The alternatives are to use less mice or to use a small amount of saline to extract toxin from the heart clot.

The mouse-protective procedure may also be adapted for ascertaining the type of botulism by protection of different groups of mice with specific types of antitoxin. Reilly and Boroff (1967) used this method and found that types of C_α and C_β antitoxin gave protection, thereby proving that the cause of a New Jersey epornitic was C_β (see page 102). Type E *C. botulinum* toxin was identified in the blood of loons and gulls during the 1963 Lake Michigan die-off by the mouse toxin-antitoxin neutralization technique (Kaufmann and Fay, 1964).

In cases where antitoxin is not available, a preliminary diagnosis may be made by dividing the serum into 2 portions, 1 of which is heated in a boiling water bath for 20 minutes and the other unheated. Inoculation of the heated portion into 1 group of mice and the unheated portion in another group should result in the death of only the recipients of the unheated serum, since *C. botulinum* toxin is heat labile. Reliance on this technique alone could lead to erroneous results and it should be supplemented with other tests. The blood of a bird, for example, could contain the etiologic agent of avian cholera which would be killed by heating, while the unheated bacteria could kill mice on injection.

The fluorescent antibody technique has been used successfully for the identification of *C. botulinum* vegetative cells (Bulatova and Kabanova, 1960; Kalitina, 1960). Walker and Batty (1964) and Boothroyd and Georgala (1964) differentiated 3 groups of *C. botulinum*—that is, proteolytic types A, B, and F; nonproteolytic C and D; and nonproteolytic E. Midura et al. (1967) also separated the proteolytic from the nonproteolytic types of fluorescent antibody, and in addition were able to distinguish types A and B. Hunter and Rosen (1967) obtained a specific fluorescence with type C vegetative cells and were able to show that conjugated antitoxin was bound to the erythrocytes of affected ducks and experimental mice in vivo.

The hemagglutination tests using formalized sheep erythrocytes may be used as a diagnostic tool, except for type E toxin which does not sensitize the red blood cells (Johnson et al., 1966).

When enough serum is available, the mouse-protection test is the serologic test of choice. If, on the other hand, there is insufficient serum, the fluorescent antibody test using conjugated antitoxin on a blood smear would be the diagnostic procedure of choice.

It is of no diagnostic consequence to isolate *C. botulinum* from the intestinal tract or internal organs of a dead bird because the organisms may be found in the tract of normal birds and postmortem invasion of the viscera by *C. botulinum* occurs readily (Boroff and Reilly, 1962).

♦ **PROGNOSIS.** A prognosis of botulism in the case of the individual bird is relative to the amount of toxin ingested. Prompt treatment with fresh water and good feed usually results in complete recovery unless the duck is in the last stages of the disease. Shorebirds, as well as some of the diving ducks such as the ruddy duck, do not respond to treatment primarily because suitable food is unavailable; thus, the prognosis would be poor.

Once the disease affects waterfowl, the degree of loss will be dependent on the persistence of environmental conditions, the measures taken to control the disease, and the severity of the epornitic. In a severe epornitic the mortality may diminish with the onset of winter with its lower temperatures. Deaths can continue through the entire winter and occasionally until the spring migration is well underway. In one instance the lower death rate with the advent of winter was just a temporary respite which was followed by a resurgence of the epornitic that reached a peak between the middle and end of February (Rosen and Cowan, 1953). Thus, it is almost impossible to forecast the outcome of an epornitic.

The same situation is applicable to pheasants on a game farm. Despite careful and continuous patrolling of pens to remove sick and dead birds, the outbreak does not decrease until the beginning of colder weather, perhaps coincidental with a decrease in fly population.

♦ **IMMUNITY.** There are 4 distinct serologic antigens of *C. botulinum*: toxin, flagellar (H), vegetative cell somatic (O), and spore. The toxins have been used to differentiate the organism into 6 serologic types, A, B, C, D, E, and F, with some cross-neutralizations occurring between types C

and D (Bengston, 1924). The nontoxigenic strains have been difficult to classify (Lynt et al., 1967). Considerable cross-reactivity occurs between the O antigens of the toxigenic types (Evancho et al., 1967). However, the H antigens are not only type-specific but strain-specific (Lynt et al., 1967). Spores have a common antigen among all 6 types (Evancho et al., 1967). Although 15 subgroups of the main toxigenic types have been separated (Gunnison and Meyer, 1929), and other serologic studies have been reported (McCoy and McClung, 1938), the primary concern in immunology is identification of toxin, which is accomplished easily.

It is necessary to consider both active and passive immunity with botulism. Furthermore, to elucidate the subject, it is essential to separate the 2 experiences that confer acquired active immunity—namely, the assault by the etiologic agent resulting in disease, and the parenteral administration of a nonpathogenic antibody stimulus.

One of the postulates in immunology states that an overt clinical infection, particularly with exotoxic diseases, generally confers an immunity which is of a higher level and more durable than artificially induced resistance. Botulism is an exception to that postulate since it does not appear to protect the recovered individual bird from a second attack of the disease. Intoxication can recur almost immediately following convalescence from a prior affliction. The author has observed ducks which have suffered as many as 3 attacks of botulism within a single season. It is possible that the 2nd or 3rd experience with the toxin could have been of less serious consequence to the bird, due to the presence of some neutralizing antibody.

Artificially induced immunity through vaccination has been somewhat successful in protecting both ducks and pheasants against experimental botulism (Boroff and Reilly, 1959) and in an actual outbreak among pheasants (Rosen, 1959). Prophylactic toxoid-induced immunity may serve a good purpose on a pheasant farm; however, it is not feasible for use in the wild bird. Passive protection of captive pheasants and ducks by the administration of antitoxin is of limited value because of its short duration.

Native resistance to botulism is of interest. The turkey vulture is able to resist 100,000 times as much type C toxin as is required to kill a pigeon (Kalmbach, 1939). Chickens are susceptible to oral poisoning with types A and C but not B (Graham and Schwarze, 1921). Although monkeys are highly sensitive to type A toxin given orally (Dack and Wood, 1928), they are resistant to large doses of C toxin (Gunnison and Meyer, 1928, 1930). There have been 2 reports of botulism in man with type C from unidentified sources (Meyer et al., 1953; Prevot et al., 1955).

The lack of reports on human type C botulism indicates that man may be fairly resistant, particularly in comparison to types A, B, and E. During the period from 1899 through 1964 in the United States and Canada, there have been 651 outbreaks of botulism with 1,670 cases of which 1,008 died (Meyer and Eddie, 1965). Of these outbreaks, 247 sources were typed and the distribution was 67% type A, 17% type B, 13% type E, 2% mixed A and B, and less than 0.5% type C. This is of epidemiological significance in light of the former practice of market hunters augmenting their supply of ducks with birds suffering from botulism. Moreover, one reason for the precipitous decline in numbers of sick ducks being rescued at Tulare Lake was the opening of the waterfowl season, with hunters taking home afflicted birds. Despite the opportunity for hunters to contract this disease, no evidence of human involvement from ingesting botulism-afflicted birds has been documented.

◆ **TREATMENT.** A large variety of remedies such as potassium permanganate, castor oil, and mineral oil have been tried as treatments for botulism in birds, but they were either useless or of little value.

Fresh water given orally is a useful treatment and it serves 2 purposes: dilution of toxin, and of more importance, flushing

FIG. 12.6. Antitoxin being inoculated intraperitoneally in a pintail with botulism.

of the intestinal tract to remove unabsorbed toxin. This is good supportive treatment to the administration of antitoxin (Fig. 12.6).

The use of antitoxin in the treatment of sick birds does have merit. First, however, it has no power to reverse the effect of the toxin on the myoneural synapse but will neutralize toxin in the general circulation. Second, it is effective for a short time only; therefore, it must be supported by measures to remove unabsorbed toxin. The removal of the sick bird from a contaminated environment and exposure to inclement weather and predators, plus providing fresh water, cover, and food, will result in a high percentage of recoveries. The recovery rate may be increased a little by the use of antitoxin. When considering a therapeutic program, an evaluation must be made of the economic considerations incumbent on physically rescuing the bird, its chances of survival with or without antitoxin treatment, and the necessity of maintaining space and manpower necessary to nurse the bird back to a condition of self-sufficiency (Fig. 12.7). More birds will be saved by efforts expended to prevent or control an outbreak of botulism.

◆ **CONTROL AND PREVENTION.** The ultimate objective of disease research is the eradication or prevention of the disease. There are several different approaches toward preventing or controlling botulism, and these encompass the source of the disease and the susceptible population.

The source of botulism involves the total environment and varies from vast expanses of marshes, ponds, lakes, and

FIG. 12.7. Sick ducks moved into hospital pens. When able to walk and swim they are transferred to a large enclosure with no top wire so they can fly out when convalescence is complete. These pens are at Tule Lake National Wildlife Refuge.

flooded fields to the microenvironment within the water margins and adjacent mudflats. At first glance this would seem to preclude manipulation of problem areas that encompass many miles. However, in this day of large mechanical devices, heavy equipment, and fully controlled water impoundments, it is not impractical either physically or economically to change a site of recurrent duck disasters to one of waterfowl habitat free of botulism.

The United States Fish and Wildlife Service has expended large quantities of money on building levees and dikes and cutting channels, all aimed at the single purpose of controlling botulism by management of water at Tule Lake. Land planes have been used to level an area prior to flooding to obviate hummocks that would have become shallow islands following inundation. Draglines have been used to construct steep-sided levees, thereby eliminating gradually sloping marginal water edges as potential botulism sites (Kalmbach and Gunderson, 1934; Quortrup and Sudheimer, 1942; Sperry, 1947). On permanent waterfowl areas contour levees provide for continually flowing water which serves to oxygenate the water and disperse preformed toxin whether free or contained within aquatic invertebrates. Dikes have also been constructed on the Bear River marshes in Utah to control water movement and flooding that resulted from wind action.

Tulare Lake is a reclaimed area now devoted to agricultural pursuits such as cotton, safflower, and grain production. It is a basin into which several rivers flowed in the past. Dams and diversions have been constructed to control water for irrigation. About once each decade, unusually heavy snowpacks with high water content form in the Sierra Nevada Mountains, and when this melts, the rapid runoff floods the basin and other lands to the south. This entire region may have as much as 200 sections under water and as many as 3.5 million waterfowl. In 1941, with 2 million ducks at Tulare Lake, an estimated quarter of a million perished from botulism. Four years later, with a population of about 3 million, only 2 ducks were observed that might have had botulism (McLean, 1946). The difference between these 2 years could be attributed to water manipulation in which contour flooding was practiced, with water being rapidly drained from one cell to another and no water standing more than 5 days. In 1952 water control was lost through record snowfalls. The emphasis was placed on other preventive measures such as discing and/or burning grain stubble prior to flooding, maintaining levees as far as possible, employing pumps to move water and using it for preirrigation on lands that would be unaffected by floodwaters, and diverting water through channels leading out of the trouble area. These measures reduced the severity of the outbreak of botulism.

The important points of control through environmental manipulation are: (1) Remove organic matter such as straw, algal mats, or duck carcasses, which may provide a medium for *C. botulinum* either directly or indirectly by supplying nutrients for aquatic invertebrates and fly larvae. (2) Alter gradual sloping edges and maintain minimum water depths of 18 to 24 inches against levees. (3) Keep water flowing through impoundments, preferably with a rapid fluctuation of water levels. (4) Use channels for water delivery rather than allowing a gradual rise of water over a broad expanse. (5) Reduce pond areas to small contoured cells for better control on water flow and drainage.

When control of the water is lost, control measures must be shifted to the population. Sometimes waterfowl may be herded from the danger areas (Kalmbach and Gunderson, 1934; Quortrup and Sudheimer, 1942). This method was carried out successfully, supplemented by distributing 130 tons of feed in a safe location and providing land and water areas for the ducks (Rosen and Bischoff, 1953).

Herding waterfowl from danger areas can also be accomplished by opening of special waterfowl hunting seasons (Rosen and Bischoff, 1953). This was tried at Colusa Wildlife Refuge, but one mistake partially negated the experiment. Little effort was made to pick up carcasses, and hunters propped up the heads of dead geese to decoy birds; consequently, after shooting hours large flocks were attracted by these decoys and returned to the toxic marsh.

For years the greatest effort expended on botulism in waterfowl was "duck rescue." In 1941 at Tulare Lake, when a quarter of a million ducks died, 5,711 were treated and 4,912 recovered and were released. This effort was responsible for saving 86% of the birds rescued; however, in reality, 9 men working 14 hours a day for 10 weeks saved less than 2% of the ducks that contracted botulism. By comparison, changing irrigation practices prevented botulism completely in 1945, and herding of birds to a safe area saved 99% in 1952.

Botulism in wild pheasants is a difficult problem to control. More of the sick birds seek heavy cover lining irrigation ditches. Management of this type of environment to reduce the threat of botulism is not feasible. A late release of game-farm pheasants serves the dual purpose of insuring better survival of the birds as well as limiting the number of pheasants frequenting the contaminated areas.

In game farms an occurrence of botulism usually is the result of poor management. The cannibalistic trait of pheasants has led game farmers into producing heavy cover crops in their pens to allow the birds to escape feather picking by their penmates. In such an environment a carcass is not easily detected and soon has a mass of maggots which becomes a potential focal point of intoxication for all birds within the pen (Bishopp, 1923). If cover crops are grown in rows or cut in strips, the birds are still able to escape the cannibalistic tendencies of others, and at the same time the caretaker is able to see and promptly remove a carcass. Other potential sources of botulism are the watering devices and the feed hoppers. Spilled moist feed can become a site for the development of fly larvae. Leaking water devices in pens where fecal deposits have accumulated through the years can create an organic sump in which maggots are produced.

When a continual history of botulism is evident despite efforts at good management practices, it would be advisable to immunize the pheasants at an early age with toxoid. The addition of 0.5 to 0.6% formalin converts toxin into toxoid, and adsorption with aluminum phosphate is one of the more common methods of the production of commercially available products (Sterne and Wentzel, 1950; Appleton and White, 1959; Rosen, 1959; Wright et al., 1960).

Vaccination with toxoid established a resistance in ducks to 2,000 LD_{50} intramuscular doses of toxin and 1,000 LD_{50} in pheasants (Boroff and Reilly, 1959). Immunized pheasants were protected against more than 400 LD_{50} intraperitoneal doses of toxin (Rosen, 1959). In a botulism epornitic, 17% of unvaccinated birds died compared to 4.7% of the vaccinates. Pheasants were immunized as 12-day-old chicks with 0.5 ml subcutaneously and again at 34 days of age with the same amount of toxoid by the same route. It may be concluded that the best immune response is toxoid with adjuvant, and 2 immunizations are necessary at about 3-week intervals. The active immunity lasts at least for 8 to 10 months. However, toxin ingested by the birds from natural sources is tremendously more potent than laboratory-prepared products. The induced levels of immunity will not completely protect pheasants from sources of botulism in nature (Fish et al., 1967).

It should be emphasized that prevention of botulism both in pheasants and waterfowl is not only possible but preferred to attempts at control once the epornitic is existent.

♦ REFERENCES

Abrams, A., Kegeles, G., and Hottle, G. A. The purification of toxin *Clostridium botulinum* type A. *J. Biol. Chem.* 164:63, 1946.

Ambache, N. Peripheral action of botulinum toxin. *J. Physiol.* 108:127, 1949.

Appleton, G. S., and White, P. G. Field evaluation of *Clostridium botulinum* type C toxoids in mink. *Am. J. Vet. Res.* 20:166, 1959.

Batson, H. C. Western duck sickness (botulism) in South Dakota. *S. Dak. Cons. Digest* 7:6 and 11, 1940.

Batty, I., and Walker, P. D. Colonial morphology and fluorescent labelled antibody staining in the identification of species of the genus *Clostridium*. *J. Appl. Bacteriol.* 28:112, 1965.

Bell, J. F., Sciple, G. W., and Hubert, A. A. A microenvironment concept of the epizoology of avian botulism. *J. Wildlife Management* 19:352, 1955.

Bengston, I. A. Preliminary note on a toxin-producing anaerobe isolated from the larvae of *Lucilia caesar*. *Public Health. Rept.* 37:164, 1922.

———. Studies on organisms concerned as causative factors in botulism. *USPHS Hyg. Lab. Bull. 136*, 1924.

Bishopp, F. C. Limberneck of fowls produced by fly larvae. *J. Parasitol.* 9:170, 1923.

Blaker, D. An outbreak of botulinus poisoning among waterbirds. *The Ostrich* 38:144, 1967.

Bonventre, P. F., and Kemp, L. L. Physiology of toxin production by *Clostridium botulinum* types A and B. I. Growth, autolysis, and toxin production. *J. Bacteriol.* 79:18, 1960.

Boothroyd, M., and Georgala, D. L. Immunofluorescent identification of *Clostridium botulinum*. *Nature* 202:515, 1964.

Boroff, D. A. Study of the toxins of *Clostridium botulinum*. III. Relation of autolysis to toxin production. *J. Bacteriol.* 70:363, 1955.

Boroff, D. A., and Reilly, J. R. Studies of the toxin of *Clostridium botulinum*. V. Prophylactic immunization of pheasants and ducks against avian botulism. *J. Bacteriol.* 77:142, 1959.

———. Studies of the toxin of *Clostridium botulinum*. VI. Botulism among pheasants and quail, mode of transmission and degree of resistance offered by immunization. *Intern. Arch. Allergy Appl. Immunol.* 20:306, 1962.

Boroff, D. A., Raynaud, M., and Prevot, A. R. Studies on the toxin of *Clostridium botulinum* type D. *J. Immunol.* 68:503, 1952.

Bott, T. L., Deffner, J. S., Foster, E. M., and McCoy, E. Ecology of *C. botulinum* in the Great Lakes. In *Botulism, Proc. Symp. USPHS*, Pub. 999-FP-1, p. 221, 1964.

Bott, T. L., Johnson, J., Jr., Foster, E. M., and Sugiyama, H. Possible origin of the incidence of *Clostridium botulinum* type E in an inland bay (Green Bay of Lake Michigan). *J. Bacteriol.* 95:1542, 1968.

Breed, R. S., Murray, E., and Smith, N. R. *Bergey's manual of determinative bacteriology*, 7th ed. Baltimore: Williams & Wilkins, 1957.

Brooks, V. B. The action of botulinum toxin on motor nerve filaments. *J. Physiol.* 123:501, 1964.

Bulatova, T. I., and Kabanova, Y. A. Identification of the botulism pathogen with luminescent sera. *J. Microbiol. Epidemiol. Immunobiol.* 31:403, 1960.

Burke, G. S. The occurrence of *Bacillus botulinus* in nature. *J. Bacteriol.* 4:541, 1919.

Cartwright, T. E., and Lauffer, M. A. Temperature effects on botulinum A toxin. *Proc. Soc. Exptl. Biol. Med.* 98:327, 1958.

Cheatum, E. L., Reilly, J. R., and Fordham, S. C., Jr. Botulism in game farm pheasants. *Trans. N. Am. Wildlife Conf.* 22:170, 1957.

Clarke, Frank C. Preliminary report upon the disease occurring among the ducks of the southern San Joaquin Valley during the fall of 1913. *Condor* 15:214, 1913.

Coale, H. K. Enormous death rate among waterfowl near Salt Lake City, Utah, fall of 1910. *Auk* 28:274, 1911.

Coburn, D. R., and Quortrup, E. R. The distribution of botulinus toxin in duck sickness area. *Trans. N. Am. Wildlife Conf.* 3:869, 1938.

Dack, G. M., and Wood, W. L. Serum therapy of botulism in monkeys. *J. Infect. Diseases* 42:209, 1928.

Davis, J. B., Malliman, L. H., and Wiley, M. *Clostridium botulinum* in a fatal wound infection. *J. Am. Med. Assoc.* 146:646, 1951.

Dolman, C. E. The influence of bacterial mutation upon type E botulinus toxin production. *Can. J. Public Health* 48:27, 1957.

———. Botulism as a world problem. In *Botulism, Proc. Symp. USPHS*, Pub. 999–FP–1, p. 5, 1964.

Dolman, C. E., and Chang, H. The epidemiology and pathogenesis of type E fish-borne botulism. *Can. J. Public Health* 44:231, 1953.

Dolman, C. E., and Iida, H. Type E botulism: Its epidemiology, prevention and specific treatment. *Can. J. Public Health* 54:293, 1963.

Dolman, C. E., and Murakami, L. *Clostridium botulinum* type F with recent observations on other types. *J. Infect. Diseases* 109:107, 1961.

Eklund, M. W., Wieler, D. I., and Poysky, F. T. Outgrowth and toxin production of nonproteolytic type B *Clostridium botulinum* at 3.3 to 5.6 C. *J. Bacteriol.* 93:1461, 1967.

Esty, J. R., and Meyer, K. F. The heat resistance of the spores of *B. botulinus* and allied anaerobes. XI. *J. Infect. Diseases* 31:650, 1922.

Evancho, G. M., Keene, J. H., and Holtman, D. F. Antigenic relationships between vegetative cells and spores of *Clostridium botulinum* types A–F. *Bacteriol. Proc.* 67:6, 1967.

Fahraeus, John. *Botulinum bacilli* and their occurrence in Sweden. Tryckeri A. B. Allehanda, Trellebord, 1949.

Fay, L. D. Type E botulism in Great Lakes water birds. *Trans. N. Am. Wildlife Nat. Res. Conf.* 31:139, 1966.

Fay, L. D., Kaufmann, O. W., and Ryel, L. A. Mass mortality of water-birds in Lake Michigan 1963–64. *Great Lakes Res. Div.*, Univ. Mich. Pub. 13, p. 36, 1965.

Fish, N. A., Mitchell, W. R., and Barnum, D. A. A report of natural outbreak of botulism in pheasants. *Can. Vet. J.* 8:10, 1967.

Foster, E. M., and Sugiyama, H. Recent developments in botulism research. Presentation at 94th meeting APHA, 1966.

Gerwing, J., Dolman, C. E., Reichmann, M. E., and Bains, H. S. Purification and molecular weight determination of *Clostridium botulinum* type E toxin. *J. Bacteriol.* 88:216, 1964.

Giltner, L. T., and Couch, J. F. Western duck sickness and botulism. *Science* 72:660, 1930.

Graham, R., and Schwarze, H. Avian botulism (type A) or limberneck. *J. Infect. Diseases* 28:317, 1921.

Gunnison, J. B., and Meyer, K. F. Susceptibility of *Macacus rhesus* monkeys to botulinum toxin types B, C, and D. *Proc. Soc. Exptl. Biol. Med.* 26:89, 1928.

———. Cultural study of an international collection of *Clostridium botulinum* and *parabotulinum*. XXXVIII. *J. Infect. Diseases* 45:119, 1929.

———. Susceptibility of monkeys, goats and small animals to oral administration of botulinum toxin, types B, C, and D. *J. Infect. Diseases* 46:335, 1930.

Gunnison, J. B., Cummings, J. R., and Meyer, K. F. *Clostridium botulinum* type E. *Proc. Soc. Exptl. Biol. Med.* 35:278, 1936.

Hampson, C. R. A case of probable botulism due to wound infection. *J. Bacteriol.* 61:647, 1951.

Herman, C. M. Diseases of birds. In *Recent studies in avian biology*, p. 450. Urbana: Univ. Ill. Press, 1955.

———. Significance of bird losses on Lake Michigan during November and December, 1963. *Great Lakes Res. Div.*, Univ. Mich. Pub. 11, p. 84, 1964.

Hobmaier, M. Duck disease caused by the poison of the *Bacillus botulinus*. *Calif. Fish Game* 16:285, 1930.

———. Conditions and control of botulism (duck disease) in waterfowl. *Calif. Fish Game* 18:5, 1932.

Hunter, B. F., and Rosen, M. N. Detection of *Clostridium botulinum* type C cells and toxin by the fluorescent antibody technique. *Avian Diseases* 11:345, 1967.

Hunter, B. F., Clark, W., Perkins, P., and Coleman, P. *Applied botulism research including management recommendations. Progress report.* Sacramento: Calif. Dept. Fish and Game, 1970.

Jensen, W. I., and Allen J. P. A possible relationship between aquatic invertebrates and avian botulism. *Trans. N. Am. Wildlife Nat. Res. Conf.* 25:171, 1960.

Johnson, H. M., Brenner, K., Angelotti, R., and Hall, H. E. Serological studies of types A, B, and E botulinal toxins by passive hemagglutination and bentonite flocculations. *J. Bacteriol.* 91:967, 1966.

Kalitina, T. A., The detection of *Clostridium botulinum* by means of luminescent antibodies. Communication I. The production of specific luminescence in *Clostridium botulinum* by treatment with a luminescent immune serum. *Bull. Biol. Med. Exp.* 49:81, 1960.

Kalmbach, E. R. Western duck sickness produced experimentally. *Science* 72:758, 1930.

Kalmbach, E. R. American vultures and the toxin of *Clostridium botulinum*. *J. Am. Vet. Med. Assoc.* 94:187, 1939.

Kalmbach, E. R., and Gunderson, M. F. Western duck sickness a form of botulism. *USDA Tech. Bull.* 411, 1934.

Katitch, R. V. Sur une technique d'extraction de la tovine de *C. botulinum* (C) a partir des corps microbiens. *Rev. Immunol.* 16: 309, 1952.

Kaufmann, O. W., and Crecelius, E. M. Experimentally induced immunity in gulls to type E botulism. *Am. J. Vet. Res.* 128:1857, 1967.

Kaufmann, O. W., and Fay, L. D. *Clostridium botulinum* type E toxin in tissues of dead loons and gulls. *Quart. Bull. Mich. Agr. Exp. Sta.* 47:236, 1964.

Lamanna, C. The most poisonous poison. *Science* 130:763, 1959.

Lamanna, C., McElroy, O. E., and Eklund, H. W. The purification and crystallization of *Clostridium botulinum* type A toxin. *Science* 103:613, 1946.

Lee, V. H., Vadlamudi, S., and Hanson, R. P. Blow fly larvae as a source of botulinum toxin for game farm pheasants. *J. Wildlife Management* 26:411, 1962.

Leuchs, J. Beitrage zur Kenntnis des toxins undantitoxins des *Bacillus botulinus* Z. *Hyg. Infektionskrankh.* 65:55, 1910.

Locke, L. Personal communication, 1967.

Lynt, R. K., Solomon, H. M., Kautter, D. A., and Lilly, T. Serological studies of *Clostridium botulinum* type E and related organisms. *J. Bacteriol.* 93.27, 1967.

McCoy, E., and McClung, L. S. Serological relations among spore-forming anaerobic bacteria. *Bacteriol. Rev.* 2:47, 1938.

McLean, D. D. Duck disease at Tulare Lake. *Calif. Fish Game* 32:71, 1946.

Meyer, K. F., and Dubovsky, B. The occurrence of the spores of *B. botulinus* in Belgium, Denmark, England, the Netherlands, and Switzerland. VI. *J. Infect. Diseases* 31: 600, 1922.

Meyer, K. F., and Eddie, B. *Sixty-five years of human botulism in the United States and Canada*. Berkeley: Univ. Calif. Press, 1965.

Meyer, K. F., and Gunnison, J. B. *C. botulinum* type D, n. sp. *Proc. Soc. Exptl. Biol. Med.* 26:88, 1928.

———. South African cultures of *Clostridium botulinum* and *parabotulinum*. XXXVII. (With a description of *C. botulinum* type D, n. sp.) *J. Infect. Diseases* 45:106, 1929.

Meyer, K. F., Eddie, B., York, G. K., Collier, C. P., and Townsend, C. T. *Clostridium botulinum* type C and human botulism.

Proc. 6th Intern. Congr. Microbiol. 4:123, 1953.

Midura, T. F., Inouye, Y., and Bodily, H. L. Use of immunofluorescence to identify *Clostridium botulinum* types A, B, and E. *Public Health Rept.* 82:275, 1967.

Moeller, V., and Scheibel, I. Preliminary report on the isolation of an apparently new type of *C. botulinum*. *Acta Pathol. Microbiol. Scand.* 48:80, 1960.

Pfenninger, W. Toxico-immunologic and serologic relationship of *B. botulinus* type C and *B. parabotulinus* "Seddon." XXII. *J. Infect. Diseases* 35:347, 1924.

Prevot, A. R., and Brygoo, E. R. Nouvelles recherches sur le botulisme et ses cinq types toxiniques. *Ann. Inst. Pasteur* 85:544, 1950.

Prevot, A. R., Terrasse, J., Daumail, J., Cavaroc, M., Riol, J., and Sillioc, R. Existence en France du botulisme humain de type C. *Bull. Acad. Nat. Med.* 21–22, 355, 1955.

Pullar, E. Enzootic botulism amongst wild birds. *Australian Vet. J.* 10:128, 1934.

Quortrup, E. R. An improved method of testing for botulinus toxin by the use of penicillin. *J. Am. Vet. Med. Assoc.* 59:214, 1946.

———. Personal communication, 1953.

Quortrup, E. R., and Sudheimer, R. L. Research notes on botulism in western marsh areas with recommendations for control. *Trans. 7th N. Am. Wildlife Conf.* 7:284, 1942.

———. Detection of botulinus toxin in the blood stream of wild ducks. *J. Am. Vet. Med. Assoc.* 102:264, 1943.

Raynaud, M., Second, L. Extraction des toxins botuliniques a patrir des corps microbiens. *Ann. Inst. Pasteur* 77:316, 1949.

Raynaud, M., Prevot, A. R., Brygoo, J., and Turpin, A. Purification de la toxine botulinque C. *Atti 6th Congr. Intern. Microbiol.* 4:135, 1953.

Reilly, J. R., and Boroff, D. A. Botulism in a tidal estuary in New Jersey. *Bull. Wildlife Disease Assoc.* 3:26, 1967.

Roberts, T. A., and Ingram, M. The resistance of spores of *Clostridium botulinum* type E to heat and radiation. *J. Appl. Bacteriol.* 28:125, 1965.

Rosen, M. N. Botulism. *Wasmann Collector* 2:8, 28, 1938.

———. Immunization of pheasants with botulinum toxoid. *Calif. Fish Game* 45:343, 1959.

Rosen, M. N., and Bankowski, R. A. A diagnostic technique and treatment for lead poisoning in swans. *Calif. Fish Game* 46:81, 1960.

Rosen, M. N., and Bischoff, A. I. A new approach toward botulism control. *Trans. 18th N. Am. Wildlife Conf.* 18:191, 1953.

Rosen, M. N., and Cowan, J. B. Winter botulism: A sequel to a severe summer outbreak. *Trans. Western Assoc. Game Fish Comm.* 33:1, 1953.

Rosen, M. N, and Mathey, W. J., Jr. Some new pheasant diseases in California. *Trans. N. Am. Wildlife Conf.* 20:220, 1955.

Seddon, H. R. Bulbar paralysis in cattle due to the action of a toxicogenic bacillus, with a discussion on the relationship of the condition to forage poisoning (botulism). *J. Comp. Pathol. Therap.* 35:147, 1922.

Segner, W. P., Schmidt, C. F., and Boltz, J. K. Effect of sodium chloride and pH on the outgrowth of spores of type E *Clostridium botulinum* at optimal and suboptimal temperatures. *Appl. Microbiol.* 14:49, 1964.

Shaw, P. A. Duck disease studies. III. Salt content of soils in disease and nondisease areas. *Proc. Soc. Exptl. Biol. Med.* 27:275, 1930.

Shillinger, J. E., and Morley, L. C. Diseases of upland game birds. *USDA Farmers' Bull. 1781,* 1937.

Sperry, C. C. Botulism control by water manipulation. *Trans. N. Am. Wildlife Conf.* 12:228, 1947.

Sterne, M., and Wentzel, L. M. A new method for the large-scale production of high-titre botulinum formol-toxoid types C and D. *J. Immunol.* 65:175, 1950.

Theiler, A. The cause and prevention of lamziekte. *Union S. Africa Dept. Agr. J.* 1:221, 1920.

Theiler, A., and Robinson, E. M. Der Botu-lismus der Haustiere. *Z. Infektionskrankh. Hyg. Haustiere* 31:165, 1927.

Treadwell, P. E., Jann, G. J., and Salle, A. J. Studies on factors affecting the rapid germination of spores of *Clostridium botulinum. J. Bacteriol.* 76:549, 1958.

Vadlamudi, S., Lee, V. H., and Hanson, R. P. Botulism type C outbreak on a pheasant game farm. *Avian Diseases* 3:344, 1959.

Van Ermengem, E. Ueber einen neuen anaeroben Bacillus und seine Beziehungen zum Botulismus. *Z. Hyg. Infektionskrankh.* 26:1, 1897.

Vinet, G., and Raynaud, M. Production et purification de la toxine botulique type C. *Rev. Can. Biol.* 22:119, 1963.

———. Botulism type C toxin: Production in cellophane tubes. *Rev. Can. Biol.* 23:227, 1964.

Walker, P. D., and Batty, I. Fluorescent studies in the genus *Clostridium*. II. A rapid method for differentiating *Clostridium botulinum* types A, B, and F, types C, D, and type E. *J. Appl. Bacteriol.* 27:140, 1964.

Wetmore, A. Mortality among waterfowl around Great Salt Lake, Utah. *USDA Bull. 217,* 1915.

———. The duck sickness in Utah. *USDA Bull. 672,* 1918.

Wright, G. G., Duff, J. T., Fiock, M. A., Devlin, H. B., and Soderstrom, R. L. Studies on immunity to toxins of *Clostridium botulinum.* V. Detoxification of purified type A and type B toxins, and the antigenicity of univalent and bivalent aluminum phosphate adsorbed toxoids. *J. Immunol.* 84:384, 1960.

13 ♦ CHLAMYDIOSIS (ORNITHOSIS-PSITTACOSIS)

● ROBERT L. BURKHART
● LESLIE A. PAGE

SYNONYMS: Psittacosis, ornithosis, parrot fever, parrot disease, and ornithotic pneumonia.

CHLAMYDIOSIS is a naturally occurring, systemic, contagious, occasionally fatal disease of birds and mammals caused by bacteria of the genus *Chlamydia*.

Chlamydiosis is a broad term needed to supplant specific disease names such as psittacosis (Morange, 1895), a disease of man and psittacine birds caused by an agent carried by psittacine birds, and ornithosis (Meyer, 1940), which was used to describe the same disease in nonpsittacine birds.

♦ **HISTORY.** The majority of reports on wild psittacine birds was published between 1934 and 1942. Wild nonpsittacine bird reports appeared from 1938 to 1942 and from 1947 to 1966. In review, there is an understandable sequence of events. For more than 30 years, almost all of the investigations were motivated by an effort to prevent the acute infection in man, and as a secondary objective, domestic birds. Unfortunately, successful control in domestic bird flocks did not end the disease outbreaks and chlamydiosis continued to occur sporadically in widely scattered geographic areas. This led to the belief that wild birds were a reservoir.

Until 1930 all evidence suggested that chlamydiosis was principally an infection of large parrots. Shortly thereafter, the disease was found in the smaller psittacines and in a few captive finches (Meyer and Eddie, 1933; Burnet, 1934; Merrillees, 1934; Meyer and Eddie, 1934b). Both wild and captive birds were found to be carriers and shedders of the disease organisms. Early limited attempts to explore the role of wild bird species as a source of infection were unsuccessful. Bedson and Western (1930) failed to experimentally infect pigeons. Eddie and Francis (1942) conducted a serologic survey in wild ducks, pheasants, and partridge, but found no reactors by complement fixation.

The discovery of ornithosis in fulmars (*Fulmarus glacialis*) in the Faeroe Islands (Rasmussen, 1938) drew attention to the possibility that the infection might be distributed in many species of different climatic areas. In the period from 1942 to 1964, a large number of epizootiological studies were conducted in many countries of the world. These were initiated by chlamydial outbreaks in domestic pigeon, duck, goose, pheasant, and turkey flocks. Some of these investigations were extended to determine the role of wild birds in the vicinity of the farms as a reservoir of infection (Eddie and Francis, 1942; Strauss et al., 1957; Basova et al., 1960; Chervonskii et al., 1960; Sery et al., 1960; Illner, 1962; Gabrashanski, 1963; and Terskikh, 1964). Of these studies, outbreaks associated with pigeons, ducks, and geese have provided the most information on chlamydial infections of wild birds. During the same period, extensive surveys of feral pigeon populations of major cities in 21 countries established this species as an important reservoir of chlamydiosis (Table 13.1).

Since 1942 sporadic reports show that the host range of *Chlamydia* includes wild mammals, domestic mammals, and arthropods (Meyer, 1967), illustrating the ubiquitous nature of the infection.

Studies of chlamydiosis in wild birds,

TABLE 13.1. Incidence of Chlamydiosis in Feral Pigeons *(Columba livia)*

Country (no. studies)	Years	Serology*	Isolation†
Australia (3)	1953–62	58/100	36/11
Brazil (1)	1952	57/7	NT‡
Bulgaria (1)	1957	29/230	4/73
Canada (3)	1946–55	21/155	58/24
Denmark (1)	1954	31/52	NT
Finland (1)	1960	28/646	NT
France (1)	1951	48/149	33/12
Germany (5)	1955–60	24/104	9/112
Great Britain (4)	1943–59	29/143	NT
Greece (1)	1956	24/304	NT
Ireland (1)	1950	31/49	NT
Israel (2)	1952–56	25/100	NT
Italy (2)	1953–56	27/417	NT
Mexico (3)	1951–55	5/398	NT
New Zealand (1)	1959	68/27	60/15
Norway (1)	1957	51/63	NT
Switzerland (1)	1951	21/103	NT
United States (1)	1941–62	37/1012	11/686
USSR (1)	1960	39/38	8/12
Yugoslavia (1)	1958	47/104	NT
Totals 20 countries (34)	. . .	30/4201	13/945

SOURCE: Adapted with permission from table by K. F. Meyer (1965).
* Direct or indirect complement-fixation test; the numerator is the percent of serologic positives/over the denominator, the total sample tested.
† The numerator is the percent of positive isolations/over the denominator, the total sample tested.
‡ NT = Not tested.

unrelated to domestic animal or human outbreaks, have been sporadic and attempted by only a few investigators. One of the earliest investigations was conducted in Australian parrots (Burnet, 1934, 1935, 1939). The complement-fixation test, used in a survey of shorebirds in Texas, gave presumptive evidence of infection in 9 of 13 species (Pollard, 1947). Isolation of chlamydiae from willets *(Catoptrophorus semipalmatus)* in Texas (Pollard et al., 1947) and snowy egrets *(Leucophoyx thula)* in Louisiana (Rubin et al., 1951) supported the conclusion that infection of shorebirds occurred. A serologic and isolation study of colonial birds in islands off the coast of Great Britain demonstrated infection in herring gulls *(Larus argentatus)* and the lesser black-backed gull *(Larus fuscus)* (Miles and Shrivaston, 1951). Extensive serologic and isolation surveys of aquatic birds along the shores of the Caspian Sea, USSR, demonstrated that chlamydial infections occur in several species of ducks, geese, gulls, terns, herons, egrets, and hawks (Terskikh, 1964).

Other surveys of wild bird populations were less successful. In a desert region of western Utah, no complement-fixation test positives were found in 122 birds, representing 19 species (Sidwell et al., 1964). An isolation study of 809 individuals of 61 species in freshwater pond areas of southern Bohemia yielded only 2 positive mallard ducks *(Anas platyrhynchos)* (Rehn and Sobeslavsky, 1965).

These investigations did, however, provide a basis and a stimulus for further studies to define the role of wild birds as hosts and transmitters of chlamydiosis.

♦ **DISTRIBUTION.** Chlamydial infections are found in domestic or wild birds and mammals throughout the world. Historically, epidemiologic studies indicate relative incidence in the following animal groups in descending order:

1. Pet birds (psittacines, finches, and pigeons)
2. Domestic fowl (ducks, geese, turkeys, and chickens)
3. Feral pigeons in cities
4. Wild birds (particularly psittacines, finches, waterfowl, and shorebirds)
5. Domestic or semidomestic mammals (cats, primates, pigs, goats, dogs, sheep, cattle, laboratory mice, rats, hamsters, and guinea pigs)
6. Wild mammals (rodents, rabbits, opossums, and seals)
7. Ectoparasites (mites, chiggers, and ticks from wild and domestic animals)

Current and future studies may alter this order. For example, prevalence of outbreaks in pet birds and domestic fowl since 1960 is considerably lower than that of the previous three decades. This is due chiefly to awareness of the disease, effective government controls, domestic breeding of psittacine birds, and application of chemotherapeutic measures. Chlamydial infections of wild mammals, mostly from North America, are summarized in an excellent review by Meyer (1967). Excluding experimental infections, the species are:

1. Snowshoe rabbit *(Lepus americanus)*
2. California ground squirrel *(Citellus beecheyi)*
3. Valley pocket gopher *(Thomomys bottae)*
4. Kangaroo rat *(Dipodomys sp.)*
5. Neotropical water rat *(Nectomys squamipes)*
6. Desert wood rat *(Neotoma lepida)*
7. Dusky-footed wood rat *(Neotoma fuscipes)*
8. White-footed mouse *(Peromyscus truci)*
9. Deer mouse *(Peromyscus maniculatum)*
10. Muskrat *(Ondatra zibethicus)*
11. Common opossum *(Didelphis paraguayensis)*
12. Wooly opossum *(Caluromys laniger)*
13. Brown-marked opossum *(Metachirus nudicaudatus)*
14. Northern fur seal *(Callorphimus ursinus)*

Transfer of chlamydial agents between avian and mammalian hosts may occur (Page, 1966).

The occurrence of chlamydiae in ectoparasites of wild and domestic animals has also been reviewed by Meyer (1967). Isolations were reported from mites, chiggers, free-living arthropods, ticks, lice, and fleas.

Of all known hosts, the feral city pigeon *(Columba livia)* is the most common and consistent source of infection (Terskikh, 1964). However, it must be noted that this is the only species that has been studied extensively enough to establish a reliable incidence rate. The incidence of positive cases in 20 countries averages 30% by complement fixation and 13% by isolation methods (Table 13.1). The perpetuation of this high infection rate may be partly explained by the high concentration in relatively small areas and the behavior pattern of the species—namely, colonial breeding in confined unsanitary areas, and feeding of the young by regurgitation. Although the feral pigeon is a potential reservoir of human infection, there is little evidence to date of transmission to wild birds.

Chlamydial infections have been found in a total of 139 species of wild birds, representing 15 orders, and are distributed by continent of origin as follows: North America, 12 (9%); South America, 19 (13%); Europe, 26 (19%); Africa, 4 (3%); Asia, 56 (40%); and Australia, 22 (16%) (Table 13.2). The majority of species (76%) are contributed by 4 orders: Psittaciformes, Passeriformes, Charadriiformes, and Anseriformes which were the most extensively studied (Table 13.3). Most of the chlamydial infections of psittacine and finch species were determined by isolation methods on wild captive imported birds. Although some of the infections may have resulted from contact during confinement, it is probable that the majority had latent infections at the time of capture (Meyer and Eddie, 1933, 1934a, 1934b, 1939). Two-thirds of the waterfowl and shorebird infections were identified by demonstration of complement-fixing antibody and the remainder by both complement-fixation and

TABLE 13.2. Reported Chlamydial Infections of Wild Birds

Order, Scientific Name	Common Name	Diagnostic Method*	Reference	Bird Origin
ANSERIFORMES				
Anser anser	graylag goose	CF	Terskikh, 1964	USSR
Anser albifrons	white-fronted goose	CF	Terskikh, 1964	Not stated
Anser erythropus	lesser white-fronted goose	CF	Terskikh, 1964	USSR
Anas platyrhynchos	mallard	CF	Gabrashanski, 1963	Bulgaria
Anas strepera	gadwall	CF	Terskikh, 1964	USSR
Anas acuta	pintail	CF	Gabrashanski, 1963	Bulgaria
		I, CF	Terskikh, 1964	USSR
Anas crecca	common teal	I, CF	Gabrashanski, 1963	Bulgaria
Anas querquedula	garganey	I, CF	Terskikh, 1964	USSR
		CF	Gabrashanski, 1963	Bulgaria
Mareca penelope	European widgeon	CF	Terskikh, 1964	USSR
Spatula clypeata	shoveler	CF	Gabrashanski, 1963	Bulgaria
Nyroca ferina	European pochard	CF	Terskikh, 1964	USSR
Bucephala clangula	common goldeneye	I, CF	Terskikh, 1964	USSR
Aythya fuligula	tufted duck	CF	Terskikh, 1964	USSR
Aythya marila	greater scaup	CF	Terskikh, 1964	USSR
Oidemia nigra	common scoter	CF	Terskikh, 1964	Not stated
Mergus albellus	smew	CF	Terskikh, 1964	Not stated
CHARADRIIFORMES				
Vanellus vanellus	lapwing	I	Gabrashanski, 1963	Bulgaria
		I	Terskikh, 1964	USSR
Pluvialis apricuria	golden plover	CF	Terskikh, 1964	USSR
Charadrius hiaticula	ringed plover	CF	Terskikh, 1964	USSR
Catoptrophorus semipalmatus	willet	CF	Pollard, 1947	United States
Crocethia alba	sanderling	CF	Pollard, 1947	United States
Philomachus pugnax	ruff	CF	Terskikh, 1964	USSR
Lobipes lobatus	northern phalarope	CF	Terskikh, 1964	USSR
Burhinus oedicnemus	stone curlew	CF	Terskikh, 1964	USSR
Numenius arquata	long-billed curlew	CF	Terskikh, 1964	Not stated
Stercorarius parasitius	parasitic jaeger	CF	Terskikh, 1964	USSR
Stercorarius longicaudus	long-tailed jaeger	CF	Terskikh, 1964	Not stated
Larus marinus	great black-backed gull	I, CF	Terskikh, 1964	USSR
Larus fuscus	lesser black-backed gull	CF	Terskikh, 1964	USSR
		CF	Miles and Shrivaston, 1951	Great Britain
Larus argentatus	herring gull	I, CF	Terskikh, 1964	USSR
		I	Miles and Shrivaston, 1951	Great Britain
Larus canus	mew gull	I, CF	Terskikh, 1964	Not stated
Larus atricilla	laughing gull	CF	Pollard, 1947	United States
Larus minutus	little gull	I, CF	Terskikh, 1964	USSR
Larus ridibundus	black-headed gull	I	Strauss et al., 1957	Czechoslovakia
Sterna albifrons	least tern	CF	Pollard, 1947	United States
Sterna hirundo	common tern	CF	Terskikh, 1964	USSR
			Pollard, 1947	United States
Gelochelidon nilotica	gull-billed tern	CF	Pollard, 1947	United States
Thalasses maximus	royal tern	CF	Pollard, 1947	United States
Rhynchops nigra	black skimmer	CF	Pollard, 1947	United States
CICONIFORMES				
Ardeola grayii	pond heron	I	Pavri et al., 1968	India
Ardea cinerea	gray heron	CF	Terskikh, 1964	USSR
Egretta alba	large white heron	CF	Terskikh, 1964	USSR
Egretta garzetta	little egret	I, CF	Terskikh, 1964	USSR
Leucophoyx thula	snowy egret	I, CF	Rubin et al., 1951	United States
Casmerodius albus	American egret	CF	Rubin et al., 1951	United States
Plegadis falanellus	glossy ibis	CF	Pollard, 1947	United States

* I = Chlamydiae isolated.   CF = complement fixation.
† Captive wild imported bird.

TABLE 13.2. Reported Chlamydial Infections of Wild Birds *(cont.)*

Order, Scientific Name	Common Name	Diagnostic Method*	Reference	Bird Origin
COLUMBIFORMES				
Columba livia	rock dove or feral pigeon	I, CF	Meyer, 1965	Worldwide
Streptopelia decoato†	dove	I	Tomlinson, 1942	Not stated
Streptopelia semitorquata†	dove	I	Tomlinson, 1942	Not stated
Streptopelia risoria†	ringed turtle dove	I	Meyer and Eddie, 1952	United States
Galli columba cruenta†	bleeding heart dove	I	Meyer and Eddie, 1952	Asia
CORACIIFORMES				
Coracias garrulus	European roller	CF	Terskikh, 1964	USSR
Upupa epops	hoopoe	CF	Terskikh, 1964	USSR
FALCONIFORMES				
Aegypius monachus	black vulture	CF	Terskikh, 1964	USSR
Milvus korchum	kite	CF	Terskikh, 1964	USSR
Falco timunculus	common kestrel	CF	Terskikh, 1964	USSR
Circus cyaneus	marsh hawk	CF	Terskikh, 1964	USSR
Circus aeruginosus	marsh harrier	I, CF	Terskikh, 1964	USSR
Buteo buteo	common buzzard		Terskikh, 1964	USSR
GALLIFORMES				
Alectoris graeca	chukar partridge	CF	Terskikh, 1964	USSR
Phasianus colchicus	ring-necked pheasant	CF	Terskikh, 1964	USSR
		CF	Meyer, 1965	United States
Perdix daurica	partridge	CF	Terskikh, 1964	USSR
Perdix perdix	gray partridge	CF	Terskikh, 1964	USSR
GRUIFORMES				
Otis tetrax	bustard	CF	Basova et al., 1960	USSR
Fulica atra	coot	CF	Terskikh, 1964	USSR
PASSERIFORMES				
Galerida cristata	crested lark	CF	Terskikh, 1964	USSR
Melanocorypha calandra	calandra lark	CF	Terskikh, 1964	USSR
Lanius minor	lesser gray shrike	CF	Terskikh, 1964	USSR
Parus sp.	titmouse	CF	Meyer and Eddie, 1952	United States
Parus major	great tit	CF	Terskikh, 1964	Not stated
Spinus spinus	pine siskin	CF	Terskikh, 1964	Not stated
Carduelis carduelis†	European goldfinch	I	Meyer, 1940	Europe
Carduelis major†	goldfinch	I	Meyer, 1940	Europe
Chrysomitris tristis†	goldfinch	I	Meyer, 1940	Asia
Serinus cenaria†	canary	I	Meyer, 1940	Europe
Pyrrhula europaeca†	bullfinch	CF	Terskikh, 1964	Not stated
		I	Meyer, 1940	Europe
Pyrrhula pyrrhula	British bullfinch	CF	Terskikh, 1964	Not stated
Passina cirus	painted bunting	I	Meyer, 1940	United States
Erythrina mexicana†	Mexican grassfinch	CF	Terskikh, 1964	Not stated
Loxia curvirostra	red crossbill	CF	Terskikh, 1964	Not stated
Passer domesticus	English or house sparrow	I	Beech and Miles, 1953	Australia
		I	Dane, 1955	Australia
		I	Illner, 1961	Germany
		CF	Terskikh, 1964	USSR
Passer hispaniolensis	Spanish sparrow	CF	Terskikh, 1964	USSR
Padda oryzivora†	Java rice bird	I	Meyer, 1940	Java
		CF	Terskikh, 1964	Not stated
Poephila marabilis†	Lady Gould finch	I	Meyer, 1940	Australia
Poephila gouldiae†	Lady Gould finch	I	Meyer, 1940	Australia
Poephila acuticanda†	Lady Gould finch	I	Meyer, 1940	Australia
Lagonosticta senegala†	firefinch	I	Meyer, 1940	Asia
Zonaeginthus guttatus†	diamond sparrow	I	Meyer, 1940	Australia

* I = Chlamydiae isolated.   CF = complement fixation.
† Captive wild imported bird.

TABLE 13.2. Reported Chlamydial Infections of Wild Birds *(cont.)*

Order, Scientific Name	Common Name	Diagnostic Method*	Reference	Bird Origin
PASSERIFORMES *(cont.)*				
Uroloncha striata†	Bengalese finch	I	Meyer, 1940	Asia
Sturnis roseus†	rosy pastor	CF	Terskikh, 1964	Not stated
Oriolus oriolus	oriole	CF	Terskikh, 1964	Not stated
Pica pica	black-billed magpie	CF	Terskikh, 1964	USSR
Nucifraga caryocatactes	nutcracker	CF	Terskikh, 1964	USSR
Corvus frigelaus	rook	CF	Basova et al., 1960	USSR
Corvus corax	raven	CF	Terskikh, 1964	USSR
PELECANIFORMES				
Phalacrocorax carbo sinensis	great cormorant	CF	Boldyrev, 1961	USSR
Phalacrocorax pygamaeus	pigmy cormorant	CF	Terskikh, 1964	USSR
PICIFORMES				
Ramphastas ariel†	toucan	CF	Terskikh, 1964	Not stated
PROCELIARIFORMES				
Fulmarus glacialis	fulmar	I	Rasmussen, 1938	Faeroe Islands
		I	Haagan and Mauer, 1938	
		I	Bedson, 1940	Iceland
		CF	Miles and Shrivaston, 1951	Vidoy Island
Puffinus puffinus	manx shearwater		Terskikh, 1964	Not stated
Puffinus tenuirostris	short-tailed shearwater	I	Mykytowycz et al., 1955	Australia
PSITTACIFORMES				
Trichoglossus chloroleptidotus†	lorikeet	I	Meyer, 1940	Australia
Thaematod moluccanus†	lorikeet	I	Meyer, 1940	Australia
Kakatoe rosicapilla	galah or pink parrot	I	Burnet and Macnamara, 1936	Australia
Kakatoe galerita†	sulfur-crested cockatoo	CF	Meyer and Eddie, 1939	Australia
Kakatoe sanguinea†	bare-eyed cockatoo	I	Meyer and Eddie, 1939	Australia
Nymphicus hollandicus	cockatiel or quarrian	I	Burnet, 1934	Australia
Ara macao†	scarlet macaw	I, CF	Meyer and Eddie, 1939	S. America
Aratinga pertinax tortugensis†	paroquet	I	Meyer, 1940	S. America
Aratinga pertinax margaritensis†	parakeet	I	Meyer, 1940	S. America
Aratinga aeruginasus†	brown-throated parakeet	I	Meyer, 1940	S. America
Nandayus nanday†	black-headed parrot	I	Meyer and Eddie, 1939	S. America
Myiopsitta monachus†	green paroquet	I	Meyer and Eddie, 1939	S. America
Forpus passerinus spengali†	Spengel's parrotlet	I	Meyer and Eddie, 1939	S. America
Forpus conspicillatus†	parrotlet	I	Meyer, 1940	S. America
Graydidascalus brachyurus†	short-tailed parrot	I	Meyer, 1940	S. America
Pionus menstrus†	blue-headed parrot	I	Meyer and Eddie, 1939	S. America
Amazona aestiva†	blue-fronteal parrot	I	Meyer and Eddie, 1939	S. America
Amazona festiva†	festive parrot	I	Meyer and Eddie, 1939	S. America
Amazona barbadensis†	yellow-shouldered parrot	I	Meyer and Eddie, 1939	S. America
Amazona ochrocephala†	yellow-headed parrot	I	Meyer and Eddie, 1939	S. America
Amazona albafrons†	spectacled parrot	I	Meyer and Eddie, 1939	S. America
Psittacus erithacus†	gray parrot	I	Meyer, 1942	Africa
		I	Drachman, 1953	Africa
Psittacula krameri manillensis†	parrotlet	I	Meyer, 1940	S. America

* I = Chlamydiae isolated.   CF = complement fixation.
† Captive wild imported bird.

TABLE 13.2.   Reported Chlamydial Infections of Wild Birds *(cont.)*

Order, Scientific Name	Common Name	Diagnostic Method*	Reference	Bird Origin
PSITTACIFORMES *(cont.)*				
Psittacula eupatria†	parakeet	I	Meyer, 1940	S. America
Psittacula conspicillata†	spectacled parrotlet	I	Meyer and Eddie, 1934a	S. America
Psittacula spengeli†	Spengel parrotlet	I	Meyer and Eddie, 1934a	S. America
Polytelis anthropeplus†	regent parrot	I	Meyer, 1942	Australia
Alisterus scapularis†	king parrot	I	Burnet, 1939	Australia
		I	Meyer, 1942	Australia
Agapornis roseicollis†	rosy-faced lovebird	I	Meyer, 1942	Africa
Agapornis personata†	African lovebird	I	Meyer, 1942	Africa
Platycercus adelaide	Adelaide rosella	I	Burnet, 1934	Australia
Platycercus eximus	eastern rosella	I	Burnet, 1934	Australia
Platycercus elegans	crimson parrot	I	Burnet, 1934	Australia
Platycercus zonarius†	yellow-banded parrot	I	Meyer and Eddie, 1939	Australia
Platycercus adiscitus†	blue-cheeked parrot	I	Meyer and Eddie, 1939	Australia
Psephatus haematonatus†	red-backed parrot	I	Burnet, 1934	Australia
		I	Beech and Miles, 1953	Australia
Melopsittacus undulatus†	budgerigar	I	Meyer and Eddie, 1934b	Australia
STRIGIFORMES				
Asio flammeus	short-eared owl	CF	Terskikh, 1964	USSR

* I = Chlamydiae isolated.   CF = complement fixation.
† Captive wild imported bird.

TABLE 13.3.   Summary of Reported Chlamydial Infections of Wild Birds

Order	Common Description	Species		Bird Origin* Free	Captive	Diagnostic Method CF	I	Investigators
		num-ber	per-cent	species	species	species	species	
Anseriformes	waterfowl	16	11.5	16	...	11	5	3
Charadriiformes	shorebirds, gulls, alcids	23	15.8	23	...	16	7	5
Cicoiiformes	herons and allies	7	5.0	7	...	4	3	4
Columbiformes	pigeons and doves	5	3.6	1	4	...	5	58
Coraciiformes	kingfishers	2	1.4	2	...	2	...	1
Falconiformes	vultures, hawks, falcons	6	4.3	6	...	5	1	1
Galliformes	gallinaceous birds	4	2.9	4	...	4	...	2
Gaviiformes	loons	1	0.7	1	...	1	...	1
Gruiformes	cranes and allies	2	1.4	2	...	2	...	2
Passeriformes	perching birds	30	21.7	16	14	19	11	7
Pelicaniformes	pelicans and allies	2	1.4	2	...	2	...	2
Piciformes	toucan	1	0.7	1	...	1	...	1
Procellariformes	tubenoses	3	2.2	3	...	1	2	6
Psittaciformes	parrots	37	26.7	6	31	1	36	4
Strigiformes	owls	1	0.7	1	...	1	...	1
Totals		140	...	91 (65%)	49 (35%)	70 (50%)	70 (50%)	...

* Bird origin at time of examination.
† CF = complement fixation; I = chlamydial isolated.

isolation methods (Terskikh, 1964).

The reported distribution of chlamydiosis in wild birds indicates that infection may be detected in populations of any climatic region or environment. Of the 15 orders reported, 8 are primarily terrestrial, representing 62% of the species, and the remaining 7 orders are aquatic. With the exception of the Falconiformes, infections of the terrestrial species would tend to be maintained within these populations, due to their limited migration and intraspecie contacts. Aquatic species, with their habits of extensive migrations, colonizing, and intraspecie contacts, are prime suspects as disseminators of chlamydia.

This rationale prompted Terskikh to initiate studies in aquatic birds of the USSR in 1951. She concluded that gulls and waterfowl were a principal source of infection for both domestic and wild birds (Terskikh, 1964).

◆ **ETIOLOGY.** The etiologic agent of chlamydiosis in wild birds is an obligately intracellular bacterium *Chlamydia psittaci*. This species designation was proposed by Page (1968) and has been approved by the Taxonomy Subcommittee on Chlamydiaceae of the American Society for Microbiology.

Numerous strains of *C. psittaci* have been found in different bird species (Meyer, 1967) and are known to vary in their pathogenicity for avian and mammalian hosts (Page, 1967). Other strains of the same species cause abortion, pneumonitis, arthritis, encephalomyelitis, or conjunctivitis in domestic cattle and sheep.

Chlamydia psittaci is one of two species of the genus, the other being *C. trachomatis*. Both species have similar morphology, developmental cycle, and group antigen, but they can be differentiated in the laboratory on the basis that *C. trachomatis* (1) forms compact, intracytoplasmic microcolonies which produce glycogen detectable by staining the colonies with iodine (Gordon and Quan, 1965), and (2) is susceptible to a standardized dose (1 mg/embryo) of sodium sulfadiazine during growth in the chicken embryo yolk sac (Lin and Moulder, 1966). In contrast, *C. psittaci* forms loosely bound intracytoplasmic microcolonies with no glycogen and is insensitive to sodium sulfadiazine.

For a detailed description of the morphology, developmental cycle, biochemistry, antigenic composition, and taxonomy of the chlamydiae, the reader is referred to reviews by Moulder (1966) and Page (1968). The latter article describes the tests for identification of each species.

◆ **TRANSMISSION.** Although knowledge on transmission of chlamydiosis in wild birds is limited, the extensive studies in domestic fowl (Bankowski and Page, 1959; Page, 1959; Moore and Watkins, 1960; Illner, 1962; Lehnert, 1962; Terskikh, 1964; Meyer, 1965) or psittacines (Meyer, 1942) provide facts to project a hypothesis. The distribution of chlamydiae in wild birds is worldwide and appears in a broad spectrum of orders, genera, and species. This suggests that transmission of the infection in nature occurs by a relatively simple process and usually does not cause widespread mortality.

● **Factors of Transmission.** The principal factors which affect success and rate of transfer are susceptibility of the host, virulence of the strain, latent infection, stress, the shedding state, and environment.

Susceptibility is primarily a function of age (Meyer, 1942). Birds with latent infections or those with a history of previous exposure have a degree of resistance. In general, birds are most susceptible early in life—that is, during the period of maximum growth. Morbidity and mortality is highest at this time.

It would appear from the distribution of chlamydiosis by species (Table 13.3) that psittacines, ducks, geese, and shorebirds (gulls, herons, and allies) are the most susceptible. However, the range of susceptibility in wild birds by species cannot be defined with available knowledge. One can only say that differences have been noted between species and in individuals within a species.

Isolates of chlamydiae vary in virulence. A highly virulent strain, lethal to mice, was isolated from snowy egrets (Rubin et al., 1951). Field strains of high and low virulence in domestic turkeys are cited by Bankowski and Page (1959). Virulent strains associated with high morbidity and mortality are characterized by a very high concentration of organisms in excreta or exudates. Production of toxins may aid in the rapid invasion of many tissues. The resulting incubation period may be only 48 hours. Strains of low virulence are associated with latent infection.

Meyer (1942) indicated that the great majority of chlamydial infections were "silent," tended to persist in tissues, and small quantities of chlamydiae were excreted. Stress factors which may influence the severity of the disease are crowding, breeding, nesting, rearing of young, molting, fluctuation of ambient temperature, extremes of heat or cold, malnutrition or starvation, and concurrent infections.

The shedding state is one of the principal factors contributing to transmission. High concentrations of chlamydiae are found in the lungs, cloaca, and kidneys (Meyer, 1942; Moore et al., 1959); therefore, it is not surprising that nasal exudates and feces are the principal sources of infection. Following recovery from acute infections, chlamydiae may be shed for several months.

Environment may increase the rate and degree of infection. Chlamydiosis in wild psittacines is not perpetuated by nest infection, but nest infections do occur in pigeons where young birds may be contaminated with feces from infected parents (Meyer, 1965). The nesting habits of many wild birds are conducive to infection; the close arboreal colonial nesting of herons provides an environment in which cross-contamination of species probably occurs. Bridge and barn nesting sites of feral pigeons are invariably unsanitary and in close contact. Nasal aerosols or fecal dust

sources of infections are more readily transmitted under nesting environments of still or limited air spaces such as deep burrows in the earth or rocks, which are preferred by shearwaters and petrels.

● **Route of Transmission.** A variety of routes have been successful—namely, oral, inhalation of aerosols, intratracheal, intramuscular, intraperitoneal, intra-air sac, intravenous, and intracerebral. Natural transmission probably occurs by ingestion or inhalation. Congenital transfer via the egg may also occur, but based on experimental evidence this is rare (Page and Bankowski, 1959). Transmission by bloodsucking arthropods has been overlooked for many years. However, recent evidence (Eddie et al., 1962) indicates that nest mites and avian lice may play an important role in intraflock transmission of chlamydiae.

Experimental oral infections in turkeys caused few signs and a weak serologic response, yet chlamydiae were excreted in feces and transmitted to other birds (Page, 1959). The oral route of infection may be one cause of a latent shedding state in wild birds. The crop and crop fluid of birds may contain high levels of chlamydiae. This has been shown experimentally in herons and egrets (Moore et al., 1959), turkeys (Page, 1959), and pigeons (Meyer, 1965). Oral transmission from parent to young may occur in species which feed their young by regurgitation of food from their crops. This is a common practice in pigeons, cormorants, pelicans, spoonbills, ibis, egrets, herons, and woodpeckers. Some passerine species feed their young by regurgitation for only a brief initial period.

The pattern of rearing young may also affect the chances of oral transfer of chlamydiae. Some species are nidifugous or able to feed themselves when hatched—namely, turkeys, grouse, pheasants, rails, gillinules, coots, plovers, surfbirds, and turnstones. Most other species are nidicolous (reared by adults in the nest) and this would increase the chances of oral transfer of chlamydiae from parents to young. Oral transmission is more likely to occur in bird species which habitually feed together in flocks.

Infection by the respiratory tract under experimental or captive conditions results in a high infectivity rate, rapid spread, and relatively high mortality—for example, turkeys (Page, 1959), pigeons (Monreal, 1958), and captive psittacines (Meyer, 1965). The source of inhalation infection may be either nasal exudates, expired aerosol droplets, fecal aerosol droplets, or dry fecal particles. Dense nesting populations with an environment of accumulating feces favor inhalation transmission. Transmission by inhalation of aerosol droplets may occur under natural conditions. Some nesting environments of humid, still air would favor persistence of droplets in the air.

The evidence for transmission of chlamydiae in birds via the egg is not conclusive. Ovaries of parakeets were found to be infected (Meyer, 1965). Egg transmission was reported in the black-headed gull *(Larus ridibundus)* (Illner, 1962) and in domestic ducks (Lehnert, 1962). Attempts to transmit chlamydiae via the egg were unsuccessful in turkeys (Davis et al., 1957; Page and Bankowski, 1959) and pigeons (Davis, 1955; Fritzsche et al., 1956).

The role of ectoparasites in the transmission of chlamydiae has not yet been clearly defined. In 1962 Eddie et al. reported the isolation of chlamydiae from the shaft louse *(Menopen gallinae)* of chickens and from mites found in the litter of infected turkeys. These mites were identified as members of the following families of Acarina: Parasitidae, Ameroseiidae, Laelapidae, Macronyssidae, Cheyletidae, Acaridae, and Glycyphagidae.

The evidence of ectoparasite transmission in wild birds is only suggestive. Three of 13 species of shorebirds—laughing gull *(Larus atricilla),* willet *(Catoptrophorus semipalmatus),* and black skimmer *(Rynchops nigra)*—had the highest percentage of serologic reactors and also the highest incidence of ectoparasites (Pollard, 1955).

Infected chigger mites (Trombiculidae) were found on the little shearwater *(Puffinus baroli)* (Terskikh et al., 1961). Since ectoparasites are so common in wild bird populations, they may prove to be an important factor in transmission.

◆ **SIGNS.** Chlamydial infections may be acute, subacute, or latent. In wild birds most infections tend to be latent, or asymptomatic. There are almost no reports of signs of the disease in wild birds except for psittacines, in spite of records of significant lesions, high complement-fixation titers, and isolations (Rasmussen, 1938; Meyer, 1942; Pollard, 1947). The signs of acute or subacute infections in birds are those associated with many systemic diseases. In the acute or peracute form of the disease mortality is highest in the young or preadult bird. Adults develop a subacute form, characterized by a series of intermittent attacks of clinical illness which may persist for several weeks. The incubation period tends to be variable and is based primarily on experimental infections. In psittacines the range is from 5 to 98 days (Meyer, 1942). In turkeys signs appeared as early as 2 to 4 days and death occurred within 8 to 15 days (Page, 1959).

The acute form of the disease tends to be rapidly fatal. Signs begin with a serous or purulent exudate of the eye or nose. Anorexia and inactivity appear early. Diarrhea follows and the feces may be gray or rust colored, with blood. As the infection progresses, birds assume a fixed position with little movement, and respiratory distress may be observed. The protracted form of the disease is characterized by signs similar to the above but less pronounced, and death, if it occurs, is delayed. Signs may subside and reappear at weekly intervals. This results in growth retardation, weight loss, and in time, marked emaciation.

Rice birds, finches, and canaries seem to have a relatively high susceptibility. Signs are very transitory and death occurs in a relatively short time. The carrier and shedder state is not common in these species (Meyer, 1942).

Infections of psittacine species may be acute (rapidly fatal) or subacute (a protracted course) (Merrillees, 1934). In the wild, infected Australian king parrots were observed to fall from trees and die within a few minutes (Burnet, 1939). Sudden deaths were also noted in parakeets (Meyer, 1942).

Conjunctivitis is often seen in one or both eyes of pigeons (Coles, 1940). Squabs may be undersized, feeble, and have gray-green concretions on the vent. Mortality is high and adults may die suddenly. The syndrome begins with a serous exudative conjunctivitis, followed by respiratory rales, rhinitis, anorexia, uncoordinated flight, blue skin over pectoral muscles, and finally, quietly posturing in a corner (Meyer, 1965).

Domestic ducks tend to continue eating during the devolpment of the disease. Egg laying terminates and is depressed following recovery. Mortality in ducklings may be high (Grimpet, 1964). Growth is often retarded, leg weakness is reflected in an unbalanced gait, and serous or purulent yellow exudates may be noted in the conjunctiva and nasal or aural orifices. Conjunctivitis may be followed by cornea involvement and lead to blindness (Strauss, 1956). Geese and turkeys have signs similar to ducks (Sery et al., 1960).

♦ **PATHOGENESIS.** Although the pathogenesis of chlamydiosis has not been studied in wild birds, the multiplication and spread of a virulent *C. psittaci* strain in turkeys, starting with an infectious aerosol, has been traced by Page. This might illustrate the path of the agent in the case of a wild bird. Titration of 13 different tissues in birds killed at various intervals after infection revealed that the chlamydiae multiplied primarily in the lungs, air sacs, and pericardial sac. Chlamydiae were found on the air sacs and mesentery within 4 hours after inhalation and titered more than 10^9 organisms per gram of lung or air

sac tissue within 24 hours after exposure. Within 48 hours chlamydiae had spilled over from the multiplication sites and were detected in low numbers in the blood, liver, spleen, and kidney. They were present in high numbers in the turbinates within 24 hours and in the cloacal contents within 72 hours, both sites representing portals of exit of the organisms. The organisms multiplied slowly on the surface of the heart and in the pericardial membrane, causing a severe inflammatory response. Fibrin plaques were observed on the heart within 48 hours after exposure.

Multiplication of the organism in the lungs caused a severe inflammatory response with evidence of destruction of tissue and occlusion of air cells with cellular debris and fibrinous exudate. The thoracic cavity filled with a transudate. As passive congestion increased, the heart enlarged to 2 to 4 times normal size and became encrusted with fibrin. Death was probably caused by heart failure, with gross lesions of severe pericarditis, pneumonitis, perihepatitis, peritonitis, and airsaculitis, an overwhelming systemic chlamydial infection. At death all tissues contained greater than 10^8 organisms per gram.

The pathogenesis after ingestion of the disease organisms was also studied. Turkeys were fed chlamydiae-containing capsules designed to release their contents into the gizzard. Titration of tissues of birds killed at intervals produced only one isolation of chlamydiae—from the jejunum contents of 1 bird on the 5th day postinfection. The remaining birds were examined weekly for bacteremia and for serum antibodies. After 2 weeks a new series of events occurred in the birds. The route of exposure of the birds became clear as each bird in turn became infected and developed bacteremia and disease identical to the birds exposed by aerosol. The birds had excreted the orally administered agent in their droppings; these droppings dried, became dust, and were inhaled as infectious dust several weeks later. This conclusion was supported by the fact that chalmydiae were recovered from droppings on the turkey runway floors during the course of the experiment.

Such a pathogenesis might be characteristic of an epizootic caused by a virulent disease agent in a crowded aviary of wild birds. It is likely, however, that most bird exposures are insidious and of a low order over a long period of time, thereby selecting for resistant birds who become chronic carriers.

◆ **PATHOLOGY.** The degree of pathology found in chlamydial infections appears to be dependent on a number of factors—namely, the virulence of the strain, the susceptibility of the host, the route of exposure, and concurrent bacterial infections. Necrotizing lesions are more likely to occur if the chlamydiae are virulent and the host is highly susceptible. Conversely, low virulence and a less susceptible host favor the development of proliferative pathology (Sprunt, 1955). With natural infections, the lung tissue of birds seldom shows pathologic changes. However, air-sac membranes may be thickened and at times also show fibropurulent exudate. *Mycoplasma* sp. infection also causes similar gross lesions and is an infection common to both avian and mammalian hosts.

The principal gross lesions may be seen in the spleen, liver, and pericardium. One of the most common findings is plastic, sticky, or fibropurulent exudates, which cover serosal surfaces. Elementary bodies may be found in the cytoplasm of cells in these exudates. Pronounced enlargement of the spleen and liver is common. This may be a result of intense vascular congestion, which in some cases leads to subcapsular hemorrhage and rupture of the spleen and may account for the occasional reports of sudden deaths (Hughes, 1947). Proliferation of lymphoid tissue around the bile ducts occurs early. As it progresses, the bile ducts become compressed, the ducts are plugged, necrosis of the duct wall occurs, and rupture follows. As the liver cells become infiltrated with bile, hepatic necrosis occurs. Erythrocyte destruction in both

liver and spleen is suggested by the large collection of hemosiderin in these organs (Sprunt, 1955). Parenchymatous changes are observed in the kidney.

These changes occur in varying degrees in acute or subacute forms of the disease in most species. A few specific pathologic changes in certain species demonstrate the variation of pathology that may be encountered.

● **Pigeons.** Occasionally lungs were edematous. Swollen spleens appeared sometimes pink or purple and soft. Enlarged livers had rounded edges and presented a mottled appearance. Microscopically, vascular congestion was observed, and some of the parenchymal cells showed cloudy swelling or necrosis. Elementary bodies were observed sometimes intercellularly or in the cytoplasm of monocytes. In a few, catarrhal or plastic exudates were seen in the lumen of the small or large intestines. In some cases the cloaca was filled with an accumulation of ureates. Hughes (1947) reported the pancreas was enlarged and grayish, with extensive pinhead necrotic foci.

● **Ducks.** The lesions described for ducks are generally similar to pigeons; however, some of the reported pathology is unusual. Eye lesions in particular were common. Conjunctivitis was associated with abundant serous or purulent exudate. The pathologic process extended to the cornea and resulted in blindness (Sery et al., 1957). Enlarged livers stained saffron yellow and histologically numerous necrotic degenerated parenchymatous cells were seen, with evidence of acute atrophy. The Kupffer cells had elementary bodies. Necrotic, tumor-like nodules were seen in some spleens. Myocardial changes were characterized as fatty disorganization of the fiber (Furst et al., 1957). Inflammation of the oviducts and oophoritis were also noted (Illner, 1962).

● **Turkeys.** Experimental infections have been induced by contact, aerosol inhalation, oral administration, or injection methods. These studies have provided some interesting detailed pathologic data (Page, 1959; Pierce et al., 1964; Pierce and Moore, 1965). Pathology included a fibrinopurulent meningoencephalitis, a diffuse pneumonia and pulmonary edema, extensive heart lesions, and an enlarged liver with biliary stasis.

● **Psittacines.** Perhaps the most striking pathology in these species, especially the large parrots, is acute biliary cirrhosis. This may progress to bile duct plugging, rupture, and infiltration of liver cells (Sprunt, 1955). Occasionally livers are observed with necrotic foci, and some may have infarcts (Tremain, 1938). In one report pneumonia was noted in parrots (Merrillees, 1934).

● **Other Wild Birds.** Gulls have enlarged spleens and fibrinous exudates on the pericardium and costal air sacs (Illner, 1962). Sparrows *(Passer domesticus)* captured in the wild, were experimentally infected in two studies (Davis, 1947; Page, 1965, 1966). The degree and extent of lesions observed were affected by the infection route and the origin of the *Chlamydia.* Davis used only pigeon-origin *Chlamydia* and infected by intracranial, intraperitoneal, and oral routes. Deaths occurred in intracranially and orally infected birds, but no pathology was observed. Intraperitoneally infected birds had enlarged soft spleens and areas of focal necrosis in the liver. Page infected sparrows by the intraperitoneal route with a pigeon isolate and noted swollen livers and spleens as well as thickened air sacs. Fibrinous exudates covered both air sacs and viscera (Fig. 13.1). *Chlamydia* of sheep origin produced similar but less extensive lesions.

♦ **DIAGNOSIS.** The diagnosis of chlamydiosis depends upon the recovery and identification of the etiologic agent and upon the serologic response, clinical signs, and gross and microscopic lesions in the infected host. The diagnostician must also

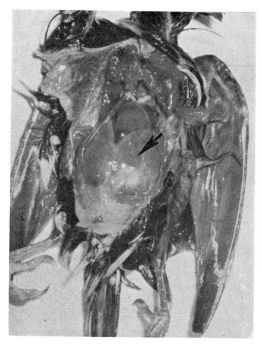

FIG. 13.1. Gross lesions of *C. psittaci* in English sparrow *(Passer domesticus).* *Arrow* points to an enlarged liver encased in fibrin. Fibrinous exudates were also found on the heart and air sacs of this bird which died 30 days after inoculation with small numbers of *C. psittaci* originally isolated from a sparrow in California.

take into consideration the stage of the disease, presence of other microbes, and the number of individual hosts needed for examination.

Chlamydiosis in wild birds is primarily a chronic infection showing few signs and lesions, although acute disease resulting in fatalities may arise under conditions described below. Investigators studying the carrier state in birds have concentrated their efforts on the parakeet and pigeon, since these birds often are symptomless carriers which excrete chlamydiae into the environment of susceptible human beings (Meyer, 1967). If an infected bird's appearance, appetite, and excretions are normal, the disease agent may best be detected by its isolation from or identification in the excretions of the live bird or from the spleen or kidney tissues of the euthanized bird. While reliable identification of the agent in these tissues may be made by the use of specific fluorescent antibody tagging or by phase contrast microscopy, these methods are feasible only if a reasonably large number of organisms is present. Therefore, it is more practical in the case of inapparent infections to isolate the organisms and cause them to multiply to a point where they can be (more) readily identified by tests based on morphology or antigenicity.

● **Isolation Procedures.** If specimens of excrement or heavily contaminated tissues are collected for isolation of chlamydiae, the samples should be homogenized, centrifuged at 500 to 1,000 rpm for 10 minutes to remove debris, and treated with a combination of antibiotics (streptomycin sulfate 2 mg/ml, tyrothricin 0.02 mg/ml, kanamycin 1 mg/ml of broth or saline buffered at pH 7.2) for 2 days at 4° C. After removal of contaminating bacteria is assured, the suspension is inoculated into mice (3 to 4 weeks of age, intraperitoneal, subcutaneous, or intracerebral route), guinea pigs (3 to 6 weeks of age, intraperitoneal route), chicken embryos (6 to 7 days of incubation, yolk sac route), or tissue cultures for primary isolation of chlamydiae. It is usually helpful to inoculate at least 2 species of the above experimental hosts.

If liver, spleen, or kidney tissues of the host are collected aseptically for isolation of chlamydiae, the tissues should be homogenized and suspended to a concentration of 10 to 20% in tryptose broth, pH 7.2, and inoculated into laboratory animals or tissue cultures as stated above.

● **Signs and Lesions of Chlamydial Infection in Laboratory Animals**

Mice. Clinical signs and gross lesions typical of chlamydial infection appear in mice within 5 to 15 days, depending upon the number and virulence of the organisms inoculated (Page, 1959, 1966). Organisms of high virulence will produce a severe systemic infection, causing the mouse to appear ruffled, anorectic, and inactive, with

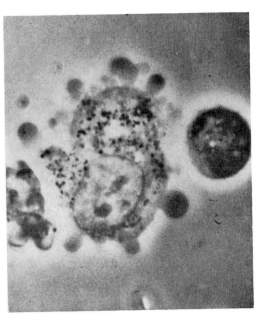

FIG. 13.2. Photomicrograph of an infected mononuclear cell from the peritoneal exudate of a mouse inoculated with *C. psittaci*. Large (1.0μ diam.) forms and small (0.3μ diam.) forms of chlamydiae can be observed distributed throughout the cytoplasm of the cell. ×4,500. (From Page, 1967.)

occasional signs of conjunctivitis. Death may occur in 5 to 7 days. Necropsy reveals hyperemic organs, especially lungs, enlarged spleen and liver, and a sticky exudate in the peritoneal and thoracic cavities. A fibrin film may cover or encase the liver and spleen. All of these exudates characteristically contain large numbers of mononuclear cells, many of which have intracytoplasmic chlamydiae. These organisms are readily visible in fresh, unstained coverslip preparations, using phase contrast microscopy at magnifications of 800 diameters or more (Fig. 13.2).

If the chlamydial agent is of low virulence, the mouse may not die but will develop lesions similar to those in Figure 13.3 (Page, 1966). The infectious agent causes damage to the vascular endothelium, producing leakage of plasma from the capillaries of the peritoneal serosa so that fibrinous fluids containing inflammatory cells accumulate in the peritoneal cavity. Mon-

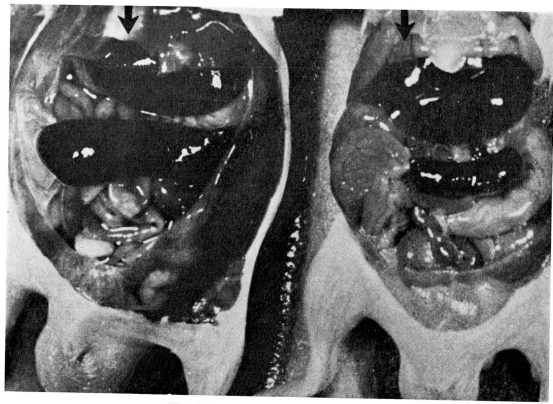

FIG. 13.3. Appearance of viscera of mouse infected intraperitoneally with *C. psittaci* (left) compared with viscera of normal mouse (right). Infected mouse has spleen enlarged ×4 and its peritoneal cavity is filled with fibrinous exudate, causing the mouse to appear bloated. (From Page, 1966.)

onuclear cells in these fluids usually are heavily infected with chlamydiae. The organisms can be recognized by phase contrast microscopy, or specifically identified by the use of fluorescein-labeled chlamydial antibodies, thereby affording a conclusive diagnosis. If labeled antibody preparations are not available, other methods described below must be used to identify the isolated organisms.

Guinea pigs. The response of guinea pigs to chlamydial agents from birds is similar to that of mice except that some strains of low virulence do not cause lesions. However, a diagnostic advantage of using guinea pigs is that their blood may be more easily drawn for serologic testing before and after infection, thereby adding sero-

logic confirmation of chlamydial infection in positive cases.

Chicken embryos. The 6- to 7-day-old chicken embryo is useful because it serves as a sensitive medium for the isolation of all strains of chlamydiae. Infected embryos usually die within 5 to 12 days after inoculation of the yolk sac. Up to 0.5 ml of the original tissue suspension may be inoculated by this route. Infected embryos and yolk sac membranes appear congested if not actually hemorrhagic. Capillaries are vaguely outlined, not sharply demarcated. Impression smears of saline-washed yolk sac membranes may be examined for intracellular chlamydiae by phase contrast microscopy, but small particles of yolk are similar in size and shape to chlamydiae and may result in misdiagnosis. Smears stained by Giemsa's, Macchiavello's, or Castaneda's methods are even more difficult to interpret. At this point, the best way to ascertain that the yolk sac is infected is to triturate the yolk sac membrane with sand and broth to make a 20% suspension and prepare it as an antigen for reaction with positive chlamydial antiserum in a complement-fixation (CF) test. If the boiled and phenolized yolk sac antigen, diluted 1:8 or more, fixes complement with positive chlamydial antiserum and does not fix complement with negative serum, then the presence of a chlamydial agent in the infected yolk sac is conclusively determined. Details of these and other tests for identification of chlamydial agents are reviewed by Meyer and Eddie (1964) and Page (1968).

If no embryos die in the first passage in eggs of suspect avian tissue homogenates, the yolk sacs are harvested at the 10th to 14th day postinoculation, triturated with sand and broth, and inoculated into another group of 6-day-old embryos. Three blind passages with no specific embryo deaths are needed to conclude that the original suspect tissue did not contain *C. psittaci*.

Tissue cultures. Numerous investigators have studied the growth of chlamydial agents in cell cultures of various tissues; for example, human liver (Officer and Brown, 1960), human embryonic skin, muscle, or lung (Pearson et al., 1965), chick embryo (Piraino and Abel, 1964; Gordon and Quan, 1965), and mouse cells of the McCoy line (Tanami et al., 1961). Most strains of *C. psittaci* isolated from birds multiply in cultured tissue cells and produce cytopathogenicity sufficient to demonstrate plaque formation (Kozikowski and Hahon, 1964; Piraino and Abel, 1964). No special combination of ingredients or media is required. Procedures normal to the routine growth of obligate intracellular organisms in tissue cells are followed. Growth of chlamydiae usually requires at least 2 days, sometimes as long as 4 to 7 days before intracellular microcolonies of

the organisms can be seen microscopically. In many systems cytopathogenicity is sufficient to destroy the cell monolayer.

Convincing evidence that chlamydiae are present in the cell culture can be obtained in two ways: (1) preparing an infected cell culture as an antigen and demonstrating in a CF test that the antigen and chlamydial antiserum fix complement; (2) reacting the infected cell culture with fluorescein-labeled chlamydial antibodies and demonstrating specific intracytoplasmic fluorescence. The latter method was claimed by Ross and Borman (1963) to be more sensitive for detecting chlamydial antigens than the CF method.

● **Serologic Diagnosis**

Methods. A variety of serologic methods (complement fixation, indirect complement fixation, agglutination, passive hemagglutination) have been studied for the detection of chlamydial antibodies in serums of birds, but the CF test has been the one most commonly used (Meyer and Eddie, 1964). The direct CF method may be used for all mammals and pigeons, whereas the indirect method of Karrer et al. (1951) is used for all other bird species. Direct CF methods for detecting antibodies in the serums of all species of birds have been developed (Benedict and McFarland, 1956; Brumfield and Pomeroy, 1957), but these have been used primarily for experimental purposes. The CF antigen is easily prepared by harvesting infected yolk sacs, homogenizing and diluting them to make a 20% suspension, boiling the suspension for 30 minutes, cooling, and adding phenol to make a final dilution of 0.5% phenol. The antigen is ready to use within 48 hours. Serial dilutions of the antigen are then tested for potency in a CF test against serial dilutions of a high titered chlamydial antiserum of mammalian origin and against a control negative serum. Once the potency is ascertained, the antigen may be used at a dilution known to contain at least 4 CF units per unit volume to test bird serums. The Karrer indirect CF method and the Brumfield direct CF method require use of carefully titrated special reagents, thereby presenting added difficulties. But both tests satisfactorily detect antibody responses in birds infected with chlamydiae (Page and Bankowski, 1960).

Interpretation of serologic results. Normally, CF antibodies appear in birds within 7 to 10 days after chlamydial infection, although they may appear earlier if the bird is exposed to a large infective dose, or later if the dose is small (Page and Bankowski, 1960). Chronically infected birds, such as pigeons, often have high titers because they have been antigenically stimulated over a long period of time. On the other hand, in acutely diseased birds in which the initial infection has progressed rapidly to serious disease and debilitation, no serologic response may be detected.

Agglutination antigens such as those developed by Mason (1959) may detect antibodies as early as 3 days after initial infection of the avian host (Page and Bankowski, 1960).

Most investigators consider that a fourfold rise in serum antibody titer of a host represents good evidence of recent chlamydial infection, if not disease. Many wild birds have been exposed to chlamydial agents at one time or another so that the normal incidence of 1 to 10% positives in a group is not surprising. The incidence of serologically positive pigeons may range as high as 80%. Therefore, determination that an individual bird has a positive titer is of little consequence, except that it indicates that the bird was, at one time, exposed to a chlamydial antigen. The height of the titer is also of little significance except to indicate the strength of the antigenic stimulus.

The serologic diagnosis of chlamydiosis in individual birds requires proof of a fourfold rise in circulating antibody titer. On a flock basis, however, if 80% or more of the birds show titers, with half of the titers ranging as high as 1:64 or more, this is reasonable evidence that the birds are currently infected with *C. psittaci*, and the likelihood of recovering chlamydiae is high.

● **Acutely Diseased Birds.** Infected birds become acutely diseased under either of two circumstances: when chronically infected birds are subjected to stress factors such as poor nutrition, crowding, excessive breeding, unusual temperature fluctuations, or complicating infections; or, if the birds are infected with an unusually virulent strain of *C. psittaci*. In the first circumstance, the organisms residing in the infected host multiply to large numbers and cause cell destruction during the host's period of lowered resistance. In the second case, multiplication of the organisms and extensive cell destruction begin soon after the disease agent gains entrance into the host.

In both cases the acutely diseased birds show signs of depression, inactivity, inappetence, diarrhea (yellow-green gelatinous droppings), and elevated temperature (2° to 3° C above normal). Mortality rates may range from 1 to 40% in naturally infected poultry. In wild birds mortality rates are difficult to ascertain since the total number of living birds is rarely known.

Gross lesions in acutely diseased birds vary according to the virulence of the disease agent and the length of time the bird has ben infected. These lesions are discussed in the section on pathology.

◆ **PROGNOSIS.** Chlamydiae isolates may vary from relatively nonvirulent (some chicken strains) to highly virulent isolates (turkey or egret strains). Similarly, the range of host resistance is wide and includes highly resistant (chicken) to highly susceptible (Java rice birds) species.

Routes of infection may affect morbidity or mortality. Oral administration or ingestion of chlamydiae is more likely to result in latent infection, while inhalation favors the development of acute infections. In addition, environmental or physical stressors may significantly alter the disease process. It is not surprising that under field conditions outbreaks may occur in many different forms—namely, asymptomatic or subclinical (slow rate of growth), mild signs lasting only a few days with no deaths, moderate signs persisting for 2 to 3 weeks and low mortality, moderate signs with a protracted course of illness over several weeks and low to high mortality, rapid onset and pronounced signs with few deaths, pronounced signs over a few days with high mortality, mild signs, and a short illness with high mortality.

● **Pigeons.** Chlamydial infection of a pigeon flock under natural conditions spreads rapidly and the prevalence ranges from 4 to 80% (Meyer, 1965). Mortality in the young is high, especially under crowded conditions. Concurrent infection with *Salmonella* sp. increases the death rate. Adult birds usually survive infection with few signs, but become carriers and shedders.

● **Ducks.** Mortality in ducklings has been reported at 60 to 100% of large flocks (Strauss, 1956). Flock death rates in fully matured birds have ranged from 3 to 15%. Grimpet (1964) reported cessation of egg laying in adult ducks and failure of egg laying in young ducks.

● **Turkeys.** Field infections show a considerable difference in mortality rates, which has been attributed to the virulence of the chlamydia isolated. Outbreaks in flocks located in areas inhabited by herons, egrets, and gulls tend to have mortalities of 20 to 30%. In contrast, flock infections in other areas generally reported lower losses, some totaling less than 1.0% (Bankowski and Page, 1959).

● **Psittacines.** Parakeets are less susceptible than most parrots and frequently become carriers (Levinthal, 1935). Parakeet morbidity and mortality are usually low (10% or less), complete recovery seldom occurs, and approximately 10% of the birds remain infected (Meyer, 1965). However, adult parakeets are less apt to be carriers than the immature bird (Meyer et al., 1942a). Infected parrots exposed to the

stress of shipping in one case had high morbidity but few deaths. In a subsequent shipment morbidity was followed by 50% mortality (Meyer and Eddie, 1934b).

● **Other Wild Birds.** Chlamydiosis in wild birds, with the possible exception of parrots, tends to cause low mortality with a significant percentage of latent infection. Infection of canaries and finches is usually associated with high mortality. Sparrows *(Passer domesticus)* experimentally infected with chlamydiae isolated from a pigeon resulted in a 33% mortality by the oral route (Davis, 1947). Sparrows infected with approximately 10 million chlamydiae isolated from an aborted ovine fetus had a 50% mortality.

◆ **IMMUNITY.** Both genetic resistance and acquired active immunity are important disease-preventing factors in wild bird populations, but the relative importance of each is unknown. The presence of complement-fixing antibody is indicative of prior infection and a degree of immunity. Thus the serological evidence of chlamydiosis in wild birds serves both as an indication of the incidence of infection and immunity (Table 13.3). Chlamydiae isolated from different species of birds, in general, show cross protection, but highly virulent isolates are more likely to protect against a heterologous species isolate than strains of low virulence (Meyer, 1965).

Acquired active immunity follows recovery from subclinical, acute, or subacute infections. Any of these infections may result in persistence of chlamydiae in tissues and are usually associated with a degree of immunity which may last for a long period of time. Latency may be a sequel to incomplete or delayed autosterilization. Active immunity in pigeons was noted after oral or intramuscular administration of chlamydiae (Bedson and Western, 1930). Finches and thrushes were described as aberrant hosts which have a lasting resistance following experimental infection (Meyer, 1942). Immunity as indicated by complement-fixing antibody was found to prevent successful isolation of chlamydiae in parakeets and rice birds (Meyer et al., 1942b). Although latent infection provides immunity, under stressful conditions it may be provoked to an acute infection. When this occurs, immunity may have waned sufficiently to be overwhelmed by the rapidly developing infection.

Acquired passive immunity to chlamydiae in birds has not been explored, but it theoretically could occur by the transfer of parental antibody via the yolk sac. This type of immunity is well documented for avian Newcastle disease and infectious bronchitis (Biester and Schwarte, 1965). In chlamydial infections of cattle (bovine pneumonitis) there is evidence of antibody transfer in the colostrum milk (Baker, 1958).

Efforts to develop a vaccine have resulted in only partial success. Live chlamydial vaccines provide solid immunity but are inherently dangerous. Killed vaccines failed to evoke a consistent and substantial immune response due to insufficient antigenic mass or an adverse effect of the inactivating agent. Multiple vaccine injections were necessary to elicit sufficient immunity to resist only modest challenge doses administered by a homologous route. In general, success was indicated principally in terms of survival. Little efficacy was evident in prevention of lesions or elimination of chlamydiae from tissues (Meyer, 1965). In spite of the limited success, these studies provide a basis for further vaccine research.

◆ **TREATMENT.** The development and application of effective treatment procedures for chlamydiosis in domestic birds have helped to reduce or eliminate this reservoir of infection for wild birds. They also provide useful procedures for research on captive wild birds. Since 1950 investigators have evaluated chlortetracycline,[1] oxytetracycline,[2] and tetracycline antibiotics against chlamydiosis outbreaks in pigeons,

psittacines, and turkeys. The antibiotics were administered by feed, water, or injection in relatively high repeated doses. The objective of treatment was to prevent morbidity, mortality, pathology, and chlamydiae in the tissues.

● **Pigeons.** Under experimental infection conditions, 80 g of chlortetracycline per gallon of drinking water, administered for 1 month, markedly reduced mortality and prevented infection of squabs. The procedure applied to commercial pigeon flocks resulted in suppression of infection but did not eliminate the carrier state (Shipkowitz et al., 1958).

● **Psittacines.** Tetracycline or chlortetracycline at intramuscular dosages of 2.5 to 5 mg per bird, given at 3-day intervals for a total of 2 to 3 injections, was effective in eliminating chlamydiae from tissues of parakeets (Bussell and Pollard, 1958; Hines and Williams, 1958; Meyer et al., 1958). Drinking water administration of tetracyclines at 0.6 to 1.2 mg per bird for 14 days to parakeets was only partially effective (Meyer et al., 1958). Hulled millet seeds impregnated with 5 mg of chlortetracycline per g, given for 14 consecutive days, were well accepted and efficacy of treatment was good to excellent as judged by a marked reduction of mortality, cessation of diarrhea, improvement of color and vitality, and elimination of chlamydiae from tissues in the majority of young and adult parakeets (Meyer et al., 1958).

Chlamydiae were eliminated from the tissues of parrots with 10 mg of chlortetracycline per g of cooked mash given for a total treatment period of 45 days (Arnstein and Meyer, 1966). The above-described medicated hulled millet seed treatment of parakeets and medicated mash treatment of large parrots have been accepted by the U.S. Federal Drug Administration for the treatment of psittacine birds suspected or known to be infected with chlamydiae.

● **Turkeys.** Under experimental conditions dosage levels of 100 to 800 g of chlortetracycline per ton of feed were fed for 2

---

1. Aureomycin[(R)] chlortetracycline is a trademark of American Cyanamid Co., Princeton, N.J.
2. Terramycin[(R)] oxytetracycline is a trademark of Chas. Pfizer & Co., Brooklyn, N.Y.

to 3 weeks. Feed levels of 100 g/ton of feed controlled mortality; 200 g/ton of feed completely suppressed mortality and signs, but 400 g/ton of feed were necessary to prevent lesions and eliminate chlamydiae from tissues. Antibody response to infection was completely suppressed at the 200 and 400 g/ton level (Davis and Watkins, 1959; Moore and Watkins, 1960). The use of antibiotic treatment at high levels for a few weeks did not result in drug-resistant chlamydiae (Meyer, 1965).

◆ **CONTROL.** Continued effective control of chlamydiosis in domestic birds reduces a potential source of infection for wild birds and this in turn reduces the potential source of infection for wild birds and this in turn reduces the potential of recycling the disease back into the wild population. It appears that little can be done about the infection once it is established in the wild bird population. One possible exception may be the feral pigeon or rock dove. Programs to reduce feral pigeon populations in cities include shooting, poison baits, elimination of nesting areas, and baiting with chemosterilants.

There is no conclusive evidence that the disease causes disseminating mortality in any wild species. There is presumptive evidence of sporadic mortality among Australian psittacines which may be due to chlamydiosis and environmental stressors. However, more information is needed on the prevalence and transmission of the disease in certain species, as indicated in the section on distribution and transmission.

From the human and domesticated mammal health aspect, a more thorough understanding of wildlife chlamydiosis would be useful in planning preventive programs. Specifically, prevalence rates in wild birds should be obtained in widely scattered geographic areas. Special attention should be given to those species which are numerous and are permanent residents of human or domestic animal populated areas. To facilitate this program, improved techniques are needed for rapid and accurate detection of chlamydiae in tissue samples.

When a definite estimate of chlamydial prevalence in wild birds is established, periodic monitoring would be indicated. Control of highly infected populations would include reduction of numbers and reproductive rates by appropriate humane measures.

◆ **REFERENCES**

Arnstein, P., and Meyer, K. P. Psittacosis-ornithosis. In R. W. Kirk, ed., *Current veterinary therapy 1966–1967*, p. 543. Philadelphia: W. B. Saunders, 1966.

Baker, J. A. Infections in mammals caused by members of the psittacosis group of viruses. In F. R. Beaudette, ed., *Progress in psittacosis research and control*. New Brunswick: Rutgers Univ. Press, 1958.

Bankowski, R. A., and Page, L. A. Studies of two epornitics of ornithosis caused by agents of low virulence. *Am. J. Vet. Res.* 20:935, 1959.

Basova, N. N., Suchkov, Y. G., Gusev, V. M., and Rudnev, M. M. Ornithosis in wild and domestic birds. *J. Microbiol. Epidemiol. Immunobiol.* 3:341, 1960.

Bedson, S. P. Virus diseases acquired from animals. *Lancet* 239:578, 1940.

Bedson, S. P., and Western, G. T. A disease of parrots communicable to man (psittacosis) aetiology—experimental observations. *Rept. Public Health Med. Subj.* 61:59, 1930.

Beech, M. D., and Miles, J. A. R. Psittacosis among birds in South Australia. *Australian J. Exptl. Biol. Med. Sci.* 31:473, 1953.

Benedict, A. A., and McFarland, C. Direct complement fixation test for diagnosis of ornithosis in turkeys. *Proc. Soc. Exptl. Biol. Med.* 92:768, 1956.

Biester, H. E., and Schwarte, L. H. *Diseases of poultry*, 5th ed. Ames: Iowa State Univ. Press, 1965.

Boldyrev, S. T. Detection of complement-fixing antibodies to ornithosis virus in the blood of the cormorant *(Phalacrocorax carbo sinensis)*. *Probl. Virol.* 6:538, 1961.

Brumfield, H. P., and Pomeroy, B. S. Direct complement fixation in turkey and chicken serum viral systems. *Proc. Soc. Exptl. Biol. Med.* 94:146, 1957.

Burnet, F. M. Psittacosis in Australian parrots. *Med. J. Australia* 2:743, 1934.

———. Enzootic psittacosis amongst wild Australian parrots. *J. Hyg.* 35:412, 1935.

———. A note on the occurrence of fatal psittacosis in parrots living in the wild state. *Med. J. Australia* 1:545, 1939.

Burnet, F. M., and Macnamara, J. Human

psittacosis in Australia. *Med. J. Australia* 2:84, 1936.

Bussell, R. H., and Pollard, M. Treatment of psittacosis-infected parakeets with chlortetracycline. In F. R. Beaudette, ed., *Progress in psittacosis research and control.* New Brunswick: Rutgers Univ. Press, 1958.

Chervonskii, V. I., Kareva, M. P., Dormidontow, R. V., Gromyko, A. I., Obukhovskaya, N. M., Kozlyakova, A. I., and Tazulakhova, E. B. Natural and secondary ornithosis focus in Zavidovsky District, Kalinin Oblast. *Vopr. Virusol.* 6:93, 1960.

Coles, J. D. W. A. Psittacosis in domestic pigeons. *Onderstepoort J. Vet. Sci. Animal Ind.* 15:141, 1940.

Dane, D. S. Some observations on the complement fixation test for the psittacosis-lymphogranuloma venerium group of viruses. *Med. J. Australia* 1:428, 1955.

Davis, D. E., and Watkins, J. R. The effect of chlortetracycline on the immunological response of turkeys infected with ornithosis. *J. Infect. Diseases* 104:56, 1959.

Davis, D. E., Delaplane, J. P., and Watkins, J. R. The role of turkey eggs in the transmission of ornithosis. *Am. J. Vet. Res.* 18: 409, 1957.

Davis, D. J. Susceptibility of the English sparrow *(Passer domesticus)* to infection with psittacosis virus of pigeon origin. *Proc. Soc. Exptl. Biol. Med.* 66:77, 1947.

———. Psittacosis in pigeons. In F. R. Beaudette, ed., *Psittacosis: Diagnosis, epidemiology, and control.* New Brunswick: Rutgers Univ. Press, 1955.

Drachman, T. S. A recent outbreak of psittacosis in upper Westchester County, N.Y. *Am. J. Public Health* 43:165, 1953.

Eddie, B., and Francis, T., Jr. Occurrence of psittacosis-like infection in domestic and game birds of Michigan. *Proc. Soc. Exptl. Biol. Med.* 50:291, 1942.

Eddie, B., Meyer, K. F., Lambrecht, F. L., and Furmen, D. P. Isolation of ornithosis bedsoniae from mites collected in turkey quarters and from chicken lice. *J. Infect. Diseases* 110:231, 1962.

Fritzsche, K., Lippelt, H., and Weyer, F. Beitrage zur Epidemsiologic, Diagnose and Therapie der Ornithose bei Tauben. *Berlin. Muench. Tieraerztl. Wochschr.* 69:61, 1956.

Furst, G., Kovac, W., and Moritsch, H. Enten als Virus-reservoir fur Ornithoseer Krankungen des Menschen. *Wien. Klin. Wochschr.* 69:223, 1957.

Gabrashanski, P. Wild birds and psittacosis. I. In ducks. II. Studies on fauna, biotypes and ecological physiology. *Nauchni Tr. Visshya Med. Inst. Prof. G. Pavlov* 11:163 and 13:155, 1963.

Gordon, F. B., and Quan, A. L. Occurrence of glycogen in inclusions of the psittacosis-lymphogranuloma venereum-t r a c h o m a agents. *J. Infect. Diseases* 115:186, 1965.

Grimpet, J. Outbreak of psittacosis in ducks. *Bull. Acad. Vet. France* 449:49, 1964.

Haagen, E., and Mauer, G. Ueber eine auf den Menschen ubertragbare Viruskrankheit bei Sturmvogeln und ihre Beziehung zur Psittakose. *Zentr. Bakteriol. Parasitenk. Abt. I. Orig.* 143:81, 1938.

Hines, M. P., and Williams, R. Treatment of psittacosis in parakeets with Aureomycin injections. Personal communication (RLB), 1958.

Hughes, D. L. Ornithosis (psittacosis) in a pigeon flock. *J. Comp. Pathol.* 57:67, 1947.

Illner, F. Ueber das Vorkommen das Ornithosevirus beim Haussperling *(Passer domesticus). Monatsh. Veterinaermed.* 16:933, 1961.

———. Ein Beitrag zur Enten-Ornithose und ihrer Epizootiologie. *Monatsh. Veterinaermed.* 17:141, 1962.

Karrer, H., Meyer, K. F., and Eddie, B. The complement fixation inhibition test and its application to the diagnosis of ornithosis in chickens and ducks. I. Principles and techniques of the test. *J. Infect. Diseases* 87:13, 1951.

Kozikowski, E. H., and Hahon, N. Plaque formation by psittacosis virus. *J. Bacteriol.* 88: 533, 1964.

Lehnert, C. Zur Frage der Uebertragung des Ornithose Virus ueber das Bruter bei Enten. *Berlin. Muench. Tieraerztl. Wochschr.* 75: 441, 1962.

Levinthal, W. Recent observations on psittacosis. *Lancet* 1:1207, 1935.

Lin, H., and Moulder, J. W. Patterns of response to sulfadiazine, d-cycloserine, and d-alanine in members of the psittacosis group. *J. Infect. Diseases* 116:372, 1966.

Mason, D. M. A capillary tube agglutination test for detecting antibodies against ornithosis in turkey serum. *J. Immunol.* 83:661, 1959.

Merrillees, C. R. Psittacosis in Australia. *Med. J. Australia* 3:320, 1934.

Meyer, K. F. Psittacosis. *Auk* 57:330, 1940.

———. The ecology of psittacosis and ornithosis. *Medicine* 21:175, 1942.

———. Ornithosis. In H. E. Biester and L. H. Schwarte, eds., *Diseases of poultry,* 5th ed. Ames: Iowa State Univ. Press, 1965.

———. The host spectrum of psittacosis-lymphogranuloma venereum (PL) agents. *Am. J. Ophthalmol.* 65:199, 1967.

Meyer, K. F., and Eddie, B. Spontaneous psittacosis infections of the canary and butterfly finch. *Proc. Soc. Exptl. Biol. Med.* 30:481, 1933.

————. Latent psittacosis and *Salmonella* psittacosis infection in South American parrotlets and conures. *Science* 79:546, 1934a.

————. Psittacosis in native South Australian budgerigars. *Proc. Soc. Exptl. Biol. Med.* 31:917, 1934b.

————. Psittacosis in importations of psittacine birds from the South American and Australian continents. *J. Infect. Diseases* 65:234, 1939.

————. Reservoirs of the psittacosis agent. *Acta Trop.* 9:204, 1952.

————. Psittacosis-lymphogranuloma venereum group *(Bedsonia* infections). In *Diagnostic procedures for viral and rickettsial diseases,* 3rd ed. New York: Am. Public Health Assoc., Inc., 1964.

Meyer, K. F., Eddie, B., and Yanamura, H. Y. Ornithosis (psittacosis) in pigeons and its relation to human pneumonitis. *Proc. Exptl. Biol. Med.* 49:609, 1942a.

————. Active immunization to the microbacterium multiforme psittacosis in parakeets and ricebirds. *J. Immunol.* 44:211, 1942b.

Meyer, K. F., Eddie, B., Richardson, J. H., Shipkowitz, N. L., and Muir, J. Chemotherapy in the control of psittacosis in parakeets. In F. R. Beaudette, ed., *Progress in psittacosis research and control.* New Brunswick: Rutgers Univ. Press, 1958.

Miles, J. A. R., and Shrivaston, J. B. Ornithosis in certain sea birds. *J. Animal Ecol.* 20:195, 1951.

Monreal, G. Untersuchungen und Beobachtungen zur Verbreitung und Klinik der Ornithose der Tauben. *Zentr. Veterinaermed.* 14:78, 1958.

Moore, R. W., and Watkins, J. R. The comparative effects of chlortetracycline and oxytetracycline in the treatment of turkeys with ornithosis. *J. Am. Vet. Med. Assoc.* 136:565, 1960.

Moore, R. W., Watkins, J. R., and Dixon, J. R. Experimental ornithosis in herons and egrets. *Am. J. Vet. Res.* 20:884, 1959.

Morange, A. De la psittacose ou infection speciale determinee par des perruches. Thesis, Paris, 1895.

Moulder, J. W. The relation of the psittacosis group (Chlamydiae) to bacteria and viruses. *Ann. Rev. Microbiol.* 20:107, 1966.

Mykytowycz, R., Dane, D. A., and Beech, M. Ornithosis in the petrel, *Puffinus tenuirostris. Australian J. Exptl. Biol. Med. Sci.* 33:639, 1955.

Officer, J., and Brown, A. Growth of psittacosis virus in tissue culture. *J. Infect. Diseases* 107:283, 1960.

Page, L. A. Experimental ornithosis in turkeys. *Avian Diseases* 3:51, 1959.

————. High body temperature of pigeons and sparrows as a factor in their resistance to an agent of the psittacosis group. *Bull. Wildlife Disease Assoc.* 1:49, 1965.

————. Interspecies transfer of psittacosis-IGV-trachoma agents: Pathogenicity of two avian and two mammalian strains for eight species of birds and mammals. *Am. J. Vet. Res.* 27:397, 1966.

————. Comparison of "pathotypes" among chlamydial (psittacosis) strains recovered from diseased birds and mammals. *Bull. Wildlife Disease Assoc.* 3:166, 1967.

————. Proposal for the recognition of two species in the genus *Chlamydia* Jones, Rake, and Stearns 1945. *Intern. J. Systematic Bacteriol.* 18:51, 1968.

Page, L. A., and Bankowski, R. A. Measurement of pathogenicity of turkey ornithosis agents for mice. *Avian Diseases* 3:23, 1959.

————. Factors affecting the production and detection of ornithosis antibodies in infected turkeys. *Am. J. Vet. Res.* 21:971, 1960.

Pavri, K. M., Rajagopalan, P. K., and Arnstein, P. Isolation of ornithosis bedsoniae from paddy birds *(Ardeola grayii)* in Mysore State, India. To be published in *Indian J. Med. Res.,* 1968.

Pearson, J. W., Duff, J. T., Gearinger, N. F., and Robbins, M. L. Growth characteristics of three agents of the psittacosis group in human diploid cell cultures. *J. Infect. Diseases* 115:49, 1965.

Pierce, K. R., and Moore, R. W. Meningoencephalitis in turkeys experimentally infected with ornithosis. *Avian Diseases* 9:266, 1965.

Pierce, K. R., Carroll, L. H., Moore, R. W. Experimental transmission of ornithosis from sheep to turkeys. *Am. J. Vet. Res.* 25:977, 1964.

Piraino, F., and Abel, C. Plaque assay for psittacosis virus in monolayers of chick embryo fibroblasts. *J. Bacteriol.* 87:1503, 1964.

Pollard, M. Ornithosis in seashore birds. *Proc. Soc. Exptl. Biol. Med.* 64:200, 1947.

————. Psittacosis in seashore birds. In F. R. Beaudette, ed., *Psittacosis: Diagnosis, epidemiology, and control.* New Brunswick: Rutgers Univ. Press, 1955.

Pollard, M., Caplovitz, C. D., and Swausch, C. D. The identification of an ornithosis virus from the willet. *Texas Rept. Biol. Med.* 5:337, 1947.

Rasmussen, R. F. Ueber eine durch Sturmovogel ubertragbare Lungenerkrankung auf den Faroern. *Zentr. Bakteriol. Parasitenk. Abt. I. Orig.* 143:89, 1938.

Rehn, F., and Sobeslavsky, O. Demonstration of ornithosis in wild birds. *J. Hyg. Epidemiol. Microbiol. Immunol.* 9:483, 1965.

Ross, M. R., and Borman, E. K. Direct and indirect fluorescent-antibody techniques for the psittacosis-lymphogranuloma venereum-trachoma group of agents. *J. Bacteriol.* 85:851, 1963.

Rubin, H., Kessling, R. E., Chamberlain, R. W., and Eidson, M. E. Isolation of a psittacosis-like agent from the blood of snowy egrets. *Proc. Soc. Exptl. Biol. Med.* 78:696, 1951.

Sery, V., Strauss, J., Eric, M., and Kleinbauer, V. An epidemic of ornithosis in east Bohemia. *Cesk. Epidemiol. Mikrobiol. Immunol.* 6:24, 1957.

Sery, V., Strauss, J., Krizove, J., Vratne, M., and Mikesove, F. M. Ornithosis and salmonellosis in wild birds in a nature reservation and in poultry and human beings in adjacent surroundings. *Vet. Med.* 33:799, 1960.

Shipkowitz, N. L., Meyer, K. F., and Eddie, B. Unpublished data (1958) cited in Chap. 23. In H. E. Biester and L. H. Schwarte, eds., *Diseases of poultry*, 5th ed. Ames: Iowa State Univ. Press, 1965.

Sidwell, R. W., Lundgren, D. L., Thorpe, B. D. Psittacosis complement-fixing antibodies in sera from fauna of the Great Salt Lake Desert of Utah. *Am. J. Trop. Med. Hyg.* 13:591, 1964.

Sprunt, D. H. The pathology of psittacosis. In F. R. Beaudette, ed., *Psittacosis: Diagnosis, epidemiology, and control.* New Brunswick: Rutgers Univ. Press, 1955.

Strauss, J. Virological demonstration of ornithosis in men and ducks in Czechoslovakia. *Cesk. Epidemiol. Mikrobiol. Immunol.* 5:281, 1956.

Strauss, J., Bednar, B., and Sery, V. The incidence of ornithosis and salmonellosis in the black-headed gull *(Larus ridibundus). Cesk. Epidemiol. Mikrobiol. Immunol.* 6:152, 1957.

Tanami, Y., Pollard, M., and Starr, T. J. Replication pattern of a psittacosis virus in a tissue culture system. *Virology* 15:22, 1961.

Terskikh, I. I. Problems of medical virology, ornithosis. *First All Union Symp.,* Vol. 10, published by the Ivanovsky Institute of Virology, Acad. Med. Sci. USSR, Moscow, 1964.

Terskikh, I. I., Shel'tsov-Bebutov, A. M., Kuborina, L. N., and Keleinikov, A. A. Studies on orthinosis in birds and its focal distribution. *Vopr. Virusol.* 6:131, 1961.

Tomlinson, C. T. Ornithosis in doves. *Public Health Dept.* 56:1073, 1942.

Tremain, A. R. Some aspects of psittacosis and the isolation of virus. *Med. J. Australia* 2:417, 1938.

14 ◆ ERYSIPELOTHRIX

● RICHARD D. SHUMAN

ERYSIPELAS refers to a specific disease caused by the bacterium *Erysipelothrix rhusiopathiae*. This organism affects a wide variety of animals, both domestic and wild, and causes a septicemia of varying severity. Of economic importance is the effect on the domestic pig, turkey, sheep, duck, and pheasant raised in captivity. The disease also can pose a problem to those responsible for the management of zoos and the procurement of specimens for aviaries.

◆ **HISTORY AND DISTRIBUTION.** The identification of the organism causing erysipelas began with the discovery by Koch in 1878 of an organism he called the "bacillus of mouse septicemia." Loeffler, in 1881–86, and Pasteur and Thuillier, in 1882 –83, related this organism to "Schweinerotlauf" and "roget du porc" respectively, or swine erysipelas. Its relationship to human wound infection, called erysipeloid (not human erysipelas), was recognized by Rosenbach in 1887. Erysipelas infection in domesticated birds was first recognized in a male turkey by Jarosch (1905). Although it was known that a variety of animals, domestic and wild, were susceptible to experimental infection with *E. rhusiopathiae,* the first report of the isolation of this organism from wild birds following natural infection was by Jarmai (1919). In a zoological garden in Hungary, he isolated the organism from birds, including the thrush, quail, and parrot. During the ensuing years *E. rhusiopathiae* has been found to have worldwide distribution, and in addition to affecting a wide variety of animals, it has been associated with marine and freshwater fish. It has been isolated from a variety of ectoparasites, sewage from abattoirs, processed meat, decomposing animal carcasses, and streams. Relatively few studies have been made on erysipelas in other than domestic animals (pig, turkey, and sheep), and a source of supplemental information has been the incidence reports from diagnostic laboratories.

Levine (1965) has reviewed the reported incidence of erysipelas in various species of birds, such as the mallard, pigeon, quail, peacock, goose, greenfinch, ring-necked parakeet, white stork, herring gull, and crane. In addition, Goret and Joubert (1947) isolated the organism from a guinea hen. Urbain (1947) mentioned that on repeated occasions enzootics had been experienced involving the turtle-dove *(Streptopelia turtur),* undulating parakeet *(Melopsittacus undulatus),* greenfinch *(Carduelis chloris),* European blackbird *(Turdus merula),* goldfinch *(Carduelis carduelis),* and finch of the tree *(Fringilla coelebs).* Casamagnaghi (1949) isolated the organism from a pet terutero *(Belonopterus chilensis cayennensis),* a common bird of South America. An *E. rhusiopathiae* infection in a pigeon and her 4-day-old squab was described by Van Dorssen and Donker-Voet (1953). Bigland (1957) isolated the organism from the body organs of a normal-appearing golden eagle *(Aquila chrysaetos canadensis)* that was clubbed to death while escaping from a granary. The erysipelas organism was isolated by Nowak (1957) from a dead pheasant and an African crowned crane *(Balearica pavonina)* several days after their transfer from another zoo. McDiarmid (1962) isolated the organism from wild wood pigeons and noted that Taylor did also from a Scottish wood grouse. Lasalle and Nouvel (1964) isolated the erysipelas organism from a North American wood duck *(Aix sponsa),* African crowned crane *(B. pavonina),* and penguins *(Eudyptes cristatus* and *Pygosceles papua).* Richter et al. (1964) reported on an outbreak of erysipelas in a commercial flock of pheasants. Deaths among a variety of wild birds due to erysipelas, which occurred in a "sick room" and in one of several outside pens, were described by Blackmore and Gallagher (1964). The loss of an entire shipment of short-tailed parrots *(Agapornis roseicollis)* within 4 days after being received was reported by Jadin and Beckers (1965). In addition to demonstrating listeriosis and erysipelas in rodents, Zhukova et al. (1966) isolated *E. rhusiopathiae* from the wood grouse *(Tetrao urogallus).* Ungureanu et al. (1966) reported on deaths attributed to *E. rhusiopathiae* among a consignment of birds that had been subjected to poor handling during transportation to a zoological garden—that is, heat, lack of water, close confinement, and excitement. The organism was isolated from an Australian black swan *(Cygnus atratus),* a great crested grebe *(Podiceps cristatus),* a red-necked grebe *(P. grisegena),* a great cormorant *(Phalacrocorax carbo),* and a mallard *(Anas platyrhynchos).* Parasitism, warm summer temperature, and a lowering of resistance were believed by Brack and Stoll (1967) to be contributing factors in the death from erysipelas of birds in a zoological garden. Affected were 3 dabchicks or little grebes *(Podiceps ruficollis),* 2 pheasant-tailed jacanas *(Hydrophasianus chirurgus),* an oystercatcher *(Haematopus ostralegus),* and a greenshank *(Tringa nebularia).* Naturally occurring erysipelas infection in starlings *(Sturnus vulgaris)* was reported by Faddoul et al. (1968). Five of 97 starlings examined during a 3-year survey were affected and were described as being "immature."

◆ **ETIOLOGY.** *Erysipelothrix rhusiopathiae (E. insidiosa)* (Breed et al., 1957) is gram-positive (but easily decolorized), nonmotile, nonsporeforming, and non-acid-fast, and although the filamentous forms resemble mycelia, branching does not occur. Granules may be seen and thus suggest spe-

cies of diphtheroids. Short rods measure from 1 to 2μ and the filamentous forms 4 to 15μ or more in length. Colonies are classified into smooth (S), rough (R), and intermediate (S-R) forms. Typical S colonies are circular, with entire edges, and have a smooth convex surface. Typical R colonies are also circular, but are apt to be irregular with curled edges, and have a flattened rough surface. The intermediate colonies have some characteristics of the R and S types and can assume a wide variety of formations. After 24 and 48 hours' growth on solid medium, typical colonies are bluish gray in diffuse light, becoming somewhat opaque as they age. Characteristically, granules are present, from a few in number to dense concentration. Young colonies are quite small and can easily be overlooked, especially when either few in number or mixed with faster-growing colonies of other organisms; a hand lens ($\times 10$) or the widefield microscope are most useful in this regard.

The organism is a facultative aerobe and grows best at 37° C within a pH range of 7.4 to 7.8; the addition of serum to the medium will enhance the growth. Useful, but presumptive evidence, for its identity is (1) the characteristic appearance of colonies, (2) the morphologic appearance of the organism, (3) the characteristic growth in liquid medium that has been best described by Smith (1885) as "a faint opalescence, which, on shaking, was resolved for a moment into delicate rolling clouds," (4) the "test tube brush" appearance in gelatin stab cultures, and (5) the production of hydrogen sulfide. Fermentation reactions in carbohydrate media can be variable, and to avoid confusion, White and Shuman (1961) recommend familiarity with the general pattern of fermentation reactions of known strains of the organism in a medium routinely used.

◆ **TRANSMISSION.** It is not specifically known how the disease is transmitted under natural conditions, but it seems reasonable to assume that it results either from ingestion of the organism or from wound infection. *Erysipelothrix rhusiopathiae* may persist in the presence of organic matter, but there is no specific evidence that it can exist as a soil saprophyte. Blackmore and Gallagher (1964) described a significant association of soil in an outside pen with the sporadic death of birds and one deer within 10 months after being placed in the pen. Many of the birds had been in the sick room during the original occurrence of erysipelas. *Erysipelothrix rhusiopathiae* was demonstrated in the soil of the pen by infecting mice with suspensions of soil and subsequently isolating the organism from the heart blood. The hypothesis of a "carrier" mammal or bird as the source of the organism seems most probable.

Erysipelas in commercial turkey flocks has been commonly associated with maturing males and with females during the breeding season, and appears to be directly related to wound infection. Richter et al. (1964) associated an epizootic in a commercial flock of pheasants with a high incidence of cannibalism caused by improper feeding.

In 1881 Gaffky (Wellmann, 1954) infected 3 sparrows through wound infection with the "septicemia agent" (rotlauf bacillus). Wellmann (1954) was able to induce the disease readily in house sparrows by intramuscular injection, inoculation of skin abrasions, and adding a culture of the organism to the feed. Although he reported the experience to be unusual, he was also able to induce the disease in doves by feeding the erysipelas organism. Blackmore and Gallagher (1964) found budgerigars to be very susceptible to infection by either intraperitoneal or intracutaneous routes. The fact that Grenci (1943) was able to isolate *E. rhusiopathiae* from 2 samples of fish meal illustrates a possible source of the agent, even though turkeys in her experiments were refractory to infection with feed containing the organism. Strains that may be virulent for pigs, white mice, and pigeons are not necessarily virulent for turkeys. Age is a factor that is related to transmission. Meloni (Van Es and Mc-

Grath, 1936) observed that although old geese, ducks, and common fowls could not be infected, the reverse was experienced when young birds were selected. Shuman (1950) and Malik (1962) experienced similar results following the experimental exposure of chickens. The latter reported also that older chickens were susceptible to infection by the intrapalpebral route.

◆ **SIGNS AND PATHOLOGY.** There are no specific signs associated with erysipelas in wild birds, and one is presented with the signs suggestive of an acute illness (diarrhea, listlessness, prostration) or a history of sudden death.

The pathologic lesions (including those of turkeys and pheasants) that have been associated with the subsequent isolation of *E. rhusiopathiae* are those of septicemia and are not of a strictly pathognomonic nature.

◆ **DIAGNOSIS.** Diagnosis will depend upon the isolation of *E. rhusiopathiae*. It may be necessary to examine contaminated material and the following have been useful ways for isolating the organism: (1) subcutaneous injection or inoculation of the superficially scarified ears of mice, (2) intramuscular injection of pigeons, (3) refrigeration of a tissue sample in liquid medium at 4° to 5° C for 4 to 5 weeks, followed by subculture onto Packer's medium (Packer, 1943), and (4) use of a liquid antibiotic selective medium (Wood, 1965) coupled with the use of Packer's medium. A serum-protection test can be helpful in confirming the identification of the erysipelas organism if virulent for mice; otherwise, repeated intravenous inoculation of rabbits for subsequent testing of the serum for specific agglutinins can be conducted. Fluorescent antibody testing can be applied to *E. rhusiopathiae* and has been used for rapid tentative identification or confirmation of results of other tests. The test is not, however, essential for identification of the organism. The methods given by Cherry et al. (1961) are applicable. When performing postmortem examinations, it should be remembered that human infection (erysipeloid) can take place easily through small abrasions of the skin.

♦ **IMMUNITY.** No specific information is available concerning immunity in wild birds, although by analogy one can assume that infection (clinical or subclinical) can induce immunity. Aluminum hydroxide adsorbate bacterin has been useful in commercial turkey flocks, but it is not known whether this biologic is of value in other avian species. Richter et al. (1964) used a lysate bacterin in pheasants with apparent success; to our knowledge, however, there are no reports of controlled experiments on the use of this product except in pigs.

♦ **TREATMENT AND CONTROL.** Specific information is lacking for the treatment of wild birds. Penicillin, however, has been used successfully in treating turkeys and captive pheasants and thus probably would be suitable for other birds. A second injection of the antibiotic may be necessary.

In circumstances where captive birds are involved, strict attention must be given to sanitation of food and quarters and protection from unconfined rodents and flies. Regular observations must be made for deviations from the usual attitude. Newly acquired specimens from any source should be placed in isolation for at least 30 days.

With regard to the use of chemical disinfectants, the remarks of Mallman (1958) are worthwhile: "disinfectants cannot be poured in excess concentrations on soiled surfaces to destroy disease-producing microorganisms successfully . . . the properties of a good disinfectant generally include penetrability, but the property of passing through organic soil to attack microorganisms is nil in most compounds."

♦ **REFERENCES**

Bigland, C. H. Isolation of *Erysipelothrix rhusiopathiae* from a golden eagle. *Can. J. Comp. Med.* 21(8):290, 1957.

Blackmore, D. K., and Gallagher, G. L. An outbreak of erysipelas in captive wild birds and mammals. *Vet. Rec.* 76(42):1161, 1964.

Breed, R. S., Murray, E. G. D., and Smith, N. R. In *Bergey's manual of determinative bacteriology*, 7th ed., p. 599. Baltimore: Williams & Wilkins, 1957.

Brack, M., and Stoll, L. Erysipelothrix bei Zoovoegeln. *Kleintier-Praxis* 12(4):109, 1967.

Casamagnaghi, A. El rouget o erisipela del cerdo. *Revista Med. Vet.* 25:887, 1949.

Cherry, W. B., Goldman, M., and Carski, T. R. Fluorescent antibody techniques in the diagnosis of communicable diseases. *PHS Publication no. 729*, USGPO, Washington, D.C., 1961.

Faddoul, G. P., Fellows, G. W., and Baird, J. Erysipelothrix infection in starlings. *Avian Diseases* 12(1):61, 1968.

Goret, P., and Joubert, L. Isolement du bacille du rouget chez une pintade. *Bull. Acad. Vet. France* 20(10):463, 1947.

Grenci, C. M. The isolation of *Erysipelothrix rhusiopathiae* and experimental infection in turkeys. *Cornell Vet.* 33(1):56, 1943.

Jadin, J. M., and Beckers, A. *D'Erysipelothrix rhusiopathiae* chez *Agapornis roseicollis.* *Bull. Soc. R. Zool. Anvers.* 36:17, 1965.

Jarmai, K. Orbanczbaczillusok elofordulasa madarakban. *Allatorvosi Lapok (Veterinarius)* 42(8):57, 1919.

Jarosch, W. L. Ueber Septikaemie der Truthuehner. *Oesterreichische Monatsschr. Tierheilk.* 30(29):197, 1905.

Lassalle, J., and Nouvel, J. Septicemie a bacille du rouget chez des manchots en captivite. *Rec. Med. Vet.* 140(1):33, 1964.

Levine, N. D. Erysipelas. In H. E. Biester and L. H. Schwarte, eds., *Diseases of poultry*, 5th ed., p. 461. Ames: Iowa State Univ. Press, 1965.

McDiarmid, A. Diseases of free-living wild animals. *FAO Agr. Studies* 57:34, 1962.

Malik, Z. Pokusy s experimentalnou vnimavostou kurciat voci mikrobu *Erysipelothrix rhusiopathiae.* *Vet. Casopis.* 11:89, 1962.

Mallman, W. L. Theory and principles of cleaning and disinfection. *Proc. Tbc. Erad. Conf.*, June 16–20, p. 91. ARS, USDA, 1958.

Nowak, B. Rozyca u ptakou. *Med. Weterynar.* 13(5):272, 1957.

Packer, R. A. The use of sodium azide (NaN₃) and crystal violet in a selective medium for streptococci and *Erysipelothrix rhusiopathiae. J. Bacteriol.* 46(4):343, 1943.

Richter, S., Karlovic, M., and Grmovsek, P. Prikaz epizootije vrbanca u. fazana. *Vet. Arhiv.* 34(3–4):101, 1964.

Shuman, R. D. *Rept. Chief Bur. Anim. Ind.*, p. 46. Washington, D.C., 1950.

Smith, T. *Second Ann. Rept. Bur. Anim. Ind.*, p. 187. Washington, D.C., 1885.

Ungureanu, C., Jordache, A., Ghitescu, N., and Danescu, A. Izolorea unor tulpini de *Erysipelothrix rhusiopathiae* de la pasari Salbatice tinute in captivitatae. *Bucharest. Inst. Cercet. Vet. Bioprep.* "Pasteur" *Lucrarile* 3(1):219, 1966.

Urbain, A. Infection spontanee d'oiseaux de voliere par le bacille du roget. *Bull. Acad. Vet. France* 20(5):201, 1947.

Van Dorssen, C. A., and Donker-Voet, J. Spontane *Erysipelothrix rhusiopathiae*-infectie bij duiven. *Tijdschr. Diergeneesk.* 78:501, 1953.

Van Es, L., and McGrath, C. B. Swine erysipelas. *Nebr. Agr. Exp. Sta. Res. Bull.* 84, p. 8, 1936.

Wellmann, G. Rotlaufinfektionsversuche an wilden Mauesen, Sperlingen, Huehnern, und Puten. *Tieraerztl. Umschau.* 15/16:269, 1954.

White, T. G., and Shuman, R. D. Fermentation reactions of *Erysipelothrix rhusiopathiae*. *J. Bacteriol.* 82(4):595, 1961.

Wood, R. L. A selective liquid medium utilizing antibiotics for isolation of *Erysipelothrix insidiosa*. *Am. J. Vet. Res.* 26(115):1303, 1965.

Zhukova, L. N., Konshina, T. A., and Popugailo, V. M. Listeriosis and erysipeloid infection of rodents in the Sverdlovsk region. *J. Microbiol. Epidemiol. Immunol.* 43(7): 18, 1966.

15 ◆ LISTERIOSIS

● WARREN C. EVELAND

Synonyms: Listeric infection, circling disease.

LISTERIOSIS is a febrile, infectious, endemic food- and water-borne disease which may be expressed in a number of syndromes. According to its clinical course, the disease may be classified as (1) acute to hyperacute (fulminant), (2) subacute, (3) chronic, and (4) abortive. It may be present also as an inapparent infection in birds which may serve as a source of human infection (Felsenfeld, 1951).

◆ **HISTORY.** The second isolation of *Listeria monocytogenes* from a wild source was made from a bird 15 years after the first isolation had been made from wild gerbils *(Tatera lobengulae)* (Pirie, 1927). In Sweden, Lilleengen (1942) reported the isolation of the organism from a wood grouse *(Tetrao urogallus)* and described some of the first pathology of the disease process in birds. Only one earlier description of the disease was made from studies of chickens with a disease characterized by massive necrosis of the myocardium (Seastone, 1935). Subsequent studies of listeriosis in fowls are reported in an excellent review by Gray (1958).

◆ **DISTRIBUTION.** While the isolation of *L. monocytogenes* among domestic fowl has been reported practically on a worldwide basis, that from wild birds has been limited to Europe—with one exception. Table 15.1 summarizes the sources of isolations made from wild birds according to the literature to date.

◆ **ETIOLOGY.** *Listeria monocytogenes* is a small, gram-positive, nonsporeforming, extremely resistant diphtherialike rod, with a peculiar tumbling motility at room temperature, but usually nonmotile at 37° C. It is aerobic to microaerophilic. Colonies on blood agar incubated 18 to 24 hours at 37° C are round, 0.2 to 0.8 mm in diameter, slightly raised, with an entire margin, and usually show a narrow zone of beta hemolysis. Hemolysins and hemagglutinins have been described in pathogenic strains (Jenkins et al., 1964, 1967; Watson et al., 1967). Cultures are easily confused with hemolytic streptococci and often mistaken for and discarded as "contaminating diphtheroids." Further distinctive characteristics of the organism have been described recently by Wetzler et al. (1968).

◆ **TRANSMISSION.** As with wild mammals, isolations of *L. monocytogenes* have been made from either diseased or carrier birds in which the organisms could have been acquired as a result of their eating other infected animals. Reed (1955) reported the isolation of *L. monocytogenes* from the intestinal tract of an apparently healthy snowy owl, which had been shot in northern Ontario, Canada. This species is known to prey on lemmings which have been reported to be carriers of the organism (Plummer and Byrne, 1950). Only one instance of the disease in birds has been associated with infected domestic animals. McDiarmid (1962) described an outbreak in partridges associated with infected sheep. No instance of a listeric outbreak can be traced to the association of birds and their ectoparasites or of any other insect vectors. More than likely, therefore, any other outbreaks of listeriosis, or even single cases of the disease, are probably a result of the birds' contact with infected soil, water, or feces.

TABLE 15.1. Isolation of *Listeria monocytogenes* from Wild Birds

Species	Country	References
Crane	Finland	Stenberg, 1961
Grouse		
Tetrao urogallus	Sweden	Lilleengen, 1942
	Denmark	Larsen, 1967b
Gull	Denmark	Larsen, 1967b
House sparrow	Denmark	Larsen, 1963; Larsen 1967b
Lapwing	Denmark	Larsen, 1967b
Magpie	USSR	Kaplinskii et al., 1962
Partridge		
Aletoris rufa and	France	Lucas et al., 1962
A. graeca chukar		
"Partridge"	England	McDiarmid, 1962
	Denmark	Larsen, 1963
Pheasant	France	Lucas et al., 1962
Ptarmigan	Finland	Stenberg, 1961
Snowy owl	Canada, Ontario	Reed, 1955
Starling	Denmark	Larsen, 1963; Larsen, 1967b
Whitethroat	England	Jennings, 1955
Wild duck	Sweden	Nystrom and Karlsson, 1961
Zoo birds		
Diamond dove	Netherlands	Zwart and Donker-Voet, 1959
Eagle	Germany	Schultz, 1950
Partridge	Netherlands	Donker-Voet, 1963
Sarus crane	Netherlands	Donker-Voet, 1963
Swainson's lorikeet	Netherlands	Donker-Voet, 1963

SOURCE: Modified from Gray (1964).

◆ **SIGNS.** While reports on the clinical picture of the disease in wild birds are rare since actual cases are not often observed, the signs of primary listeriosis in domestic fowl might offer some comparisons. As in mammalian species, young fowl appear to be more susceptible to listeric infection than older birds. Outbreaks are usually sporadic and mortality in the individual flock may vary from a few birds to as many as 40% of the flock (Paterson, 1937; Pallaske, 1951; Schoop, 1951; Thompson, 1954; Csontos et al., 1955). There are no pathognomonic signs or lesions in birds with listeriosis. Paterson (1937) reported that adult chickens usually died suddenly, while young birds exhibited a slow wasting before death. In contrast, Csontos et al. (1955) stated that among geese, the very young died suddenly, often within a few hours after the onset of signs. Older geese survived somewhat longer and displayed torticollis, spasms, and other nervous signs before death.

In most instances *L. monocytogenes* plays a secondary role in disease of birds. It has been associated with other bacterial, viral, and parasitic diseases and has also been isolated from apparently normal birds (Jennings, 1955; Reed, 1955). The blue eagle from which Schultz (1950) isolated the organism did not appear ill immediately before death. However, it had been treated over a long period for an abscess of the abdominal wall. It is known that *L. monocytogenes* may be associated with abscess formation, and this may actually have been the primary focus of infection in this bird.

Lucas et al. (1962), who have isolated *L. monocytogenes* from the largest number of free-living birds, found no pathognomonic signs or lesions. They found a variety of primary conditions and rarely necrotic foci; they concluded that most listeric infections in wild birds are either secondary or latent and that birds constitute the most important reservoir of infection. Certainly, *L. monocytogenes* should be given consideration whenever gram-positive rods are isolated from free-living birds.

◆ **PATHOGENESIS.** As with the wild mammals, very little is known with respect to the pathogenesis of these organisms.

Since the oral-fecal route of infection is highly suspected from inferences in the literature and discussions with various researchers in the field, it is possible that numbers of organisms, pathogenicity of the strains, host factors, and environmental factors may all or individually have a definite role. In the concluding remarks of the review by Gray and Killinger (1966) the statement is made, "The pathogenesis of the disease is not known. Infections resulting in disturbances of the central nervous system appear to have a different pathogenesis from those producing abortion or other disturbances of pregnancy." Further research is definitely needed in this area.

◆ **PATHOLOGY.** Little has been observed with respect to the pathology present in wild birds. Lilleengen (1942) observed fatty degeneration and necrosis of the hepatic cells in liver sections from a wood grouse which at necropsy had necrosis in the ceca, a swollen spleen, and grayish discoloration of the liver. Again some common facts may exist between what has been observed in domestic fowl and wild birds. The best observations of the pathologic processes in chickens were made by Pallaske (1951), who distinguishes between small, medium, and large myocardial foci. The first involved only a few fibrils within a muscle bundle. These stained a bit more deeply with eosin and the nuclei showed pycnosis and karyorrhexis. Moderate fatty changes were also evident. The medium foci involved several bundles with complete necrosis at the center and coagulation necrosis at the periphery and some proliferation of histiocytes. The large foci were characterized by complete destruction of extensive areas of the heart, edema, marked proliferation of histiocytes, and infiltration of monocytes, lymphocytes, and plasma cells. These often formed a marked cuff around the capillaries and small vessels, which is characteristically found in the brain of cattle with listeriosis. Many of the erythrocytes in these vessels showed degenerative changes in the nuclei. In Gram-stained sections, the bacteria were always

found at the periphery rather than at the center of the lesion.

Additional descriptions of the pathology of the infection are given in the excellent review by Gray (1958). His summary of a review of about 21 authors states that primary listeriosis in birds is commonly manifested by a septicemia and the organisms can be isolated from most of the viscera, particularly the liver and spleen, and occasionally the brain. Usually the most conspicuous lesions are massive areas of myocardial degeneration, with marked engorgement of the cardiac vessels, pericarditis, and an increased amount of pericardial fluid. In some instances the heart may show varying numbers of well-defined grayish white foci of necrosis, ranging in size from pinpoint to 5 mm in diameter. Focal hepatic necrosis without cardiac alterations also is common in naturally infected birds. Sometimes these foci are seen also in the spleen and lungs. Other lesions frequently encountered include splenomegaly, nephritis, peritonitis, enteritis, ulcers in the ileum and ceca, generalized or pulmonary edema, inflammation of the air sacs, and conjunctivitis.

◆ **DIAGNOSIS.** The diagnosis of *L. monocytogenes* infections, as with most bacterial diseases, should entail the isolation of the specific organism and its confirmation by biochemical and serological tests. Although it grows well on most media *after* isolation, it may be difficult to isolate initially, with the consequence that isolations are many times missed. The bacteria are often confined in the focal lesions of infected tissue, frequently intracellularly; hence, it is necessary to release them by a maceration technique. Diluents for this process should be either distilled water or broth, since salt solution seems to be inhibitory—especially when the organisms are few in number. It has been suggested by certain authors (Suchanova et al., 1958; Solomkin, 1959; Sword and Pickett, 1961) that L-forms of the organism may play a role in the disease process. Other studies have shown that L-forms can be induced and isolated (Suchanova and Patocka, 1957; Brem and Eveland, 1967), so if the organism is present in that form in the animal body, it would be necessary to use special media for its isolation and conversion to the standard vegetative form.

Suspect tissue should be macerated in a mortar, tissue grinder, or blender, with sufficient distilled water or tryptose broth to well cover the material in the tube or bottle in which it is to be stored. Initial platings should be made on tryptose agar, trypticase soy agar, or McBride's agar and the remaining suspension incubated at 4° C. Body fluids and swabs should be plated, tryptose broth added, and then stored. Feces should be emulsified in enough tryptose broth to well cover the specimen and stored at 4° C for at least a week before plating. Storage in the cold, besides enhancing the growth of this somewhat psychrophilic organism, tends to destroy most of the gram-negative organisms which might be present in the specimen. Smears or impression smears should be made from the original material for staining by fluorescent antibody methods, if specific labeled antiserum is available (Biegeleisen, 1963; Eveland, 1963; Smith and Metzger, 1963; Eveland and Baublis, 1967). After 18 to 24 hours incubation at 37° C, colonies on the inoculated clear agar, when examined with a scanning microscope or a hand lens with the plate resting on a laboratory tripod, using obliquely transmitted light, are a characteristic and distinctive blue-green color. The above schema has been outlined in detail by Gray (1962) and Gray and Killinger (1966).

If the initial culture fails to reveal *L. monocytogenes* after 72 hours incubation, the refrigerated material should be replated at intervals of several weeks for at least up to 3 months and possibly as long as 6 months. An additional type of enrichment recently reported by Lehnert (1964) and evaluated by McCrum et al. (1967) has shown the value of a 3.75% potassium thiocyanate broth in early isolations of the organism. Recent evaluations of the cold storage holding technique by Larsen

(1967a) and others have shown that it enhances the probability of isolating *L. monocytogenes* by 31%. A diagnosis of listeric infection cannot be eliminated merely by failure to isolate the organism on initial culture attempts.

A number of isolations of *L. monocytogenes* have been made by the intraperitoneal inoculation of suspect material into mice (Olsufev and Emelyanova, 1951; Olsufev and Petrov, 1959; Solomkin, 1959; Gray, 1960). In this country and in Canada several isolations have been made from mice inoculated intracerebrally with suspended brain tissue (Frappier et al., 1967). It is possible that these techniques may be more effective for initial isolation of the organism than the use of ordinary bacteriologic medium.

Usually the liver and/or spleen are cultured for detection of carriers of *L. monocytogenes*. Ponomareva et al. (1962) claim that swabbing the pharynx is the most effective method with the common rat. By this technique one isolation has been made in our laboratory from a pet dog. Perhaps the most potentially rewarding source, feces, has been completely overlooked. Artificially infected animals excrete large numbers of the organisms in the feces. Recent studies on deer (McCrum et al., 1967) and on man and domestic animals (Larsen, 1967b) have shown the presence of clinically healthy carriers in these groups.

Serologic tests have not been a very satisfactory aid to diagnosis of *L. monocytogenes* infections. Standard agglutination and complement-fixation tests (Seeliger, 1961) and refined antigen agglutination tests (Osebold et al., 1965) have been used to determine the presence of antibodies, but care must be exercised in their interpretation because of cross-reactions that occur between *L. monocytogenes* and such other organisms as *Staphylococcus aureus* and *Streptococcus fecalis*. Recent evaluation, in our laboratory, of the live antigen agglutination test (Potel and Degen, 1960) has shown it to be quite sensitive and specific. Further work is certainly needed in this area.

Biologic tests as an aid to the identification of *L. monocytogenes* cultures have been discussed by Gray and Killinger (1966). These tests include: (1) the production of a monocytosis in rabbits by inoculation of a standardized live culture intravenously and the observation of up to a 30% increase in circulating monocytes, and (2) the conjunctival instillation or Anton test by inoculation of a few drops of an 18- to 24-hour broth culture into the conjunctival sac of a rabbit, guinea pig, or mouse, with the production of a severe conjunctivitis in a few days. Both tests have been used in clinical laboratories in various areas of the world.

◆ **PROGNOSIS.** Since the disease appears to be self-limiting among wild animals and probably birds, and since listeric infection among fowl has often been complicated by some other disorder, coupled with the relative difficulty of artificially infecting healthy birds, it is suggested that wild animals, birds, and fowl possess a rather high degree of natural resistance to the disease. If this is so, it might explain why the reports indicate that the disease may be present in all variations from the carrier to single cases to those of epizootic proportions.

◆ **IMMUNITY.** Nothing is known with respect to the immunity conferred by the organism to wild birds, since no studies have been done to determine the presence of antibodies in the serum or of the role of circulating antibodies in protection against the disease.

◆ **TREATMENT.** Treatment of listeric infection in man and domestic animals is done best by the use of broad-spectrum antibiotics. The present widespread use of poultry feeds containing antibiotics may have prophylactic value against listeric infection in domesticated birds, and since this was initiated several years ago, reports of the disease in poultry have become rare. It could be assumed that this type of treatment would be effective in wild birds.

◆ **CONTROL.** One of the concluding remarks made by Gray and Killinger (1966) was: "Listeric infection is widespread in both domesticated and wild animals, but few definite figures are available on its incidence. It is not known with certainty whether affected or carrier animals constitute a source of infection for man." Until such time as more information is available about the distribution of *L. monocytogenes* among wildlife, and the ways this distribution affects the spread of the disease, we can only hope to check the outbreaks as they occur. Final control will come only when we have a better understanding of the epizootiology of this organism.

◆ **REFERENCES**

Biegeleisen, J. Z. Fluorescent antibody studies on *Listeria monocytogenes.* In M. L. Gray, ed., *Proc. 2nd Symp. Listeric Infect.,* Aug. 1962, Bozeman, Mont., p. 183, 1963.

Brem, A., and Eveland, W. C. Inducing L-forms in *Listeria monocytogenes* types 1 through 7. *Appl. Microbiol.* 15:1510, 1967.

Csontos, L., Derzsy, D., and Baranyi, I. T. Listeriosis in young geese. *Acta. Vet. Hung.* 5:261, 1955. Also: Listeriosis fiatal libakban. *Magy. Allatorv. Lapja* 10:110, 1955.

Donker-Voet, J. Listeric infection in animals in The Netherlands. In M. L. Gray, ed., *Proc. 2nd Symp. Listeric Infect.,* Aug. 1962, Bozeman, Mont., p. 30, 1963.

Eveland, W. C. Fluorescent antibody studies on *Listeria monocytogenes.* In M. L. Gray, ed., *Proc. 2nd Symp. Listeric Infect.,* Aug. 1962, Bozeman, Mont., p. 186, 1963.

Eveland, W. C., and Baublis, J. V. Two case reports of the association of human and canine listeriosis. *Proc. 3rd Intern. Symp. Listeriosis,* July 1966, Bilthoven, The Netherlands, p. 269, 1967.

Felsenfeld, O. Diseases of poultry transmissible to man. *Iowa State Coll. Vet.* 13:89, 1951.

Frappier, C. L., Becker, M. E., and Keahey, K. K. Listeriosis in animals submitted for rabies diagnosis. *Proc. 3rd Intern. Symp. Listeriosis,* July 1966, Bilthoven, The Netherlands, p. 259, 1967.

Gray, M. L. Listeriosis in fowls—a review. *Avian Diseases* 2:296, 1958.

――――. The isolation of *Listeria monocytogenes* from oat silage. *Science* 132:1767, 1960.

――――. *Listeria monocytogenes* and listeric infection in the diagnostic laboratory. *Ann. N.Y. Acad. Sci.* 98:686, 1962.

————. Infections due to *Listeria monocytogenes* in wildlife. *Trans. 29th N. Am. Wildlife Nat. Resources Conf.*, p. 202, 1964.

Gray, M. L., and Killinger, A. H. *Listeria monocytogenes* and listeric infection. *Bacteriol. Rev.* 30:309, 1966.

Jenkins, E. M., Njoku-Obi, A. N., and Adams, E. W. Purification of the soluble hemolysin of *Listeria monocytogenes*. *J. Bacteriol.* 88:418, 1964.

Jenkins, E. M., Adams, E. W., and Watson, B. B. Further investigations on the production and nature of the soluble hemolysins of *Listeria monocytogenes*. *Proc. 3rd Intern. Symp. Listeriosis*, Bilthoven, The Netherlands, p. 109, 1967.

Jennings, A. R. Diseases in wild birds. *Bird Study* 2:69, 1955.

Kaplinskii, M. B., Burganskii, B. Kh., Kortev, A. I., Malyarchikova, G. S., Ananev, I. T., and Karasev, A. G. On listeriosis in the Urals. (In Russian.) *Mater. Sci. Conf.*, Tomsk, p. 106, 1962.

Larsen, H. E. Listeric infection among animals in Denmark. In M. L. Gray, ed., *Proc. 2nd Symp. Listeric Infect.*, Aug. 1962, Bozeman, Mont., p. 27, 1963.

————. Isolation technique for *Listeria monocytogenes*. Primary cultivation and cold incubation technique. *Proc. 3rd Intern. Symp. Listeriosis*, Bilthoven, The Netherlands, p. 43, 1967a.

————. Epidemiology of listeriosis. The ubiquitous occurrence of *Listeria monocytogenes*. *Proc. 3rd Intern. Symp. Listeriosis*, Bilthoven, The Netherlands, p. 295, 1967b.

Lehnert, C. Bakteriologische, serologische und tierexperimentelle untersuchungen zur Pathogenese, Epizootologie und Prophylaxe der Listeriose. *Arch. Exptl. Veterinaermed.* 18 (5):981; 18(6):1247, 1964.

Lilleengen, K. Listerellos hos tjaeder. *Skand. Vet. Tidskr.* 23:458, 1942.

Lucas, A., Laroche, M., Hamel, J., and Chauvrat, J. L'infection naturelle a *Listeria monocytogene* chez le canard, la perdrix, le faisan, le pigeon. *Rec. Med. Vet.* 138:31, 1962.

McCrum, M. W., Eveland, W. C., Wetzler, T. F., and Cowan, A. B. *Listeria monocytogenes* in the feces of white-tailed deer (*Odocoileus virginianus*). *Bull. Wildlife Disease Assoc.* 3:98, 1967.

McDiarmid, A. Diseases of free-living wild animals. *FAO UN Agr. Studies* 57:34, 1962.

Nystrom, K. G., and Karlsson, K. A. Sensitivity of *Listeria monocytogenes* in vitro to different antibiotics and chemotherapeutics. *Acta Paediat.* 50:113, 1961.

Olsufev, N. G., and Emelyanova, O. S. Discovery of *Listerella* infection from wild rodents, insectivores and *Ixodes* ticks. (In Russian.) *Zh. Mikrobiol. Epidemiol. Immunobiol.* 22 (6):67, 1951.

Olsufev, N. G., and Petrov, V. G. Detection of *Erysipelothrix* and *Listeria* in stream water. (In Russian.) *Zh. Mikrobiol. Epidemiol. Immunobiol.* 30:89, 1959.

Osebold, J. W., Aalund, O., and Chrisp, C. E. Chemical and immunological composition of surface structure of *Listeria monocytogenes*. *J. Bacteriol.* 89:84, 1965.

Pallaske, G. Listerella-infektion bei huehnern in Deutschland. *Berlin. Muench. Tieraerztl. Wochschr.* 37:441, 1951.

Paterson, J. S. Listerella infection in fowls. Preliminary note on its occurrence in East Anglia. *Vet. Rec.* 49:1533, 1937.

Pirie, J. H. H. A new disease of veld rodents "Tiger River Disease." *S. African Inst. Med. Res.* 3:163, 1927.

Plummer, P. J. G., and Byrne, J. L. *Listeria monocytogenes* in lemming. *Can. J. Comp. Med.* 14:214, 1950.

Ponomareva, T. N., Yushchenko, G. V., Rodkevich, L. V., Kovaleva, R. V., and Ogneva, N. S. Comparative data on the isolation of bacterial cultures by means of examination of the tissues of the internal organs and of pharyngeal washings in rodents. (In Russian.) *Zh. Mikrobiol. Epidemiol. Immunobiol.* 33(9):116, 1962.

Potel, J., and Degen, L. Zur Serologie und Immunobiologie der Listeriose. *Zentr. Bakteriol. Parasitenk.* 130:61, 1960.

Reed, R. W. Listeriosis in man. *Can. Med. Assoc. J.* 73:400, 1955.

Schoop, G. *Listeria monocytogenes* ein Krankheitserreger unserer Haustiere. *Deut. Tieraerztl. Wochschr.* 35/36:293, 1951.

Schultz, W. Listerellose bei einem Adler. *Mh. Vet. Med.* 5:200, 1950.

Seastone, C. V. Pathogenic organisms of the genus *Listerella*. *J. Exptl. Med.* 62:203, 1935.

Seeliger, H. P. R. *Listeriosis*, p. 224. New York: Hafner, 1961.

Smith, C. W., and Metzger, J. F. Identification of *Listeria monocytogenes* in experimentally infected animal tissue by immunofluorescence. In M. L. Gray, ed., *Proc. 2nd Symp. Listeric Infect.*, Aug. 1962, Bozeman, Mont., p. 179, 1963.

Solomkin, P. S. Listerellez selskokhozyaistvennikh zhivotnikh. *State Publish Agr. Lit. Moskva*, 1959.

Stenberg, H. Einige beobachtungen ueber die Listeriose in Finnland, 1946–1960. *Zentr. Bakteriol. Parasitenk. Abt. I. Orig.* 182:485, 1961.

Suchanova, M., and Patocka, F. Pokus o dox-
azeni L forem *Listeria monocytogenes.*
Czech. Epidemiol. Mikrobiol. Immunol. 6:
133, 1957.

Suchanova, M., Mencikova, E., and Patocka, F.
Experimentelle Listeriose der Kaninchen.
Verlauf der experimentalen Infektion und
Studium ihrer Übertragung von der Mutter
auf die Frucht. *Zentr. Bakteriol. Parasitenk.
Abt. I. Orig.* 170:547, 1958.

Sword, C. P., and Pickett, M. J. Isolation and
distribution of bacteriophages from *Listeria
monocytogenes. J. Gen. Microbiol.* 25:241,
1961.

Thompson, C. H. Unusual pathological changes in a case of fowl listeriosis. *Am. J. Vet.
Res.* 15:130, 1954.

Watson, B. B., and Jenkins, E. M. Further
studies on the heat-stable lipolytic activity
associated with *Listeria monocytogenes.
Bacteriol. Proc. 1967 M. 98,* p. 77, 1967.

Wetzler, T. F., Freeman, N. R., French, M. LV.,
Renkowski, L. A., Eveland, W. C., and Car-
ver, O. J. Biological characterization of
Listeria monocytogenes for clinical bacteriology laboratories. *Health Lab. Sci.* 5:46,
1968.

Zwart, P., and Donker-Voet, J. Listeriosis by
in gevangenschap gehouden dieren. *Tijdschr. Diergeneesk.* 84:712, 1959.

16 ◆ ASPERGILLOSIS

- ● DAVID C. O'MEARA
- ● J. FRANKLIN WITTER

SYNONYMS: Brooder pneumonia, pseudotuberculosis, mycosis, cytomycosis, bron-
chomycosis, chick fever, pneumonie
de la conveuse, Schimmelpilzerkran-
kung, aspergillose, mucormykose.

ASPERGILLOSIS is an acute or chronic infection of avian species, usually of the respiratory tract and frequently of the peritoneum and abdominal organs, characterized by the formation of yellow or gray-green plaques, and caused by the fungus *Aspergillus fumigatus*.

◆ **HISTORY.** As early as 1813 Montague described blue mold in the air sac of a scaup duck, and Mayer and Emmert (1815) reported similar findings in a jay. There have been a number of good reviews and bibliographies on aspergillosis prepared by Urbain and Guillot (1938), Halloran (1955), and Chute et al. (1962), the latter bibliography containing annotated remarks. The history of aspergillosis is discussed by Chute (1965), Raper and Fennell (1965), and McDiarmid (1969).

◆ **DISTRIBUTION.** The literature cites aspergillosis in a variety of both captive and free-living species. Waterfowl and game birds represent the majority of the free-living hosts cited (Table 16.1). Whether this actually represents the prevalence of the disease or is merely an indication that aspergillosis is more obvious in game birds processed for eating is unknown.

Since spores of *Aspergillus* species are widely distributed throughout the world and seem to be capable of both a saprophytic and parasitic way of life, all free-living birds undoubtedly have numerous opportunities to contact this agent. Published reports, some over a century old, indicate worldwide occurrence of aspergillosis, with the Antarctic the greatest exception. The frequency of aspergillosis reports is more likely to be indicative of specific interests in a particular area or species rather than a real difference in area incidence. Fatal systemic fungous infections among wild birds in captivity are reported often from many different geographic areas.

◆ **ETIOLOGY.** *Aspergillus fumigatus* Fresenius is the chief pathologic agent involved. Raper and Fennell (1965), in their complete reference to aspergilli, regard the following species as synonyms for *A. fumigatus: A. aviarius, A. bronchiolis, A. calyptratus, A. cellulosae, A. glaucoides, A. lignieresi, A. nigrescens, A. pulmonum, A. ramosus, A. septatus, A. synecephalis, A. viridogriseus,* and several *A. fumigatus* varieties.

The identification and relationship of the *Aspergillus* become a specialty, and Raper and Fennell (1965) should be consulted by anyone seriously attempting identification of members of this genus.

Growth on Sabouraud's dextrose agar is rapid at 37° to 45° C; colonies are gray-blue to green at first and darken as they age. They are of velvety to powdery texture, with a nearly flat top and no pigment on the underside of the colony substrate. The hyphae are septate and branched. The conidiophores are compact, 0.5 mm or less in length, and have a smooth stalk and inverted flask-shaped vesicle. Single rows

---

All photos in this chapter by D. C. O'Meara unless otherwise indicated.

TABLE 16.1. Aspergillosis Reported from Free-living or Recent Captive Avian Species

Common Name	Scientific Name	Captive C	Locality	Reference
Common loon	*Gavia immer*		Florida	Hartman, 1946
Manx shearwater	*Puffinus puffinus*		Wales	Dane, 1948
Humboldt penguin	*Spheniscus humboldtii*	C	California	Conti, 1938
King penguin	*Aptenodytes patogonica*	C	France, Eng.	Urbain and Nouvel, 1954; Appleby, 1962
Gentoo penguin	*Pygoscelis papua*	C	France, Eng.	Urbain and Nouvel, 1954; Appleby, 1962
Ringed penguin	*Pygoscelis antarctica*	C	England	Appleby, 1962
Maccaroni penguin	*Eudyptes chryaolophus*	C	England	Appleby, 1962
Blackfoot penguin	*Spheniscus demersus*	C	England	Appleby, 1962
Magellan penguin	*Spheniscus magellanicus*	C	England	Appleby, 1962
Whistling swan	*Olor columbianus*		Calif., Utah	Rosen, 1964; Quortrup and Shillinger, 1941
Canada goose	*Branta canadensis*		Ill., Mo.	Christianson, 1932; Graham and Thorp, 1931; McDougle and Vaught, 1968
Mallard duck	*Anas platyrhynchos*		Calif., Colo., Wash., N.Y.	Herman, 1943; Neff, 1955; Stock, 1961; Torrey et al., 1934
Pin-tailed duck	*Anas acuta*		Calif., Utah	Van Roekel, 1929; Quortrup and Shillinger, 1941
Green-winged teal	*Anas carolinensis*		Utah	Quortrup and Shillinger, 1941
Cinnamon teal	*Anas cyanoptera*		Utah	Quortrup and Shillinger, 1941
Shoveler	*Spatula clypeata*		Utah	Quortrup and Shillinger, 1941
Wood duck	*Aix sponsa*		Illinois	Bellrose et al., 1945
Canvasback	*Aythya valisineria*		N.Y., Calif.	Graham and Thorp, 1931; Rosen, 1964
Lesser scaup	*Aythya affinis*		N.Y., Calif.	Graham and Thorp, 1931; Rosen, 1964
Falcon	*Falco rufus*		Germany	Mueller, 1842
Bald eagle	*Haliaeetus leucocephalus*	C	Missouri	Coon and Locke, 1968
Ruffed grouse	*Bonasa umbellus*		Conn., Maine	Gross, 1925; O'Meara, 1968
Sage grouse	*Centrocercus urophasianus*		Wyoming	Honess and Winters, 1956
Capercaillae	*Tetrao urogallus*	C and wild	Sweden	Huelphers et al., 1941
Black grouse	*Lyrurus tetrix*		Sweden	Huelphers et al., 1941
Willow ptarmigan	*Lagopus lagopus*		Norway	Sorum, 1950
Gambel's quail	*Lophortyx gambelii*		Nevada	Gullion, 1957
Ring-necked pheasant	*Phasianus colchicus*	C	Maine	O'Meara, 1968
Great blue heron	*Ardea herodias*		Ohio	O'Meara, 1968
Flamingo	*Phoenicopterus ruber*	C	Pa., France, Wash., D.C.	Leidy, 1875; Mohler and Buckley, 1904; Saez, 1961
American coot	*Fulica americana*		California	Rosen, 1964
Herring gull	*Larus argentatus*	C	Mass., N.J., Maine	Davis and McClung, 1940; Beaudette, 1945; O'Meara, 1968
Glaucous gull	*Larus hyperboreus*		California	Herman and Bolander, 1943
Thayer gull	*Larus thayeri*		Canada	Cowan, 1945
Wood pigeon	*Columba palumbus*		G. Britain	McDiarmid, 1960

NOTE: No reports were included from long-captive zoo birds, cage birds, game-farm birds, domestic swans, or if culture confirmation was not stated.

TABLE 16.1. Aspergillosis Reported from Free-living or Recent Captive Avian Species *(cont.)*

Common Name	Scientific Name	Captive C	Locality	Reference
Snowy owl	*Nyctea scandiaca*	C	New York	Meade and Stone, 1942
Barn owl	*Strix myctea*		Germany	Mueller, 1842
Common raven	*Corvus corax*		Maine	O'Meara, 1968
Common crow	*Corvus cryptoleucus*		Maine	O'Meara, 1968
Jackdaw	*Corvus monedula spermologus*		England	McDiarmid, 1955
Robin	*Turdus migratorius*		Calif., Maine	Rosen, 1964; O'Meara 1968
Varied thrush	*Ixoreus naevius*		California	Rosen, 1964
Audubon's warbler	*Dendroica auduboni*		California	Rosen, 1964
House sparrow	*Passer domesticus*		Md., Maine	Locke, 1965; O'Meara, 1968
Common grackle	*Quiscalus quiscula*		Md., Maine	Clark, 1960; O'Meara, 1968
Brown-headed cow-bird	*Molothrus ater*		Md., Maine	Clark, 1960; O'Meara, 1968
White-crowned sparrow	*Zonatrichia leucophrys*		California	Rosen, 1964
Song sparrow	*Melospiza melodia*	C	New York	Manwell, 1954

of sterigmata occur only on the upper half of the vesicles. These vesicles are un-branched chains 20 to 30μ long and usually colored. The conidia are dark green, 2.0 to 3.5μ in diameter, and have heavy surface markings. Spores which are elliptical with no surface markings may be a variety of *A. ellipticus*. If sclerotia or cleistothecia are found, the *Aspergillus* is not *A. fumigatus*, but may be *A. fisheri*.

The spores of *A. fumigatus* are produced in tremendous numbers within a few days under favorable conditions, compatible food, and high oxygen supply, and are very resistant to unfavorable environmental conditions.

Proof that the isolate obtained caused the infection observed is usually based upon the reasoning that this isolate will establish a similar infection in susceptible birds of the same species. However, no reported studies have been found on experimental infectivity of free-living bird species. There is need of repositories for pathogenic strains isolated from free-living avian species. Future research in avian species' susceptibility to various isolates can be done only if such viable strains are available. Continuous subculturing can alter the pathogenic character of the strains.

◆ **TRANSMISSION.** The typical respiratory aspergillosis most common in avian species is usually the result of inhaling spores and perhaps hyphal fragments of *A. fumigatus*. Since the studies of O'Meara and Chute (1959), few controlled experiments using the inhalation method of transmission have been reported, and none for wild birds.

Studies on spore counts in the upper air strata and on moldy hay (Gregory and Lacey, 1963) suggest interesting possibilities for spore transmission by air currents and their release by raindrops (Hirst and Stedman, 1967). Ainsworth and Austwick (1959) and Vanbreuseghem (1958) state the possibility of universal exposure because the spores are so widely distributed and it is so easy to culture *A. fumigatus* from apparently healthy respiratory tracts. The number of spores present in the air, the length of bird exposure, the age of the bird, and its physiologic state are all related to the transmission potential. A marked increase in resistance to infection occurs in chickens between 2 and 7 days after hatching (O'Meara and Chute, 1959). If similar conditions exist in free-living birds, the type of nesting materials, degree of nest reuse, nesting population density, and the regional or seasonal occurrence of favorable humidity and temperature conditions would seem to potentially play a large role in the incidence of aspergillosis in newly hatched birds.

Beyond this critical period of the first few days of the bird's life, infections most likely occur during periods of physiologic stress. As an example of either the effects of stress or species susceptibility, herring gulls which appeared healthy when trapped developed aspergillosis while housed under low *Aspergillus* spore density conditions, while chickens housed in the same room remained free of this infection (O'Meara, 1968). Inspired air or spore-contaminated aerosols from food or water are the most likely routes of transmission in adult birds. Transmission can also occur from puncture wounds contaminated with hyphal fragments or spores, especially if the wounds enter air sacs.

Davis and McClung (1940) postulated that the high incidence of *Aspergillus* in herring gulls in the Boston area could be related to dump feeding habits of these birds.

In domestic birds there is an efficient clearing mechanism operating in the avian respiratory tract, consisting of a sheet of mucus which is moved upward in the bronchi and trachea by means of cilia. This mucous sheet is constantly being augmented by the secretions of mucous gland cells lining the airways. Under humidity conditions of greater than 10%, this sheet of mucus acts as an effective belt conveyor for moving the spores to the outside faster than they can germinate. This very effective device may also be operating in free-living birds. In poultry, severe dust with low humidity causes impairment of this system, providing further evidence that the environment can alter susceptibility (O'-Meara, 1968). This type of research needs confirmation in wild birds.

◆ **SIGNS.** Usually both domestic and wild birds with a fungus infection show signs of gasping, droopiness, and emaciation. Often the dyspnea is not accompanied by

gurgling sounds of mucous movements in the trachea as is the case with some of the common viral respiratory diseases. In the later stages of infection, diarrhea is common. Occasionally ataxia and other nervous signs develop. Some infected birds appear to be healthy and yet show lesions at necropsy. The added stress of a bacterial, viral, or protozoan infection may provide the fungus the role of an opportunist invader and thus obscure the real cause of the mortality.

◆ **PATHOGENESIS.** *Aspergillus fumigatus* becomes established in domestic birds in several ways. Massive fungal exposures of susceptible young birds can cause death before any classical cellular changes or plaques are formed. Usually the exposure is more gradual and the bird survives for a week or more, allowing the development of typical lesions. In the lungs the mycelia penetrate the bronchial walls and adjacent parenchyma. At first there is a cellular infiltration, including giant cells, and a wall is built around the center of radiating hyphae to form a nodule similar to a tubercle. If the lesion develops in the air sacs or over the pleural or peritoneal surfaces, the true plaque will form and sometimes the fruiting organs of the fungus develop. Often these are seen in waterfowl as large green or bluish plaques, with surfaces resembling bread mold.

The tremendous cellular response to the few hyphal strands seen in a single plaque reflects the severity of the bird's reaction to this fungus. Plaque formation results in both loss of tissue effectiveness and in actual tissue damage caused by the fungus hyphae. It is difficult to separate these effects when evaluating infection in a bird.

Not all fungus infections are fatal. Regression of infections following experimental exposures of several strains of domestic chickens occurred by the second week. Plaques have been examined which were histologically typical of fungal lesions, but from which fungus cultures could not be obtained and in which there was not any reaction to the Gridley staining method.

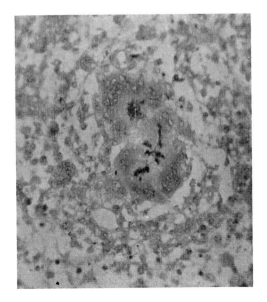

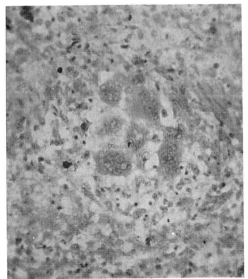

FIGS. 16.1 and 16.2. Different plaque forms in experimental *A. fumigatus* infection of 3-week-old chickens, 7 and 15 days after aerosol exposure. ×200.

There is no indication that the widespread occurrence of plaques in lungs, air sacs, liver, and spleen represents the result of a single infection, wave-distributed via the circulatory system, or that these lesions represent a metastasis of an earlier infection.

◆ **PATHOLOGY.** Lesions in both domestic and wild species occur most frequently in the lungs and air sacs but can occur in any organ or tissue. Great variation in numbers of plaques has been reported, ranging from one to dozens (Figs. 16.1, 16.2). Air sac lesions are more apt to have the typical fruiting bodies, with gray-green to almost black velvety growth apparent on gross examination (Fig. 16.3). Other lesions are light yellow to orange in color. The plaques vary from pinhead size to several millimeters in diameter, and from spongy soft to hard. The form of the plaques varies from a nearly spherical tubercle to flattened discs. Some lesions are surrounded by fluid exudate. Lesions can be firmly attached within or on the surface of organs, or very loosely attached as is usual in the mesentery (Figs. 16.4, 16.5, 16.6).

Extensive plaque formation and the associated severe cellular reaction can pro-

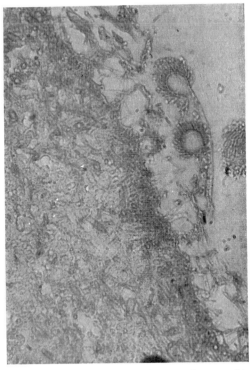

FIG. 16.3. Herring gull air sac plaque with conidia of *A. fumigatus* (not stained). ×200.

FIG. 16.4. Herring gull with a variety of firm plaques involving lungs, air sac, and peritoneum.

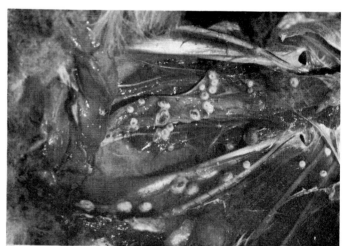

FIG. 16.5. Canada goose with air sac plaques. (Photo by M. Friend, Vet. Science Dept., Univ. of Wis.)

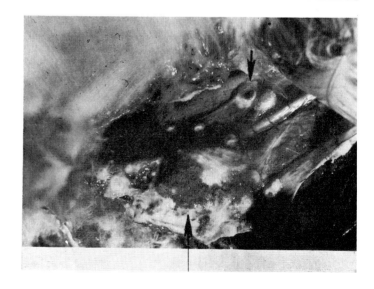

FIG. 16.6. Canada goose with dark, powdery sporulation of aspergillosis on air sac plaques. (Photo by M. Friend, Vet. Science Dept., Univ. of Wis.)

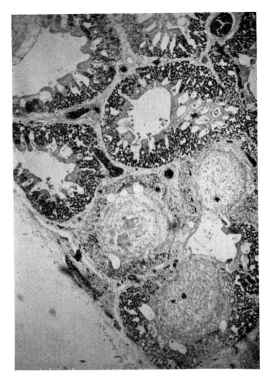

FIG. 16.7. Herring gull with lower three tertiary bronchi occupied by plaques. H & E stain. ×50.

duce pleurisy, lung hepatization and abscesses, thickening of the air sacs, and peritonitis with adhesions (Fig. 16.7).

The morbidity from aspergillosis in wild birds is difficult to appraise, but in severe hatchery-acquired infections, up to 100% of the domestic chicks can be affected. Mortality is extremely variable, being highest in domestic chicks the first week to 10 days of age, and is influenced by severity and duration of the exposure and the stress of associated viral, bacterial, and protozoan diseases.

Observations of lesions in mature wild birds suggest that the infection becomes chronic and extends over a period of weeks or longer, often resulting in weakness and emaciation, leading to death. Prognosis is dependent upon the severity of the infection and the age of the bird. Spontaneous recovery does occur in chickens.

The ability of certain fungi to produce toxins while growing in feeds is well docu-

mented (Crawford, 1962; Wogan, 1965). The effects of isolated fungal toxins on poultry have been reported by Chute et al. (1965). Fungal toxins can produce both degeneration and hyperplasia in the liver with no signs of illness. Other species might show severe signs and high mortality with the same degree of exposure. Forgacs and Carll (1962) describe hemorrhagic conditions from mycotoxins. There are no reports on the effects of fungal toxins on free-living birds; however, it seems logical that the use of moldy feed or the storage of wild bird feed under conditions conducive to molding should be avoided.

♦ **DIAGNOSIS.** The detection of plaques or nodules in birds is usually diagnostic and this observation can be strengthened by observing hyphae on an open plaque under magnification or by histologic techniques. Austwick (1965) should be consulted for methods, laboratory hazards, and a working bibliography on the pathogenic aspergilli.

The presence of hyphae can be demonstrated in the plaque by treating with 2 to 20% sodium hydroxide (Fig. 16.8). Lacto

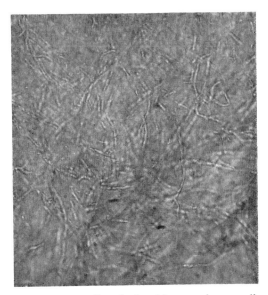

FIG. 16.8. Sodium-hydroxide-treated aspergillosis plaque from a herring gull. Wet mount unstained. ×200.

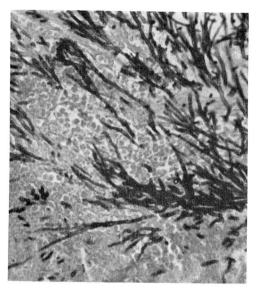

FIG. 16.9. Acute systemic *A. fumigatus* infection in liver of a herring gull with septate branching hyphae. (Gridley-stained tissue supplied by M. Friend, Vet. Science Dept., Univ. of Wis.) ×100.

cotton phenol blue will stain the hyphae in a crushed plaque. For histologic examination, fixation of tissue in 10% formal saline will permit subsequent dehydration and embedding in paraffin for sectioning. Gridley stain (1953) colors the hyphae a deep rose against a yellow background of the plaque (Fig. 16.9). The use of fungus-positive tissue sections for control staining is recommended.

Confirmation of the diagnosis should be made by obtaining growth of the fungus on differential media. This can be accomplished by treating an isolated plaque with 1% tincture of iodine for 10 to 20 seconds, rinsing in sterile water or saline, and placing the washed plaque on fungous growth media. The iodine treatment will not kill the hyphae in the plaque but will insure the elimination of other microorganisms which could grow on the media and mask the true causative agent. Pieces of tissue for culture should be obtained aseptically as rapidly as possible and placed firmly against the agar surface of the media. Sabouraud's medium is very satisfactory and can be stored for years in powder form

and prepared in either plates or slants. As soon as growth is noted on the culture media, transfers should be made to agar slants in screw-capped vials suitable for mailing to a mycologist for identification. The viable storage of cultures is enhanced by the use of an inert substrate in the vials. Sterile sand, loam, filter paper, or unglazed porcelain can be added to solidified media. When the cultures have sporulated, shaking the vials will coat the inert material with spores which will then survive for a much longer period than in the regular media. Lowered temperature, drying, and use of inert gases will also prolong shelf life.

Since fungi can be cultured from apparently healthy tissue or tissue damaged by other agents, confirmation of the pathogenicity of the isolate must be made. A suspension of spores and hyphae fragments washed off a pure culture with sterile saline containing a wetting agent has been used by some workers to inject into the thoracic air sacs of susceptible birds to evaluate the pathogenicity of the isolate (Chute and O'Meara, 1958; Herman and Sladen, 1958; Clark, 1960). This method can be criticized because of the use of a wetting agent and the unnatural route of exposure, but comparative studies between natural inhalation versus thoracic air sac injection exposure have shown the air sac injection route to result in a much greater number of infections (O'Meara, 1968).

When working with fungus cultures, caution should always be used to prevent accidental release of these potential human pathogens in the laboratory.

◆ **IMMUNITY.** Serologic reactions to measure antibody response to aspergillosis have not been satisfactory diagnostic aids. An extensive review of the serology and immunology of the mycoses has been made by Salvin (1963).

◆ **TREATMENT AND CONTROL.** There is no practical method of treatment for free-living birds. Treatment of game-farm and captive birds has been somewhat successful by using nystatin (Mycostatin-20, Squibb) either in the feed or injected. Commercial poultrymen rarely treat their flocks but rely upon culling sick birds and subsequently removing all of the litter from the contaminated house and applying disinfectants or fungicides after thoroughly washing away all organic matter. These sanitation principles for preventing continued exposure of birds to sources known to be contaminated with *A. fumigatus* can certainly be applied to most captive or propagated birds and might be applied to nesting sites of free-living birds.

The use of moldy feed, especially corn, is potentially dangerous as demonstrated with pheasants (Rosen, 1964), and the frequent cleaning of feed and water utensils to prevent mold accumulation is helpful. Game-farm incubators need to be thoroughly cleaned between hatches to reduce the risk of a buildup of fungus. Eggs being incubated should be periodically candled to remove infertiles and dead embryos and thus eliminate favorite sites for rapid fungus growth.

♦ REFERENCES

Ainsworth, G. C., and Austwick, P. K. C. Fungal diseases of animals, *Commonwealth Agr. Bur.*, Farnham Royal Bucks, England, 1959.

Appleby, E. C. Mycosis of the respiratory tract in penguins. *Proc. Zool. Soc. London* 139: 495, 1962.

Austwick, P. K. C. Pathogenicity. In K. B. Raper and D. I. Fennell, eds., *The genus Aspergillus*, p. 82. Baltimore: Williams & Wilkins, 1965.

Beaudette, F. R. Aspergillosis and parasitism in a gull. *Bird Banding* 16 (3):99, 1945.

Bellrose, F. C., Hanson, H. C., and Beamer, P. D. Aspergillosis in wood ducks. *J. Wildlife Management* 9 (5):325, 1945.

Christenson, R. O. An epizootic in wild geese due to nematode and fungus infections. *N. Am. Vet.* 13 (11):57, 1932.

Chute, H. L. Diseases caused by fungi. In H. E. Biester and L. H. Schwarte, eds., *Diseases of poultry,* 5th ed., p. 384. Ames: Iowa State Univ. Press, 1965.

Chute, H. L., and O'Meara, D. C. Experimental fungous infections in chickens. *Avian Diseases* 2:154, 1958.

Chute, H. L., O'Meara, D. C., and Barden, E. S. A bibliography of avian mycosis. *Me. Agr. Exp. Sta. Bull.* 655, 1962.

Chute, H. L., Hollander, S. L., Barden, E. S., and O'Meara, D. C. The pathology of certain fungi in chickens. *Avian Diseases* 9 (1): 57, 1965.

Clark, G. M. Aspergillosis in naturally infected cowbirds and grackles. *Avian Diseases* 4:94, 1960.

Conti, L. F. A generalized aspergillus infection in penguins. *J. Bacteriol.* 36:453, 1938.

Coon, N. C., and Locke, L. N. Aspergillosis in a bald eagle *(Haliaeetus leucocephalus) Bull. Wildlife Disease Assoc.* 4 (2):51, 1968.

Cowan, I. McT. Aspergillosis in a thayer gull. *Murrelet* 24 (2):29, 1945.

Crawford, M. Mycotoxicosis in veterinary medicine. *Vet. Bull.* 32 (7):415, 1962.

Dane, S. D. A disease of manx shearwaters *(Puffinus puffinus). J. Animal Ecol.* 17:158, 1948.

Davis, W. A., and McClung, L. S. Aspergillosis in wild herring gulls. *J. Bacteriol.* 40 (2):321, 1940.

Forgacs, J., and Carll, W. T. Mycotoxicosis. *Advan. Vet. Sci.* 7:273, 1962.

Graham, R., and Thorp, F. A laryngotracheitis syndrome in a wild goose associated with pneumomycosis. *Am. Vet. Med. Assoc.* 79:90, 1931.

Gregory, P. H., and Lacey, M. E. Mycological examination of dust from mouldy hay associated with farmer's lung disease. *J. Gen. Microbiol.* 30:75, 1963.

Gridley, M. F. A stain for fungi in tissue sections. *Am. J. Clin. Pathol.* 23:303, 1953.

Gross, A. O. Diseases of ruffed grouse. *Auk* 42:423, 1925.

Gullion, G. W. Gambel quail disease and parasite investigation in Nevada. *Am. Midland Naturalist* 40:414, 1957.

Halloran, P. O. A bibliography of references to diseases of wild mammals and birds. *Am. J. Vet. Res.* 16 (61):465, 1955.

Hartman, F. Notes on the pathology of a loon and a pelican. *Auk* 63:588, 1946.

Herman, C. M. An outbreak of mycotic pneumonia in mallards. *Calif. Fish Game* 29 (4): 204, 1943.

Herman, C. M., and Bolander, G. Fungus disease in a glaucous-winged gull. *Condor* 45 (4):160, 1943.

Herman, C. M., and Sladen, W. J. L. Aspergillosis in waterfowl. *Trans. N. Am. Wildlife Conf.* 23:187, 1958.

Hirst, J. M., and Stedman, O. J. Long distance spore transport. *J. Gen. Microbiol.* 48 (3): 329, 1967.

Honess, R. F., and Winters, K. B. Diseases of wildlife in Wyoming. *Wyo. Game Fish Comm. Bull.* 9:279, 1956.

Huelphers, G., Lilleengen, K., and Henricson, T. Aspergillosis in hares, ducks, capercailzie, and blackcock. *Svensk Jaaroverz.* 6:250, 1941.

Leidy, J. On a fungus in a flamingo. *Proc. Acad. Nat. Sci. Phila.* 27:11, 1875.

Locke, L. N. Additional records of aspergillosis among passerine birds in Maryland and the Washington D.C. metropolitan area. *Chesapeake Sci.* 6 (2):120, 1965.

McDiarmid, A. Aspergillosis in free-living wild birds. *J. Comp. Pathol. Therap.* 65 (3):246, 1955.

———. Diseases of free-living wild animals. *Animal Health Bur. F.A.O. Rome,* p. 36, 1960.

———. *Diseases of free-living wild animals.* New York: Academic Press, 1969.

McDougle, H. C., and Vaught, R. W. An epizootic of aspergillosis in Canada geese. *J. Wildlife Management* 32 (2):415, 1968.

Manwell, R. D. A case of aspergillosis in a song sparrow. *J. Parasitol.* 40 (2):231, 1954.

Mayer, A. C., and Emmert. Verschimmelung (Mucedo) im lebenden Korper. *Deut. Arch. Anat. U. Physical (Meckel)* 1:310, 1815.

Meade, G. M., and Stone, D. Aspergillosis in a snowy owl. *Auk* 59 (4):577, 1942.

Mohler, J. R., and Buckley, J. S. Pulmonary mycosis of birds. *Twentieth Ann. Rept. Animal Industry 1903. USDA Circ.* 58, p. 122, 1904.

Montague, G. Supplement to the ornithological dictionary. London: Woolman, 1813.

Mueller, J. R. Ueber Parasitischen Bildunger. *Mueller Arch. (Anat. u. Physiol.)* 198, 1842.

Neff, J. A. Outbreak of aspergillosis in mallards. *J. Wildlife Management* 19:415, 1955.

O'Meara, D. C. Unpublished data, 1968.

O'Meara, D. C., and Chute, H. L. Aspergillosis experimentally produced in hatching chicks. *Avian Diseases* 3:404, 1959.

Quortrup, E. R., and Shillinger, J. E. Autopsies on 3000 wild birds on western lake areas. *J. Am. Vet. Med Assoc.* 99:382, 1941.

Raper, K. B., and Fennell, D. I. *The genus Aspergillus.* Baltimore: Williams & Wilkins, 1965.

Rosen, M. N. Aspergillosis in wild and domestic fowl. *Avian Diseases* 8:1, 1964.

Saez, H. Quelques cas d'aspergillose aviare observesau. Park Zoologique de Paris. *Ann. Parasitol. Human Comp.* 36:154, 1961.

Salvin, S. B. Immunologic aspects of the mycosis. *Progr. Allergy* 7:220, 1963.

Sorum, L. Fugleviltundersokelser pa laboratoriet. *N.J.F.F.,* p. 55, 1950.

Stock, B. L. Case report: Generalized granulomatous lesions in chickens and wild ducks caused by *Aspergillus* species. *Avian Diseases* 5 (1):89, 1961.

Threlfall, W. Diseases and pathological conditions of the herring gull *(Larus argentatus* Pontopp.) excluding helminth infestations. *Bull. Wildlife Disease Assoc.* 3 (2):62, 1967.

Torrey, J. L., Thorpe, F., and Graham, R. Note on pathological changes encountered in wild ducks. *Cornell Vet.* 24:289, 1934.

Urbain, A., and Guillot, G. Les aspergilloses aviares. (The aspergillosis of birds.) *Rev. Pathol. Gen. Comparee* 38 (503):929, 1938.

Urbain, A., and Nouvel, J. Infestations parasitaires mortelles observees sur des manchots recemment impartes des Iles Kerguelen. *Paris Mus. d'Hist. Nat. Bull.* 26 (2):188, 1954.

Vanbreuseghem, R. *Mycoses of man and animals.* Springfield: Charles C Thomas, 1958.

Van Roekel, H. Diseases observed in game bird raising. *Calif. Fish Game* 15 (4):301, 1929.

Wogan, G. N., ed. *Mycotoxins in food stuffs.* Cambridge: Mass. Inst. Tech., 1965.

17 ◆ CANDIDIASIS

- **DAVID C. O'MEARA**
- **J. FRANKLIN WITTER**

SYNONYMS: Thrush, crop mycosis, levuroses, moniliasis, muguet, soor, sour crop.

CANDIDIASIS is a mycotic infection caused by *Candida albicans,* usually of the digestive tract of birds and characterized by the formation of necrotic membranous patches with some ulceration.

◆**HISTORY.** Fungal infections of the digestive tract were first recognized in man by Langenbeck (1839) and in chickens and turkeys by Eberth (1858) and Schlegel (1912). However, Jungherr's (1934) detailed description of this disease in birds placed new emphasis on its pathology, distribution, and importance.

Recent reviews on the history of this group of fungal infections have been made by Lodder and Van Rij (1952), Skinner and Fletcher (1960), Emmons et al. (1963), Winner and Hurley (1964), and McDiarmid (1969).

◆ **DISTRIBUTION.** Candidiasis has been reported from domestic chickens, turkeys, geese, and pigeons, as well as pheasants *(Phasianus colchicus),* ruffed grouse *(Bonasa umbellus),* quail *(Colinus virginianus),* and herring gulls *(Larus argentatus).* The infection in man and avian species has worldwide distribution (Vanbreuseghem, 1958).

McDiarmid (1960) mentions pigeons, pheasants, and grouse as the wild birds being most often infected in England. He also reports a jackdaw case. Kawakita and Van Uden (1965) isolated *C. albicans* from the digestive tracts of gulls and terns, although it was cultured less frequently than

All photos by D. C. O'Meara.

four other yeastlike fungi. Threlfall (1967) found that herring gulls in Wales frequently had the infection in the esophagus. Keymer and Austwick (1961) reported on an outbreak of moniliasis in game-farm partridges in England. The reports on infections in free-living wild birds are so infrequent that no specific statement can be made on the prevalence of candidiasis in wild bird populations.

◆ **ETIOLOGY.** The fungus *Candida albicans* is the recognized etiologic agent. It has also been called *Oidium albicans, Mycotorula albicans, Monilia candida,* and *Monilia albicans.* Conant et al. (1954) reported that there are 172 synonyms in the literature.

This fungus has both yeastlike and mycelial forms. A streak inoculation made on Sabouraud's glucose agar and grown in aerobic conditions at 37° C will produce colonies in 24 to 48 hours which are white to cream in color, with smooth surfaces and edges, moist and viscous. With age, colonies become rough surfaced. Colony growth on eosin methylene blue agar media can be spidery, with several fingerlike projections radiating out from the central mass (Bacle and Bigland, 1962). Colonies tend to be more circular when inoculated by stab technique than when streaked. Filaments, which are often constricted at the septae, may be seen after 48 hours growth along the colony edges (Fig. 17.1). Microscopic examination of a wet mount in Lugol's iodine of a portion of a young colony will reveal circular elliptical cells 2 to 6μ in size, with buds on some (Fig. 17.2). From older colonies and along colony edges, there can be seen mycelia with

FIG. 17.1. Pseudomycelia growing from edges of 4-day-old colonies of *C. albicans* at 25° C on cornmeal agar media. ×150.

FIG. 17.3. *C. albicans* colonies 3 days old on Difco chlamydospore agar. ×4.

thick-walled, round chlamydospores 7 to 9μ in diameter which usually arise at the ends of the mycelial strand (Fig. 17.3). A maize (cornmeal) agar (Difco, 1966), reduced oxygen, less than 37° C incubating temperature, and aging colonies tend to promote the characteristic chlamydospore development. A pure culture of *C. albicans*

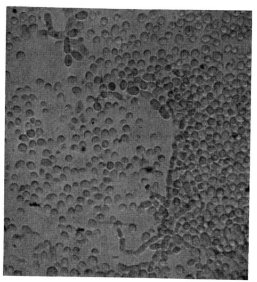

FIG. 17.2. *C. albicans* smear showing a variety of yeastlike cells. Wet mount. ×100.

will ferment glucose, maltose, and levulose at 37° C; saccharose is fermented more slowly (Vanbreuseghem, 1958).

♦ **TRANSMISSION.** Ingestion of *C. albicans* on food or in the water is the most likely route of transmission (Van Uden, 1960). Van Uden and Branco (1963), Ainsworth and Austwick (1955), and Bacle and Bigland (1962) report the wide distribution of these organisms in nature. Wild birds frequenting dumps, poultry operations, and areas contaminated with human waste could have ample chance for acquiring this fungus.

Respiratory infections could conceivably be caused by the inhalation of dust contaminated with *C. albicans.* Although there have not been documental reports of puncture wounds as a means of transmission, they are possible routes. In domestic fowl, experimental infections with *C. albicans* are much more difficult to establish than with *A. fumigatus* (O'Meara, 1968).

♦ **SIGNS.** There are no specific signs to indicate candidiasis infection. Typical lesions can be found in both healthy- and unthrifty-appearing birds.

◆ **PATHOGENESIS.** There is no clear-cut understanding of the pathogenesis of candidiasis in free-living bird species. In domestic poultry, experimental candidiasis is difficult to produce, but factors such as prolonged antibiotic treatments, feeding high levels of carbohydrate, vitamin deficiencies, and hormone additives seem to predispose the birds to a *C. albicans* infection (Jeoffery et al., 1960; Kemp and Reid, 1966; O'Meara, 1968).

Balish and Phillips (1966) reported hyphal development of *C. albicans* in bacteria-free chicks exposed to *Candida* cultures and no hyphae in "normal" chicks exposed similarly but having a multispecies bacterial intestinal flora. Ainsworth and Austwick (1959) cautioned against claiming a pathogenic status for *C. albicans* even when it is found in a diseased host. Hinshaw (1965) and Chute (1965) presented aspects of candidiasis in poultry which resembled problems commonly encountered on game farms. Young poultry were found more severely affected by candidiasis (Jungherr, 1933a, 1934; Chute, 1965). Kuprowski (1956) reported candidiasis as a possible complicating factor in blackhead (histomoniasis) of capercaillie, although Kemp and Reid (1966) stated that *Histomonas meleagridis* was the only etiologic agent of blackhead.

The screening of isolates of *C. albicans* and other yeastlike forms from wild birds for their potential pathogenicity is needed to resolve the question of species pathogenicity. The testing of isolates for chicken embryo tissue invasiveness (Meyer and Ordal, 1946; Norris et al., 1948) could serve as a preliminary classification of the fungus, and infected chicken embryos could provide a reliable inoculum for subsequent wild bird exposure trials (Fig. 17.4).

Vanbreuseghem (1958) stated that the intravenous injection of *C. albicans* in rabbits caused death in 4 to 5 days and produced lesions in the viscera, kidney, and brain. *Candida tropicalis* was less virulent for the rabbit, and other *Candida* species were not pathogenic. Emmons et al. (1963) suggested the use of white rats and mice for testing pathogenicity, but Ajello et al.

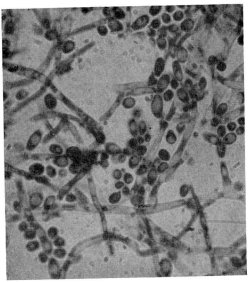

FIG. 17.4. *C. albicans* mycelia showing constrictions at septae. Attached and separated chlamydospores (larger bodies) and blastospores. Paraffin section Masson's trichrome stain from inoculated 10-day chicken embryo. ×200.

(1963) did not favor this method. Hasenclever and Mitchell (1961) compared the pathogenicity of various antigenic strains of *C. albicans* in mice and rabbits. Tissue invasion by the fungus is basic to the evaluation of pathogenicity and this can be ascertained by demonstrating hyphae in the tissues. However, tissue invasion and lesions do not necessarily jeopardize the health of birds. Threlfall (1967) reported lesions of up to 7 mm in diameter in herring gull esophagi, which seemed to have very little if any effect on the birds' well-being.

Research on age, sex, physiologic state, and species reaction to experimental infections of *C. albicans* is needed to clarify the possible pathogenic role of this fungus in wild birds.

◆ **PATHOLOGY.** Lesions may be present in the mucosa of the mouth, proventriculus crop, or intestine of the infected bird. These lesions are thickened, off-white or light-colored areas of the mucosa, and are frequently corrugated or have a turkish-towel-like loose adhering surface. The lesion may or may not be accompanied by gross inflammation of the surrounding tissue (Jungherr, 1933a, b; Threlfall, 1967; Underwood, 1955). Aortic changes associated with *C. albicans* were found in domestic turkeys by Tripathy et al. (1965). Once hyphae become established in tissues, a local reaction ensues and chronic inflammation with giant cells and abscess formation usually occurs (Conant et al., 1954).

Lesions in the trachea and lungs could be mistaken for other granulomas. They would not, however, be confused with the firm discreet plaques of aspergillosis.

◆ **DIAGNOSIS.** The gross detection of the characteristic mucosal lesions, such as patches in the mouth, crop, and proventriculus, should be followed by cultural and histologic examination of some of the lesions to confirm the diagnosis of candidiasis (Fig. 17.4). After removing the loose necrotic surface from a lesion, a scraping of the deeper tissue should be treated with 10 to 20% potassium hydroxide on a microscope slide as a wet crush mount. A tentative identification of *C. albicans* can be based upon the presence of yeastlike cells, with some budding and possibly mycelial strands (Figs. 17.1 and 17.2). Histologic preparations of these fungi stain poorly with hematoxylin and eosin; periodic acid-Schiff stain, or Grocott's technique are recommended by Kemp and Reid (1966). The Gridley (1953) stain is practical for routine diagnosis. Fors (1962) reported on a Luxol fast blue PAS hematoxylin stain which differentiates *Candida* as red and *Aspergillus* as blue in tissue sections of rabbits. Metzger et al. (1962) and Hamid and Haberman (1966) have reported on a method of immunofluorescence diagnosis for *C. albicans* detection in tissues.

The use of a panendoscope by Underwood (1955) permitted crop examination of live poultry for *Candida* lesions. This could be a useful tool to assess the gross occurrence of *Candida* in live wild birds.

The presence of *C. albicans* in suspected lesions should be confirmed by isolation techniques. After removing the surface tissue of the lesion, the site to be cultured is treated with 2% iodine to reduce surface contaminants. The tissue is then excised and pressed into the surface of a Sabouraud's glucose agar plate or slant. Streak and stab inoculations could also be made but should not replace the tissue fragment culture. Antibiotics such as penicillin, streptomycin, and Aureomycin in low concentrations aid in restricting competing bacterial growth (Bacle and Bigland, 1962). Eosin methylene blue agar can also be used as a second isolation medium. After colonies develop it is best to restreak from single typical colonies and incubate until growth is sufficient to use for sugar inoculation.

Bakerspigel (1954), Hayes and Thompson (1963), Ajello et al. (1963), Conant et al. (1954), and the Air Force Manual (1963) are all useful for information on working techniques and identification of candidae. Bonfanti and Barroeta (1968) made use of a plasma medium method for identification in which *C. albicans* forms germ tubes within 2 to 4 hours. Because of the increasing interest in *Candida* infections in man, prepared media kits are available and hospital laboratories are routinely engaged in culture and identification of *Candida*.

The preservation of viable pure culture isolates from wild birds is necessary if there is to be significant research on candidiasis in wild species. Screw-capped or flame-sealed vials for long storage are a necessity. Inert atmosphere and lowered temperature and humidity help to retain viability during long storage. Since these isolates are potential human pathogens, great care should be used in working with lesions and cultures of *C. albicans*.

◆ **IMMUNITY.** The great medical interest in *Candida* type infections of man during recent years has resulted in much research and resulting publications on the immune response and serology (Salvin, 1963; Taschdjian et al., 1967). These sources should be consulted by anyone contemplating a serologic study of wild birds for candidiasis. A capillary precipitation method by Trimble (1957) might be of use as a field-screening technique. No reports of immunologic studies of candidiasis in wild birds have been found in the literature.

◆ **TREATMENT AND CONTROL.** Treatment of free-living wild birds for candidiasis seems impractical at present. Game-bird farms, zoo birds, and loosely confined wild bird flocks do offer some practical opportunities for candidiasis control.

If the affected birds are being given antibiotics, these drugs should be discontinued as an aid in the control of candidiasis (Sieburth and Roth, 1954). Sayedain and Kenzy (1960) found that a vitamin A deficiency resulted in an increased candidiasis in chickens; therefore, increased vitamins A and B in the feed could be helpful as a treatment. A reduction of the carbohydrate level of the feed would also help limit *Candida* problems. Gentry et al. (1960), Kahn and Weisblatt (1963), and Kahn and Slocum (1966) reported that Nystatin given with feed was an effective treatment for chickens and turkeys. Yacowitz et al. (1959) used Mycostatin in feed to control candidiasis in turkeys, and Wind and Yacowitz (1960) reported treatment via drinking water. Trials with these drugs in wild birds have not been reported.

In game farms, a careful cleanup of equipment and quarters is important to prevent a buildup of *C. albicans* in the environment. Jungherr (1933b) suggested that overcrowding and unsanitary conditions could be contributing factors to a candidiasis outbreak. Litter should be dry and of a material having a low sugar content so as not to provide a source of energy for the fungi. Isolation or quarantine of new stock and of suspected or known infected birds and taking care of these birds after attending the rest of the flock will limit transmission. Washing and disinfection of footwear between flock visitations will aid in preventing the spread of candidiasis.

◆ **REFERENCES**

Ajello, L., George, L. K., Kaplan, W., and Kaufman, L. Laboratory manual for medical mycology. *Public Health Serv. Pub. 994*, USGPO, Washington, D.C., 1963.

Ainsworth, G. C., and Austwick, P. K. C. Fungal diseases of animals. *Commonwealth Agr. Bur.*, p. 16. Farnham Royal Bucks, England, 1959.

Air force manual, laboratory procedures in clinical mycology. AFM, 160–53, Dept. Air Force, USGPO, Washington, D.C., 1963.

Bacle, J. F., and Bigland, C. H. Avian mycologic survey in Alberta. *J. Am. Vet. Med. Assoc.* 141 (4):476, 1962.

Bakerspigel, A. A preferred method for the routine identification of *Candida*. *J. Infect. Diseases* 94:141, 1954.

Balish, E., and Phillips, A. W. Growth, morphogenesis, and virulence of *Candida albicans* after oral inoculation in the germ-free and conventional chick. *J. Bacteriol.* 91: 1736, 1966.

Bonfanti, R., and Barroeta, S. Development and evaluation of a rapid identification test for *Candida albicans*. *Mycopathol. Mycol. Appl.* 34 (1):33, 1968.

Chute, H. L. Diseases caused by fungi. In H. E. Biester and L. H. Schwarte, eds., *Diseases of poultry*, 5th ed., p. 504. Ames: Iowa State Univ. Press, 1965.

Conant, N. F., Smith, D. T., Baker, R. D., Callaway, J. L., and Martin, D. S. *Manual of clinical mycology*, p. 169. Philadelphia: W. B. Saunders, 1954.

Difco manual, 9th ed., reprinted. Difco Laboratories, Detroit, 1966.

Eberth, J. Einige Beobachtungen von Pflanzlichen Parasiten bei Thieren. *Arch. Pathol. Anat. Physiol.* 13:522, 1858.

Emmons, C. W., Chapman, H. B., and Utz, J. P. *Medical mycology*, p. 131. Philadelphia: Lea and Febiger, 1963.

Fors, B. Techniques of staining *Aspergillus* and *Candida* in tissues. *Acta Pathol. Microbiol. Scand.* Suppl., p. 184, 1962.

Gentry, R. F., Bubash, G. R., and Chute, H. L. *Candida albicans* in turkeys. *Poultry Sci.* 39:1252, 1960.

Gridley, M. F. A stain for fungi in tissue sections. *Am. J. Clin. Pathol.* 23:303, 1953.

Hamid, R. R., and Haberman, S. The use of immunofluorescence for identification of yeast-like fungi in human infections. *Am. J. Clin. Pathol.* 46:433, 1966.

Hasenclever, H. F., and Mitchell, W. A. Antigenic studies of *Candida*. I. *J. Bacteriol.* 82:570, II. 574, III. 578, 1961.

Hayes, A., and Thompson, J. R. Identification of *Candida albicans*. *Am. J. Clin. Pathol.* 40:553, 1963.

Hinshaw, W. R. Diseases of the turkey. In H. C. Biester and L. H. Schwarte, eds., *Diseases of poultry*, 5th ed., p. 1267. Ames: Iowa State Univ. Press, 1965.

Jeoffery, S., Sayedain, M., and Kenzy, S. G. Nutritional factors influencing experimental *Candida albicans* infection in chickens. I. Effect of vitamin A deficiency. *Avian Diseases* 4 (2):138, 1960.

Jungherr, E. L. Observations on a severe outbreak of mycosis in chicks. *J. Agr. Res.* 46 (2):169, 1933a.

———. Studies on yeast-like fungi from gallinaceous birds. *Storrs Agr. Exp. Sta. Bull. 188,* 1933b.

———. Mycosis in fowl caused by yeast-like fungi. *J. Am. Vet. Med. Assoc.* 37 (3):500, 1934.

Kahn, S. G., and Slocum, A. Water miscible amphotericin for the treatment of crop mycosis in chicks. *Poultry Sci.* 45:761, 1966.

Kahn, S. G., and Weisblatt, H. A comparison of nystatin and copper sulfate in experimental moniliasis of chickens and turkeys. *Avian Diseases* 7 (3):304, 1963.

Kawakita, S., and Van Uden, N. Occurrence and population densities of yeast species in the digestive tracts of gulls and terns. *J. Gen. Microbiol.* 39 (1):125, 1965.

Kemp, R. L., and Reid, W. M. Studies on the etiology of blackhead disease: The roles of *Histomonas meleagridis* and *Candida albicans* in the United States. *Poultry Sci.* 45 (6):1296, 1966.

Keymer, I. F., and Austwick, P. K. C. Moniliasis in partridges *(Perdix perdix). Sabouraudia* 1:22, 1961.

Kuprowski, M. O moniliasie u gluszow i o enter-hepatitis. (Moniliasis in capercaillie in relation to blackhead.) *Med. Weterynar.* 12:201 (In Polish. Summ. in G. and R.), 1956.

Langenbeck, B. Contribution a l'etude du champignon du muguet. *Arch. Med. Exp. Anat. Pathol.* 12:145, 1839.

Lodder, J., and Van Rij, J. W. K. *The yeasts: A taxonomic study.* Amsterdam: N. Holland Pub. Co., 1952.

McDiarmid, A. Diseases of free-living wild animals. Animal Health Branch, Monogr. 1, p. 41, 1960.

———. *Diseases of free-living wild animals.* New York: Academic Press, 1969.

Metzger, J. F., Kase, A., and Smith, C. W. Identification of pathogenic fungi in surgical and autopsy specimens by immunofluorescence. *Mycopathologia* 17:335, 1962.

Meyer, E., and Ordal, Z. J. Pathogenicity of *Candida* species for the chick embryo. *J. Bacteriol.* 52:615, 1946.

Norris, R. F., Shorey, W. K., and Bongiovanni, A. M. Lesions produced in chick embryos by *Candida (Monilia) albicans. Arch. Pathol.* 45:504, 1948.

O'Meara, D. C. Unpublished data, 1968.

Salvin, S. B. Immunologic aspects of the mycoses. Progress in allergy. *Fortschr. Allergielehre* 7:223, 1963.

Sayedain, J. S. M., and Kenzy, S. G. Nutritional factors influencing experimental *C. albicans* infections in chickens. I. Effect of vitamin A deficiency. *Avian Diseases* 4:138, 1960.

Schlegel, M. Soorkrankheit bei huhnern. *Berlin. Muench. Tieraerztl. Wochschr.* 56:63, 1912.

Sieburth, J. McN., and Roth, F. J., Jr. The effect of Aureomycin and Terramycin on *Candida albicans* in the fecal microflora of chicks and turkey poults. *J. Bacteriol.* 67 (4):460, 1954.

Skinner, C. E., and Fletcher, D. W. A review of the genus *Candida. Bacteriol. Rev.* 24:397, 1960.

Taschdjian, C. L., Kozinn, P. J., Akas, A., Caroline, L., and Halle, M. A. Serodiagnosis of systemic candidiasis. *J. Infect. Diseases* 117 (2):180, 1967.

Threlfall, W. Diseases and pathological conditions of the herring gull *(Larus argentatus* Pontopp.) excluding helminth infestations. *Bull. Wildlife Disease Assoc.* 3:62, 1967.

Trimble, J. R. The use of a precipitin test to differentiate *C. albicans* from *C. stellatoidea. J. Invest. Dermatol.* 28:349, 1957.

Tripathy, S. B., Mathey, W. J., and Kenzy, S. G. Study of aortic changes associated with candidiasis of turkeys. *Avian Diseases* 9 (4):520, 1965.

Underwood, P. C. Detection of crop mycosis (moniliasis) in chickens and turkey poults with a panendoscope. *J. Am. Vet. Med. Assoc.* 127:229, 1955.

Vanbreuseghem, R. *Mycoses of man and animals,* p. 166. Springfield: Charles C Thomas, 1958.

Van Uden, H. The occurrence of *Candida* and other yeasts in the intestinal tracts of animals. *Ann. N.Y. Acad. Sci.* 89 (1):59, 1960.

Van Uden, N., and Branco, R. Distribution and population densities of yeast species in Pacific water, air animals, and kelp of southern California. *Limnol. Oceanog.* 8 (3):323, 4 tables, 1963.

Wind, S., and Yacowitz, H. Use of Mycostatin in the drinking water for the treatment of crop mycosis in turkeys. *Poultry Sci.* 39:904, 1960.

Winner, H. I., and Hurley, R. *Candida albi-* *cans.* Boston: Little, Brown, 1964.

Yacowitz, H., Wind, A., Jambor, W. P., Willett, N. P., and Pagano, J. F. Use of Mycostatin for the prevention of moniliasis (crop mycosis) in chicks and turkeys. *Poultry Sci.* 38: 653, 1959.

18 ♦ Q (QUERY) FEVER

● J. FREDERICK BELL

Q FEVER is a generalized febrile rickettsial infection characterized in man by absence of rash and usually by pneumonitis. It occurs worldwide in a great variety of parasitic arthropods and in homiothermic vertebrates in widely diverse habitats.

♦ **HISTORY.** The causative organism was discovered at about the same time in slaughterhouse workers and in bandicoots *(Isoodon)* in Queensland and in ticks *(Dermacentor)* in Montana. After the identity of isolates from those sources was established, the disease or its agent was identified in many countries.

♦ **ETIOLOGY.** The Q fever rickettsia is the only species of the genus *Coxiella* in the tribe Rickettsieae, family Rickettsiaceae. The species designation has been changed several times *(Rickettsia diaporica, R. burneti, Coxiella burnetii);* the preferred form at present is *C. burneti.*

The organism is rod-shaped, diplobacillary or coccoid, and filterable (through Berkefeld N & W and Seitz EK filters). It has not yet been cultivated in cell-free media but is readily propagated in embryonated hens eggs and in several kinds of cells in culture. When propagated in eggs it loses an antigenic component, thus transforming from Phase I to Phase II. Reversion to Phase I occurs when laboratory animals are infected. Reproduction is by transverse binary fission. It is remarkably durable in fomites such as tick feces and wool and is exceptionally resistant to chemical and physical agents, properties of significance in isolation, sterilization, and epidemiology. Culture of the rickettsia is favored by its ability to grow in the presence of antibiotics in concentrations sufficient to inhibit

some contaminants. Isolation of the organism is usually accomplished by inoculation of suspect material into guinea pigs. However, isolation of the agent is dangerous to personnel and, in addition, may yield misleading results unless strict precautions are taken to prevent cross infection in the animal colony. Other methods useful for survey and for diagnosis are the skin test and serologic tests such as fluorescent antibody complement fixation, neutralization, capillary agglutination, and radioisotope precipitation. For individual diagnosis paired serum specimens are necessary. Infection with *R. burneti* does not result in the formation of humoral antibodies to Proteus OX bacteria. Details of useful techniques may be found in the book *Diagnostic Procedures for Viral and Rickettsial Diseases* (Lennette and Schmidt, 1964).

Natural transmission is by aerosol and by ingestion as well as by arthropod vectors.

In comparison with the infection in mammals, coxiellosis in birds appears to be of minor importance. A 1965 textbook on diseases of poultry does not even mention the disease. Nevertheless, there is good evidence that *Coxiella* can invade and persist in birds, can serve as a source of infection, and in some species there is typical diagnostic antibody reaction to the infection.

Babudieri and Moscovici (1952) inoculated domestic fowl and pigeons parenterally. None of the birds showed clinical evidence of disease, but after 1 month the complement-fixation (CF) test was positive with goose *(Anser)* and pigeon *(Columba)* blood. They also inoculated pigeons, sparrows *(Passer)*, and goldfinches *(Chrysomitris)* orally, and rickettsias were found in the kidneys for as long as 40 days in some birds. In general the CF test yielded erratic results that were inconsistent with isolation tests: birds were found to have negative CF tests or to become seronegative while their tissues were infected.

Shestochenko (1960) reached a similar conclusion regarding the CF test as applied to bird serums. He studied the experimental infection in domestic chickens *(Gallus)* and pigeons. Agglutinating antibodies were readily demonstrated and a skin test (ST) yielded satisfactory results. The ST was applied by subcutaneous injection of 0.1 ml of antigen in the wattle. Contrary to the results of antigen injection in mammals, in which the reaction is typically of the delayed type, the reaction in chickens is of the Arthus type, reaching a maximum in 6 hours.

Serums from birds obtained in areas of Italy where cases of Q fever in man had not been reported were negative in the CF test, whereas several serums from pigeons and one from a goose from another area with recent human cases were seropositive. Coxiellosis was transmitted from a seropositive pigeon to a cavy 160 days later. In an area of high incidence of infection of livestock in France, serums of 3 of 17 alpine crows *(Corvus)* had significant titers of antibodies (Seigneurin and Seigneurin, 1968). In Czechoslovakia serologic evidence of *Coxiella* infection was found in 10 species of wild birds and the organism was isolated from the spleens and kidneys of 3 (Zdrodovskii and Golinevich, 1960). Rehn and Radvan (1967) demonstrated the infection serologically in the pheasant *(Phasianus)* in Bohemia. Karulin (1960) assigns a participating role of birds (and reptiles) in the transmission of *Coxiella* in natural foci in the desert, and ticks and mites taken from bird nests have been found to be infected (Syrucek and Raska, 1956).

Coxiella burneti has also been isolated from eggshells and from tissues of hens (Zhmaeva and Pchelkina, 1957). The organism may persist for 5 months in spleens and kidneys of chickens. Feces are infectious up to 42 days (Sobeslovsky and Syrucek, 1959), a possible source of infection to man and domestic animals.

Vest et al. (1965) failed to find *Coxiella* or antibodies to it among numerous birds of several species in an enzootic area in Utah. Marchette (1965) did not find CF antibodies at the 1:8 level in 44 birds in an area of Malay, where seropositive reactions were frequent in mammals.

In a survey of Q fever in Ontario, McKiel et al. (1962) observed the development of a CF titer in guinea pigs inoculated with tissues from a barn swallow *(Hirundo)* and from rodents.

In spite of the demonstrated potential of a role for birds in the domestic and sylvatic ecology of *Coxiella,* they do not seem to be essential or even major reservoirs.

◆ REFERENCES

Babudieri, B., and Moscovici, C. Experimental and natural infection of birds by *Coxiella burneti. Nature* 169:195, 1952.

Karulin, B. E. The geographic-ecological analysis of foci of Q fever. *J. Microbiol. Epidemiol. Immunobiol.* USSR 31 (part 2):1597, 1960.

Lennette, E. H., and Schmidt, N. J. Diagnostic procedures for viral and rickettsial diseases, 3rd ed. New York: American Public Health Assoc., 1964.

Marchette, N. J. Rickettsiosis (tick typhus, Q-fever, urban typhus) in Malaya. *J. Med. Entomol.* 2:339, 1965.

McKiel, J. A., Elder, R. H., Hall, R. R., and Millar, A. M. Q fever in Ontario. *Can. J. Public Health* 53:358, 1962.

Rehn, F., and Radvan, R. Contribution to the problem of the occurrence of natural foci of Q fever. *J. Hyg. Epidemiol. Microbiol. Immunol.* 11:192, 1967.

Seigneurin, R., and Seigneurin, J. M. Le corbeau des Alpes est infecte par *Rickettsia burneti. Bull. Acad. Natl. Med.* 152:5, 1968.

Shestochenko, M. A. A study of the methods of diagnosis of Q fever in birds. *J. Microbiol. Epidemiol. Immunobiol.* USSR 31 (part 2): 1604, 1960.

Sobeslovsky, O., and Syrucek, L. Transovular transmission of *C. burneti* in the domestic fowl *(Gallus gallus domesticus). J. Hyg. Epidemiol. Microbiol. Immunol.* 3:458, 1959.

Syrucek, L., and Raska, K. Q fever in domestic and wild birds. *Bull. World Health Organ.* 15:329, 1956.

Vest, E. D., Lundgren, D. L., Parker, D. D.,

Johnson, D. E., Morse, E. L., Bushman, J. B., Sidwell, R. W., and Thorpe, B. D. Results of a five-year survey for certain enzootic diseases in the fauna of western Utah. *Am. J. Trop. Med. Hyg.* 14:124, 1965.

Zdrodovskii, P. F., and Golinevich, E. H. *The rickettsial diseases.* New York: Pergamon Press, 1960.

Zhmaeva, Z. M., and Pchelkina, A. A. Domestic birds as carriers of the rickettsia of Q fever in the Turkmen, SSR. *J. Microbiol.* (Moscow) 28:347, 1957.

PART THREE

PARASITIC INFECTIONS

19 ◆ FLEAS AND LICE

● E. C. TURNER, JR.

ALTHOUGH detailed and excellent treatises have been written on the phylogeny and taxonomy of fleas and lice, little comprehensive work has been done on the biology and pathogenicity of these ectoparasites on wild hosts. Debilitant losses caused by species of lice and fleas have been reported on certain domestic animals. Such information is not easy to obtain with wild animals such as birds. Probably any losses are not widespread enough to be detected except in exceptional circumstances. Practically all such cases have been reported to occur on the very young or on individuals that have been injured or weakened in some way.

FLEAS
(Order: Siphonaptera)

Fleas generally infest mammals. Of the 1,800 described species, only about 100 have been reported on birds. This suggests that there has been a transfer of certain species from mammals to birds. Species of fleas associated with nest-dwelling mammals are also associated with birds that nest in a similar environment. Rothschild (1952) pointed out that of the 55 or more species of bird fleas described at that time, 27 were from birds that return to the same nesting site each year, 19 were from ground- or hole-nesting birds, 9 were from islands, and the others were mostly from birds which used mud in nest construction.

◆ DISTRIBUTION (Host and Geographic). Fleas are free-living in all but the adult stage. They frequently exhibit preference for certain habitats rather than their hosts. *Ceratophyllus gallinae* (Schrank), the common hen flea (Fig. 19.1), is usually found in dry, elevated nests in hen houses and in the nests of sparrows, starlings, and swallows. On the other hand, a related species, *C. garei*, the duck flea, prefers low, wet, swampy conditions.

Although relatively few species attack birds, their preference is scattered throughout the class Aves. Rothschild and Clay (1952) have outlined the biology and host associations of fleas in Britain. Hopkins (1957) has carefully reviewed the host association and distribution of all fleas, including bird fleas. But the records in many

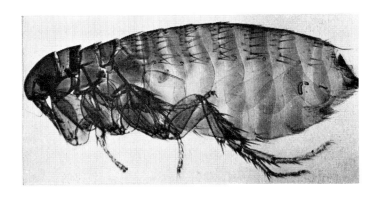

FIG. 19.1. *Ceratophyllus gallinae* (Schrank). (Actual size approximately 3.7 mm.)

TABLE 19.1. List of Bird Flea Genera and Their General Host Distribution

Family, Geographic Region, and Genera	Host(s)
Ceratophyllidae—Holarctic	
Orneacus	*Delichon, Columba*
Micotenopsylla	probably *Rissa*
Ceratophyllus	wide variety of birds, species sometimes specific to type of host nest
Dasypayllus	wide variety of birds having nests in low situations, Passeriformes
Leptopsyllidae—Holarctic	
Frontopsylla (Orfrontia)	*Oenanthe,* Hirundinidae, *Riparia, Delichon*
Pulicidae—Worldwide	
Ornithopsylla	*Puffinus puffinus*
Acetenopsylla	*Ptychoramphus aleuticus*
Echidnophaga	*Gallus domesticus*
Xenopsylla	*Petrochelidon, Puffinus*
Pygiopsyllidae Australian	
Stivalius	pronotal combs characteristic of birds' fleas (limited records)
Notiopsylla	burrow-nesting Procellariiformes
Rhopalopsyllidae—Neotropical	
Listronius	limited records only
Parapsyllus	Sphenisciformes
Tungidae—Neotropical	
Hectopsylla	wide selectivity (limited records)

Sources: Hopkins (1957); Holland (1964).

cases are still too scanty to permit definite conclusions on host distribution of these parasites. Table 19.1 lists the genera of bird fleas and their general host distribution.

◆ **TRANSMISSION AND DEVELOPMENT.** Bird fleas have a broad host range. In addition they have developed the ability to fast for long periods when a host is not available. They remain in old nests and transfer to new hosts that occupy or come near the nest. Many species also tend to leave the nests and remain in cracks of bark, rubbish, etc., until a suitable host is available. Fleas can be transmitted or disseminated in a number of ways. They can simply hop on a passing host bird, or if the bird is quite gregarious, they can be disseminated by direct contact. Birds occupying abandoned nests of former infested hosts may inherit the fleas of the former occupant.

These insects undergo complete metamorphosis. Depending on the species, adults lay up to 500 eggs at random, usually in small batches on the host. Some eggs stick, but most of them drop to the floor of the nest or dwelling. The eggs hatch into brown or lemon-colored eruciform larvae which have sparse long hairs on each segment. These immature forms are negatively phototropic, moving into cracks and crevices and feeding on organic matter, dried blood from the host, or feces from adult fleas. Exarate pupae are formed and enclosed in a semitransparent cocoon in which bits of soil and debris are brought together by silken threads. After a period of time which varies with the species and environmental temperature, the adults emerge. The complete life cycle may vary from 3 weeks to 20 months, depending on the above factors.

◆ **CLINICAL SIGNS.** Clinical signs are difficult to detect on wild birds, and to the author's knowledge, have not been reported.

◆ **PATHOLOGY.** According to research reports, fleas do not transmit pathogenic

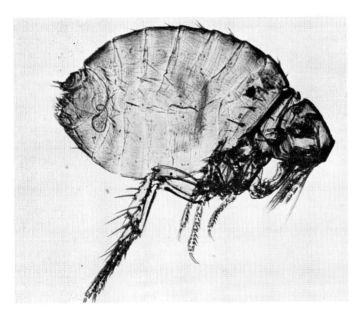

FIG. 19.2. *Echidnophaga gallinacea* (Westwood). (Actual size approximately 1.9 mm.)

organisms to wild birds. The sticktight flea, *Echidnophaga gallinacia* (Westwood), on domestic poultry (Fig. 19.2), causes weight loss, reduction in egg production, and even death due to loss of blood. Authors have occasionally reported the presence of thousands of fleas in individual bird nests containing young birds and it is possible that this is a contributing cause of death among the young. On the other hand, Rothschild (1965) reported that young animals seem to survive in nests containing thousands of fleas. Her experiments indicated that animals 2 to 6 weeks of age are apparently unattractive to the parasites. Thus it appears that the effect of fleas on young birds is difficult to evaluate. Little serious study has been made on the possible losses of birds caused by these ectoparasites.

◆**DIAGNOSIS.** Most bird fleas crawl through the feathers of their host but are generally not found there. Therefore examination of the nest of the host is important in determining the species and relative numbers infesting the host. The sticktight flea, however, remains embedded in the skin of the host, usually about the head.

Collection of fleas from birds usually requires additional skill in hunting or trapping. In most areas, a permit should be obtained from state or local conservation officials before this is done. After the birds are captured, they must be placed quickly in individual containers or bags to avoid the mixing of the fleas of one host with those of another and to prevent escape of the insects. A small amount of chloroform or ethyl acetate added to the container will kill the bird and its ectoparasites. The fleas can then be brushed onto a clean surface. Sometimes it is more convenient to place the killed hosts and their parasites in individual plastic bags for storage in deep freeze. Examination can then be made later. Often it is not desirable nor necessary to kill the captured birds. The application of a small amount of insecticide dust such as pyrethrum or rotenone will cause most of the fleas to drop from the birds.

Whenever possible, the nests of hosts should be collected and placed in covered battery jars or larger containers. The fleas can be collected as they become mature. These nests can also be placed in Berlese funnels for about 48 hours. This will permit evaporation of moisture and have a maximum effect in driving the fleas into the collecting jars below.

Preliminary identification of fleas can be made from liquid mounts, but it is usually more satisfactory to mount them individually as permanent microscopic whole mounts. Holland (1949), after evaluating various techniques, decided that the following method was most consistent and satisfactory. Fleas are placed in 10% potassium hydroxide solution for about 24 hours, or somewhat longer in the case of heavily sclerotized species. Once cleared to the extent that the internal structure has become clearly visible, the specimens then must stand overnight in water. Acetic acid is added to neutralize any potassium hydroxide that might still be present. The specimens are transferred to a 95% ethyl alcohol solution for at least 1 hour, but preferably overnight. Then they are placed in absolute alcohol for at least ½ hour. For final clearing, fleas are placed in oil of wintergreen for 15 minutes and mounted directly on slides in Canada balsam.

◆ **TREATMENT   AND   CONTROL.** Much is known about the control of fleas attacking domestic poultry. Little, however, is known about the control of fleas on wild birds. Insecticide treatment of the bird and nest, using materials such as 10% DDT or 5% malathion dust, would probably result in effective control, but the use of insecticides cannot be recommended without toxicologic investigations of host animals. It is doubtful if such insecticide treatment would be practicable on a large scale. It is recommended that management practices be employed that would maintain the health and well-being of the host animal.

BITING LICE
(Order: Mallophaga)

Lice of birds are confined to the order Mallophaga. It is believed that the ancestors of this group probably lived in the bark of trees, feeding on organic matter. Gradually they began feeding on the skin debris of reptiles. When these reptiles, which were ancestors of birds, began to evolve feathers, a new source of shelter and protection was available to these parasites. They then evolved with their host. It is generally thought that biting lice subsequently spead to mammals.

◆ **SYNONOMY.** Ferris (1951) outlined the taxonomic history and synonomy of lice. He pointed out the state of confusion that has existed and still exists in the taxonomic status of the two major groups. Part of this concern was whether the biting and sucking lice should be placed in the orders Mallophaga and Anoplura, respectively, or placed as suborders under the order Phthiraptera, as British workers had suggested (Hopkins, 1949). This writer has chosen to agree with Ferris (1951) in that they appear to be two distinct groups, but the rank assigned to them (order or suborder) becomes a matter of opinion. Thus the sucking lice will be placed in the order Anoplura and the biting lice in the order Mallophaga.

◆ **DISTRIBUTION.** Mallophaga are very host-specific—so much so that it is nearly always possible to determine from the species of lice at least the order to which the host animal belongs. Thus the species distribution of biting lice generally coincides with the distribution of their hosts. Clay (1957) has extensively analyzed the host distribution of bird lice. An outline of this is shown in Table 19.2.

◆ **TRANSMISSION   AND   DEVELOPMENT.** Intraspecific transmission of bird lice is done mainly during host-mating, breeding of the young, roosting of gregarious species, and by using common dusting baths. Interspecific transmission rarely occurs. The difficulties of such a transfer are due to (1) physical structure of the feathers, (2) chemical composition of blood and feathers, (3) temperature differences, and (4) competition with normal lice populations already established. Generally lice die on

TABLE 19.2. Partial List of the Genera of Mallophaga and Their Host Distribution on Birds

Classification (Suborder, Family, Genera)	Bird Host(s)
AMBLYCERA	
Menoponidae	
Actornithophilus	Procellariiformes, Gruiformes
Ardeiphilus	Ciconiiformes
Austromenopon	Procellariiformes, Pelecaniformes, Charadriiformes
Carrikeria	OPISTHOCOMI
Ciconiphilus	Ciconiiformes, Anseriformes
Clayia	Galliformes
Colpocephalum	Piciformes, Ciconiiformes, Falconiformes, Passeriformes, Columbiformes, Cuculiformes, Strigiformes
Culculiphilus	Falconiformes, Cuculiformes
Dennyus	Apodiformes
Dicteisia	Anseriformes
Eidmaniella	Pelecaniformes
Eomenopon	Psittaciformes
Eucolpocephalum	Cicconiiformes
Eureum	Anseriformes
Hoazineus	OPISTHOCOMI
Hohrstiella	Columbiformes
Holomenopon	Anseriformes
Kelerimenopon	Galliformes
Kurodaia	Falconiformes, Strigiformes
Longimenopon	Procellariiformes, Charadriiformes
Machaerilaemus	Passeriformes
Menacanthus	Tinamiformes, Galliformes, Passeriformes, Coraciiformes, Piciformes
Menopon	Galliformes
Microctenia	Tinamiformes
Myrsidea	Trogoniformes, Passeriformes, Piciformes
Neomenopon	Columbiformes
Nosopon	Falconiformes
Numidicola	Galliformes
Osborniella	Cuculiformes
Plegadiphilus	Ciconiiformes
Pseudomenopon	Podicipediformes, Gruiformes
Psittacomenopon	Psittaciformes
Somaphantus	Galliformes
Trinoton	Anseriformes
Turacoeca	Culiformes
Laemabothriidae	
Laemobothrion	Ciconiiformes, Falconiformes, OPISTHOCOMI
Ricinidae	
Ricinus	Apodiformes, Passeriformes
ISCHNOCERA	
Philopteridae	
Acidoproctus	Anseriformes
Anaticola	Anseriformes
Anatoecus	Anseriformes
Aquanirmus	Podicipediformes
Ardeicola	Ciconiiformes
Auricotes	Columbiformes
Austrogonoides	Sphenisciformes
Bothriometopus	Anseriformes
Bruelia	Trogoniformes, Coraciiformes, Passeriformes Piciformes
Campanulotes	Columbiformes
Chelopistes	Galliformes
Colilipeurus	Coliiformes
Coloceras	Columbiformes
Columbicola	Columbiformes

TABLE 19.2. Partial List of the Genera of Mallophaga and Their Host Distribution on Birds *(cont.)*

Classification (Suborder, Family, Genera)	Bird Host(s)
Craspedonirmus	Gaviiformes
Craspedorrynchus	Falconiformes
Cuclotogaster	Galliformes
Cuculoecus	Cuculiformes
Dahlemhornia	Casuariiformes
Degeeriella complex	Piciformes, Coraciiformes, Trogoniformes
	Falconiformes, Gruiformes, Passeriformes
Falcoecus	Falconiformes
Falcolipeurus	Falconiformes
Goniocotes	Galliformes
Ibidoecus	Ciconiiformes
Kodocephalon	Columbiformes
Lagopoecus	Galliformes
Lipeurus	Galliformes
Mulcticola	Caprimulgiformes
Neophilopterus	Ciconiiformes
Nesiotinus	Sphenisciformes
Osculotes	OPISTHOCOMI
Otidoecus	Galliformes, Gruiformes
Oxylipeurus	Galliformes
Pectinopygus	Pelecaniformes
Penenirmus	Piciformes, Passeriformes
Philoceanus complex	Procellariiformes
Philopterus	Passeriformes, Coraciiformes, Piciformes
Physconelloides	Columbiformes
Pseudolipeurus	Tinamiformes
Quadraceps	Gruiformes, Ciconiiformes
Rallicola	Apterygiformes
Rhynonirmus	Galliformes
Saemundssonia	Charadriiformes, Pelecaniformes
	Gruiformes, Procellariiformes
Strigiphilus	Cuculiformes
Sturnidoecus	Passeriformes
Struthiolipeurus	Struthioniformes, Rheiformes
Syrrhaptoecus	Columbiformes
Tinamotaecola	Tinamiformes, Gruiformes
Turnicola	Gruiformes
Vernoniella	Cuculiformes
Wilsoniella	OPISTHOCOMI
Heptapsogasteridae	
Heptapsogaster complex	Tinamiformes, Gruiformes

SOURCES: Genera and host distribution from Clay (1957); Hopkins and Clay (1952). Bird classification after Wetmore (1951).

the death of their host unless they can transfer quickly to another individual of the same species. In such cases they will approach any warm or rough-textured object. There have been numerous reports of phoresy in which Mallophaga attach to louse flies, fleas, mosquitoes, dragon flies, bumblebees, and butterflies.

Lice undergo simple metamorphosis. The differences in life history of each species are due to the host and its environment. A composite life cycle is given as follows: The eggs are laid in rows, usually on the flight feathers and usually in areas relatively safe from the bill of the host. The location of these eggs varies with the species. After 3 or 4 days the young nymphs hatch and undergo growth and development, including 3 instars about a week apart. At the end of the 4th week, the adult lice emerge. The total life cycle is about 30 to 36 days. Lice from the suborder Ischnocera are generally feather feeders only and feed in sharply defined areas. Lice belonging to the suborder Amblycera take blood and serum in addition to feathers. Some species of the latter puncture feathers in the quill to take blood from the central pulp in the growing feather.

◆ **CLINICAL SIGNS.** A bird severely infested with lice exhibits signs not unlike that of molting. The movement of lice is intensely irritating and the bird may damage itself by excessive scratching and preening. Feather shafts can be denuded, and the punctures made in quills may inhibit further development of the feathers.

◆ **PATHOGENESIS.** Sick birds tend to be more heavily infested with lice than healthy birds. The birds in a weakened condition apparently are unable to keep the ectoparasites in check by preening. A heavy infestation is extremely irritating and can seriously affect the host. Many workers have reported losses in weight and egg production in domestic poultry. Olson (1935), conducting experiments in which chickens were heavily infested with 4 species of biting lice, reported that a slight anemia was noted in the infested group of birds. Thrombocytosis and moderate leukocytosis were also observed in this group after they had been hosts to the parasites for at least 30 days. However, Olson was not sure of the significance of these 2 phenomena.

In nature the size of the population of lice on a host is variable and does not seem to be seasonal. In a survey of wild birds in Britain, Keymer et al. (1962) found that of 2,044 birds examined only 9 carried a parasite burden that could be considered pathogenic.

◆ **DIAGNOSIS.** Mallophaga can be distinguished from other arthropods by their flattened appearance and large, broad head (Fig. 19.3). They can be seen crawling rapidly over the body of the host. Size varies from 1 to 9 mm in length, depending on the species. The color of lice also varies with the species. Rothschild and Clay (1952) cite numerous examples in which light-colored hosts are infested with light-colored lice and vice versa.

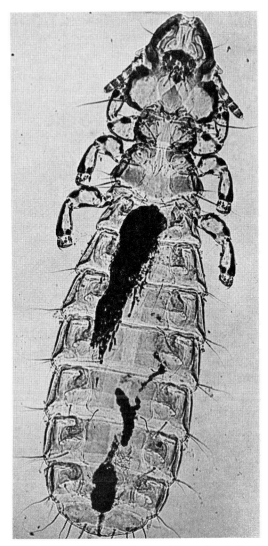

FIG. 19.3. *Bruelia nebulosa* (Burmeister) from Starling. (Photo by W. G. Mitchell.)

Lice can be collected from hosts by brushing them from the body onto a clean white surface. Other methods of collecting and counting lice on birds have been reported by entomologists working on control of poultry lice (Harshbarger and Raffensperger, 1959). A more satisfactory method of collecting from wild birds has been outlined by Malcomson (1960). This method causes little or no injury to the bird. A safe and quick-acting insecticidal dust such as pyrethrum is ruffled through the feathers of the bird; care is taken not to get dust in its eyes. The bird is then placed in a cardboard carton inverted over white paper and allowed to flutter for about 5 minutes. The lice crawl to the edge of the feathers and drop to the paper beneath. The bird can be released and the lice collected and preserved in 70% alcohol.

Positive identification of lice, particularly with unknown groups, can be made only with microscopic whole mounts. Hoyer's solution is used for temporary mounts, but most workers have adopted the following method: The lice are soaked in 10% potassium hydroxide. The abdomen is punctured with a sharp needle and all the soft body parts are liquified. The dissolved parts are then squeezed out gently with a blunt needle. The specimens are passed through 50, 70, 90, and 100% ethyl alcohol, then oil of cloves, and mounted on slides in Canada balsam. Staining is usually unnecessary.

Quantitative evaluations of lice on domestic poultry have been made, but little has been done with wild birds. The use of a coding system such as outlined by Harshbarger and Raffensperger (1961) could be adopted. Handling wild birds requires special techniques, depending on the size of the bird and infestation of the parasites.

◆ TREATMENT AND CONTROL. It has been widely reported that healthy birds do not become as heavily infested by lice as sick or injured birds. Obviously management practices ensuring healthy birds are the best ways to control lice. Insecticide treatment of the nests of birds might be effective temporarily. There is little information on insecticidal control of bird lice or the effect of insecticides on the birds.

◆ REFERENCES

● Fleas

Alicata, J. E., Kartman, L., and Fisher, H. J. Wild birds as possible carriers of poultry parasites. *Univ. Hawaii Agr. Exp. Sta., Biennial Rept.*, p. 104, 1948.

Allan, R. M. Fleas (Siphonaptera) from birds in northeast Scotland. *Scot. Naturalist* 62: 34, 1950.

Ash, J. S. Siphonaptera bred from birds nests. *Entomol. Monthly Mag.* 88:217, 1952.

Bates, J. K. Host selection in bird fleas. *Brit. Ecol. Soc. Aut. Meetings. J. Animal Ecol.* 25:475, 1956.

Bates, J. K., and Rothschild, M. Field studies on the behavior of bird fleas. I. Behavior of the adults of three species of bird fleas in the field. *Parasitology* 52:113, 1962.

Benton, A. H., and Cerwonka, R. H. Host relationship of some eastern Siphonaptera. *Am. Midland Naturalist* 63(2):383, 1960.

Benton, A. H., and Shatrau, V. Notes on a collection of bird fleas from Grand Manan, New Brunswick. *Can. Entomologist* 94(7): 743, 1962.

———. The bird fleas of eastern North America. *Wilson Bull.* 77(1):76, 1965.

Eads, R. B. Ectoparasites from swallow nests, with the description of a new Ceratophyllid flea. *J. Parasitol.* 42:73, 1956.

Grebenyub, R. V., and Shwarts, E. A. Fleas as parasites of birds of Kirghizia (Aphaniptera, Siphonaptera). *Akad. Nauk Kirgizskoi SSR, Inst. Zool.*, 1961 [from *Bibliog. Agr.* 27(6)].

Holland, G. P. The Siphonaptera of Canada. *Can. Dept. Agr. Tech. Bull. No. 70*, 1949.

———. Notes on some bird fleas, with the description of a new species of *Ceratophyllus*, and a key to the bird fleas known from Canada (Siphonaptera: Ceratophyllidae). *Can. Entomologist* 83(11):281, 1951.

———. The crow flea, *Ceratophyllus rossittensis* Dampf, in North America (Siphonaptera: Ceratophyllidae). *Can. Entomologist* 86(7): 334, 1954.

Hopkins, G. H. E. Host associations of Siphonaptera. *First Symp. Host Specificity Among Parasites of Vertebrates*, p. 64. Univ. Neuchatel, Switzerland, 1957.

Jordan, K. Further records of North American bird-fleas, with a list of the Nearctic birds from which fleas are known. *Novit. Zool.* 35:89, 1929.

Rothschild, M. A collection of fleas from the bodies of British birds, with notes on their distribution and host preferences. *Bull. Brit. Museum Entomol.* 2(4):185, 1952.

———. The bird fleas of Fair Isle. *Parasitology* 48:382, 1958.

———. Remarks on the life-cycles of fleas (Siphonaptera). *Congr. Parasitol., Rome, Italy* (mimeo. copy), 1965.

Rothschild, M., and Clay, T. *Fleas, Flukes and Cuckoos*. London: Collins, 1952.

Smit, F. G. A. M. Identification of fleas. *World Health Organ. Mono. Ser.* 22:648, 1952.

Stansfield, G. The collection of bird fleas from Fair Isle in 1956. *Parasitology* 51(3&4):367, 1961.

Thompson, G. B. The parasites of British birds and mammals. XXIV. Sand martins' fleas. *Entomol. Monthly Mag.* 88:177, 1952.

——. The parasites of British birds and mammals. XXVI. Further notes on sand martins' fleas. *Entomol. Monthly Mag.* 89:224, 1953.

Trembly, H. L., and Bishopp, F. C. Distribution and hosts of some fleas of economic importance. *J. Econ. Entomol.* 33(4):701, 1940.

● **Biting Lice**

Ash, J. S. A study of the Mallophaga of birds with particular reference to their ecology. *Ibis* 102(1):93, 1960.

Boyd, E. M. The external parasites of birds. A review. *Wilson Bull.* 63(4):363, 1951.

Brown, J. H., and Wilk, A. L. Mallophaga of Alberta: A list of species with hosts. *Can. Entomologist* 76:127, 1944.

Clay, T. A preliminary key to the genera of the Menoponidae (Mallophaga). *Proc. Zool. Soc. London* 117:457, 1947.

——. An introduction to classification of the avian Ischnocera (Mallophaga): Part 1. *Trans. Roy. Entomol. Soc. London* 102(2): 171, 1951.

——. Revisions of the genera of Mallophaga. I. The *Rallicola* complex. *Proc. Zool. Soc. London* 123:563, 1953.

——. Revisions of the genera of Mallophaga. *Colilipeurus* and a new genus. *Trans. Roy. Entomol. Soc. London* 107:169, 1955.

——. The Mallophaga of birds. *First Symp. Host Specificity Among Parasites of Vertebrates,* p. 120. Univ. Neuchatel, Switzerland, 1957.

Corbet, G. B. The phoresy of Mallophaga on a population of *Ornithomyia fringellina*. *Entomol. Monthly Mag.* 92:207, 1956.

Cowan, I. M. Death of a trumpeter swan from multiple parasitism. *Auk* 63(2):248, 1946.

Emerson, K. C. Records of Mallophaga from Oklahoma hosts. *Can. Entomologist* 72(5): 104, 1940.

Ewing, H. E. The taxonomy of the mallophagan family Trichodectidae with special reference to the New World fauna. *J. Parasitol.* 22:233, 1936.

Ferris, G. F. The sucking lice. *Mem. Pac. Coast Entomol. Soc.* 1:1, 1951.

Geist, R. M. Additional Mallophaga from Ohio birds. *Ohio J. Sci.* 31:505, 1931.

Harrison, L. The genera and species of Mallophaga. *Parasitology* 9 (1):1, 1916.

Harshbarger, J. C., and Raffensperger, E. M. A method for collecting and counting populations of the shaft louse. *J. Econ. Entomol.* 52 (6):1215, 1959.

——. An evaluation of coding systems for estimating populations of the shaft louse, *Menopon gallinae. J. Econ. Entomol.* 54 (1):74, 1961.

Hopkins, G. H. E. The host-associations of the lice of mammals. *Proc. Zool. Soc. London* 119 (2):387, 1949.

Hopkins, G. H. E., and Clay, T. *A check list of the genera and species of Mallophaga.* Trustees of the British Museum, London, 1952.

Johnson, T. H., and Harrison, L. A census of Australian Mallophaga. *Proc. Roy. Soc. Queensland* 24:1, 1912a.

——. A list of Mallophaga found on introduced domestic animals in Australia. *Proc. Roy. Soc. Queensland* 24:17, 1912b.

Kellogg, V. L. A list of biting lice (Mallophaga) taken from birds and mammals of North America. *U.S. Natl. Museum* (1183) 22:39, 1900.

——. The Mallophaga of the world: Systematic summary. *Psyche* 15 (1):11, 1908a.

——. Mallophaga. *Genera Insectorum* (66), 1908b.

Keymer, I. F., Rose, J. H., Beesley, W. H., and Davies, S. F. M. A survey and review of parasitic diseases of wild and game birds in Great Britain. *Vet. Rec.* 74 (33):887, 1962.

Malcomson, R. O. Mallophaga from birds of North America. *Wilson Bull.* 72 (2):182, 1960.

Martin, M. Life history and habits of pigeon louse *Columbicola columbae* (Linn.). *Can. Entomologist* 66:6, 1934.

Meinertzhagen, R., and Clay, T. List of Mallophaga collected from birds brought to the society's prosectorium. *Proc. Zool. Soc. London* 117 (4):675, 1948.

Mohr, C. O., and Stumpf, W. A. Relation of ectoparasite load to host size and home area in small mammals and birds. *Trans. 27th N. Am. Wildlife Conf.*, p. 174, 1962.

Olson, C. The effect of certain ectoparasites on the cellular elements and hemoglobin of the blood of the domestic chicken. *J. Am. Vet. Med. Assoc.* 87:559, 1935.

Peters, H. S. A list of external parasites from birds of the eastern part of the United States. *Bird Banding* 7 (1):9, 1936.

Steward, M. W. Dispersal of the sticktight flea of hens *(Echidnophaga gallinacea)* (Westwood). *J. Econ. Entomol.* 25:164, 1932.

Stirrett, G. M. Mallophaga collected from birds in Ontario. *Can. Entomologist* 84:205, 1952.

Thompson, G. B. The Praget collection of Mallophaga. Part I. *Ann. Mag. Nat. Hist. Ser. 10,* 20 (115):19, 1937.

——. The Praget collection of Mallophaga. Part II. *Ann. Mag. Nat. Hist. Ser. 11,* 1 (3): 268, 1938a.

——. The Praget collection of Mallophaga. Part III. *Ann. Mag. Nat. Hist. Ser. 11,* 1(5):493, 1938b.

——. The Praget collection of Mallophaga. Part IV. *Ann. Mag. Nat. Hist. Ser. 11,* 2 (1): 339, 1938c.

——. The Praget collection of Mallophaga. Part V. *Ann. Mag. Nat. Hist. Ser. 11,* 2 (12): 607, 1938d.

——. The Praget collection of Mallophaga. Part VI. *Ann. Mag. Nat. Hist. Ser. 11,* 3 (16): 417, 1938e.

——. The Praget collection of Mallophaga. Part VII. *Ann. Mag. Nat. Hist. Ser. 11,* 4 (19):139, 1939.

——. Contributions toward a study of the ectoparasites of British birds and mammals. No. 3 *Ann. Mag. Nat. Hist.* 7 (12):438, 1954.

——. The parasites of British birds and mammals. XXXV. The ectoparasites of the swallow *(Hirundo rustica* L.). *Entomol. Monthly Mag.* 97:79, 1962.

Tuff, D. W. The Mallophaga of the Ciconiiformes of America north of Mexico. Ph.D. dissertation, Texas A & M Univ., 1963 [from *Dissertation Abstr.* 25 (1), 1964].

Van Den Brock, E., and Jansen, J., Jr. Parasites of animals in the Netherlands. Suppl. 1: Parasites of wild birds. *Ardea* 52:111 [from *Ibis* 107 (1), 1965].

Warren, D. C. The value of DDT for the control of the common chicken louse. *Poultry Sci.* 24:473, 1945.

Warren, D. C., Eaton, R., and Smith, H. Influence of infestations of body lice on egg production in the hen. *Poultry Sci.* 27:641, 1948.

Werneck, F. C. Os Malofagos de *Cervus elaphus, Dama dama,* e *Capreolus capreolus. Rev. Brasil. Biol.* 7 (4):403, 1947.

Wetmore, A. A revised classification for the birds of the world. *Smithsonian Inst. Misc. Collections* 117 (4), 1951.

Wilson, F. H. A louse feeding on the blood of its host. *Science* 77:490, 1933.

——. The life cycle and bionomics of *Lipeurus heterographus* Nitzsch. *J. Parasitol.* 20: 304, 1934.

——. The life cycle and bionomics of *Lipeurus caponis* (Linn.). *Ann. Entomol. Soc. Am.* 32:318, 1939.

——. The slender lice of American pigeons and doves with descriptions of two new species. *J. Parasitol.* 27:259, 1941.

B. ENDOPARASITES

20 ♦ NEMATODES

● EVERETT E. WEHR

THE LIFE CYCLES and pathogenicity of most nematode parasites of wild birds have not been elucidated or are poorly known. However, some species occur in both wild and domestic birds and studies of their development and pathogenicity in domestic birds have been possible. Information from such studies has been incorporated freely in this chapter.

The rearing of pheasants in captivity has met with considerable difficulty because of the disease syngamiasis caused by the gapeworm *(Syngamus trachea)*. This tracheal nematode has caused great losses among pen-raised pheasants in the United States and elsewhere.

The crop worm *(Capillaria contorta)* occurs naturally in the bobwhite quail *(Colinus virginianus)* and the pheasant *(Phasianus colchicus)*. It also parasitizes the turkey *(Meleagris gallopavo)* and the domestic duck *(Anas boschas domestica)*. Experimental infections in domestic birds, as well as those in young quail, have added greatly to the knowledge of this nematode.

The cecal strongyle *(Trichostrongylus tenuis)* has been associated with losses in the grouse *(Lagopus lagopus scoticus)* in England and Scotland (Cobbold, 1873; Shipley, 1909; Clapham, 1935a, 1936), and has been especially destructive in pen-raised partridges in Denmark (Madsen, 1952). In the United States it has been found especially abundant in the Canada goose *(Branta canadensis)* (Herman and Wehr, 1953).

To conform more closely to the theme of the book, each parasite has been discussed under the parasitic or invasive disease caused by it. The name of the disease has been derived from the generic name of the causative agent with the addition of the suffix "iasis." For example, amidostomiasis is a disease caused by *Amidostomum* spp., and syngamiasis is a disease caused by *Syngamus* spp.

As a rule, the diagnosis of a specific parasitic disease in the living animal is based primarily on the clinical signs and on the presence of the parasite in the host. Since clinical signs exhibited by animals infected with the various parasites are so similar— loss of appetite, dullness, emaciation, etc.— it is impossible in most cases to identify the particular disease involved. The methods most commonly used in the diagnosis of helminthiasis in the living animal are (1) recovery of whole or fragments of worms in feces; (2) recovery of eggs in the feces; and (3) recovery of larvae in feces. However, a postmortem examination of sick birds is the surest and most reliable method and should be resorted to in all outbreaks of parasitic diseases.

Prompt and correct remedial measures for any parasitic disease can be made only after identifying the causative agent and obtaining complete information on its development and transmission. Compulsory therapeusis and prophylaxis are the measures most often employed in combating helminthiasis in animals. However, in the case of most nematodes found in wild birds, treatment would probably be impractical, but where artificial propagation is being carried out, especially for valuable breeding birds, it might be desirable and worthwhile. The employment of a mash medicated with thiabendazole holds excellent promise for the reduction of the gapeworm *(Syngamus trachea)* in pen-raised pheasants (Wehr, 1967). Such measures as the prompt removal of droppings or the raising of birds on wire-bottomed runs may be effective in preventing infections of parasites with direct life cycles or even those with indirect life cycles. Measures should be devised to reduce the number of intermediate hosts which may feed on droppings even at considerable distances from the birds.

CAPILLARIASIS

Capillariasis is a parasitic disease caused by a group of roundworms known as hairworms, threadworms, or capillarids. These roundworms, although they belong to a single genus, *Capillaria,* constitute a diversified group of parasites. The development and habits of some of the species vary greatly. The adult worms inhabit not only the digestive tract of man and different kinds of animals, including birds, but they have been found in such unusual places as the urinary bladder and the liver.

Capillariasis in poultry has long been recognized as a possible source of economic loss, and with the use of more intensive methods of rearing these birds, the problem has assumed even greater importance.

The esophagus and crop are the preferred sites of *C. contorta,* and the small intestine is preferred by *C. obsignata,* the two species discussed in this chapter.

Capillaria obsignata Madsen 1945

SYNONYMS: *Capillaria columbae* of Graybill 1924; *C. dujardini* Travassos 1914 of Travassos 1915.

◆ **DISTRIBUTION.** Galliformes: *Gallus gallus domesticus, Meleagris gallopavo domesticus, Pavo cristatus.* Columbiformes: *Columba livia domestica.*

◆ **TRANSMISSION AND DEVELOPMENT.** The life cycle is direct. The eggs are passed in the feces and require from 6 to 8 days at room temperature to reach the infective stage in which fully developed embryos are found. The embryo does not hatch from the egg and has not been observed to molt while inside the egg. A susceptible avian host becomes infected by swallowing the embryonated eggs with food or water. All larval stages have been found in the intestinal tract of experimentally infected birds, and mature worms were recovered from the small intestine as early as 19 days after infection. Eggs were found in the feces of infected birds 26 days after infection (Wehr, 1939).

◆ **CLINICAL SIGNS.** Heavily infected birds show signs of emaciation, diarrhea, listlessness, anorexia, and reduced water consumption. Death frequently results from such infections. The infected birds spend much of their time huddled on the ground, with the head drawn back close to the body, and with the eyes closed. The feathers appear ruffled and soiled around the vent, and the skin and visible mucous membranes are pale. According to Levine (1938), much pinkish material was noticed in the feces of infected birds on the 12th day after the feeding of embryonated eggs. During the next 4 days the feces of the birds were watery. A number of birds lost weight, became extremely emaciated, and died.

◆ **PATHOLOGY.** Intensive intestinal inflammation, with almost complete destruction of intestinal mucosa, has been reported. In severe cases, masses of sloughed mucosa constrict the lumen of the large intestine and prevent large quantities of fluid from escaping. In nonfatal experimental cases, a moderate thickening of the mucosa was observed. It contained pinhead hemorrhagic spots to extensive diffuse hyperemia. In some cases the mucosa was covered with much catarrhal exudate which ranged in color from "opaque white to translucent salmon color" (Levine, 1938). All stages of the worm penetrate the intestinal mucosa, the larvae being found somewhat deeper than the adults.

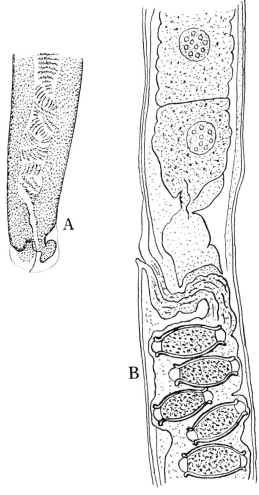

FIG. 20.1. *Capillaria obsignata.* *(A)* Male tail. *(B)* Vulvar region of female. (After Graybill, 1924.)

◆ **DIAGNOSIS.** The presence of sexually mature forms may be detected by examination of the feces for the presence of the lemon-shaped eggs (Fig. 20.1). Each egg is about 0.050 to 0.062 mm in size, and the innermost shell bends to a low collar. Incidentally, this is the only capillarid that has been found in the pigeon of the United States.

◆ **TREATMENT AND CONTROL.** The results of recent studies by Wehr et al. (1967) indicated that a 5% aqueous solution of methyridine injected subcutaneous-

ly beneath the wing was an effective anthelmintic for the removal of threadworms from pigeons. Doses ranged from 23 mg (0.5 ml) to 45 mg (1.0 ml) per bird. There was a slight edema at the site of the injection and a transitory incoordination was observed in some of the treated birds. However this failure of muscular incoordination disappeared within 2 or 3 hours and the birds returned to normal. Injections in the amount of 35 to 45 mg methyridine per bird were 99 to 100% effective against *C. obsignata* in naturally infected birds, but doses of 23 mg per bird removed only 62% of the worms. The anthelmintic action of the drug was relatively rapid, as indicated by the elimination of the majority of the worms within 24 hours after treatment.

Hendriks (1962, 1963) and Thienport and Mortelmans (1962) have shown that methyridine is an excellent drug for the removal of *C. obsignata* from chickens.

Capillaria contorta
(Creplin 1839) Travassos 1915

SYNONYMS: *Trichosoma contortum* Creplin 1839; *Thominx contorta* (Creplin 1839) Travassos 1915; *Capillaria vanelli* Yamaguti 1935.

◆ **DISTRIBUTION.** Anseriformes: *Anas boschas, A.b. domesticus, A. querquedula* (syn. *A. circia*), *Chaulelasmus streperus* (syn. *Anas streperus*), *Dafila acuta, Nettion crecca* (syn. *Anas crecca*), *Spatula clypeata* (syn. *Anas clypeata*), *Tadorna tadorna* (syn. *T. cornuta*). Charadriiformes: *Alle alle, Charadrius hiaticula* (syn. *Aegialitis hiaticula*), *Gelochelidon nilotica* (syn. *Sterna anglica*), *Larus canus, L. cachinnans, L. ridibundus, Philomachus pugnax* (syn. *Machetes pugnax, Pavoncella pugnax, Tringa pugnax*), *Recurvirostra avosetta, Sterna hirundo* (syn. *S. fulviatilus*), *Thalasseus maximus* (syn. *Sterna maxima*), *Uria grylle, Vanellus vanellus* (syn. *V. cristatus*). Falconiformes: *Accipiter nisus* (syn. *Astur nisus, Nisus communis*), *Buteo buteo* (syn. *B. vulgaris, Falco buteo*). Galliformes:

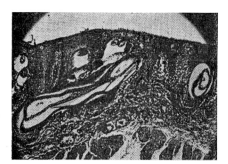

FIG. 20.2. *Capillaria annulata.* Esophagus of turkey. Worm and eggs in mucosa. (From Hung, 1926.)

Bonasa umbellus, Colinus virginianus, Crossoptilon mantchuricum, Lophortyx californica, Meleagris gallopavo, Oreortynx picta, Perdix perdix, Phasianus colchicus torquatus. Passeriformes: *Coloeus monedula* (syn. *Corvus monedula*), *Corvus brachyrhynchos* (syn. *C. americanus*), *C. cornix, C. corone* (syn. *Corone corone*), *Corvus frugilegus* (syn. *Trypanocorax frugiliguso*), *Erithacus rubecula* (syn. *Lusciola rubecula, Rubecula familiaris*), *Oenanthes oenanthe* (syn. *Saxicola oenanthe*), *Phoenicurus ochrurus* (syn. *Lusciola tithys, Ruticilla tithys*), *Sturnus vulgaris.*

◆ **TRANSMISSION AND DEVELOPMENT.** The eggs (Fig. 20.2) are deposited in burrows in the crop and esophageal walls. As the mucosa sloughs, the eggs drop into the lumen of the crop and esophagus and reach the exterior in the feces. Approximately 1 month's exposure to exterior weather conditions is required for the eggs to become infective. Susceptible hosts become infected by swallowing the infective eggs, or by feeding on invertebrates (earthworms, etc.) that have ingested the eggs with their food. So far as is known, no development of the larva takes place within the invertebrate host. Worms mature and eggs are found in the feces of infected birds in 1 to 2 months after experimental infection. Attempts to observe the early stages of the invasion of *C. contorta* have been futile (Madsen, 1952).

◆ **CLINICAL SIGNS.** Affected birds become droopy, weak, and emaciated. These birds move only when disturbed and then very slowly and with an unsteady gait. Occasionally an infected bird will fall back on its hock joints and assume a penguinlike position (Wehr, 1948). Others extend and retract their heads and necks as if attempting to swallow or remove an obstruction. Heavily infected quail were observed to squat, with their legs folded underneath their bodies.

◆ **PATHOLOGY.** When present in large numbers, there is marked thickening and inflammation of the crop and esophageal walls, with flocculent exudate covering the mucosa (Fig. 20.2). In natural infections in domestic turkeys, the crops of the most severely affected birds were filled with a fetid liquid which was prevented from draining into the alimentary tract by the thickened walls caused by the invasion of numerous worms. There is also sloughing of the mucosa. The crops of heavily infected quail were observed to be greatly thickened, inflamed, and usually empty.

◆ **DIAGNOSIS.** The identification of the species of *Capillaria* by the structure of the egg is difficult and requires the services of a specialist. The identification of the species involved and the exact location of the parasite is possible only by necropsy. If the worms, assuming them to be *Capillaria*, are located in the crop and esophageal wall, they are likely to be either *annulata* or *contorta*, although other species have occasionally been reported from this location (Cram, 1936). *Capillaria annulata* is readily differentiated from *C. contorta* by the presence of a cuticular inflation around the head. Madsen (1951) considered *C. annulata* as a synonym of *C. contorta*, but the author believes that sufficient evidence is still unavailable to demonstrate this synonymy.

◆ **TREATMENT AND CONTROL.** Numerous workers have reported that methyridine (2-[B-methoxyethyl] pyridine) is effective against *Capillaria obsignata* of the intestinal tract of poultry. Colglazier et al. (1967) found that 3 separate doses of 35 to 45 mg per bird of a 5% aqueous solution of methyridine, spaced at 4- to 5-day intervals, were highly efficacious in removing *C. contorta* from infected quail and resulted in less toxicity and mortality among the treated birds than single doses of 68 mg per bird. The necessity of handling each bird 3 times over a 9- or 10-day period, however, seems to reduce this regimen's practicality for use with wild birds, except in cases of a few birds that may be easily captured.

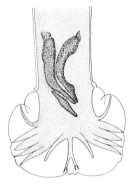

FIG. 20.3.   *Trichostrongylus tenuis*. Male bursa. (After Railliet, 1893.)

TRICHOSTRONGYLIASIS

Two species belonging to the genus *Trichostrongylus* have been described from the ceca of birds—namely, *T. pergracilis* (Cobbold 1875) Railliet and Henry 1909 and *T. tenuis* (Mehlis 1846) Railliet and Henry 1909. *Trichostrongylus pergracilis* is considered a synonym of *T. tenuis* (Cram and Wehr, 1934). *Trichostrongylus pergracilis* was originally described from the red grouse in England by Cobbold, and he may have overlooked the description of *T. tenuis*.

This parasite was reported for the first time in the United States in the bobwhite quail *(Colinus virginianus)* by Cram (1925). Since then, it has been collected from the pheasant *(Phasianus colchicus)*, blue goose *(Chen caerulescens)*, Canadian goose *(Branta canadensis)*, domestic goose *(Anser anser domesticus)*, and experimentally in other gallinaceous birds in this country.

Trichostrongylus tenuis
(Mehlis 1846) Railliet and Henry 1909

SYNONYMS: *Strongylus tenuis* Mehlis 1846 (in Creplin, 1846); *S. pergracilis* Cobbold 1873; *S. serratus* Linstow 1876; *Trichostrongylus pergracilis* (Cobbold 1873) Railliet and Henry 1909.

◆ **DISTRIBUTION.** Anseriformes: *Anas platyrhynchos, A. p. domesticus, Anser albifrons, A. anser, A. a. domesticus, Branta canadensis, Chen caerulescens.* Galliformes: *Gallus gallus, Lagopus scoticus, Meleagris gallopavo, Numida meleagris, Perdix perdix, Phasianus colchicus, Colinus virginianus.* Otidiformes: *Otis tarda.* Africa (South Africa [Natal]); Asia (Russian Turkestan); Europe (France, Germany, Great Britain, Scotland, Denmark, USSR); and North America (United States).

◆ **TRANSMISSION AND DEVELOPMENT.** The worm (Fig. 20.3) has a direct life cycle. The eggs are deposited in the morula stage and the 1st stage larva hatches within 36 to 48 hours later. In 4 or 5 days the larva molts to the 2nd stage and it is during this stage that the mouth capsule gradually disappears and the esophagus lengthens. It is very active at this stage and migrates to vegetation. Here it coils up and is resistant to changes in temperature and moisture. The 3rd stage larva, when swallowed by a grouse, completes the second molt, reaches the ceca, and after two more molts becomes adult (Leiper, 1910). Eggs may be produced and passed in the droppings of the bird 4 to 7 days after infection.

◆ **CLINICAL SIGNS.** According to Clapham (1935b), the contents of the ceca under disease conditions were yellowish white, dry, caked, and of cheesy consistency. The birds showed evidence of malnutrition and emaciation. Mature birds frequently weighed only 5 to 6 ounces as compared with a normal weight of 13 to 14 ounces. Portal and Collinge (1932) stated that diseased birds possessed dark plumage.

◆ **PATHOLOGY.** Cobbold (1873) discovered that *T. tenuis* was associated with the disease which decimated the red grouse population in Scotland. Clapham (1935b) stated that typical lesions were noticed in certain birds and a fatal dose was as low as 500 infective larvae. The ceca were distended and congested. The cecal contents were solid. The mucosae of the ceca were inflamed and the ridges were greatly thickened. There is some evidence that *T. tenuis* can be fatal to young goslings under certain conditions (Cram and Cuvillier, 1934). The trichostrongyles were present in large numbers in the ceca, and the mucosae of the ceca were ulcerated and darkly stained with blood pigments.

Heaviest mortality occurs in the fall, mainly in young birds of that year's hatching, and again in the spring. These two periods are apparently not isolated epidemics but are rather the peaks of a disease which continues in a chronic form the entire year. Heavy infections with this parasite have caused serious pathological changes.

◆ **DIAGNOSIS.** A postmortem examination of a diseased bird and the presence of the worm in the ceca are necessary to establish the extent of infection and damage.

ORNITHOSTRONGYLIASIS

Many worm infections are chronic in nature, but ornithostrongyliasis caused by *Ornithostrongylus quadriradiatus* usually appears suddenly in a highly acute form, with many fatalities.

The etiologic agent of this disease normally occurs in the upper part of the small intestine. The adults (Fig. 20.4) are very slender, spirally coiled, and red in color.

The disease is common in pigeons in the United States.

Ornithostrongylus quadriradiatus
(Stevenson 1904) Travassos 1914

SYNONYMS: *Strongylus quadriradiatus* Stevenson 1904; *Trichostrongylus quadriradiatus* (Stevenson 1904) Shipley 1909; *Cephalostrongylus quadriradiatus* (Stevenson 1904) Irwin-Smith 1920.

◆ **DISTRIBUTION.** Columbiformes: *Columba livia domestica, Zenaidura macroura carolensis.* North America (United States); South Africa; Cuba; Brazil; and Australia.

◆ **TRANSMISSION AND DEVELOPMENT.** The life cycle is direct. The thin-shelled, oval eggs are voided in the feces. Considerable oxygen and moisture are needed for further development of the eggs; dessication is detrimental to them. Eggs develop larvae which may hatch as early as 20 hours and as late as 9 days after being passed in the feces. Escaped larvae molt twice before reaching the infective stage. When the infective larva is swallowed by a pigeon or other susceptible host, it molts twice again and develops to maturity in the small intestine. The female worm begins to deposit eggs in 5 to 6 days following ingestion.

◆ **CLINICAL SIGNS.** Birds heavily infected with *O. quadriradiatus* become droopy, with ruffled feathers and neck retracted. They squat and seldom move; when disturbed they attempt to move but frequently tip forward. Anorexia is a common characteristic, and if food is accepted, it is frequently regurgitated, along with bile-stained fluid; water consumption, on the other hand, is somewhat increased. There is pronounced greenish diarrhea, and the bird gradually wastes away. Difficult and rapid breathing usually precedes death.

◆ **PATHOLOGY.** *Ornithostrongylus quadriradiatus* is a bloodsucking parasite and loss of blood through hemorrhages into the lumen of the intestine and through sucking by the worms causes a pronounced

FIG. 20.4. *Ornithostrongylus quadriradiatus.* *(A)* Male tail, bursa. *(B)* Anterior end, showing inflation around head. *(C)* Eggs. (After Stevenson, 1904.)

anemia. The intestines of fatally infected birds are markedly hemorrhagic and contain a greenish mucoid content, with masses of sloughed epithelium. There is considerable desquamation of the intestinal mucosa, the proventriculus is highly inflamed, and the mucosa is covered with an exudate. The duodenum is somewhat enlarged and lacking in muscular tone.

Cuvillier (1937) stated that a microscopic examination of sections of the duodenum revealed that larvae had penetrated almost to the basal muscular layer of the glands and that the tissue surrounding them had dissolved. The adult worms were tangled in the mass of mucus and were deeply embedded in the mucosa of the intestine. Fatal cases showed extensive destruction of the mucosa and an abundance of mucus, which was stained a bright green. The damaged tissue had sloughed into the lumen. In nonfatal experimental infections, the parasite caused a less severe reaction. Damage to the mucosa, other than numerous petechial hemorrhages, was not present. The feces returned to normal within a few days and the birds recovered.

◆ **DIAGNOSIS.** This is the only strongyloid nematode that occurs in the intestine of the pigeon, at least in the United States. Therefore the presence of thin-shelled eggs, usually in the morula stage when deposited in the feces, is diagnostic.

◆ **TREATMENT AND CONTROL.** The development of the eggs and larvae require considerable oxygen and moisture. Therefore the maintenance of dry conditions is considered one of the best preventive measures to check the spread of the parasite. Dry litter tends to absorb moisture from the droppings and aids in reducing the incidence of infection.

Leibovitz (1962) fed 0.05% thiabendazole in the feed for 10 days and reported that the output of ova in the feces was "markedly reduced" within 24 hours after treatment and fecal samples were free of ova after 72 hours of medication. None of the treated birds died, they ate well, and the greenish diarrhea disappeared. Single oral doses of 75 mg daily per bird for 4 days were not as effective as incorporation of the drug in the feed.

AMIDOSTOMIASIS

This disease may be caused by several species of the genus *Amidostomum*. The causative agent *(Amidostomum anseris)* of this disease in geese localizes in the gizzard and inhibits the growth and development of these birds, particularly young birds, and there may be considerable mortality.

Amidostomum anseris (Zeder 1800)
Railliet and Henry 1909 (Fig. 20.5)

SYNONYMS: *Strongylus anseris* Zeder 1800 in part; *Amidostomum nodulosum* (Rudolphi 1803) Seurat 1918; *Ascaris mucronata* Froelich 1791, not Schrank 1780; *Strongylus nodulosus* Rudolphi 1803; *Strongylus monodon* Linstow 1882.

◆ **DISTRIBUTION.** Anseriformes: *Anas acuta, A. penelope, A. platyrhynchos, A. querquedula, Anser albifrons, A. a. domesticus, A. cinereus, A. clangula, A. erythropus, A. fatalis, A. strepera, Branta canadensis, B. c. interior, Chloephaga poliocephala, Cyngus olor, Fuligula cristata, F. marila,*

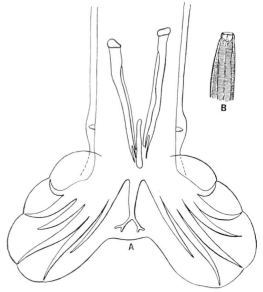

FIG. 20.5. *Amidostomum anseris. (A)* Anterior end. (After Wedl, 1856.) *(B)* Male bursa. (From Gedoelst, 1916, after Railliet, 1893.)

Gallinula chloropus, Glaucionetta clangula, Melinitta nigra, Mereca penelope, Nettion crecca, Nyroca clangula, Oidema fusca, Somateria mollisima, S. spectabilis, Spatula clypeata.

◆ **TRANSMISSION AND DEVELOPMENT.** Eggs are deposited by the female worm in the lumen of the gizzard and subsequently pass out in the droppings. Under optimal conditions of temperature and moisture, active embryos develop in the eggs within 24 to 48 hours. Larvae must molt twice before becoming infective to the definitive host. If a suitable bird ingests these infective larvae while feeding or drinking, the larvae reach the gizzard, remain in the lumen for a few days, and then enter the submucosa where they feed on the host tissue, particularly at the esophageal and intestinal junctures where the lining is soft. Eggs were detected in the feces of experimentally infected birds 14 to 25 days after exposure (Cowan, 1955).

◆ **CLINICAL SIGNS.** Young birds are most seriously affected. Dullness, loss of appetite, and emaciation are the most pronounced signs. These signs are apparently due to loss of blood and to the toxic effect of the worms on the host, and partly to digestive disturbances resulting from improper functioning of the gizzard. Death is frequently the end result of heavy infection. Of the Canada geese examined from the Pea Island National Wildlife Refuge, North Carolina, there were those in which the occurrence of these parasites alone could account for weakness or ultimate death. Many of these birds, however, also harbored other parasites which obscured the picture. The parasite burden, added to adverse conditions of habitat and competition among winter populations of Canada geese, places *A. anseris* more in the category of a contributing factor to, than the primary cause of, the losses (Herman and Wehr, 1954).

◆ **PATHOLOGY.** In the Canada goose extensive pathologic changes were frequently observed in the gizzard. The mucosa was overlaid with a dark brown coating, which often appeared in patches. The surface of such an area is ruffed and filled with worms. Although some erosion of the gizzard lining was evident even in light infections, extensive and sometimes complete erosion was usually present in heavy infections.

◆ **DIAGNOSIS.** Laboratory diagnosis consists of detecting eggs in the feces. Due to the fact that only an expert or specialist can identify the eggs of *Amidostomum,* it is usually necessary to make a postmortem examination for the presence of this parasite in the gizzard.

◆ **TREATMENT AND CONTROL.** Ershov (1956) has recommended carbon tetrachloride for the control of amidostomiasis in domestic geese. The dosage is 1 ml for goslings 21 days old, 4 ml for birds 3 to 4 months old, and 5 to 10 ml for adults. The dehelminthization process is carried out in a confined area. After treatment the birds

are kept in the inclosed area for at least 3 days. The excreta is collected and sterilized or disposed of properly. Following this procedure the birds are transferred to clean quarters while the vacated quarters are thoroughly cleaned and sterilized.

SYNGAMIASIS

In the United States *Syngamus trachea* is the causative agent of this disease in chickens, turkeys, peacocks, and pheasants. It parasitizes the trachea, and less frequently the bronchi of these birds. Members of the genus *Cyathostoma,* which has recently been made a synonym of the genus *Syngamus* (Yamaguti, 1961), have been found in geese of this country. Ershov (1956) stated that syngamiasis of the domestic fowl in Russia is caused by *Syngamus skrjabinomorpha* and is limited to western Georgia.

Only in artificial rearing of pheasants is gapes a serious menace among these birds in the United States. The author has visited many pheasant-rearing farms in the last few years on which losses have occurred because of this disease.

The following discussion of gapes in wild birds is based on our knowledge of *S. trachea* infections in chickens and pheasants.

Syngamus trachea
(Montagu 1811) Chaplin 1925

SYNONYMS: *Fasciola trachea* Montagu 1811; *Syngamus furcatus* Theobold 1896; *S. mucronatus* Schlotthauber 1860; *S. primitivus* Molin 1861; *S. pugionatus* Schlotthauber 1860; *S. sclerostomum* Molin 1861; *S. trachealis* Siebold 1836; *Strongylus pictus* Creplin 1849.

◆ **DISTRIBUTION.** In Galliformes and Passeriformes, rarely in Anseriformes, Ardeiformes, Pelecaniformes, Otidiformes, Piciformes, and Cypseliformes. Europe;

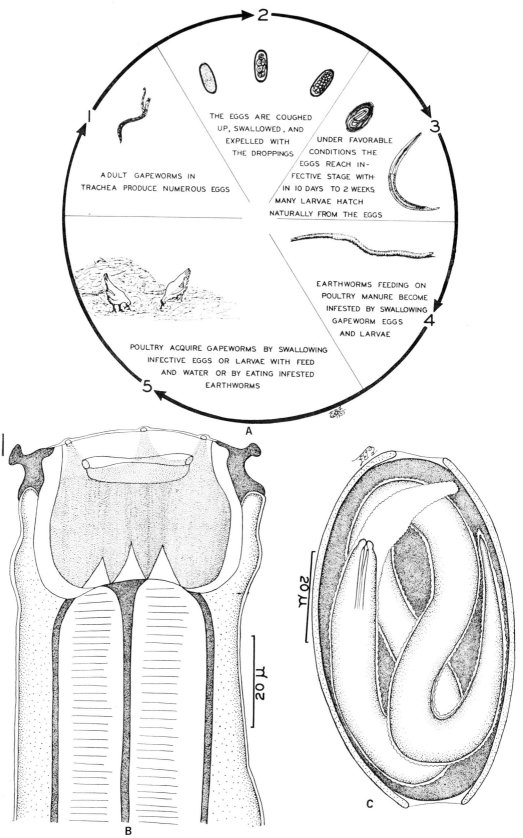

FIG. 20.6. *Syngamus trachea.* (A) Life cycle chart. (B) Anterior end, enlarged, showing teeth at base. (C) Egg, larvated. (After Wehr, 1937b.)

India; South America; North America; Australia; and Africa.

◆ **TRANSMISSION AND DEVELOP-MENT.** Eggs (Fig. 20.6C) deposited in the trachea by the female worms are carried into the mouth cavity by the ciliated epithelium and swallowed. They pass through the alimentary canal without undergoing any change and are passed to the exterior with the feces. These eggs become infective within approximately 2 weeks, the larvae undergoing two molts inside the eggshells. Infective larvae often hatch from the eggs before ingestion by an avian host.

The transfer of the infective eggs or larvae from one host to another is successfully accomplished experimentally, and presumably in nature as well, either indirectly by the ingestion of parasitized earthworms *(Eisenia foetida, Helodrilus caliginosus,* etc.) or other invertebrate hosts, or directly by swallowing the embryonated eggs or larvae with the food or water (Fig. 20.6A). Earthworms and other invertebrate hosts feed on the soil or organic material and ingest the eggs and larvae of *S. trachea* with their food. Madsen (1952) observed that those wild birds which fed extensively on earthworms had the greatest number of gapeworms.

By whatever method the embryonated eggs or free larvae are procured by the susceptible avian host, the larvae reach the lungs unchanged within a few hours after experimental infection. Within the lungs the larvae develop quite rapidly, molting twice again. They reach the 4th stage within 3 or 4 days and the immature adult stage by the 6th and 7th days. The immature male and female worms copulate in the lungs and then migrate to the trachea (Fig. 20.7). Some reach there by the 7th day. Within 12 to 14 days after inoculation, the larvae attain sexual maturity and eggs appear in the feces.

◆ **CLINICAL SIGNS.** Young birds are most seriously affected. The rapidly growing gapeworms obstruct the lumen of the trachea and cause the birds to suffocate and

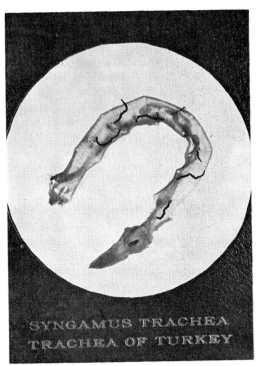

FIG. 20.7. *Syngamus trachea.* Trachea of infected bird, showing attached gapeworms.

die. The inability to breathe normally causes the bird to "gape," which is one of the early signs of the disease. Affected birds constantly emit short, whistling sounds and jerk their heads as if to free themselves of some obstruction that has become lodged in their throats.

For about 1 week after experimental infection the birds feed normally and appear healthy. Very soon after this they begin to refuse feed, cease moving, and usually assume a squatting position. The wings droop and the plumage appears ruffled. Heavily infected birds show extreme emaciation and difficult breathing. Death usually results.

◆ **PATHOLOGY.** The parasites attach themselves to the wall of the trachea. The head of the male penetrates deeply into the mucous membrane of the trachea and causes a reactive proliferation of the cartilaginous material, and a pea-sized nodule or lesion may develop at the site of the proliferation. A cross section of the nodule reveals the anterior end of the male. Because of this peculiar behavior, it is believed that the male worm remains permanently attached to the tracheal wall, while the female attaches and detaches several times for the purpose of securing sufficient blood for egg production. Blood clots and an abundance of mucus are usually found in the trachea.

◆ **DIAGNOSIS.** The detection of the eggs in the feces is one of the most reliable methods of determining the presence of gapeworms. The eggs are irregularly oval, approximately 90μ long and 50μ wide, and have "plugs" or opercula at the poles (Fig. 20.6C). They are thin-shelled and are usually in the four- or eight-celled cleavage stage at the time of deposition. Signs of gaping are also an indication of gapeworms. However, other diseases such as bronchitis and laryngotracheitis may also cause birds to gape, thus a postmortem examination of one or more affected birds is necessary. An inspection of the trachea of the live bird for the presence of the parasites may be made. The bird is held at eye level before a strong light, the beak is opened, and the head and neck are stretched so that the light passes through the trachea. The red parasites, if present in the upper half or two-thirds of the trachea, may be seen with the naked eye; however, if they are located farther down in the trachea or in the lungs, their presence will not be detected.

◆ **TREATMENT AND CONTROL.** Barium antimonyl tartrate successfully removes a high percentage of gapeworms when administered as an inhalant. For treatment with this drug, however, the birds must be confined in a tight box or enclosure of some sort. The drug, which is a fine powder and capable of remaining suspended in the air for some time, is introduced into the container by means of a dust gun or other suitable gadget at some distance above the heads of the birds. As the dust-laden air is breathed in by the infected birds, the fine particles of barium antimonyl tartrate apparently adhere to the moist surfaces of the worms and act as a contact poison.

Although barium antimonyl tartrate is effective in removing the gapeworm, it causes certain undesirable side effects such as eye irritation. The method of administration is also rather cumbersome and unsuitable for use in wild birds.

Recently several workers have reported thiabendazole to be effective against the gapeworm when administered in the feed to naturally and experimentally infected birds. The drug was added to the feed at levels of 0.05 to 0.5% for 4 to 14 days. In those experiments in which the birds were necropsied and worm counts made, the drug proved to be remarkably effective in controlling the parasite (Wehr and Hwang, 1967).

HETERAKIASIS

This disease is caused by members of the genus *Heterakis* of which *H. gallinarum*, *H. isolonche*, and *H. bonasae* are parasites of wild birds in the United States. They parasitize the cecum and sometimes the small intestine.

Heterakis gallinarum is also a well-known parasite of the domestic fowl and rarely of geese and ducks.

Heterakis gallinarum
(Schrank 1788) Madsen 1949

SYNONYMS: *Ascaris teres* Goeze 1782; *A. gallinarum* Schrank 1788; *A. gallinae* Gmelin 1790; *A. vesicularis* Froelich 1791; *Heterakis vesicularis* (Froelich 1791) of Dujardin 1845; *H. longicaudata* v. Linstow 1879; *H. papillosa* (Bloch 1782) of Railliet 1885; *H. parisi* Blanc 1913; *H. gallinae* (Gmelin 1790) of Freeborn 1923 et auctt. nov., *H. gallinae* (Gmelin 1790) of Madsen 1941; *H. gallinae* (Gmelin 1790) of Lopez-Neyra 1947.

◆ **DISTRIBUTION.** Galliformes: *Alectoris graeca chukar, A. graeca saxatilis, A. rufa, Bonasa umbellus, Centrocercus urophasianus, Colinus virginianus, Coturnix coturnix, Lagopus mutus helveticus, Lagopus scoticus, Lyrurus tetrix, Pedioecetes phasianellus, Perdix perdix, Phasianus colchicus, Tetrao urogallus, Tetrastes bonasia, Tympanuchus cupido,* also in *Otis tarda* and geese in captivity. Cosmopolitan. Most frequent of the nematodes in pheasant, partridge, and black grouse in Denmark (Madsen, 1952).

◆ **TRANSMISSION AND DEVELOPMENT.** The life history is direct. The eggs pass out with the feces in a noninfective stage. Two weeks or less, under favorable conditions of temperature and moisture, are required for the eggs to reach the 2nd or infective stage. When the latter are swallowed by a susceptible host, the infective larvae hatch from the eggs and develop to the adult worms in the ceca. Earthworms ingest the eggs of the cecal worm and may be the means of causing an infection.

Roberts (1937) stated that the egg hatches in the upper part of the intestine, and within 24 hours the majority of the larvae have reached the ceca. Uribe (1922) maintained that the larvae spend a short period (2 to 5 days) in the cecal mucosa, after which the entire life cycle is spent in the lumen of the cecum. At necropsy the majority of the worms are found in the tips or blind ends of the ceca.

◆ **CLINICAL SIGNS.** Ershov (1956) stated that the first clinical signs to appear in the infected fowl are gastric disturbances, anorexia, diarrhea, and emaciation. In young birds the disease causes stunting of growth and development, and in adult birds a cessation of egg laying. Although this parasite occurs in many species of wild birds, the infections are usually light and no severe signs of illness have been reported.

◆ **PATHOLOGY.** Cram (1931c) observed no pathologic changes in the ceca of quail as the direct result of the presence of *Heterakis gallinarum.* She did observe, however, cases of blackhead, and it is possible that the cecal worm may have been responsible for them.

In poultry this parasite has been associated with signs of malnutrition, unthriftiness, digestive disturbances, marked inflammation, and thickening of the cecal walls.

Clapham (1936) stated that *H. gallinarum* occurred frequently in the ceca of partridges, but the pathologic changes associated with its presence were insignificant from the point of view of disease.

The chief economic importance of the cecal worm lies in its role as a carrier of the blackhead organism, *Histomonas meleagridis.* Graybill and Smith (1920) demonstrated experimentally for the first time that blackhead may be produced in susceptible birds by feeding them embryonated eggs of *H. gallinarum.*

Cram (1931c) stated that *Heterakis bonasae* was collected from several quail which died of blackhead, so the possibility of this species serving in a manner similar to that of *H. gallinarum* in the transmission of blackhead should be kept in mind. However, in investigations of parasitic diseases of ruffed grouse by Allen and Gross (1926), *H. bonasae* was not found in birds which had died of blackhead, all cases of the latter disease being in birds raised in captivity, either with bantam hens or on ground where chickens had ranged.

◆ **DIAGNOSIS.** Diagnosis is based on clinical signs of the disease and on the presence of the parasites (Fig. 20.8) in infected birds. The detection of ascaridlike eggs in the feces is not proof that *Heterakis* worms are present, since the eggs of *Ascaridia* are similar to those of *Heterakis.*

◆ **TREATMENT AND CONTROL.** McCulloch and Nicholson (1940) reported that phenothiazine, either in single or repeated doses, was effective in the removal of the cecal worm from chickens. Doses ranging between 0.05 and 0.5 g were found to be

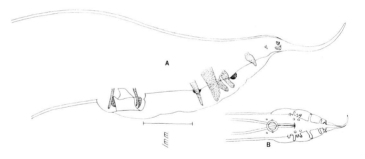

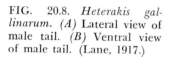

FIG. 20.8. *Heterakis gallinarum.* *(A)* Lateral view of male tail. *(B)* Ventral view of male tail. (Lane, 1917.)

the most satisfactory individual doses. These authors found repeated doses and the administration of the drug in individual capsules slightly more satisfactory than flock medication.

Sloan et al. (1954), Shumard and Eveleth (1955), Shumard (1956), and others found that piperazine possessed some anthelmintic action against *Heterakis.* Colglazier et al. (1960) found phenothiazine effective against *Heterakis,* but their data suggested that the dosage level necessary to achieve maximum efficacy against the cecal worm was probably above 0.5 g per bird. They also found that a single 1-g dose of a 7:1 mixture of phenothiazine and piperazine removed a high percentage of both *Ascaridia* and *Heterakis* in chickens.

Birds given phenothiazine should be confined, if possible, to the house. Feed should be withheld for a few hours or until the birds become quite hungry. After treatment the house should then be thoroughly dry-cleaned, and clean litter added. Birds given access to yards or the range during treatment should be removed to new soil not later than 1 week after treatment, and if possible the contaminated soil should be exposed to action of the sun and wind for several months.

ASCARIASIS

One of the best known ascarids of wild birds is *Ascaridia columbae* of the common pigeon *(Columba livia domestica).* This roundworm is a common parasite of the small intestine and is the only ascarid that occurs in this bird in the United States.

A large accumulation of adults, which frequently occurs in experimental infections, may cause obstruction and even rupture of the intestine.

The disease frequently causes death or stunting.

Ascaridia columbae
(Gmelin 1790) Travassos 1913

SYNONYMS: *Ascaris columbae* Gmelin 1790; *A. maculosa* Rudolphi 1802; *Heterakis maculosa* Schneider 1860; *H. columbae* (Gmelin 1790) Railliet 1885; *Fusaria maculosa* Zeder 1803.

◆ **DISTRIBUTION.** Columbiformes: *Columba arquatrix, C. domestica, C. d. laticauda, C. gutterosa, C. livia, C. picui, C. rosoria, C. speciosa, C. talpacoti, Crocopus phoenicopterus, Phlogoenas luzonica, Leucosarcia* sp., *Stictoenas arquatrix, Turtur sylvaticus.*

◆ **TRANSMISSION AND DEVELOPMENT.** The parasite has a direct life cycle. The pigeon or other susceptible host is infected by swallowing the infective eggs. Wehr and Hwang (1964) reported that the 2nd stage larva is the infective stage and the first molt takes place inside the egg. No further development of the larva takes place until after its ingestion by a susceptible host. Within the bird's body, 2nd stage larvae are encountered in the liver (Fig. 20.9) of nearly all infected birds. However, periodic examinations of larvae from the livers of infected birds, killed every few days for 50 days after infection, revealed

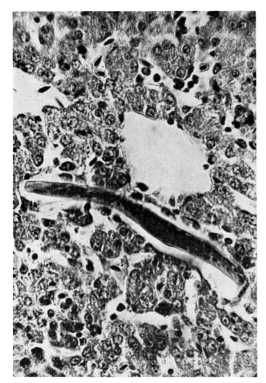

FIG. 20.9. *Ascaridia columbae*. Section, larva in liver tissue.

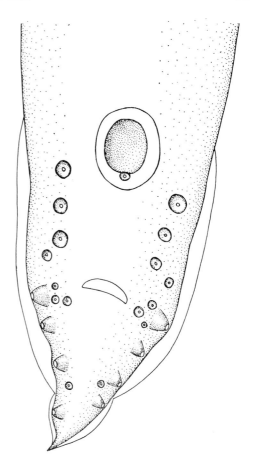

FIG. 20.10. *Ascaridia columbae*. Male tail. Ventral view.

that no development takes place in the liver. All stages of development of the parasite from 2nd stage larvae to mature forms were observed by these authors within the small intestine. Therefore, a path of migration through the liver is improbable and certainly not essential for the completion of development. The molt to the 3rd stage occurs between the 3rd and 6th days after infection, to the 4th stage between the 11th and 15th days, and to the 5th stage (Fig. 20.10) between the 16th and 19th days. Eggs appear in the feces of the avian host 37 to 42 days after infection (Wehr and Hwang, 1964).

A true invasion of the intestinal wall by the larvae has not been observed and is apparently not an essential part of the life cycle.

◆ **CLINICAL SIGNS.** Diseased birds manifest diarrhea or constipation, lethargy, and exhaustion. Anemia of the mucosal membranes, diminution of appetite, and emaciation have been observed. Heavily infected birds often die.

◆ **PATHOLOGY.** Through destruction of the mucosa by the worms, the wall of the intestine becomes thin and transparent. In heavily infected birds, the worms are distinctly visible through the intestinal wall. With a large accumulation of worms, which often occurs in experimental infections, the intestine becomes greatly distended and feels hard and solid to the touch. The author has necropsied experimentally infected birds in which the intestine was greatly distended and almost completely filled with immature and mature worms. It was indeed puzzling how any

FIG. 20.11. *Ascaridia colum-bae.* Spots on liver caused by larval penetration.

solid food could get through the alimentary tract.

Wehr and Shalkop (1963) observed numerous microscopic, pinpoint-sized lesions (Fig. 20.11) on the surface of the liver of experimentally infected pigeons. Microscopic sections of these lesions revealed larvae of *A. columbae.* A histopathologic study of these lesions also revealed that the progress of these granulomatous lesions coincided with degenerative changes in invading larvae. Little or no evidence of inflammatory reaction was visible in lesions containing viable larvae. It was only when the parasites began to degenerate that a pronounced eosinophilic reaction was observed. The eosinophils surrounded and became intimately associated with the degenerating parasite. The final stage was the development of foreign body giant cells.

◆ **DIAGNOSIS.** The presence of gravid females may be determined by an examination of the feces for eggs. Since this is the only species of *Ascaridia* known to occur in the pigeon, the presence of ascarid eggs in the feces would immediately suggest this worm.

◆ **TREATMENT AND CONTROL.** The piperazine compounds are excellent drugs for the removal of *Ascaridia galli* of chick-

ens. Attempts to remove *A. columbae* with these compounds have been disappointing. The results of unpublished data indicate that thiabendazole-medicated mash possesses remarkable anthelmintic properties against *A. columbae* of the pigeon. The medicated mash contains 0.5% thiabendazole and is fed continuously for 7 to 13 days. Earlier tests, using this same drug against unrelated parasites, indicate that thiabendazole may be used in the feed at a lower percentage and with the same results.

Periodic sterilization of the premises and equipment is essential in case of an outbreak.

SUBULURIASIS

Nematodes collected by Dikmans from the cecum of a turkey in Puerto Rico were identified by Cram as *Subulura brumpti.* This was the first report of a species of *Subulura* from birds in North America (Cram, 1926a). Also Cram (1927a) reported for the first time *Subulura strongylina* from chickens in North America (Puerto Rico). The latter species has subsequently been found in the bobwhite quail in Georgia and North Carolina (Cram, 1931c). The life history of this species, as well as most of the other species of the genus, is not known, but is presumed to involve an

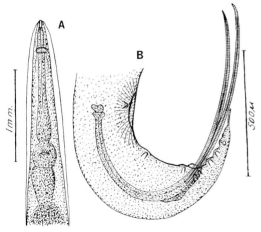

FIG. 20.12. *Subulura brumpti.* *(A)* Anterior end. *(B)* Lateral view, male tail. (After Lopez-Neyra, 1922.)

intermediate host as does *S. brumpti.*

Several other species of the genus *Subulura* have been reported from wild birds, but nothing is known about them.

Subulura brumpti (Lopez-Neyra 1922)
Cram 1926 (Fig. 20.12)

SYNONYMS: *Allodapa brumpti* Lopez-Neyra 1922; *A. suctoria* (Molin 1860) Seurat 1914; *Heterakis suctoria* Molin 1860; *Subulura suctoria* (Molin 1860) Railliet and Henry 1914.

◆ **DISTRIBUTION.** *Alectoris graeca, Anas* sp., *Colinus virginianus, Gallus gallus, Meleagris gallopavo, Numida* sp., *Perdix perdix.* Europe; Sudan; Palestine; Cyprus; Cuba; Puerto Rico; Panama; North America; Hawaii; Africa.

◆ **TRANSMISSION AND DEVELOPMENT.** Eggs pass from the definitive host in cecal droppings. At this time they contain embryos which are infective to the intermediate host. Beetles *(Alphitobius disperinus, Tribolium castaneum, Dermestes vulpinus, Gonocephalum seriatum, Ammorphorus insularis)*, grasshoppers *(Conocephalus saltator, Oxya chinensis)*, and earwig *(Euborella annulipes)* have been reported as intermediate hosts. When the eggs are ingested by a susceptible intermediate host, the larvae hatch in 4 to 5 hours, penetrate the intestinal wall, and enter the body cavity where they develop. The first larval molt occurs on the 4th or 5th day after infection, and by the 7th or 8th day the larva encapsulates on the intestinal wall. The molt to the 2nd stage occurs between the 13th and 15th days after infection and shortly thereafter the larva contracts and coils up within the capsule. It is now in the 3rd or infective stage. When the definitive host swallows an infected intermediate host, the larvae migrate to the cecum and develop to the 4th stage within about 2 weeks. The final molt takes place on about the 18th day after infection. The young adults continue to grow and develop, and eggs appear in the cecal droppings of the infected chickens about 6 weeks after infection (Cuckler and Alicata, 1944).

Abdou and Selim (1957) found beetles *(Ocnera hispida* and *Blaps polycresta)* were intermediate hosts of *"Subulura suctoria"* in Egypt.

◆ **PATHOLOGY.** Cuckler and Alicata (1944) reported that sections of the cecum showed no evidence of larval penetration or extensive inflammatory reactions.

Ortlepp (1937) considered *Subulura suctoria* (Molin 1860), *Subulura differens* (Sonsino 1890), and *Subulura brumpti* (Lopez-Neyra 1922) to be conspecific. *Subulura differens* is reported from *Francolinus bicalcaratus, Perdix perdix canescens, Alectoris graeca, Centropus phasianus,* and *Coturnix coturnix.*

Subulura bolivaria (Lopez-Neyra 1922)
Lopez-Neyra 1934

SYNONYM: *Allodapa bolivari* Lopez-Neyra 1922.

◆ **DISTRIBUTION.** *Athene noctua.* Spain.

◆ **TRANSMISSION AND DEVELOP-
MENT.** According to Chabaud (1954), the
life cycle involves an intermediate host.
The larvae in intermediate hosts are free
in large spherical capsules, are presumably
in connective tissue, and are about 250μ in
width. The body is extremely curved and
contracted dorsally so that the head comes
in contact with the tail, making the diameter of the middle portion much greater.
This contraction does not change when
one places the larva in water or heats it
slightly. The description of this larva corresponds closely with the description of the
3rd stage larva of *S. brumpti* as given by
Alicata (1939). The only difference detected between the two larvae is the position of the nerve ring. In *S. bolivari*, it is
on the same level as the excretory pore, and
in *S. brumpti*, it is behind the excretory
pore (Chabaud, 1954).

Gonocephalum rusticum and *Blaps
pinguis* were experimentally infected with
larvae of *S. bolivari*. Seventeen days after
infection, these beetles yielded larvae enclosed in large capsules attached to the intestinal wall. The avian host apparently
becomes infected by swallowing the intermediate hosts (beetles) or some other invertebrates that serve as intermediate hosts
in nature.

HETEROCHEILIASIS

The members of the genera *Contracaecum* and *Porrocaecum* are common parasites of fish-eating vertebrates. The larval
forms lack many of the adult features, and
for this reason are difficult to identify.
They have been observed in the musculature, mesentery, liver, and body cavity of
many species of fish. Therefore, both larvae and adults may be assumed to be cosmopolitan in distribution.

The larvae are able to survive suitable
conditions for long periods of time. Van
Thiel et al. (1960) have recently reported
that man can become infected by eating
slightly salted or marinated herring.

Contracaecum spiculigerum
(Rudolphi 1809) Railliet and Henry 1912

SYNONYMS: *Ascaris spiculigera* Rud. 1809; *Ascaris variegata* Rud. 1809; Hart-
wich (1964) gives to this species a
new name. *Contracaecum rudolphi.*

◆ **DISTRIBUTION.** *Alca torda, Anas
elangula, Carbo brasiliensis, C. cormora-
nus, C. cristatus, C. dilophus, C. graculus,
C. pygmaeus.*

◆ **TRANSMISSION AND DEVELOP-
MENT.** This parasite has an indirect life
cycle. Huizinga (1965) stated that the eggs
pass in the bird's feces and develop to free-
living, 2nd stage larvae in about 7 days at
21° to 24° C in lake or sea water. The 1st
stage cuticular sheath is retained by the
free-living larvae which attach to the substrate and move actively. Experimental
evidence shows that the copepod (*Cyclops
vernalis*) feeds readily on larvae of *C. spiculigerum*. The larvae remain in the intestine for only a few minutes (about 15
minutes) where the 1st stage sheath is shed.
After 30 minutes the 2nd stage larvae penetrate the intestinal wall into the hemocoel
(body cavity). The larvae remain alive and
active within the copepod for several
months, and indications are that little
growth takes place within this invertebrate.
It is likely that a species of copepod serves
as intermediate or transport host in nature.
Young guppies ingest infected copepods,
after which the larvae are freed in the intestine. Within an hour, they penetrate the
intestinal wall and reach the coelomic
cavity where they encyst on the mesentery.
The larvae grow rapidly within the fish
and by the 10th day they increase to ten
times in size. The larvae remain encysted
on the mesentery and nutrition is apparently absorbed from the host through the
cyst wall. In most cases, however, the
larvae, when fed to guppies, do not shed
their sheaths, but pass unchanged and un-
digested through the intestine. Fish ingest
the larvae directly (Thomas, 1937a, 1937b;

1940). The 3rd stage larvae penetrate the intestinal wall of the fish and enter the body cavity where they encyst. Within the cyst, the larva increases in size, develops, and remains alive for an indeterminate length of time. The bird acquires its infection by ingesting an infected fish. The larval stages develop in a wide variety of marine and freshwater fishes. In other words, three hosts may be involved in the life history of *C. spiculigerum*—that is, (1) copepod, (2) plankton-eating fish, and (3) piscivorous bird.

The life cycles of other species of the genus *Contracaecum* of birds are apparently not well elucidated. Several species of fishes have been incriminated as intermediate hosts of *C. microcephalum*, but it is not known whether larvae found in these fish belong to this species. Dubinin contends that *Ascaris squalii* Linstow from *Leuciscus schmidtii* is a stage in the life cycle of *C. microcephalum*. He obtained adults of *C. microcephalum* from the heron as a result of feeding larvae from *Alburnus alburnus* and *Scardinius erythropthalmus*.

◆ **CLINICAL SIGNS.** Unreported.

◆ **PATHOLOGY.** In the black-crowned night heron *(Nycticorax nycticorax)*, the American merganser *(Mergus americanus)*, and the brown pelican *(Pelecanus occidentalis)*, the worms were found within the lumen of the proventriculus or were burrowing within the mucosa. Frequently they were attached to the wall of the proventriculus by means of their lips, and pinpoint hemorrhages were seen in the mucosa. Mechanical damage and denudation of mucosal epithelium were observed at points where nematodes had tunneled part way through the mucosa. The worms also had burrowed into and were feeding upon flesh of the ingested fish in the proventriculus.

Larval *C. spiculigerum* have been given to guinea pigs, and the damage done by the actively migrating larvae was mechanical. Macroscopically, inflammation and

hemorrhages were seen, but microscopically, there was the usual infiltration of leukocytes and macrophages surrounding the larvae (Myers, 1963).

◆ **TREATMENT AND CONTROL.** Nothing is known about the control of this parasite in birds. Thorough cooking of fish before eating kills the larvae and renders the meat fit for human consumption.

Porrocaecum ensicaudatum
(Zeder 1800)

SYNONYMS: *Fusaria ensicaudata* Zeder 1800; *Fusaria crenata* Zeder 1800; *Ascaria ensicaudata* (Zeder 1800) Rudolphi 1809; *Ascaria crenata* (Zeder 1800) Rud. 1809.

◆ **DISTRIBUTION.** *Turdus merula, T. iliacus, T. pilaris, T. philomelos, T. torquatus, T. viscivorus, T. musicus, T. musicus coburni, T. magellanicus, Sturnus vulgaris, Pastor roseus, Mimus polyglottus, Molothrus ater, Quiscalus quiscalus, Motacilla alba, Charadrius dubuis.* Europe; North America.

◆ **TRANSMISSION AND DEVELOPMENT.** Levin (1957) experimentally infected *Lumbricus terrestris* and *Octolasium lacteum* by feeding the infective eggs of *P. ensicaudatum*. The larvae were found in the ventral blood vessel and hearts of these invertebrates. He fed parasitized *Lumbricus* to chickens, robins, and starlings and observed within an hour after ingestion that the larvae had penetrated the horny lining of the gizzard, had exsheathed between the horny lining and the muscle wall of the gizzard, had migrated to the duodenum, and had penetrated the wall. The molt to the 3rd stage took place in the intestinal tissue. Subsequent growth took place after the larvae emerged from the intestinal wall.

Osche (1959) stated that *P. ensicaudatum* lived as 1st to 3rd stage larvae in the blood vessels of *Lumbricus* and penetrated through the horny lining of the muscular stomach (gizzard) after the invasion of the definitive host. They then grew as 4th stage larvae in the small intestine, where a histotropic phase was interpolated, and reached maturity after a final molt.

According to Mozgovi (1952) and Hartwich (1959), *Porrocaecum crassum* and *P. semiteres* apparently have life cycles similar to that of *P. ensicaudatum*. Other species, such as *P. angusticolle* and *P. depressum*, possibly utilize insectivores or rodents as intermediate hosts. The larvae lie in thin, connective tissue capsules in the outer wall of the intestine or in the mesentery of the intermediate host. However, for many *Porrocaecum* species for which a vertebrate has been observed as the intermediate host, the possibility of an earlier developmental stage in an invertebrate cannot be excluded (Osche, 1958). For example, the heron parasite *(Porrocaecum ardae)*, also found in the flamingo, has been listed as having fish as intermediate hosts. The heron, which eats mainly crustacea, has been infected by feeding it parasitized *Lumbricus*. *Porrocaecum depressum* occurs in birds of prey and is reported to have insectivores as intermediate hosts. These birds have been infected by feeding parasitized *Lumbricus* (Osche, 1958).

◆ **CLINICAL SIGNS.** Subnormal weight, loss of plumage, reluctance to move, listlessness, frequent vomiting and foamy discharges from the nose, and increased feeding have been reported.

◆ **PATHOLOGY.** In this infection the hemoglobin content was below normal level. The number of red blood cells dropped as much as 50% accelerated blood sedimentation rate. There was increased maximal and minimal osmotic resistance of erythrocytes, decreased hemocytolic index (ratio of lymphocytes to segmented forms), and morphologic changes in the cells. The pernicious effects of infection in ducks were expressed in quantitative and qualitative changes in the blood, indicating inhibition of the hemopoietic organs, with marked

anemia. The hemopoietic index in diseased ducks showed that invasions of worms inhibited both the hemopoietic organs and the central nervous system (Ryzhkova, 1953).

CHEILOSPIRURIASIS

This disease is caused by species of the genus *Cheilospirura* which normally occur beneath the horny lining of the gizzard, usually in the cardiac and/or the pyloric regions where the lining is soft and pliable.

Only 4 species of the genus *Cheilospirura*—namely, *C. hamulosa* (Diesing 1851), *C. spinosa* Cram 1927, *C. cyanocitta* Boyd 1956, and *C. centrocerci* Simons 1939—occur in North American birds. Yamaguti (1962) includes the 4 above-mentioned species in the genus *Acuaria* Bremser 1811.

Cheilospirura hamulosa is quite harmful to domestic birds, often in heavy infections causing the wall of the gizzard to be weakened to such an extent that it ruptures.

Cheilospirura spinosa Cram 1927

◆ **DISTRIBUTION.** Galliformes: *Bonasa umbellus, Centrocercus urophasianus* (see Wehr, 1933), *Colinus virginianus, Pedioecetus phasianellus camprestris* (see Boughton, 1937). Cram suggested that the range of this parasite in quail corresponds to the range of the ruffed grouse and that it has spread from grouse to quail.

◆ **TRANSMISSION AND DEVELOPMENT.** Cram (1931a) found that the grasshopper *(Melanoplus femurrubrum)* served experimentally as an intermediate host. Larvae encysted in the muscles of the legs and in the inner surface of the body wall. Quail were infected by feeding them grasshoppers with encysted larvae.

◆ **PATHOLOGY.** Allen and Gross (1926) reported that in ruffed grouse the parasite caused little damage, although if present in large numbers, the wall of the gizzard

adult; the sexes are distinguishable by the form of the caudal point which is much finer in the male.

The infective larva is capable of reencapsulating in different vertebrates (tadpoles of *Discoglossus pictus,* and in Cyprinidae related to *Barbus*).

Bubulcus ibis were experimentally infected by feeding them ostracods. At necropsy of an infected bird, young adults as well as mature adults, which correspond to an infection of 15 days, and 4th stage larvae, which correspond to an infection of 6 days, were found under the horny lining of the gizzard. The third molt takes place before the 6th day and the fourth molt before the 15th day, since at this date the females have already matured.

The larvae of the 4th stage have four slender, nonspinous, nonrecurrent cephalic cordons which anastomose on lateral surfaces. There are large tricuspid deirids and bicuspid postdeirids. The female genital apparatus, which is monodelphic (the vulva is situated preanally), already has the characteristics of the adult.

The life cycle is remarkable for its extreme rapidity. The larvae reach the infective stage within 13 days in the intermediate host, and in 15 days in the final host the worms are mature.

CYRNIASIS

One of the causative agents of this disease, *Cyrnea colini,* is common in the bobwhite quail, turkey, prairie chicken, and sharp-tailed grouse of the United States. This species has not been reported elsewhere.

The nematode localizes in the wall of the proventriculus, usually at its junction with the gizzard.

Cyrnea colini Cram 1927 (Fig. 20.14)

SYNONYM: *Seurocyrnea colini* Strand 1929.

◆ **DISTRIBUTION.** *Colinus virginianus, Meleagris gallopavo, Pedioecetus phasianel-* *lus, Tympanuchus americanus.* The United States.

◆ **TRANSMISSION AND DEVELOP-MENT.** The larvae hatch in the digestive tract of the cockroach *(Blatella germanica)* and develop in the body cavity. They do not appear to encyst but develop to the 3rd stage larvae among the tissues, from which they quickly emerge when the cockroach is dissected. These larvae are 3.2 to 3.3 mm long. The head end is bluntly rounded and without lips, but the structure underlying the cuticle suggests the primordia of the lips. The larvae are apparently fully grown at the end of 18 days, as they do not change in size or appearance between the 18th and 45th days. However it is only at the end of the 45th day that their infectivity for the final host has been tested. The definitive host becomes infected by ingesting infected cockroaches. Two more molts take place inside the definitive host. Specimens collected from quail at the end of 13 days were composed of 4th stage larvae and immature adults; those collected from this same host 41 days after experimental feeding had apparently completed their development. The eggs of the female were embryonated and were shown to be infective by experimental feeding to cockroaches (Cram, 1931a).

◆ **PATHOLOGY.** No pathologic conditions which could be attributed definitely to this species could be found, although occasionally slight hemorrhagic areas which may have resulted from the presence of this parasite were noted (Cram, 1931a).

◆ **PREVENTION.** Methods which prevent quail from ingesting the intermediate hosts will be effective in eliminating infections with this parasite (for example, prompt removal of droppings or the raising of quail on wire-bottomed runs).

This is the only species of the genus whose life cycle has been elucidated.

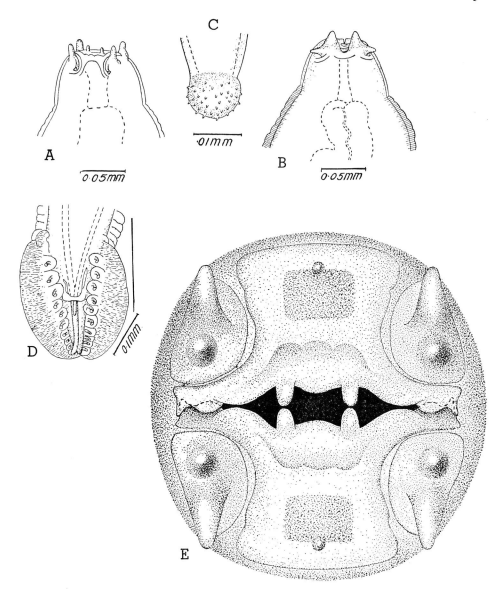

FIG. 20.14. *Cyrnea colini.* *(A)* Head, oblique lateral view. *(B)* Head, ventral view. *(C)* Tail of third-stage larva. *(D)* Male tail. *(E)* Head. En face view, semidiagrammatic. (After Cram, 1927.)

SICARIASIS

Sicarius dipterum is a parasite of the small intestine of the hoopoe. Although this parasite has been placed in the subfamily Habronematinae, the location of the parasite in the small intestine of its avian host is puzzling in that all or nearly all other species of this subfamily have been collected from the proventriculus or stomach.

Sicarius dipterum (Popova 1927) Li 1934

SYNONYM: *Habronema dipterum* Popova 1927.

◆ **DISTRIBUTION.** *Upupa epops.* Russia; Turkestan; and North China.

◆ **TRANSMISSION AND DEVELOPMENT.** The larvae penetrate rapidly into the body cavity of coleopterans (for example, *Asida sericea, A. jurinei* var. *marmottani, Phylan abbreviatus,* and *Tentyria mucronata*) and grow slowly. The first molt occurs about the 20th day after experimental infection, and the immature 2nd stage larva measures about 480μ. The larva then triples its length in 10 days and ultimately attains a length of 1,500μ in 31 days. The second molt takes place about this time and the larva of the 3rd stage does not undergo additional growth while in the insect. The larva may remain free in the body cavity for a long time. It is only toward the end of the 2nd stage that one observes some larvae enclosed in small capsules with thin walls, situated generally against the intestine.

About 10 larvae removed 41 days after infection were fed to an adult cock, but worms were not recovered from the animal at autopsy (Chabaud, 1954).

DISPHARYNXIASIS

The spiral stomach worm (*Dispharynx nasuta*) occurs in the glandular stomach of its host and may be the cause of marked pathologic changes. It has been considered the most important helminth parasite of the ruffed grouse by Goble and Kutz (1945b) and Madsen (1952). The incidence in young birds is significantly greater than in adults. Bump (1935) stated that this worm was the most important parasite recovered from wild game birds in New York, and Allen (1925) expressed the belief that this worm was the chief cause of the grouse disease in northeastern United States. Heavy infections of this parasite resulted in the death of many pigeons in southern United States (Cram, 1928; Hwang et al., 1961).

Dispharynx nasuta (Rudolphi 1819)

SYNONYMS: *Spiroptera nasuta* Rudolphi 1819; *Dispharagus spiralis* Molin 1858; *Acuaria spiralis* (Molin 1858) Rail-

liet, Henry, and Sisoff 1912; *Dispharagus nasutus* (Rud. 1819) Dujardin 1844; *Filaria nasuta* (Rud. 1819) Schneider 1866; *Dispharagus tentaculatus* Colucci 1893; *Dispharagus spiralis columbae* Bridre 1910; *Acuaria nasuta* (Rud. 1819) Railliet, Henry, and Sisoff 1912; *Cheilospirura nasuta* (Rud. 1819) Ransom 1916; *Dispharynx stonae* Harwood 1933.

◆ **DISTRIBUTION.** Passeriformes: *Coracias garrula, Corvus brachyrhynchos, Dumetella carolensis, Molothrus ater, Passer domesticus, Quiscalis versicolor, Sialia sialis, Sturnus vulgaris, Thryothorus ludovicianus, Turdus migratorius.* Galliformes: *Alectoris barbara, Bonasa umbellus, Chrysolophus pictus, Colinus virginianus, Gallus gallus, Numida meleagris, Meleagris gallopavo, Pavo cristatus, Perdix perdix, Phasianus colchicus.* Columbiformes: *Columba livia.* Europe (Austria, France, Italy, Spain, Denmark); Asia (Russian Turkestan, Uzbekistan, Kazakhstan); Africa (Tunisia, Algeria, Belgian Congo); South America (Brazil); Australia; North America (United States, Canada); Guam; Puerto Rico.

◆ **TRANSMISSION AND DEVELOPMENT.** *Dispharynx nasuta* requires an intermediate host for its development. The pill bug (*Armadillidium vulgare*) and the sow bug (*Porcellia scaber*) served as intermediate hosts in experimental infections by Cram (1931a). Infective or 3rd stage larvae recovered from these two species of isopods were fed to young bobwhite quail and pigeons (*Columba livia domestica*), and fully developed worms were recovered from these birds about 27 days later. The eggs were embryonated at the time of deposition. Within 4 days after the above isopods ingested the embryonated eggs, larvae were found among tissues of the body cavity. Development of larvae to the infective stage in the intermediate host is completed within 1 month. No further development takes place until the infected intermediate host is swallowed by a susceptible bird. The larvae reach the adult stage and the female worms begin to deposit embryonated eggs 1 month after infection.

◆ **CLINICAL SIGNS.** According to Goble and Kutz (1945b) and Madsen (1952), *D. nasuta*, in areas where it occurs, has been found in approximately one-third of the ruffed grouse (birds-of-the-year) examined during the fall and winter months. The incidence in juvenile birds is significantly greater than in adults. Madsen (1941) observed that the parasite was encountered most often in largest numbers in young partridges and only in chicks of pheasants. Infected birds become droopy and usually die as a result of the infection.

◆ **PATHOLOGY.** The parasite occasionally lies free on the inner surface of the proventriculus, but more often attaches by the head end to mucous and epithelial cells (Fig. 20.15). The formation of ulcers is often observed in the proventriculi of infected birds. In heavy infections the wall of the proventriculus is tremendously thickened and macerated as to occlude entirely the opening and prevent the passage of food. Tissue layers are indistinguishable, and the parasites become almost completely concealed beneath the proliferating tissue.

A histopathologic study of a severe case of proventriculitis in the pigeon due to this nematode showed that "the sections of worms were surrounded by a myxomatous-like exudate that was essentially acellular. The exudate was probably of mucous origin intermixed with strands of fibrous tissue" (Hwang et al., 1961). Marked vesicular congestion was occasionally noted. Briefly, the infected proventriculi showed primarily a catarrhal type of inflammation characterized by epithelial desquamation, papillary proliferation, hypersecretion of mucus, congestion, and secondary bacterial invasion of the superficial mucosa.

◆ **DIAGNOSIS.** The detection of eggs in the feces indicates that the worms are present. The eggs are embryonated, small,

thick-shelled, and about 40μ by 20μ in size. The identification of the species involved and the exact location of the parasite is only possible by necropsy. The worms are less than one-half inch in length, and on microscopic examination have four wavy cuticular bands originating at the base of the lips and extending for a short distance posteriorly, then turning forward for a short distance (Fig. 20.16). The body is usually coiled or rolled in a spiral shape.

◆ **TREATMENT AND CONTROL.** Nothing is known.

ECHINURIASIS

Species of the genus *Echinuria*, causative agents of the disease known as echinuriasis, form tumorlike or ulcerlike growths in the wall of the proventriculus. This is particularly true of *E. uncinata*. The worms burrow deeply into the mucosa of the proventriculus with their anterior ends. A large number of specimens of *E. uncinata* were collected by the writer from nodules near the union of the proventriculus and the ventriculus of a mallard duck received from the National Zoological Park, Washington, D.C.

Echinuria uncinata (Rudolphi 1819)
Soloviev 1912 (Fig. 20.17)

SYNONYMS: *Spiroptera uncinata* Rudolphi 1819; *Dispharagus uncinatus* (Rud. 1819) Railliet 1893; *Acuaria (Hamannia) uncinata* (Rud. 1819) Railliet, Henry, and Sisoff 1912; *Hamannia uncinata* (Rud. 1819) Stiles and Hassall 1912; *Echinuria jugadornata* Soloviev 1912.

◆ **DISTRIBUTION.** *Anas boschas domestica, A. penelope, A. rubripes, Anser cinereus domesticus, Cynus olor domesticus, Mareca americana, Nettion carolinensis.* Europe; Africa; North America; Afghanistan; India.

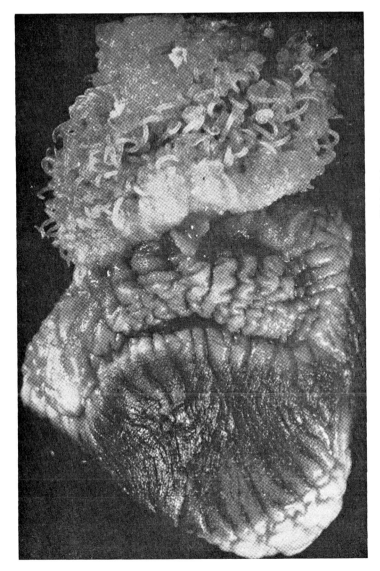

FIG. 20.15. *Dispharynx nasuta.* Proventriculus showing parasites in situ. (Hwang et al., 1961.)

♦ **TRANSMISSION AND DEVELOPMENT.** The mature female worm deposits well-developed embryonated eggs which pass to the exterior with the feces. If the excrement of the infected bird is dropped in water where the crustacean, *Daphnia pulex,* abounds, the eggs are ingested by these crustaceans. The larvae hatch in the intestine, burrow through the intestinal wall, and enter the body cavity. Here they continue their development and ultimately reach a length of approximately 2 mm (Hamann, 1893). At this time they are presumably in the 3rd stage of development. The definitive host is infected by ingesting infected *Daphnia pulex.* The larvae are freed as the *Daphnia* are ingested and the young worms burrow into the walls of the esophagus and proventriculus, leaving their tail ends protruding into the lumen or cavity of this organ. Mating takes place and the females lay thousands of eggs which pass out with the droppings.

♦ **PATHOLOGY.** This parasite has been reported to have caused deaths among

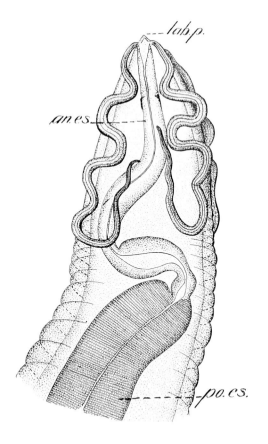

FIG. 20.16. *Dispharynx nasuta.* Anterior end, showing cordons, labial papillae (lab.p.), anterior esophagus (an.es.), and posterior esophagus (po.es.).

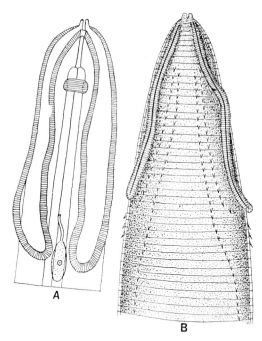

FIG. 20.17. *Echinuria uncinata.* (*A*) Head end, ventral view. (Seurat, 1919.) (*B*) Head end, dorsal view. (Schneider, 1866.)

ducks, especially young birds (Hamann, 1893). The disease usually makes its appearance in midsummer when the weather is warm. Young birds of the late hatches suffer the most, while the breeding stock and the first hatches in the spring are rarely severely affected. Affected birds at first appear listless and take little food. Ultimately they become emaciated and may reject food completely. Death from starvation may result.

Postmortem examinations of infected birds show that the worms form tumors or nodules in the affected areas. Sometimes the tissue reaction to the presence of the young adult worms is so severe that masses of tissue are built up. The result is a fibrous tumor which may grow until the passage through the stomach is blocked and the bird starves to death.

◆ **PREVENTION.** Young ducks in contaminated areas must be protected from infection by withholding them from entering ponds known to contain the intermediate host. Likewise old ducks must not be permitted to use ponds containing *Daphnia pulex.* It is assumed that if such a procedure is followed during the summer months little trouble from this parasite will be encountered (Hamann, 1893).

TETRAMERIASIS

Nematodes of the genera *Tetrameres* and *Microtetrameres* are noted for their extreme sexual dimorphism. The male is a small white worm of filiform appearance, with or without spines along the median

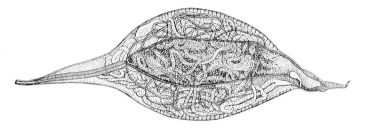

FIG. 20.18. *Tetrameres confusa.* Female. (After Travassos, 1919.)

and lateral lines. The body of the female is technically described as globular and fusiform *(Tetrameres)* (Fig. 20.18), or with the long axis spirally coiled *(Microtetrameres)* (Fig. 20.19 B and C). The bulk of the body is swollen into a globe mostly occupied by the uterus, which contains an enormous number of thin-shelled eggs in various stages of development. However, it tapers to a point at each end, and is termed fusiform (Fig. 20.19 A and D).

These worms are found in the proventriculus of birds.

Tetrameres crami Swales 1933

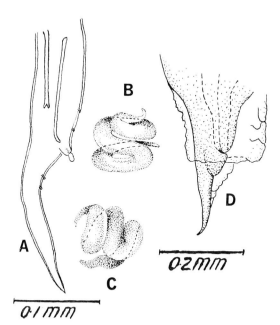

FIG. 20.19. *Microtetrameres helix.* (A) Male tail, lateral view. (B) and (C) Female. (D) Female tail. (Cram, 1927.)

SYNONYM: *Tropisurus crami* (Swales 1933) Yamaguti 1961.

◆ **DISTRIBUTION.** *Anas boschas domesticus, A. platyrhynchos, A. rubripes, Chaulelasmus streperus, Dafila acuta, Glaucionetta clangula, Mareca americana, Nettion carolensis, Nyroca marila, N. affinis, Querquedula discors, Spatula clypeata.* North America.

◆ **TRANSMISSION AND DEVELOPMENT.** The eggs contain fully developed embryos when laid and the embryos are infective to the intermediate host. These ova are readily ingested by the amphipods *Gammarus fasciatus* and *Hyalella knickerbockeri.* The larvae enter the intestine, penetrate the intestinal wall, and enter the body cavity. They molt twice within the body cavity, forming the 3rd stage larvae. It is the general rule (Swales, 1936) for the 2nd stage larvae to encyst, but occasionally in experimentally infected amphipods a molt to the 3rd stage prior to encystment occurs. Usually the second molt occurs after the encystment of the 2nd stage larvae. These latter migrate to various parts of the body and encyst commonly in the coxae, or inner surface of the dorsal shield, and occasionally in the leg muscles. The encysted larvae grow rapidly but do not molt. Experimental evidence (Swales, 1936) seems to indicate that the 3rd stage larvae require some time for growth in their encysted state before becoming infective. Each larva has a rounded tail adorned with a circle of nine spines and other spines in the center of this ring. Infection of the definitive host occurs when the intermediate host containing 3rd stage larvae is ingested. The larvae escape from the crustacean in the crop and make their way to the proventriculus. The third molt takes place and the 4th stage larvae are found in the crypts of Lieberkuehn. While a fourth molt is probable, it has not been observed (Swales, 1936; Olsen, 1962). Only adult males and 3rd stage larvae have been found in the mucus of the proventriculus; apparently the 4th larval stage exists entirely in the crypts and only the adult males return to the lumen.

The female of *T. americana,* a closely related species, occurs in the glands of the glandular stomach of chickens, ducks, and bobwhite quail. It utilizes grasshoppers (*Melanoplus femurrubrum, M. differentialis, Scyllina cyanips*) and the cockroach (*Blatella germanica*) as intermediate hosts. The males are seldom observed elsewhere than on the surface of the mucosa of the proventriculus. However the males of some of the species of *Tetrameres* occurring in wild birds have been found with the females in the same glands (Wehr, 1934a). When the males of *Tetrameres* spp. enter the glands of the proventriculus, they apparently do so only long enough to mate with the females.

Tetrameres fissispina, another closely related species known as the globular stomach worm of poultry and wild birds, has a life cycle similar to *T. crami* and *T. americana.* Investigations by various authors have incriminated two crustaceans (*Grammarus pulex* and *Daphnia pulex*), four species of grasshoppers (*Pternoscirta sauteri, Heteropternis respondens, Gastrimargus transversus,* and *Atractomorpha bedelli*), two species of cockroaches (*Periplaneta americana* and *P. australasiae*), and two species of earthworms (*Perichaeta candida* and *Allolobophora foetida*) as intermediate hosts of *T. fissispina.*

When embryonated eggs are ingested by the grasshopper (*Pternoscirta sauteri*), they hatch in the intestinal tract, and the larvae pass into the body cavity, then penetrate the tissues, and become loosely encysted. In 20 days the larvae are infective to the final host.

♦ **PATHOLOGY.** The following changes have been associated with the infection of *T. crami:* emaciation, with atrophy of thoracic musculature, anemic mucosa, proventriculus enlarged, proventricular wall thickened, mucosa swollen and sown with round structures of reddish color resembling hematomas; stomach wall with pale tissue covered by reddish brown oval and round inclusions of larger size than similar structures on mucosa; contents of stomach of mashlike consistency; small intestine with liquid of greenish hue due to presence of large amounts of bile; intestinal mucosa swollen and covered with mucus; proliferation and desquamation of the mucosal epithelium and the compound glands of the submucosal layer partially or almost completely atrophied; and muscular layer edematous with serous layer friable. These latter alterations lead to dysfunction and markedly impaired digestion, then to emaciation and finally death (Popova, 1954).

Swales (1936) found that in infections involving the presence of 100 or more females of *T. crami,* the host was always in rather poor condition. In the few cases studied from this aspect by Swales, sections of the crypts revealed adult parasites enclosed within thin fibrous cysts around which little or no evidence of acute inflammatory processes was seen. However, the crypt was greatly distended, and owing to mechanical discharge, the secretory glands could not function. As the function of the proventriculus is to bathe the passing food with gastric juice and pepsin, and thus break down protein, severe infections probably impair this process to some extent. This effect alone may account for the failure of the parasitized birds to gain weight normally.

Cram (1930) noted that *T. americana* produced a catarrhal condition associated with a thickening of the walls of the proventriculus in infected chickens. In 1931b she observed that this parasite did not produce damage in naturally infected quail. However, the infections in the bobwhite were light.

Diarrhea and loss of appetite have been observed in infections of *T. fissispina* in ducks and chickens. In ducks naturally infected with *T. fissispina*, large-scale invasions of the disease lead to emaciation, anemia, and frequently death. Ducklings are particularly susceptible.

Rust (1908) and Eber (1918) reported ulcers in the gastric mucosa of ducks infected with *Tetrameres*. Grosso (1914) reported slight atrophy of the glandular epithelium as a result of pressure by the parasite and some distension of the glands as well as slight infiltration of eosinophils into the connective tissue of the glandular surface. Travassos (1915) described merely Lieberkuehn gland epithelial atrophy. Bittner (1924) noted a compression of the individual tubules of the glands and slight degeneration of the epithelium. Lesbouyries (1941) noted cysts coinciding with the primary cavities of the glandular lobes. These cysts contained *Tetrameres* and were surrounded by a collagenic membrane internally lined by a layer of granular cells containing larger nuclei and dispersed without order in the tissue, later being replaced by mucous cells. Tissue around cysts was infiltrated with leukocytes.

The females of the genus *Tetrameres* are known to feed on blood, and the intake of blood for food requirements must be fairly extensive in egg-producing females. The toxic action described in *T. fissispina* of pigeons by Timon-David (1932) may also play a part in this disease.

◆ **DIAGNOSIS.** Diagnosis of the disease is based on the presence of the parasites in the proventriculus. The red female worms may be observed through the wall of the unopened proventriculus. Young birds seem to be more severely affected than adults (Wehr and Herman, 1954).

Microtetrameres helix Cram 1927
(Fig. 20.19)

◆ **DISTRIBUTION.** *Corvus americanus, C. brachyrhynchos, C. frugilegus.* North America and Russia.

◆ **TRANSMISSION AND DEVELOPMENT.** Infective eggs were fed to arthropods and annelids and 3rd stage larvae were recovered 26 to 68 days later from several grasshopper nymphs (*Melanoplus* spp.), 2 adult grasshoppers (*Melanoplus femurrubrum* and *M. bivittatus*), and a cockroach (*Blatella germanica*). The larvae, coiled in thick-walled, semitransparent cysts, were found chiefly among the tissues of the body cavity, less frequently in muscles of the legs and head. When released from the cysts, the larvae became very active. Pigeons proved to be susceptible to invasion with 3rd stage larvae. Immature adults of both males and females of *M. helix* were recovered from the pigeon (*Columba livia domestica*) 35 days after ingestion of larvae (Cram, 1934a).

Schell (1953) fed eggs of *Microtetrameres corax* to cockroaches (*Blatella germanica*) and larvae of the mealworm (*Tenebrio* sp.) and recovered what were assumed to be 3rd stage larvae of this species from the cockroach. These larvae were later fed to 1-day-old chicks but no worms were found in them 50 to 56 days later.

◆ **PATHOLOGY.** As members of this genus inhabit the glands of the proventriculus, it is assumed that the damage done to the definitive host is similar to that of *Tetrameres* spp.

EUSTRONGYLIDIASIS

The genus *Eustrongylides* is closely related to *Dioctophyme* and *Hystrichis*. The larvae of *Eustrongylides* occur in the connective tissue or body cavity of fishes, and adults are parasitic in glands of the proventriculus of piscivorous birds.

Eustrongylides ignotus Jagerskiold 1909
(Fig. 20.20)

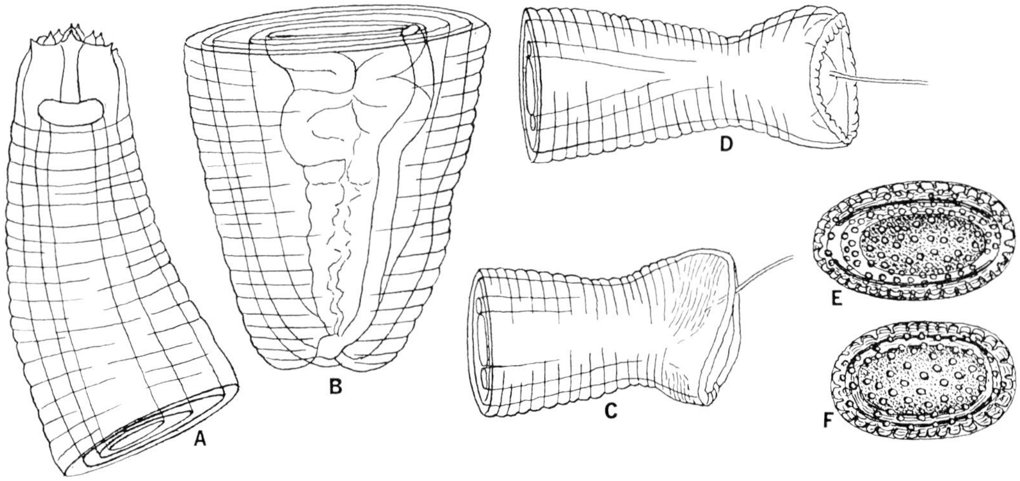

FIG. 20.20. *Eustrongylides ignotus.* *(A)* Head end. *(B)* Female tail. *(C)* and *(D)* Male tail. *(E)* and *(F)* Egg. (After Jagerskiold, 1909.)

SYNONYMS: *Filaria cystica* Rudolphi 1819; *Aga-monema cysticum* (Rud. 1819) Die-sing 1851; *Eustrongylus papillosus* Diesing 1851 in part; *Hystrichis papillosus* Molin 1861 in part; *Eustrongylus tubifex* Schneider 1866 in part; *Spiroptera bicolor* Linstow 1899.

◆ **DISTRIBUTION.** *Ardea* sp., *A. herodias, Botaurus* sp., *Casmerodius albus, Nycticorax nycticorax hoactli.* Europe; North America.

◆ **TRANSMISSION AND DEVELOPMENT.** The life cycle of no species of *Eustrongylides* has been elucidated but it may be similar to that of *Dioctophyme renale* and *Hystrichis tricolor* which are related species. According to Karmanova (1959), the 1st stage larva of *D. renale* (a parasite of carnivores) develops to the infective stage in the blood vessels of *Lumbriculus variegatus.* The definitive host becomes infected by ingesting oligochaetes containing infective larvae, but fish may serve as transport hosts.

Hystrichis tricolor, of the proventriculus of ducks, develops in the blood vessels of *Criodrilus lacuum* and *Allolobophora dubiosa pontica* (Karmanova, 1956). The definitive host becomes infected by ingesting infected oligochaetes. The larvae bore into the proventricular wall, molt the fourth time, and develop to maturity.

◆ **PATHOLOGY.** Bowdish (1948) reported fatal cases of verminous peritonitis in a black-crowned night heron *(Nycticorax nycticorax)* and in a great blue heron *(A. herodias)* in New Jersey. Locke (1961) reported that *Eustrongylides ignotus,* a common parasite of the peritoneal cavity of birds, was the cause of death in a great blue heron and American egrets *(Casmerodius albus)* in Maryland and Delaware, respecively (Fig. 20.21). His findings were as follows: The peritoneal cavity contained a "shieldlike" mass of red worms, adhered intestines, and ingesta. The intestines were so tightly entwined with the fibrous tubes containing the worms that they could not be separated without damage to worms and the intestine. In the heron, 2 nematodes had entered the liver and the fibrous coils containing the worms looped out of the liver and reentered several times. In the egret, none of the nematodes had penetrated the liver, but the coils had made impressions on the liver surface.

Microscopically, the sections of the peritoneal lesion showed that the fibrous tube

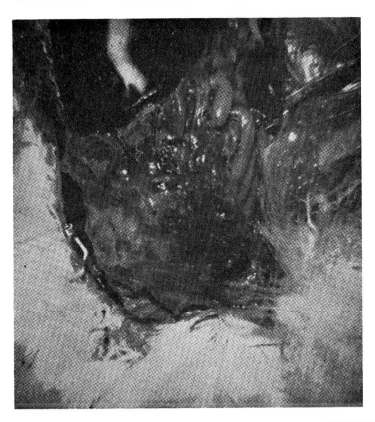

FIG. 20.21. *Eustrongylus ignatus.* Verminous peritonitis in an American egret. (Locke, 1961.)

surrounding the worm was highly vascular, indicating that a severe inflammatory reaction had set up. Closer to the nematode, many granulocytes were observed, but the most conspicuous cells in this zone were erythrocytes. Immediately adjacent to the worm was a necrotic area.

SPLENDIDOFILARIASIS

The life cycle of a species of the genus *Splendidofilaria,* causative agent of the disease known as splendidofilariasis, was first elucidated by Anderson (1956a). He was successful in getting the microfilariae of *S. fallisensis* to develop to the infective stage in blackflies (Simuliidae) and in recovering the adult worms in Pekin ducklings after infective larvae had been injected into them.

Splendidofilaria fallisensis (Anderson 1954)
(Fig. 20.22)

SYNONYM: *Ornithofilaria fallisensis* Anderson 1954.

◆ **DISTRIBUTION.** *Anas rubripes, Anas boschas domestica.* Canada.

◆ **TRANSMISSION AND DEVELOPMENT.** This filarioid nematode develops in *Simulium venustum, S. parassum, S. rugglesi,* and *S. anatinum. Simulium venustum* and *S. parassum,* although serving as intermediate hosts for the development of the larval stages, are unlikely hosts for the transmission of spendidofilariasis under natural conditions because they are not ornithophilic. *Simulium anatinum* is active during the early part of the blackfly season, whereas *S. rugglesi* is active during the latter part of May, June, and July. Both these species feed on waterfowl. The development of the microfilariae to the infective stage takes place in the body cavity of the blackfly, usually in the abdominal cavity,

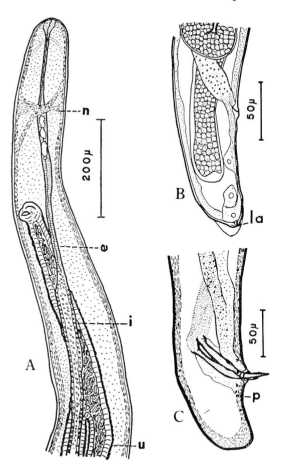

FIG. 20.22. *Splendidofilaria fallisensis.* *(A)* Anterior end, female, ventral view. *(B)* Caudal end, female, lateral view. *(C)* Caudal end, male, lateral view. *(i)* intestine; *(la)* lateral appendage; *(n)* nerve ring; *(e)* esophagus; *(p)* pedunculate papilla; *(u)* uterus. (After Anderson, 1954.)

after they have penetrated the stomach wall. During the development to the infective stage, the microfilaria assumes a sausagelike stage and undergoes two molts; the first molt occurs as early as the 4th day and the second molt as early as the 6th day after ingestion. The tail of the 3rd or infective stage larva is provided with two rounded, lateral protuberances. When development is completed, the 3rd stage larvae migrate from the abdomen to the head where they accumulate in the mouth parts, eyes, and muscles. The definitive host becomes infected at the time infected flies feed on it and ingest its blood, the infective larvae escaping into the puncture made by the mouth parts of the insect. The microfilariae show a pronounced periodicity, being most numerous during the daytime when the vectors are most active.

There is evidence to show that infected birds become resistant to reinfection. Microfilariae appear in the blood of ducks 30 to 36 days after infection.

◆**DIAGNOSIS.** The microfilaria is provided with a delicate sheath which is closely applied to the body of the worm and is perceptible only at the extremities and at points of constriction of the body. The body is comparatively short, and the tail is short and blunt.

AVIOSERPENSIASIS

Avioserpens taiwana, the etiologic agent of this avian disease, is a parasite of the connective tissue or mucous membrane of the mouth and pharynx of birds. The para-

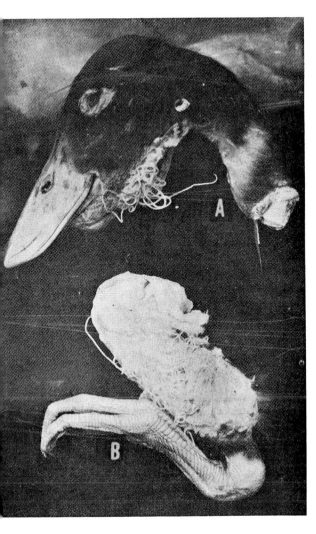

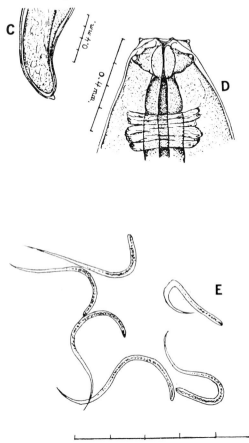

FIG. 20.23. *(A) Avioserpens taiwana* (Sugimoto, 1919) in the chin of a domestic duck. Natural size. *(B) Avioserpens taiwana* (Sugimoto, 1919) in the thigh of a domestic duck. Natural size. *(C)* Tail of female *Avioserpens taiwana* (Sugimoto, 1919). *(D)* Head of female *Aviosperpens taiwana* (Sugimoto, 1919). *(E)* Embryos of *Avioserpens taiwana* (Sugimoto, 1919). (After Sugimoto, 1934.)

0·5 mm.

site produces tumors on the inferior mandible and chin. These tumors, which in the beginning are soft and painless but later become hard and painful, are a mass of entangled parasites. They interfere with swallowing, especially in the latter stages of infection, and may cause asphyxiation.

Avioserpens taiwana (Sugimoto 1919)
(Fig. 20.23)

SYNONYMS: *Filaria taiwana* Sugimoto 1919; *Oshimaia taiwana* (Sugimoto 1919) Sugimoto 1934; *Avioserpens denticulophasma* Wehr and Chitwood 1934; *Petroviprocta vigissi* Schachtschtinskaja 1951.

◆ **DISTRIBUTION.** *Anas boschas domestica, A. fulvigula, Anhinga anhinga,*

Cairina moschata, Casmerodius albus egretta, Egretta thula. Formosa; Indochina; and North America.

◆ **TRANSMISSION AND DEVELOPMENT.** The life cycle is probably similar to that of *Dracunculus medinensis* as reported by Moorthy (1938). The free-swimming 1st stage larva of *D. medinensis* is ingested by species of *Cyclops* and reaches the infective stage in the body cavity. The definitive host, in this case dog, man, etc., becomes infected by swallowing infected *Cyclops*. The larva is freed in the gut, reaches the body cavity, and grows to adulthood. After copulation the males disappear and the females migrate to the subcutaneous tissues. Larvae are produced in 8 or 9 months.

Brackett (1938) interpolated a tadpole into the life cycle of *Dracunculus ophidensis* of snakes and stated that it may serve as a transport host although it was not essential to the life cycle.

◆ **PATHOLOGY.** According to Truong-Tan-Ngog (1937), this parasite occurs in young ducks in January, February, March, and April (dry season), living in marshy regions. It is observed only occasionally in the rainy season. The parasite produces tumors on the inferior mandibles and chin (Fig. 20.22A). Initially this tumor is painless and soft and contains a mass of entangled parasites. When the parasites attain their maximum development (after about 1 month) the tumor becomes hard, voluminous, and painful. It attains the size of a large nut. It occasionally impedes and hinders swallowing. The disease may cause asphyxiation or inanination after several days.

In the benign form of the disease, the tumor is small; it is slowly resorbed and replaced by fibrous tissue.

There exists a general form of the disease, which is rare. In this form, in addition to the tumor of the throat, one observes shoulder tumors (very rare) or tumors on the inferior region of the shank

near the tibiotarsal articulation which may impede locomotion. In this case, if a sick bird is in the water, it swims with the uninfected leg.

The duration of the malady is about $1\frac{1}{2}$ months from the appearance of the tumor to its disappearance.

As a general rule, the female worms pierce the projecting end of the tumor to provide an opening for the release of larvae. This orifice is generally slowly scarred over without complications although the tumor sometimes abscesses. The parasites may die in the tumor and the resulting abscess is longer in healing.

In the generalized form, the tumors of the shanks advance under the skin of the feet toward the palms of the toes, or perforate the skin and escape to the exterior. There is left, after their escape, a fistula which scars very slowly, and fatal infections often result.

Ducks with this infection are thin, and their growth is retarded. Infections are acquired early in life.

◆ **DIAGNOSIS.** Tumors, in which are found masses of worms, are present under the inferior mandible and on the chin, especially in young ducklings which are raised in marshes.

◆ **TREATMENT AND PREVENTION.** Parasites should be removed by making an incision in the most salient part of the tumor and applying an antiseptic (permanganate solution, boric acid solution, or phenol solution; bathing with tincture of iodide; dusting with pulverized boric acid). In general, there are no complications.

When contemplating an increase in ducks, one should arrange for the ducklings to hatch during the rainy season or in a month before the season when the water is brackish (December). Ducklings born during the dry season should be on the floor and be given clean water which has not been contaminated.

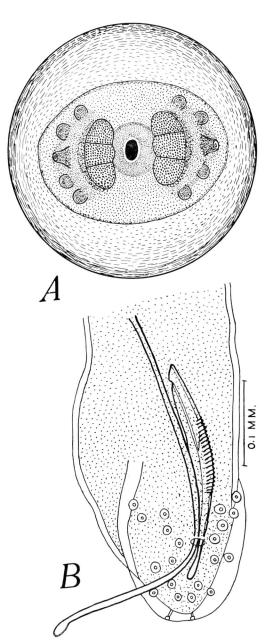

A

B

FIG. 20.24 *Serratospiculum amaculata.* *(A)* En face view. *(B)* Male tail, showing spicules and caudal papillae. (After Wehr, 1938a.)

SERRATOSPICULIASIS

The members of the genus *Serratospiculum* live in the air sacs of birds, princi-

pally hawks. Only one of these species *(S. amaculata)* occurs in birds of North America, so far as is known at present.

The worms accumulate, and in heavy infections become entangled in the connective tissue of the abdominal and thoracic air sacs. Since the air sacs connect with the upper respiratory passages via the bronchi, the eggs of this parasite probably pass from the air sacs into the lungs, up the trachea, and are swallowed and passed in feces.

Serratospiculum amaculata Wehr 1938
(Fig. 20.24)

◆ **DISTRIBUTION.** Prairie falcon *(Falco mexicanus mexicanus)* and peregrine falcon *(Falco peregrinus anatum)*. United States (Montana, Oregon, North Dakota, and California); Canada (Alberta).

◆ **TRANSMISSION AND DEVELOPMENT.** Unknown. This parasite presumably requires an arthropod other than a bloodsucking one as an intermediate host. In common with species of other closely related filarioid nematodes such as *Dicheilonema, Diplotriaena,* and *Hamatospiculum,* the species of *Serratospiculum* produce thick-shelled eggs which are assumed to pass through the lungs, up the trachea, and out in the feces. Insects and other arthropods feeding on the feces-contaminated forage may become infected and serve as intermediate hosts.

◆ **CLINICAL SIGNS.** Not well known. Liquid instead of solid feces, turning green and watery just before death, have been reported. Anorexia, dessication, excitability, and death have been reported by investigators who have trained birds for falconry.

◆ **PATHOLOGY.** Heavy accumulation of worms entwined in the connective tissue of the abdominal and thoracic cavities (air sacs) has been reported by Wehr (1938b) and Bigland et al. (1964) (Fig. 20.25). The latter authors reported multiple yellow necrotic foci in the liver and spleen, pericardi-

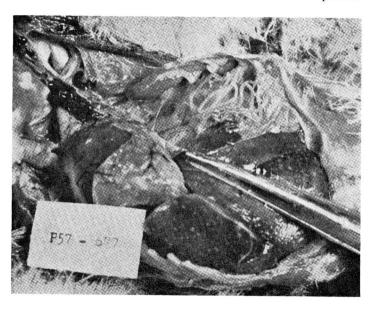

FIG. 20.25. *Serratospiculum amaculata* in situ in the air sac of a prairie falcon. (Biglund, Liu, and Perry, 1964.)

tis with attached yellow caseous material in one case, and a large necrotic lesion involving the crop and esophagus in another. Histopathologic findings include hyperplasia and hyperemia of the proventriculus; occlusion of the bile ducts and congestion of the hepatic veins of the liver; hyperplasia and sloughing of columnar epithelium and mesothelium; an accumulation of mononuclear leukocytes, plasma cells, and macrophages in the connective tissue spaces of the air sacs; and general hyperemia and atelectasis of air spaces, with dilation of the parabronchi of the lungs. Embryonated ova were present in all areas. Degenerative changes in the collagen-muscle layer of the air sacs were also observed.

◆ **DIAGNOSIS.** Embryonated eggs may be seen in the feces, but they resemble those of other nematodes of this group, having thick-shelled eggs with differentiated larvae. The necropsy of an infected bird, the location of the worms in the connective tissue of the thoracic and abdominal regions, and the microscopic identification of the parasite are the only reliable means of diagnosing the infection.

◆ **TREATMENT AND CONTROL.** Unknown. Until information regarding the

life cycle of this parasite is available, progress in this field of investigation will be slow.

DIPLOTRIAENIASIS

The members of the genus *Diplotriaena* have chitinized tridents (tridentlike structures present on lateral sides of the head) and are parasites of the air sacs of birds.

Diplotriaena agelaius (Walton 1927) (Fig. 20.26)

SYNONYMS: *Diplotriaenoides agelaius* Walton 1927; *Diplotriaenoides translucidus* Anderson 1956.

◆**DISTRIBUTION.** *Seiurus aurocapillus, Agelaius phoeniceus, Ostinops decumanus.* North and South America.

◆ **TRANSMISSION AND DEVELOPMENT.** The life cycle of this species has been partly elucidated by Anderson (1957a). The eggs are embryonated at the time of deposition. They are expelled by the female in the air sacs and lungs and are conveyed through the trachea into the mouth cavity. They are then swallowed and pass

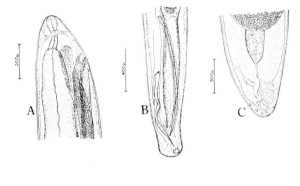

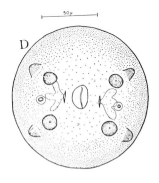

FIG. 20.26. *(A)* Anterior end, female, lateral view of allotype. *(B)* Caudal end, male, ventral view of holotype. *(C)* Caudal end, female, lateral view of allotype. *(D)* Anterior end, female, en face view of paratype. Tridents semidiagrammatic, based on sketches of tridents at various depths of focus under oil immersion. (Anderson, 1956.)

to the exterior with the feces. When fed experimentally to grasshoppers *(Camnula pellucida),* the embryonated eggs hatch in the intestine and the larvae burrow through the wall and enter the hemocoel. Two molts occur and the 3rd stage larvae are found free or encysted in the hemocoel about 1 month after the eggs are ingested. Infection of the vertebrate host presumably occurs when the infected intermediate host harboring 3rd stage larvae is ingested. Since grasshoppers are apparently not a regular part of the diet of oven birds *(Seiurus aurocapillus),* some other arthropod perhaps serves as the intermediate host of *D. translucidus* in nature (Anderson, 1957a). As no oven birds were available to which to feed the 3rd stage larvae collected from the grasshopper, Anderson fed them to a white-crowned sparrow, but no worms were found at necropsy of the bird.

The life cycle of *Diplotriaena monticelliana* (Stossich 1890) of *Sylvia atricapilla* is believed to take place in coprophagous insects, but this has not been experimentally verified (Chabaud, 1956).

◆ **PATHOLOGY.** Nothing is known of the pathology and control of this parasite.

◆ **REFERENCES**

Abdou, A. H., and Selim, M. K. On the life cycle of *Subulura suctoria,* a cecal nematode of poultry in Egypt. *Z. Parasitenk.* 18:20, 1957.

Abel Malik, Emile. Life cycle studies on the nematode *Subulura brumpti* (Lopez-Neyra, 1922) Cram, 1926, and its distribution in the Sudan. *J. Parasitol.* 44 (suppl.):31, 1958.

Alicata, J. E. The life history of the gizzard worm *(Cheilospirura hamulosa)* and its mode of transmission to chickens, with special reference to Hawaiian conditions. *Livro Jub. Pr. L. Travassos,* p. 11, 1938.

———. Preliminary note on the life history of *Subulura brumpti,* a common cecal nematode of poultry in Hawaii. *J. Parasitol.* 25: 179, 1939.

Allen, A. A. The grouse disease in 1924. *Am.*

Game Bull. Am. Game Protect. Assoc. 14:11, 1925.

Allen, A. A., and Gross, A. O. Ruffed grouse investigations. Season of 1925–1926. Am. Game Bull. Am. Game Protect. Assoc., p. 3, 1926.

Anderson, R. C. Ornithofilaria fallisensis n. sp. (Nematoda: Filarioidea) from the domestic duck with descriptions of Microfilariae in waterfowl. Can. J. Zool. 32:125, 1954a.

———. The development of Ornithofilaria fallisensis Anderson, 1954, in Simulium venustum Say. J. Parasitol. 40 (suppl.):12, 1954b.

———. Black flies (Simuliidae) as vectors of Ornithofilaria fallisensis Anderson, 1954. J. Parasitol. 41 (suppl.):45, 1955.

———. The life cycle and seasonal transmission of Ornithofilaria fallisensis Anderson, a parasite of domestic and wild ducks. Can. J. Zool. 34:485, 1956a.

———. Two new filarioid nematodes from Ontario birds. Can. J. Zool. 34:213, 1956b.

———. Observations on the life cycles of Diplotriaenoides translucidus Anderson and members of the genus Diplotriaena. Can. J. Zool. 35:15, 1957a.

———. The life cycles of dipetalonematid nematodes (Filarioidea, Dipetalonematidae): The problem of their evolution. J. Helminthol. 31:203, 1957b.

———. Possible steps in the evolution of filarial life cycles. Proc. 6th Intern. Congr. Trop. Med. Malaria 2:5, 1958.

———. Corrections to a previous paper. Can. J. Zool. 38:677, 1960.

———. Splendidofilaria wehri n. sp. with a revision of Splendidofilaria and related genera. Can. J. Zool. 39:201, 1961.

———. On the development, morphology, and experimental transmission of Diplotriaena bargusinica (Filarioidea: Diplotriaenidae). Can. J. Zool. 40:1175, 1962.

———. The simuliid vectors of Splendidofilaria fallisensis of ducks. Can. J. Zool. 46:610.

Anderson, R. C., and Chabaud, A. G. Remarques sur la classification des Splendidofilariinae (1). Ann. Parasitol. Human Comp. 34: 53, 1959.

Bangham, R. V. Parasites of Centrachidae from southern Florida. Trans. Am. Fish Soc. (68th Ann. Meeting, Asheville, N.C., June 23–24, 1938):263, 1939.

———. Parasites of fresh water fish of southern Florida. Proc. Florida Acad. Sci. (1940) 5:289, 1941.

Baudet, E. A. R. F. Cyathostoma phenisci n. sp., parasite de la trachee d'un pingouin. Ann. Parasitol. Human Comp. 15:218, 1937.

Baylis, H. A. The life-histories of some nematodes. J. Quekett Microscop. Club 16:107, 1929.

Beaudette, F. R. Heterakis isolonche Linstow, 1906 in a pheasant with remarks on tuberculosis and gapeworms. J. Am. Med. Assoc. 101:274, 1942.

Beaudette, F. R. Distribution of Tetrameres americana in New Jersey. J. Parasitol. 19: 302, 1933.

Beer, J. Parasites of the blue grouse. J. Wildlife Management 8:91, 1944.

Bigland, C. H., Si-Kwang, Lui, and Perry, M. L. Five cases of Serratospiculum amaculata (Nematoda: Filarioidea) infection in prairie falcons (Falco mexicanus). Avian Diseases 8:412, 1964.

Bittner, H. Schistogonimus rarus (Braun), ein seltener Trematode in der Bursa Fabricii einer an Tetramereinvasion gestorbenen Hausente. Arch. wissenchaftische praktische Tierheilkunde 50:253, 1924.

Boughton, R. V. Endoparasitic infestations in grouse, their pathogenicity and correlation with metero-topographical conditions. Tech. Bull. Minn. Agr. Exp. Sta. 121:1, 1937.

Bowdish, B. S. Heron mortality caused by Eustrongylides ignotus. Auk 65:602, 1948.

Boyd, E. M. A survey of parasitism of the starling Sturnus vulgaris L. in North America. J. Parasitol. 37:56, 1951.

Brackett, Sterling. Description and life history of the nematode Dracunculus ophidensis n. sp., with a description of the genus. J. Parasitol. 24:353, 1938.

Brand, T. von. Physiological observations upon a larval Eustrongylides. VI. Transmission to various cold-blooded intermediate hosts. Proc. Helminthol. Soc. Wash. D.C. 11:23, 1944.

Brand, T. von, and Cullinan, R. F. Physiological observations upon a larval Eustrongylides. V. The behavior in abnormal warm-blooded hosts. Proc. Helminthol. Soc. Wash. D.C. 10:29, 1943.

Brugger, L. A survey of the endoparasites of the digestive and respiratory tracts of the Hungarian partridge. Anat. Record 81:134, 1941.

Bump, G. Ruffed grouse in New York State during the period of maximum abundance. Trans. 21st Am. Game Conf. 364, 1935.

Caballero, E. Contribucion al conocimiento de los nematodes de las aves de Mexico. IV. Ann. Inst. Biol. Univ. Mex. 8:397, 1937.

Cahall, W. C. A parasite of the bird's brain. J. Nerv. Ment. Diseases 14:361, 1889.

Cameron, T. W. M. Animal parasites. Trans. Am. Game Conf. 21:412, 1935.

Campbell, J. W. Gapeworm (Syngamus) in wild birds. J. Animal Ecol. 4:208, 1935.

Canavan, W. P. N. Nematode parasites of vertebrates in the Philadelphia Zoological Garden and vicinity. I. Parasitology 21:63, 1929a.

———. Some observations on the distribution of parasites in mammals with the report of some new forms. *Arch. Pathol.* 8:1021, 1929b.

———. Nematode parasites of vertebrates in the Philadelphia Zoological Garden and vicinity. II. *Parasitology* 23:196, 1931.

Chabaud, A. G. A propos du cycle evolutif d'un *Synhimantus* (Nematoda: Acuariidae). Recherche des lois qui regissent la vitesse du developpement suivant la place zoologique du parasite et la biologie del l'hôte intermediaire. *Bull. Soc. Zool.* 74:342, 1949.

———. Cycle evolutif de *Synhimantus (Desportesius) spinulatus* (Nematoda: Acuariidae). *Ann. Parasitol. Human Comp.* 25:150, 1950.

———. Cycle evolutif chez des coleopteres tenebrionides de deux especies de nematodes Habronematinae (genre *Sicarius* et genre *Hadjelia*) parasites de *Upupa epops* L. a Banyuls. *Compt. Rend. Acad. Sci.* 232:564, 1951.

———. Identite de *Petroviprocta vigissi* Schachtactinskaja, 1951, et d'*Avioserpens galliardi* Chabaud et Campana, 1949. *Ann. Parasitol. Human Comp.* 27:482, 1952.

———. Sur le cycle evolutif des spirurides et de nematodes ayant une biologie comparable. Valeur systematique des caracteres biologiques. *Ann. Parasitol. Human. Comp.* 29:42, 1954.

———. Remarques sur le cycle evolutif des filaires du genre *Diplotriaena* et redescription de *D. monticelliana* (Stossich, 1890). *Vie Milieu* 6:342, 1956.

———. Sur la systematique des nematodes du sous-ordre des Ascaridina parasites des vertebres. *Bull. Soc. Zool.* 82:243, 1957.

———. Remarques sur l'evolution et la taxonomie chez les nematodes parasites de vertebres. *15th Intern. Congr. Zool. Sect. 8, Paper 27*, p. 1, 1958a.

———. Essai de classification des nematodes Habronematinae. *Ann. Parasitol. Human Comp.* 33:445, 1958b.

———. Phenomene d'evolution regressive des structures cephaliques et classification des nematodes Spiruroidea. *Parassitologia* 1:11, 1959a.

———. Remarques sur la systematique des nematodes Trichostrongyloidea. *Bull. Soc. Zool.* 84:473, 1959b.

Chabaud, A. G., and Campana, Y. *Avioserpens galliardi* n. sp., parasite de l'aigrette *Egretta garzetta* L. *Ann. Parasitol. Human Comp.* 24:67, 1949.

Chabaud, A. G., and Petter, A. J. Essai de classification des nematodes Acuariidae. *Ann. Parasitol. Human Comp.* 34:331, 1959.

Chabaud, A. G., and Rogeaux, M. Remarques sur la dentition de *Syngamus trachea* (Montagu) et sur la place systematique des syngames. *Ann. Parasitol. Human Comp.* 32:264, 1957.

Chabaud, A. G., Campana, Y., and Truong-Tan-Ngoc. Note sur les dracunculids d'oiseaux. *Ann. Parasitol. Human Comp.* 25:335, 1950.

Chaddock, T. T. Some facts relative to disease as found in wildlife. *N. Am. Vet.* 29:560, 1948.

Chakravarty, G. K. On the nematode worms in the collection of the zoological laboratory, Univ. of Calcutta. I. Families Heterakidae and Kathlaniidae. *J. Dept. Sci. Calcutta Univ.* 4:70, 1938.

Chandler, A. C. Some new genera and species of nematode worms, Filarioidea, from animals dying in the Calcutta Zoological Gardens. *Proc. Smithsonian Inst.* 75:1, 1929.

———. A new genus and species of Subulurinae (nematodes). *Trans. Am. Microscop. Soc.* 54: 33, 1935.

Chapin, E. A. *Eustrongylides ignotus* Jagersk. in the U. S. *J. Parasitol.* 13:86, 1926.

Chitwood, B. G. Nematodes parasitic in, and associated with, Crustacea, and descriptions of some new species and a new variety. *Proc. Helminthol. Soc. Wash. D.C.* 2:93, 1935.

Ciurea, I. Sur une infestation massive des poissons rapaces du lac greaca par les larves d'*Eustrongylides excisus* Jagerskiold (recherches experimentales). *Grigore Antipa. Hommage a son oeuvre Bucuresti*, p. 149, 1938.

Clapham, P. A. On nodules occasioned by gapeworms in pheasants. *J. Helminthol.* 13:9, 1935a.

———. Some helminth parasites from partridges and other English birds. *J. Helminthol.* 13:139, 1935b.

———. Further observations on the occurrence and incidence of helminths in British partridges. *J. Helminthol.* 14:61, 1936.

———. New records of helminths in British birds. *J. Helminthol.* 16:47, 1938a.

———. Are there host strains within the species of *Syngamus trachea*? *J. Helminthol.* 16:49, 1938b.

———. On a sex difference in the infection rate of birds with *Syngamus trachea*. *J. Helminthol.* 17:192, 1939a.

———. On the larval migration of *Syngamus trachea* and its causal relationship to pneumonia in young birds. *J. Helminthol.* 17:159, 1939b.

Clarke, C. H. D. The dying of the ruffed grouse. *Trans. Am. Game Conf.* 21:402, 1935a.

———. Fluctuations in numbers of ruffed grouse *(Bonasa umbellus* Linne) with special reference to Ontario. *Univ. Toronto Studies Biol.* 41, 1935b.

Cleland, J. B. The parasites of Australian birds. *Trans. Roy. Soc. S. Australia* 46:85, 1922.

Cobbold, T. S. On *Sclerostoma syngamus* and the disease it occasions in birds. *J. Linn. Soc.* 5:304, 1861.

——. Remarks on the entozoa of the common fowl and game birds in their supposed relation to grouse disease. *Rept. Brit. Assoc.* 37:80, 1867.

——. *The grouse disease. A statement of facts tending to prove the parasite origin of the epidemic,* 1873.

Colglazier, M. L., Foster, A. O., Enzie, F. D., and Thompson, D. E. The anthelmintic action of phenothiazine and piperazine against *Heterakis gallinae* and *Ascaridia galli* in chickens. *J. Parasitol.* 46:267, 1960.

Colglazier, M. L., Wehr, E. E., Burtner, R. H., and Wiest, L. M., Jr. Preliminary observations on the anthelmintic activity of methyridine against *Capillaria contorta* in quail. *Proc. Helminthol. Soc. Wash. D.C.* 34:219, 1967.

Collinge, W. E. A parasite of pheasants. *Country Life,* London 72:109, 1932.

——. Note on the life cycle of *Trichostrongylus tenuis* (Mehlis), Nematoda. *Ann. Mg. Nat. Hist.* 12:783, 1945.

Cowan, A. B. Some preliminary observations on the life history of *Amidostomum anseris* Zeder, 1800. *J. Parasitol.* 41 (suppl.):43, 1955.

Cowan, I. M. Two apparently fatal grouse diseases. *J. Wildlife Management* 4:311, 1940.

Cram, E. B. New records of economically important nematodes in birds. *J. Parasitol.* 12:113, 1925.

——. *Subulura brumpti* from the turkey in Porto Rico. *J. Parasitol.* 12:164, 1926a.

——. A parasitic disease of the esophagus of turkeys. *N. Am. Vet.* 7:46, 1926b.

——. A parasitic nematode as the cause of losses among domestic geese. *N. Am. Vet.* 7:27, 1926c.

——. New records of nematodes of birds. *J. Parasitol.* 12:180, 1926d.

——. Bird parasites of the nematode suborders Strongylata, Ascaridata, and Spirurata. *Bull. U.S. Nat. Mus.* (140), 1927a.

——. New records of distribution for various nematodes. *J. Parasitol.* 14:70, 1927b.

——. Nematodes of pathological significance found in some economically important birds in North America. *U.S. Dept. Agr. Bull.* 49, 1928.

——. The life history of the gizzard worm of the ruffed grouse and the bobwhite quail. *J. Parasitol.* 15:285, 1929a.

——. New ideas and discoveries. *U.S. Dept. Agr. Official Record,* p. 5, 1929b.

——. Pathological conditions ascribed to nematodes in poultry. *U.S. Dept. Agr. Circ.* 126:1, 1930.

——. Developmental stages of some nematodes of the Spiruroidea, parasitic in poultry and game birds. *U.S. Dept. Agr. Tech. Bull.* 227, 1931a.

——. A comparison of the internal parasites of the ruffed grouse of Labrador with those of the ruffed grouse of the United States. *J. Parasitol.* 18:48, 1931b.

——. Nematodes (roundworms) in quail. In H. L. Stoddard, ed., *The bobwhite quail, its habits, preservation, and increase.* New York: Scribner's, p. 240, 1931c.

——. Recent findings in connection with parasitisms in game birds. *Trans. Am. Game Conf.* 18:243, 1932.

——. *Eustrongylides ignotus* from the blackcrowned night heron. *J. Parasitol.* 20:71, 1933a.

——. A new species of *Tetrameres* from the bobwhite quail. *J. Parasitol.* 19:245, 1933b.

——. Ornithostrongylosis, a parasitic disease of pigeons. *U.S. Dept. Agr. Bur. An. Ind. Vet.* 9:1, 1933c.

——. *Habronema incerta* (Smith, Fox and White, 1908) Gendre, 1922 in a new bird host and in a new locality. *J. Parasitol.* 20: 74, 1933d.

——. Orthopterans and pigeons as secondary and primary hosts, respectively, for the crow stomach worm, *Microtetrameres helix* (Nematoda: Spiruridae). *Proc. Helminthol. Soc. Wash. D.C.* 1:50, 1934a.

——. Species of *Capillaria* parasitic in the upper digestive tract of domestic and game birds. *J. Parasitol.* 20:334, 1934b.

——. Species of *Capillaria* parasitic in the upper digestive tract of birds. *U.S. Dept. Agr. Tech. Bull.* 516, 1936.

——. A species of Orthoptera serving as intermediate host of *Tetrameres americana* of poultry in Puerto Rico. *Proc. Helminthol. Soc. Wash. D.C.* 4:24, 1937.

——. Redescription and emendation of the genus *Aproctella* (Filariidae) nematodes from gallinaceous birds. *Proc. Helminthol. Soc. Wash. D.C.* 6:94, 1939.

Cram, E. B., and Cuvillier, E. *Ornithostrongylus quadriradiatus* of pigeons: Observations on its life history, pathogenicity, and treatment. *J. Parasitol.* 18:116, 1931.

——. Ornithostrongylosis of the pigeon (*Columba livia dom.*). *Atti del V Congresso Mondiale di Pollicoltura organizzato dal Ministero del'Agricoltura e delle Foreste,*

Roma, 6–15, Settembre, 1933. 3a Sezione, N. 75, 1933.

———. Observations on *Trichostrongylus tenuis* infestation in domestic and game birds in the United States. *Parasitology* 26:340, 1934.

Cram, E. B., and Jones, M. F. Parasitologist of Bureau of Animal Industry demonstrates complete life cycle of gizzard worm of grouse and quail. *U.S. Dept. Agr. Official Record* 8:5, 1929.

———. Parasitism in game birds. *Trans. Am. Game Conf.* 17:203, 1930.

Cram, E. B., and Wehr, E. E. The status of the species of *Trichostrongylus* of birds. *Parasitology* 26:335, 1934.

Cram, E. B., Jones, M. F., and Allen, E. A. Internal parasites and parasitic diseases of the bobwhite. In H. L. Stoddard, *The bobwhite quail, its habits, preservation and increase.* New York: Scribner's, p. 229, 1931.

Cuckler, A. C., and Alicata, J. E. The life history of *Subulura brumpti*, a cecal nematode of poultry in Hawaii. *Trans. Am. Microscop. Soc.* 63:345, 1944.

Cullinan, R. P. The larvae of *Eustrongylides ignotus* in *Fundulus heteroclitus. J. Parasitol.* 31:109, 1945.

Cuvillier, E. A new intermediate host of *Cheilospirura hamulosa*, the gizzard worm of poultry. *J. Parasitol.* 19:244, 1933.

———. The nematode, *Ornithostrongylus quadriradiatus*, a parasite of the domestic pigeon. *U.S. Dept. Agr. Tech. Bull.* 569, 1937.

Davies, T. I., and Evans, R. Report on helminths collected from an Indian chukar with descriptions of two new species of *Raillietina* Fuhrman, 1920. *Parasitology* 30:419, 1939.

Dikmans, G. *Ascaridia numidae*, a parasite of the guinea hen, *Numida meleagris*, in Louisiana. *J. Parasitol.* 17:230, 1931.

Dotsenko, T. K. Determination of the biological cycle of the nematode, *Cheilospirura hamulosa*, parasite of gallinaceous birds. (Russian text.) *Dokl. Akad. Nauk SSSR*, n.s. 88:583, 1953.

Dubinin, V. B. Experimental investigation on the cycle of development of several parasitic worms of animals of the Volga district. *Parazitol. Sb. Akad. Nauk SSSR Zool. Inst. 11*, p. 126, 1949.

Eber, A. Darmentzuendung, verursacht, durch starken Befall mit Haarwuermern *(Trichosoma retusum)*, Tod durch Lungenentzuenung bei einem jungen Puter. *Deut. Tieraerztl. Wochschr.* 26:46, 1918.

Elsea, J. R. An unsuccessful attempt to establish *Eustrongylides* in the black-crowned night heron, *Nycticorax nycticorax hoactli. J. Parasitol.* 40:362, 1954.

Ershov, V. S. Parasitology and parasitic diseases of livestock, Moscow, 1956. Published for Nat. Sci. Found. and USDA by The Israel Program for Scientific Translators, 1960.

Fahmy, M. A. M. New records of ecto- and endo-parasites of chickens in Egypt with special reference to the taxonomy of *Subulura brumpti. J. Parasitol.* 32:184, 1952.

Flakes, K. Wildlife pathology studies. *Wisc. Wildlife Res.* 9:84, 1950.

Fox, H. Disease in captive wild mammals and and birds; incidence, description and comparison. Philadelphia: Lippincott, 1923.

Freire, J. J. Ornithostrongylose em pombos correio. *Bol. Dir. Prod. Animal Sec. Agr. Ind. e Com. Porto Alegre* 4:12, 1948.

French, G. H. Worms in the brain of a bird. *Science* 21:304, 1893.

Garzia, G. Una nuova specie di *Ascaridia trovata* nei sacchi aerei di uno struzzo. *Nuova Ercol.* 43:81, 1938.

Geller, P. R., and Babich, L. A. Life cycle of *Contracaecum bidentatum* (Linstow, 1899). *Raboty Gel'mintol. 75-Let. Skrjabin*, p. 133, 1954.

Ghesquiere, J. Note sur quelques parasites des oiseaux de basse-cour au Congo Belge. *Bull. Agr. Congo Belge* 12:727, 1921.

———. Sur la repartition geographique de deux vers syngames au Congo Belge. *Compt. Rend. Soc. Biogeograph.* 89:10, 1934.

Gilfillian, G. H. Treatment for wireworm and tapeworm in ostrich chicks. *Rhodesia Agr. J.* 3:298, 1906.

Goble, F. C., and Kutz, H. L. Notes on the gapeworm (Nematoda: Syngamidae) of galliform and passeriform birds in New York State. *J. Parasitol.* 31:394, 1945a.

——— The genus *Dispharynx* (Nematoda: Acuariidae) in galliform and passeriform birds. *J. Parasitol.* 31:323, 1945b.

Gower, W. C. Host-parasite catalogue of the helminths of ducks. *Am. Midland Naturalist* 22:580, 1939.

Graham, G. L. *Capillaria* infestations in New Jersey pheasants. *J. Parasitol.* 21:61, 1925.

Graybill, H. W. *Capillaria columbae* (Rud.) from the chicken and turkey. *J. Parasitol.* 10:205, 1924.

Graybill, H. W., and Smith, T. Production of fatal blackhead in turkeys by feeding embryonated eggs of *Heterakis papillosa. J. Exptl. Med.* 31:647, 1920.

Green, R. G. Disease in relation to game cycles. *Trans. Am. Game Conf.* 18:109, 1931.

———. Pathological report on miscellaneous specimens. *Minn. Wildlife Disease Invest.* 2:39, 1935.

Griffiths, H. J., Leary, R. M., and Fenstermacher, R. A new record of gapeworm (*Cyathostoma bronchialis*) infection of domestic geese in North America. *Am. J. Vet. Res.* 15:298, 1954.

Gross, A. O. Disease of the ruffed grouse. *Auk* 42:423, 1925.

———. Progress report of the Wisconsin prairie chicken investigations. *Wisconsin Conserv. Committee* 1:112, 1930a.

———. Report of the New England ruffed grouse investigations. *New England Game Conf.*, p. 58, 1930b.

———. Parasites and disease in ruffed grouse. *Matamek Conf.*, p. 245, 1931.

Grosso, G. Ueber die *Tropidocerca fissispina* im Vormagen der Ente. *Zentr. Bakteriol. Abt. I. Orig.* 74:272, 1914.

Guilhon, J. Un nouvel anthelmintique: le diethylene diamine. *Bull. Acad. Vet. France* 24:243, 1951.

Hallberg, C. W. *Dioctophyma renale* (Goeze, 1782), a study of the migration routes to the kidneys of mammals and resultant pathology. *Trans. Am. Microscop. Soc.* 72:351, 1953.

Halloran, P. O. A bibliography of references to diseases in wild mammals and birds. *Am. J. Vet. Res.* 16:315, 1955.

Hamann, O. Die Filarienseuche der Enten und der Zwischenwirt von *Filaria uncinata* R. *Zentr. Bakteriol. Parasitenk.* 14:555, 1893.

Hamerton, A. E. Report on the deaths occurring in the society's gardens during 1932. *Proc. Zool. Soc. London* 1933:451, 1933.

———. Reports on the deaths occurring in the society's gardens during 1937. *Proc. Zool. Soc. London* 108:489, 1938.

———, and Rewell, R. E. Report of the pathologist for the year 1946. *Proc. Zool. Soc. London* 117:663, 1947.

Hamilton, C. M. *Capillaria annulata* in Hungarian partridges. *J. Am. Vet. Med. Assoc.* 78:865, 1931.

Hanson, H. C. A three-year survey of *Ornithofilaria* sp. microfilaria in Canada geese. *J. Parasitol.* 42:543, 1956.

Hanson, H. C., and Gilford, J. H. The prevalence of some helminth parasites in Canada geese wintering in southern Illinois. *Trans. Ill. State Acad. Sci.* 54:41, 1961.

Hartwich, G. Revision der vogelparasitischen Nematoden Mitteleuropas. I. Die Gattung *Porrocaecum* Railliet & Henry, 1912 (Ascaridoidea). *Mitt. Zool. Mus.* 35:107, 1959.

———. Revision der vogelparasitischen Nematoden Mitteleuropas. II. Die Gattung *Contracaecum* Railliet & Henry, 1912 (Ascaridoidea). *Mitt. Zool. Mus.* 40:15, 1964.

Hendriks, J. The use of Promintic as anthelmintic against experimental infections of *Capillaria obsignata* Madsen, 1945, in chickens. *Tijdschr. Diergeneesk.* 88:314, 1962.

———. Methyridine in the drinking water against *Capillaria obsignata* Madsen, 1945, in experimentally infected chickens. *Tijdschr. Diergeneesk.* 88:418, 1963.

Herman, C. M. Parasites obtained from animals in the collection of the New York Zoological Park. *Zoologica* 24:481, 1939.

———. Gapeworm in California quail and chukar partridge. *Calif. Fish Game* 31:68, 1945.

Herman, C. M., and Kramer, R. Control of gapeworm infection in game farm birds. *Calif. Fish Game* 36:13, 1950.

Herman, C. M., and Rosen, M. N. Disease investigations on mammals and birds by the California Division of Fish and Game. *Calif. Fish Game* 35:193, 1949.

Herman, C. M., and Wehr, E. E. Progress report of 1950–1952 investigations on Canada goose losses at Pea Island, N.C. Mimeo., 1953.

———. The occurrence of gizzard worms in Canada geese. *J. Wildlife Management* 18:509, 1954.

Hinwood, K. A. A subcutaneous avian parasite. *Emu* 30:131, 1930.

Houdemer, F. E. Parasites des animaux domestiques ou sauvages du Tonkin. *Bull. Soc. Pathol. Exotique* 18:343, 1925.

Huizinga, H. W. Studies on the life cycle and histopathology of the nematode parasite, *Contracaecum spiculigerum,* in fish-eating birds. Mimeo., *Northeast Fish Wildlife Conf.*, Harrisburg, Pa., Jan., p. 17, 1965.

Hung, S. L. Pathological lesions caused by *Capillaria annulata*. *N. Am. Vet.* 7:49, 1926.

Hutcheon, D. Worms in ostriches. *Agr. J. Cape Town* 14:677, 1899.

Hwang, J. C., and Wehr, E. E. Occurrence of *Capillaria obsignata* Madsen, 1945, in the peafowl and its transmission to chickens. *J. Parasitol.* 45 (suppl.):47, 1945.

———. Occurrence of *Capillaria obsignata* Madsen, 1945, in peafowl, with a note on systematic relationship to some other species of *Capillaria* in domestic birds. *Libro Homenaje al Caballero y Caballero,* p. 475, 1960.

Hwang, J. C., McLoughlin, D. K., and Wehr, E. E. Removal of ascarids from pigeons. *Vet. Med.* 53:263, 1958.

Hwang, J. C., Tolgay, N., Shalkop, W. T., and Jaquette, D. S. Case report—*Dispharynx nasuta* causing severe proventriculitis in pigeons. *Avian Diseases* 5:60, 1961.

Inglis, W. G. The comparative anatomy of the subulurid head (Nematoda), with a consideration of its systematic importance. *Proc. Zool. Soc. London* 130:577, 1958.

Karmanov, E. M. An interpretation of the biological cycle of the nematode *Hystrichis tricolor* Dujardin, 1845, a parasite of domestic and wild ducks. (Russian text.) *Dokl. Akad. Nauk SSSR* 3:245, 1956.

———. On the biology of nematodes of the suborder Dioctophymata. (Russian text.) *Raboty Gel'mintol. 80–Let. Skrjabin*, p. 148 (authorized for publication Nov. 24, 1958), 1959.

Kelley, G. W. Removal of *Syngamus trachea*, gapeworm, from pheasants with subcutaneously injected disophenol. *Poultry Sci.* 41:1358, 1962.

Komarov, A., and Beaudette, F. R. *Ornithostrongylus quadriradiatus* in squabs. *J. Am. Vet. Med. Assoc.* 79:393, 1931.

Kreis, H. A. Beitrage zur Kenntnis parasitischer Nematoden. III. *Contortospiculum filiformis* n. sp. ein neuer parasitischer Nematode aus dem Nandu, *Rhea americana* L. *Rev. Suisse Zool.* 43:647, 1936.

Lal, M. B. *Heterakis tragoponis*, a new species of the genus *Heterakis* from the intestine of a crimson-horned pheasant. *Current Sci.* 11:388, 1942.

Layman, E. M. The postembryonal development of the representatives of the family Heterocheilidae and their life cycle. *Uch. Zap. Mosk. Gos. Univ.* (4):129, 1935.

Layman, E. M., and Andronova, A. V. A new nematode from the heron. *Rab. Parasitol. Lab. Mosk. Univ.* 1926:47, 1926.

Leibovitz, L. Thiabendazole therapy of pigeons affected with *Ornithostrongylus quadriradiatus. Avian Diseases* 6:380, 1962.

Leigh, W. H. Some parasites of the prairie chickens of Illinois. *Trans. Ill. Acad. Sci.* 31:233, 1938.

———. Preliminary studies on parasites of upland game birds and fur-bearing mammals in Illinois. *Bull. Ill. Nat. Hist. Sur.* 21:185, 1940.

Leiper, R. T. Exhibition of the larval stages of *Trichostrongylus pergracilis*, the causal factor of grouse disease, etc. *Proc. Zool. Soc. London* 1910:387, 1910.

Le Roux, P. L. Helminths collected from the domestic fowl *(Gallus domesticus)* and the domestic pigeon *(Columba livia)* in Natal. *11th–12th Rept. Director Vet. Educ. Res. Dept. Agr. Union S. Africa, Pretoria, Pt. 1*, Sept., p. 209, 1926.

Lesbouyries, G. *La pathologie des oiseaux*, 1941.

Letulle, M., and Marotel, G. Nodules parasitaires des caecums chez la faisan. *Bull. Soc. Centr. Med. Vet.* 55:268, 1901.

———. Etudes des typhlitis parasitaires; nodules des caecum parasitaires chez le faisan (1). *Arch. Parasitol.* 12:361, 1909.

Levin, N. L. Life history studies on *Porrocaecum ensicaudatum*, an avian nematode. *J. Parasitol.* 43(suppl):47, 1957.

Levine, P. P. Infection of chicken with *Capillaris columbae* (Reed). *J. Parasitol.* 24:45, 1938.

Lewis, E. A. Helminths of wild birds found in the Aberystwyth area. *J. Helminthol.* 4:7, 1926.

———. Observations on the morphology of *Syngamus* of some wild and domestic birds. *J. Helminthol.* 6:99, 1928.

Locke, L. N. Heron and egret losses due to verminous peritonitis. *Avian Diseases* 5:135, 1961.

Lordello, L. G. E., and Pinto Monteiro, F. Larvas de nematodeos do genero *Eustrongylides* parasitando "pintado" do rio piracicaba (Dioctophymidae). *Rev. Agr. Sao Paulo* 5:37, 1959.

Loveridge, A. Notes on East African birds (chiefly nesting habits and endoparasites) collected 1920–1923. *Proc. Zool. Soc. London* 1923:899, 1923.

Lucet, A., and Henry, A. La typhlite verrugueuse des faisans et son parasite (*Heterakis isolonche* v. Linstow). *Bull. Soc. Centr. Med. Vet.*, 1911.

Madsen, D. E. Report on sage grouse survey with reference to parasites and disease. *Misc. Publ. Utah Agr. Exp. Sta.*, p. 22, 1933.

Madsen, H. The occurrence of helminths and coccidia in partridge and pheasants in Denmark. *J. Parasitol.* 27:29, 1941.

———. The species of *Capillaria* (Nematoda: Trichinelloidea) parasitic in the digestive tract of Danish gallinaceous and anatine birds, with a revised list of species of *Capillaria* in birds. *Danish Rev. Game Biol.* 1:1, 1945.

———. Notes on the species of *Capillaria* Zeder, 1800, known species from gallinaceous birds. *J. Parasitol.* 37:257, 1951.

———. A study on the nematodes of Danish gallinaceous game birds. *Danish Rev. Game Biol.* 2:1, 1952.

Malek, E. A. Life cycle studies on the nematode *Subulura brumpti* (Lopez-Neyra, 1922) Cram, 1926, and its distribution in the Sudan. *J. Parasitol.* 44(suppl.):31, 1958.

Margolis, L., and Butler, T. H. An unusual and heavy infection of a prawn, *Pandalus borealis* Kroyer, by a nematode, *Contracaecum* sp. *J. Parasitol.* 40:649, 1954.

Markowski, St. Ueber die Entwicklungsgeschichte und Biologie des Nematoden *Contracaecum aduncum* (Rud., 1802). *Bull. Intern. Acad. Polon. Sc. et Latt., Cracovie, Cl. Sc. Math. et Nat., s. B: Sc. Nat.* (11), (5–7):227, 1937.

Mawson, P. M. Filariid nematodes from Canadian birds. *Can. J. Zool.* 35:213, 1957.

McClure, H. E. The eyeworm (*Oxyspirura petrowi*) in Nebraska pheasant. *J. Wildlife Management* 13:304, 1949.

McCulloch, E. C., and Nicholson, L. G. Phenothiazine for the removal of *Heterakis gallinae* from chicken. *Vet. Med.* 35:398, 1940.

Micke, H. W. A nematode parasite in the Chinese ringnecked pheasant *(Phasianus torquatus)* in the vicinity of Greeley, Colorado. *J. Colo.-Wyo. Acad. Sci.* 1:77, 1934.

Moore, E. J. The parasite problem in game birds. *Atlantic Sportsman* 2:28, 1933.

Moorthy, V. N. Observations on the development of *Dracunculus medinensis* larvae in cyclops. *Am. J. Hyg.* 27:437, 1938.

Morehouse, N. F. Life cycle of *Capillaria caudinflata*, a nematode parasite of the common fowl. Thesis. Iowa State Coll., 1942.

——. Life cycle of *Capillaria caudinflata*, a nematode parasite of the common fowl. *Iowa State Coll. J. Sci.* 18:217, 1944.

Morgan, B. B., and Hamerstrom, F. M. Notes on the endoparasites of Wisconsin pinnated and sharp-tailed grouse. *J. Wildlife Management* 5:194, 1941.

Morgan, B. B., and Clapham, P. A. Some observations on tapeworms in poultry and game birds. *J. Helminthol.* 12:63, 1934.

Mozgovi, A. A. The biology of *Porrocaecum crassum*—nematode of aquatic birds. (Russian text.) *Tr. Gel'minthol. Lab. Akad. Nauk SSSR* 6:114, 1952.

Mueller, J. F. Some parasites newly recorded for the ruffed grouse, *Bonasa umbellus*, in the United States. *Proc. Helminthol. Soc. Wash. D.C.* 8:14, 1941.

Myers, J. B. On morphology and life history of *Phocanema decipiens* (Krabbe, 1878) Myers, 1959 (Nematoda: Anisakinae). *Can. J. Zool.* 28:331, 1960.

——. The migration of *Anisakis*-type larvae in experimental animals. *Can. J. Zool.* 41:147, 1963.

Nagel, W. O. Relationships between diet and extent of parasitism in bobwhite quail. *Wilson Bull.* 41:147, 1934.

Olivier, L. Acquired resistance to the gapeworm, *Syngamus trachea*, in the turkey and ringnecked pheasant. *J. Parasitol.* 28 (suppl.): 20, 1942.

——. Acquired resistance in chickens, turkeys and ringnecked pheasants to the gapeworm, *Syngamus trachea*. *J. Parasitol.* 30:69, 1944.

Olsen, O. W. *Avioserpens bifidus*, a new species of nematode (Dracunculidae) from ducks. *Trans. Am. Microscop. Soc.* 71:150, 1952.

——. Animal parasites. Their biology and life cycles. Minneapolis, 1962.

Ortlepp, R. J. South African helminths. *Onderstepoort J. Vet. Sci.* 9:311, 1937.

——. South African helminths. V. Some avian and mammalian helminths. *Onderstepoort J. Vet. Sci.* 11:63, 1938.

Osche, G. Ueber Entwicklung, Zwischenwirt und Bau von *Porrocaecum talpae*, *P. ensicaudatum* und *Habronema mansoni* (Nematoda). *Z. Parasitenk.* 17:144, 1955.

——. Beitrage zur Morphologie, Oekologie und Phylogonie der Ascaridoidea (Nematoda) parallelen in der Evolution von Parasit und Wirt. *Z. Parasitenk.* 18:479, 1958.

——. Ueber Zwischenwirt, Fehlwirte und die Morphogenese der Lippenregion bei *Porrocaecum*—und *Contracaecum*—Arten (Ascaridoidea Nematoda). *Z. Parasitenk.* 19:458, 1959.

Perez Vigueras, I. Una enfermedad parasitaria epizootica de las Palomas. *Agr. Zootec.* 8: 167, 1929.

Peters, B. G. *Paronchocerca circoniarum* n. g., n. sp. from the saddle-billed stork in West Africa. *J. Helminthol.* 14:1, 1936.

Pollard, H. B. Pheasants and parasites. *Country Life*, London 62:1614, 1927.

Popova, Z. D. Pathological-morphological changes in the glandular stomach of the duck caused by *Tetrameres fissispina* (Diesing, 1961). Russian text.) *Raboty Gel'mintol. 75-Let. Skrjabin*, p. 547 (authorized for publication Nov. 25, 1953), 1954.

Portal, M., and Collinge, W. E. Partridge disease and its causes, including the report and suggestions of the country life committee of inquiry into the diseases of partridges during the season 1931–32, 1932.

Rademeyer, C. W. Worms in ostriches. Treatment with bluestone. *Agr. J. Cape Town* 35:232, 1909.

Rankin, J. S. Helminth parasites of birds and mammals in western Massachusetts. *Am. Midland Naturalist* 35:756, 1946.

Refuerzo, P. G. Arthropod intermediate hosts of *Acuaria hamulosa* in the Philippines. *Nat. Appl. Sci. Bull. Univ. Philippines* 7:407, 1940.

Reibisch, J. *Trichosomum strumosum* n. sp., ein Parasit aus dem Epithel des Oesophagus von *Phasianus colchicus*. *Arch. Naturg. Berlin* 59:331, 1893.

Riley, W. A. Reported killing of grouse of Minnesota by parasitic disease. *J. Parasitol.* 11: 229, 1925.

Robert, Roger. L'helminthiase intestinale de la

poule et du pigeon, son traitement par le bromhydrate d'arecaidine. *These Vet. Alfort,* 1932.

Roberts, F. H. S. Studies on the life history and economic importance of *Heterakis gallinae* (Gmelin, 1790; Freeborn, 1923), the cecal worm of fowls. *Australian J. Exptl. Biol. Med. Sci.* 15:429, 1937.

Romanova, N. P. Diagnosis of *Cyathostoma* infection in the emu. *Tr. Moshovak. Zooparka.* 3:136, 1946.

Rose, J. H., and Keymer, I. F. An outbreak of ornithostrongylosis in domestic pigeons. *Vet. Rec.* 70:932, 1938.

Rust, K. B. Entenerkrankung durch tropidocerca fissispina. [Abstract.] *Veroeffentl.* a.d. *J. Vet. Ber. d. beamt Tieraerzte Preuss.* 6:30, 1908.

Ryzhikov, K. M. Reservoir parasitism among helminths. (Russian text.) *Tr. Gel'mintol. Lab. Akad. Nauk SSSR* 7:200, 1953.

Sambon, W. Note on a *Filaria* of the red grouse. *J. Trop. Med. Hyg.* 10:304, 1907.

Schachtachtinskaja, Z. Un nouveaux nematode, *Petroviprocta vigissi,* nov. gen., nov. sp., de la cavite thoracique du bihoreaux. *Tr. Gel'mintol. Lab. Akad. Nauk SSSR* 5:162, 1951.

Schell, S. C. Four new species of *Microtetrameres* (Nematoda: Spiruroidea) from North American birds. *Trans. Am. Microscop. Soc.* 72:227, 1953.

Schwartz, B. Occurrence of nodular typhlitis in pheasants due to *Heterakis isolonche* in North America. *J. Am. Vet. Med. Assoc.* 65:622, 1924a.

———. *Heterakis isolonche* in pheasants from Pennsylvania. *J. Parasitol.* 11:109, 1924b.

Seurat, L. G. Sur un nouveaux parasite de la perdix rouge d'Algerie (*Perdix rubra* Bresson). *Bull. Soc. Pathol. Exotique* 10:701, 1914.

Shaw, J. N. Some parasites of Oregon wildlife. *Bull. Oregon Agr. Exp. Sta. 11,* 1947.

Shillinger, J. E. Parasites and wildlife. *Vet. Med.* 31:12, 1936.

Shillinger, J. E., and Coburn, D. R. Diseases of game birds. *Vet. Med.* 35:124, 1940.

Shillinger, J. E., and Morley, L. C. Diseases of upland game birds. *Circ. Fish Wildlife Serv. Wash. D.C.* 21, 1942.

Shipley, A. E. Internal parasites of birds allied to the grouse. *Proc. Zool. Soc. London* (2): 363, 1909.

———. Parasites of the willow grouse. *Field* 115:519, 1910.

Shumard, R. F. The anthelmintic activity of powdered and liquid parvex against *Ascaridia galli* and *Heterakis gallinae. J. Parasitol.* 42 (suppl.):13, 1956.

Shumard, R. F., and Eveleth, D. F. A preliminary report on the anthelmintic action of piperazine citrate on *Ascaridia galli* and *Heterakis gallinae* in hens. *Vet. Med.* 50:203, 1955.

Simon, F. *Cheilospirura centrocerci,* a new nematode from the sage grouse, *Centrocercus urophasianus. Trans. Am. Microscop. Soc.* 58:78, 1939.

———. The parasites of the sage grouse. *Wyoming Univ. Publ.* 7:77, 1940.

Singh, S. N. Studies on the helminth parasites of birds in Hyderabad state. Nematoda I. *J. Helminthol.* 22:77, 1948a.

———. Studies on the helminth parasites of birds in Hyderabad state. Nematoda II. *J. Helminthol.* 22:199, 1948b.

———. Studies on the helminth parasites of birds in Hyderabad state. Nematoda III. *J. Helminthol.* 23:25, 1949.

Skrjabin, K. I. Neue Nematoden der Gattung *Oxyspirura* Drasche aus dem Vogelauge. *Z. Parasitenk.* 3:726, 1931.

Sloan, J. E. N., Kingsbury, P. A., and Jolly, D. W. Preliminary trials with piperazine adipate as a veterinary anthelmintic. *J. Pharm. Pharmacol.* 6:718, 1954.

Stafseth, H. J., and Kotlan, S. Report of investigations on an alleged epizootic of ruffed grouse in Michigan. *J. Am. Vet. Med. Assoc.* 20:210, 1925.

Stevenson, E. C. A new parasite (*Strongylus quadriradiatus* n. sp.) found in the pigeon. Preliminary report, *U.S. Dept. Agr. Bur. Animal Ind. Circ. 47,* 1904.

Sugimoto, M. On a nematode parasite (*Filaria* sp.) from Formosan ducks. *J. Agr. Formosa,* no. 108, p. 63, 1914.

———. List of zooparasites of the domesticated animals in Formosa, 1919.

———. On a new species of the genus Eustrongylidae from Formosan herons. *J. Japan. Soc. Vet. Sci.* 12:29, 1933.

———. On the *Filaria* from the Formosan domesticated birds. *J. Japan. Soc. Vet. Sci.* 13:261, 1934a.

———. Study of a nematode (*Oshimaia taiwana*) (Sugimoto, 1919) from Formosan duck, and filariasis of the duck. *J. Soc. Trop. Agr. Taihoku Imp. Univ.* 6:437, 1934b.

———. On the *Filaria* from domestic fowls in Formosa. *J. Centr. Soc. Vet. Med. Tokyo* 48:277, 1935.

Sugimoto, M., and Nashiyama, S. On the nematode, *Tropisurus fissispinus* (Diesing, 1835), and its transmission to chickens in Formosa. *J. Japan. Soc. Vet. Sci.* 16:305, 1937.

Swales, W. E. A review of Canadian helminthology. I. The present status of knowledge of the helminth parasites of domesticated and semidomesticated mammals and economically important birds in Canada, as determined from work published prior to 1933. *Can. J. Res.* 8:468, 1933.

Swales, W. E. *Tetrameres crami* Swales, 1933, a nematode parasite of ducks in Canada. Morphological and biological studies. *Can. J. Res. D.* 14:151, 1936.

Swanson, L. A note on the parasitic fauna of the Hawaiian Islands. *Proc. Helminthol. Soc. Wash. D.C.* 6:29, 1939.

Tauber, A. H., and Benbrook, E. A. Parasites and diseases of wild animals, with special emphasis on the pheasant, quail and wild rabbit. *Rep. Agr. Res. Iowa State Conserv. Commission,* Project no. 570, 1944.

Teixeira de Freitas, J. H. *Capillaria rudolphii* n. sp. parasita do intestino delgado *Tinamus solitarius* Vieill. *Mem. Inst. Oswaldo Cruz* 28:259, 1934.

Teixeira de Freitas, J. H., and Lins de Almeida, J. Sobre os nematoda capillariinae parasitas de esophago e papo de aves. *Mem. Inst. Oswaldo Cruz* 30:123, 1935.

Theil, P. H. van, Kuipers, F. C., and Roskam, R. Th. A nematode parasitic to herring, causing acute abdominal syndromes in man. *Trop. Geograph. Med.* 12:97, 1960.

———. A nematode parasitic to herring, causing acute abdominal syndromes in man. *Acta Leidensia* 30:143, 1960.

Thienport, D., and Mortelmans, J. Methyridine in the control of intestinal capillariasis in birds. *Vet. Rec.* 74:850, 1962.

Thomas, E. *Capillaria annulata* in quail. *J. Am. Vet. Med. Assoc.* 76:95, 1930.

Thomas, J. L. On the life cycle of *Contracaecum spiculigerum* (Rud.). *J. Parasitol.* 23:429, 1937a.

———. Further studies on the life cycle of *Contracaecum spiculigerum.* *J. Parasitol.* 23:572, 1937b.

———. Life cycle studies on *Contracaecum spiculigerum* a nematode from the cormorant, *Phalacrocorax auritus,* and other fish-eating birds. 3. *Intern. Congr. Microbiol. Rep. Proc.* 458, 1940.

Timon-David, Jean. Les kystes a tetrameres du pigeon. *Ann. Parasitol.* 10:425, 1932.

Travassos, L. Sobre as especies brazileiros de genero *Tetrameres* Creplin, 1846. (Nota previa) *Brasil-Med. Rio de Jan.* 29:297, 1915.

———. *Ascaridia pintoi* n. sp., parasite de la perdix. *Compt. Rend. Soc. Biol.* 112:1475, 1933.

Truong-Tan-Ngog. Filariose du canard domestique en Cochinchine due a *Oshimaia taiwana* (Sugimoto, 1919). *Bull. Soc. Pathol. Exotique* 30:775, 1937.

Uribe, C. Observations on the development of

Heterakis papillosa Bloch in the chicken. *J. Parasitol.* 8:167, 1922.

Van Cleave, H. J. Worm parasites and their relation to wildlife investigations. *J. Wildlife Management* 1:21, 1937.

Vaz, Z. Redescription of *Tetracheilonema quadrilabiatum* (Molin, 1858) a filariid worm-parasite of South American Tinamiformes birds. *Ann. Trop. Med. Parasitol.* 28:21, 1934.

Vaz, Z., and Pereia, C. Some new Brazilian nematodes. *Trans. Am. Microscop. Soc.* 54:36, 1935.

Venard, C. Helminths and coccidia from the Ohio bobwhite. *J. Parasitol.* 19:205, 1933.

Ward, J. W. Parasite studies of quail, *Colinus virginianus* and *Colinus virginianus texanus* in Texas. *J. Parasitol.* 31 (suppl.):23, 1945a.

———. A new locality for five species of helminth parasites of the bobwhite quail. *Proc. Helminthol. Soc. Wash. D.C.* 12:71, 1945b.

Webster, J. D., and Addis, C. J. Helminths from the bobwhite quail in Texas. *J. Parasitol.* 37:322, 1945.

Wehr, E. E. A nematode pathogenic to the sage grouse. *J. Parasitol.* 16:168, 1930.

———. Occurrence of *Desmidocercella numidica* in herons in the United States. *J. Parasitol.* 17:231, 1931a.

———. A new species of nematode worm from the sage grouse. *Proc. U.S. Nat. Mus.* 79:1, 1931b.

———. Occurrence of a nematode, *Cheilospirura spinosa* Cram, 1927, as a parasite of the sage grouse of western United States. *J. Parasitol.* 19:90, 1932.

———. A new nematode from the rhea. *Proc. U.S. Nat. Mus.* 82:1, 1933a.

———. Occurrence of *Ascaridia lineata* in California valley quail. *J. Parasitol.* 19:252, 1933b.

———. Coexistence of adult male and female *Tetrameres* (Nematoda: Spiruridae) in proventriculus of the Florida grackle. *Proc. Helminthol. Soc. Wash. D.C.* 1:50, 1934a.

———. A new host for the bird dracunculid, *Avioserpens denticulophasma.* *Proc. Helminthol. Soc. Wash. D.C.* 1:11, 1934b.

———. Relative abundance of crop worms in turkeys. Microscopic differentiation of species. *Vet. Med.* 6:230, 1937a.

———. Observations on the development of the poultry gapeworm *Syngamus trachea.* *Trans. Am. Microscop. Soc.* 56:72, 1937b.

———. New genera and species of the nematode superfamily Filarioidea. I. *Serratospiculum amaculata,* n. sp. *Proc. Helminthol. Soc. Wash. D.C.* 5:59, 1938a.

———. A new species of crop worm, *Gongylonema phasianella,* from the sharp-tailed grouse. *Livro Jubilaire Prof. L. Travassos,* p. 523, 1938b.

————. Studies on the development of the pigeon capillarid, *Capillaria columbae. U.S. Dept. Agr. Tech. Bull. 679,* 1939.

————. Nematodes of domestic fowls transmissible to wild game birds. *Vet. Med.* 35:52, 1940a.

————. A new intestinal roundworm from the ruffed grouse *(Bonasa umbellus)* in the United States. *J. Parasitol.* 26:373, 1940b.

————. A cropworm, *Capillaria contorta,* the cause of death in turkeys. *Proc. Helminthol. Soc. Wash. D.C.* 15:80, 1948.

————. Recent studies on transmission of *Capillaria* spp. of poultry, with special reference to *C. contorta. J. Parasitol.* 38 (suppl.):17, 1952.

————. Nematodes and acanthocephalids of poultry. In H. E. Biester and L. H. Schwarte, *Diseases of poultry.* Ames: Iowa State Univ. Press, 1965.

————. Thiabendazole as an anthelmintic for the control of gapeworm *(Syngamus trachea)* in the pheasant *(Phasianus colchicus). J. Parasitol.* 53:792, 1967.

Wehr, E. E., and Chitwood, B. G. A new nematode from birds. *Proc. Helminthol. Soc. Wash. D.C.* 1:10, 1934.

Wehr, E. E., and Herman, C. M. Age as a factor in acquisition of parasites by Canada geese. *J. Wildlife Management* 18:239, 1954.

Wehr, E. E., and Hwang, J. C. The life cycle and morphology of *Ascaridia columbae* (Gmelin, 1790) Travassos, 1913 (Nematoda: Ascarididae) in the domestic pigeon *(Co-lumba livia domestica). J. Parasitol.* 50:131, 1964.

————. Anthelmintic activity of thiabendazole against the gapeworm *(Syngamus trachea)* in turkeys. *Avian Diseases* 11:44, 1967.

Wehr, E. E., and Shalkop, W. T. *Ascaridia columbae* infection in pigeons: a histopathologic study of liver lesions. *Avian Diseases* 7:206, 1963.

Wehr, E. E., Colglazier, M. L., Burtner, R. H., and Wiest, L. M., Jr. Methyridine, an effective anthelmintic for intestinal threadworm, *Capillaria obsignata,* in pigeons. *Avian Diseases* 11:322, 1967.

Wells, M. J., and Hunter, W. S. Helminths of the yellow-throat, *Geothlypis trichas,* during migration. *J. Parasitol.* 46:623, 1960.

Wetzel, R., and Enigh, K. Gehaufte Todesfalle von Nandus *(Rhea americana)* durch Helminthenbefall. *Sitzber. Ges. Naturf. Fr. Berl.* (1–3), p. 19, 1938.

Woodhead, A. E. Life history cycle of the giant kidney worm, *Dioctophyma renale* (Nematoda), of man and many other mammals. *Trans. Am. Microscop. Soc.* 69:21, 1950.

Yamaguti, S. Studies on the helminth fauna of Japan. XII. Avian nematodes. *Japan J. Zool.* 6:403, 1937.

————. Systema helminthicum. III. The nematodes of vertebrates. Part 1, p. 1; Part 2, p. 681, 1962.

Yamashita, J. *Subulura olympioi* Barreto, 1918, a nematode of the Indian peacock, *Pavo cristatus,* Linn. *Oyo Dobutsugaku Zasshi,* Tokyo 10:22, 1938.

C. PROTOZOA

21 ◆ COCCIDIA OF ANSERIFORMES, GALLIFORMES, AND PASSERIFORMES

- **KENNETH S. TODD, JR.**
- **DATUS M. HAMMOND**

COCCIDIA are widespread and important parasites of vertebrates. They cause a disease known as coccidiosis, which is a serious problem in poultry, sheep, and cattle. Most coccidia are unusual in having a relatively high degree of host-specificity and in the frequency of occurrence of several different species in the same host. The most common genus is *Eimeria;* more than 500 species of this genus have been described. *Eimeria* spp. are frequently found in anseriform and galliform birds but *Eimeria* spp. are rare in Passeriformes.

◆ **TAXONOMY.** The coccidia proper belong to the suborder Eimeriina, order Eucoccida, subclass Coccidia, class Telosporea, subphylum Sporozoa, phylum Protozoa. The suborder Eimeriina is characterized by independent development of the sexual stages. Also, each microgametocyte produces many microgametes, the zygote is immotile, and the sporozoites are surrounded by a membrane to form the sporocyst. The coccidia considered in this chapter belong to the family Eimeriidae or to the family Lankesterellidae. In the former family the species have a single host; development of the endogenous stages occurs within the host cells to produce a resistant stage, the oocyst; sporulation of oocysts usually takes place outside the host. The oocysts of different genera have a character-

istic number of sporocysts, each with 1 or more sporozoites. In species of the Lankesterellidae, there are 2 hosts, but all development occurs in the vertebrate host, terminating in the formation of sporozoites, which enter red blood cells. These are ingested by an invertebrate (a leech or a mite) and in this way are transferred to another individual of the vertebrate host. The sporozoites, which lie free in the oocyst, number 32 or more in the genus *Lankesterella,* which is the only member of the family occurring in birds.

In the family Eimeriidae, 5 genera are known to occur in the birds herein considered. The species of the genus *Eimeria,* which constitute the largest number, have oocysts with 4 sporocysts, each containing 2 sporozoites. The species of the genus *Isospora* have oocysts with 2 sporocysts, each containing 4 sporozoites. The species of the genus *Dorisiella* have oocysts with 2 sporocysts, each with 8 sporozoites. The species of the genus *Wenyonella* have oocysts with 4 sporocysts, each with 4 sporozoites. The genus *Tyzzeria* includes species having oocysts with 8 naked sporozoites.

◆ **MORPHOLOGY.** Because taxonomy is usually based upon the morphology of the sporulated oocyst stage, this is described in detail here. A typical eimerian oocyst is illustrated in Fig. 21.1.

The oocyst has an outer covering consisting of one or two layers, although three are present in rare instances. An inner lining membrane sometimes occurs. At one end of the oocyst, the wall may be thinner or otherwise differentiated to form

We wish to thank Drs. John Ernst, Paul R. Fitzgerald and Norman D. Levine for comments on the manuscript. William P. Bischoff and Sammy K. Allen assisted with the literature. The work was supported in part by a National Science Foundation Research Grant, GB 5667X and Training Grant AI-00033 from the National Institutes of Health.

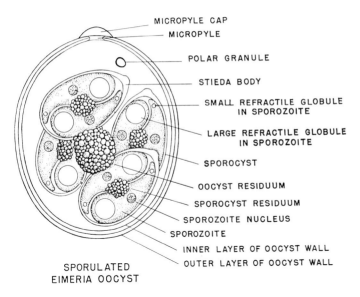

MICROPYLE CAP
MICROPYLE
POLAR GRANULE
STIEDA BODY
SMALL REFRACTILE GLOBULE
IN SPOROZOITE
LARGE REFRACTILE GLOBULE
IN SPOROZOITE
SPOROCYST
OOCYST RESIDUUM
SPOROCYST RESIDUUM
SPOROZOITE NUCLEUS
SPOROZOITE
INNER LAYER OF OOCYST WALL
OUTER LAYER OF OOCYST WALL
SPORULATED
EIMERIA OOCYST

FIG. 21.1. Structures of sporulated *Eimeria* oocysts. (From Levine, 1961.)

a micropyle, through which the sporozoites excyst. This area is sometimes covered by a micropylar cap. Associated with the micropyle, a structure known as Allen's operculum may occur in some species.

The space within the oocyst is filled with a colorless fluid in which the sporocysts are suspended. In many species there are one or more polar granules, which are small refractile structures, presumably representing the polar bodies associated with meiosis. An oocyst residuum, composed of scattered or compact granules or globules, may also occur.

The sporocysts have a relatively thin wall with a knoblike enlargement, the Stieda body, at one end. In some species a pluglike substiedal body lies immediately below the Stieda body. Within the sporocysts are the sporozoites, and frequently a scattered or compact granular residuum. The sporozoites are usually spindle-shaped with one end wider than the other, and they vary in location within the sporocyst. Often a nucleus and one or more prominent refractile bodies may be distinguished within each sporozoite.

The characteristics of the sporulated oocysts, including measurements, are usually sufficient to diagnose species of coccidia. Other features of importance in dis-

tinguishing species are duration of patent and prepatent periods, time required for sporulation, host-specificity, location in the host, morphology of the endogenous stages, relationship of these to the host cell, and pathogenicity.

◆ **LIFE CYCLES.** The life cycles of the members of the Eimeriidae are similar. Infection may be initiated by the ingestion of sporulated oocysts. These contain the infective stages, the sporozoites, which usually excyst in the intestine of the host. The free sporozoites are motile and penetrate cells lining the lumen of the digestive tract. The intracellular sporozoite transforms into a rounded stage, the trophozoite, which grows rapidly at the expense of the host cell. During this growth, the nucleus of the parasite divides a number of times, and the host cell may become enlarged. The schizont stage, which begins after the occurrence of nuclear multiplication, terminates in the formation of merozoites. These resemble the sporozoites in general form and motility. They are released by the disintegration of the host cell and penetrate new cells in the same or a lower region of the digestive tract.

The time required for development of

the sporozoite to the merozoite stage is generally 1 or more days. This cycle is usually repeated at least once. Coccidia generally have 2 or 3 generations of schizonts, but some species have 4 generations. These repeated generations of schizonts result in a great increase in numbers of coccidia in the host. The last generation of merozoites enters new host cells and develops into gametocytes, of which there are 2 kinds. The macrogamete has a prominent nucleus, which does not divide, and special granules are developed in its cytoplasm; these later participate in formation of the oocyst wall. In the microgametocytes, nuclear multiplication occurs, and a number of flagellated microgametes are produced. These are motile when liberated and fertilize the macrogametes. After fertilization the oocyst wall is formed around the zygote. The protoplasm at first fills all the space within the oocyst wall, but by the time the oocyst has been discharged in the feces of the host, the protoplasm has usually contracted to a spheroidal mass, the sporont, occupying only half to two-thirds of the internal space. The interval from ingestion of oocysts until daughter oocysts are discharged varies from a few days to a week or more. Oocyst discharge usually continues for 10 days or longer. Unless additional oocysts are ingested, infections last for only a few weeks.

Under favorable conditions of moisture, temperature, and availability of oxygen, the discharged oocysts undergo sporulation. This process, which is meiotic in nature, usually requires several days. The sporont nucleus divides to form a haploid cell and polar body. The former divides into 4 sporoblasts, each of which forms a surrounding wall to become a sporocyst. Then another division occurs, resulting in the formation of 2 sporozoites within each sporocyst. The sporulated oocysts are resistant to unfavorable conditions and may survive for months or years.

The life cycle of *Eimeria tenella* from the domestic chicken has been described in detail and is illustrated in Figure 21.2.

◆ **EPIDEMIOLOGY.** Coccidia are usually transmitted from one individual to another in food or water contaminated with feces. Thus, when animals of a particular species are crowded together, coccidiosis is much more likely to be a problem than when they are not. For this reason, wild animals do not have as much trouble from coccidian infections as do domestic animals, except when reared under game-farm conditions. With respect to wild birds, gregarious species are more likely to have large numbers of coccidia than those which are not gregarious.

In animals in which coccidiosis is a serious problem, immunity usually plays an important role. In the majority of species for which information is available, infections of light or moderate intensity stimulate the development of resistance to additional infections. Such immunity is of variable duration and degree in different species and hosts. Older animals often have some degree of immunity as a result of previous infections, so they are less susceptible to infection than young animals of the same species. Such older animals may, however, have light infections and discharge oocysts, thus acting as a source of infection for associated young animals. Farm-reared game birds are likely to have developed some immunity by the time they are mature and may transmit infections to wild birds after they are released.

Coccidian species are typically able to infect only one host species. However, some species are transmissible to one or more additional host species within the same genus, and some instances of cross-generic transmission are known. One species, *Isospora lacazei,* has been described from many species belonging to different genera of passeriform and other birds, but further investigation is needed to determine the true host range of this species (Levine and Mohan, 1960). A number of instances of mistaken identity have occurred as a result of the description of new species based on the finding in fecal samples of oocysts which had passed through

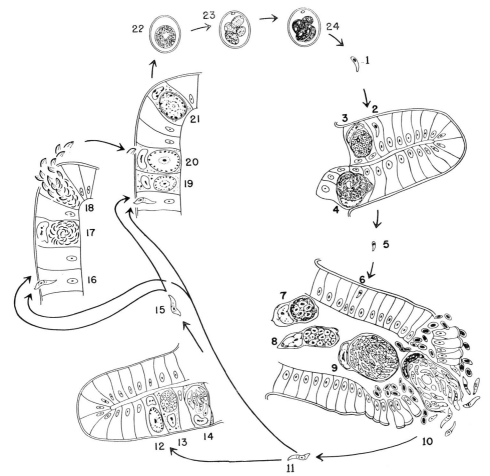

FIG. 21.2. Life cycle of the chicken coccidium, *Eimeria tenella*. A sporozoite *(1)* enters an intestinal endothelial cell *(2)*, rounds up, grows, and becomes a first generation schizont *(3)*. This produces a large number of first generation merozoites *(4)*, which break out of the host cell *(5)*, enter new intestinal endothelial cells *(6)*, round up, grow, and become second generation schizonts *(7, 8)*. These produce a large number of second generation merozoites *(9, 10)*, which break out of the host cell *(11)*. Some enter new host intestinal endothelial cells and round up to become third generation schizonts *(12, 13)*, which produce third generation merozoites *(14)*. The third generation merozoites *(15)* and the great majority of second generation merozoites *(11)* enter new host intestinal endothelial cells. Some become microgametocytes *(16, 17)*, which produce a large number of microgametes *(18)*. Others turn into macrogametes *(19, 20)*. The macrogametes are fertilized by the microgametes and become zygotes *(21)*, which lay down a heavy wall around themselves and turn into young oocysts. These break out of the host cell and pass out in the feces *(22)*. The oocysts then sporulate. The sporont throws off a polar body and forms 4 sporoblasts *(23)*, each of which forms a sporocyst containing 2 sporozoites *(24)*. When the sporulated oocyst *(24)* is ingested by a chicken, the sporozoites are released *(1)*. (From Levine, 1961.)

the digestive tract of a host after ingestion without causing an infection.

◆ **PATHOGENESIS.** Little is known as to how coccidia cause pathologic changes in wild birds. In chickens the 9 recognized species of *Eimeria* differ considerably in pathogenicity, and each of the pathogenic species produces changes characteristic of that species. Generally the affected portion of the intestine undergoes destruction of the epithelium, hemorrhage occurs, and the lumen is filled with sloughed tissue and blood. In some species cores of fibrinous and necrotic material form in the lumen. The intestine is often thickened and congested. Usually a marked diarrhea, which may be bloody, occurs, depending upon the severity of the infection and the species involved. Dehydration often accompanies coccidiosis. An inflammatory reaction occurs and the epithelium regenerates after termination of the infection. Animals that survive severe infections suffer retardation of growth.

◆ **DIAGNOSIS.** Coccidiosis is generally diagnosed by the finding of oocysts in fecal samples. Because the oocysts may be present in relatively low numbers, it is generally advisable to use a method for concentrating the oocysts. The most practicable procedure is sugar flotation. A method recommended by Levine (1961), which is suitable for most purposes, is as follows:

1. Make a rather heavy suspension of feces in physiologic salt solution in a shell vial or other container.
2. Strain through two layers of cheesecloth into a test tube or centrifuge tube, filling the tube almost half full. The lip of the tube must be smooth, or an air bubble will form under the cover slip following centrifugation (#6 below).
3. Add an equal volume of Sheather's sugar solution, leaving a small air space at the top. Cover with a plastic cover slip or small piece of card and invert tube repeatedly to mix.
4. Add enough additional Sheather's sugar

solution to bring the surface of the liquid barely above the top of the tube.
5. Cover with a round cover slip.
6. Centrifuge for 5 minutes. (If a centrifuge is not available, let stand for 45 minutes to 1 hour.)
7. Remove the cover slip, place it on a slide, and examine under the microscope.
   (If desired, Steps 2 and 4 can be modified by straining the fecal suspension into a second shell vial, mixing with an equal volume of Sheather's sugar solution, and then filling the centrifuge tube with the mixture.)

Sheather's sugar solution is prepared by mixing 500 g of sucrose to 320 g of distilled water, and adding 6.5 g of phenol, which has been melted in a water bath, as a preservative.

Another method of sugar flotation involves the use of McMaster slides. In this method a suspension of the fecal sample is prepared as described above. One ml of this is mixed with 2 ml of Sheather's solution, and part of the mixture is transferred to a McMaster slide. This consists of 2 glass slides mounted one above the other, forming a chamber 1.5 mm deep; the upper slide has a 1 sq cm grid etched on its under surface. After allowing the preparation to stand for 15 minutes or more to allow the oocysts to accumulate at the upper surface of the fluid, the slide is examined under the microscope. This method gives quantitative information, which may be useful in evaluating the seriousness of the coccidian infection.

Examinations for endogenous stages are conducted by taking samples of intestinal contents, scrapings of intestinal mucosa, or histologic sections of the intestinal wall, and examining these for oocysts, gamonts, or schizonts.

◆ **TREATMENT AND CONTROL.** Because of the self-limiting nature of coccidian infections, and their tendency to cause problems only when host animals are living in crowded conditions, treatment is generally not necessary in wild birds.

Treatment may be needed to control coccidiosis on game-bird farms, but if the birds are reared under proper hygienic conditions, severe coccidian infections should not occur. Coccidiostats such as Zoalene and Amprolium have been found to be effective for preventing coccidiosis in pheasants, and various sulfonamides are helpful in reducing losses in infected birds. However, each coccidian species responds differently to drugs.

In the following sections coccidia from wild and game-farm or zoo birds (which are usually found in the wild state) of the orders Anseriformes, Galliformes, and Passeriformes are discussed. The coccidia are listed under the genus from which they were first described, even though the parasite may have subsequently been described from additional genera. Bird names follow the American Ornithologists' Union *Check-List of North American Birds* (1957) or Peters' (1931–1967) *Check-List of the Birds of the World*.

ANSERIFORMES

Hanson et al. (1957) reviewed the literature on the coccidia of wild geese and swans. Several species of *Eimeria* and *Tyzzeria anseris* have been found in both domestic and wild geese. *Tyzzeria anseris* is widely distributed in wild geese and has been reported from the whistling swan. Five of the *Eimeria* species from geese are highly unusual in that they are found in both *Anser* and *Branta* species. Some species seem to be restricted to each genus, but Hanson et al. (1957) thought future study might show that some species which have not been found in both genera might be present in both *Anser* and *Branta*.

Anas

Eimeria anatis Scholtyseck 1955

◆ **DISTRIBUTION AND INCIDENCE.** Five of 32 mallards (*Anas platyrhynchos platyrhynchos*), Germany.

◆ **DEVELOPMENT.** The sporulation time is 4 days. Endogenous development takes place in the small intestine.

◆ **CLINICAL SIGNS.** Unknown.

◆ **PATHOGENESIS.** Unknown.

◆ **DIAGNOSIS.** The oocysts are ovoid and measure 14 to 19μ by 11 to 16μ (mean 16.8μ by 14.1μ). The oocyst wall is smooth, about 0.7 to 1.0μ thick, and composed of two layers. A collar is present around the micropyle. A plug, Allen's operculum, similar to that in *Eimeria phasiani*, is located interior to the micropyle. No oocyst residuum is present. The sporocysts are oval and have indistinct Stieda bodies. The sporocyst residuum consists of a few granules which are located between the sporozoites.

Eimeria boschadis Walden 1963

◆ **DISTRIBUTION AND INCIDENCE.** Two of 27 mallards (*Anas platyrhynchos platyrhynchos*), Sweden.

◆ **DEVELOPMENT.** Endogenous development takes place in the kidney.

◆ **CLINICAL SIGNS.** Unknown.

◆ **PATHOGENESIS.** Both cases observed by Walden were light infections and of little importance.

◆ **DIAGNOSIS.** Oocysts are bottle-shaped and slightly asymmetrical (Fig. 21.3). The oocyst wall is colorless and slightly rough. A micropyle at the narrow end of the oocyst measures 2 to 3μ in width. Oocysts measure 18 to 27μ by 12 to 13μ (mean 23.9μ by 12.7μ).

Tyzzeria pellerdyi Bhatia and Pande 1966

◆ **DISTRIBUTION AND INCIDENCE.** One of 2 gadwalls (*Anas strepera*) and 2 of 4 white-eyed pochards (*Aythya nyroca*) from India.

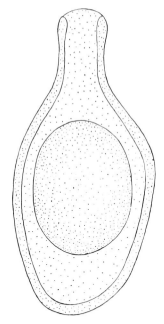

FIG. 21.3. Oocyst of *Eimeria boschadis.* ×3,000. (From Walden, 1963.)

◆ **DEVELOPMENT.** Unknown.

◆ **CLINICAL SIGNS.** Unknown.

◆ **PATHOGENESIS.** Unknown.

◆ **DIAGNOSIS.** Oocysts (Fig. 21.4) are subspherical to ovoid and measure 11 to 16μ by 8 to 11μ (mean 13μ by 10μ). The oocyst wall is smooth, colorless, and 0.5 to 0.7μ thick. No micropyle is present. As in other species of *Tyzzeria,* a distinct oocyst residuum is present. The polar granule is

FIG. 21.4. Oocyst of *Tyzzeria pellerdyi.* (From Bhatia and Pande, 1966.)

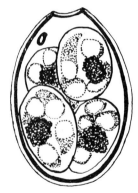

FIG. 21.5. Oocyst of *Wenyonella pellerdyi.* (From Bhatia and Pande, 1966.)

absent. Sporozoites measure 8.0 to 10.0μ by 1.7 to 2.2μ (mean 8.5μ by 2.0μ).

Wenyonella pellerdyi
Bhatia and Pande 1966

◆ **DISTRIBUTION.** Two of 4 blue-winged teal *(Anas querquedula),* India.

◆ **DEVELOPMENT.** Sexual stages were found by Bhatia and Pande in epithelial cells of the villi of the "middle intestinal region." Sporulation time is 2 days.

◆ **CLINICAL SIGNS.** Unknown.

◆ **PATHOGENESIS.** Unknown.

◆ **DIAGNOSIS.** Oocysts (Fig. 21.5) are ellipsoidal or ovoidal and measure 13 to 19μ by 10 to 13μ (mean 17.6μ by 12.7μ). The oocyst wall is colorless, consists of two layers, and is about 1.0 to 1.3μ thick. A micropyle, 2.0 to 2.5μ in diameter, is present. A single polar granule is present, but an oocyst residuum is absent. Sporocysts are ovoid and measure 7 to 9μ by 4 to 8μ (mean 8.0μ by 5.7μ). No Stieda body is present. Sporozoites measure 5 to 7μ by 2 to 3μ (mean 6.0μ by 2.5μ) and contain a compact sporocyst residuum.

◆ **REMARKS.** *Tyzzeria perniciosa* has been described from the domestic duck and is pathogenic to ducklings (Allen, 1936). *Eimeria battakhi* Dubey and Pande 1963 and *Wenyonella anatis* Pande, Bhatia, and Srivastava 1965 have also been described from domestic ducks. Two species that are pathogenic to domestic ducks but have not been reported from wild ducks are *Eimeria danailovi* Graefner, Graubmann, and Betke 1965 and *Eimeria saitamae* Inoue 1967.

Anser

Eimeria anseris Kotlan 1932, emend. Kotlan 1933

◆ **DISTRIBUTION AND INCIDENCE.** Domestic geese *(Anser anser)*, Europe; 3 of 73 snow geese *(Chen hyperborea)* and blue geese *(Chen caerulescens),* Ontario; 2 of 6 Richardson's Canada geese *(Branta canadensis hutchinsi)*, Manitoba.

◆ **DEVELOPMENT.** In the domestic goose endogenous development takes place in the epithelial cells of the villi of the small intestine; it may also occur in the lamina propria (Pellerdy, 1965). In heavy infections Klimes (1963) found gametocytes throughout the intestine and ceca. The parasites are most numerous in the lower portion of the small intestine. According to Pellerdy (1965) mature schizonts are 12 to 20μ and contain 15 to 25 merozoites. Pellerdy reported that several asexual generations might occur and that in mild infections the sexual stages are usually in the epithelial cells, but in heavy infections they are also in the lamina propria of the villi. According to Klimes (1963) macrogametes are 11 to 24μ by 10 to 18μ (mean 18.5μ by 13.4μ); microgametocytes are slightly larger than the macrogametes. The sporulation time is 1 to 2 days and the prepatent period is 7 days.

◆ **CLINICAL SIGNS.** Unknown.

◆ **PATHOGENESIS.** Unknown in wild geese. In domestic geese the parasite may cause severe intestinal coccidiosis, sometimes resulting in death.

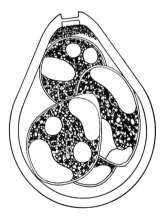

FIG. 21.6. Oocyst of *Eimeria anseris.* ×2,300. (From Hanson et al., 1957. Reproduced by permission of the National Research Council of Canada.)

◆ **DIAGNOSIS.** The description of oocysts by Kotlan (1933) is incomplete. The following description is that of Hanson et al. (1957). Oocysts (Fig. 21.6) are pyriform or shaped like a sphere with a truncate cone and have a length to width ratio of 1.1 to 1.4 (mean 1.27). Oocysts measure 20 to 24μ by 16 to 19μ (mean 21.7μ by 17.2μ). The oocyst wall is smooth, colorless, composed of one layer, measures about 1μ thick and has a distinct micropyle. No polar granule is present, but an oocyst residuum occurs adjacent to the micropyle. Sporocysts are ovoid. The sporocyst wall is slightly thickened at the small end, but does not form a distinct Stieda body. A large sporocyst residuum is present. Sporocysts measure 10 to 12μ by 7 to 9μ.

Eimeria clarkei Hanson, Levine, and Ivens 1957

◆ **DISTRIBUTION AND INCIDENCE.** One of 73 blue geese *(Chen caerulescens)* and lesser snow geese *(Chen hyperborea)*, Ontario.

◆ **DEVELOPMENT.** Unknown.

◆ **CLINICAL SIGNS.** Unknown.

◆ **PATHOGENESIS.** Unknown.

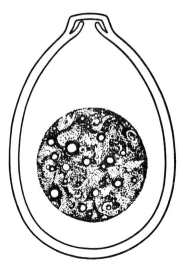

FIG. 21.7. Oocyst of *Eimeria clarkei.* ×2,300. (From Hanson et al., 1957. Reproduced by permission of the National Research Council of Canada.)

◆ **DIAGNOSIS.** Completely sporulated oocysts have not been observed. Oocysts (Fig. 21.7) are shaped like a round-bottomed flask with a short narrow neck and have a length to width ratio of 1.3 to 1.5 (mean 1.42). Oocysts are 25 to 30μ by 18 to 21μ (mean 27.3μ by 19.3μ). The oocyst wall is smooth, colorless, and about 1μ thick. A micropyle is present. The oocyst wall is composed of one layer, except that two layers are present around the micropyle. The outer layer forms a cap over the micropyle and the inner layer forms a ring around the micropyle. Partially sporulated oocysts do not have an oocyst residuum or polar granule.

Eimeria farri
Hanson, Levine, and Ivens 1957

◆ **DISTRIBUTION AND INCIDENCE.** One of 6 white-fronted geese *(Anser albifrons frontalis),* California.

◆ **DEVELOPMENT.** Unknown.

◆ **CLINICAL SIGNS.** Unknown.

◆ **PATHOGENESIS.** Unknown.

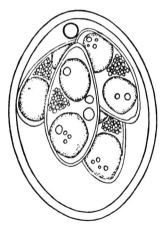

FIG. 21.8. Oocyst of *Eimeria farri.* ×2,300. (From Hanson et al., 1957. Reproduced by permission of the National Research Council of Canada.)

◆ **DIAGNOSIS.** Oocysts are ellipsoidal or slightly ovoid and sometimes slightly asymmetrical (Fig. 21.8). Oocysts measure 22 to 23μ by 17 to 20μ (mean 22.8μ by 18.0μ) and have a length to width ratio of 1.2 to 1.3 (mean 1.27). The oocyst wall is smooth, colorless to very pale yellow, composed of a single layer, and about 0.9μ thick. A polar granule is present, but an oocyst residuum is absent. Sporocysts are elongate-ovoid, 12 to 13μ by 6μ, and have small Stieda bodies. The sporocyst residuum contains both coarse and fine granules.

Eimeria nocens Kotlan 1933

◆ **DISTRIBUTION.** Domestic geese *(Anser anser),* Europe; snow geese *(Chen hyperborea)* and blue geese *(Chen caerulescens),* North America.

◆ **DEVELOPMENT.** Sporulation time is 60 hours at 20° C. In experimental infections of the domestic goose, Klimes (1963) found gametocytes throughout the entire small intestine, with the heaviest infection in the lower small intestine. Isolated gametocytes were found in the cecum and large intestine. Kotlan (1933) found schizonts are 15 to 30μ in diameter and contain 15 to 35 merozoites; macrogametes are 20

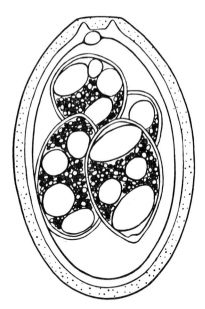

FIG. 21.9. Oocyst of *Eimeria nocens.* ×2,300. (From Hanson et al., 1957. Reproduced by permission of the National Research Council of Canada.)

to 25μ by 16 to 20μ and microgametocytes are 28 to 36μ by 23 to 31μ.

◆ **CLINICAL SIGNS.** Unknown.

◆ **PATHOGENESIS.** Unknown in wild geese. In domestic geese, Klimes (1963) stated that *E. nocens* was pathogenic to young geese, particularly in combination with *E. anseris,* but was relatively nonpathogenic to older geese.

◆ **DIAGNOSIS.** Kotlan (1933) did not describe sporulated oocysts, but he gave the measurements of oocysts as 25 to 33μ by 17 to 24μ. The following description is from Hanson et al. (1957). Oocysts (Fig. 21.9) are ovoid, flattened at the micropylar end, measure 29 to 33μ by 19 to 24μ (mean 31.0μ by 21.6μ) and have a length to width ratio of 1.3 to 1.7 (mean 1.45). The oocyst wall is smooth and composed of two layers; the outer layer is pale yellow and 1.3μ thick, and the inner layer is colorless and 0.9μ thick. A prominent micropyle is present, and the inner layer of the oocyst

wall is absent at the micropyle. An oocyst residuum and polar granule are absent. Sporocysts measure 10 to 14μ by 8 to 10μ (mean 12.1 by 9.1μ). A small Stieda body is present, as well as a large amount of sporocyst residual material, which is packed between the sporozoites.

Eimeria truncata
(Railliet and Lucet 1891) Wasielewski 1904

SYNONYM: *Coccidium truncatum* Railliet and Lucet 1891.

◆ **DISTRIBUTION AND INCIDENCE.** Domestic geese *(Anser anser),* North America and Europe; graylag geese *(Anser anser),* Denmark and Sweden; Canada geese *(Branta canadensis interior)* 34% of 450 from North Carolina, 9% of 43 from Maryland, Sweden; 1 of 3 Ross' geese *(Chen rossi),* California; 13% of 16 Moffit's Canada geese *(Branta canadensis moffitti),* California; 4 of 4 mute swans *(Cygnus olor),* Denmark; domestic ducks *(Anas platyrhynchos platyrhynchos),* Bulgaria and Czechoslovakia; common eiders *(Somateria mollissima mollissima),* Denmark and Sweden.

◆ **DEVELOPMENT.** The sporulation time given by various authors varies from 1 to 5 days. Pellerdy (1965) speculated that after excystation the sporozoites penetrate the intestinal wall, enter the bloodstream, and are carried to the kidney, where endogenous development takes place in the epithelial cells of the tubules. According to Pellerdy (1965), mature schizonts measure about 13μ in diameter and contain 20 to 30 merozoites. Macrogametes are 15 to 17μ in diameter and have both eosinophilic and basophilic granules. Microgametocytes measure 6 to 13μ by 4 to 7μ. Oocysts are discharged through the ureters into the cloaca where they are passed in the feces.

◆ **CLINICAL SIGNS.** Unknown in wild birds; in domestic geese there is a loss of appetite, depression, and a loss of coordination. Affected birds may drink more water than usual.

◆ **PATHOGENESIS.** Little is known of the pathogenicity of *E. truncata* in wild birds, but it is probably pathogenic to young birds. In domestic goslings *E. truncata* is pathogenic and may cause a high mortality. In infected birds the kidneys are enlarged with white nodules and streaks which contain uric acid salts, parasites, and cellular debris.

◆ **DIAGNOSIS.** Descriptions of oocysts given by different authors do not agree, and the following is a composite of several descriptions. The shape of the oocysts varies considerably from ellipsoidal or ovoid to asymmetrical, but usually oocysts have a smaller truncate end, which has a micropyle. A micropylar cap may be present or absent. Oocysts measure 14 to 27μ by 12 to 22μ. The oocyst wall is smooth and is easily shrunken by hypertonic solutions. No oocyst residuum is present. Sporocysts measure 8μ by 5μ and do not contain a sporocyst residuum.

◆ **REMARKS.** That *E. truncata* occurs in ducks is questionable. Tiboldy (1934) failed to infect domestic ducks with *E. truncata* from geese.

Tyzzeria parvula
(Kotlan 1933) Klimes 1963

SYNONYMS: *Tyzzeria* sp. Levine 1951, and 1952; *Tyzzeria anseris* Nieschulz 1947; *Eimeria parvula* Kotlan 1932; *Eimeria parvula* Kotlan 1933. The taxonomy of species of *Tyzzeria* from birds is uncertain. Allen (1936) defined the genus and described the type species *(T. perniciosa)* from the domestic duck *(Anas domesticus)*. Other species are *T. alleni* Chakravarty and Basu 1946 from the cotton teal *(Cheniscus* [syn. *Nettapus*] *coromandelianus); T. anseris* Nieschulz 1947 from the domestic goose *(Anser anser anser); T. pellerdyi* Bhatia

and Pande 1966 from the gadwall *(Anas strepera)* and the common white-eyed pochard *(Aythya nyroca)*. All of the species of *Tyzzeria* from birds have a similar structure and size. Nieschulz (1947) was unable to infect a single duck with oocysts of *T. anseris* from domestic geese; Farr (1953) infected domestic geese with *Tyzzeria* sp. from the Canada goose *(Branta canadensis interior);* Farr (1965) inoculated 4 ducks ("mallard crosses") with *Tyzzeria* sp. from the lesser scaup duck *(Aythya affinis)* and reported that a few unsporulated oocysts were discharged on the 5th day. Klimes (1963) was unable to infect ten 14-day-old domestic ducks with *Tyzzeria* from the domestic goose. Hanson et al. (1957) thought it best to use the name *T. anseris* for the species of *Tyzzeria* from geese and swans until cross-transmission studies determine the status of *Tyzzeria* from birds. From Klimes' (1963) work, it appears that the species in domestic geese and domestic ducks may be distinct.

◆ **DISTRIBUTION AND INCIDENCE.** Domestic geese *(Anser anser domesticus)*, Maryland, Holland, Czechoslovakia; 15% of 13 whistling swans *(Olor columbianus)*, Maryland; white-fronted geese *(Anser albifrons frontalis)*, 56% of 9 from Missouri, 19% of 21 from California; blue geese *(Chen caerulescens)* and snow geese *(Chen hyperborea)*, 8% of 73 from Ontario, 57% of 14 from California; snow geese *(Chen hyperborea)*, 75% of 8 from North Carolina, 4% of 28 from Quebec; Ross' geese *(Chen rossi)*, 45% of 7 from California, 50% of 6 from Northwest Territories; Canada geese *(Branta canadensis interior)*, North Carolina, Michigan, 47% of 43 from Maryland, 28% of 136 from Illinois, 18% of 17 from Ontario, 45% of 7 from Manitoba; Moffit's Canada geese *(Branta canadensis moffitti)*, 20% of 5 from Oregon, and 38% of 16 from California; a Taverner's Canada goose *(Branta canadensis taver-*

neri), California; cackling Canada geese *(Branta canadensis minima),* 7% of 14 from Oregon, 43% of 7 from California; Atlantic brant *(Branta bernicla hrota),* 25% of 8, Quebec.

◆ **DEVELOPMENT.** In experimental infections of domestic geese, Klimes (1963) reported that endogenous stages were found in epithelial cells at the tips of the villi of the small intestine. Most parasites occurred in the middle small intestine, but a few were located in the large intestine and ceca. Schizonts had 16 to 32 merozoites; those with 16 merozoites measured 12 by 9μ. From Klimes's description it appears that more than one asexual generation may occur. The prepatent period was 5 days and the patent period lasted from 3 to more than 14 days. Sporulation time was 24 hours.

◆ **CLINICAL SIGNS.** Unknown.

◆ **PATHOGENESIS.** Unknown in wild birds; experimental studies in domestic geese indicate that *T. anseris* is probably not pathogenic.

◆ **DIAGNOSIS.** Oocysts (Fig. 21.10) described by Levine (1952) from Canada geese were ellipsoidal and had a length to width ratio of 1.0 to 1.4 (mean 1.2). The oocyst

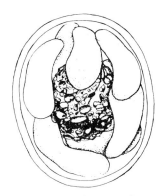

FIG. 21.10. Oocyst of *Tyzzeria parvula* (= *Tyzzeria* sp. Levine 1951). ×4,100. (From Levine, 1952.)

wall was smooth, colorless, and about 0.6μ thick; no micropyle was present. Oocysts measured 11 to 15μ by 9 to 12μ (mean 12.8μ by 10.8μ). Often the eight sporozoites surrounded a large, irregular, granular, residual body. Oocysts described by Klimes (1963) from domestic geese were similar to those described by Levine. The oocysts measured 12 to 17μ by 11 to 15μ (mean 14.8μ by 12.8μ) and had a length to width ratio of 1.16. Oocysts described by Nieschulz (1947) from domestic geese were 12 to 16μ by 10 to 12μ (mean 14.0μ by 15.5μ).

◆ **REMARKS.** The following species of coccidia have been reported from domestic geese, but not from wild geese: *E. stigmosa* Klimes 1963 and *E. kotlani* Graefner and Graubmann 1964.

Aythya

Eimeria aythyae Farr 1965

◆ **DISTRIBUTION.** Lesser scaup *(Aythya affinis),* Minnesota, Wisconsin, and Iowa.

◆ **DEVELOPMENT.** Unknown.

◆ **CLINICAL SIGNS.** Unknown.

◆ **PATHOGENESIS.** Farr (1965) suspected that *E. aythyae* was responsible for two die-offs of lesser scaup ducks.

◆ **DIAGNOSIS.** Oocyst shape varies from a shouldered round-bottomed urn to broadly elliptical (Fig. 21.11); measurements are 15 to 24μ by 11 to 18μ (mean 20.1μ by 15.5μ). The length to width ratio is 1.17 to 1.56 (mean 1.32). The oocyst wall is pale yellow to colorless, smooth or slightly rough, and 0.6 to 0.9μ thick. A prominent micropyle, 2.2 to 4.3μ (mean 3.6μ) in diameter, and a micropylar cap are present. No polar granule or oocyst residuum is present. Each sporocyst has a small Stieda body and compact sporocyst residuum.

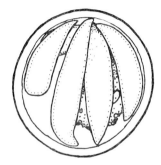

FIG. 21.12. Oocyst of *Tyzzeria* sp. (From Farr, 1965.)

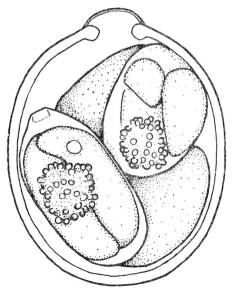

FIG. 21.11. Oocysts of *Eimeria aythyae*. (From Farr, 1965.)

Tyzzeria sp. Farr 1965

SYNONYM: *Tyzzeria anseris* Farr (1959).

◆ **DISTRIBUTION.** Lesser scaup *(Aythya affinis)*, Minnesota and Wisconsin.

◆ **DEVELOPMENT.** Farr (1965) inoculated 4 ducks ("mallard crosses") which discharged a few unsporulated oocysts 5 days after inoculation.

◆ **CLINICAL SIGNS.** Unknown.

◆ **PATHOGENESIS.** Unknown.

◆ **DIAGNOSIS.** Oocysts measure 11 to 14μ by 9 to 12μ and have a subspherical to ellipsoidal shape (Fig. 21.12). The oocyst wall is smooth and colorless. No micropyle is present. Eight free sporozoites and a large compact residual body are found in sporulated oocysts.

◆ **REMARKS.** Bump (1937) reported unidentified oocysts from 2 lesser scaup ducks in New York.

Branta

Eimeria brantae Levine 1953

◆ **DISTRIBUTION AND INCIDENCE.** One of 4 lesser Canada geese *(Branta canadensis parvipes)*, Northwest Territories; Richardson's Canada geese *(Branta canadensis hutchinsi)*, Manitoba.

◆ **DEVELOPMENT.** Unknown.

◆ **CLINICAL SIGNS.** Unknown.

◆ **PATHOGENESIS.** Unknown.

◆ **DIAGNOSIS.** Oocysts (Fig. 21.13) are ovoid and measure 18μ by 23μ; the length to width ratio is 1.3. The oocyst wall is

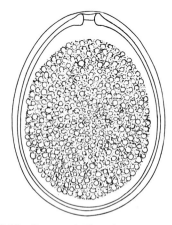

FIG. 21.13. Oocyst of *Eimeria brantae*. ×4,000. (From Levine, 1953.)

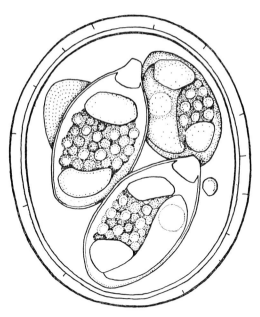

FIG. 21.14. Oocyst of *Eimeria crassa*. (From Farr, 1963.)

composed of two colorless layers with the outer layer slightly thicker than the inner. A micropyle is present. Completely sporulated oocysts have not been described.

Eimeria crassa Farr 1963

◆ **DISTRIBUTION.** Canada geese *(Branta canadensis interior)*, Maryland.

◆ **DEVELOPMENT.** The prepatent period is 5 days.

◆ **CLINICAL SIGNS.** Unknown.

◆ **PATHOGENESIS.** Unknown.

◆ **DIAGNOSIS.** Oocysts (Fig. 21.14) are broadly elliptical to ovoid and measure 24 to 28μ by 19 to 24μ (mean 25.8μ by 21.2μ) with a length to width ratio of 1.1 to 1.4 (mean 1.23). The oocyst wall consists of an outer pale yellow layer about 0.9μ thick and a colorless inner layer about 0.4μ thick. Oocysts have 1 large and 1 to 3 small polar granules but no micropyle or oocyst residuum. Sporocysts are 13 to 16μ by 8

to 10μ (mean 14.1μ by 8.2μ) and have large Stieda bodies. The sporocyst residuum is coarsely granular.

Eimeria fulva Farr 1953

HOMONYM: *Eimeria fulva* Seidel 1954.

◆ **DISTRIBUTION AND INCIDENCE.** Canada goose *(Branta canadensis interior)*, North Carolina, New York, Michigan; domestic goose *(Anser anser)*, experimental; 3% of 73 snow geese *(Chen hyperborea)* and blue geese *(Chen caerulescens)*, Ontario.

◆ **DEVELOPMENT.** Farr (1953) experimentally infected domestic and Canada geese. Sporulation time was 72 to 96 hours at room temperature. Endogenous development took place throughout the small intestine, but parasites were most abundant in the anterior portion. At approximately 144 hours after inoculation, schizonts measuring 13μ by 15μ and having 16 to 30 merozoites were present in epithelial cells on the tips and sides of the villi; however, some were later found in the lamina propria and the intestinal glands. At 193 hours after inoculation, gametocytes were present along the basement membrane and in the lamina propria. Microgametocytes were 29 to 38μ by 35 to 46μ and macrogametes were 20 to 24μ by 26 to 30μ. The prepatent period was 9 days.

◆ **CLINICAL SIGNS.** Unknown.

◆ **PATHOGENESIS.** In severe experimental infections, Farr (1953) found a thickening and congestion of the intestinal wall and an accumulation of greenish mucus in the small intestine.

◆ **DIAGNOSIS.** Oocysts are broadly ovoid, rarely pyriform, and have a flattened micropylar end (Fig. 21.15). The oocysts measure 26 to 32μ by 20 to 25μ (mean 29.7μ by 21.6μ). The length to width ratio is 1.18 to 1.56. The outer layer of the oocyst wall

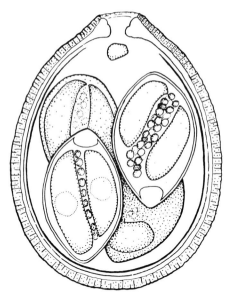

FIG. 21.15.   Oocyst of *Eimeria fulva*. (From Farr, 1953.)

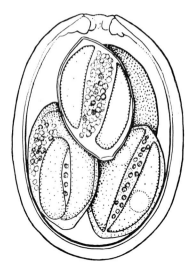

FIG. 21.16.   Oocyst of *Eimeria hermani*. (From Farr, 1953.)

is yellow, rough, and 1μ thick, but is thinner in the region of the micropyle; the inner layer is colorless and 0.6μ thick, except for the area near the micropyle, which is thicker. The micropyle is 3.3 to 4.0μ in diameter. A large polar granule is present, but no oocyst residuum has been observed. The sporocysts are 14 to 15μ by 8 to 10μ and each has a prominent Stieda body as well as a coarsely granular sporocyst residuum.

Eimeria hermani Farr 1953

◆ **DISTRIBUTION AND INCIDENCE.** Canada geese *(Branta canadensis interior)*, North Carolina and Michigan; 14% of 14 cackling geese *(Branta canadensis minima)*, Oregon; domestic geese *(Anser anser)*, experimental; 12% of 73 snow geese *(Chen hyperborea)* and blue geese *(Chen caerulescens)*, Ontario.

◆ **DEVELOPMENT.** Sporulation time is 48 hours at room temperature. In *Anser anser* endogenous development takes place throughout the small intestine and oocysts first appear in the feces 5 days after inoculation.

◆ **CLINICAL SIGNS.** Unknown.

◆ **PATHOGENESIS.** Unknown.

◆ **DIAGNOSIS.** Oocysts are ovoid and slightly flattened at the micropylar end; the micropyle is 3.2μ in diameter (Fig. 21.16). The oocyst wall consists of two colorless layers. The outer layer is smooth and 1.0μ thick; the inner layer is 0.4μ thick and forms irregular lobes around the micropyle. Oocysts measure 24 to 28μ by 18 to 20μ (mean 27.6μ by 18.9μ) and have a width to length ratio of 1.32 to 1.56 (mean 1.41). An oocyst residuum and polar granule are absent. Sporocysts are slightly pointed at both ends and have an inconspicuous Stieda body at one end. Sporocysts measure 8 to 9μ by 14μ. A finely granular sporocyst residuum is present.

Eimeria magnalabia Levine 1951

SYNONYM: *Eimeria striata* Farr 1953.

◆ **DISTRIBUTION AND INCIDENCE.** Canada geese *(Branta canadensis interior)*, 5% of 43 birds from Maryland, 4.5% of 136 from Illinois, 24% of 17 from Ontario, 14% of 7 from Manitoba, and also in

Canada geese from North Carolina and Michigan; 3 of 6 Richardson's Canada geese *(Branta canadensis hutchinsi)*, Manitoba; cackling Canada geese *(Branta canadensis minima)*, 21% of 14 from Oregon, 14% of 12 from California; 44% of 9 whitefronted geese *(Anser albifrons frontalis)*, Missouri; domestic geese *(Anser anser)*, experimental.

◆ **DEVELOPMENT.** Using oocysts from the domestic goose *(Anser anser)*, Farr (1953) found the sporulation time is 72 hours at room temperature. In this host the endogenous stages are located in the small intestine, and the prepatent period is 5 days.

◆ **CLINICAL SIGNS.** Unknown.

◆ **PATHOGENESIS.** Unknown.

◆ **DIAGNOSIS.** Oocysts (Fig. 21.17) are ovoid and measure 22 to 24μ by 15 to 17μ (mean 16.3μ by 22.3μ); length to width ratio is 1.3 to 1.5 (mean 1.4). The oocyst wall is about 1.8μ thick and consists of two layers. The outer layer is rough, brownish yellow, and the inner layer is thinner and colorless. There is a prominent micropyle, around which the oocyst wall is thickened. The polar granule and oocyst residuum are absent. Sporocysts measure approximately 12μ by 8μ and each contains a large granular residuum. No Stieda body is present.

◆ **REMARKS.** Farr (1953) reported that *E. striata* differed from *E. magnalabia* by the presence of one or more polar granules and small Stieda bodies, and by the nature of the oocyst wall. The original description of *E. magnalabia* was based on relatively few oocysts. Hanson et al. (1957) studied oocysts of *E. magnalabia* from several hosts and concluded that *E. striata* was a synonym of *E. magnalabia*.

Eimeria pulchella Farr 1963

◆ **DISTRIBUTION.** Canada geese *(Branta canadensis interior)*, Maryland.

◆ **DEVELOPMENT.** The prepatent period is 5 days.

◆ **CLINICAL SIGNS.** Unknown.

◆ **PATHOGENESIS.** Unknown.

◆ **DIAGNOSIS.** Oocysts (Fig. 21.18) are ovoid and have a length to width ratio of 1.39 to 1.92 (mean 1.67). They measure 20 to 28μ by 12 to 18μ (mean 24.3μ by 14.8μ). A small micropyle is present in some oocysts. The outer layer of the oocyst wall is colorless to pale yellow and about 0.6μ thick; the inner layer is colorless and about 0.3μ thick. An oocyst residuum is absent, but one or two polar granules are present. The mean sporocyst measurements are 6.0μ by 11.9μ. A small Stieda body and a finely granular sporocyst residuum are present.

Bucephala

Eimeria bucephalae
Christiansen and Madsen 1948

◆ **DISTRIBUTION.** Common golden eye *(Bucephala clangula)*, Denmark.

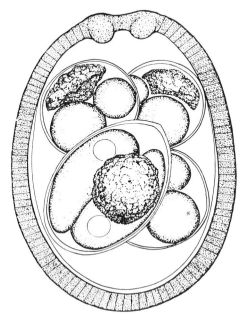

FIG. 21.17. Oocyst of *Eimeria magnalabia*. ×4,100. (From Levine, 1952.)

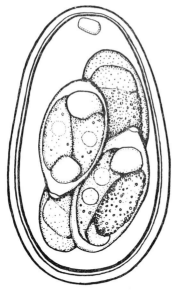

FIG. 21.18.   Oocyst of *Eimeria pulchella*. (From Farr, 1963.)

◆ **DEVELOPMENT.** Sporulation time is 4 days at room temperature. Endogenous development takes place in the small intestine.

◆ **CLINICAL SIGNS.** Birds which die from coccidiosis are emaciated.

◆ **PATHOGENESIS.** Christiansen and Madsen (1948) reported that the intestinal mucosa of infected birds was congested and thickened and a catarrhal or fibrous exudate was present. A bloody diarrhea occurred in some cases. There was an increase in leukocytes and eosinophils in the interglandular tissues.

◆ **DIAGNOSIS.** The shapes of the oocysts vary considerably; they are usually ovoidal, but sometimes ellipsoidal or kidney-shaped. Oocysts measure 25 to 39μ by 13 to 20μ (mean 30.3μ by 15.6μ) and have a length to width ratio of 1.5 to 2.5 (mean 2.0). The oocyst wall is light brown and has a small micropyle. The oocyst residuum is absent. Polar granules are present within [*sic*] the micropyle. The sporocysts measure 15μ by 7μ and each contains a sporocyst residuum.

Cheniscus

Tyzzeria alleni
Chakravarty and Basu 1946

◆ **DISTRIBUTION.** A cotton teal (*Cheniscus* [syn. *Nettapus*] *coromandelianus*), India.

◆ **DEVELOPMENT.** The sporulation time is 48 hours.

◆ **CLINICAL SIGNS.** Unknown.

◆ **PATHOGENESIS.** Unknown.

◆ **DIAGNOSIS.** The oocysts are oval and measure 14 to 17μ by 10 to 12μ. No micropyle is present. An oocyst residuum, about 6.4μ in diameter, is present. Sporozoites measure 5.4 to 6.5μ in length.

◆ **REMARKS.** The morphology of the oocysts from the description by Chakravarty and Basu (1946) does not clearly distinguish them from other species of *Tyzzeria* reported from waterfowl and until cross-transmission studies have been performed the taxonomic status of *T. alleni* will remain in question.

Olor

Eimeria christianseni Walden 1963

SYNONYM: Walden (1963) considered that *E. truncata,* described by Christiansen (1952) from mute swans, was identical to *E. christianseni.*

◆ **DISTRIBUTION AND INCIDENCE.** Mute swans (*Cygnus olor*), 12 of 12 from Denmark, 2 of 16 from Sweden.

◆ **DEVELOPMENT.** Endogenous stages are in the kidney.

◆ **CLINICAL SIGNS.** Unknown.

◆ **PATHOGENESIS.** The form found by Christiansen (1952) could cause death.

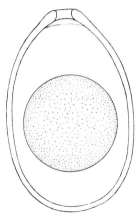

FIG. 21.19. Oocyst of *Eimeria christianseni.* ×3,000. (From Walden, 1963.)

◆ **DIAGNOSIS.** The oocysts are oval, smooth, and have a micropyle (Fig. 21.19). Oocysts measure 14 to 21μ by 10 to 14μ (mean 17.3μ by 11.3μ). The oocysts resemble *E. truncata* except that the micropylar end is not flattened.

Somateria

Eimeria somateriae Christiansen 1952

◆ **DISTRIBUTION AND INCIDENCE.** Twenty of 21 common eiders *(Somateria mollissima),* Denmark; oldsquaws *(Clangula hyemalis),* Sweden.

◆ **DEVELOPMENT.** The sporulation time is 3 days. The endogenous stages are located in the kidney.

◆ **CLINICAL SIGNS.** Unknown.

◆ **PATHOGENESIS.** Christiansen (1952) reported that the species was nonpathogenic; however, Walden (1963) stated that *E. somateriae* may be pathogenic to *Clangula hyemalis.*

◆ **DIAGNOSIS.** The oocysts are ellipsoidal and sometimes asymmetrical, with the micropylar end drawn out like the neck of a bottle. Oocysts measure 21 to 41μ by 11 to 19μ (mean 31.9μ by 13.9μ). The oocyst wall is colorless and smooth. No oocyst residuum is present. Sporocysts are 11μ by 6μ. Oocysts described by Walden (1963) are 25 to 39μ by 13 to 17μ (mean 34μ by 15μ).

GALLIFORMES

Alectoris

Eimeria alectoreae
Ray and Hiregaudar 1959

◆ **DISTRIBUTION AND INCIDENCE.** Two of 2 chukars *(Alectoris graeca),* Calcutta Zoological Gardens, India.

◆ **DEVELOPMENT.** Sporulation time is 24 to 48 hours.

◆ **CLINICAL SIGNS.** Unknown.

◆ **PATHOGENESIS.** In 2 dead birds containing large numbers of oocysts, the ceca were enlarged and filled with blood.

◆ **DIAGNOSIS.** The oocysts are usually ellipsoidal with a few being ovoidal or spherical. Oocysts measure 23.6 $\pm$ 2.4μ by 15.6 $\pm$ 1.5μ and 26.2 $\pm$ 2.5μ by 17.4 $\pm$ 1.9μ from the second bird. The length to width ratio is 1.43 to 1.50. The oocyst wall is pale yellowish brown, and a few small granules are present near an inconspicuous micropyle. A polar granule is present. Sporocysts are pyriform, 8 to 10μ by 4 to 6μ and have a Stieda body and sporocyst residuum.

Eimeria kofoidi
Yakimoff and Matikaschwili 1936

◆ **DISTRIBUTION.** Oocysts were found in the feces of the chukar *(Alectoris graeca* [syn. *Caccabis chukar])* and the gray partridge *(Perdix perdix)* in the Leningrad Zoological Gardens, USSR. Since the birds were in the same cage, it is not known which species the parasites were from.

◆ **DEVELOPMENT.** Unknown.

◆ **CLINICAL SIGNS.** Unknown.

◆ **PATHOGENESIS.** Unknown.

◆ **DIAGNOSIS.** The oocysts are oval or spherical and have a length to width ratio of 1.03 to 1.44 (mean 1.19). Oocysts measure 16 to 25μ by 14 to 20μ (mean 20.0μ by 17.6μ). Spherical oocysts measure 17.6μ in diameter. The oocyst wall is composed of two layers. A polar granule is present, but an oocyst residuum is absent. The sporocysts measure 8 to 10μ by 6 to 7μ and each contains a sporocyst residuum.

Eimeria legionensis Cordero del Campello and Pla Hernandez 1966

◆ **DISTRIBUTION.** Red-legged partridges *(Alectoris rufa)*, Spain.

◆ **DEVELOPMENT.** Sporulation time is 72 hours at 20° C.

◆ **CLINICAL SIGNS.** Unknown.

◆ **PATHOGENESIS.** Unknown.

◆ **DIAGNOSIS.** Oocysts are ellipsoidal with the poles nearly symmetrical. Oocysts measure 18 to 24μ by 12 to 16μ (mean 21.3μ by 14.6μ). A micropyle and oocyst residuum are present. Sporocysts measure 9.5 to 10.6μ by 6.3μ [*sic*]. A sporocyst residuum and Stieda body are present.

Bonasa

Eimeria angusta Allen 1934

◆ **DISTRIBUTION AND INCIDENCE.** Ruffed grouse *(Bonasa umbellus)*, Alaska, Labrador, 4 of 560 from Minnesota; spruce grouse *(Canachites canadensis)*, Alaska; 1 of 62 sharp-tailed grouse *(Pedioecetes phasianellus)*, Minnesota; sage grouse *(Centrocercus urophasianus)*, Wyoming.

◆ **DEVELOPMENT.** Unknown.

◆ **CLINICAL SIGNS.** Unknown.

◆ **PATHOGENESIS.** Unknown.

◆ **DIAGNOSIS.** Allen (1934) described oocysts as elliptical to oval and 27 to 33μ by 17 to 18μ. An operculum (micropyle?) was present. Oocysts found by Boughton (1937b) were 27 to 33μ by 15 to 17μ (mean 16.1μ by 30.1μ). Those described by Honess and Post (1955) were 25 to 34μ by 16 to 22μ (mean 29.6μ by 18.8μ).

Eimeria bonasae Allen 1934

◆ **DISTRIBUTION.** Ruffed grouse *(Bonasa umbellus)*, Alaska and Labrador; willow ptarmigan *(Lagopus lagopus)*, Labrador; sharp-tailed grouse *(Pedioecetes phasianellus)*; spruce grouse *(Canachites canadensis)*.

◆ **DEVELOPMENT.** Unknown.

◆ **CLINICAL SIGNS.** Unknown.

◆ **PATHOGENESIS.** Unknown.

◆ **DIAGNOSIS.** Oocysts are subspherical and measure approximately 21μ in diameter. The oocyst wall consists of four colorless layers. No micropyle is present. Completely sporulated oocysts have not been described.

Centrocercus

Eimeria centrocerci Simon 1939

◆ **DISTRIBUTION.** Sage grouse *(Centrocercus urophasianus)*, Wyoming.

◆ **DEVELOPMENT.** Unknown.

◆ **CLINICAL SIGNS.** Unknown.

◆ **PATHOGENESIS.** Unknown.

◆ **DIAGNOSIS.** Oocysts are ellipsoidal and measure 21 to 25μ by 17 to 18μ (mean

22.6μ by 17.1μ), according to Simon. Honess and Post (1955) reported the oocysts to be 17 to 25μ by 13 to 18μ (mean 21.2μ by 15.0μ). Simon gave the sporocyst size as 11 to 13μ by 6.6 to 7.1μ [*sic*] (mean 11.8μ by 7.6μ); an indistinct micropylar cap, small oocyst residuum, sporocyst residuum, and Stieda body are present. The oocysts observed by Honess and Post (1955) were similar except that there was a thinning of the oocyst wall at the micropylar end.

Eimeria pattersoni Honess and Post 1955

◆ **DISTRIBUTION.** Sage grouse *(Centrocercus urophasianus)*, Wyoming.

◆ **DEVELOPMENT.** Unknown.

◆ **CLINICAL SIGNS.** Unknown.

◆ **PATHOGENESIS.** Unknown.

◆ **DIAGNOSIS.** Oocysts are ellipsoidal and measure 18 to 23μ by 12 to 15μ (mean 20.2μ by 13.5μ). The oocyst wall consists of two layers and has an indistinct micropyle. No polar body or oocyst residuum is present. Sporocysts are ovoidal.

Eimeria spp.

Several authors have reported *Eimeria* sp. from sage grouse (see Braun and Willers, 1967).

Chrysolophus

Isospora sp. Pavlov 1943

◆ **DISTRIBUTION.** Golden pheasants *(Chrysolophus pictus)*, Bulgaria.

◆ **DEVELOPMENT.** Unknown.

◆ **CLINICAL SIGNS.** Unknown.

◆ **PATHOGENESIS.** Unknown.

◆ **DIAGNOSIS.** The oocysts are 20 to 28μ in diameter.

Colinus

Eimeria dispersa Tyzzer 1929

◆ **DISTRIBUTION.** Bobwhites *(Colinus virginianus)*; ring-necked pheasants *(Phasianus colchicus)*; turkeys *(Meleagris gallopavo)*; ruffed grouse *(Bonasa umbellus)*; sharp-tailed grouse *(Pedioecetes phasianellus)*, North America; quail *(Coturnix coturnix)*; gray quail *(Perdix perdix)*, experimental; chickens *(Gallus domesticus)*, experimental.

◆ **DEVELOPMENT.** Sporulation time is 48 to 72 hours. In the bobwhite the parasites are found throughout the small intestine, with the heaviest infection in the upper part. Endogenous stages are found above and below the host cell nuclei of epithelial cells in the villi. The prepatent period is 4 days in the bobwhite and 5 or 6 days in pheasants and turkeys.

◆ **CLINICAL SIGNS.** Unknown.

◆ **PATHOGENESIS.** Tyzzer (1929) quoted Stoddard who reported many wild and game-farm quail were heavily infected and appeared normal. Heavy infections in young quail could be fatal, causing severe diarrhea and emaciation. Whether species other than *E. dispersa* were present in such birds is not known.

◆ **DIAGNOSIS.** Oocysts from quail are ovoid and measure 22 to 26μ by 15 to 17μ (mean 22.8μ by 18.8μ). Those from pheasants measure 20 to 23μ by 14 to 15μ (mean 20μ by 18μ). No polar granule or sporocyst residuum is present.

◆ **REMARKS.** Tyzzer (1929) described *E. dispersa* from the bobwhite and pheasant and was able to transmit the strain from bobwhites to turkeys; he also established light infections in chickens and possibly in pheasants. Hawkins (1952) found *E. dispersa* in naturally infected turkeys. Hawkins infected bobwhites and gray partridges with the strain from turkeys, but was not successful in infecting pheasants or chickens. Moore and Brown (1952) infected bobwhites with a turkey strain, but Moore (1954) could not establish infections in pheasants. Vernard (1933) and Patterson (1933) inoculated chickens with the bobwhite strain but the chickens did not become infected.

Eimeria spp.

Vernard (1933) reported *E. tenella* and *E. acervulina* from the bobwhite and transmitted *E. tenella* from bobwhites to chickens; Tyzzer (1929) could not infect bobwhites with *E. acervulina* from chickens. Patterson (1933) was unable to infect bobwhites with *E. tenella*, *E. acervulina*, *E. mitis*, or *E. maxima* from chickens. In view of the above evidence, Levine (1953) concluded that several species of coccidia, one of which is *E. dispersa*, occur in quail. Further study of the coccidia in quail is needed to determine what species are present.

Coturnix

Eimeria bateri
Bhatia, Pandey, Pande 1965

◆ **DISTRIBUTION AND INCIDENCE.** Fifteen of 29 quail *(Coturnix coturnix)*, India.

◆ **DEVELOPMENT.** Sporulation time in 2% potassium dichromate is 24 hours. Endogenous stages are located above the host cell nuclei in the epithelial cells of the villi, chiefly in the lower half of the small intestine. Schizonts measure 7 to 15μ by 7 to 12μ (mean 11.5μ by 9.0μ) and have 20 to 25 merozoites. Mature microgametocytes are 12 to 20μ by 9 to 19μ (17.0μ by 13.4μ) and contain centrally located residual material. Macrogametes measure 13 to 21μ by 10 to 14μ (mean 18μ by 12μ).

◆ **CLINICAL SIGNS.** Unknown.

◆ **PATHOGENESIS.** Bhatia et al. (1965) reported that congested, edematous lesions,

containing gamonts and oocysts, were present in the small intestine.

◆ **DIAGNOSIS.** Oocysts are ellipsoidal, ovoid, or rarely spherical, and measure 15 to 28μ by 14 to 23μ (mean 23μ by 18μ). The length to width ratio is 1.03 to 1.7 (mean 1.26). The oocyst wall is 1.2μ thick, smooth, and composed of an outer yellowish and an inner bluish or violet layer. A micropyle, micropylar cap, and oocyst residuum are absent. A polar granule is present. Sporocysts measure 9 to 13μ by 5 to 8μ (mean 12μ by 7μ) and have a Stieda body and residuum.

Eimeria coturnicus
Chakravarty and Kar 1947

◆ **DISTRIBUTION.** Quail *(Coturnix coturnix)*, India.

◆ **DEVELOPMENT.** Unknown.

◆ **CLINICAL SIGNS.** Unknown.

◆ **PATHOGENESIS.** Unknown.

◆ **DIAGNOSIS.** The oocysts are oval and measure 26 to 39μ by 20 to 26μ (Fig. 21.20). The oocyst wall is composed of two layers. No micropyle or oocyst residuum is present. Sporocysts are pyriform and have a pointed end with a "small knob" (Stieda

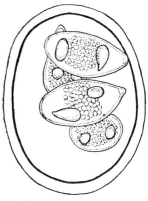

FIG. 21.20. Oocyst of *Eimeria coturnicus.* ×1,600. (From Chakravarty and Kar, 1947.)

body?). Sporocysts measure 13 to 17μ by 9 to 11μ. A sporocyst residuum is present.

Wenyonella bahli Misra 1944

◆ **DISTRIBUTION AND INCIDENCE.** Five of 24 quail *(Coturnix coturnix)*, India.

◆ **DEVELOPMENT.** The sporulation time is 4 or 5 days.

◆ **CLINICAL SIGNS.** Unknown.

◆ **PATHOGENESIS.** Unknown.

◆ **DIAGNOSIS.** Oocysts are subspherical or ovoid and measure 16 to 18μ by 15 to 16μ. A micropyle and oocyst residuum are absent. The sporocysts are 7μ by 4μ and have no "lensiform knob" (Stieda body?) or residuum.

Crax

Eimeria mutum Grecchi 1939

◆ **DISTRIBUTION.** Curassows *(Crax fasciolata)*, South America.

◆ **DEVELOPMENT.** The sporulation time is 14 days.

◆ **CLINICAL SIGNS.** Unknown.

◆ **PATHOGENESIS.** Unknown.

◆ **DIAGNOSIS.** The oocysts are ovoid and have mean measurements of 24μ by 22μ. The oocyst wall is colorless, smooth, and composed of two layers. A polar granule is present, but an oocyst residuum and micropyle are absent. The sporocysts measure 13μ by 7.7μ and have a Stieda body and residuum.

Francolinus

Eimeria teetari Bhatia, Pandey, and Pande 1966

◆ **DISTRIBUTION AND INCIDENCE.** Gray partridges *(Francolinus pondiceri-*

anus); 3 of 3 black partridges *(Francolinus francolinus)*; India.

◆ **DEVELOPMENT.** Bhatia et al. (1966) reported the sporulation time was 3 days for oocysts from gray partridges and 1 day for oocysts from black partridges. Endogenous development took place in the upper half of the small intestine, especially in the duodenum. The parasites were located above the nuclei of epithelial cells in the villi. Schizonts had 12 to 15 merozoites and measured 9 to 14μ by 7 to 10μ (mean 11.4μ by 8.3μ). Mature microgametocytes were 21 to 35μ by 17 to 28μ (mean 29.0μ by 24.8μ). Macrogametes which contained prominent eosinophilic granules were 17 to 24μ by 17 to 21μ (mean 20.7μ by 18.0μ).

◆ **CLINICAL SIGNS.** Unknown.

◆ **PATHOGENESIS.** Bhatia et al. (1966) found a thickening of the mucosa and edema in lesions which contained endogenous stages.

◆ **DIAGNOSIS.** Oocysts vary from ellipsoidal to ovoidal and measure 21 to 29μ by 18 to 23μ (mean 24μ by 20μ). The oocyst wall is composed of two layers and measures 1.4μ in thickness. The outer layer is light green and the inner layer is dark blue. One to three polar granules are present. A micropyle and oocyst residuum are absent. Sporocysts measure 11 to 15μ by 6 to 8μ (mean 13μ by 7μ). Sporocysts have a plug-like Stieda body and a sporocyst residuum.

Gennaeus

Eimeria gennaesscus Ray and Hiregaudar 1959

◆ **DISTRIBUTION.** Kalij pheasants *(Gennaeus horsfieldii)*, Calcutta Zoological Garden, India.

◆ **DEVELOPMENT.** The sporulation time is 24 to 36 hours.

◆ **CLINICAL SIGNS.** Unknown.

◆ **PATHOGENESIS.** Unknown.

◆ **DIAGNOSIS.** The oocysts are subspherical, measure $21.2 \pm 1.5\mu$ by $18.3 \pm 2.0\mu$ and have a length to width ratio of 1.16. The oocyst wall is pale yellowish brown and composed of two layers, with the inner wall being thicker. Sporocysts are 7 to 8μ by 4 to 5μ and have a pyriform shape. A Stieda body and sporocyst residuum are present.

Lagopus

Eimeria brinkmanni Levine 1953

◆ **DISTRIBUTION AND INCIDENCE.** One of six rock ptarmigans *(Lagopus mutus rupestris)*, Canada.

◆ **DEVELOPMENT.** Unknown.

◆ **CLINICAL SIGNS.** Unknown.

◆ **PATHOGENESIS.** Unknown.

◆ **DIAGNOSIS.** Oocysts (Fig. 21.21) are ellipsoidal and measure 18 to 20μ by 26 to 30μ (mean 18.8μ by 28.6μ). The oocyst wall consists of two layers, the outer being slightly rough. One or two polar granules are present. An oocyst residuum and mi-

cropyle are absent. Sporocysts are pyriform and have large Stieda bodies. Sporocysts measure 13μ by 7μ. No sporocyst residuum is present.

Eimeria fanthami Levine 1953

◆ **DISTRIBUTION AND INCIDENCE.** One of six rock ptarmigans *(Lagopus mutus rupestris)*, Canada.

◆ **DEVELOPMENT.** Unknown.

◆ **CLINICAL SIGNS.** Unknown.

◆ **PATHOGENESIS.** Unknown.

◆ **DIAGNOSIS.** Oocysts (Fig. 21.22) are ellipsoidal and measure 18 to 20μ by 27 to 29μ (mean 18.8μ by 28.3μ). The oocyst wall consists of two layers. No oocyst residuum or micropyle is present, but there are one to three polar bodies. Sporocysts have Stieda bodies but no residual material.

Eimeria lagopodi Galli-Valerio 1929

◆ **DISTRIBUTION.** Rock ptarmigans *(Lagopus mutus)*, Switzerland.

◆ **DEVELOPMENT.** Unknown.

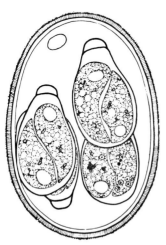

FIG. 21.21. Oocyst of *Eimeria brinkmanni.* ×4,000. (From Levine, 1953.)

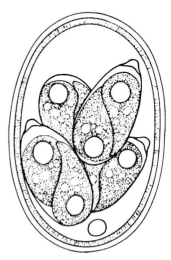

FIG. 21.22. Oocyst of *Eimeria fanthami.* ×4,000. (From Levine, 1953.)

◆ **CLINICAL SIGNS.** Unknown.

◆ **PATHOGENESIS.** Unknown.

◆ **DIAGNOSIS.** Oocysts are ovoid to ellipsoidal and measure 24μ by 15μ. A micropyle is present.

◆ **REMARKS.** The description of this species is incomplete but differs from other species described from ptarmigans by the presence of a micropyle.

Eimeria spp.

Fantham (1910) reported *Coccidium (Eimeria) avium* from the red grouse *(Lagopus scoticus)* and the willow ptarmigan *(Lagopus lagopus)*. Brinkmann (1927) reported *E. avium* from the ptarmigans *Lagopus mutus* and *Lagopus mutus hyperboreus* from Norway. Until Tyzzer's (1929) work, many species of coccidia from different birds were described as *E. avium,* a name which is no longer considered valid.

Lophortyx, Oreortyx

Eimeria spp.

◆ **DISTRIBUTION AND INCIDENCE.** Henry (1931) reported that three species of coccidia *(E. tenella, E. acervulina,* and *E. mitis)* were present in California quail *(Lophortyx californicus)* and mountain quail *(Oreortyx pictus)* from game farms in California. She reported that these coccidia could be transmitted to chickens. Herman (1949) found at least five species of *Eimeria* in wild and game-farm California quail but was unable to transmit four of the species to chickens. Herman et al. (1942) reported that 92.6% of adult female and 83.8% of adult male California quail were infected with coccidia. Herman et al. (1943) found a lower intensity of infection during summer months when the birds were eating seeds than during the rest of the year when the birds were eating green material.

◆ **DEVELOPMENT.** Unknown.

◆ **CLINICAL SIGNS.** Unknown.

◆ **PATHOGENESIS.** Coccidiosis in California quail can cause death.

◆ **DIAGNOSIS.** The oocysts have never been adequately described.

◆ **REMARKS.** Because species of *Eimeria* are usually host-specific and because of Herman's (1949) unsuccessful attempts to transmit quail coccidia to chickens, it is doubtful if the species in quail are the chicken coccidia listed by Henry (1931).

Lyrurus

Eimeria lyruri Galli-Valerio 1927

SYNONYM: pro parte *Eimeria dendrocopi* Levine 1953.

◆ **DISTRIBUTION.** Black grouse *(Lyrurus tetrix)*, Switzerland and USSR; capercaillies *(Tetrao urogallus)*, USSR.

◆ **DEVELOPMENT.** Unknown.

◆ **CLINICAL SIGNS.** Unknown.

◆ **PATHOGENESIS.** Unknown.

◆ **DIAGNOSIS.** According to Galli-Valerio (1927) oocysts are elongate cylindrical and measure 24 to 27μ by 15μ. The oocyst wall is thin, and an indistinct micropyle is present. Sporoblasts (sporocysts?) are 10μ by 6μ. Yakimoff and Gousseff (1936a) redescribed *E. lyruri* from the same host. Their measurements of oocysts were 22 to 37μ by 12 to 20μ (mean 28μ to 16μ). The oocyst wall was thin and colorless, and the oocyst shape was cylindrical. An oocyst residuum and polar body were present. Sporocysts contained no residual material and measured 10μ by 4μ.

◆ **REMARKS.** Yakimoff and Gousseff (1936a) also described *E. lyruri* from *Tetrao urogallus.* Their description of oocysts from *T. urogallus* is similar to that of oocysts they found in *L. tetrix*, except that the sporocysts measured 14μ by 5 to 9μ, no micropyle was present, and an oocyst residuum was not present. Because of these morphological differences, it is questionable whether the species present in *Lyrurus* is identical with that in *Tetrao*. Yakimoff and Gousseff (1936a) also considered a coccidium they found in a woodpecker *(Dendrocopos* [syn. *Dryobatis]* major*) to be *E. lyruri*. Because of the high degree of host specificity of *Eimeria* species, Levine (1953) reserved the name *Eimeria dendrocopi* for the form from *Dendrocopus major*.

Eimeria nadsoni
Yakimoff and Gousseff 1936

♦ **DISTRIBUTION.** Black grouse *(Lyrurus tetrix),* USSR.

♦ **DEVELOPMENT.** Unknown.

♦ **CLINICAL SIGNS.** Unknown.

♦ **PATHOGENESIS.** Unknown.

♦ **DIAGNOSIS.** The oocysts are spherical to subspherical. Subspherical forms measure 21 to 29μ by 17 to 24μ (mean 24.9μ by 21.3μ) and have a length to width ratio of 1.05 to 1.30 (mean 1.16). The oocyst wall is 1.5μ thick and does not have a micropyle. Spherical forms measure 20 to 26μ (mean 22.1μ) in diameter. Polar bodies are present. No oocyst residuum is present, and the presence of a sporocyst residuum is questionable.

Eimeria tetricis Haase 1939

♦ **DISTRIBUTION.** Black grouse *(Lyrurus* [syn. *Tetrao]* tetrix),* Germany.

♦ **DEVELOPMENT.** Sporulation time is 24 to 36 hours at room temperature.

♦ **CLINICAL SIGNS.** Unknown.

♦ **PATHOGENESIS.** Unknown.

♦ **DIAGNOSIS.** Oocysts are ellipsoidal and the sides are flat and nearly parallel. The oocysts measure 30 to 31μ by 14 to 15μ (mean 30.6μ by 15.3μ) and the length to width ratio is 2.00 to 2.08. The oocyst wall is smooth, composed of two layers, and 1.2μ thick. A micropyle and polar body are present, but an oocyst residuum is absent. Each sporocyst has a Stieda body and sporocyst residuum.

♦ **REMARKS.** Haase (1939) reported that oocysts of *E. tetricis* and *E. procera* had a nearly similar structure. He stated that they might be identical species.

Isospora lyruri Galli-Valerio 1931

♦ **DISTRIBUTION AND INCIDENCE.** A black grouse *(Lyrurus tetrix)* and the capercaillie *(Tetrao urogallus),* Switzerland.

♦ **DEVELOPMENT.** Unknown.

♦ **CLINICAL SIGNS.** Unknown.

♦ **PATHOGENESIS.** Unknown.

♦ **DIAGNOSIS.** The oocysts are spherical and have a diameter of 15μ. A micropyle is present. The sporozoites are 6μ by 3μ.

Phasianus

Although seven species of *Eimeria* have been described from pheasants, most reports have been concerned only with oocyst structure, and description of pathology has largely been limited to experimental infections. Coccidiosis is an important disease in game-farm pheasants (Jones 1964, 1966), but the importance of coccidia in wild birds is unknown. M'Fadyean (1894) first described coccidiosis in young pheasants. Jones (1964, 1965b, 1966) found coccidiosis in 12%, 33%, and 33%, respectively, of wild pheasants examined in England, and Ormsbee (1939) found a yearly incidence of 38% in 37 wild pheasants from Washington, with the highest incidences in October and April. Madsen (1941) found coccidia in 82% of 169 adults and 73% of 67 chicks of *Phasianus colchicus* from Denmark. Christiansen (1935) indicated that coccidiosis was a well-known cause of disease in both wild and pen-reared pheasant chicks in Denmark. Immunity to coccidia is probably established in older birds. Because of the high mortality of pheasants caused by hunting and natural factors however, the summer and fall populations are largely composed of young, presumably susceptible birds.

Although coccidiostats are impracticable for wild pheasants, their use in combination with proper hygienic methods may be important to game-farm breeding. Sulfaquinoxaline is evidently a fairly effective drug in controlling all of the species of *Eimeria* in pheasants that have been tested. Jones (1964) has discussed the use of coccidiostats for game birds.

Eimeria colchici Norton 1967

SYNONYMS: On the basis of oocyst size, Norton (1967b) considered that the species described as *Coccidium oviforme* by M'Fadyean (1894) and as *Eimeria* sp. by Davies et al. (1963) may have been *E. colchici*.

◆ **DISTRIBUTION.** Ring-necked pheasants *(Phasianus colchicus)*, England; turkeys *(Meleagris gallopavo)*, experimental.

◆ **DEVELOPMENT.** In experimental infections, Norton (1967b) found that 96% of oocysts had sporulated after 48 hours in 2% potassium dichromate at 26° C. In 3-day-old coccidia-free pheasants, 1st-generation schizonts were present in the small intestine 48 hours after inoculation of oocysts. Second-generation schizonts were first observed in the small intestine at 60 hours after inoculation, and 3rd-generation schizonts were found deep in cecal crypts 96 hours after inoculation. Gametocytes were present in epithelial cells of the cecal crypts at 96 hours and oocysts were observed in the lumen of the cecal crypts at 144 hours. The prepatent period was 6 days.

◆ **CLINICAL SIGNS.** (Experimental infections). Norton (1967b) reported that when 320,000 oocysts were given to 10 coccidia-free pheasants, anorexia, depression, and weight loss occurred on the 4th day; on the 5th day all birds died. In birds given 80,000 oocysts, signs and weight loss were less severe than those described above. On the 6th day, 6 of the 10 birds died. Two birds died on the 7th day and the last died on the 9th day. Ten pheasants of the same age that were given 20,000 oocysts appeared normal when compared with noninfected controls on the 4th day, but a slight depression was noted on the 6th day and 1 bird died on the 7th and 8th days of the infection.

PATHOGENESIS. Norton (1967b) reported that the small intestine of birds inoculated with 5,000, 20,000, and 80,000 oocysts appeared normal when the birds were killed on the 5th day, except that the ceca were thickened. Birds which died on the 5th day after inoculation with 320,000 oocysts appeared in good condition except for a general intestinal hyperemia; the lower intestine and ceca were thickened and contained a core of necrotic intestinal debris, granular leukocytes, and food material.

◆ **DIAGNOSIS.** Oocysts (Fig. 21.23) are elongate ellipsoidal and often slightly asymmetrical; they measure 19 to 34μ by 13 to 20μ (mean 27.4μ by 16.7μ). The oocyst wall is 1.3μ thick and has an inconspicuous micropyle. A polar granule was present in 81% of the oocysts. Sporocysts measure 12 to 17μ by 6 to 8μ (mean 14.6μ by 6.6μ). A sporocyst residuum and prominent Stieda body are present.

◆ **TREATMENT.** Zoalene and amprolium were effective as coccidiostats when ad-

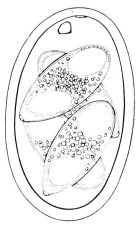

FIG. 21.23. Oocyst of *Eimeria colchici.* (From Norton, 1967b.)

ministered 2 days before inoculation and continued for 16 days after inoculation of 3-week-old pheasants with 80,000 oocysts. Sulfaquinoxaline was somewhat less effective under the same conditions. When different sulfa compounds were given 3, 4, and 5 days after inoculation, the weight gain was less than when Amprolium, sulfaquinoxaline, and Zoalene were given prior to inoculation.

Eimeria duodenalis Norton 1967

◆ **DISTRIBUTION.** Ring-necked pheasants *(Phasianus colchicus),* England.

◆ **DEVELOPMENT.** Norton (1967a) found complete sporulation of 92% of oocysts in 2% potassium dichromate at 27° C after 44 hours. When 3-week-old coccidia-free pheasants were experimentally infected, mature 1st-generation schizonts were present after 48 hours in the epithelial cells of villi, mainly in the duodenum and upper small intestine. Second-generation schizonts were present in the same part of the intestine at 72 hours after inoculation. After 96 hours, mature schizonts, presumably of a 3rd generation, and gametocytes were present in the upper small intestine. The prepatent period was 5 days.

◆ **CLINICAL SIGNS.** Norton (1967a) found no signs in 3-week-old coccidia-free

pheasants experimentally inoculated with 5,000 oocysts; birds inoculated with 50,000 oocysts exhibited anorexia on the 4th day after inoculation and anorexia and slight depression on the 5th and 6th days. In birds given 500,000 oocysts, anorexia was noted from the 3rd to 7th days and depression on days 5 and 6.

◆ **PATHOGENESIS.** Norton (1967a) found that no birds died when given 5,000 oocysts; however, in birds given 50,000, 500,000, and 5,000,000 oocysts the mortality rate was 30%, 40%, and 70%, respectively. In birds which died 4 days after receiving 5,000,000 oocysts, the small intestine was congested; in lesions in the upper small intestine, the mucosa was edematous and covered with a pink mucoid exudate. In birds that died 5 days after inoculation, more prominent lesions and a mucoid exudate were seen in the small intestine, and the ceca were filled with a yellow foamy fluid. Experimental birds had decreased weight gains proportionate to the dosage of oocysts given.

◆ **DIAGNOSIS.** The oocysts (Fig. 21.24) are subspherical and measure 18 to 24μ by 15 to 21μ (mean 21.2μ by 18.6μ); no micropyle or polar granule is present. Sporocysts are ellipsoidal and measure 10 to 15μ by 6 to 9μ (mean 12.8μ by 7.3μ). A prominent Stieda body is present, as well as a granular sporocyst residuum.

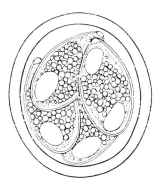

FIG. 21.24. Oocyst of *Eimeria duodenalis.* (From Norton, 1967a.)

◆ **TREATMENT.** Norton (1967a) found that when birds were given coccidiostats 2 days prior to inoculation with 500,000 oocysts and the treatment was continued for 12 days, sulfaquinoxaline and Zoalene prevented infection, but Amprolium was less effective. Treatment with 4 different sulfonamides 2, 3, and 4 days after inoculation with 500,000 oocysts caused a decrease in oocyst discharge and birds had a larger weight gain than that of nontreated controls.

Eimeria langeroni
Yakimoff and Matschoulsky 1937

◆ **DISTRIBUTION.** Ring-necked pheasants *(Phasianus colchicus gordius* and *P. colchicus turcestanicus)*, Tashkent Zoological Garden, USSR.

◆ **DEVELOPMENT.** Unknown.

◆ **CLINICAL SIGNS.** Unknown.

◆ **PATHOGENESIS.** Unknown.

◆ **DIAGNOSIS.** The oocysts are oval or elongate oval and measure 30 to 36μ by 16 to 20μ (mean 32.5μ by 18.4μ). The oocyst length to width ratio is 1.49 to 2.13 (mean 1.75). The oocyst wall is about 1μ thick and composed of two layers. No polar granule or oocyst residuum is present. Sporocysts are 6 to 14μ by 6μ. There are no Stieda bodies.

Eimeria megalostomata Ormsbee 1939

◆ **DISTRIBUTION AND INCIDENCE.** Two of 37 pheasants *(Phasianus colchicus)*, Washington.

◆ **DEVELOPMENT.** The sporulation time is 48 hours at 20° C.

◆ **CLINICAL SIGNS.** Unknown.

◆ **PATHOGENESIS.** Unknown.

◆ **DIAGNOSIS.** Oocysts are ovoid, measure 21 to 29μ by 16 to 22μ (mean 24μ by

FIG. 21.25. Oocyst of *Eimeria megalostoma.* (From Ormsbee, 1939.)

19μ) and have a length to width ratio of 1.27 (Fig. 21.25). The oocyst wall is smooth, light yellowish brown, and 2μ thick. The wall is composed of three layers. A micropyle and polar granule are present, but the oocyst residuum is absent.

Eimeria pacifica Ormsbee 1939

◆ **DISTRIBUTION AND INCIDENCE.** Four of 37 pheasants *(Phasianus colchicus)*, Washington.

◆ **DEVELOPMENT.** Ormsbee (1939) reported a sporulation time of 48 hours at 20° C. He found endogenous stages throughout the upper intestine and ceca of a pheasant passing oocysts only of *E. pacifica*. Schizonts were located both above and below the host cell nuclei of epithelial cells. Although Ormsbee stated that he was working with a pure infection (based on oocyst discharge), some of the endogenous stages he observed may have been those of other species.

◆ **CLINICAL SIGNS.** Unknown.

◆ **PATHOGENESIS.** Unknown.

◆ **DIAGNOSIS.** The oocysts (Fig. 21.26) are ovoid and measure 17 to 26μ by 14 to 20μ (mean 22μ by 18μ). The length to width ratio is 1.23. The oocyst wall is smooth, light yellow, 1.8μ thick, and composed of 2 layers. Two or three polar bodies are present.

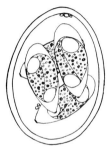

FIG. 21.26. Oocyst of *Eimeria pacifica*. (From Ormsbee, 1939.)

Eimeria phasiani Tyzzer 1929

SYNONYM: *Eimeria phasiana* Tyzzer 1929.

◆ **DISTRIBUTION AND INCIDENCE.** Pheasants *(Phasianus colchicus),* 3 of 37, Washington; 3 of 5, Germany; 56% of 70, England.

◆ **DEVELOPMENT.** The sporulation time is 24 hours at room temperature (Tyzzer, 1929) or 52 hours at 20° C (Trigg, 1967a). Tyzzer (1929) and Haase (1939) reported some details on the life cycle of *E. phasiani,* but Trigg (1967a) gave a detailed description as follows: mature 1st-generation schizonts were present below or to the side of nuclei of epithelial cells of the upper small intestine 48 hours after inoculation. Second-generation schizonts were also located in the small intestine, but the infection extended to a lower level than that of the 1st generation. Mature 2nd-generation schizonts, which were present below the host cell nuclei, were first seen 66 hours after inoculation. Most 3rd-generation schizonts were located below the host cell nuclei of the lower small intestine and the terminal halves of the ceca. Mature 3rd-generation schizonts were first present 96 hours after inoculation and oocysts were observed in the feces at 112 hours. The mean prepatent period was 117 hours. Tyzzer (1929) reported that the prepatent period was 5 days and that endogenous stages were located in the terminal part of the small intestine and in the constricted portion of the ceca.

◆ **CLINICAL SIGNS.** In experimentally infected coccidia-free pheasants, Trigg (1967b) found that symptoms and mortality depended on the number of oocysts given. In birds inoculated with 10,000 oocysts, no signs of coccidiosis were noted except for diarrhea. When 100,000 or more oocysts were given, a decreased food intake was noted on the 4th day, as well as a ruffling of feathers, unsteady gait, and liquid feces which contained mucus. By the 5th day, birds passed mucus with small amounts of blood, large numbers of 3rd-generation merozoites, and cellular debris. At the end of the 5th day, the liquid feces contained immature gametocytes, oocysts, and cellular debris. *Eimeria phasiani* infections caused a decreased weight gain in infected chicks as compared with that of noninfected controls.

◆ **PATHOGENESIS.** At the end of the 4th day in birds infected with 100,000 or more oocysts, petechial hemorrhages were present on the serosal and mucosal surfaces of the upper half to two-thirds of the small intestine. In the area of hemorrhage, the mesenteric blood vessels were congested, and the intestinal wall was thickened and edematous. The lumen contained mucus, blood, and cellular debris. By the 5th day the ceca were slightly congested and contained clots, consisting of parasites, mucus, and cellular debris. After the invasion of the intestine by the parasites, there was an immediate increase of leukocytes, chiefly eosinophils, in the lamina propria of the villi. An alteration in numbers of erythrocytes and leukocytes in the peripheral blood was not observed.

◆ **DIAGNOSIS.** Oocysts have been described by Tyzzer (1929), Haase (1939), Ormsbee (1939), and Trigg (1967a). Because Trigg's description is most complete and does not differ greatly from that of the other authors, it has been used for the following description. The oocysts (Fig. 21.27) are ellipsoidal and measure 20 to 31μ by 14 to 21μ (mean 24.7μ by 17.1μ). The length to width ratio is 1.44. The two-layered oocyst wall is smooth and 1.6μ thick. No

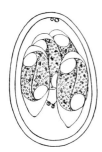

FIG. 21.27. Oocyst of *Eimeria phasiani*. (From Ormsbee, 1939.)

micropyle or oocyst residuum is present. There are one to three polar granules. Sporocysts measure 13 to 16μ by 6 to 7μ (mean 14.3μ by 6.7μ). A Stieda body is present, but the sporocyst residuum is absent.

◆ **TREATMENT.** Trigg (1967b) gave three coccidiostats to experimentally infected birds 2 days prior to inoculation and continued treatment throughout the infection. Sulfaquinoxaline completely suppressed oocyst production, and weight gain was similar to that of noninfected controls. Zoalene and Amprolium suppressed oocyst output and inoculated birds had a greater weight gain than that of nontreated birds, but these drugs were less effective than sulfaquinoxaline.

Polyplectron

Eimeria bhutanensis
Ray and Hiregaudar 1959

◆ **DISTRIBUTION.** Peacock pheasants *(Polyplectron bicalcaratum)*, Calcutta Zoological Garden, India.

◆ **DEVELOPMENT.** Sporulation time is 24 to 36 hours.

◆ **CLINICAL SIGNS.** Unknown.

◆ **PATHOGENESIS.** Unknown.

◆ **DIAGNOSIS.** Oocysts are spherical to subspherical and measure 16 to 17μ by 15 to 17μ. The oocyst wall is yellowish and composed of two layers. A polar granule is present. Sporocysts are bean-shaped and measure 6 to 7μ by 3 to 4μ. Each sporocyst has a Stieda body and a small amount of residual material.

Pternistis

Eimeria pternistis
Agostinucci and Bronzini 1956

◆ **DISTRIBUTION.** Partridges *(Pternistis leucoscepus)*, Rome Zoological Garden. The host was originally from Italian Somaliland.

◆ **DEVELOPMENT.** Average sporulation time was 4 days at 20° C.

◆ **CLINICAL SIGNS.** Unknown.

◆ **PATHOGENESIS.** Unknown.

◆ **DIAGNOSIS.** The oocysts are oval, measure 18.6 ± 0.95μ by 14.5 ± 0.50μ and have a length to width ratio of 1.27 ± 0.03. The oocyst wall is yellowish, smooth, composed of two layers, and about 0.4μ thick. A micropyle and polar granule are present, but an oocyst residuum is absent. Sporocysts measure 8.9 ± 0.53μ by 5.0 ± 0.48μ, and each has a Stieda body and a small residuum.

Tetrao

Eimeria ventriosa Haase 1939

SYNONYM: *Eimeria ventricosa* lapsus in Reichenow (1949).

◆ **DISTRIBUTION.** Capercaillies *(Tetrao urogallus)*, Germany.

◆ **DEVELOPMENT.** Sporulation time is 48 hours at 23° C.

◆ **CLINICAL SIGNS.** Unknown.

◆ **PATHOGENESIS.** Unknown.

◆ **DIAGNOSIS.** Oocysts are ellipsoidal and flattened on two sides and measure 32 to 34μ in length by 20 to 23μ or 16 to 17μ in width. The oocysts have a length to width ratio of 1.47 to 2.17. The oocyst wall is smooth, colorless, composed of 2 layers, and 1μ thick. A micropyle and polar bodies are present, but an oocyst residuum is absent. The sporocysts are bottle-shaped and each has a sporocyst residuum.

Eimeria procera Haase 1939

◆ **DISTRIBUTION.** Capercaillies *(Tetrao urogallus);* gray partridges *(Perdix perdix);* Germany.

◆ **DEVELOPMENT.** Sporulation time is 20 to 24 hours at 23° C.

◆ **CLINICAL SIGNS.** Unknown.

◆ **PATHOGENESIS.** Unknown.

◆ **DIAGNOSIS.** Oocysts are ellipsoidal, have a length to width ratio of 1.79 to 1.92, and measure 29 to 31μ by 16 to 17μ (mean 30.0μ by 16.8μ). The oocyst wall is rough, composed of two layers, and about 1.5μ thick. A micropyle is not apparent in freshly passed oocysts, but is visible in sporulated oocysts. A polar granule is present, but the oocyst residuum is absent. The sporocysts are ovoid and each has a Stieda body.

Eimeria yakisevi
(Yakimoff and Gousseff 1936)
Hardcastle 1943

SYNONYMS: *Eimeria brumpti* Yakimoff and Gousseff 1936; pro parte *Eimeria nonbrumpti* Levine 1953; homonym *Eimeria brumpti* Cauchemez 1921.

◆ **DISTRIBUTION.** Capercaillies *(Tetrao urogallus),* USSR.

◆ **DEVELOPMENT.** Unknown.

◆ **CLINICAL SIGNS.** Unknown.

◆ **DIAGNOSIS.** Oocysts are spherical and measure 20μ in diameter. No polar granule or oocyst residuum is present. Sporocysts measure 11μ by 5μ.

◆ **REMARKS.** The name *E. brumpti* Cauchemez 1921 had priority over the name *E. brumpti* Yakimoff and Gousseff 1936, which was described from *Tetrao urogallus* and a woodpecker *(Dendrocopus [Dryobatis] major).* Because of the high degree of host specificity of eimerian species, Levine (1953) renamed the form from *D. major* as *E. nonbrumpti.*

Questionable Species

Eimeria caucasica
Yakimoff and Buewitsch 1932

◆ **DISTRIBUTION AND INCIDENCE.** The species was described from two "Berghuehner" of unknown genus and species from the USSR.

◆ **DEVELOPMENT.** Sporulation time is 24 hours.

◆ **CLINICAL SIGNS.** Unknown.

◆ **PATHOGENESIS.** Unknown.

◆ **DIAGNOSIS.** The oocysts are usually elongate cylindrical, but may be ovoid. Oocysts measure 25 to 36μ by 14 to 22μ (mean 32.7μ by 19.0μ) and the length to width ratio is 1:0.50 to 0.70 (mean 1:0.58). The oocyst wall is composed of two layers, is colorless, and has no micropyle. A polar granule is present, but the oocyst residuum is absent. Sporocysts measure 9 to 13μ by 6 to 7μ and each has a Stieda body and residuum.

PASSERIFORMES

Dorisiella aethiopsaris
Chakravarty and Karr 1947

◆ **DISTRIBUTION.** Jungle mynahs *(Acridotheres* [syn. *Aethiopsar] fuscus fuscus)*, India.

◆ **DEVELOPMENT.** Unknown.

◆ **CLINICAL SIGNS.** Unknown.

◆ **PATHOGENESIS.** Unknown.

◆ **DIAGNOSIS.** Oocysts are subspherical or oval. The subspherical forms measure 29 to 31μ by 24 to 26μ and the oval forms are 33 to 39μ by 24 to 26μ. The oocyst wall is composed of two layers and is about 2μ thick. No micropyle is present. The sporocysts measure 20 to 22μ by 11 to 13μ and have a sporocyst residuum.

Dorisiella hareni
Chakravarty and Kar 1944

◆ **DISTRIBUTION.** Black-headed munias *(Munia malacca malacca);* red munias *(Amandava amandava);* munias *(Munia atricapilla atricapilla);* white-throated munias *(Uroloncha malabarica);* spotted munias *(Uroloncha punctulata punctulata);* India.

◆ **DEVELOPMENT.** Endogenous stages are located in the small intestine. The sporulation time is 3 to 4 days.

◆ **CLINICAL SIGNS.** Unknown.

◆ **PATHOGENESIS.** Unknown.

◆ **DIAGNOSIS.** Oocysts are spherical and measure 19 to 23μ (mean 20.6μ) in diameter (Fig. 21.28). The oocyst wall is composed of two layers and about 2μ thick. No micropyle is present. The sporocysts are pyriform, measure 14 to 19μ by 9 to 10μ and contain a diffuse sporocyst residuum.

Eimeria balozeti
Yakimoff and Gousseff 1938

◆ **DISTRIBUTION.** Starlings *(Sturnus vulgaris)*, USSR.

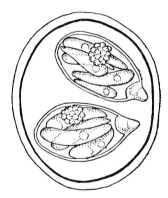

FIG. 21.28. Oocyst of *Dorisiella aethioparis.* ×1,600. (From Chakravarty and Kar, 1947.)

◆ **DEVELOPMENT.** Unknown.

◆ **CLINICAL SIGNS.** Unknown.

◆ **PATHOGENESIS.** Unknown.

◆ **DIAGNOSIS.** Oocysts are ovoid and measure 20 to 31μ by 17 to 27μ. The oocyst wall is composed of two layers. A micropyle, polar granule, and oocyst residuum are absent. The sporocysts measure 12 to 14μ by 7 to 9μ.

Eimeria lucknowensis Misra 1947

SYNONYM: *Eimeria lacknowensis* Misra 1947 lapsus in Pellerdy (1956).

◆ **DISTRIBUTION.** Pied wagtails *(Motacilla alba)*, India.

◆ **DEVELOPMENT.** Endogenous stages were found in the small intestine. Sporulation time is 3 to 4 days.

◆ **CLINICAL SIGNS.** Unknown.

◆ **PATHOGENESIS.** Unknown.

◆ **DIAGNOSIS.** Oocysts are ovoid and measure 21 to 25μ by 17 to 19μ. The oocyst wall is colorless and composed of two layers. A micropyle, oocyst residuum, and polar body are absent. Sporocysts are ovoid and measure 9μ by 6μ. A sporocyst residuum is present.

Eimeria malaccae
Chakravarty and Kar 1944

◆ **DISTRIBUTION.** Black-headed munias *(Munia malacca malacca)*, India.

◆ **DEVELOPMENT.** Unknown.

◆ **CLINICAL SIGNS.** Unknown.

◆ **PATHOGENESIS.** Unknown.

◆ **DIAGNOSIS.** Oocysts are broadly to elongate oval and measure 27 to 31μ by 16 to 19μ. There is no oocyst residuum. A micropyle is present. Sporocysts measure 12μ by 10μ and have a sporocyst residuum and Stieda body.

Isospora ampullacea Schwalbach 1959

◆ **DISTRIBUTION.** Garden warblers *(Sylvia borin)*, Germany.

◆ **DEVELOPMENT.** Sporulation time is 57 hours at 16° C.

◆ **CLINICAL SIGNS.** Unknown.

◆ **PATHOGENESIS.** Unknown.

◆ **DIAGNOSIS.** The oocysts are spherical and measure 19 to 28μ (mean 27μ). The oocyst wall is about 1μ thick. The sporocysts are flask-shaped, measure 21μ by 12μ, and have a Stieda body and large diffuse residuum.

Isospora anthi Schwalbach 1959

◆ **DISTRIBUTION.** Meadow pipits *(Anthus pratensis)*, Germany.

◆ **DEVELOPMENT.** The sporulation time is 52 hours at 16° C.

◆ **CLINICAL SIGNS.** Unknown.

◆ **PATHOGENESIS.** Unknown.

◆ **DIAGNOSIS.** Oocysts are bluntly ellipsoidal to subspherical and measure 19 to 30μ by 19 to 26μ (mean 25.6μ by 21.6μ). The oocyst wall is about 0.9μ thick. A polar granule is present, but an oocyst residuum and micropyle are absent. The sporocysts are ellipsoidal and measure 16μ by 9μ. Each sporocyst has a Stieda body, substiedal body, and compact sporocyst residuum.

Isospora corviae
Ray, Shivnani, Oommen, and Bhaskaran 1952

◆ **DISTRIBUTION.** Common Himalayan crows *(Corvus macrorhynchos intermedius)*, India.

◆ **DEVELOPMENT.** The sporulation time is 36 to 48 hours at room temperature.

◆ **CLINICAL SIGNS.** Unknown.

◆ **PATHOGENESIS.** Unknown.

◆ **DIAGNOSIS.** The oocysts are subspherical to spherical and measure 15 to 23μ by 14 to 22μ (mean 17.7μ by 20.0μ). The oocyst wall is composed of two layers and is grayish pink. One or two residual granules, which may or may not have a polar position, are present. The sporocysts measure 8 to 13μ by 6 to 9μ (mean 7.8μ by 10.8μ) and contain a compact sporocyst residuum.

Isospora chloridis Anwar 1966

◆ **DISTRIBUTION.** House sparrows *(Passer domesticus)*; greenfinches *(Carduelis* [syn. *Chloris] chloris)*; chaffinches *(Fringilla coelebs)*; England.

◆ **DEVELOPMENT.** The life cycle was described by Anwar (1966). The endogenous stages are located above the nuclei of epithelial cells in the villi of the duodenum. Schizogony takes 72 to 84 hours. Mature 1st-generation schizonts measure 9μ

by 8μ and 2nd-generation schizonts are 17μ by 14μ. Second-generation schizonts give rise to either gametocytes or another asexual generation. Mature microgametocytes are 15μ by 12μ, and mature macrogametes measure 17μ by 13μ. The sporulation time is 62 to 72 hours at 25° C.

◆ **CLINICAL SIGNS.** Unknown.

◆ **PATHOGENESIS.** Unknown.

◆ **DIAGNOSIS.** Oocysts are ellipsoidal and measure 17 to 33μ by 17 to 30μ (mean 25.4μ by 22.3μ). The oocyst wall is smooth, colorless, composed of one layer, and about 0.8μ thick. A micropyle and oocyst residuum are absent. Two or more polar granules are present. The sporocysts measure 14 to 19μ by 8 to 12μ (mean 15.3μ by 9.4μ). The sporocysts have a Stieda body and compact sporocyst residuum, which becomes scattered in older sporocysts.

Isospora dilatata Schwalbach 1959

◆ **DISTRIBUTION.** Meadow pipits *(Anthus pratensis);* garden warblers *(Sylvia borin);* whitethroats *(Sylvia communis);* blackcaps *(Sylvia atricapilla);* starlings *(Sturnus vulgaris);* Germany.

◆ **DEVELOPMENT.** Sporulation time is 54 hours at 16° C.

◆ **CLINICAL SIGNS.** Unknown.

◆ **PATHOGENESIS.** Unknown.

◆ **DIAGNOSIS.** The oocysts are spherical and measure 19 to 29μ (mean 24.3μ). The oocyst wall is about 1μ thick. Two or three granules are present in the oocyst. Sporocysts measure 18 by 11μ and each has a compact sporocyst residuum, Stieda body, and substiedal body.

Isospora ficedulae Schwalbach 1959

◆ **DISTRIBUTION.** Pied flycatchers *(Ficedula hypoleuca),* Germany.

◆ **DEVELOPMENT.** The sporulation time is 48 hours at 16° C.

◆ **CLINICAL SIGNS.** Unknown.

◆ **PATHOGENESIS.** Unknown.

◆ **DIAGNOSIS.** The oocysts are spherical and measure 16μ by 24μ (mean 20.5μ) in diameter. The oocyst wall is about 0.9μ thick. A polar granule is present, but a micropyle is absent. Sporocysts measure 17μ by 11μ and each has a compact residuum, Stieda body, and substiedal body.

Isospora fringillae
Yakimoff and Gousseff 1938

◆ **DISTRIBUTION.** Chaffinches *(Fringilla coelebs),* USSR.

◆ **DEVELOPMENT.** Unknown.

◆ **CLINICAL SIGNS.** Unknown.

◆ **PATHOGENESIS.** Unknown.

◆ **DIAGNOSIS.** The oocysts are spherical or oval. Spherical forms measure 16 to 24μ (mean 21.2μ) and oval forms are 20 to 28μ by 16 to 22μ (mean 24.1μ by 19.4μ). The length to width ratio of oval forms is 1.18 to 1.56 (mean 1.27). No oocyst residuum or micropyle is present, but a polar granule and sporocyst residuum are present. Sporocysts measure 12 to 14μ by 8 to 10μ.

Isospora garrulae
Ray, Shivnani, Oommen, and
Bhaskaran 1952

◆ **DISTRIBUTION.** Streaked laughing thrushes *(Garrulax lineatus lineatus),* India.

◆ **DEVELOPMENT.** Sporulation time is 24 to 36 hours at room temperature.

◆ **CLINICAL SIGNS.** Unknown.

◆ **PATHOGENESIS.** Unknown.

◆ **DIAGNOSIS.** Oocysts are spherical to subspherical and measure 20 to 23μ by 18 to 21μ (mean 20.6μ by 19.8μ). The oocyst wall is composed of two layers and has a brownish color. A polar granule is present. Sporocysts are pyriform and measure 10 to 16μ by 8 to 13μ (mean 13.4μ by 8.5μ). A Stieda body and compact sporocyst residuum are present.

Isospora garrulusae
Ray, Shivnani, Oommen, and
Bhaskaran 1952

◆ **DISTRIBUTION.** Himalayan jays (*Garrulus glandarius bispecularis*), India.

◆ **DEVELOPMENT.** The sporulation time is 48 to 72 hours at room temperature.

◆ **CLINICAL SIGNS.** Unknown.

◆ **PATHOGENESIS.** Unknown.

◆ **DIAGNOSIS.** Oocysts are oval to subspherical and measure 25 to 28μ by 20 to 25μ (mean 25.2μ by 21.2μ). The oocyst wall is grayish, composed of two layers, and has a micropyle. One or two granules are present in sporulated oocysts. Sporocysts are pyriform and measure 13 to 18μ by 8 to 10μ (mean 16.1μ by 9.6μ). A sporocyst residuum and distinct Stieda body are present.

Isospora ginginiana
Chakravarty and Kar 1944

SYNONYM: *Isospora ginginiana* var. *tristis* Chakravarty and Kar 1947.

◆ **DISTRIBUTION.** Mynahs (*Acridotheres ginginianus*); common mynahs (*Acridotheres tristis tristis*); India.

◆ **DEVELOPMENT.** Endogenous stages are located in the intestine.

◆ **CLINICAL SIGNS.** Unknown.

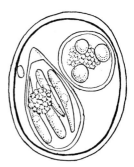

FIG. 21.29. Oocyst of *Isospora ginginiana.* ×1,600. (From Chakravarty and Kar, 1947.)

◆ **PATHOGENESIS.** Unknown.

◆ **DIAGNOSIS.** In the original description, the oocysts are described as spherical and 22 to 24μ in diameter (Fig. 21.29). No oocyst residuum or micropyle is present. Sporocysts are pyriform and measure 15 to 18μ by 11μ. In a later description the oocysts are described as 26 to 31μ by 24 to 26μ. A small, spherical oocyst residuum is present.

◆ **REMARKS.** Chakravarty and Kar (1947) described *I. ginginiana* var. *tristis.* The oocysts are oval to spherical and measure 24 to 28μ by 20 to 24μ. The oocyst wall is composed of two layers and has a micropyle. No oocyst residuum is present. Sporocysts are pyriform and measure 15 to 18μ by 9 to 11μ. A compact sporocyst residuum is present. Because this description is similar to that of *I. ginginiana* and the two forms are from the same host genus, we consider *I. ginginiana* var. *tristis* a synonym of *I. ginginiana.*

Isospora hirundinis Schwalbach 1959

◆ **DISTRIBUTION.** Swallows (*Hirundo rustica*); redstarts (*Phoenicurus phoenicurus*); black redstarts (*Phoenicurus ochruros*); Germany.

◆ **DEVELOPMENT.** Sporulation time is 42 hours at 16° C.

◆ **CLINICAL SIGNS.** Unknown.

◆ **PATHOGENESIS.** Unknown.

◆ **DIAGNOSIS.** Oocysts are ellipsoidal and measure 24 to 33μ by 20 to 29μ (mean 28.0μ by 22.6μ). The oocyst wall is about 0.9 to 1.0μ thick. A polar granule is present, but an oocyst residuum is absent. Sporocysts measure 19μ by 11μ. Each sporocyst has a Stieda body and substiedal body, as well as a sporocyst residuum.

Isospora lacazei (Labbe 1893)

Synonyms: *Diplospora lacazii* Labbe 1893; *Diplospora rivoltae* Labbe 1893; *Isospora passerum* Sjboring 1897; *Isospora communis passerum* Sjboring 1897.

◆ **DISTRIBUTION.** *Isospora lacazei* has been reported from over 50 species of passeriform and other birds throughout the world. Boughton (1937b) and Scholtyseck and Przygodda (1956) have listed many of the hosts from which *I. lacazei* has been reported.

◆ **DEVELOPMENT.** The endogenous development has been reported by several authors (Laveran, 1898; Wasielewski, 1904; Wenyon, 1926; Hosoda, 1928; Chakravarty and Kar, 1944a; and Anwar, 1964, 1966). The sporulation time ranges from 2 to 6 days. Anwar (1966) described endogenous stages as follows: Endogenous stages are located in epithelial cells of the duodenum. Mature first-generation schizonts are present 72 hours after inoculation. These measure 8μ by 7μ and have 10 to 12 merozoites. Second-generation schizonts are 16μ by 10μ and have 14 to 16 merozoites. Mature microgametocytes measure 15μ by 13μ and mature macrogametes are 16μ by 13μ. No plastic granules are present in macrogametes.

◆ **CLINICAL SIGNS.** Unknown.

◆ **PATHOGENESIS.** Unknown.

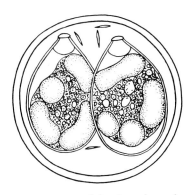

FIG. 21.30. Oocyst of *Isospora lacazei*. ×2,000. (From Levine and Mohan, 1960.)

◆ **DIAGNOSIS.** The description of oocysts of *I. lacazei* differs considerably. The size of oocysts described by Labbe (1893) was 23 to 35μ in diameter. In the same paper Labbe described *Diplospora rivoltae* whose oocysts were 18 to 19μ in diameter. Labbe (1896) considered *D. rivoltae* to be a synonym of *D. lacazei*. Boughton (1930, 1933, 1937b) found that oocysts of *I. lacazei* in English sparrows were 16 to 32μ by 13 to 29μ. A micropyle is present according to some authors, but others say it is absent. For detailed descriptions of oocysts see Scholtyseck (1954), Levine and Mohan (1960) (Fig. 21.30), and Anwar (1966). Scholtyseck (1954) found two sizes of oocysts in English sparrows; he considered the larger forms to be *I. lacazei* and the smaller forms to be *I. passerum*.

◆ **REMARKS.** Because of the large numbers of hosts from which *I. lacazei* has been reported, Levine and Mohan (p. 739, 1960) stated, "The best way to minimize confusion would be to retain for the present only the name *I. lacazei* for all those forms of *Isospora* from passeriform birds customarily referred to this species and for morphologically similar forms from other birds, recognizing that it may very well be a complex of several species. If future investigations justify it, one or more species might be split off from this complex, and when this is done they should be given new and uncompromised names." Schwalbach (1959) studied the coccidia of birds and named several new species on the basis of sporogony and type of Stieda body (micropyle) in sporocysts. Schwalbach also considered the amount and location of glycogen in the sporocysts to be an important diagnostic character.

Isospora lickfeldi Schwalbach 1959

◆ **DISTRIBUTION.** Blackcaps *(Sylvia atricapilla);* garden warblers *(Sylvia borin);* whitethroats *(Sylvia communis);* Germany.

◆ **DEVELOPMENT.** Sporulation time is 72 hours at 16° C.

◆ **CLINICAL SIGNS.** Unknown.

◆ **PATHOGENESIS.** Unknown.

◆ **DIAGNOSIS.** Oocysts are spherical and average 24.3μ in diameter. The oocyst wall is about 1.2μ thick. An oocyst residuum and polar body are absent. Sporocysts measure 18μ by 10μ and have both ends pointed. A Stieda body and sporocyst residuum are present.

Isospora monedulae Yakimoff and Matschoulsky 1936

SYNONYM: *Isopora* sp. Nemeseri 1949.

◆ **DISTRIBUTION.** Collared jackdaws *(Corvus* [syn. *Coloeus] monedula),* Tashkent Zoological Garden, USSR.

◆ **CLINICAL SIGNS.** Unknown.

◆ **PATHOGENESIS.** Unknown.

◆ **DIAGNOSIS.** The oocysts are spherical or oval. Spherical forms are 16 to 20μ (mean 18μ) in diameter and oval forms are 16 to 22μ by 14 to 18μ (mean 20μ by 18μ). The length to width ratio of oval forms is 1.11 to 1.23 (mean 1.16). A polar granule is present, but an oocyst residuum is absent. The sporocysts are pyriform, measure

12 to 16μ by 6 to 8μ and have a sporocyst residuum.

Isospora muniae Chakravarty and Kar 1944

◆ **DISTRIBUTION.** Black-headed munias, *(Munia malacca malacca),* India.

◆ **DEVELOPMENT.** Endogenous stages are located in the small intestine. The sporulation time is 48 hours.

◆ **CLINICAL SIGNS.** Unknown.

◆ **PATHOGENESIS.** Unknown.

◆ **DIAGNOSIS.** Oocysts are broadly to elongate oval and measure 25 to 31μ by 14 to 19μ. The oocyst wall is about 1 to 2μ thick, composed of two layers, and has a micropyle. No oocyst residuum is present. The sporocysts are pyriform and measure 14 to 17μ by 10μ. A scattered sporocyst residuum is present.

Isospora nucifragae Galli-Valerio 1933

◆ **DISTRIBUTION.** Nutcrackers *(Nucifraga caryocatactes),* Switzerland.

◆ **CLINICAL SIGNS.** Unknown.

◆ **PATHOGENESIS.** Unknown.

◆ **DIAGNOSIS.** Oocysts are ovoid, but narrow near the micropylar end, and measure 24μ by 21μ. Sporoblasts are 11μ by 9μ.

Isospora parusae Ray, Shivnani, Oommen, and Bhaskaran 1952

SYNONYM: *Isospora lophophuriae* Ray, Shivnani, Oommen, and Bhaskaran 1952.

◆ **DISTRIBUTION.** Brown-crested tits *(Parus dichrous),* India.

◆ **DEVELOPMENT.** Sporulation time is 48 hours at room temperature.

◆ **CLINICAL SIGNS.** Unknown.

◆ **PATHOGENESIS.** Unknown.

◆ **DIAGNOSIS.** The oocysts are oval to subspherical and measure 23 to 28μ by 20 to 23μ (mean 24.2μ by 20.8μ). The oocyst wall is two-layered, yellowish, and has a micropyle. Two granules are present in sporulated oocysts. The sporocysts are pyriform and measure 10 to 18μ by 10μ (mean 15μ by 10μ). A prominent Stieda body and compact sporocyst residuum are present.

Isospora perronciti Carpano 1937

◆ **DISTRIBUTION.** Bullfinches *(Pyrrhula europea)*, Egypt.

◆ **DEVELOPMENT.** Carpano (1937) described endogenous stages which were present in the small intestine.

◆ **CLINICAL SIGNS.** Unknown.

◆ **PATHOGENESIS.** Unknown.

◆ **DIAGNOSIS.** Oocysts are spherical to subspherical and have a mean measurement of 15 to 25μ. The oocyst wall is smooth and no micropyle is present. There is no oocyst residuum, but a sporocyst residuum is present.

Isospora phoenicuri Schwalbach 1959

◆ **DISTRIBUTION.** Pied flycatchers *(Ficedula hypoleuca)*; redstarts, *(Phoenicurus phoenicurus)*; Germany.

◆ **DEVELOPMENT.** Sporulation time is 42 hours at 16° C.

◆ **CLINICAL SIGNS.** Unknown.

◆ **PATHOGENESIS.** Unknown.

◆ **DIAGNOSIS.** The oocysts are ellipsoidal and measure 23 to 35μ by 16 to 27μ (mean 30.6μ by 20.0μ). The oocyst wall is

0.9 to 1.0μ thick. Sporocysts are pyriform and have a mean measurement of 21.6μ by 10.0μ. A compact sporocyst residuum and substiedal body are present.

Isospora rochalimai
Yakimoff and Gousseff 1936 emend.

SYNONYM: *Isospora rocha-limai* Yakimoff and Gousseff 1936; *Isospora* sp. in the black-billed magpie *(Pica pica hudsonia)* was reported by Todd et al. (1967); because they could not distinguish the oocysts from *I. lacazei* and found no features that distinguish *I. rochalimai* from *I. lacazei,* they thought *I. rochalimai* should probably be considered as a synonym of *I. lacazei.*

◆ **DISTRIBUTION.** Magpies *(Pica pica),* USSR, Hungary.

◆ **DEVELOPMENT.** Nemeseri (1949) reported the sporulation time was 48 to 60 hours.

◆ **CLINICAL SIGNS.** Unknown.

◆ **PATHOGENESIS.** Unknown.

◆ **DIAGNOSIS.** According to Yakimoff and Gousseff (1936b) the oocysts are subspherical and measure 23 to 25μ by 18 to 23μ (mean 23.9μ by 19.9μ). The length to width ratio is 1.08 to 1.33 (mean 1.20). The oocyst wall is colorless. No micropyle is present. Sporocysts are ovoid and measure 15μ by 19μ. An oocyst and sporocyst residuum are present.

Isospora rodhaini
Yakimoff and Matschoulsky 1938

◆ **DISTRIBUTION AND INCIDENCE.** A raven *(Corvus* sp.), Leningrad Zoological Garden, USSR.

◆ **DEVELOPMENT.** The sporulation time is 72 to 96 hours.

◆ **CLINICAL SIGNS.** Unknown.

◆ **PATHOGENESIS.** Unknown.

◆ **DIAGNOSIS.** Oocysts are spherical, subspherical, or ovoidal. Spherical forms measure 17 to 25μ (mean 22.9μ) and the subspherical or ovoidal forms are 19 to 27μ by 17 to 25μ (mean 24.9μ by 22.6μ). The oocyst wall is smooth and an oocyst residuum may be present or absent. A polar granule is present. Sporocysts measure 11 to 15μ by 8 to 11μ and have a Stieda body and compact residuum.

Isospora seicercussae Ray, Shivnani, Oommen, and Bhaskaran 1952

SYNONYM: *Isopora cryptolophae* Ray, Shivnani, Oommen, and Bhaskaran 1952.

◆ **DISTRIBUTION.** Gray-headed warblers *(Seicercus xanthoschistos)*, India.

◆ **DEVELOPMENT.** Sporulation time is 48 hours at room temperature.

◆ **CLINICAL SIGNS.** Unknown.

◆ **PATHOGENESIS.** Unknown.

◆ **DIAGNOSIS.** Oocysts are spherical to subspherical and measure 23 to 30μ by 20 to 25μ (mean 24.8μ by 23.3μ). The oocyst wall is two-layered and a micropyle is present. Two granules are present in sporulated oocysts. Sporocysts are pyriform and measure 10 to 18μ by 9 to 11μ (mean 10.3μ by 14.2μ). A sporocyst residuum and Stieda body are present.

Isospora sturniae
Chakravarty and Kar 1947

◆ **DISTRIBUTION.** Gray-headed mynahs *(Sturnus [syn. Sturnia] malabaricus)*, India.

◆ **DEVELOPMENT.** Chakravarty and

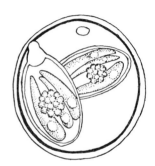

FIG. 21.31. Oocyst of *Isospora sturniae*. ×1,600. (From Chakravarty and Kar, 1947.)

Kar (1947) described endogenous stages but did not give their location in the intestine.

◆ **CLINICAL SIGNS.** Unknown.

◆ **PATHOGENESIS.** Unknown.

◆ **DIAGNOSIS.** The oocysts are spherical to subspherical and measure 22 to 29μ in diameter (Fig. 21.31). The oocyst wall is composed of two layers and has a micropyle. No oocyst residuum is present but a polar granule has been illustrated. Sporocysts are pyriform and measure 18 to 20μ by 11 to 13μ. A prominent Stieda body and compact sporocyst residuum are present.

Isospora sylviae Schwalbach 1959

◆ **DISTRIBUTION.** Blackcaps *(Sylvia atricapilla)*; garden warblers *(Sylvia borin)*; whitethroats *(Sylvia communis)*, Germany.

◆ **DEVELOPMENT.** Sporulation time is 46 hours at 16° C.

◆ **PATHOGENESIS.** Unknown.

◆ **DIAGNOSIS.** The oocysts are spherical to subspherical and have a mean measurement of 29.7μ by 27.0μ. There is no oocyst residuum, but a few polar granules are present. Sporocysts measure 22μ by 14μ and have a substiedal body.

Isospora sylvianthina Schwalbach 1959

♦ **DISTRIBUTION.** Meadow pipits *(Anthus pratensis)*; garden warblers *(Sylvia borin)*; whitethroats *(Sylvia communis)*; blackcaps *(Sylvia atricapilla)*, Germany.

♦ **DEVELOPMENT.** Sporulation time is 59 hours at 16° C.

♦ **CLINICAL SIGNS.** Unknown.

♦ **PATHOGENESIS.** Unknown.

♦ **DIAGNOSIS.** The oocysts are 19 to 35μ by 18 to 33μ (mean 27.0μ by 24.3μ). The oocyst wall is 1.2μ thick. No oocyst residuum is present, but two polar granules are present. The sporocysts are 19μ by 11μ and have a Stieda body and large diffuse sporocyst residuum.

Isospora temenuchii
Chakravarty and Kar 1944

♦ **DISTRIBUTION.** Brahmin mynahs *(Sturnus* [syn. *Temenuchus] pagodarum)*, India.

♦ **DEVELOPMENT.** Unknown.

♦ **CLINICAL SIGNS.** Unknown.

♦ **PATHOGENESIS.** Unknown.

♦ **DIAGNOSIS.** Oocysts are usually subspherical, but a few are slightly ovoid. Oocysts measure 22 to 24μ by 20 to 22μ. The oocyst wall is about 2μ thick, composed of two layers, and has a micropyle. No oocyst residuum is present. Sporocysts are oval, with one end somewhat bluntly pointed, and measure 15 to 18μ by 11μ. A Stieda body and compact sporocyst residuum are present.

Isospora turdi Schwalbach 1959

♦ **DISTRIBUTION.** Blackbirds *(Turdus merula)*, Germany.

♦ **DEVELOPMENT.** Sporulation time is 21 hours at 20° C.

♦ **CLINICAL SIGNS.** Unknown.

♦ **PATHOGENESIS.** Unknown.

♦ **DIAGNOSIS.** The oocysts are oval with sharply rounded ends and measure 16 to 23μ by 15 to 19μ (mean 18.9μ by 16.2μ). The oocyst wall is 0.8 to 0.9μ thick. A micropyle is absent. A polar granule, compact sporocyst residuum, and substiedal body are present.

Isospora volki Boughton 1937

♦ **DISTRIBUTION.** Lawes' six-plumed bird of paradise *(Parotia lawesi lawesi)*; greater bird of paradise *(Paradisaea apoda apoda)*; Count Salvadori's bird of paradise *(Paradisaea apoda salvadori)*; Emperor of Germany's bird of paradise *(Paradisaea guilelmi)*; lesser bird of paradise *(Paradisaea minor minor)*; Prince Rudolph's bird of paradise *(Paradisaea rudolphi rudolphi)*; long-tailed bird of paradise *(Epimachus meyeri meyeri)*; twelve-wired bird of paradise *(Seleucides melanoleucus melanoleucus)*; lesser superb bird of paradise *(Lophorina superba minor)*; red bird of paradise *(Paradisaea* [syn. *Uranornis] rubra)*; blue manucode *(Manucodia chalybatus)*. All of the above records are from the New York Zoological Garden. With the exception of *M. chalybatus*, which was imported from the Papuan Islands, all of the birds were originally from New Guinea.

♦ **DEVELOPMENT.** The sporulation time is 48 hours at room temperature.

♦ **CLINICAL SIGNS.** Unknown.

♦ **PATHOGENESIS.** Unknown.

♦ **DIAGNOSIS.** Oocysts are broadly ovoid when passed, but the thin wall collapses around the sporocysts after sporulation. The oocysts measure 14 to 21μ by 14 to 20μ (mean 18μ by 16μ). There is no micropyle. Sporocysts are ellipsoid with a Stieda body at the pointed end. A globule (polar body?) is present between the sporocysts, and a sporocyst residuum is present.

Isospora wurmbachi Schwalbach 1959

◆ **DISTRIBUTION.** Whinchats *(Saxicola rubetra)*; blackcaps *(Sylvia atricapilla)*; garden warblers *(Sylvia borin)*; whitethroats *(Sylvia communis)*; willow warblers *(Phylloscopus trochilus)*; pied flycatchers *(Ficedula hypoleuca)*; meadow pipits *(Anthus pratensis)*, Germany.

◆ **DEVELOPMENT.** Sporulation time is 72 hours at 16° C.

◆ **CLINICAL SIGNS.** Unknown.

◆ **PATHOGENESIS.** Unknown.

◆ **DIAGNOSIS.** Oocysts are spherical and have a mean measurement of 21.6μ in diameter and the oocyst wall is 1.2μ thick. Scattered granules are present in the oocyst. Sporocysts are ovoid, measure 18μ by 10μ, and have a Stieda body and sporocyst residuum.

Isospora zosteropis Chakravarty and Kar 1947

◆ **DISTRIBUTION.** Indian white-eyes *(Zosterops palpebrosa palpebrosa)*; brown-headed barbets *(Megalaima* [syn. *Thereiceryx] zeylanica caniceps)*; India.

◆ **DEVELOPMENT.** Unknown.

◆ **CLINICAL SIGNS.** Unknown.

◆ **PATHOGENESIS.** Unknown.

◆ **DIAGNOSIS.** Oocysts are oval and measure 18 to 22μ by 13 to 20μ (Fig. 21.32). The oocyst wall is composed of two layers and does not have a micropyle. An oocyst residuum was present in forms from *M. zeylanicus caniceps* but not in those from *Z. p. palpebrosa*. Sporocysts are oval and measure 15 to 18μ by 11μ. A compact sporocyst residuum is present.

FIG. 21.32. Oocyst of *Isospora zosteropis.* ×1,600. (From Chakravarty and Kar, 1947.)

Lankesterella

Avian toxoplasmosis has been reported by many authors. Although *Toxoplasma gondii* does infect birds, many of the reported cases of avian toxoplasmosis are probably caused by a different organism. Garnham (1950) established the genus *Atoxoplasma* for avian forms. Lainson (1959) discovered that *Atoxoplasma* was a synonym of *Lankesterella*. Because Lainson (1960) experimentally transmitted *Lankesterella* from sparrows to canaries, the specific status of all species is in question and further work needs to be done to resolve the matter (see also p. 309).

Lankesterella adiei (Aragao 1933) Lainson 1959

SYNONYMS: The species was described by Adie (1908) but was not named; *Haemogregarina adiei* Aragao 1933; *Lankersterella passeris* Raffaele 1938; *Lankesterella garnhami* Lainson 1959; *Lankesterella serini* Lainson 1959; *Lankesterella* sp. Box 1966 and Box 1967.

◆ **DISTRIBUTION AND INCIDENCE.** All of 99 adults and 150 fledgling house sparrows *(Passer domesticus)*, England; also in *P. domesticus* from New York and Illinois, 30 of 41 from Massachusetts, 24% of 128 young and 17% of 150 adults from Texas, all of 58 adults and 14 of 18 young from Poland; canaries *(Serini canaris).*

◆ **DEVELOPMENT.** Lainson (1959) found sporozoites in lymphocytes and monocytes; occasionally extracellular forms were seen in the blood. Schizogony took place in the lymphoid-macrophage cells of the spleen, bone marrow, and liver; gametogony occurred in the lymphoid-macrophage cells of the liver, lungs, and kidney. Young birds can be infected by the mite *Dermanyssus gallinae* (Lainson 1960).

◆ **CLINICAL SIGNS.** Unknown.

◆ **PATHOGENESIS.** Lainson (1958) reported that *L. adiei* may cause congestion, hemorrhage, and inflammatory foci of the liver and lungs in English sparrows.

◆ **DIAGNOSIS.** Lainson (1959) found that sporozoites in circulating blood cells are oval or sausage-shaped. The parasites are in a vacuole and often in close proximity to the host cell nucleus. The position and shape of the parasite nucleus varies. Sporozoites measure 3.6 to 5.4μ by 1.8 to 3.6μ (mean 5μ by 3μ). Two types of schizonts are present. One has 10 to 30 (mean 16) oval merozoites which measure 3.6μ by 2.3μ. The second type of schizont has a smaller number of merozoites with one pointed end; these merozoites measure 5.7μ by 3.5μ. Mature macrogametes measure 14.5μ in diameter and have a large karyosome. Mature microgametocytes have about 60 to 100 microgametes. The zygote nucleus of oocysts undergoes repeated division to form large numbers of sporozoites which are about 3.6μ by 1.8μ.

Lankesterella argyae
(Garnham 1950) Lainson 1959

SYNONYM: *Atoxoplasma argyae* Garnham 1950.

◆**DISTRIBUTION.** Chatterers *(Turdoides* [syn. *Argya*] *rubiginosus)* and shrikes *(Lanius collaris);* East Africa.

◆ **DEVELOPMENT.** Schizogony and gametogony evidently take place in the lungs and possibly in the liver and spleen.

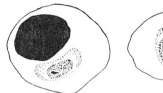

FIG. 21.33. Sporozoites of *Lankesterella argyae.* ×2,000. (From Garnham, 1950.)

◆ **CLINICAL SIGNS.** Unknown.

◆ **PATHOGENESIS.** Unknown.

◆ **DIAGNOSIS.** In the peripheral blood the sausage-shaped sporozoites chiefly inhabit lymphocytes. The parasite is closely associated with the nucleus so as to indent the nucleus or in some cases cause it to fragment into two parts (Fig. 21.33). Oval forms, 7.5μ by 3.0μ, were also found in blood smears. In the lungs the parasites are usually in large monocytes and are not closely associated with the nuclei.

Lankesterella corvi Baker, Lainson, and Killick-Kendrick 1959

◆ **DISTRIBUTION AND INCIDENCE.** Rooks *(Corvus frugilegus),* England. Parasites were present in 36 of 196 fledglings less than 1 year old, but were not found in 25 nestlings or 38 adults.

◆ **DEVELOPMENT.** Baker et al. (1959) found sporozoites in erythrocytes, thrombocytes, neutrophils, monocytes, and lymphocytes. Gametocytes were present in tibiotarsal marrow smears. The mite, *Ornithonyssus sylviarum,* was considered to be a possible vector.

◆ **CLINICAL SIGNS.** Unknown.

◆ **PATHOGENESIS.** Unknown.

◆ **DIAGNOSIS.** The blood forms are bean-shaped to oval. The nucleus forms a band across the center of the parasites, but the remainder of the sporozoites is nearly clear. The mean measurements are 6.2μ

by 2.5μ. In smears of bone marrow, macrogametes are round to oval and measure 14 to 18μ by 15 to 18μ. The nucleus is indistinct, but the cytoplasm contains dark areas about 1.5μ in diameter.

Lankesterella paddae
(Laveran 1900) Lainson 1959

SYNONYMS: *Haemamoeba danilewskyi* Laveran 1900; *Haemogregarina paddae* Aragao 1933; *Toxoplasma avium* Marullaz 1913; *Atoxoplasma paddae* Laird 1959 .

♦ **DISTRIBUTION.** *Padda oryzivora;* silvereyes *(Zosterops flavifrons, Z. lateralis, Z. rennelliana, Woodfordia superciliosa)* and a rail *(Gallirallus australis)* from islands in the South Pacific; silvereyes *(Zosterops palpebrosa),* Argentina.

♦ **DEVELOPMENT.** Laird (1959) observed sporozoites in peripheral blood in large lymphocytes where binary fission may produce as many as four daughter organisms. These stages cause an indentation of the host cell nucleus. Later stages occur in lymphocytes and monocytes and do not indent the host cell nucleus. In view of the life cycle of *L. adiei* that was reported by Lainson (1959), binary fission probably does not take place in peripheral blood cells. The two or four parasites that were present in some lymphocytes observed by Laird (1959) were probably the result of multiple invasion of parasites, and not the result of binary division of the sporozoites within the host cell.

♦ **CLINICAL SIGNS.** Unknown.

♦ **PATHOGENESIS.** Unknown.

♦ **DIAGNOSIS.** According to Laird (1959) the early forms in blood cells are round or pyriform and measure 2.5 to 4.3μ (mean 3.2μ) in diameter. The "later stages" described by Laird are oval or sausage-shaped

and measure 3.0 to 5.9μ (mean 4.2μ) by 2.3 to 3.8μ (mean 2.9μ).

Wenyonella mackinnoni Misra 1947

♦ **DISTRIBUTION.** Pied wagtails *(Motacilla alba),* India.

♦ **DEVELOPMENT.** Endogenous development takes place in the small intestine. Schizogonic stages have not been observed. Mature microgametocytes have an average measurement of 21μ by 16μ and each contains a central residuum. Mature macrogametes are ellipsoidal and measure 23μ by 20μ. The sporulation time is 4 to 6 days.

♦ **CLINICAL SIGNS.** Unknown.

♦ **PATHOGENESIS.** Unknown.

♦ **DIAGNOSIS.** Oocysts are spherical to ovoid. The spherical forms measure 19 to 23μ and the ovoid forms are 24 to 26μ by 18 to 22μ. The oocyst wall is composed of two layers. The outer layer is thin and colorless and the inner layer is thicker and brownish (illustrations show the outer layer is thicker). An oocyst residuum, polar granule, and micropyle are absent. Sporocysts measure 10μ by 7μ and have a residuum.

♦ **REFERENCES**

Adie, J. R. Note on a parasite in the sparrow. *Indian Med. Gaz.* 43:176, 1908.
Adler, H. E., and Moore, E. W. Renal coccidiosis and gizzard worm infection in geese. *J. Am. Vet. Med. Assoc.* 112:154, 1948.
Agostinucci, G., and Bronzini, E. *Eimeria pternistis* n. sp. parassita del francolino somalo *(Pternistis leucoscepus* Er.). *N. Ann. Ig. Microbiol.* 6:449, 1955.
Allen, E. A. The occurrence of *Eimeria truncata* in the United States. *J. Parasitol.* 20:73, 1933.
——. *Eimeria angusta* sp. nov. and *Eimeria bonasae* sp. nov. from grouse, with a key to the species of *Eimeria* in birds. *Trans. Am. Microscop. Soc.* 53:1, 1934.
——. *Tyzzeria perniciosa* gen. et sp. nov., a

coccidium from the small intestine of the Pekin duck, *Anas domesticus* L. *Arch. Protistenk.* 87:262, 1936.

Anonymous. *Check-list of North American birds,* 5th ed. American Ornithologists Union, 1957.

Anwar, M. Types of schizogony in *Isospora* infections of the greenfinch *(Chloris chloris).* Abstr. *Parasitology* 54:9p, 1964.

———. *Isospora lacazei* (Labbe, 1893) and *I. chloridis* sp. n. (Protozoa: Eimeriidae) from the English sparrow *(Passer domesticus),* greenfinch *(Chloris chloris)* and chaffinch *(Fringilla coelebs). J. Protozool.* 13:84, 1966.

Aragao, H. B. Considerations sur les hemogregarines des oiseaux. *Compt. Rend. Soc. Biol.* 113:214, 1933.

Baidalin, A. J. Epizootologie, therapy and prophylaxis against kidney coccidiosis in geese. (In Russian). *Veterinaria* 35(5):43, 1958.

Baker, J. R., Lainson, R., and Killick-Kendrick, R. *Lankesterella corvi* n. sp., a blood parasite of the English rook, *Corvus frugilegus frugilegus. J. Protozool.* 6:233, 1959.

Bhatia, B. B., and Pande, B. P. On two new species of coccidia from wild Anatidae. *Acta Vet. Acad. Sci. Hung.* 16:335, 1966.

Bhatia, B. B., Pandey, T. P., and Pande, B. P. *Eimeria bateri* n. sp. from Indian common grey quail *(Coturnix coturnix coturnix). Indian J. Microbiol.* 5:61, 1965.

———. *Eimeria teetari* n. sp. (Eimeriidae: Sporozoa) in Indian partridges. *Acta Vet. Acad. Sci. Hung.* 16:329, 1966.

Bhatia, B. L. *Protozoa: Sporozoa.* In *The Fauna of British India.* London: Taylor and Francis, 1938.

Boughton, D. C. The value of measurements in the study of a protozoan parasite *Isospora lacazei* (Labbe). *Am. J. Hyg.* 11:212, 1930.

———. Diurnal gametic periodicity in avian *Isospora. Am. J. Hyg.* 18:161, 1933.

———. *Isospora volki* n. sp., a new avian coccidian. *J. Parasitol.* 23:97, 1937a.

———. Notes on avian coccidiosis. *Auk* 54:500, 1937b.

Boughton, D. C., and Volk, J. Avian hosts of eimerian coccidia. *Bird Banding* 9:139, 1938a.

Boughton, D. C., Boughton, R. B., and Volk, J. Avian hosts of the genus *Isospora. Ohio J. Sci.* 38:149, 1938b.

Boughton, R. V. Endoparasitic infestations in grouse, their pathogenicity and correlation with meteoro-topographical conditions. *Minn. Agr. Exp. Sta. Tech. Bull.* 121, 1937.

Box, E. D. Blood and tissue protozoa of the English sparrow *(Passer domesticus domesticus)* in Galveston, Texas. *J. Protozool.* 13: 204, 1966.

———. Influence of *Isospora* infections on patency of avian *Lankesterella (Atoxoplasma,* Garnham, 1950). *J. Parasitol.* 53:1140, 1967.

Braun, C. E., and Willers, W. B. The helminth and protozoan parasites of North American grouse (Family: Tetraonidae): A checklist. *Avian Diseases* 11:170, 1967.

Brinkmann, A. Coccidiosen hos lirypen. *Bergen's Mus. Aarb. (1926),* p. 71, 1927.

Bump, G. *Bureau of Game 26th Annual Report, New York Conservation Department (1936),* p. 288, 1937.

Carpano, M. Sui coccidi deglie uccelli e su di una particolare *Isospora* osservata nelle pirrule *(Isospora perronciti,* n. sp.). *Riv. Parass.* 1:259, 1937.

Cauchemez, L. Frequence de la coccidie du porc *(Eimeria brumpti,* n. sp.), en France. *Bull. Soc. Pathol. Exotique* 14:645, 1921.

Chakravarty, M., and Basu, S. P. On a new coccidium *Tyzzeria alleni* n. sp. from the intestine of the bird cotton teal. *Sci. Culture* 12:106, 1946.

Chakravarty, M., and Kar, A. B. Studies on coccidia of Indian birds. I. On the life-history of *Isospora lacazei* (Labbe). *J. Dept. Sci. Calcutta Univ.* 1:78, 1944a.

———. Studies on the coccidia of Indian birds. II. Observations on several species of coccidia of the sub-families Cyclosporinae and Eimeriinae. *Proc. Indian Acad. Sci.* 20B: 102, 1944b.

———. A study on the coccidia of Indian birds. *Proc. Roy. Soc. Edinburgh* 62B:225, 1947.

Christiansen, M. De vigtigste smitsomme sygdomme hos vildtet. *Maanedsskr. Dyrl.* 47: 353, 1935.

———. Nyrecoccidiose hos vildtlevende andefugle (Anseriformes), *Eimeria somateriae* n. sp. hos ederfugl *(Somateria mollissima* [L]). *Nord. Vet. Med.* 4:1173, 1952.

Christiansen, M., and Madsen, H. *Eimeria bucephalae* n. sp. (Coccidia) pathogenic in goldeneye *(Bucephala clangula* L.) in Denmark. *Danish Rev. Game Biol.* 1:61, 1948.

Cordero del Campillo, M., and Pla Hernandez, M. Sobre las coccidiosis de las perdices, con description de *Eimeria legionensis* n. sp., parasita de *Alectoris rufa* L. y una clave para su diferenciacion. *Rev. Iber. Parasitol.* 26:27, 1966.

Cram, E. B., A comparison of internal parasites of ruffed grouse of Labrador with those of ruffed grouse of the United States. *J. Parasitol.* 18:48, 1931.

Critcher, S. Renal coccidiosis in Pea Island Canada geese. *Wildlife in N. Carolina* 14:14, 1950.

Davies, S. F. M. An outbreak of duck coccidiosis in Britain. *Vet. Rec.* 69:1051, 1957.

Davies, S. F. M., Joyner, L. P., and Kendall, S. B. *Coccidiosis.* Edinburgh and London: Oliver and Boyd, 1963.

Dubey, J. P., and Pande, B. P. A preliminary note on *Eimeria battakhi* n. sp. (Protozoa: Eimeriidae) from domestic duck *(Anas platyrhynchos domesticus).* Current Sci. 32:329, 1963.

Fantham, H. B. Experimental studies on avian coccidiosis, especially in relation to young grouse, fowls, and pigeons. *Proc. Zool. Soc. London* 2:708, 1910.

Farr, M. M. Three new species of coccidia from the Canada goose, *Branta canadensis* (Linne, 1758). *J. Wash. Acad. Sci.* 43:336, 1953.

———. Coccidiosis of lesser scaup ducks *(Nyroca affinis).* Abstr. *Proc. 11th Ann. Meet. Soc. Protozool.* 6:7, 1959.

———. Two new species of coccidia, *Eimeria crassa* and *E. pulchella* (Sporozoa: Eimeriidae) from the Canada goose, *Branta canadensis* (L). *Proc. Helminthol. Soc. Wash. D.C.* 30:155, 1963.

———. Coccidiosis of the lesser scaup duck, *Aythya affinis* (Eyton, 1838), with a description of a new species, *Eimeria aythyae. Proc. Helminthol. Soc. Wash. D.C.* 32:236, 1965.

Farr, M. M., and Wehr, E. E. *Eimeria truncata* associated with morbidity and death of domestic goslings. *Cornell Vet.* 42:185, 1952.

Gallagher, B. A. Coccidia as a cause of quail disease. *J. Am. Vet. Med. Assoc.* 59:85, 1921.

Galli-Valerio, B. Notes de parasitologie et de technique parasitologique. *Zentr. Bakteriol. Parasitenk. Abt. I. Orig.* 103:177, 1927.

———. Notes de parasitologie. *Zentr. Bakteriol. Parasitenk. Abt. I. Orig.* 112:54, 1929.

———. Notes de parasitologie. *Zentr. Bakteriol. Parasitenk. Abt. I. Orig.* 120:98, 1931.

———. Notes de parasitologie et de technique parasitologique. *Zentr. Bakteriol. Parasitenk. Abt. I. Orig.* 125:129, 1932.

———. Notes parasitologiques et de technique parasitologique. *Zentr. Bakteriol. Parasitenk. Abt. I. Orig.* 129:422, 1933.

Garnham, P. C. C. Blood parasites of East African vertebrates, with a brief description of exo-erythrocytic schizogony in *Plasmodium pitmani. Parasitology* 40:328, 1950.

Glover, J. S. Poultry diseases laboratory service. *Rept. Ontario Vet. Coll.* (1946–47):60, 1947.

Graefner, G., and Graubmann, H.-D. *Eimeria kotlani* n. sp., eine neue pathogene Kokzidienart bei Gaensen. *Monatsh. Veterinaermed.* 19:819, 1964.

Graefner, G., Graubmann, H.-D., and Betke, P. Duenndarmkokzidiose bei Hausenten, verursacht durch eine neue Kokzidienart, *Eimeria danailovi* n. sp. *Monatsh. Veterinaermed.* 20:141, 1965.

Grecchi, D. Sobre uma *Eimeria* do mutum. *Rev. Soc. Paulista Med. Vet.* 5:171, 1939.

Haase, A. Untersuchungen ueber die bei deutschen Wildhuehnern vorkommenden *Eimeria*—Arten. *Arch. Protistenk.* 92:329, 1939.

Hadley, P. B. Studies in avian coccidiosis. III. Coccidiosis in the English sparrow and other wild birds. *Zentr. Bakteriol. Parasitenk. Abt. I. Orig.* 56:522, 1910.

———. *Eimeria avium:* A morphological study. *Arch. Protistenk.* 23:7, 1911.

Hanson, H. C., Levine, N. D., and Ivens, V. Coccidia (Protozoa: Eimeriidae) of North American wild geese and swans. *Can. J. Zool.* 35:715, 1957.

Hardcastle, A. B. A check list and host-index of the species of the protozoan genus *Eimeria. Proc. Helminthol. Soc. Wash. D.C.* 10:35, 1943.

Hawkins, P. A. Coccidiosis in turkeys. *Mich. Agr. Exp. Sta. Tech. Bull.* 226, 1952.

Henry, D. P. Species of coccidia in chickens and quail in California. *Univ. Calif. Publ. Zool.* 36:157, 1931.

Herman, C. M. Coccidiosis in native California valley quail and problems of control. *Ann. N.Y. Acad. Sci.* 52:621, 1949.

Herman, C. M., Jankiewicz, H. A., and Saarni, R. W. Coccidiosis in California quail. *Condor* 44:168, 1942.

Herman, C. M., Chattin, J. E., and Saarni, R. W. Food habits and intensity of coccidian infection in native valley quail in California. *J. Parasitol.* 29:206, 1943.

Hilbert, K. F. Renal coccidiosis in a goose on Long Island. *Cornell Vet.* 41:54, 1951.

Honess, R. F., and Post, G. *Eimeria* of grouse (Family: Tetraonidae), with a description of *Eimeria pattersoni* n. sp. from the sage grouse. *Wyo. Game Fish Comm. Bull.* 8:5, 1955.

Hosoda, S. Experimentelle Studien ueber die Entwicklung des *Eimeria avium. Fukuoka Ikwadaigaku Zasshi* 21:777, 1928.

Inoue, I. *Eimeria saitamae* n. sp.: A new cause of coccidiosis in domestic ducks *(Anas platyrhyncha var. domestica). Japan. J. Vet. Sci.* 29:209, 1967.

Jones, M. B. Survey of game bird diseases. *Rept. Game Res. Assoc.* 3:13, 1964.

———. Coccidiosis and coccidiostats. *Rept. Game Res. Assoc.* 4:75, 1965a.

———. Survey of game bird diseases. *Rept. Game Res. Assoc.* 4:45, 1965b.

———. Survey of game bird diseases. *Rept. Game Res. Assoc.* 5:34, 1966.

Klimes, B. Coccidia of the domestic goose *(Anser anser dom.)*. *Zentr. Veterinaermed.* 10B: 427, 1963.

Kotlan, S. Adatok a vizimadarak (kacsa, liba) coccidiosisanak ismeretehez. *Allatorvosi Lapok* 55:103, 1932.

———. Zur Kenntnis der Kokzidiose des Wassergefluegels. Die Kokzidiose der Hausgans. *Zentr. Bakteriol. Parasitenk. Abt. I. Orig.* 129:11, 1933.

Labbe, A. Sur les coccidies des oiseaux. *Compt. Rend. Acad. Sci.* 117:407, 1893.

———. Recherches zoologiques, cytologiques et biologiques sur les coccidies. *Arch. Zool. Exptl. Gen.* 4:517, 1896.

Lainson, R. *Atoxoplasma* Garnham, 1950, in an English sparrow *(Passer domesticus domesticus* Linn.). *Trans. Roy. Soc. Trop. Med. Hyg.* 52:15, 1958.

———. *Atoxoplasma* Garnham, 1950, as a synonym for *Lankesterella* Labbe, 1899. Its life cycle in the English sparrow *(Passer domesticus domesticus,* Linn.). *J. Protozool.* 6:360, 1959.

———. The transmission of *Lankesterella* (= *Atoxoplasma)* in birds by the mite *Dermanyssus gallinae. J. Protozool.* 7:321, 1960.

Laird, M. *Atoxoplasma paddae* (Aragao) from several South Pacific silvereyes (Zosteropidae) and a New Zealand rail. *J. Parasitol.* 45:47, 1959.

Laveran, M. Sur les modes de reproduction d'*Isospora lacazei. Compt. Rend. Soc. Biol.* 50:1139, 1898.

———. Au sujet de l'hematozoaire endoglobulaire de *Padda oryzivora. Compt. Rend. Soc. Biol.* 52:19, 1900.

Lerche, M. Nierencoccidiose bei Hausgaensen. *Z. Hyg. Infektionskrankh.* 25:122, 1924.

Levine, N. D. *Tyzzeria* and *Eimeria* from the Canada goose. Abstr. *Proc. Am. Soc. Protozool.* 2:17, 1951.

———. *Eimeria magnalabia* and *Tyzzeria* sp. (Protozoa: Eimeriidae) from the Canada goose. *Cornell Vet.* 42:247, 1952.

———. A review of the coccidia from the avian orders Galliformes, Anseriformes and Charadriiformes, with descriptions of three new species. *Am. Midland Naturalist* 49:696, 1953.

———. *Protozoan Parasites of Domestic Animals and of Man.* Minneapolis: Burgess, 1961.

Levine, N. D., and Mohan, R. N. *Isospora* sp. (Protozoa: Eimeriidae) from cattle and its relationship to *I. lacazei* of the English sparrow. *J. Parasitol.* 46:733, 1960.

Levine, N. D., Morrill, C. C., and Schmittle, S. C. Renal coccidiosis in an Illinois gosling. *N. Am. Vet.* 31:738, 1950.

Lindquist, W. D., Belding, R. C., and Hitchcock, D. J. A report on the presence of renal coccidiosis in Michigan. *Mich. St. Coll. Vet.* 12:19, 1951.

M'Fadyean, J. Some observations regarding the *Coccidium oviforme. J. Comp. Pathol. Therap.* 7:131, 1894.

McNutt, S. H. Renal coccidiosis of geese. *J. Am. Vet. Med. Assoc.* 75:365, 1929.

Madsen, H. The occurrence of helminths and coccidia in partridges and pheasants in Denmark. *J. Parasitol.* 27:29, 1941.

Manwell, R. D. Avian toxoplasmosis with invasion of the erythrocytes. *J. Parasitol.* 27: 245, 1941.

Marullaz, M. Au sujet d'un toxoplasme des oiseaux. *Bull. Soc. Pathol. Exotique* 6:323, 1913.

Misra, P. L. On a new coccidian *Wenyonella bahli* n. sp. from the common grey quail, *Coturnix communis* Bonn. *Proc. Nat. Inst. Sci. India* 10:203, 1944.

———. On three coccidian parasites *Wenyonella mackinnoni* n. sp., *Eimeria lucknowensis* n. sp., and *Isospora* sp., from the intestine of the wagtail *Motacilla alba* Linn. (Passeriformes, Montacillidae). *Proc. Indian Acad. Sci.* 25B:75, 1947.

Moore, E. N. Species of coccidia affecting turkeys. *Am. Vet. Med. Assoc., Proc. 91st Ann. Meeting,* p. 300, 1954.

Moore, E. N., and Brown, J. A. A new coccidium of turkeys, *Eimeria innocua* n. sp. (Protozoa: Eimeriidae). *Cornell Vet.* 42:395, 1952.

Morgan, B. B., and Hawkins, P. A. *Veterinary protozoology.* Minneapolis: Burgess, 1948.

Morse, G. B. Quail disease in the United States. *U. S. Dept. Agr., Bur. Animal Ind. Circ.* 109, 1907.

Nemeseri, L. Studies on coccidia of birds with special reference to the genus *Isospora* (in Hungarian). *Diss. Budapest.* 1949. Cited in Pellerdy (1965).

Nieschulz, O. Eine neue Kokzidienart bei der Hausgans. *Zentr. Bakteriol. Parasitenk. Abt. I. Orig.* 152:74, 1947.

Norton, C. C. *Eimeria duodenalis* sp. nov. from English covert pheasants *(Phasianus* sp.). *Parasitology* 57:31, 1967a.

———. *Eimeria colchici* sp. nov. (Protozoa: Eimeriidae), the cause of cecal coccidiosis in English covert pheasants. *J. Protozool.* 14: 772, 1967b.

Ormsbee, R. A. Field studies on coccidiosis in the ring-necked pheasants of Eastern Washington. *Parasitology* 31:389, 1939.

Pande, B. P., Bhatia, B. B., and Srivastava, K. M. N. *Wenyonella anatis,* n. sp. (Protozoa: Eimeriidae) from Indian domestic duck. *Sci. Culture* 31:383, 1965.

Patterson, F. D. Cross-infection experiments with coccidia of birds. *Cornell Vet.* 23:249, 1933.

Pavlov, P. Coccidienbefunde bei Saeugetieren und Voegeln in Bulgarien. *Zentr. Bakteriol. Parasitenk. Abt. I. Orig.* 149:317, 1943.

Pellerdy, L. P. Catalogue of the genus *Eimeria* (Protozoa: Eimeriidae). *Acta Vet. Acad. Sci. Hung.* 6:75, 1956.

———. *Catalogue of Eimeriidae* (Protozoa: Sporozoa. Budapest: Akademiai Kiado, 1963.

———. *Coccidia and coccidiosis.* Budapest: Akademiai Kiado, 1965.

Peters, J. L. *Check-list of birds of the world,* vols. 1–7, 9, 10, 12, 15. Cambridge: Harvard Univ. Press and Museum of Comparative Zoology, 1931–1967.

Raffaele, G. Evoluzione di *Plasmodium, Toxoplasma* ed altri microrganismi negli organi interni dei vertebrati. *Riv. Malariol. Rome* 17:85, 1938.

Railliet, A., and Lucet, A. Note sur quelques especes de coccidies encore peu etudiees. *Bull. Soc. Zool. France* 16:246, 1891.

Ramisz, A. The occurrence of *Lankesterella* Labbe in birds of the family Fringillidae in Wroclaw. *Acta Parasitol. Pol.* 12:297, 1964.

Ray, D. K., Shivnani, G. A., Oommen, M., and Bhaskaran, R. A study on the coccidia of some Himalayan birds. *Proc. Zool. Soc. Bengal* 5:141, 1952.

Ray, H., and Hiregaudar, L. S. Coccidia from some birds at the Calcutta Zoo. *Bull. Calcutta School Trop. Med.* 7:111, 1959.

Reichenow, E. *Lehrbuch der Protozoenkunde.* Jena: Gustav Fischer, 1949.

Rothschild, M., and Clay, T. *Fleas, flukes and cuckoos.* New York: Macmillan, 1957.

Scholtyseck, E. Untersuchungen ueber die bei einheimischen Vogelarten vorkommenden Coccidien der Gattung *Isospora. Arch. Protistenk.* 100:91, 1954.

———. *Eimeria anatis* n. sp., ein neues Coccid aus der Stockente *(Anas platyrhynchos). Arch. Protistenk.* 100:431, 1955.

Scholtyseck, E., and Przygodda, W. Die Coccidiose der Voegel. *Die Vogelwelt* 77:161, 1956.

Schwalbach, G. Untersuchungen und Beobachtungen an Coccidien der Gattungen *Eimeria, Isospora* und *Caryospora* bei Voegeln mit einer Beschreibung von sechzehn neuen Arten. *Arch. Protistenk.* 104:431, 1959.

———. Die Coccidiose der Singvoegel. I. Der Ausscheidungsrhythmus der Isospora-Oocysten beim Haussperling *(Passer domesticus). Zentr. Bakteriol. Parasitenk. Abt. I. Orig.* 178:263, 1960.

———. Die Coccidiose der Singvoegel. II. Beobachtungen an Isospora-Oocysten aus einem Weichfresser *(Parus major)* mit besonderer Beruecksichtigung des Ausscheidungsrhythmus. *Zentr. Bakteriol. Parasitenk. Abt. I. Orig.* 181:264, 1961.

Seidel, E. Einiges ueber neue Parasitenfunde beim Sumpfbiber. *Deutsch. Pelztierzuechter* 28:190, 1954.

Simon, F. *Eimeria centrocerci* n. sp. du *Centrocercus urophasianus* (cog de bruyere). *Ann. Parasitol.* 17:137, 1939.

Sjboering, N. Beitraege zur Kenntnis einiger Protozoen. *Zentr. Bakteriol. Parasitenk. Abt. I. Orig.* 22:675, 1897.

Skidmore, L. B. The incidence of coccidia in the common English sparrow *(Passer domesticus). J. Parasitol.* 20:331, 1934.

Spiegl, A. Nieren-Kokzidiose bei Hausgaensen. *Z. Hyg. Infektionskrankh.* 22:263, 1921.

Stoddard, H. L. *The bobwhite quail.* New York: Charles Scribner's & Sons, 1931.

Tiboldy, B. Experimental researches on the specificity of coccidiosis of domestic birds. (In Hungarian.) *Koezl. Osszehas. Elet-es Kort.* 26:173, 1934.

Todd, K. S., Jr., Ernst, J. V., and Hammond, D. M. Parasites of the black-billed magpie, *Pica pica hudsonia* (Sabine, 1823) from northern Utah. *Bull. Wildlife Disease Assoc.* 3:112, 1967.

Trigg, P. I. *Eimeria phasiani* Tyzzer, 1929—A coccidium from the pheasant *(Phasianus colchicus).* I The life cycle. *Parasitology* 57: 135, 1967a.

———. *Eimeria phasiani* Tyzzer, 1929—A coccidium from the pheasant *(Phasianus colchicus).* II. Pathogenicity and drug action. *Parasitology* 57:147, 1967b.

Tyzzer, E. E. Coccidiosis in gallinaceous birds. *Am. J. Hyg.* 10:269, 1929.

Vernard, C. Helminths and coccidia from Ohio bobwhite. *J. Parasitol.* 19:205, 1933.

Walden, H. W. Observations on renal coccidia in Swedish anseriform birds, with notes concerning two new species, *Eimeria boschadis,* and *Eimeria christianseni* (Sporozoa, Telosporidia). *Arkiv. Zool.* 15:97, 1963.

Wasielewski, T. von. *Studien und Mikrophotogramme zur Kenntnis der pathogenen Protozoen,* vol. 1. Leipzig: Barth, 1904.

Wenyon, C. M. *Protozoology. A manual for medical men, veterinarians and zoologists,* 2 vols. New York: William Wood, 1926.

Wickware, A. B. Notes on miscellaneous diseases of geese. *Can. J. Comp. Med.* 5:21, 1941.

Yakimoff, W. L., and Buewitsch, B. I. Zur Frage der Coccidien wildlebender Voegel in Aserbaidschan (Transkaukasus). *Arch. Protistenk.* 77:187, 1932.

Yakimoff, W. L., and Gousseff, W. F. A propos des coccidies des oiseaux sauvages. *Ann. Parasitol.* 14:449, 1936a.

———. *Isospora rocha-limai* n. sp. parasita da pega *(Pica pica* L.). *Arch. Inst. Biol. Sao Paulo* 7:189, 1936b.

———. *Eimeria balozeti* n. sp., coccidie nouvelle de *Sturnus vulgaris. Arch. Inst. Pasteur Tunis* 27:282, 1938.

Yakimoff, W. L., and Matikaschwili, I. L. Coccidiosis of the grey and stone partridge. *Parasitology* 28:146, 1936.

Yakimoff, W. L., and Matschoulsky, S. N. Eine Kokzidie der Dohle. *Berlin. Muench. Tieraerztl. Wochschr.* 87:603, 1936.

———. Nouvelle coccidie du faisan. *Ann. Parasitol.* 15:162, 1937.

———. Les coccidies du corbeau. *Ann. Soc. Belge Med. Trop.* 18:527, 1938.

22 ◆ TRICHOMONIASIS

- ● RICHARD M. KOCAN
- ● CARLTON M. HERMAN

NONPATHOGENIC TRICHOMONADS frequently invade the organs of the body, the cecum being the most common site of infection. Three known pathogenic species, however, invade the upper digestive tract and genitalia. These are *Trichomonas gallinae,* a parasite of the upper digestive tract of birds, the only species proved to cause mortality in wildlife; and *T. vaginalis* and *Tritrichomonas foetus,* parasites of the genital tracts of primate and bovine species. Probably the earliest known parasitic disease of wildlife was trichomoniasis caused by *T. gallinae* in Columbiformes and other birds. This disease has undoubtedly been known to falconers and pigeon raisers for many centuries. Early books and journals on falconry referred to the characteristic caseous lesions as frounce (a term still used) or as canker or roup. Stabler (1954) refers to a work published in England in 1619 which discusses the lesions and their treatment. It was recognized at that time that captive hawks became infected by eating infected pigeons.

◆ **DISTRIBUTION.** The domestic or common pigeon *(Columba livia)* is usually considered the primary host of *T. gallinae,* although the parasite occurs naturally in a wide variety of birds throughout the world. Occurrence in North American birds has been reviewed by Stabler and Herman (1951). Stabler (1954) provides several references to reports from other parts of the world and further distribution records are presented by Dams (1966). Recent references include Morgan (1943), Locke and Kiel (1960), Locke, (1961), Locke et al. (1961), Locke and James (1962), Hayse and James (1964), and Sileo and Fitzhugh (1969).

◆ **CLASSIFICATION**
Phylum: Protozoa
S. Phylum: Sarcomastigophora
Super Class : Mastigophora
Class: Zoomastigophorea
Order: Trichomonadida
Family: Trichomonadidae
Genera: *Pentatrichomonas* (5 flagella)
 Trichomonas (4 flagella)
 Tritrichomonas (3 flagella)

Trichomonas gallinae (Rivolta 1878)
Stabler 1938

SYNONYMS: *Cercomonas gallinae* Rivolta 1878; *C. hepaticum* Rivolta 1878; *T. diversa* Volkmar 1930; *T. halli* Yakimoff 1934.

Trichomonas columbae, used by many authors to designate this parasite, has no valid taxonomic status. The reader is referred to Stabler (1954) for a complete review of the taxonomic position of this flagellate.

◆ **MORPHOLOGY.** *Trichomonas gallinae* is a flagellated protozoan varying from pear-shaped to rounded. It measures 6.2 to 18.9μ by 2.3 to 8.5μ (mean 10.5μ by 5.2μ). There are four free anterior flagella and a fifth flagellum which trails posteriorly along the undulating membrane for about one-half to two-thirds of the body length. An axostyle extends along the long axis of the cell and beyond the posterior end for 1 to 2μ. Various cytoplasmic bodies can be seen which vary somewhat, depending on the medium in which the organism has been growing. For detailed morphology see Stabler (1941a).

◆ DIAGNOSIS AND CLINICAL SIGNS.

Trichomonas gallinae infections may be inapparent except for the presence of the organism, or may produce very severe organ necrosis, caseation, and organ invasion, resulting in death as early as 4 days postinfection. Mildly pathogenic strains may produce little more than excessive salivation and inflammation of the mucosa of the mouth and throat. More virulent strains can produce cankers in the mouth, throat, and crop, with invasion of the head sinuses, skull, and skin of the neck. Some highly pathogenic strains produce lesions only in the head, neck, and crop, while others also invade the liver, lungs, pericardium, peritoneum, air sacs, and pancreas. Experimental evidence (Jaquette, 1950) shows that invasion of the internal organs is not via the intestine, since esophagotomized pigeons readily develop visceral lesions similar to those in intact birds. It has been suggested that invasion is via the bloodstream. No evidence for the presence of *T. gallinae* in the intestinal tract posterior to the proventriculus has been presented.

In cases where severe caseation of the mouth and throat occur, death can result from starvation caused by blockage of the esophagus or from respiratory failure caused by blockage of the trachea, rather than from destruction of various tissues.

Infection in birds which have recovered from the disease, and in symptomless carriers, can be detected only by demonstrating the presence of the parasite. This can be done by examining smears of throat or crop swabs or by culturing material from these locations. When the organism is abundant, direct examination of swabs is sufficient; however, when the level of infection is low, cultures or multiple swabbings are helpful. It should be noted here that organisms other than *T. gallinae* may appear in cultures (Toepfer, 1964; Kocan, 1968). The most frequent contaminants which might cause confusion are yeasts and various free-living protozoa. Most protozoology and parasitology texts list the various media which will support growth of *T. gallinae*. Diamond (1954) lists 28 types

of suitable media and an improved medium (1957).

When lesions occur in the oral region, they are easily recognized. They may be located on either the floor or roof of the mouth, or in the pharyngeal region, and appear as well-circumscribed, yellowish masses. Early in the infection, the lesions may be small and flush with the surface of the epithelium, but as the disease progresses, they rise above the surface of the normal tissue. At such times the surfaces of the lesions become quite irregular and often have small spurlike projections in their centers. As the caseation progresses, the lesions may coalesce and form large, cheesy masses in the mouth and throat. These often completely block the passage of grain, and the bird soon becomes emaciated and dies of starvation.

Lesions resulting from infection by virulent *T. gallinae* are superficially similar to those characteristic of aspergillosis or fowlpox. Before a definite diagnosis can be made, the causative organism must be isolated in pure culture and must be proved capable of producing lesions in known clean birds. If this is not done, there is no way of knowing that the trichomonads seen accompanying the lesions are not a nonvirulent strain growing in a bird which also had pox or aspergillosis.

Birds which have recovered from trichomoniasis caused by a lesion-producing strain of *T. gallinae* may be recognized by examining the pharyngeal folds in the back of the throat. These folds are often eroded away by necrosis during the course of infection, and the absence of these folds, therefore, is often suggestive of previous disease.

Mesa et al. (1961) and Frost and Honigberg (1962) give excellent histologic descriptions of the lesions occurring in both natural and experimental hosts. The earliest phase of infection is characterized by a palisading of trichomonads on the epithelial surface of the oral mucosa. At this time no inflammation is noted. As the disease progresses, leukocyte infiltration can be seen below the trichomonad layer. Soon after this infiltration, the lesions become macroscopically visible. As more leukocytes invade the mucosa and die, the lesions become larger, with the trichomonads remaining between the necrotic area and normal tissue. In experimentally infected animals and in those infected by the viscera-invading forms, necrotic foci are established and surrounded by a layer of trichomonads. Leukocyte infiltration continues, progressing from the surrounding normal tissue toward the invading organisms. It is believed that necrosis results from proliferation of the organisms followed by invasion and death of phagocytic cells. The dead and dying white cells provide a more suitable substrate for trichomonad proliferation, and the cycle continues. If the cellular defenses cannot contain the parasite, death from massive organ destruction results. When infections are limited to the mouth and head sinuses, death can result from invasion of the skull and brain, from starvation following occlusion of the esophagus, or from respiratory failure caused by blockage of the trachea.

Some reports indicate that the lungs and viscera other than the liver may also be involved. The location of the lesions is apparently determined by the host. Kocan (1969b) has shown that primary lesions in mourning doves occur in the lungs, while in pigeons the liver is the primary site of lesions. The pericardium, peritoneum, and other organs probably become involved by metastatic growth of the lesions. When extensive visceral involvement occurs, a plasmalike fluid containing numerous trichomonads often fills the abdominal cavity.

There is as yet no knowledge of the nature of the invasive or virulent factors present in various strains of *T. gallinae*. There is also no satisfactory explanation for the mechanism of lesion production, although hypersensitivity has been ruled out because of the early appearance of the canker.

◆ **TRANSMISSION.** The regurgitational method of feeding of young among the columbiform birds and the primary location of the trichomonads in the upper digestive tract provide a mechanism for direct transmission to squabs from infected parents. That this is truly the situation is borne out both by field surveys and by experiments which show that newly hatched squabs can be infected at their first feeding. No evidence for transovarial transmission was obtained when eggs from infected parents were incubated, hatched, and reared by uninfected adults (Stabler, 1954). Therefore the primary route of transmission is via direct transfer per os of trichomonads to newly hatched squabs.

Neither resting stages nor cysts have been described for trichomonads, and since the trichomonads are extremely sensitive to desiccation, they die rapidly if dried. This indicates that transmission is either direct or via some vehicle.

There have been reports of adults acquiring infection from other adults. Transmission is either via direct contact between infected and uninfected individuals during courtship, or by the ingestion of contaminated grain or water. The courtship behavior of columbiform birds involves cross-feeding and billing and provides a ready route of infection. Water has been suggested as the best medium for adult-to-adult transmission. Recent data (Kocan, 1969c) show that *T. gallinae* remains alive and motile in distilled water for as long as 20 minutes and for up to several hours in 0.01% NaCl. There is also evidence that some moist grains can maintain viable *T. gallinae* for at least 5 days.

Even without transmission within a wild dove or pigeon flock it is probable that these birds would constantly be reinfected by other feral pigeons. The rate of infection in common pigeons is often quite high, and since they may frequent the same watering and feeding areas as wild columbids, the opportunity is present for transfer of *T. gallinae* through water or grain.

Feral pigeons are also a source of infection for domestic pigeons and poultry. Several severe outbreaks of trichomoniasis in domestic poultry have been attributed to contamination of their feed or water by wild columbids. There is some speculation that the massive die-offs of mourning doves in 1950 reported by Haugen (1952) and Haugen and Keeler (1952) were due to transmission of virulent *T. gallinae* from feral pigeons to doves in feedlots. This hypothesis remains to be proved, but the disease does rank high among the possible causes of dove mortality.

The very nature of the disease enhances adult-to-adult transmission. Birds with lesions in their throats are unable to swallow larger pieces of grain. These are picked up, contaminated with the organism, and then dropped back to the ground. When doves are feeding in large flocks in feedlots and fields, it is highly probable that another bird will pick up the contaminated grain, thereby being exposed to the organism. Even when doves and pigeons do not have severe caseation of the throat, they are observed to drop many of the pieces of grain which they pick up. This behavioral characteristic could be a means of transmitting the less virulent and the visceral strains of trichomonads which produce minimal lesions in the upper digestive tract.

Naturally occurring infections of *T. gallinae* have been reported in raptors, and it is believed that these birds acquire their infections by eating infected pigeons (Stabler, 1941b; Stone and James, 1969). The large number of feral pigeons in many areas of the country makes an excellent source of *T. gallinae* for birds of prey. There has been some speculation that the decline of certain raptorial species may be directly related to their shift in diet from other wild birds to feral pigeons. Although there is no definite proof of this, the presence of naturally occurring trichomoniasis is worthy of consideration when studying the population dynamics of birds of prey. It has also been suggested that *T. gallinae* may have been a contributing factor in the demise of the passenger pigeon.

◆ **IMMUNITY.** The response of the host to infection by *T. gallinae* is poorly understood. The histologic studies by Mesa et al. (1961) and Frost and Honigberg (1962) show that leukocyte infiltration occurs at the site of lesion formation. This response is similar to that observed in any case of inflammation and is probably a primary defense measure of the host. The effectiveness of this response differs, depending on the strain of *T. gallinae* involved. For nonvirulent and mildly virulent strains, phagocytosis of the trichomonads themselves or their products is apparently sufficient to arrest the disease. Highly virulent strains, however, appear to be unaffected by this defense measure.

The nature of humoral antibodies and antibodies produced in situ has received scant attention. Definite proof of humoral antibody production has appeared recently (Kocan, 1970; Kocan and Herman, 1970) but the mode of action of this antibody is unknown. It may either lyse the trichomonads after they penetrate the epithelium of the upper digestive tract, or inhibit their penetration of the epithelium. Whatever the case, the protection can be transferred from immune to nonimmune birds via the plasma or serum. The role of phagocytosis in immune birds is unknown.

Immunologic studies on *Tritrichomonas foetus* in cattle (Robertson, 1963) have shown that three types of antibodies are produced in response to the *Tr. foetus* antigen. These include (1) a circulating antibody produced in response to natural infection, implantation of *Tr. foetus* antigen in the uterus, and intramuscular injection of *Tr. foetus;* (2) an antibody produced by the cells of the uterus in response to infection or implantation of the antigen; and (3) a vaginal antibody produced by cells of the vagina in response to infection or antigen implantation. The humoral antibody plays no role as a defense mechanism, while the uterine and vaginal antibodies may be capable of ridding the organs of low-level infections. All three of the above types of antibodies are rapidly lost after the elimination of trichomonads from the genital tract. Stabler (1954) also feels that immunity to trichomoniasis in pigeons is lost soon after loss of the parasite from the throat and crop. The authors, however, have evidence that pigeons and mourning doves retain their resistance to trichomoniasis for well over 1 year following the elimination of the parasite from the upper digestive tract (Kocan, 1969a; Kocan and Knisley, 1970). This would indicate that a sterilizing immunity results from recovery from trichomoniasis and that the trichomonads surviving in the lumen of the throat and crop play little or no role in the maintenance of immunity.

Stabler (1948, 1951) has shown the presence of a strong cross-immunity between nonvirulent and virulent strains of *T. gallinae* in pigeons. Infection by a nonlesion-producing strain, or recovery from infection by a pathogenic strain, confers resistance to disease when a highly pathogenic strain is superimposed on the primary infection. This raises some question as to the nature of the "virulence factor" in certain strains of *T. gallinae*. Although no actual disease results when a virulent strain is superimposed on a nonvirulent strain, the bird is capable of acting as a carrier for both strains. Of further interest is the observation that the same carrier may transmit the nonvirulent strain on one occasion and the virulent strain on another.

Immunity to trichomoniasis may be the result of destruction of the causative organism, or the result of a suppression or deactivation of the "virulence factor" possessed by certain strains. The nature of the cross-resistance makes one wonder if the "virulence factor" is not some normal component present in all strains of *T. gallinae* but altered in some way in the virulent forms to make it pathogenic for the host without altering its antigenicity. This would explain the cross-immunity between pathogenic and nonpathogenic strains.

◆ **TREATMENT.** The successful treatment of canker caused by *T. gallinae* is feasible only when the infected birds are in captivity. The reason for this is that the chemotherapeutic agents must be administered orally. This can be done by force-feeding or by treatment of food and water. Since the chemicals most effective are not palatable, the birds must be forced to ingest them; hence the need for confinement.

Many compounds have been tried in the past, primarily by falconers. These were usually worthless or gave highly questionable results. The greatest use has been made of copper sulfate, primarily for the treatment of domestic pigeons. Jaquette (1948) carried out experiments with this compound and found it to be effective if given to nonbreeders for 20 days at a concentration of 100 mg/100 cc of water. Lower concentrations were less effective and higher concentrations were toxic to the birds. He concluded that even the optimal dosage caused some liver damage. Stabler and Mellentin (1951, 1953) reported excellent anti-*T. gallinae* properties for Enheptin® (2 amino-5-nitrothiazole). The drug was capable of curing all carriers and reversing the effects of the more virulent strains, even when given late in the course of infection. Recently a new drug, Emtryl® (1,2-dimethyl-5-nitroimidazole), has been tested and shown to be effective in the treatment of canker (Devos et al., 1965; McLoughlin, 1966) and frounce (Stabler and Kitzmiller, 1967).

One problem with all of these compounds, as mentioned earlier, is that the birds will not readily drink treated water. They must be confined and their sole water supply treated. Then they will drink, but water consumption is reduced. The compound can also be administered by intubation of the crop when immediate attention is required for a near-terminal case.

High concentrations of Enheptin® become toxic and many birds are lost when 90 mg/kg/day are used for 7 days. Fortunately, the effective dose range (9 to 14 mg/kg/day for 7 days) is well below the toxic level for pigeons.

Treatment of wild populations with chemotherapeutic agents is not feasible at this time. The ready supply of untreated water eliminates the best vehicle for administration. A second major drawback to treating wild birds is the production of nonimmune young. Columbiformes denuded of their parasites produce uninfected, nonimmune young, and these non-immune individuals in the population increase the risk of an epidemic.

◆ OTHER TRICHOMONADS OF WILD BIRDS.

As mentioned in the opening paragraph of this chapter, *T. gallinae* is the only trichomonad known to be pathogenic for wild birds. Many other trichomonads have been described from wild species but most have proved nonpathogenic or of questionable effect. The following list of species covers the better known of these nonpathogenic forms.

Tritrichomonas eberthi (Martin and Robertson 1911) Kofoid 1920

Host: chicken *(Gallus domesticus)*; turkey *(Meleagris gallopavo)*; mallard duck *(Anas platyrhynchos)*
Disease: none (unknown?)
Location: ceca

Tr. beckeri (Travis 1936)

Host: yellow-billed cuckoo *(Coccyzus americanus)*
Disease: none (unknown?)
Location: large intestine

Tr. porzanae (Travis 1936)

Host: sora rail *(Porzana carolina)*
Disease: none (unknown?)
Location: ceca

Tr. chordeilis (Travis and Hamerstrom 1934)

Host: nighthawk *(Chordeiles minor)*
Disease: none (unknown?)
Location: intestine

Tr. bonasae (Tanabe 1926)

Host: ruffed grouse *(Bonasa umbellus)*
Disease: none (unknown?)
Location: ceca

Trichomonas gallinarum (Martin and Robertson 1911)

Host: chicken *(Gallus domesticus)*; turkey *(Meleagris gallopavo)*; ring-necked pheasant *(Phasianus colchicus)*; bobwhite quail *(Colinus virginianus)*; chukar *(Alectoris graeca)*
Disease: possibly liver lesions
Location: ceca, occasionally liver

T. anatis (Kotlan 1923)

Host: mallard duck *(Anas platyrhynchos)*
Disease: none (unknown?)

T. hoarei (DeMuro 1934)

Host: cormorant *(Phalacrocorax africanus)*
Disease: none (unknown?)
Location: intestine

T. fulicae (Travis 1936)

Host: American coot *(Fulica americana)*
Disease: none (unknown?)
Location: ceca

T. coccyzi (Travis 1936)

Host: yellow-billed cuckoo *(Coccyzus americanus)*
Disease: none (unknown?)
Location: large intestine

T. hegneri (Travis 1936)

Host: European partridge *(Perdix perdix)*; California quail *(Lophortyx californicus)*
Disease: none (unknown?)
Location: ceca

T. floridanae (Hegner 1929)

Host: bobwhite quail *(Colinus virginianus)*
Disease: none (unknown?)
Location: ceca

T. ortyxsis (Hegner 1929)

Host: valley quail *(Lophortyx califor-nicus vallicola)*
Disease: none (unknown?)
Location: ceca

T. phasiana (Travis 1932)

Host: ring-necked pheasant *(Phasianus colchicus);* bobwhite quail *(Colinus virginianus)*
Disease: none (unknown?)
Location: ceca

T. pisobiae (Travis and Hamerstrom 1934)

Host: least sandpiper *(Erolia minutilla);* pectoral sandpiper *(Erolia melanotos);* semipalmated sandpiper *(Ereunetes psillus)*
Disease: none (unknown?)
Location: intestine

T. iowensis (Travis and Hamerstrom 1934)

Host: nighthawk *(Chordeiles minor)*
Disease: none (unknown?)
Location: intestine

T. oti (Tanabe 1926)

Host: screech owl *(Otis asio)*
Disease: none (unknown?)
Location: ceca

T. lanceolata (da Cunha and Muniz 1926)

Host: Brazilian bird
Disease: none (unknown?)
Location: ceca

T. avium (da Cunha and Muniz 1925)

Host: smooth-billed ani *(Crotophaga ani)*
Disease: none (unknown?)
Location: ceca

T. anseri (Hegner 1929)

Host: Canada goose *(Branta canadensis)*
Disease: none (unknown?)
Location: ceca

Pentatrichomonas sp. (Allen 1936)

Host: nighthawk *(Chordeiles minor)*
Disease: none (unknown?)
Location: intestine

◆ REFERENCES

Allen, E. A. A *Pentatrichomonas* associated with certain cases of enterohepatitis or "blackhead" of poultry. *Trans. Am. Microscop. Soc.* 55:315, 1936.

da Cunha, A. M., and Muniz, J. Sur les flagelles, parasites des oiseaux du Bresil. *Compt. Rend. Soc. Biol. Paris* 95:1459, 1925.

———. Contribuicao para o conhecimento das flagellados parasitas do intestino das aves do Brasil. *Sciencia Med.* 4:430, 1926.

Dams, R. La trichomonose du pigeon. Un nouvel agent chimioprophylactique et therapeutique: le metronidazol. Thesis, l'Ecole Nationale Veterinaire de Lyon, 1966.

DeMuro, P. *Trichomonas hoarei* sp. nov., a new intestinal flagellate from a cormorant *(Phalacrocorax africanus africanus). Ann. Trop. Med. Parasitol.* 28:171, 1934.

Devos, A., Viaene, N., and Staelens, M. Behandeling van de Trichomonas besmelting bij duiven met thiazol en imidazol derivaten. (Treatment of trichomonas infection in pigeons with thiazol and imidazole derivatives). *Vlaams Diergeneesk. Tijdschr.* 34:241, 1965.

Diamond, L. S. A comparative study of 28 culture media for *Trichomonas gallinae. Exptl. Parasitol.* 3:251, 1954.

———. The establishment of various trichomonads of animals and man in axenic cultures. *J. Parasitol.* 43:488, 1957.

Frost, J. K., and Honigberg, B. M. Comparative pathogenicity of *Trichomonas vaginalis* and *Trichomonas gallinae* to mice. II. Histopathology of subcutaneous lesions. *J. Parasitol.* 48:898, 1962.

Haugen, A. O. Trichomoniasis in Alabama mourning doves. *J. Wildlife Management* 15:164, 1952.

Haugen, A. O., and Keeler, J. Mortality of mourning doves from trichomoniasis in Alabama during 1951. *Trans. 17th N. Am. Wildlife Conf.,* p. 141, 1952.

Hayse, F. A., and James, P. *Trichomonas gallinae* isolated from the white-fronted dove

(*Leptotila verreauxi*). *J. Parasitol.* 50:89, 1964.

Hegner, R. W. The infection of parasite-free chicks with intestinal protozoa from birds and other animals. *Am. J. Hyg.* 10:33, 1929.

Jaquette, D. S. Copper sulfate as a treatment for subclinical trichomoniasis in pigeons. *Am. J. Vet. Res.* 9:206, 1948.

———. Hepatic trichomoniasis in esophagotomized pigeons. *Poultry Sci.* 29:157, 1950.

Kocan, R. M. Probable origin of ciliates seen in oral swabbings of doves and pigeons. *J. Parasitol.* 54:1033, 1968.

———. A method for producing healthy carriers of the Jones' Barn strain of *Trichomonas gallinae*. *J. Parasitol.* 55:397, 1969a.

———. Different organ preferences by the same strain of *Trichomonas gallinae* in different host species. *J. Parasitol.* 55:1003, 1969b.

———. Various grains and liquid as potential vehicles of transmission for *Trichomonas gallinae*. *Bull. Wildlife Disease Assoc.* 5:148, 1969c.

———. Passive immunization of pigeons against trichomoniasis. *J. Protozool.* (in press), 1970.

Kocan, R. M. ,and Herman, C. M. Serum protein changes in immune and nonimmune pigeons infected with various strains of *Trichomonas gallinae*. *J. Wildlife Diseases* 6:43, 1970.

Kocan, R. M., and Knisley, J. O. Challenge infection as a means of determining the rate of disease-resistant *Trichomonas gallinae*-free birds in a population. *J. Wildlife Diseases* 6:13, 1970.

Kotlan, A. Zur Kenntnis der Darmflagellaten aus der Hausente und anderen Wasservögeln. *Zentr. Bakteriol. Parasitenk. Abt. I. Orig.* 90:24, 1923.

Locke, L. N. The susceptibility of the cardinal, *Richmondena cardinalis* (L.), to *Trichomonas gallinae* from a mourning drove, *Zenaidura macroura* (L.). *J. Parasitol.* 47:76, 1961.

Locke, L. N., and James, P. Trichomonad canker in the Inca dove, *Scardafella inca.* (Lesson). *J. Parasitol.* 48:497, 1962.

Locke, L. N., and Kiel, W. H., Jr. Isolation of *Trichomonas gallinae* from the white-winged dove, *Zenaida a. asiatica. Proc. Helminthol. Soc. Wash. D.C.* 27:128, 1960.

Locke, L. N., Locke, Frances S., and Reese, D. H. Occurrence of *Trichomonas gallinae* in the ground dove, *Columbigallina passerina* (L.). *J. Parasitol.* 47(sec. 1):532, 1961.

McLoughlin, D. K. Observations on the treatment of *Trichomonas gallinae* in pigeons. *Avian Diseases* 10:288, 1966.

Martin, C. H., and Robertson, M. Further observations on the caecal parasites of fowls, with some references to the rectal fauna of other vertebrates. Part 1. *Quart. J. Microscop. Sci.* 57:53, 1911.

Mesa, C. P., Stabler, R. M., and Berthrough, M. Histopathologic changes in the domestic pigeon infected with *Trichomonas gallinae* (Jones' Barn strain). *Avian Diseases* 5:48, 1961.

Morgan, B. B. Host list of the genus *Trichomonas* (Protozoa: Flagellata). Part 2, Host-parasite list. *Trans. Wis. Acad. Sci. Arts Letters* 35:235, 1943.

Robertson, M. Antibody response in cattle to infection with *Trichomonas foetus*. In P. C. C. Garnham, ed., *Immunity to protozoa*, p. 336. Philadelphia: F. A. Davis, 1963.

Sileo, L., and Fitzhugh, E. L. Incidence of trichomoniasis in the band-tailed pigeons of southern Arizona. *Bull. Wildlife Disease Assoc.* 5:146, 1969.

Stabler, R. M. The morphology of *Trichomonas gallinae (= columbae) J. Morphol.* 69:501, 1941a.

———. Further studies on trichomoniasis in birds. *Auk* 58:558, 1941b.

———. Protection in pigeons against virulent *Trichomonas gallinae* acquired by infection with milder strains. *J. Parasitol.* 34:150, 1948.

———. Effect of *Trichomonas gallinae* from diseased mourning doves on clean domestic pigeons. *J. Parasitol.* 37:473, 1951.

———. *Trichomonas gallinae*: A review. *Exptl. Parasitol.* 3:368, 1954.

Stabler, R. M., and Herman, C. M. Upper digestive tract trichomoniasis in mourning doves and other birds. *Trans. 16th N. Am. Wildlife Conf.*, p. 145, 1951.

Stabler, R. M., and Kitzmiller, N. J. Emtryl in the treatment of trichomoniasis in pigeons and hawks. *J. N. Am. Falconers Assoc.* 7:47, 1967.

Stabler, R. M., and Mellentin, R. W. Treatment of *Trichomonas gallinae* infections in domestic pigeons with Enheptin. *Anat. Record* 111:169, 1951.

———. Effect of 2-amino-5-nitro-thiazole (Enheptin) and other drugs on *Trichomonas gallinae* infections in the domestic pigeon. *J. Parasitol.* 39:637, 1953.

Stone, W. B., and Jones, D. E. Trichomoniasis in captive sparrow hawks. *Bull. Wildlife Disease Assoc.* 5:147, 1969.

Tanabe, M. Morphological studies on *Trichomonas. J. Parasitol.* 12:120, 1926.

Toepfer, E. W. *Colpoda steinii* in oral swabbings from mourning doves (*Zenaidura macroura* L.). *J. Parasitol.* 50:703, 1964.

Travis, B. V. *Trichomonas phasiani*, a new flagellate from the ring-necked pheasant, *Phasianus torquatus* Gmelin. *J. Parasitol.* 18:285, 1932.

————. Studies on some trichomonad flagellates from birds with descriptions of five new species and two new varieties. *Iowa State College J. Sci.* 10:115, 1936.

Travis, B. V., and Hamerstrom, F. N., Jr. Three new trichomonads from birds. *Iowa State College J. Sci.* 8:537, 1934.

● ROBERT S. COOK

PARASITES of this genus are found only in birds. They derived their name from the belief that gametocytes occupied only blood leukocytes. However, Cook (1954) and Desser (1967) have shown that gametocytes occupy and develop in erythrocytes as well as in leukocytes.

The life history is essentially similar to that of *Plasmodium* and *Haemoproteus*. The mature gametocytes in blood cells of the avian host are ingested by the intermediate host, the blackfly. Gametogenesis occurs in the insect stomach immediately after ingestion. Fertilization follows, with the production of motile zygotes (ookinetes) which rest for several hours. The ookinetes then penetrate and develop as oocysts within and on the outer surface of the fly stomach until the sporozoites are released. The sporozoites travel to the salivary gland and are injected into the bloodstream of new hosts during subsequent feedings. Within the new host the sporozoites invade and multiply by schizogony within epithelial or reticuloendothelial cells. Resulting merozoites may enter blood cells and develop into gametocytes, or reenter tissue cells and undergo further schizogony. Schizogony does not occur in the blood cells.

Diagnosis is made by observing gametocytes in blood cells of stained smears, the presence of schizonts in tissues of internal organs, and clinical signs.

Leucocytozoonosis is common in many wild and domestic birds. Many reports list only the occurrence of a *Leucocytozoon* parasite and do not assign a species name (for example, Clarke, 1945; Hunninen and Young, 1950; Marx, 1966). A species and host-index has been compiled by Coatney (1937), and Herman (1944) lists the species

and their avian hosts occurring in North America.

Some species are pathogenic to young ducks and turkeys.

Leucocytozoon simondi
Mathis and Leger 1910

SYNONYMS: *L. anatis, L. anseris.*

◆ **DISTRIBUTION.** Levine and Hanson (1953) assembled host records that included 24 species of Anatidae, both wild and domestic ducks and geese. Leucocytozoonosis occurs commonly throughout the world where *L. simondi* is present and conditions are suitable for certain ornithophilic blackflies (Simuliidae) and waterfowl. Host-specificity studies by Fallis et al. (1954) showed the infection could be transmitted both artificially and naturally from domestic ducks to domestic geese but not to ruffed grouse *(Bonasa umbellus)*, pheasants *(Phasianus colchicus)*, turkeys *(Meleagris gallopavo)*, or chickens *(Gallus domesticus)*.

◆ **TRANSMISSION AND DEVELOPMENT.** Simuliids were first reported as natural vectors of *L. simondi* by O'Roke (1934). Later studies have shown these blackflies to be ornithophilic and probably exclusively feeding on Anatidae (Shewell, 1955; Bennett, 1960).

Transmission studies have shown certain simuliids have definite preferences regarding their feeding habitat. Bennett (1960), working primarily with *Simulium rugglesi*, found their favorite feeding area to be within 50 feet of the shoreline and very little activity farther into the forest. Fallis and Bennett (1966) found most transmission by *S. rugglesi* occurred at water level, near or at the shoreline. Birds exposed 100 to 200 yards from shore, at the shoreline but at levels 6 to 15 feet in the air, and birds in woodland showed a much lower infection level when compared to those exposed at the shoreline.

Bennett (1963) found *S. rugglesi* lives for several weeks, feeds several times during its lifetime, and can move at least 2 miles between meals. These findings are of great importance to the understanding of *Leucocytozoon* epizootics.

A report by Fallis et al. (1956) that *S. croxtoni* and *S. euryadminiculum* were vectors in Canada was later proved erroneous by Fallis and Bennett (1966), as these species were confused with *S. anatinum*. In Canada the vector in late May and early June is *S. anatinum,* and following that period to as late as August or early September the vector is *S. rugglesi* (Fallis and Bennett, 1966). The vector in Wisconsin is *S. rugglesi* (Anderson et al., 1962). Tarshis and Herman (1965) suggest *Cnephia invenusta* may be a possible vector of *L. simondi* in geese.

Sporogony in the insect vector may be completed in 3 to 4 days and viable sporozoites have been found in vectors up to 18 days following their last blood meal (Fallis et al., 1956). Desser and Fallis (1967a) found ookinetes in stomach contents of *S. rugglesi* as early as 12 hours after ingestion of gametocytes. Oocysts were found in tissues digested 36 to 72 hours after ingestion of gametocytes and the sequence of development was similar to that of *L. bonasae, L. mirandae,* and *L. fringillinarum* as described by Fallis and Bennett (1962).

The epizootiology of *L. simondi* in Algonquin Park, Canada, shows the chain of events that may lead to epizootics (Fallis and Bennett, 1966). Spring relapse in mature ducks can furnish small sources of infection for the early-emerging blackflies. These vectors carry some parasites to other adult ducks in which high parasitemias can result (Fallis et al., 1951). These adult ducks with high parasitemias are sources of infection for later-hatching blackflies that in turn infect young ducklings.

◆ **CLINICAL SIGNS.** These signs depend upon the age and condition of the bird, but a very rapid onset usually occurs in young ducklings (O'Roke, 1934). Apparently healthy ducklings may become ill and die within a 24-hour period. Signs may include inappetence, listlessness, weakness, and dyspnea. During the acute period the blood is pale and thin, with many parasitized blood cells present.

In adults the parasite induces listlessness and loss of wariness in wild birds (O'Roke, 1934). Signs appear less abruptly and usually 5 or more days are necessary before death occurs, but death is rare in older birds.

Most experimentally infected birds die between 10 and 19 days postexposure (Chernin, 1952c; Kocan and Clark, 1966a), and mortality to 100% may occur in ducklings (Chernin, 1952b; Fallis et al., 1956; Fallis and Bennett, 1966).

◆ **PATHOGENESIS.** Following the infection of a susceptible bird the sporozoites enter cells of various tissues but primary asexual development seems to occur in liver parenchyma cells (hepatic schizont) (Desser, 1967). When the hepatic schizonts rupture, some fully developed merozoites enter the bloodstream. Some of these merozoites then enter blood cells and develop into gametocytes. The usual prepatent period in artificially infected Peking ducks is 7 days (Kocan and Clark, 1966a) and a minimum of 5 days (Desser, 1967). Some merozoites from the primary hepatic schizonts may reenter liver tissue and another cycle of hepatic schizonts occurs; some may enter blood cells and form round gametocytes; and some may be phagocytized by macrophages and develop into encapsulated megaloschizonts in various body tissues (Desser, 1967; Desser and Fallis, 1967b). Among the tissues that are invaded are the lung, heart, gizzard, spleen, and intestines. Cowan (1955) recorded megaloschizonts up to 206μ in diameter, and they have been found in the brain up to a diameter of 160 to 190μ (Karstad, 1965). The host tissue may react against the megaloschizonts in a number of ways, including phagocytosis (Cowan, 1957). Surviving megaloschizonts mature and release the merozoites into the bloodstream, producing many gametocytes in the blood cells approximately 7 to 14 days following initial infection (Desser, 1967).

Primary parasitemia usually lasts about 30 days (Chernin, 1952a). The parasitemia then drops to chronic level in peripheral blood until onset of the breeding season in February and March, at which time a relapse occurs (Chernin, 1952b). The parasitemia following relapse is usually lower than that of the primary infection but can be quite high (Fallis et al., 1951).

Leucocytozoon simondi causes hypertrophy of the spleen and liver as well as anemia in its host, beginning with the appearance of gametocytes in peripheral blood (Fallis et al., 1951). Anemia lasts for the duration of the parasitemia, usually becoming most severe 1 to 5 days postpatency (Kocan and Clark, 1966b). However, in a study using 34 Peking ducklings, Kocan and Clark (1966a) concluded parasite levels were not high enough to cause the observed anemia and suggested, as did Huff (1942), that this may be the result of an auto-immune response of the host. In a later study using Peking ducklings, Kocan (1967) observed during the acute phase of infection agglutinin titers as high as 1:100 and hemolysin titers as high as 1:64 against erythrocytes of untreated birds. Serum from the acute phase of infection could produce anemia in uninfected ducklings. He concluded that anemia was the result of an antierythrocytic factor in the serum as no erythrophagocytosis was observed during the study.

Microscopic lesions are similar in young and adult birds. According to Newberne (1957), histopathologic changes in severe fatal cases include extensive and severe liver and spleen involvement with splenomegaly, proliferation of macrophages, liver necrosis, and moderate hemosiderosis in both liver and spleen.

Less severe cases include similar but more moderate pathologic signs, while no reactions are observed in light, nonfatal cases (Newberne, 1957).

◆ **CONTROL AND TREATMENT.** Control of the disease depends on control of the blackfly vector. Large-scale destruction of the vector is not feasible at the present time. Successful raising of waterfowl now depends on screening them from flies or in confining operations to vector-free areas. O'Roke (1934) used preparations of plasmoquin, quinine dihydrochloride, and quinine sulfate for treating leucocytozoonosis in ducks. He concluded that quinine may have value early in the patent period but it was not effective after the adult gametocytes appeared. Coatney and West (1937) concluded a quinacrine hydrochloride preparation had a parasiticidal effect on *Leucocytozoon* in a heavily infected greathorned owl *(Bubo virginianus)* and a juvenile red-tailed hawk *(Buteo borealis)*. Preparations of proguanil hydrochloride, quinacrine hydrochloride, and sulfamerazine were ineffective against developing and mature stages of *L. simondi* in ducks (Fallis, 1948).

Leucocytozoon bonasae
Clark 1945

◆ **DISTRIBUTION.** Ruffed grouse *(Bonasa umbellus)* is the type host (Clarke, 1935). These parasites have also been found in the following grouse: spruce grouse *(Canachites canadensis)* (Clarke, 1935), sharp-tailed grouse *(Pedioecetes phasianellus)* (Saunders, 1935), and willow and rock ptarmigan *(Lagopus lagopus* and *L. mutus rupestris)* (Allen and Levine, 1935; Clarke, 1938, respectively). *Leucocytozoon* sp. has been reported in the sooty (blue) grouse *(Dendragapus obscurus fuliginosus)* (Fowle, 1946; Adams and Bendell, 1953). The present range includes the north central United States and Canada.

Specificity was indicated by Fallis and Bennett (1958), who inoculated a duckling (species unknown but presumably white Peking) and a white-crowned sparrow (*Zonotrichia leucophrys*) with the same material that produced infection in grouse, but failed to produce a parasitemia in these hosts.

Fallis (1945) found 65 of 106 ruffed grouse infected in Ontario. Erickson (1953) found the incidence to be from 50 to 100% in Minnesota ruffed grouse, with a slightly higher incidence in young birds, over an 11-year study period. Dorney and Todd (1960) found 86% of 164 birds infected in Wisconsin during the spring season. Infection occurred in 95% of spring-trapped sharptails, but in only 31% of the fall and winter sample in Michigan (Cowan and Peterle, 1957). The relapse phenomenon occurs in grouse (Clarke, 1938; Cowan and Peterle, 1957; Dorney and Todd, 1960).

◆ **TRANSMISSION AND DEVELOPMENT.** In experimental studies Fallis and Bennett (1958) found gametocytes in the peripheral blood of grouse 12 to 13 days after injection of sporozoites. Gametocytes with rounded and pointed ends were observed in erythrocytes but may occur in leukocytes as well. Clarke (1938) found schizonts in the liver of 10-day-old grouse and observed that an increased amount of melanin in liver cells indicated an older infection. Schizonts were also observed in the absence of gametocytes in the circulating blood (Clarke, 1938).

Known vectors of *L. bonasae* in Ontario are *Simulium latipes* and *S. aureum* (Fallis and Bennett, 1958). These ornithophilic blackflies were shown experimentally to be suitable intermediate hosts. These species prefer a woodland habitat as their feeding area (Bennett, 1960).

Fallis and Bennett (1961) determined experimentally that sporogony can be completed within 5 days in *S. latipes*. The flies were maintained at an average daily temperature of 16° C. Later experiments showed the oocysts to be spherical to ovoid

in shape and diameters ranged from 8 to 16μ (av. 13μ) (Fallis and Bennett, 1962).

◆ **CLINICAL SIGNS.** None reported.

◆ **PATHOGENESIS.** Low-level parasitemias seem characteristic in ruffed grouse (Fallis and Bennett, 1958) and are of little importance to the welfare of the birds (Erickson, 1953; Fallis and Bennett, 1958; Dorney and Todd, 1960).

Leucocytozoon mansoni Sambon 1908

◆ **DISTRIBUTION.** The capercaillie (*Tetrao urogallus*), black grouse (*Lyrurus tetrix*), and hazel grouse (*Tetrastes bonasia*) are common hosts in Sweden (Borg, 1953). Incidence in the capercaillie was highest, reaching 88% during the summer. The percentage of black grouse and hazel grouse infected was slightly less than that found in the capercaillie population (Borg, 1953).

◆ **TRANSMISSION AND DEVELOPMENT.** Vectors of this parasite are unknown. Borg (1953) described three types of gametocytes: round, oval, and elongated. Host cell cytoplasm formed a tail at each end of the cell when the oval or elongated parasites occurred. No tails were present in round forms.

Schizogony was apparently restricted to liver cells of young capercaillie (Borg, 1953). Hemosiderin and melanin were observed in liver cells by Borg (1953) and were considered a result of late schizont development. Borg (1953) searched other organs besides the liver but did not find megaloschizonts.

◆ **PATHOGENESIS.** Not known.

Leucocytozoon marchouxi
Mathis and Leger 1910

SYNONYM: *L. turtur.*

◆ **DISTRIBUTION.** Levine (1954) and Levine and Kantor (1959) list 17 species of

Columbiformes as hosts of this cosmopolitan parasite. There are two reports of *L. marchouxi* in domestic pigeons *(Columba livia),* one by Jansen (1952) in South Africa, and the other by Stabler and Holt (1963) in Colorado.

Hanson et al. (1957) found a low incidence in mourning doves *(Zenaidura macroura carolinensis)* in Illinois during a 7-year survey; only 1% of 392 juveniles and 7% of the 72 adults were infected. Saunders (1959) found infection in 2 of 58 western white-winged doves *(Zenaida asiatica mearnsi)* collected in different parts of Mexico, and Stabler and Holt (1963), in Colorado, found 39 of 109 bandtail pigeons *(Columba fasciata fasciata)* infected.

◆ **TRANSMISSION AND DEVELOPMENT.** Levine (1954) described the morphology of gametocytes in mourning doves, reporting leukocytes as the host cells. Gametocytes were observed in a 14-day-old nestling. Vectors, sporogony, and schizogony are unknown.

◆ **PATHOGENESIS.** Unknown.

Leucocytozoon smithi
Laveran and Lucet 1905

◆ **DISTRIBUTION.** This species is found in both wild and domestic turkeys *(Meleagris gallopavo)* in the United States, Canada, and parts of Europe and Asia. *Leucocytozoon smithi* was first found in domestic turkeys. Its presence in wild turkeys was discovered by Mosby and Handley (1943) in Virginia. They also found the parasite in pen-reared wild and domestic turkeys. Kozicky (1948) found 5 infected wild turkeys in Pennsylvania, and McDowell (1954) reported finding a *Leucocytozoon* in some wild turkeys in the Cumberland State Forest of Virginia, after receiving reports of moribund birds in the area. Later, Byrd (1959) reported infection in all of 9 free-ranging wild adults but in none of 9 juveniles (less than 1 year old) from the Cumberland area.

There are several reports of *L. smithi* in wild birds raised in captivity and in domestic flocks; for example, Johnson et al. (1938), Travis et al. (1939), Banks (1943), Hinshaw and McNeil (1943), Savage and Isa (1945), Atchley (1951), and Glushchenko (1962).

Leucocytozoon smithi was not transmitted experimentally to chickens or ducks (Byrd, 1959).

◆ **TRANSMISSION AND DEVELOPMENT.** Byrd (1959) found a short period of infectivity in birds housed in large, open-topped, screen pens resting on the bare ground in areas of the Cumberland State Forest. The period corresponded with the presence of the blackfly, *Prosimulium hirtipes.* The fly was proved a vector experimentally by Byrd (1959). Skidmore (1932) reported *Simulium occidentale* was a vector in Nebraska. Johnson et al. (1938) and Johnson (1942) found *S. nigroparvum* to be a vector in Virginia, although later Byrd (1959) could not experimentally transmit *L. smithi* using this vector. Richey and Ware (1955) injected intramuscularly several engorged *S. slossonae* that had been ground and mixed with saline solution into domestic turkeys and produced infection, an experiment confirmed by Wehr (1962) in South Carolina. The life cycle within the intermediate host is apparently similar to that of *L. simondi,* although some of the stages have not been demonstrated.

The development within the vertebrate host has been observed only in domestic turkeys. Only one type of schizont has been reported in the liver. Megaloschizonts have not been seen (Newberne, 1955). The prepatent period is about 9 days. Gametocytes are of both the elongate type, with tapered ends, and rounded. Very young gametocyte stages were not observed (Byrd, 1959), although older ones were seen in erythrocytes. This is in agreement with the observations of Cook (1954) on *L. simondi* in ducks.

◆ **CLINICAL SIGNS.** Various signs were attributed to this parasite in domestic birds, including inappetence, droopiness, depression, and diarrhea (Wehr, 1962). Typical signs last 2 or 3 days at which time the birds either die or begin recovery (Johnson et al., 1938). Only one inconsistent sign, droopiness, occurred in experimentally infected wild birds (Byrd, 1959).

◆ **PATHOGENESIS.** Several reports outline the pathogenic nature of *L. smithi* in flocks of domestic turkeys (Skidmore, 1932; Travis et al., 1939; West and Starr, 1940; Banks, 1943; Savage and Isa, 1945). However, in a detailed critique, Borg (1953) cast some doubt upon *L. smithi* as the sole causative agent. Borg concluded, as did Byrd (1959) and several others, that the reports did not prove conclusively the pathogenic role of this parasite in the hosts described. However, Byrd (1959) did observe more severe signs in domestic poults than in pen-raised wild ones. Detailed studies will have to be conducted before *L. smithi* can be considered a serious pathogen in wild birds.

Leucocytozoon sakharoffi
Sambon 1908

SYNONYM: *L. zuccarelli* (Coatney and West, 1938; Wingstrand, 1947).

◆ **DISTRIBUTION.** Reported hosts in North America are the common crow (*Corvus brachyrhynchos*) (Coatney and West, 1938; Morgan and Waller, 1941; Fallis and Bennett, 1961) and the blue jay (*Cyanocitta cristata*) (Fallis and Bennett, 1961); in Europe the raven (*C. corax*) (Sakharoff, 1893; Sambon, 1908), rook (*C. frugilegus*) (Sakharoff, 1893; Glushchenko, 1962; Ramisz, 1962), carrion crow (*C. corone*) (Glushchenko, 1962; Ramisz, 1962), and the jackaw (*C. monedula*) (Glushchenko, 1962; Ramisz, 1962).

Morgan and Waller (1941) found 3 of 112 common crows, collected in southern Wisconsin and Iowa, infected. In the Kiev forest zone, Glushchenko (1962) found infection in 3 of 10 carrion crows, 18 of 32 rooks, and 2 of 15 jackdaws. Wingstrand

(1947) believes nearly 100% of hooded crows (*C. corone cornix*) in Sweden carry a *Leucocytozoon* infection.

◆ **TRANSMISSION AND DEVELOPMENT.** Fallis and Bennett (1961) found complete sporogony occurred in certain simuliids and that microgamete formation was similar to that of *L. simondi*. Ookinetes were seen in the stomach contents of *Simulium aureum* and oocysts were found in the stomach wall. Some oocysts found in specimens of *S. latipes* averaged 10μ in diameter. Residual bodies were present. Oocysts were only slightly larger than zygotes. Sporozoites were motile. Some specimens of *S. aureum* that had fed 18 days previously on infected crows contained oocysts with sporozoites still inside, indicating a relatively lengthy sporogenic period (Fallis and Bennett, 1961).

Coatney and West (1938) and Wingstrand (1947) have described and illustrated gametocytes in crows from Nebraska and Sweden, respectively. A karyosome lies just outside and in contact with the nucleus of the female gametocytes (Coatney and West, 1938). Wingstrand (1947) described most growth stages of the gametocytes as occurring in lymphocytes, and the parasites were usually round in form.

Schizogony stages described by Wingstrand (1947, 1948) included the presence of very large (up to 480μ in diameter) megaloschizonts that were located in the spleen, liver, pancreas, gonads, thyroid, and pituitary. Typical hepatic schizonts as found in *L. simondi* (Huff, 1942) were not found. A portion of Wingstrand's study, involving adult carrier birds, showed some schizogony occurred in liver cells and it was apparently completed before the schizonts attained the size of the host cell. Megaloschizonts were not seen in these chronic carriers. Wingstrand concluded that megaloschizonts were part of the initial infection and were present only during the acute stage of the disease.

◆ **PATHOGENESIS.** Two acutely infected young crows had enlarged, fragile spleens and slightly hypertrophied livers. Both liver and spleen contained many granules of a yellow-brown pigment within blood vessels and macrophages (Wingstrand, 1948).

◆ REFERENCES

Adams, J. R., and Bendell, J. F. A high incidence of blood parasites in a population of sooty grouse. *J. Parasitol.* 39(4 Sec. 2):11, 1953.

Allen, A. A., and Levine, P. P. A brief study of the willow ptarmigan and its relation to predators and *Leucocytozoon* disease. *Trans. Am. Game Conf.* 21:381, 1935.

Anderson, J. R., Trainer, D. O., and DeFoliart, G. R. Natural and experimental transmission of the waterfowl parasite, *Leucocytozoon simondi* M. & L., in Wisconsin. *Zoonoses Res.* 1:155, 1962.

Atchley, F. O. *Leucocytozoon andrewsi* n. sp. from chickens observed in a survey of blood parasites in domestic animals in South Carolina. *J. Parasitol.* 37:483, 1951.

Banks, W. C. *Leucocytozoon smithi* infection and other diseases of turkey poults in central Texas. *J. Am. Vet. Med. Assoc.* 102:467, 1943.

Bennett, G. F. On some ornithophilic blood-sucking diptera in Algonquin Park, Ontario, Canada. *Can. J. Zool.* 38:377, 1960.

———. Use of P$_{32}$ in the study of a population of *Simulium rugglesi* (Diptera: Simuliidae) in Algonquin Park, Ontario, Canada. *Can. J. Zool.* 41:831, 1963.

Borg, K. On *Leucocytozoon* in Swedish capercaillie, black grouse and hazel grouse. *Berlingska Boktryckeriet Lund.*, 1953.

Byrd, M. A. Observations on *Leucocytozoon* in pen-raised and free-ranging wild turkeys. *J. Wildlife Management* 23:145, 1959.

Chernin, E. Parasitemia in primary *Leucocytozoon simondi* infections. *J. Parasitol.* 38:499, 1952a.

———. The relapse phenomenon in the *Leucocytozoon simondi* infection of the domestic duck. *Am. J. Hyg.* 56:101, 1952b.

———. The epizootiology of *Leucocytozoon simondi* infections in domestic ducks in northern Michigan. *Am. J. Hyg.* 56:39, 1952c.

Clarke, C. H. D. Blood parasites of ruffed grouse, *Bonasa umbellus*, and spruce grouse, *Canachites canadensis*, with a description of *Leucocytozoon bonasae* n. sp. *Can. J. Res.* 12:646, 1935.

———. Organisms of a malarial type in ruffed grouse, with a description of the schizogony of *Leucocytozoon bonasae*. *J. Wildlife Management* 2:146, 1938.

———. Some records of blood parasites from Ontario birds. *Can. Field-Nat.* 60:34, 1945.

Coatney, G. R. A catalog and host-index of the genus *Leucocytozoon*. *J. Parasitol.* 23:202, 1937.

Coatney, G. R., and West, Evaline. Some notes on the effect of atebrine on the gametocytes of the genus *Leucocytozoon*. *J. Parasitol.* 23:227, 1937.

———. Some blood parasites from Nebraska birds—II. *Am. Midland Naturalist* 19:601, 1938.

Cook, Alice R. The gametocyte development of *Leucocytozoon simondi*. *Proc. Helminthol. Soc. Wash. D.C.* 21:1, 1954.

Cowan, A. B. The development of megaloschizonts of *Leucocytozoon simondi* Mathis and Leger. *J. Protozool.* 2:158, 1955.

———. Reactions against the megaloschizonts of *Leucocytozoon simondi* Mathis and Leger in ducks. *J. Infect. Diseases* 100:82, 1957.

Cowan, A. B., and Peterle, T. J. *Leucocytozoon bonasae* Clarke in Michigan sharp-tailed grouse. *J. Wildlife Management* 21:469, 1957.

Desser, S. S. Schizogony and gametogony of *Leucocytozoon simondi* and associated reactions in the avian host. *J. Protozool.* 14:244, 1967.

Desser, S. S., and Fallis, A. M. A description of stages in the sporogony of *Leucocytozoon simondi*. *Can. J. Zool.* 45:275, 1967a.

———. The cytological development and encapsulation of megaloschizonts of *Leucocytozoon simondi*. *Can. J. Zool.* 45:1061, 1967b.

Dorney, R. S., and Todd, A. C. Spring incidence of ruffed grouse blood parasites. *J. Parasitol.* 46:687, 1960.

Erickson, A. B. *Leucocytozoon bonasae* in ruffed grouse; its possible relationship to fluctuations in numbers of grouse. *J. Wildlife Management* 17:536, 1953.

Fallis, A. M. Population trends and blood parasites of ruffed grouse in Ontario. *J. Wildlife Management* 9:203, 1945.

———. Observations on *Leucocytozoon* infections in birds receiving paludrine, atabrine, and sulphamerazine. *Can. J. Res.* D 26:73, 1948.

Fallis, A. M., and Bennett, G. F. Transmission of *Leucocytozoon bonasae* Clarke to ruffed grouse (*Bonasa umbellus* L.) by the black flies *Simulium latipes* MG. and *Simulium aureum* Fries. *Can. J. Zool.* 36:533, 1958.

———. Sporogony of *Leucocytozoon* and *Haemoproteus* in simuliids and ceratopogonids and a revised classification of the

Haemosporidiida. *Can. J. Zool.* 39:215, 1961.

———. Observations on the sporogony of *Leucocytozoon mirandae, L. bonasae,* and *L. fringillinarum* (Sporozoa: Leucocytozoidae). *Can. J. Zool.* 40:395, 1962.

———. On the epizootiology of infections caused by *Leucocytozoon simondi* in Algonquin Park, Canada. *Can. J. Zool.* 44:101, 1966.

Fallis, A. M., Davies, D. M., and Vickers, Marjorie A. Life history of *Leucocytozoon simondi* Mathis and Leger in natural and experimental infections and blood changes produced in the avian host. *Can. J. Zool.* 29:305, 1951.

Fallis, A. M., Pearson, J. C., and Bennett, G. F. On the specificity of *Leucocytozoon. Can. J. Zool.* 32:120, 1954.

Fallis, A. M., Anderson, R. C., and Bennett, G. R. Further observations on the transmission and development of *Leucocytozoon simondi. Can. J. Zool.* 34:389, 1956.

Fowle, C. D. The blood parasites of the blue grouse. *Science* 103:708, 1946.

Glushchenko, V. V. New data on the blood parasites of domestic and wild birds in the Kiev forest zone. (Ukrainian text; English and Russian summaries.) *Dopovidi Akad. Nauk Ukrain. RSR* 10:1387, 1962.

Hanson, H. C., Levine, N. D., Kossack, C. W., Kantor, S., and Stannard, L. J. Parasites of the mourning dove *(Zenaidura macroura carolinensis)* in Illinois. *J. Parasitol.* 43:186, 1957.

Herman, C. M. The blood protozoa of North American birds. *Bird Banding* 15:89, 1944.

Hinshaw, W. R., and McNeil, Ethel. *Leucocytozoon* sp. from turkeys in California. *Poultry Sci.* 22:268, 1943.

Huff, C. G. Schizogony and gametocyte development in *Leucocytozoon simondi,* and comparisons with *Plasmodium* and *Haemoproteus. J. Infect. Diseases* 71:19, 1942.

Hunninen, A. V., and Young, M. D. Blood protozoa of birds at Columbia, South Carolina. *J. Parasitol.* 36:258, 1950.

Jansen, B. C. The occurrence of some hitherto undescribed *Leucocytozoon* and *Haemoproteus* species in South African birds. *Onderstepoort J. Vet. Res.* 25:3, 1952.

Johnson, E. P. Further observations on a blood protozoan of turkeys transmitted by *Simulium nigroparvum (Twinn). Am. J. Vet. Res.* 3:214, 1942.

Johnson, E. P., Underhill, G. W., Cox, J. A., and Threlkeld, W. L. A blood protozoon of turkeys transmitted by *Simulium nigroparvum* (Twinn). *Am. J. Hyg.* 27:649, 1938.

Karstad, L. A case of leucocytozoonosis in a wild mallard. *Bull. Wildlife Disease Assoc.* 1:33, 1965.

Kocan, R. M. Mechanism of anemia in ducks infected with *Leucocytozoon simondi. J. Protozool.* 14(suppl.):15, 1967.

Kocan, R. M., and Clark, D. T. Prepatent period and parasitemia in *Leucocytozoon simondi* infections resulting from short exposures to sporozoites. *J. Parasitol.* 52:962, 1966a.

———. Anemia in ducks infected with *Leucocytozoon simondi. J. Protozool.* 13:465, 1966b.

Kozicky, E. L. Some protozoan parasites of the eastern wild turkey in Pennsylvania. *J. Wildlife Management* 12:263, 1948.

Levine, N. D. *Leucocytozoon* in the avian order Columbiformes, with a description of *L. marchouxi* Mathis and Leger 1910 from the mourning dove. *J. Protozool.* 1:140, 1954.

Levine, N. D., and Hanson, H. C. Blood parasites of the Canada goose, *Branta canadensis interior. J. Wildlife Management* 17:185, 1953.

Levine, N. D., and Kantor, S. Check-list of blood parasites of birds of the Columbiformes. *Wildlife Diseases* 1:1, 1959.

McDowell, R. D. Unpublished report to the Virginia Commission of Game and Inland Fisheries. Filed in Va. Comm. Game and Inland Fisheries Office, Richmond, Virginia, 1954.

Marx, D. J. Some blood parasites from Minnesota and Wisconsin birds. *Bull. Wildlife Disease Assoc.* 2:6, 1966.

Morgan, B. B., and Waller, E. F. Some parasites of the eastern crow. *Bird Banding* 12:17, 1941.

Mosby, H. S., and Handley, C. O. The wild turkey in Virginia: Its status, life history and management. *Va. Comm. Game and Inland Fisheries, Richmond, Virginia,* 1943.

Newberne, J. W. The pathology of *Leucocytozoon* infection in turkeys with a note on its tissue stages. *Am. J. Vet. Res.* 16:593, 1955.

———. Studies on the histopathology of *Leucocytozoon simondi* infection. *Am. J. Vet. Res.* 18:191, 1957.

O'Roke, E. C. A malaria-like disease of ducks caused by *Leucocytozoon anatis* wickware. *Univ. Mich. School Forest Conser. Bull.* 4:1, 1934.

Ramisz, A. Protozoa of the genus *Leucocytozoon* Danilewski, 1890 in birds of the environs of Wroclaw. *Acta Parasitol. Polon.* 10:39, 1962.

Richey, D. J., and Ware, R. E. Schizonts of *Leucocytozoon smithi* in artificially infected turkeys. *Cornell Vet.* 45:642, 1955.

Sakharoff, M. N. Recherches sur les hematozoaires des oiseaux. *Ann. Inst. Pasteur* 7: 801, 1893.

Sambon, L. W. Remarks on the avian hematozoa of the genus *Leucocytozoon, Danilewsky*. *J. Trop. Med.* 11:325, 1908.

Saunders, Dorothy C. Microfilariae and other blood parasites in Mexican wild doves and pigeons. *J. Parasitol.* 45:69, 1959.

Saunders, G. B. Michigan's studies of sharp-tailed grouse. *Trans. Am. Game Conf.* 21: 342, 1935.

Savage, A., and Isa, J. M. An outbreak of *Leucocytozoon* disease in turkeys. *Cornell Vet.* 35:270, 1945.

Shewell, G. E. Identity of the black fly that attacks ducklings and goslings in Canada (Diptera: Simuliidae). *Can. Entomologist* 87: 345, 1955.

Skidmore, L. V. *Leucocytozoon smithi* in turkeys and its transmission by *Simulium occidentale* Townsend. *Zentr. Bakteriol. Parasitenk. Abt. I. Orig.* 125:329, 1932.

Stabler, R. M., and Holt, Portia A. Hematozoa from Colorado birds. I. Pigeons and doves. *J. Parasitol.* 49:320, 1963.

Tarshis, I. B., and Herman, C. M. Is *Cnephia invenusta* (Walker) a possible important vector of *Leucocytozoon* in Canada geese? *Bull. Wildlife Disease Assoc.* 1:10, 1965.

Travis, B. V., Goodwin, M. H., Jr., and Gambrell, E. Preliminary note on the occurrence of *Leucocytozoon smithi* Laveran and Lucet (1905) in turkeys in the southeastern United States. *J. Parasitol.* 25:278, 1939.

Wehr, E. E. Studies on leucocytozoonosis of turkeys, with notes on schizogony, transmission, and control of *Leucocytozoon smithi*. *Avian Diseases* 6:195, 1962.

West, J. L., and Starr, L. E. Further observations on a blood protozoan infection in turkeys. *Vet. Med.* 35:649, 1940.

Wingstrand, K. G. On some haematozoa of Swedish birds with remarks on the schizogony of *Leucocytozoon sakharoffi*. *K. Sv. Vetenskapsakad. Handlingar.* Ser. 3. 24(5):1, 1947.

———. Further studies on *Leucocytozoon sakharoffi*. *K. Sv. Vetenskapsakad. Handlingar.* Ser. 3. 24(8):1, 1948.

● ROBERT S. COOK

Haemoproteus is a blood parasite belonging to the family Haemoproteidae. The gametocytes contain pigment granules, are found within red blood cells, and are usually halter-shaped. Their shape gave them the synonym *Halteridium* Labbe 1894. Occasionally a rounded form is seen exoerythrocytically. Asexual stages occur in the vertebrate host while sexual development occurs in an intermediate insect host.

Transmission of *Haemoproteus* is by louse flies (Hippoboscidae) and midges *(Culicoides),* the known intermediate hosts (Tarshis, 1955; Fallis and Wood, 1957). Baker (1967) has reviewed the role of the Hippoboscidae as vectors of *Haemoproteus* spp. This does not mean other insects may not be vectors, as the life cycles of only a few have been studied.

The portion of the general life cycle within the intermediate host begins after the ingestion of infected blood when the microgametocytes exflagellate to form several microgametes. These fertilize macrogametes. The zygotes are motile ookinetes that penetrate the stomach wall and form oocysts within the wall or on its outer surface. Sporozoites are produced in the oocysts. These are liberated into the body cavity. They travel to the lumen of the salivary gland and are discharged when the insect feeds on the next host.

Once inside the vertebrate host, the sporozoites are carried to the endothelial cells of the blood vessels of various internal organs. In these cells a number of replications of merozoites occur; these merozoites finally enter the bloodstream, penetrate the red blood cells, and form gametocytes. The gametocytes are readily apparent in stained blood smears.

Checklists and host-indexes of the genus *Haemoproteus* have been published by Coatney (1936), Herman (1944), Levine and Kantor (1959), and others. Members of the genus occur commonly in many species of birds and in some reptiles. Many species have been described and named but too frequently they were named only on the basis of occurrence within a new host, not from detailed life history studies that are also needed to establish new species. Only those species most commonly found and described in wild birds will be discussed.

Another member of Haemoproteidae, *Leucocytozoon,* is the cause of an important disease in wild birds but differs from *Haemoproteus* in that it parasitizes certain leukocytes as well as erythrocytes, and pigment granules are usually absent in the stained parasites. The similarity of certain erythrocytic stages of *Haemoproteus* with members of the true malarial family, Plasmodiidae, can cause confusion. Only developing or mature gametocytes of *Haemoproteus* are found in red blood cells as schizogony occurs only in endothelial cells of blood vessels in the lungs, liver, spleen, and other internal organs. Schizogony occurs both in the endothelial tissue of internal organs and within erythrocytes in *Plasmodium* infection. Therefore, if only gametocyte stages are present it would be impossible to differentiate the two genera by observing blood smears.

Manwell (1952) and Levine (1961) suggested Haemoproteidae and Plasmodiidae be combined into one family. Manwell (1965) suggested that members of Haemoproteidae be included in the Plasmodiidae.

A different point of view has been advanced by Fallis and Bennett (1961). They proposed three separate families; that is, Plasmodiidae, Haemoproteidae, and Leucocytozoidae. Furthermore, Bennett et al. (1965) divided the genus *Leucocytozoon* into two genera, *Leucocytozoon* and *Akiba,* and the genus *Haemoproteus* into *Haemoproteus* and *Parahaemoproteus.* Their evidence was based on differences in the life cycles of the parasites, including the types of intermediate hosts. While established nomenclature has been used in this text, an attempt has been made to give that proposed as well.

Haemoproteus columbae Kruse 1890

SYNONYMS: *H. Maccallumi, H. melopeliae, H. turtur.*

Haemoproteus maccallumi was the name given to a morphologically indistinguishable form found in the mourning dove *(Zenaidura macroura).* This form was transmitted from the mourning dove to the pigeon by the hippoboscid fly *(Pseudolynchia canariensis* [*= maura*]) (Huff, 1932). However, Coatney (1933) could not duplicate the experiment. Levine (1961) suggested strain differences may exist between *H. columbae* and *maccallumi* but recommends *H. columbae* be used for both unless proved otherwise by further study.

♦ **DISTRIBUTION.** Originally found in the common pigeon *(Columba livia),* this parasite also occurs in many wild pigeons and doves. At least 45 columbiform species, worldwide in distribution, were recorded as hosts of *Haemoproteus* spp. by Levine and Kantor (1959). However, Levine (1962) lists only 14 host species found in 24 countries that were reported as specifically being infected with *H. columbae.*

It is a common parasite. Levine and Kantor (1959) summarized 38 reports for domestic pigeons and found a range of 28 to 100% occurrence. Saunders (1959) examined birds collected in Mexico and

found 1 of 31 red-billed pigeons *(Columba f. flavirostris),* 2 of 46 western mourning doves *(Zenaidura m. marginella),* and 3 of 58 western white-winged doves *(Zenaida asiatica mearnsi)* infected. Stabler (1961) found infection in all of 51 white-winged doves *(Zenaida a. asiatica)* from Texas. Stabler and Holt (1962) found this parasite for the first time in 4 of 4 eastern ground doves *(Columbigallina passerina passerina)* collected in Florida. Levine (1961) summarized several reports on the occurrence of *Haemoproteus* in mourning doves and found prevalence ranging from 8 to 93%.

Hanson et al. (1957) found the prevalence of the parasite increased with age in mourning doves in Illinois, ranging steadily upward from 7% in the youngest juveniles to 70% in the older adults. Coatney (1933) found the relapse of *H. columbae* in pigeons very irregular, and he concluded relapse was correlated with the intensity of the initial infection. Farmer (1962) experimentally established the relapse phenomenon in mourning doves and found it occurred irregularly also. The possibility of relapse occurring, either seasonally or irregularly, must be considered when prevalence is being interpreted.

Knisley and Herman (1967) have recently reviewed the distribution and prevalence of *Haemoproteus* in domestic pigeons and mourning doves throughout the world.

♦ **TRANSMISSION AND DEVELOPMENT.** Sexual stages of reproduction can take place in certain hippoboscid flies. Huff (1932) infected pigeons with this parasite, using *Pseudolynchia canariensis* (*= maura*) as the intermediate host. Baker (1957) demonstrated sporogony in *Ornithomyia avicularia* and successfully transmitted it to English wood-pigeons *(Columba p. palumbus),* but he could not produce infection in domestic pigeons with the infected flies (Baker, 1963). Later experiments (Baker, 1966) showed the *Haemoproteus* species that he worked with was a different strain of *H. columbae,* or possibly a new species.

A *Triatoma* sp. was also capable of transmitting *H. columbae* (Rivero, 1947).

Experimental infection in common pigeons was produced when they were directly inoculated with large amounts of whole blood or a saline suspension of tissue obtained from recently infected pigeons (Lastra and Coatney, 1950). As Levine (1961) pointed out, it is very unlikely that hippoboscids are the only vectors, as these flies are rarely found on mourning doves, yet these birds harbor *H. columbae.*

Life history studies have been reported by many workers, including Coatney (1933), Huff (1932, 1942), and Manwell and Loeffler (1961). Detailed studies of microgametogenesis have been conducted (Bradbury and Trager, 1967; Trager and Bradbury, 1967).

A detailed description of the asexual stages in the vertebrate host can be found in most parasitological reference books, including Levine (1961) and Kudo (1966). Briefly, sporozoites reach the endothelial cells of the spleen, liver, and lungs via the bloodstream. After penetrating these cells they form schizonts and undergo multiple fission, becoming cytomeres. The cytomeres enlarge and become multinucleate. Finally the host cell ruptures and the cytomeres enter the bloodstream and accumulate in the capillaries. Then merozoites form in the cytomeres. The cytomeres finally release merozoites into the bloodstream where they invade erythrocytes and become gametocytes. Mature gametocytes are C-shaped, growing along one side and over the ends of the host cell nucleus.

Relapse is common (Coatney, 1933).

◆ **PATHOGENESIS.** Not considered a severe pathogen, *H. columbae* may cause some clinical signs in heavy infections. Coatney (1933) noted abnormal behavior in one heavily infected bird. Levine (1961) listed restlessness, anorexia, and anemia from red blood cell destruction. Becker et al. (1956) found a great number of parasitized red blood cells in a pigeon whose spleen was enlarged and highly pigmented.

◆ **TREATMENT AND CONTROL.** Coatney (1935) used preparations of both quinacrine hydrochloride and plasmochin in tests on domestic pigeons. The former drug inhibited development of young gametocytes while the latter destroyed mature forms, removing them in 3 days. Neither drug affected the tissue stages.

The apparently limited pathogenicity of these parasites has provided little incentive for investigation on their treatment or control.

Haemoproteus sacharovi
Novy and MacNeal 1904

◆ **DISTRIBUTION.** Initially found in the eastern mourning dove *(Zenaidura macroura carolinensis),* it also occurs in the western mourning dove *(Z. m. marginella),* as well as in many other wild doves and pigeons. The common pigeon *(Columba livia)* is a known host, too (Coatney and West, 1940). Occurrence of these parasites has been observed throughout North America and in Italy.

In addition to the reports on prevalence summarized by Levine (1961) and Knisley and Herman (1967), Stabler and Holt (1963) in Colorado found 76 of 109 band-tailed pigeons *(C. fasciata fasciata)* and 163 of 269 western mourning doves infected. Stabler (1961) found infection in 26 of 51 eastern white-winged doves *(Z. a. asiatica)* from Texas.

◆ **TRANSMISSION AND DEVELOPMENT.** Huff (1932) succeeded in transferring this parasite from the mourning dove to domestic pigeons, using the vector *Pseudolynchia canariensis* (= *maura*). This does not necessarily prove the natural intermediate host is a louse fly. The patent period in one bird lasted until the bird was killed 3 months after exposure.

The distinguishing feature of this species is that mature gametocytes completely fill the host cell cytoplasm and cause hypertrophy of the infected red blood cells. It also contains comparatively few granules. Huff (1932), Coatney and West (1940), Levine (1961), and Farmer (1962) describe the morphology of this species.

♦ **PATHOGENESIS.** *Haemoproteus sacharovi* is reported as nonpathogenic in wild doves and pigeons. In young infected domestic pigeons, Becker et al. (1956) reported enlarged and pigmented spleens and granular gizzard muscles.

Haemoproteus danilewskii Kruse 1890

SYNONYM: The genus name *Parahaemoproteus* has been proposed (Bennett et al., 1965).

♦ **DISTRIBUTION.** *Haemoproteus danilewskii* was first found and described in the hooded crow (*Corvus cornix*) and later in many other Old World birds by Kruse (1890). Among those reporting this parasite in captive wild birds was Plimmer (1912, 1913, 1915), who found infection in an Australian shelldrake (*Casarca tadornoides*), Baer's pochard (*Aythya baeri*), red jungle fowl (*Gallus gallus*), and a cotton teal (*Cheniscus coramandelianus*) held in the London Zoo. Infection has also been reported from such common birds as the crow (*Corvus brachyrhynchos brachyrhynchos*) in Nebraska (Coatney and West, 1938), Montana (Coatney and Jellison, 1940), Wisconsin, and Iowa (Morgan and Waller, 1941), and in the English sparrow (*Passer domesticus*) in Illinois (Sachs, 1953). Without evidence of transmissibility, Levine and Hanson (1953) deem the name no longer acceptable for the parasite occurring in Anseriformes. Glushchenko (1962) lists 23 species collected in the Kiev Forest region as hosts of this parasite.

♦ **TRANSMISSION AND DEVELOPMENT.** Intermediate hosts responsible for transmission are unknown. The outstanding characteristic of the gametocytes is the occupancy of the entire host cell cytoplasm by the parasite. The parasite completely surrounds the host cell nucleus or displaces it (Coatney and West, 1938).

♦ **PATHOGENESIS.** Unknown.

Haemoproteus lophortyx O'Roke 1929

♦ **DISTRIBUTION.** This species was first found and described in California valley quail (*Lophortyx californica*) by O'Roke (1930) and later reported in San Quentin quail (*L. c. plumbea*), Gambel's quail (*L. gambelii gambelii*), and mountain quail (*Oreortyx picta*) in California by Wood and Herman (1943). Gambel's quail and scaled quail (*Callipepla squamata pallida*) in New Mexico and Arizona harbored this parasite (Campbell and Lee, 1953; Hungerford, 1955), and Wetmore (1941) found an infected bobwhite quail (*Colinus virginianus*) in the vicinity of the District of Columbia.

This parasite was found in 6 of 12 valley quail, 14 of 33 San Quentin quail, and 1 mountain quail (Wood and Herman, 1943). Eighty-four percent of 503 quail from the San Joaquin Experimental Range, California, were infected (Herman and Glading, 1942). Seventy-eight percent of 367 adults and 56% of 531 immature California valley quail were found infected during a 5-year period in California (Tarshis, 1955). One of 93 bobwhites was infected in the District of Columbia area (Wetmore, 1941). No *Haemoproteus* was found in 73 bobwhites collected in Texas at various times throughout the year (Parmalee, 1952). Gullion (1957) found 62 of 110 Gambel's quail in Nevada positive.

♦ **TRANSMISSION AND DEVELOPMENT.** Vectors are hippoboscid louse flies: *Lynchia hirsuta* (O'Roke, 1930) and *Stilbometopa impressa* (Herman and Bischoff, 1949; Tarshis, 1955). A prepatent period of 21 days occurred in a quail experimentally infected with sporozoites from *S. impressa* and patency ranged from several weeks to over 4 years (Herman and Bischoff, 1949).

The gametocyte and its staining properties are described by O'Roke (1929, 1932).

◆ **CLINICAL SIGNS.** Herman and Bischoff (1949) reported that experimentally infected quail became droopy and lost their appetite 7 days postinoculation. Death occurred on the 10th day and the carcass did not show emaciation. Peak infections, indicated by the number of parasitized red blood cells, showed seasonal variation, with greatest intensity occurring in February, March, and April.

Herman and Bischoff (1949) concluded that once a quail is infected, complete remission is doubtful. O'Roke (1932) described four types of *Haemoproteus* infection in California valley quail:

1. Mild, chronic. An inapparent infection, no external signs, gametocytes present in red blood cells.
2. Mild, acute. Bird goes "off feed" for 2 to 4 days, is restless, recovers completely.
3. Moderate, chronic. Seen commonly under field conditions. Bird is thin, anemic, weak.
4. Heavy, acute. Late spring and summer at peak of relapse. Birds do not eat, are droopy, weak, and die. These cases are rare.

◆ **PATHOGENESIS.** O'Roke (1932) reported an enlarged, blackened spleen and black pigment in the lungs and liver as fairly constant lesions. Hypertrophy of infected red blood cells, anemia, and capillary congestion were also present.

Campbell and Lee (1953) and Campbell (1954) reported no pathogenic effects in experimentally infected Gambel's quail.

Haemoproteus meleagridis Levine 1961

◆ **DISTRIBUTION.** The hosts are the wild and domestic turkey *(Meleagris gallopavo)*. Its known geographic distribution is presently confined to North America.

Kozicky (1948) was the first to report *Haemoproteus* in wild turkeys; 5 of 97 wild Pennsylvania turkeys collected during 1947 were positive. Four of the 5 positive birds had been reared in captivity. In 1953 Love et al. found 1 of 2 wild turkeys in Georgia

infected, and Cook et al. (1966) found all of 63 immature turkeys and 63% of 70 adults from southern Texas lightly infected. This parasite has also been reported in domestic turkeys.

◆ **TRANSMISSION AND DEVELOPMENT.** Unknown in wild turkeys.

◆ **CLINICAL SIGNS.** No signs have been reported for wild turkeys. Morehouse (1945) reported a heavy infection of this parasite in an anemic domestic bird from a sick flock in Texas. The only parasite found was *Haemoproteus*, and Morehouse suggested it might be the pathogen.

◆ **PATHOGENESIS.** Unknown.

Haemoproteus nettionis
(Cleland and Johnson 1909)
Coatney 1936

SYNONYMS: *H. anatis* Haiba 1946; *H. hermani* Haiba 1948. Herman (1954), on the basis of morphologic similarities, proposed *H. nettionis* as the accepted name for the species found in Anatidae and gives a comprehensive list of synonyms. Later writers have generally accepted his view (Fallis and Wood, 1957; Levine, 1961; Lund and Farr, 1965). Bennett et al. (1965) have proposed the generic name *Parahaemoproteus* which would include this species.

◆ **DISTRIBUTION.** *Haemoproteus nettionis* is a cosmopolitan parasite of waterfowl. It was found first in North American black ducks by Herman (1938a, 1938b). Summaries show at least 23 species harbor this parasite (Coatney, 1936; Herman, 1944, 1954; Levine and Hanson, 1953; Fallis and Wood, 1957; Levine, 1961).

◆ **TRANSMISSION AND DEVELOPMENT.** Herman (1954) demonstrated natural transmission at Patuxent Research Refuge, Laurel, Maryland, by exposing 2-

week-old, incubator-hatched Indian runner ducks and white domestic Chinese geese (both species unknown) in outdoor pens. No vectors were observed on these birds but parasitemias developed in both groups. He concluded the vectors could have been free-flying insects. Incubation times in the ducks were 19 to 33 days, and 23 days in the geese. Parasitemias lasted 7 to 12 days in the ducks and more than 2 weeks in the geese.

Hippoboscids were never observed on several hundred ducks used in a study of *Leucocytozoon* even though they were examined daily (Anderson, 1956). Bequaert (1953) does not consider aquatic birds as suitable hosts for Hippoboscidae.

Fallis and Wood (1957) showed that certain biting midges *(Culicoides* sp.) were suitable intermediate hosts and that these midges feed on ducks at night in contrast to blackflies that feed during the day. The prepatent period was 14 to 21 days, and gametocytes took 4 to 6 days to reach maturity.

An amended general description of the sexual stages of this parasite in red blood cells is given by Herman (1954).

◆ **PATHOGENESIS.** There is no evidence that this species is pathogenic to waterfowl.

Haemoproteus canachites
Fallis and Bennett 1960

SYNONYM: *Parahaemoproteus* has been proposed (Bennett et al., 1965).

◆ **DISTRIBUTION.** The present known range of *H. canachites* is Algonquin Park, Canada, and the type host is the spruce grouse *(Canachites canadensis).*

Fallis and Bennett (1960) experimentally infected ruffed grouse *(Bonasa umbellus),* using sporozoites from the salivary glands of *Culicoides sphagnumensis.* Their study showed that ruffed grouse are suitable hosts for this parasite. Infections were

not produced by injecting similar sporozoites into 3 domestic ducks *(Anas boschas),* 1 Java sparrow *(Padda oryzivora),* and a pigeon *(Columba livia).* A specificity for grouse was therefore indicated.

Clark (1938) described many gametocytes as surrounding the nucleus of the host cell in his study of *Haemoproteus* in ruffed grouse. In a later study most parasites of *H. canachites* did not surround the nucleus of the host cell (Fallis and Bennett, 1960), suggesting 2 species may exist in grouse.

As pointed out by Fallis and Bennett (1960), parasites of the genus *Haemoproteus* have been recorded in many species of grouse (Fantham, 1910; Clarke, 1938; Herman, 1944; Fallis, 1945; Fowle, 1946; Borg, 1953; Bendell, 1955; Dorney and Todd, 1960; Stabler et al., 1967) but were never assigned to a species of *Haemoproteus.*

◆ **TRANSMISSION AND DEVELOPMENT.** The sporogonic cycle of *H. canachites* was completed in an ornithophilic ceratopogonid, *Culicoides sphagnumensis.* That ceratopogonid was the predominant species that fed on an exposed infected spruce grouse in Algonquin Park, Canada (Fallis and Bennett, 1960). Various stages of the sporogonic cycle were reported in detail by these same workers. Exflagellation of mature gametocytes occurred 3 to 20 minutes after ingestion by *Culicoides.* Zygotes were found in the stomach contents 12 hours after ingestion of gametocytes. Ookinetes were vacuolated and movement was very slow. Oocysts were seen in the stomach walls 4 days after ingestion of gametocytes. A residual body was present. Sporozoites began reaching maturity on the 6th day following initiation of the cycle. There were approximately 20 to 30 motile sporozoites per oocyst. Sporozoites were found in the salivary glands on the 7th day.

Fallis and Bennett (1960) also found the prepatent period in ruffed grouse was 14 days. Usually gametocytes encircled about three-fourths of the host cell nucleus, although about 10% did grow completely around the nucleus. Gametocytes attained maximum size in about 6 days.

The same study showed about 1% of the red blood cells contained gametocytes in the infected spruce grouse that was the source of gametocytes for the experiment. Infection intensity did not reach that level in the experimentally infected ruffed grouse. The parasitemia peak was short.

♦ **CLINICAL SIGNS.** Fallis and Bennett (1960) reported having to force-feed the infected adult spruce grouse they captured, although they do not report any signs in the experimentally infected ruffed grouse.

♦ **PATHOGENESIS.** Unknown.

♦ **REFERENCES**

Anderson, R. C. The life cycle and seasonal transmission of *Ornithofilaria fallisensis* Anderson, a parasite of domestic and wild ducks. *Can. J. Zool.* 34:485, 1956.

Baker, J. R. A new vector of *Haemoproteus columbae* in England. *J. Protozool.* 4:204, 1957.

———. The transmission of *Haemoproteus* sp. of English wood-pigeons by *Ornithomyia avicularia. J. Protozool.* 10:461, 1963.

———. The host-restriction of *Haemoproteus* sp. indet. of the wood-pigeon *Columba p. palumbus. J. Protozool.* 13:406, 1966.

———. A review of the role played by the Hippoboscidae (Diptera) as vectors of endoparasites. *J. Parasitol.* 53:412, 1967.

Becker, E. R., Hollander, W. F., and Pattillo, W. H. Naturally occurring *Plasmodium* and *Haemoproteus* infection in the common pigeon. *J. Parasitol.* 42:474, 1956.

Bendell, J. F. Disease as a control of a population of blue grouse, *Dendragapus obscurus fuliginosus* (Ridgeway). *Can. J. Zool.* 33:195, 1955.

Bennett, G. F., Garnham, P. C. C., and Fallis, A. M. On the status of the genera *Leucocytozoon* Ziemann, 1898 and *Haemoproteus* Kruse, 1890 (Haemosporidiida: Leucocytozoidae and Haemoproteidae). *Can. J. Zool.* 43:927, 1965.

Bequaert, J. C. The Hippoboscidae or louseflies (Diptera) of mammals and birds. Part 1. Structure, physiology, and natural history. *Entomologica Americana* 33:211, 1953.

Borg, K. On *Leucocytozoon* in Swedish caper-caillie, black grouse and hazel grouse. *Berlingska Boktryckeriet Lund.*, 1953.

Bradbury, Phyllis, and Trager, W. Axoneme formation during microgametogenesis in *Haemoproteus columbae. J. Protozool.* 14 (suppl.):15, 1967.

Campbell, H. Avian malaria in relation to survival and growth of a group of young Gambel's quail in captivity. *J. Wildlife Management* 18:416, 1954.

Campbell, H., and Lee, L. Studies on quail malaria in New Mexico and notes on other aspects of quail populations. New Mexico Dept. Game and Fish, Sante Fe. *PR Report W-41-R*, 1953.

Clarke, C. H. D. Organisms of a malarial type in ruffed grouse, with a description of the schizogony of *Leucocytozoon bonasae. J. Wildlife Management* 2:146, 1938.

Coatney, G. R. Relapse and associated phenomena in the *Haemoproteus* infection of the pigeon. *Am. J. Hyg.* 18:133, 1933.

———. The effect of Atebrine and Plasmochin on the *Haemoproteus* infection of the pigeon. *Am. J. Hyg.* 21:249, 1935.

———. A check-list and host-index of the genus *Haemoproteus. J. Parasitol.* 22:88, 1936.

Coatney, G. R., and Jellison, W. L. Some blood parasites from Montana birds. *J. Parasitol.* 26:158, 1940.

Coatney, G. R., and West, Evaline. Some blood parasites from Nebraska birds—II. *Am. Midland Naturalist* 19:601, 1938.

———. Studies on *Haemoproteus sacharovi* of mourning doves and pigeons, with notes on *H. maccallumi. Am. J. Hyg.* 31:9, 1940.

Cook, R. S., Trainer, D. O., and Glazener, W. C. *Haemoproteus* in wild turkeys from the coastal bend of South Texas. *J. Protozool.* 13:588, 1966.

Dorney, R. S., and Todd, A. C. Spring incidence of ruffed grouse blood parasites. *J. Parasitol.* 46:687, 1960.

Fallis, A. M. Population trends and blood parasites of ruffed grouse in Ontario. *J. Wildlife Management* 9:203, 1945.

Fallis, A. M., and Bennett, G. F. Description of *Haemoproteus canachites* n. sp. (Sporozoa: Haemoproteidae) and sporogony in *Culicoides* (Diptera: Ceratopogonidae). *Can. J. Zool.* 38:455, 1960.

———. Sporogony of *Leucocytozoon* and *Haemoproteus* in simuliids and ceratopogonids and a revised classification of the Haemosporidiida. *Can. J. Zool.* 39:215, 1961.

Fallis, A. M., and Wood, D. M. Biting midges (Diptera: Ceratopogonidae) as intermediate hosts for *Haemoproteus* of ducks. *Can. J. Zool.* 35:425, 1957.

Fantham, H. B. Observations on the parasitic protozoa of the red grouse (*Lagopus scoticus*) with a note on the grouse fly. *Proc. Zool. Soc. London* 2:692, 1910.

Farmer, J. N. Relapse of *Haemoproteus sacharovi* infections in mourning doves. *Trans. N. Am. Wildlife Nat. Resources Conf.* 27:164, 1962.

Fowle, C. D. The blood parasites of the blue grouse. *Science* 103:708, 1946.

Glushchenko, V. V. New data on the blood parasites of domestic and wild birds in the Kiev forest zone. (Ukrainian text; English and Russian summaries) *Dopovidi Akad. Nauk Ukrain. RSR* 10:1387, 1962.

Gullion, G. W. Gambel quail disease and parasite investigations in Nevada. *Am. Midland Naturalist* 57:414, 1957.

Hanson, H. C., Levine, N. D., Kossack, C. W., Kantor, S., and Stannard, L. J. Parasites of the mourning dove (*Zenaidura macroura carolinensis*) in Illinois. *J. Parasitol.* 43:186, 1957.

Herman, C. M. The relative incidence of blood protozoa in some birds from Cape Cod. *Trans. Am. Microscop. Soc.* 57:132, 1938a.

———. *Haemoproteus* sp. from the common black duck, *Anas rubripes tristis. J. Parasitol.* 24:53, 1938b.

———. The blood protozoa of North American birds. *Bird Banding* 15:89, 1944.

———. *Haemoproteus* infections in waterfowl. *Proc. Helminthol. Soc. Wash. D.C.* 21:37, 1954.

Herman, C. M., and Bischoff, A. I. The duration of *Haemoproteus* infection in California quail. *California Fish Game* 35:293, 1949.

Herman, C. M., and Glading, B. The protozoan blood parasite *Haemoproteus lophortyx* O'Roke in quail at the San Joaquin Experimental Range, California. *California Fish Game* 28:150, 1942.

Huff, C. G. Studies on *Haemoproteus* of mourning doves. *Am. J. Hyg.* 16:618, 1932.

———. Schizogony and gametocyte development in *Leucocytozoon simondi*, and comparisons with *Plasmodium* and *Haemoproteus. J. Infect. Diseases* 71:18, 1942.

Hungerford, C. R. A preliminary evaluation of quail malaria in southern Arizona in relation to habitat and quail mortality. *Trans. N. Am. Wildlife Conf.* 20:209, 1955.

Knisley, J. O., and Herman, C. M. *Haemoproteus*, a blood parasite, in domestic pigeons and mourning doves in Maryland. *Chesapeake Sci.* 8:200, 1967.

Kozicky, E. L. Some protozoan parasites of the eastern wild turkey in Pennsylvania. *J. Wildlife Management* 12:263, 1948.

Kruse, W. Ueber Blutparasiten. *Virchows Arch.* 121:359, 1890.

Kudo, R. R. *Protozoology*, 5th ed. Springfield: Charles C Thomas, 1966.

Lastra, I., and Coatney, G. R. Transmission of *Haemoproteus columbae* by blood inoculation and tissue transplants. *J. Nat. Malaria Soc.* 9:151, 1950.

Levine, N. D. *Protozoan parasites of domestic animals and of man.* Minneapolis: Burgess, 1961.

———. Geographic host distribution of blood parasites in columboid birds. *Trans. Illinois State Acad. Sci.* 55(2):92, 1962.

Levine, N. D., and Hanson, H. C. Blood parasites of the Canada goose, *Branta canadensis interior. J. Wildlife Management* 17:185, 1953.

Levine, N. D., and Kantor, S. Check-list of blood parasites of birds of the order Columbiformes. *Wildlife Diseases* 1:1, 1959.

Love, G. J., Wilkin, S. A., and Goodwin, M. H., Jr. Incidence of blood parasites in birds collected in southwestern Georgia. *J. Parasitol.* 39:52, 1953.

Lund, E. E., and Farr, M. M. Protozoa. *Haemoproteus* infections. In H. E. Biester and L. H. Schwarte, eds., *Diseases of poultry*, p. 1121. Ames: Iowa State Univ. Press, 1965.

Manwell, R. D. *Haemoproteus* in wild birds. *Proc. Soc. Protozool.* 3:2, 1952.

———. The lesser Haemosporidina. *J. Protozool.* 12:1, 1965.

Manwell, R. D., and Loeffler, C. A. Glucose consumption by *Haemoproteus columbae. J. Parasitol.* 47:285, 1961.

Morehouse, N. F. The occurrence of *Haemoproteus* sp. in the domesticated turkey. *Trans. Am. Microscop. Soc.* 64:109, 1945.

Morgan, B. B., and Waller, E. F. Some parasites of the eastern crow. *Bird Banding* 12:17, 1941.

O'Roke, E. C. The morphology of *Haemoproteus lophortyx* sp. nov. *Science* 70:432, 1929.

———. The morphology, transmission and life history of *Haemoproteus lophortyx* O'Roke, a blood parasite of the California valley quail. *Univ. Calif. Publ. Zool.* 36:1, 1930.

———. Parasitism of the California valley quail by *Haemoproteus lophortyx*, a protozoan blood parasite. *Calif. Fish Game* 18:223, 1932.

Parmalee, P. W. Ecto- and endoparasites of the bobwhite: Their numbers, species, and possible importance in the health and vigor of quail. *Trans. N. Am. Wildlife Conf.* 17:174, 1952.

Plimmer, H. G. On the blood parasites found in animals in the Zoological Gardens during the four years 1908–1911. *Proc. Zool. Soc. London 1912*, p. 406, 1912.

———. Report on deaths which occurred in the Zoological Gardens during 1912, together with a list of the blood-parasites found during the year. *Proc. Zool. Soc. London 1913*, p. 141, 1913.

———. Report on the deaths which occurred in the Zoological Gardens during 1914, together with a list of the blood-parasites found during the year. *Proc. Zool. Soc. London 1915*, p. 123, 1915.

Rivero, M. D. La infeccion experimental por el *Haemoproteus columbae* Celli y Sanfelice. *Rev. Med. Mexicana* 26:197, 1947.

Sachs, I. B. Certain blood-inhabiting protozoa of birds in the vicinity of Urbana, Illinois. *Trans. Am. Microscop. Soc.* 72:216, 1953.

Saunders, Dorothy C. Microfilariae and other blood parasites in Mexican wild doves and pigeons. *J. Parasitol.* 45:69, 1959.

Stabler, R. M. A parasitological survey of fifty-one eastern white-winged doves. *J. Parasitol.* 47:309, 1961.

Stabler, R. M., and Holt, Portia A. The parasites of four eastern ground doves. *Proc. Helminthol. Soc. Wash. D.C.* 29:76, 1962.

———. Hematozoa from Colorado birds. I. Pigeons and doves. *J. Parasitol.* 49:320, 1963.

Stabler, R. M., Kitzmiller, Nancy J., Ellison, L. N., and Holt, Portia A. Hematozoa from the Alaskan spruce grouse, *Canachites canadensis*. *J. Parasitol.* 53:233, 1967.

Tarshis, I. B. Transmission of *Haemoproteus lophortyx* O'Roke of the California quail by hippoboscid flies of the species *Stilbometopa impressa* (Bigot) and *Lynchia hirsuta* Ferris. *Exptl. Parasitol.* 61:464, 1955.

Trager, W., and Bradbury, Phyllis. The fine structure of the gametes of *Haemoproteus columbae*. *J. Protozool.* 14(suppl.):15, 1967.

Wetmore, Psyche W. Blood parasites of birds of the District of Columbia and Patuxent Research Refuge vicinity. *J. Parasitol.* 27:379, 1941.

Wood, S. F., and Herman, C. M. The occurrence of blood parasites in birds from southwestern United States. *J. Parasitol.* 29:187, 1943.

25 ◆ *LANKESTERELLA (ATOXOPLASMA)*

- **EDITH D. BOX**

Lankesterella is the latest in a series of generic names given to *Toxoplasma*-like protozoa found in lymphoid-macrophage cells of birds. The parasites are most commonly encountered in peripheral blood smears in surveys of passerine birds (Fig. 25.1) but are more plentiful in cells of the lymphoid-macrophage system of the deep tissues. The parasites were first described by Laveran (1900) from the Java sparrow *(Padda oryzivora)* and named *Haemogregarina paddae* by Aragao (1911). The infection was known for many years as avian toxoplasmosis because of its morphologic resemblance to *Toxoplasma gondii*. However, while *T. gondii* is capable of infecting almost any type of cell in any warm-blooded animal, avian *Lankesterella* is restricted to cells of the lymphoid-macrophage system (with two reports of the parasites in red blood cells). In addition, *Toxoplasma* is readily transmitted from host to host by subinoculation but *Lankesterella* is not. *Lankesterella* multiples in the tissues by schizogony, whereas *Toxoplasma* multiplies

by dividing in two by a process known as endodyogyny, which is perhaps a special form of schizogony (Jacobs, 1967). Before the exoerythrocytic cycle of plasmodial infections was demonstrated, *Lankesterella* was also confused with tissue stages of bird malaria (Wolfson, 1940). In 1950, for the sake of convenience, Garnham proposed the genus name *Atoxoplasma* for these parasites. Discovery of coccodialike sexual stages in tissues of rooks *(Corvus f. frugilegus)* by Baker et al. (1959) and English sparrows *(Passer d. domesticus)* by Lainson (1959) stimulated these authors to propose inclusion of the organisms in the genus *Lankesterella* with transmission of unchanged sporozoites from bird to bird by bloodsucking mites. Lainson (1960) reported experimental transmission of the parasites from the sparrow to the canary *(Serinus canarius)* and canary to canary by a bloodsucking mite *(Dermanyssus gallinae)*, and named the organism in both birds *L. garnhami*. However, as Levine (1961) points out, the specific name *L. adiei* Aragao 1911 has priority for the sparrow parasite. Most of the knowledge of the infection comes from studies on English sparrows and domestic canaries. English sparrows frequently die of this infection when confined in the laboratory and moribund sparrows with heavily parasitized internal organs are also found in nature. Canaries are known to die of heavy infections and many wild passerines undoubtedly do also.

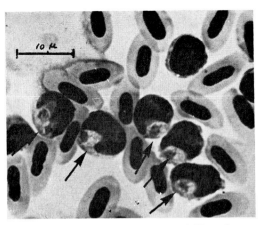

FIG. 25.1. *Lankesterella* in blood film of sparrow. May-Greenwald-tetrachrome stain.

SYNONYMS: It is uncertain at the present time whether one or many species of *Lankesterella* occur in birds. The first of these parasites was described from the Java rice bird *(Padda oryzivora)*. It was named *Haemogreg-*

arina paddae by Aragao (1911), *Toxoplasma avium* by Marullaz (1913), *Atoxoplasma avium* by Garnham (1950), and *Lankesterella paddae* by Lainson (1959). Similar parasites of *Passer domesticus* were named *Haemogregarina adiei* by Aragao (1911) and *Lankesterella garnhami* by Lainson (1959). Morphologically indistinguishable parasites of the canary *(Serinus canarius)* were named *Haemogregarina serini* by Aragao (1933), *Lankesterella serini* by Lainson (1959), and *L. garnhami* by Lainson (1960). A number of additional avian parasites morphologically similar to those listed above have been given the generic name *Haemogregarina, Toxoplasma, Atoxoplasma,* or *Lankesterella* with the species name taken from the genus of the avian host.

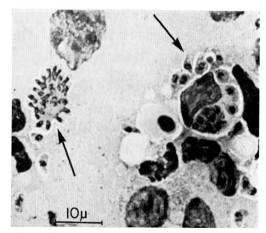

FIG. 25.2. Schizogony in spleen of sparrow nestling, showing two sizes of merozoites. Geimsa-stained touch smear.

◆ **DISTRIBUTION.** The geographic distribution of avian *Lankesterella* is worldwide. The host list is also extensive. Approximately 75 avian host species are reported in the literature; about 70 are in Passeriformes, with an occasional report in the Falconiformes, Columbiformes, and Gruiformes. Many of these were reported before *Toxoplasma gondii* was clearly distinguished from the parasite under discussion and may refer to *T. gondii,* although the latter has not been isolated frequently from birds.

◆ **TRANSMISSION AND DEVELOPMENT.** The complete life cycle of these parasites has remained a mystery for decades. Lainson (1959) studied the parasites in the English sparrow and proposed a life cycle similar to that described for *Lankesterella minima* in frogs. In this scheme, the circulating forms in the blood are sporozoites and are ingested by bloodsucking mites. The sporozoites remain unchanged in the mite and when it is ingested by another bird, sporozoites released from the mite penetrate the gut and begin an asexual cycle characterized by schizogonous

multiplication in cells of the lymphoid-macrophage system. There are two types of schizonts, one producing 10 to 30 oval merozoites with an average size of 3.6μ by 2.3μ, the second type producing a smaller number of heteropolar merozoites averaging 5.7μ by 3.5μ (Fig. 25.2). When schizogony diminishes, sporogony occurs, with male and female gametocytes similar to those of the intestinal coccidia developing in the lymphoid-macrophage cells of the liver, lungs, and kidney. After fertilization an oocyst is formed with a prominent wall. Nuclear division occurs, resulting in a large number of sporozoites measuring about 3.6μ by 1.8μ which are released into the blood by rupture of the oocyst, enter circulating lymphocytes and monocytes, and grow to an average size of 5μ by 3μ.

Schizogony in the tissues of the avian host has been well documented. The organs most commonly found infected are the spleen, liver, bone marrow, lungs, and intestine. Corradetti and Scanga (1963) also reported finding in tissues of finches *(Coccothraustes coccothraustes)* the two types of schizonts described by Lainson in English sparrows. These authors were unable to find sporogonous stages in the finches; nor have I been able to find such stages in tissue smears of English sparrows. Raffaele (1938), who pictured an *Eimeria*-like microgametocyte from the spleen of a passerine bird, and Baker et al. (1959), who found gametogonic and sporogonic stages in the bone marrow of a rook, constitute the only confirmations of the occurrence of these stages. Mite transmission has not been confirmed as yet. On the contrary, Box (1967) found heavy tissue infections in canary nestlings presumably reared free of mites in the laboratory. The birds had been infected with sporulated oocysts of *Isospora*.

Sparrows are usually infected before leaving the nest; Lainson (1959) found nestlings with light infections as early as 6 days after hatching. Apparently the parasite goes through a period of rapid multiplication in tissues of the fledgling bird, resulting in either the parasite or the host gaining the upper hand; hence, heavy infection and mortality are most commonly observed in young birds. In surveys the incidence of the parasite in both tissues and peripheral blood smears is higher in young birds.

◆ **CLINICAL SIGNS.** In many birds, for example the English sparrow, *Lankesterella* is almost invariably present, so a light infection may be considered a normal condition. When the infection becomes uncontrolled the bird appears puffed up and is usually emaciated so that the carina feels sharp on palpation.

◆ **PATHOLOGY.** In sparrows and canaries dead of the infection, the most noticeable gross lesion is an enlargement of the liver and spleen. The liver often has a mottled appearance, and microscopically an infiltration of lymphoid cells is prominent. Lainson (1958) reported considerable congestion and hemorrhage from the blood vessels in the liver and lungs and extensive inflammatory foci throughout these organs in an infected *Passer domesticus*.

◆ **DIAGNOSIS.** The usual diagnosis of the parasite is by finding it in smears of peripheral blood stained with Giemsa or another Romanowsky type of stain. The organisms are more plentiful in heart-blood films and internal organs; for example, whereas 20% of English sparrows in the Galveston, Texas, area had positive peripheral blood films, 95% of them had positive tissue smears (Box, 1966). Lainson (1959) was able to improve findings of the parasite in peripheral blood of English sparrows after concentration of the white cells by centrifugation. At autopsy of birds whose death is due to the protozoan, there is no difficulty of visualizing organisms in imprint smears wet-fixed with Bouin's fixative and stained with double-strength Giemsa's stain for several hours. They are most plentiful in the organs containing many lymphoid-macrophage cells and are seldom found in the brain. The organisms are difficult to visualize and identify in sections. In heavy infections a bit of liver or spleen mashed in physiological saline under a cover slip will reveal masses of motile organisms (Fig. 25.3). In surveys of healthy birds at autopsy, it may be necessary to examine several organs. In my experience, the parasite is most easily found in the spleen of the English sparrow. In the boat-tailed grackle *(Cassidix mexi-*

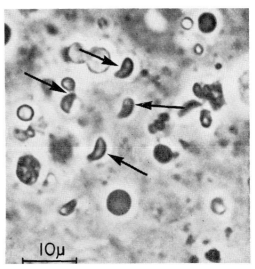

FIG. 25.3. Phase contrast photograph of motile living forms in spleen of sparrow nestling.

canus), on the other hand, the lung is most heavily infected, a finding also reported by Garnham (1950) for the chatterer *(Argya rubiginosa)*.

◆ **TREATMENT AND CONTROL.** There have been no studies on chemotherapy for this infection. In my experience with English sparrows and canaries, the chronic light infection is managed well by the host. Administration of large numbers of *Isospora* oocysts will usually result in the death of the bird, and at autopsy it will show massive tissue infection with *Lankesterella*. There is some evidence, including morphologic similarity of the 2 parasites and the effect of experimental *Isospora* infections (Box, 1967), which supports the contention of earlier authors (Coulston, 1942; Manwell et al., 1945) that *Lankesterella* may represent a tissue invasion by the coccidian parasite. Until Lainson's mite transmission is confirmed experimentally, this possibility should be kept in mind. Whatever the relationship between the 2 parasites, eliminating reinfection with *Isospora* will help control deaths due to *Lankesterella* in captive passerine birds.

◆ **REFERENCES**

Aragao, H. B. Observacoes sobre algumas Hemogregarinas das aves. *Mem. Inst. Oswaldo Cruz* 3:54, 1911.

——. Considerations sur les Hemogregarines des oiseaux. *Compt. Rend. Soc. Biol.* 113:214, 1933.

Baker, J. R., Lainson, R., and Killick-Kendrick, R. *Lankesterella corvi* n. sp., a blood parasite of the English rook, *Corvus f. frugilegus* L. *J. Protozool.* 6:233, 1959.

Box, E. D. Blood and tissue protozoa of the English sparrow *(Passer domesticus domesti-*

cus) in Galveston, Texas. *J. Protozool.* 13:204, 1966.

——. Influence of *Isospora* infections on patency of avian *Lankesterella (Atoxoplasma,* Garnham, 1950). *J. Parasitol.* 53:1140, 1967.

Corradetti, A., and Scanga, M. *Atoxoplasma coccothraustis* n. sp., Parassita del Frosone *(Coccothraustes coccothraustes)*. *Parassitologia* 5:61, 1963.

Coulston, F. The coccidial nature of avian *Toxoplasma*. *J. Parasitol.* 28:16(suppl.), 1942.

Garnham, P. C. C. Blood parasites of East African vertebrates with a brief description of exoerythrocytic schizogony in *Plasmodium pitmani*. *Parasitology* 40:328, 1950.

Jacobs, L. *Toxoplasma* and toxoplasmosis. In B. Dawes, ed., *Advances in parasitology*, vol. 5, p. 1. London and New York: Academic Press, 1967.

Lainson, R. *Atoxoplasma* Garnham, 1950, in an English sparrow *(Passer domesticus domesticus* Linn.). *Trans. Roy. Soc. Trop. Med. Hyg.* 52:15, 1958.

——. *Atoxoplasma* Garnham, 1950, as a synonym for *Lankesterella* Labbe, 1899. Its life cycle in the English sparrow *(Passer domesticus domesticus* Linn.). *J. Protozool.* 6:360, 1959.

——. The transmission of *Lankesterella (Atoxoplasma)* in birds by the mite *Dermanyssus gallinae*. *J. Protozool.* 7:321, 1960.

Laveran, A. Au sujet de l'hematozoaires endoglobulaire de *Padda orizivora*. *Compt. Rend. Soc. Biol.* 52:19, 1900.

Levine, N. D. *Protozoan parasites of domestic animals and of man*. Minneapolis: Burgess, 1961.

Manwell, R. D., Coulston, F., Binckley, E. C., and Jones, V. P. Mammalian and avian toxoplasmas. *J. Infect. Diseases* 76:1, 1945.

Marullaz, M. Au sujet d'un Toxoplasme des oiseaux. *Bull. Soc. Path. Exotique* 6:360, 1913.

Raffaele, G. Evoluzione di *Plasmodium, Toxoplasma* ed altri microorganismi negli organi interni dei vertebrati. *Riv. Malariol.* 17:85, 1938.

Wolfson, F. Organisms described as avian *Toxoplasma*. *Am. J. Hyg.* 32:88, 1940.

● VANCE L. SANGER

THE PRESENCE of the organism *Toxoplasma gondii,* the causative agent in toxoplasmosis, is extremely common in man and in wild and domestic animals and birds, but the disease is far less common (Noble and Noble, 1964).

Toxoplasmas are parasitic organisms which belong to the subphylum, Sporozoa. There is only one species, but different strains exist. They are crescent-shaped organisms about 6 to 12μ long and about half as wide. One end is rounded and one is pointed. A nucleus is located centrally (Cheng, 1964). Some reports indicate a smaller size range, 4 to 8μ long and 2 to 4μ wide (Levine, 1961).

SYNONYMS: *Toxoplasma cuniculi, T. caviae, T. canis, T. musculi, T. ratti, T. laidlawi, T. sciuri, T. pyrogenes, T. hominis* (Levine, 1961).

◆ **DISTRIBUTION.** The *Toxoplasma* organism is distributed worldwide. It infects an almost unlimited number of mammals and birds. Cold-blooded animals have been reported to be infected. The parasites invade many organs and tissues, but they seem to have an affinity for brain tissue (Cheng, 1964). According to serologic surveys, large numbers of human, animal, and pigeon populations in some sections of the country have been exposed to *Toxoplasma* organisms (Chandler and Read, 1961). Fifty-nine percent of dogs tested, 34% of cats, 48% of goats, 30% of pigs, 3 to 20% of rats, and 10 to 12% of pigeons reacted positively. In man the incidence ranges from 0% in Eskimos to 68% in the

inhabitants of Tahiti. In the United States the range is from 17 to 35%.

In man a greater incidence of infection is found in warm climates than in cold and more in moist than in dry climates.

◆ **PATHOGENICITY.** The *Toxoplasma* organism is pathogenic in a wide range of hosts. However, it frequently is found in the absence of any recognizable disease, and often exposure to it can be established only by positive serologic reactions. In this review of toxoplasmosis and the host range, the clinical signs and lesions have been summarized when they were given in the reports.

◆ **HOSTS.** In 1900 an unidentified parasite was reported in *Padda oryzivora,* which was known to be infected with *Haemamoeba danilewskyi* (Laveran, 1900). In 1913 a further study of these parasites was made by Marullaz in the padda, and they were identified as toxoplasmas. Thirty-five of 37 birds were infected. In addition the author found these parasites in some West African passerine birds and in *Estrilda phoenicatis, Lagonostica senegata, Quele aerythrops, Pyromelona franciscana,* and *Fringilla coelebs.* He suggested the name *Toxoplasma avium.* Eighteen of 24 sparrows, picked at random, had parasites in several organs and tissues (Adie, 1908). These parasites were not identified by the author but later were reported to be toxoplasmas (Herman, 1937).

Toxoplasmas were recovered from the viscera of a wild pigeon that had a serum antibody titer of 1:1024 (Feldman and Sabin, 1949). Jacobs (1952) cited reports in which epizootics of toxoplasmosis occurred in pigeons (Springer, 1942; Johnson, 1943; Wiktor, 1950). Eighty wild pigeons were examined for toxoplasmosis by antibody test and mouse inoculation (Jacobs et al., 1952). One pigeon was positive by both methods. Three were negative for antibodies, but organisms were recovered from their tissues. Six had antibodies but no organisms. In another survey, 1 of 50 pigeons was positive for organisms (Manwell and Drobeck, 1952). One of 16 wild pigeons had a dye-test titer of 1:16, and organisms were isolated from the tissues of this bird (Gibson and Eyles, 1957). Serums from 14 wild pigeons were negative for *Toxoplasma* antibodies (Morris et al., 1956). A blue-tailed fruit pigeon *(Corpophaga concinna)* from the Aru Islands was emaciated and anemic; the lungs were congested and contained exudate. Bloody fluid was present in the abdominal cavity. Organisms were recovered from the blood and lungs (Plimmer, 1915–17).

Toxoplasmas were isolated from a pool of brain tissue from 4 crows *(Corvus brachyrhynchos)*. Organisms were recovered from blood and tissue of 3 of 13 crows injected experimentally (Finlay and Manwell, 1956). Habegger (1953) reported toxoplasmosis in large numbers of wild birds. In another study of large numbers of wild birds (Herman, 1937), toxoplasmas were found in 12 families of birds, including 40 species. Some of the species listed were English sparrow *(Passer domesticus)*, catbird *(Dumatella carolinensis)*, chipping sparrow *(Spizella passerina)*, kingbird *(Tyrannus tyrannus)*, red-eyed towhee *(Pipilo erythrophthalmus)*, song sparrow *(Melospiza melodia)*, starling *(Sturnus vulgaris)*, and swamp sparrow *(Melospiza georgiana)*. The parasites were found in heart, spleen, liver, bone marrow, lung, and blood.

In a study of 571 wild birds, toxoplasmosis was found in English sparrows and canaries (Manwell and Herman, 1935). Eight hundred fifty-five birds from 17 orders and 94 species were studied for toxoplasmosis (Iygiste and Gusen, 1962). One hundred one serums of 806 tested were positive for antibodies. Organisms were isolated from the tissues of the field harrier by mouse inoculation. *Toxoplasma* organisms were isolated from a penguin from a zoological garden (Rodhain, 1937). Herman (1937) cited a report by Uegaki in which 34 of 53 *Oryzornis oryzivora* were infected (Uegaki, 1930). During a survey of parasites in wild birds, toxoplasmas were recovered from 2 house finches (Wood and Wood, 1937).

Sixty-five jackdaws *(Corvus monedula spermologus)*, 14 pigeons *(Columba palumbus palumbus)*, and 6 rooks *(Corvus frugilegus frugilegus)* were negative for the parasite (Lainson, 1957). Experimental toxoplasmosis infection was fatal in canaries, English sparrows, a song sparrow, and white ducks. Pigeons and chickens were sick but did not die (Manwell et al., 1945). Four of 16 woodpeckers were positive for toxoplasmas as proved by mouse inoculation (Pande et al., 1961). The mode of infection was not known. The authors suggested that the incidence of infection in the woodpecker population was probably about 25%.

Between 1940 and 1950, 14 recently imported adult birds died in the Philadelphia Zoological Gardens. Toxoplasmosis was diagnosed postmortem after finding organisms in the tissues (Ratcliffe and Worth, 1951).

Many reports of *Toxoplasma* infection in domestic chickens have been published. Only 3 will be mentioned here. The reason for including the domestic chicken is that this extends the host range among the avian species a little further. Toxoplasmas were isolated from 5 of a flock of 40 hens (Erichsen and Harboe, 1953). Clinical signs included anorexia, emaciation, paleness, shrunken combs, diarrhea, and blindness in a few. Gross lesions included serous pericarditis, focal or diffuse myocarditis, diffuse or focal necrotizing encephalitis, necrotizing hepatitis, and ulcerative gastroenteritis. In another report (Biering-Sorensen, 1956) toxoplasmas were found in 35 hens from 21 flocks. Eleven of the hens had necrosis of the optic chiasma, with extension of the necrosis into the brain in 1 hen. Jones et al. (1959) stated that the chicken is a natural host of *Toxoplasma gondii* but rarely shows signs of disease. Large inocula are required to produce disease in mature fowl. Young chickens survive inoculations with the same number of organisms that cause fatal disease in laboratory animals.

◆ **CLINICAL SIGNS AND LESIONS.** Animals and birds frequently harbor the *Toxoplasma* organisms with no clinical evidence of illness (Levine, 1961). Also, when the organism is present in the "pseudocyst" form, it is probably inactive. This is suggested by the fact that no tissue reaction occurs around the "pseudocysts" which are often found accidentally.

Nonavian species may show evidence of disease, but as can be seen from this review, avian species are less often suspected of having the disease. It usually is diagnosed by postmortem examination or else exposure to the organism is determined by serologic tests. Therefore, descriptions of clinical signs are infrequent, and even in some reports of experimental infections, clinical signs and lesions were not described.

In mammals, within 4 hours after experimental inoculation, organisms can be found free in the blood and various organs (Cheng, 1964). They subsequently disappear from the blood; but in rats they can be found in the liver, lungs, and spleen for several weeks and are uniformly present in the brain for at least 2 years. If a mammal shows evidence of disease (Noble and Noble, 1964), the disease usually, but not always, passes through the acute, subacute, and chronic phases. In the acute phase, fever, lymphadenitis, splenic enlargement, myocarditis, pneumonitis, hepatitis, hydrocephalus, encephalitis, and skin rash may be present. Not all these signs are necessarily present in every case. The active disease in animals may be similar to that in man.

Gross lesions vary according to the severity of the disease and the organs involved. Necrosis and hemorrhage frequently occur, and edema and ascites may also be found. Inflammatory cells usually appear in the lesions. Pneumonic lesions may be present, and consolidation of some lobes of the lung may be nearly complete.

Central nervous system signs are referable to lesions in the brain and spinal cord.

◆ **DIAGNOSIS.** Organisms may be found in microscopic examination of tissue sections. Usually pseudocysts will be found, but in acute cases the individual organisms will be lying free in the tissues.

Mouse and guinea pig inoculations, using tissue suspensions, will reveal the organisms. Toxoplasmas grow in tissue culture and chick embryos. Several serologic tests are also useful diagnostic tools.

◆ **TREATMENT.** No treatment for toxoplasmosis in avian species was found; therefore, no recommendations can be made. However, a treatment for the disease in laboratory animals has been reported (Eyles, 1959). It may be that these drugs would be useful in avian species, but research data would be needed to verify this.

◆ **CONTROL.** In the absence of good information on the mode of natural spread of toxoplasmosis, specific preventive measures can hardly be recommended; however, the measures used to control infectious diseases should be considered; namely, avoid crowding, maintain good sanitation, prevent cannibalism, make use of serologic testing, and examine all birds to determine the cause of death.

◆ **REFERENCES**

Adie, J. R. Note on a parasite in the sparrow. *Indian Med. Gaz.* 43:176, 1908.

Biering-Sorensen, Af. U. Poultry toxoplasmosis. On the occurrence of endemic toxoplasmosis (toxoplasmosis gallinarum) in Danish chicken flocks. *Nord. Vet.-Med.* 8:140, 1956 (English summary).

Chandler, A. C., and Read, C. P. *Introduction to parasitology.* New York: John Wiley, 1961.

Cheng, T. C. *The biology of animal parasites.* Philadelphia: W. B. Saunders, 1964.

Erichsen, S., and Harboe, A. Toxoplasmosis in chickens. I. An epidemic outbreak of toxoplasmosis in a chicken flock in south-eastern Norway. *Acta Pathol. Microbiol. Scand.* 33:56, 1953.

Eyles, D. E. *The treatment of toxoplasmosis. From human toxoplasmosis.* Copenhagen, Denmark: Munksgaard, p. 127, 1959.

Feldman, H. A., and Sabin, A. B. Skin reactions to toxoplasmic antigen in people of different ages without known history of infection. *Pediatrics* 4:798, 1949.

Finlay, P., and Manwell, H. D. *Toxoplasma* from the crow, a new natural host. *Exptl. Parasitol.* 5:149, 1956.

Gibson, C., and Eyles, E. Toxoplasma infections in animals associated with a case of human congenital toxoplasmosis. *Am. J. Trop. Med. Hyg.* 6:990, 1957.

Habegger, H. *Le reservoir biologique animale et sa relation avec l'infection toxoplasmique humaine.* Geneva: Ambilly-Annemasse. Imprimerie Franco-Suisse, 1953.

Herman, C. M. *Toxoplasma* in North American birds and attempted transmission to canaries and chickens. *Am. J. Hyg.* 25:303, 1937.

Iygiste, A. K., and Gusen, V. M. Toxoplasmosis of wild birds in the USSR. *Doklady Akademii Nauk SSR. Biol. Sci. Sections* 143:384, 1962.

Jacobs, L., Melton, M. L., and Jones, F. E. The prevalence of toxoplasmosis in wild pigeons *J. Parasitol.* 38:457, 1952.

Johnson, C. M. In *Ann. Rept.* Gorgas Mem. Lab., p. 15, 1943.

Jones, F. E., Melton, M. L., Lunde, M. N., Eyles, D. E., and Jacobs, L. Experimental toxoplasmosis in chickens. J. Parasitol. 45: 31, 1959.

Lainson, R. The demonstration of *Toxoplasma* in animals, with particular reference to members of the Mustelidae. *Trans. Roy. Soc. Trop. Med. Hyg.* 51:111, 1957.

Laveran, A. Au sujet de l'hematozoaire endoglobulaire de *Padda oryzivora. Compt. Rend. Soc. Biol.* 52:19, 1900.

Levine, N. D. *Protozoan parasites of domestic animals and of man.* Minneapolis: Burgess, 1961.

Manwell, R. D., and Drobeck, H. P. Mammalian toxoplasmosis in birds. *Exptl. Parasitol.* 1:83, 1952.

Manwell, R. D., and Herman, C. M. Blood parasites of birds of Syracuse (N.Y.) region. *J. Parasitol.* 21:415, 1935.

Manwell, R. D., Coulston, F., Binckley, E. C., and Jones, V. P. Mammalian and avian *Toxoplasma. J. Infect. Diseases* 76:1, 1945.

Marullaz, M. Au sujet d'un *Toxoplasme* des oiseaux. *Bull. Soc. Pathol. Exotique* 6:323, 1913.

Morris, J. A., Aulisio, C. G., and McCowan, J. M. Serological evidence of toxoplasmosis in animals. *J. Infect. Diseases* 98:52, 1956.

Noble, E. R., and Noble, G. A. *Parasitology,* 2nd ed. Philadephia: Lea and Febiger, 1964.

Pande, P. G., Sekarish, P. C., and Shukla, R. R. *Toxoplasma* from the woodpecker, a new natural host. *Trans. Roy. Soc. Trop. Hyg.* 55:277, 1961.

Plimmer, H. G. Notes on the genus *Toxoplasma,* with a description of three new species. *Proc. Roy. Soc. London,* s. B. 89: 291, 1915–17.

Ratcliffe, H. L., and Worth, C. B. Toxoplasmosis of captive wild birds and mammals. *Am. J. Pathol.* 27:655, 1951.

Rodhain, J. Une infection a *Plasmodium* chez *Sphenisens demersus* (Manchot du Cap). *Ann. Parasitol. Human Comp.* 15:253, 1937.

Springer, L. Toxoplasmose entre Pombos. *Arquiv. Inst. Biol. (Sao Paulo)* 26:74, 1942.

Uegaki, J. Untersuchungen ueber die Blutprotozoen von Voegeln der Suedsee. *Arch. Protistenk.* 72:74, 1930.

Wiktor, T. J. Toxoplasmose animale. Sur une epidemie des lapins et des pigeons a Stanleyville (Congo Belge). *Ann. Soc. Belge Med. Trop.* 30:97, 1950.

Wood, F. D., and Wood, S. F. Occurrence of hematozoa in some California birds and mammals. *J. Parasitol.* 23:197, 1937.

PART FOUR

NEOPLASTIC DISEASES

● VANCE L. SANGER

IN THIS BRIEF DISCUSSION of neoplastic diseases in wild birds, avian species have been included which have been bred in captivity for long perods of time. For example, Schlumberger (1955) suggested that the shell parakeet *(Melopsittacus undulatus)* could be considered to be domesticated. Likewise, pigeons have been bred in captivity for decades. Nevertheless, thousands of these 2 species exist today in the wild state. Also, avian species which are held captive in zoos have been included. If records on these various species were excluded, the number of cases of neoplastic diseases would be rather insignificant compared to the number of reports that are presently available in the literature. In fact, most of our records come from zoo statistics or from animal hospital or diagnostic laboratory reports where hundreds or even thousands of birds have been examined over many decades.

◆ **DISTRIBUTION.** In spite of these sources of records, the number of reports of tumors in wild birds is much smaller than the number of reports of tumors in nonavian species, both warm-blooded and cold-blooded. Furthermore, zoo records reveal that tumors occur twice as often in captive nonavian populations as in captive wild birds. Efforts to explain this include the suggestions that birds may be more resistant to tumor development than nonavian species with the exception of the shell parakeet and the domestic chicken *(Gallus domesticus).* The incidence of tumors in wild parakeets is not known but it is high in the captive population and perhaps feed and environment have some influence. Hunters seek and take a wider variety of wild mammals than wild birds;

therefore, chance influences the number of nonavian and avian species available for observation. Finally, it may be that wild birds suffer from tumors more than is realized, but they die and are never recovered. Therefore, there is no accurate record of the incidence.

◆ **ETIOLOGY.** The causes of tumors in birds are not known any more than in other species. Likewise, the types of tumors, both malignant and benign, that have been reported have not been limited to a few cell types, and tumors may originate in any of the 3 germ layers or in any part of the body. The wing is a common site for tumor formation in many species and many of the tumors that form here are of the malignant sarcomatous type (Arnall, 1961a). Tumors may be single or multiple, and metastasis frequently occurs. The most common metastatic site is the lung (Arnall, 1961b).

◆ **TRANSMISSION.** Clinical signs presented by sick birds vary with the location, type, and size of the tumor. Tumors may or may not respond to treatment. Where feasible, radiation or surgical removal can be initiated. However, recurrence following surgical removal is common in malignant neoplasms (Stone, 1960). Some avian tumors have been transplanted and tumors can be induced in parakeets with carcinogenic agents. Schlumberger (1956a) successfully transplanted 4 different malignant pituitary tumors from shell parakeets into recipients of the same species. These tumors had invaded the orbit or nasopharynx in the primary host. Transplanted tumors grew in the brains of 2 recipients of 1 tumor and 5 grew in the subcutaneous tissues from 3 other donors. One of the latter was carried through 6 passages following the initial transfer. Schlumberger (1956b) also induced tumors in shell parakeets by painting the bare skin of the left pectoral region with 20-methylcholanthrene. A 3% solution in benzene was applied 2 times weekly for 270 days. Papillomas appeared in 26 of 28 birds after 80 days. Microscopically, some cellular changes in these papillomas were characteristic of squamous cell carcinoma. One such carcinoma was successfully transplanted to other parakeets and was carried through the 6th passage. Metastasis to the spleen and kidney occurred in 1 recipient. Cell-free extracts of the transplanted tumors were prepared and applied to the scarified epidermis of other parakeets, but after 3 months no tumors had appeared.

◆ **HOST RANGE.** By far the highest incidence of tumors among all avian species, excluding the domestic chicken, occurs in shell parakeets. This species has a tumor incidence greater than any nonavian species, including man. In one report, 24.2% of all deaths in 866 parakeets were caused from neoplasia.

In contrast to this, among 55 other birds representing several species, only 2 tumors were found—a lipoma in a Roseate cockatoo (*Kakatoe rosiecapilla*) and a lymphosarcoma in a canary (*Serinus canarius*) (Beach, 1962). In a later paper Beach (1965) reported that neoplasms accounted for nearly 25% of the deaths among another group of parakeets he had examined.

Extensive records from the Zoological Society of Philadelphia revealed that the undulated grass parakeet had the highest tumor incidence among all birds (Fox, 1923; Lombard and Witte, 1959). Arnall (1958) examined 435 birds and found 67 tumors, of which 54 were in parakeets. In another report covering 22 months, 1,000 parakeets were examined or necropsied and 199 tumors were found (Frost, 1961). Likewise, a report from the Moscow Zoological Park reported a higher incidence of tumors

in shell parakeets than in other birds (Dvishkov and Zvetaeva, 1946).

From 1901 to 1932, 6,898 necropsies were performed on birds in the Philadelphia Zoo. Eighty-two tumors were found in 81 birds and 42 of these were in psittacine birds. In this series of tumors the renal-adrenal-gonad tissue combination was most often affected, while the skin and mucocutaneous junction were rarely affected (Ratcliffe, 1933). In the United States pituitary tumors were reported to be the most common type of tumor found in parakeets (Schlumberger, 1956a), but in Great Britain tumors were found most frequently in the viscera (Beach, 1965). A pituitary tumor was reported in an African parakeet (*Agapornis pullaria*) by Slye et al., 1931.

Schlumberger (1954) reported that the average age of parakeets with pituitary tumors was 2.5 years, and in his series of 50 pituitary tumors from 50 parakeets, 7 other different types of tumors were found. Only 2 had metastasized—1 to the kidney and 1 to the liver. In a report of a single tumor, probably of gonadal origin, in a 7-year-old parakeet, metastasis had occurred to the liver (Reedy, 1967). Some reports state that the most frequent tumor found in parakeets is the lipoma, sometimes accompanied by necrosis. Xanthomas were also mentioned to be frequent (Wendt, 1955; Gandal, 1959; Stone, 1967).

Records, covering 18 years, from the Gardens of the Royal Zoological Society in Scotland revealed 5 tumors among 126 parakeets (Appleby, 1958). Occasionally tumors may form 20 to 25% of the total body weight of parakeets (Edwards, 1943; Bigland, 1961). Over a 4-year period, Schlumberger (1957) examined 497 tumor-bearing parakeets. These tumors included 156 primary pituitary adenomas or carcinomas; 106 primary renal carcinomas; 159 fibrosarcomas of the skin, spleen, and liver; 37 neoplastic hemopoietic tumors; and a few other unnamed tumors.

An angiosarcoma was reported from a lesser sulfur-crested cockatoo (*Kakatoe sulphurea*) (Wadsworth, 1954). Three tumors were found during the examination of 110 pigeons—an osteogenic sarcoma and 2 papillomas (Hare, 1937). An epithelial ependymoma was found in the brain of an ostrich which died after a 4-day illness (Williamson et al., 1956).

An extensive number of references to tumors in birds can be found in *A Bibliography of References to Diseases in Wild Mammals and Birds* (Halloran, 1955). Readers are referred to this extensive bibliography for additional reading.

Published reports reveal that tumors have occurred in many of the species of birds that exist today. True, many of these are of a single tumor in a single member of a species. Nevertheless, this indicates that generally wild birds are not immune to tumor development, and as has been suggested (Schlumberger, 1954), it may be that the incidence is higher than records reveal because affected birds are rarely recovered in the wild state. Reports also reveal that like mammals, almost all tissues in wild birds are susceptible to neoplastic change. The specific types of tumors reported here are summarized in Table 27.1.

It seems reasonable that with the immense amount of research being done on cancer, the interest of the public in this subject, and the increasing interest in diseases in wild birds, more and more reports of tumors in wild birds will be published.

As this occurs, perhaps the wide gap between the reported incidence of neoplastic disease in birds and in nonavian species will be noticeably narrowed.

◆ REFERENCES

Appleby, E. C. *Proc. Brit. Small Animal Vet. Assoc. Congr.*, p. 25, 1958.

Arnall, L. Experiences with cage birds. *Vet. Rec.* 70:120, 1958.

———. Anesthesia and surgery in cage and aviary birds. *Vet. Rec.* 73:173, 1961a.

———. Anesthesia and surgery in cage and aviary birds. *Vet. Rec.* 73:188, 1961b.

Beach, J. E. Diseases of budgerigars and other cage birds. *Vet. Rec.* 74:134, 1962.

———. Some of the major problems of budgerigar pathology. *J. Small Animal Pract.* 6:15, 1965.

Bigland, C. H., Pennifold, K. S., and Graesser, F. E. Testicular tumor in a parakeet. *Can. Vet. J.* 2:269, 1961.

Dvishkov, P. P., and Zvetaeva, N. P. A contribution to the comparative pathology of tumors of animals. *Proc. Moscow Zool. Park* 3:166, 1946 (English summary).

Edwards, F. B. Cancer in a budgerigar. *Vet. Rec.* 55:64, 1943.

Fox, Herbert. *Diseases in captive wild mammals and birds: incidence, description, comparison.* Philadelphia: J. B. Lippincott, p. 480, 1923.

Frost, R. C. Experiences with pet budgerigars. *Vet. Rec.* 73:621, 1961.

Gandal, C. P., and Saunders, L. Z. The surgery of subcutaneous tumors in parakeets (*Me-*

TABLE 27.1.   Summary of the Tumors and Species Affected

Tumor	Species	No. Affected
Pituitary	shell parakeet	210
	African parakeet	1
Fibrosarcoma	shell parakeet	159
Renal carcinoma	shell parakeet	106
Hemopoietic tissue	shell parakeet	37
Papilloma	shell parakeet	26 (experimental)
	pigeon	2
Lipoma	roseate cockatoo	1
Lymphosarcoma	canary	1
Gonad (type not specified)	shell parakeet	1
Angiosarcoma	lesser sulfur-crested cockatoo	1
Osteogenic sarcoma	pigeon	1
Epithelial ependymoma	ostrich	1

lopsittacus undulatus). *J. Am. Vet. Med. Assoc.* 134:212, 1959.

Halloran, P. O'C. A bibliography of references to diseases in wild mammals and birds. *Am. J. Vet. Res.* Part 2. 16:306, 1955.

Hare, T. A study of 110 consecutive cases of disease in pigeons. *Vet. Rec.* 49:680, 1937.

Lombard, L., and Witte, E. Frequency and types of tumors in mammals and birds of the Philadelphia Zoological Garden. *Cancer Res.* 19:127, 1959.

Michigan Agricultural Experiment Station. Article 4257.

Ratcliffe, H. J. Incidence and nature of tumors in captive wild mammals and birds. *Am. J. Cancer* 17:116, 1933.

Reedy, L. M. Adenocarcinoma in a parakeet. *Vet. Med.* 62:694, 1967.

Schlumberger, H. G. Neoplasia in the parakeet. I. Spontaneous chromophobe pituitary tumors. *Cancer Res.* 14:237, 1954.

———. Spontaneous goiter and cancer in the thyroid in animals. *Ohio J. Sci.* 55:23, 1955.

———. Neoplasia in the parakeet. II. Transplantation of pituitary tumor. *Cancer Res.* 16:149, 1956a.

———. Neoplasia of the parakeet. III. Transplantable methyl-cholanthrene-induced skin carcinoma. *Cancer Res.* 16:1043, 1956b.

———. Tumors characteristic for certain animal species. A preview. *Cancer Res.* 17:823, 1957.

Slye, M., Holmes, H. F., and Wells, H. G. Intracranial neoplasms in lower animals. Studies on the incidence and inheritability of spontaneous tumors in mice. *Am. J. Cancer* 15:1387, 1931.

Stone, R. M. Pet bird practice. *J. Am. Vet. Med. Assoc.* 137:364, 1960.

———. Prevalent problems and treatment of pet birds. *Vet. Med.* 62:142, 1967.

Wadsworth, J. R. Some neoplasms of captive wild animals. *J. Am. Vet. Med. Assoc.* 125:121, 1954.

Wendt, W. E. Treatment of psittacine diseases. *Speculum,* pp. 6, 56. Columbus: Ohio State Univ. Vet. Coll., Winter, 1955.

Williamson, W. M., Simon, J., and Hatton, E. H. An epithelial ependymoma in an ostrich. *J. Am. Vet. Med. Assoc.* 128:157, 1956.

PART FIVE

TOXINS

28 ◆ EFFECTS OF TOXIC SUBSTANCES

● ROLF HARTUNG

Birds have always had contacts with numerous toxic substances. But the variety of toxic materials present in the environment has been increasing drastically during the last three decades. In addition to poisons derived from plants and animals, birds now have to cope with an increasing number of toxic materials because of the increased application of synthetic chemicals to the environment.

It is not within the scope of this brief discussion to present even an outline of the great multitude of toxic substances with which birds have contact. Instead, the discussion will center on a brief review of toxicologic principles, which will have general applicability regardless of the specific toxic substance involved. This discussion will be followed by a series of selected examples of different types of toxic materials and their interactions with birds.

The Society of Toxicology has defined toxicology as the quantitative study of the injurious effects of chemical and physical agents as observed in alterations of structure, function, and response in living systems, including evaluation of safety (5th annual meeting, March 14–16, 1966, Williamsburg, Va.). This definition is very broad. It implies, however, that toxic effects may range from transient alterations in behavior to death. The actual interaction of the toxic agent with the animal may result in structural or biochemical changes. In most cases the poison must first be absorbed and distributed before it can reach its specific site of action. The facility with which a toxic compound can be absorbed, distributed, metabolized, and excreted greatly affects its toxicity.

◆ **ABSORPTION.** Toxic materials may be absorbed through the gastrointestinal tract, the skin, the respiratory tract, or by a combination of these routes. In most cases the oral route appears to be the most important route of absorption in birds.

While some small ions may be absorbed by active transport across cell membranes, most organic molecules are absorbed by passive diffusion. The rate of absorption is greatly influenced by the molecular configuration of the compound and by the properties of the cell membranes. Since cell membranes are largely lipid in nature (Hokin and Hokin, 1965), lipid soluble materials are most readily absorbed. The relationship of lipid solubility, molecular size, and ease of absorption had already been demonstrated in 1902 by the classical work of Overton. Large organic molecules in ionized form are relatively lipid insoluble and are absorbed only with great difficulty. Many organic acids and bases may exist partly in the ionized lipid insoluble state, and partly in the un-ionized lipid soluble state, depending on the pH of the immediate environment. Thus many organic acids are in the un-ionized state at pH 1 to 2, so they can be readily absorbed from the stomach. Most organic bases, however, are highly ionized at that pH and therefore are not absorbed until they reach the higher pH found in the intestine where they become partly un-ionized and thus more lipid soluble.

◆ **DISTRIBUTION.** Once a toxic material has been absorbed, it is distributed and transported to the site of action, centers of metabolic breakdown or detoxication, storage sites, and excretory sites. Many toxic substances are transported only to a minor extent while in solution. Most are transported reversibly bound to plasma proteins. Plasma-bound materials usually must revert to the free state to be biologically active. Thus, the total amount of plasma protein available to bind and transport toxic materials plays an important role in their toxicity (Petermann, 1961).

If the degree of plasma binding is extensive, and if the rate of reversion to the free state is low, plasma proteins may also act as a storage depot. Whenever a toxic material has a pronounced affinity for certain constituents of the body, then those constituents are likely to become storage depots. Thus many chlorinated hydrocarbon pesticides are stored in the body fat, and some heavy metals such as lead are stored in bone.

There also exist barriers to the free distribution of toxic substances in the body. Transfer across capillary walls encounters similar obstacles as the original absorption of the material by the organism. The so-called blood-brain barrier presents a more formidable obstacle to the distribution of toxic substances. Most water soluble toxic chemicals are almost completely prevented from reaching the central nervous system by this barrier (Brodie and Hogben, 1957).

♦ **SITE OF ACTION.** While we frequently can name the organs and the gross functions which are injured by a specific toxic agent, it must be admitted that our present knowledge of the site and mechanism of action for the vast majority of toxic substances is unknown. Where information of this type has been uncovered—for example, for the organic phosphates—it has been extremely useful in explaining the observed toxicity of many related compounds. Thus it has been helpful and instructive to consider sites and mechanisms of action in their most fundamental terms.

The primary interaction of any toxic agent or its toxic metabolite occurs at the molecular level. The primary interaction may result in protein degradation leading to structural changes first at the subcellular, and then at the cellular and organ levels. If the interaction is profound, it may result in cell death. The early structural alterations, which have been observed electron-microscopically, are usually associated with functional changes (Millington and Finean, 1961; Dinman et al., 1963).

Interactions of toxic substances in biochemical reactions have received a great deal of study. One class of these interactions is that which inhibits various enzyme activities. Most prominent is the inhibition of cholinesterases by organic phosphates (Koelle, 1963), which results in profound changes in function of some segments of the nervous system.

The metabolic breakdown of some toxic materials may deplete an essential nutrient (Barnes et al., 1959), resulting in undesirable secondary effects.

Other toxic compounds may actually be incorporated into biochemical reactions and lead to the synthesis of ineffective or detrimental substances. This process has been termed "lethal synthesis" by Peters et al. (1953).

Some chemicals may also interact with subcellular or cellular membranes without physically damaging their structure, but nevertheless greatly affecting their function. Thus the distribution of electrical charges on membrane surfaces may be altered by the presence of foreign materials. These alterations could affect phenomena closely associated with membrane permeability, such as nerve conduction, absorption, and excretion.

As a special case of membrane interactions, toxic materials may interact directly with physiologically active sites, so-called receptor sites. They may either interact with the receptor to produce a stimulus resulting in a physiologic effect, or they may block the receptor so normal receptor interactions can no longer take place (Ariens and Simonis, 1964a, 1964b). In either event normal physiologic activities may be upset seriously.

◆ **METABOLISM.** While some compounds may act and be finally excreted without undergoing any modification, many toxic substances are at least partially metabolized. In some cases one of the metabolites may become the primary active toxic agent.

The most important organ in the metabolism of many toxic compounds is the liver. It contains enzyme systems which appear to act selectively on a large variety of compounds not normally found in the body (Conney, 1967). The metabolic breakdown of toxic materials has been termed detoxication (Williams, 1959). The overall tendency of these metabolic steps is to make the compounds more ionic in character so they can be excreted more readily. The most common of the detoxication mechanisms are oxidations and conjugations with glucuronic acid, with activated sulfates, and with a number of amino acids. Many of the oxidative reactions are carried out by the microsomal enzymes of the liver (Brodie et al., 1958). Many compounds are metabolized by a number of pathways simultaneously.

◆ **EXCRETION.** Toxic substances may be excreted unchanged and/or as metabolites. The most important route of excretion is through the kidney. Compounds may be eliminated by glomerular filtration and tubular secretion. For ionizable materials the amount of tubular reabsorption and therefore excretion is greatly influenced by pH. There is less tubular-reabsorption for the ionized material and therefore it is excreted more rapidly.

Another important route of excretion is via the bile through the feces. This is an important excretory route, especially for the heavy metals. An appreciable quantity of the material eliminated via the bile may reabsorb in the intestinal tract and may thus recycle.

A significant proportion of many volatile organic solvents and petroleum fuels is exhaled unchanged via the lungs.

Some lipid soluble materials, including many of the chlorinated hydrocarbon pesticides, are eliminated in significant quantities with the yolk during egg-laying.

◆ **MEASUREMENT OF ACUTE TOXICITY.** The acute toxicity of any substance is commonly measured as the median lethal dose (LD_{50})—that dose which kills 50% of the animals. Sometimes it is also measured as the median effective dose (ED_{50})—that dose which elicits a certain measured response in 50% of the animals. The response may be the appearance of convulsions, a loss in body weight, or any other measurable phenomenon.

Certain attributes are affected more readily than others. Often the first noticeable alterations are changes in behavior (Goldberg et al., 1964; Xintaras et al., 1966).

Other attributes which often indicate early changes due to damage by toxic agents are body weight, organ weight/body weight ratios, food consumption, histopathology, and serum enzyme levels (Rowe et al., 1959).

◆ **SUBACUTE AND CHRONIC TOXICITY.** Animals can be exposed to such low concentrations of toxic materials that no immediate symptoms will be produced by that exposure. If the animal is able to metabolize or excrete these compounds at a rate equal to the rate of intake, then it may be able to resist these long-lasting low-level exposures indefinitely.

Many animals are known to be able to adapt, within limits, to low-level exposures of some compounds. Adaptive enzymes in the liver may increase in response to exposure by some toxic agents and may in turn speed up their metabolism (Conney, 1967).

If, however, the intake of toxic materials exceeds the sum of metabolic breakdown and excretion, then these substances can accumulate. Accumulation and storage do not continue indefinitely, but appear to reach an equilibrium which is dependent on the rate of intake. While the fact of accumulation in itself need not necessarily be harmful (viz. lead in bone and DDT in body fat), it can lead to pronounced toxic symptoms when stored substances are suddenly released (Bernard, 1963). Likewise, continued low-level exposures may stress a repair mechanism until it is overwhelmed and damage becomes apparent. Many chronic exposures are very difficult to evaluate because the causative agent is usually present in only very minute quantities, and it may take months or even years for damage to become noticeable. This is especially true for effects on reproduction or on the production of malignant tumors.

◆ **FACTORS INFLUENCING TOXICITY.** A great number of factors affect the toxicity of a compound. The most obvious are differences due to species or strains. The differential toxicities of insecticides for insects compared with vertebrates, and the toxicity of herbicides for plants compared with vertebrates, are well known. Comparisons among vertebrates usually demonstrate much smaller differences.

Individual differences within a species are readily apparent whenever an acute toxicity test is made. It is probable that individual variability with respect to toxic materials is greater among heterogeneous wild populations than among closely inbred populations of some species of laboratory animals. Sex and age differences may also result in different sensitivities to toxic substances.

Additional complications can arise when an organism is exposed to two or more toxic substances. These compounds may antagonize one another, they may have an additive effect, or they may have a greater than additive effect—that is, they may potentiate one another. This phenomenon of potentiation has long been of concern to toxicologists. Many organophosphate insecticides are known to potentiate one another (DuBois, 1958).

◆ **RISK.** While toxicity is an intrinsic property in interactions between chemical substances and biological matter, the risk of being poisoned takes into account a great number of extrinsic factors which influence the likelihood of reaching an effective or lethal dose in an individual.

The level of risk is associated with many identifiable factors. Among these are (1) the location of the toxic material in relation to the territory occupied by an individual animal, (2) the time during which the toxic substance is present, (3) the concentration of the toxic material, (4) its palatability, or the palatability of materials associated with it, (5) the proportion of the toxic substance in the total diet, and (6) reactions of the animal toward the toxic material— for example: attraction, avoidance, emesis, etc. Thus the hazards posed by a toxic substance may be tempered or enhanced by many ecologic and physiologic factors whose importance is not taken into account in most acute or chronic toxicity measurements conducted within the laboratory.

◆ **IDENTIFICATION OF TOXIC AGENTS.** The investigator who is trying to determine the cause of mortalities among wild birds is in a peculiarly difficult position. He may only be able to secure specimens which have been dead for some time. Information on symptomatology may be available only from untrained eyewitnesses, and information on the past movements of the affected birds may not be known. Mortalities due to disease must be excluded. A mere history of presumed contact with a toxic agent prior to death is not sufficient proof to establish poisoning as the cause of death. A history of exposure is, however, extremely helpful as a prelude to chemical analysis of animal tissues to ascertain the identity and quantity of a toxic agent. Publications are available which list the ingredients found in many commercial products (Gleason et al., 1963) and to aid in their chemical analysis (Stewart and Stolman, 1960, 1961; Stolman, 1963, 1965).

If poisoning is suspected, but no history of exposure can be ascertained, then the search for the suspected toxic agent can be extremely complex. The gross pathology and histopathology are rarely pathognomic, but may at least assist in narrowing down the search by a process of elimination. In combination with physiologic and biochemical measurements the anatomical findings can narrow the choice of possible toxic agents considerably. Tables of symptoms and physiologic and pathologic changes such as those published by von Oettingen (1958) can be very useful. However, with all these diagnostic aids, in most cases the final diagnosis should be based on the qualitative and quantitative identification of the toxic agent.

◆ **SURVEY OF SPECIFIC TOXICANTS.**
Since it would be impossible to give a reasonably complete discussion or even a list of toxic materials within the scope of this treatise, the discussion will be limited to a few selected examples among groups of toxic materials which may be of importance to wild animals. The reader who desires more specific information should turn to the cited references.

There are a few obvious differences in diseases caused by organisms and diseases caused by chemical substances. If a chemical substance is deleterious for one vertebrate species, then it is prone to be damaging to other vertebrate species. If a chemical substance is deleterious for a number of vertebrate species which are not closely related, then the likelihood is great that it will be damaging for most vertebrates. This does not mean that there cannot be some qualitative and quantitative differences in toxicity among species, but it does mean that toxicity is not very likely to respect divisions into wild, domesticated wild, feral, and domesticated species.

Thus, wherever necessary, the literature from veterinary toxicology and laboratory toxicology will be used freely to illustrate and expand the often limited diagnostic observations on poisons in wild birds.

◆ **POISONS OF BIOLOGICAL ORI-**

GIN. Among the poisons of biological origin, the toxic proteins produced by *Clostridium botulinum* have caused the greatest mortalities among birds. Among the species affected are grebes, loons, pelicans, cormorants, herons, geese, dabbling ducks, diving ducks, mergansers, hawks, falcons, pheasants, sandpipers, jaegers, gulls, magpies, and blackbirds (Kalmbach, 1934). At times, more than 100,000 birds have been affected in a single incident. The symptoms and pathology produced by *C. botulinum* toxin are discussed in greater detail in Chapter 12 in this book and therefore will not be repeated here.

The consumption of blue-green algae appears to have caused occasional mortalities among waterfowl. Especially the alga *Nodularia spumigena* has been thought to produce diarrhea, emesis, ataxia, and death (Deem and Thorp, 1939; Pankow, 1964).

The fungus *Aspergillus flavus* produces a highly substituted coumarin called aflatoxin. This material produces parenchymal necrosis and bile duct proliferation after acute exposure (Kohler and Schumacher, 1967). Chronically, aflatoxin is a very potent hepatocarcinogen. Ducks and turkeys are highly sensitive to this material. Aflatoxin is produced readily in moldy peanuts or other grains. It has caused numerous deaths among domestic ducks and turkeys (the syndrome caused by aflatoxin was at one time described as "turkey X" disease) (Marth, 1967). At this time (October 1970) there have been no reports describing its occurrence among wild birds. However, the distribution of the fungus and the toxin appears to be widespread.

Poisonous fruits and seeds have produced some deaths among birds. Losses of quail have been reported after eating *Crotolaria* seeds (Nestler and Bailey, 1941).

American goldfinches *(Spinus tristis)* have died after consuming almond seeds *(Prunus amygdalis)*. Death was presumably due to cyanide released by hydrolysis of amygdalin, a cyanogenic glycoside (Macgregor, 1956; Tschiersch, 1967).

On the other hand, quail have ingested

large quantities of hemlock seeds (*Conium maculatum*) without displaying any toxic symptoms. The meat from such quail has been shown to be highly poisonous for dogs (Sergent, 1941).

◆ **INORGANIC CHEMICALS.** Among the inorganic chemicals, lead has caused the greatest number of poisonings among birds. Waterfowl are especially hard hit because they seem to mistake spent lead shot for seeds or grit (Bellrose, 1951). These lead shot are then ground up in the gizzard, so that the lead becomes more absorbable in the intestinal tract. Lead transport mimics that of calcium, resulting in bone storage. Most of it is excreted via the bile into the feces; excretion of lead via the kidneys is of secondary importance.

Ingestion is by far the most important route of poisoning. Machle (1940) indicated that lead absorption from bullets imbedded in muscle was minimal. He found that lead poisoning became likely when bullets were lodged in joint capsules.

Lead is able to inhibit a great number of enzymes which contain sulfhydryl groups. It also prevents the incorporation of iron into the heme moiety of hemoglobin (Cantarow and Trumper, 1944). Symptoms of birds suffering from lead poisoning include lowered food intake, weakness, weight loss, drooping wings, inability to fly, ataxia, and green diarrhea. On autopsy the birds appear severely emaciated, the gallbladder is usually greatly enlarged, and the proventriculus is often impacted with food (Jordan and Bellrose, 1951). These authors also indicated that the immediate cause of death among ducks ingesting one lead shot was starvation.

Some of the observed impaction of food in the proventriculus may be the result of direct stimulation of the smooth muscles by lead salts, resulting in abnormal contractions. Lead also affects the nervous system, producing ataxia and paralysis of extensor muscles of the most frequently used appendage (Aub et al., 1926).

The most pronounced findings in blood are increased red cell fragility, slight a-nemia, basophilic stippling of the red cells in most species, and an increased number of reticulocytes (Waldron, 1966).

In addition to this, Locke et al. (1966) found acid-fast inclusion bodies in the kidney tubules in mallards and in mourning doves (Locke and Bagley, 1967).

The frequency of occurrence of lead in ducks is significant. From his own work and his survey of the literature Hunt (1960) cited an incidence of 3.2 to 8.6% of ingested shot. In his fluoroscoped sample Hunt found that 84.4% of the ducks which contained lead shot had only one shot in each gizzard. While there can be no doubt that lead has frequently killed ducks, Hunt's extensive band returns were unable to demonstrate a significant reduction in longevity after ingestion of lead.

Among the inorganic chemicals, lead has by far the greatest impact on bird populations. The arsenicals have on occasion caused losses of birds. Frost (1938) noted a decline in bird populations after the use of lead arsenate. However, Lilly (1940) found that young pheasants were relatively resistant to arsenites. In birds the most frequently observed symptom after arsenicals is a drastic weight loss.

In their review of the toxicity of arsenicals to wildlife, Rudd and Genelly (1956) conclude that these materials generally pose a minimal threat to wildlife.

A great number of other inorganic chemicals have caused losses among birds, but many of these incidences have been local phenomena, and therefore only a few examples of these will be cited here. Coburn et al. (1950) reported on the occurrence of phosphorous poisoning in black ducks and mallards. The most evident symptoms were depression followed by terminal convulsions. In the laboratory white phosphorus (1 to 3 mg/kg) resulted in fatty degeneration of the liver, kidneys, and muscle. Chronic exposures produced blood dyscrasias.

Trainer and Karstad (1960) reported on the occurrence of salt poisoning (NaCl) due to salt spread on highways during the winter. Among others, bobwhite quail and pheasants were affected. Symptoms occurring in the field were reproduced under laboratory conditions. Depression and thirst were followed by tremors, incoordination, coma, and death. Histopathologic alterations of the cerebellum and the brainstem were observed.

◆ **ORGANIC CHEMICALS.** Organic chemicals have found steadily increasing use by man in his industrial activities. Organic pollutants of the environment have been the accidental or intentional by-products of many such activities.

The mining, manufacture, transport, and use of petroleum products have resulted in many incidents of oil pollution of surface waters. As a result, many waterbirds are killed each year by oil pollution (Hawkes, 1961; Erickson, 1963). The primary effect of oiling appears to be a drastic reduction in insulating capacity of the plumage, resulting in a greatly increased metabolic rate. The reduced buoyancy after oiling isolates the bird from his food supply. These factors then combine and lead to an "accelerated starvation" syndrome (Hartung, 1967b).

Some of the oil on the feathers is also ingested. This has been found to produce lipid pneumonia, gastrointestinal irritation, and fatty changes in the liver. Depending on the kind of oil involved, various additives may produce additional effects. Among these are acinar atrophy of the pancreas, toxic nephrosis, and in some cases, cholinesterase inhibition (Hartung and Hunt, 1966).

Rittinghaus (1956) and Hartung (1965) have also reported that small quantities of oil coated onto eggs by oiled birds reduce the hatchability of those eggs greatly.

It has been estimated that tens of thousands of waterbirds are killed by oil each year (ZoBell, 1964). In some cases oil is thought to have had a significant impact on the total populations of some species of waterbirds (Giles and Livingston, 1960).

The intentional use of organic chemicals for environmental modification has sometimes had severe side effects on birds.

Chlorinated hydrocarbon insecticides, notably DDT, have been particularly implicated in some bird mortalities (Barker, 1958; Bernard, 1963). Since insects are a major part of the diet of many species of birds, a drastic reduction in insects due to insecticides is also bound to have an effect on these bird populations because of the reduction of their food supply.

The chlorinated hydrocarbon insecticides as a group are relatively stable and have a high lipid solubility. Therefore they tend to concentrate in the fatty tissues of birds and other animals (Hartung, 1967a). The occurrence of chlorinated hydrocarbon pesticides is now widespread (Dustman, 1966; Walker et al., 1967).

The data presented by De Witt et al. (1955) indicate that on an acute basis, birds are not more sensitive to DDT than mammals. However, this situation changes when chronic effects are considered.

At times chlorinated hydrocarbons have been transported and greatly magnified through the food chain, so the final predators and scavengers had pesticide concentrations several orders of magnitude higher than the original environmental concentrations (Hunt and Bischoff, 1960; Woodwell et al., 1967). When high levels of fat-stored DDT are suddenly released by fat utilization during starvation, typical acute DDT poisoning can occur (Bernard, 1963). This is characterized by tremors which lead to convulsions and ultimately to death. The poisoning is apparently related to an increased DDT level in the brain.

Of even greater concern are the effects of some chlorinated hydrocarbon insecticides on the reproduction of birds. Walker et al. (1967) have reported on the occurrence of chlorinated hydrocarbon insecticides in bird eggs. The eggs of predators and scavengers contained the highest concentrations. Jones and Summers (1968) reported that a diet containing 200 ppm DDT did not affect hatchability of Japanese quail eggs (*Coturnix japonica*) but did increase chick mortality. Koeman et al. (1967) reported that chick mortality shortly after hatching was due to the absorption of chlorinated hydrocarbons from the yolk during the first 24 to 48 hours after hatching, during which most birds do not feed. He also observed a large loss of recently hatched sandwich terns in the field. The convulsions and subsequent tissue analyses led him to conclude that insecticides were the chief cause of death.

Recent worldwide declines in birds of prey have caused many people to relate these reductions to the chronic toxicity of chlorinated hydrocarbon insecticides (Cramp, 1963). Keith (1966) related declining reproduction in herring gulls (*Larus argentatus*) to high DDT levels (21 ppm, wet weight basis). Wurster and Wingate (1968) project that the Bermuda petrel (*Pterodroma cahow*) is threatened with extinction because of DDT contamination. Hickey and Anderson (1968) related these population declines to decreases in eggshell thickness after exposure to DDT.

Because of the persistence and also because of the adverse effects on wildlife, many of the chlorinated hydrocarbon insecticides are slowly being replaced by organophosphorous insecticides. Since the latter are readily broken down by hydrolysis, chronic toxicity is virtually unknown. Some of the organophosphates are highly toxic, with lethal doses of only a few mg/kg. Examples from this group are parathion, TEPP, Systox, Thymet, and others (Rudd and Genelly, 1956; Bunyan et al., 1968a, 1968b). Chlorthion and Malathion, among others, have a low level of toxicity, and these agents have not been implicated in any bird mortalities. Their lethal doses can exceed 1 g/kg. Acutely, all organophosphorous pesticides inhibit the enzyme cholinesterase, and this inhibition alters the transmission of nerve impulses across synapses. Most severely affected are the parasympathetic nervous system and the neuromyal junction. Symptoms are muscle fasciculations, decreased heart rate, and respiratory difficulties leading to death due to respiratory arrest (Koelle, 1963). The analysis of blood cholinesterase activity is useful in establishing a diagnosis of organophosphor-

ous poisoning. A differential diagnosis may still be required to eliminate carbamate insecticides which are mild inhibitors of cholinesterases (Baron et al., 1966).

While organophosphorous insecticides are thought to act solely on an acute basis, an exception has been found in the case of EPN (O-Ethyl O-p-nitrophenyl phenylphosphonothioate) under experimental conditions. EPN can produce characteristic foot deformities in ducklings when injected into the egg (Khera et al., 1966).

Herbicides, especially the popular chlorinated phenoxyacetic acids, have presented little or no direct hazard to wildlife. At normal application rates 2,4D and 2,4,5T are essentially nontoxic to birds. However, the indirect effects, due to profound alterations of plant communities after herbicide treatment, may have pronounced effects on bird populations.

Some chemicals which are used to treat seeds as fungicides or as repellents have on occasion produced toxic effects in birds. An example of one of these is tetramethylthiuramdisulfide (thiram). Elder (1964) found that pigeons (*Columba livia*) layed fewer and soft-shelled eggs after thiram. Wedig et al. (1968) demonstrated inhibition of ovulation in the bobwhite quail (*Colinus virginianus*) after thiram.

◆ **CONCLUSIONS.** Toxic substances have had a profound impact on some species of birds. The greatest impact has been made by pollutants and pesticides. There is some evidence that some of the pesticides have strongly contributed to declines in some predator species which may even be threatened with extinction. While increasing human population pressures will undoubtedly increase the use of chemicals in the environment, there appears to be a growing awareness of possible long-term effects, so present trends may be reversed.

For the immediate future, toxic substances will continue to present an important hazard for some species of birds. Because of this, an increasing amount of research is required to study the acute and chronic toxicity of pollutants and of chemicals used for environmental modification. These substances must be evaluated for birds in the laboratory as well as in an ecologic setting.

♦ REFERENCES

Ariens, E. J., and Simonis, A. M. A molecular basis for drug action. *J. Pharm. Pharmacol.* 16(3):137, 1964a.

———. A molecular basis for drug action. The interaction of one or more drugs with different receptors. *J. Pharm. Pharmacol.* 16(5):289, 1964b.

Aub, J. C., Fairhall, L. T., Minot, A. S., and Reznikoff, P. *Lead poisoning. Medicine monographs VII.* Baltimore: Williams & Wilkins, 1926.

Barker, R. J. Notes on some ecological effects of DDT sprayed on elms. *J. Wildlife Management* 22(3):269, 1958.

Barnes, M. M., James, S. P., and Blood, P. B. The formation of mercapturic acids. *Biochem. J.* 71(4):680, 1959.

Baron, R. L., Casterline, J. L., Jr., and Orzel, R. In vivo effects of carbamate insecticides on mammalian esterase enzymes. *Toxicol. Appl. Pharmacol.* 9(1):6, 1966.

Bellrose, F. C. Effects of ingested lead upon waterfowl populations. *Trans. 16th N. Am. Wildlife Conf.* 16:125, 1951.

Bernard, R. F. Studies on the effects of DDT on birds. *Publ. Museum Mich. State Univ., Biol. Series* 2(3):155, 1963.

Brodie, B. B., and Hogben, C. A. M. Some physiochemical factors in drug action. *J. Pharm. Pharmacol.* 9(6):345, 1957.

Brodie, B. B., Gilette, J. R., and LaDu, B. N. Enzymatic metabolism of drugs and other foreign compounds. *Ann. Rev. Biochem.* 27:427, 1958.

Bunyan, P. J., Jennings, D. M., and Taylor, A. Organophosphorus poisoning—some properties of avian esterases. *Agr. Food Chem.* 16(2):326, 1968a.

———. Organophosphorus poisoning—diagnosis of poisoning in pheasants owing to a number of common pesticides. *Agr. Food Chem.* 16(2):332, 1968b.

Cantarow, A., and Trumper, M. *Lead poisoning.* Baltimore: Williams & Wilkins, 1944.

Coburn, D. R., DeWitt, J. B., Derby, J. V., Jr., and Ediger, E. Phosphorus poisoning in waterfowl. *J. Am. Pharm. Assoc.* 39(3):151, 1950.

Conney, A. H. Pharmacological implications of microsomal enzyme induction. *Pharmacol. Rev.* 19(3):317, 1967.

Cramp, S. Toxic chemicals and birds of prey. *Brit. Birds* 56(4):124, 1963.

Deem, A. W., and Thorp, F., Jr. Toxic algae in Colorado. *J. Am. Vet. Med. Assoc.* 95 (752):542, 1939.

DeWitt, J. B., Derby, J. V., Jr., and Mangan, G. F., Jr. DDT vs. wildlife, relationship between quantities ingested, toxic effects and tissue storage. *J. Am. Pharm. Assoc.* 44(1):22, 1955.

Dinman, B. D., Hamdi, E. A., Fox, C. F., and Frajola, W. J. CCl₄ toxicity III: hepatostructural and enzymatic change. *Arch. Environ. Health* 7(6):630, 1963.

DuBois, K. P. Potentiation of the toxicity of insecticidal organic phosphates. *A.M.A. Arch. Ind. Health* 18(6):488, 1958.

Dustman, E. H. Monitoring wildlife for pesticide content. *Symp. Scientific Aspects Pest Control.* N.A.S.-N.R.C. Publ. 1402:343, 1966.

Elder, W. H. Chemical inhibitors of ovulation in the pigeon. *J. Wildlife Management* 28 (3):556, 1964.

Erickson, R. C. Oil pollution and migratory birds. *Atlantic Naturalist* 18(1):5, 1963.

Fouts, J. R. Physiological impairment of drug metabolism. *Proc. 1st Int. Pharmacol. Meeting* 6:257, 1962.

Frost, A. Effect upon wildlife of spraying for control of gypsymoths. *J. Wildlife Management* 2(1):13, 1938.

Giles, L. A., Jr., and Livingston, J. Oil pollution of the seas. *Trans. 25th N. Am. Wildlife Conf.* 25:297, 1960.

Gleason, M. N., Gosselin, R. E., and Hodge, H. C. *Clinical toxicology of commercial products.* Baltimore: Williams & Wilkins, 1963.

Goldberg, M. E., Johnson, H. E., Possani, U. C., and Smyth, H. F., Jr. Effect of repeated inhalation of vapors of industrial solvents on animal behavior. *Am. Ind. Hyg. Assoc. J.* 25(4):369, 1964.

Hartung, R. Some effects of oiling on reproduction of ducks. *J. Wildlife Management* 29(4):872, 1965.

———. An outline for biological and physical concentrating mechanisms for chlorinated hydrocarbon pesticides. *Papers Mich. Acad. Sci., Arts, Letters* 52:77, 1967a.

———. Energy metabolism in oil-covered ducks. *J. Wildlife Management* 31(4):798, 1967b.

Hartung, R., and Hunt, G. S. Toxicity of some oils to waterfowl. *J. Wildlife Management* 30(3):564, 1966.

Hawkes, A. L. A review of the nature and extent of damage caused by oil pollution at sea. *Trans. N. Am. Wildlife Nat. Resources Conf.* 26:343, 1961.

Hokin, L. E., and Hokin, M. R. The chemistry of cell membranes. *Scientific American* 213(4):78, 1965.

Hunt, E. G., and Bischoff, A. I. Inimical effects of periodic DDD applications to Clear Lake. *Calif. Fish Game* 46(1):91, 1960.

Hunt, G. S. Lead poisoning among ducks wintering on the lower Detroit River. *Trans. 25th N. Am. Wildlife Conf.* 25:162, 1960.

Jones, F. J. S., and Summers, D. D. B. Relation between DDT in diets of laying birds and viability of their eggs. *Nature* 217(5134): 1162, 1968.

Hickey, J. J., and Anderson, D. W. Chlorinated hydrocarbons and eggshell changes in raptorial and fish-eating birds. *Science* 162:271, 1968.

Jordan, J. S., and Bellrose, F. C. Lead poisoning in waterfowl. *Biol. Notes No. 26, Illinois Natural History Survey,* 1951.

Kalmbach, E. R. Western duck sickness a form of botulism. *U.S. Dept. Agr. Tech. Bull. 411,* 1934.

Keith, J. A. Reproduction in a population of herring gulls *(Larus argentatus)* contaminated by DDT. *J. Appl. Ecol.* 3(suppl.):57, 1966.

Khera, K. S., Lattam, Q. N., Ellis, C. F. G., Zawidzka, Z. A., and Grice, H. C. Foot deformity in ducks from injection of EPN during embryogenesis. *Toxicol. Appl. Pharmacol.* 8(3):540, 1966.

Koelle, G. B. Cholinesterases and anticholinesterase agents. *Handbuch der experimentellen Pharmakologie. Ergaenzungswerk,* vol. 15. Berlin: Springer Verlag, 1963.

Koeman, J. H., Oudejans, R. C. H. M., and Huisman, E. A. Danger of chlorinated hydrocarbon insecticides in birds' eggs. *Nature* 215(5105):1094, 1967.

Koehler, H., and Schumacher, A. Licht- und elektronenoptische Untersuchungen zur Leberzirrhose nach experimenteller Aflatoxinvergiftung bei Entenkueken. *Zentr. Veterinaermed.* 14:395, 1967.

Lilly, J. H. The effect of arsenical grasshopper poisons upon pheasants. *J. Econ. Entomol.* 33(3):501, 1940.

Locke, L. N., Bagley, G. E., and Irby, H. D. Acid-fast intranuclear inclusion bodies in the kidneys of mallards fed shot. *Bull. Wildlife Disease Assoc.* 2(4):127, 1966.

Locke, L. N., and Bagley, G. E. Lead poisoning in a sample of Maryland mourning doves. *J. Wildlife Management* 31(3):515, 1967.

Macgregor, W. G. Cyanide poisoning of songbirds by almonds. *Condor* 58(2):370, 1956.

Machle, W. Lead absorption from bullets lodged in the tissues. *J. Am. Med. Assoc.* 115 (18):1536, 1940.

Marth, E. H. Aflatoxins and other mycotoxins in agricultural products. *J. Milk Food Technol.* 30(6):192, 1967.

Millington, P. F., and Finean, J. B. Electron microscope and x-ray diffraction studies of the effects of mercuric chloride on the structure of nerve myelin. *J. Ultrastructure Res.* 5(5):470, 1961.

Nestler, R. B., and Bailey, W. W. The toxicity of *Crotolaria spectabilis* seeds for quail. *J. Wildlife Management* 5(3):309, 1941.

Oettingen von, W. F. *Poisoning.* Philadelphia: W. B. Saunders, 1958.

Overton, E. Veitrage zur allgemeinen Muskel- und Nervenphysiologie. Archiv fuer die gesammte Physiologie des Menschen und der Thiere *Pfluger's Arch. Physiol.* 92:115, 1902.

Pankow, H. Bemerkungen ueber die Schaedlichkeit von Blaualgenwasserblueten fuer Tiere. *Naturwissenschaften* 51(6):146, 1964.

Petermann, M. L. Plasma protein abnormalities in cancer. *Med. Clin. N. Am.* 45(3): 537, 1961.

Peters, R. A., Wakelin, R., Rivett, D., and Thomas, L. Fluoroacetate poisoning: comparison of synthetic fluorocitric acid with the enzymatically synthesized fluorotricarboxylic acid. *Nature* 171:1111, 1953.

Rittinghaus, H. Etwas ueber die indirekte Verbreitung der Oelpest in einem Seevogelschutzgebiete. *Ornithologische Mitteilungen* 8(3):43, 1956.

Rowe, V. K., Wolf, M. A., Weil, C. S., and Smyth, H. F., Jr. The toxicological basis of threshold limit values: 2 pathological and biochemical criteria. *Am. Ind. Hyg. Assoc. J.* 20(5):346, 1959.

Rudd, R. L., and Genelly, R. E. Pesticides: their use and toxicity to wildlife. *Calif. Dept. Fish Game,* Bull. 7, 1956.

Sergent, E. Les cailles empoisonneuses dans la bible, et en Algerie des nos jours. *Arch. Inst. Pasteur Algerie* 19 (2):161, 1941.

Stewart, C. P., and Stolman, A. *Toxicology— mechanisms and analytical methods.* Academic Press, vol. 1, 1960; vol. 2, 1961.

Stolman, A. *Progress in chemical toxicology.* Academic Press, vol. 1, 1963; vol. 2, 1965.

Trainer, D. O., and Karstad, L. Salt poisoning in Wisconsin wildlife. *J. Am. Vet. Med. Assoc.* 136 (1):14, 1960.

Tschiersch, B. Blausaeure und Blausaeureglykoride. *Die Pharmazie* 22 (2):76, 1967.

Waldron, H. A. The anaemia of lead poisoning: a review *Brit. J. Ind. Med.* 23 (2):83, 1966.

Walker, C. H., Hamilton, G. A., and Harrison, R. B. Organochloride insecticide residues in wild birds in Britain. *J. Sci. Food Agr.* 18 (2):123, 1967.

Wedig, J., Cowan, A. B., and Hartung, R. Some of the effects of tetramethylthiuram disulfide (TMTD) on reproduction of the bobwhite quail *(Colinus virginianus). Toxicol. Appl. Pharmacol.* 12 (2):293, 1968.

Williams, R. T. *Detoxication mechanisms.* John Wiley & Sons, 1959.

Woodwell, G. M., Wurster, C. F., Jr., and Isaacson, P. A. DDT residues in an East Coast estuary: a case of biological concentration of a persistent insecticide. *Science* 156 (3776):821, 1967.

Wurster, C. F., Jr., and Wingate, D. B. DDT residues and declining reproduction in the Bermuda petrel. *Science* 159 (3818):979, 1968.

Xintaras, C., Johnson, B. L., Ulrich, E. E., Terrill, R. E., and Sobechi, M. F. Application of the evoked response technique in air pollution toxicology. *Tox. Appl. Pharmacol.* 8 (1):77, 1966.

ZoBell, C. E. The occurrence, effects and fate of oil polluting the sea. *Advan. Water Pollution Res.* 3:85, 1964.

◆ INDEX